Contemporary European Playwrights

Contemporary European Playwrights presents and discusses a range of key writers that have radically reshaped European theatre by finding new ways to express the changing nature of the continent's society and culture, and whose work is still in dialogue with Europe today.

Traversing borders and languages, this volume offers a fresh approach to analysing plays in production by some of the most widely performed European playwrights, assessing how their work has revealed new meanings and theatrical possibilities as they move across the continent, building an unprecedented picture of the contemporary European repertoire. With chapters by leading scholars and contributions by the writers themselves, the chapters bring playwrights together to examine their work as part of a network and genealogy of writing, examining how these plays embody and interrogate the nature of contemporary Europe.

Written for students and scholars of European theatre and playwriting, this book will leave the reader with an understanding of the shifting relationships between the subsidised and commercial, the alternative and the mainstream stage, and political stakes of playmaking in European theatre since 1989.

Maria M. Delgado is Professor of Theatre and Screen Arts at The Royal Central School of Speech and Drama, University of London, UK. Her publications include *'Other' Spanish Theatres* (2003, revised Spanish-language edition, 2017), *Federico García Lorca* (2008) and ten co-edited volumes.

Bryce Lease is Reader in Theatre and Performance Studies at Royal Holloway, University of London, UK and Co-Editor of *Contemporary Theatre Review*. His publications include *After '89: Polish Theatre and the Political* (2016) and *A History of Polish Theatre* (2021).

Dan Rebellato is a playwright and Professor of Contemporary Theatre at Royal Holloway University of London, UK. His publications include *1956 and All That* (1999), *Theatre and Globalization* (2009), and the Cambridge *Companions to British Theatre 1945* and *Contemporary British Plays and Playwriting* (2020).

Contemporary European Playwrights

Edited by
Maria M. Delgado, Bryce Lease and
Dan Rebellato

LONDON AND NEW YORK

First published 2020
by Routledge
2 Park Square, Milton Park, Abingdon, Oxon OX14 4RN

and by Routledge
52 Vanderbilt Avenue, New York, NY 10017

Routledge is an imprint of the Taylor & Francis Group, an informa business

© 2020 selection and editorial matter, Maria M. Delgado, Bryce Lease and
Dan Rebellato; individual chapters, the contributors

The right of Maria M. Delgado, Bryce Lease and Dan Rebellato to be
identified as the authors of the editorial material, and of the authors for their
individual chapters, has been asserted in accordance with sections 77 and 78
of the Copyright, Designs and Patents Act 1988.

All rights reserved. No part of this book may be reprinted or reproduced or
utilised in any form or by any electronic, mechanical, or other means, now
known or hereafter invented, including photocopying and recording, or in
any information storage or retrieval system, without permission in writing
from the publishers.

Trademark notice: Product or corporate names may be trademarks or registered
trademarks, and are used only for identification and explanation without
intent to infringe.

British Library Cataloguing-in-Publication Data
A catalogue record for this book is available from the British Library

Library of Congress Cataloging-in-Publication Data
Names: Delgado, Maria M., editor. | Lease, Bryce, editor. | Rebellato,
Dan, editor.
Title: Contemporary European playwrights / edited by Maria M. Delgado,
Bryce Lease and Dan Rebellato.
Description: Abingdon, Oxon ; New York : Routledge 2020. |
Includes bibliographical references and index.
Identifiers: LCCN 2020001676 (print) | LCCN 2020001677 (ebook)
Subjects: LCSH: European drama--21st century--Themes and motives. |
Theater--Europe--History--21st century. | Theater and society--Europe--
History--21st century. | Literature and society--Europe--History--
21st century. | Dramatists, European--21st century.
Classification: LCC PN1861.2 C66 2020 (print) | LCC PN1861.2 (ebook) |
DDC 809.2/051--dc23
LC record available at https://lccn.loc.gov/2020001676
LC ebook record available at https://lccn.loc.gov/2020001677

ISBN: 978-1-138-08421-6 (hbk)
ISBN: 978-1-138-08422-3 (pbk)
ISBN: 978-1-315-11194-0 (ebk)

Typeset in Bembo
by Taylor & Francis Books

Contents

List of figures	viii
Acknowledgements	x
List of contributors	xii
Foreword	xvii
TIAGO RODRIGUES	

Introduction   1
MARIA M. DELGADO, BRYCE LEASE AND DAN REBELLATO

1   European playwriting and politics, 1945–89   21
DAN REBELLATO

2   Elfriede Jelinek and Werner Schwab: *Heimat* critique and
dissections of right-wing populism and xenophobia   44
KAREN JÜRS-MUNBY

3   Weronika Szczawińska and Agnieszka Jakimiak: Dramaturg as a
figure of transition   66
BRYCE LEASE

4   András Visky and Matéi Visniec: Challenging boundaries of
cultural specificity   76
JOZEFINA KOMPORALY

5   Lars Norén and Jon Fosse: Nordic grey or theatre innovators?   95
RIKARD HOOGLAND

6   Martin Crimp and Simon Stephens: British playwrights as
European playwrights   112
DAVID BARNETT

vi   *Contents*

7   Marius von Mayenburg and Roland Schimmelpfennig: Dissecting
    European lives under global capitalism   129
    PETER M. BOENISCH

8   Sarah Kane and Mark Ravenhill: The 'blood and sperm'
    generation   150
    ANDREW HAYDON

9   Vasilii Sigarev and the Presniakov Brothers: Staging the new
    Russia   168
    NOAH BIRKSTED-BREEN

10 Paweł Demirski and Dorota Masłowska: Painful pasts,
    transformative presents   185
    BRYCE LEASE

11 Jordi Galceran and Juan Mayorga: Unravelling the present,
    narrativising the past   203
    MARIA M. DELGADO

12 Ivan Vyrypaev and Natalia Vorozhbyt: Language, memory, and
    cultural mythology in Russian and Ukrainian new drama   226
    MOLLY FLYNN

13 Enda Walsh and Martin McDonagh: Reimagining Irish theatre   244
    PATRICK LONERGAN

14 Yasmina Reza and Florian Zeller: The art of success   261
    DOMINIC GLYNN

15 Lena Kitsopoulou and Yannis Mavritsakis: Greek theatre at the
    antipodes of crisis   277
    ELIZABETH SAKELLARIDOU

16 Emma Dante and Fausto Paravidino: Families, national identity,
    and international audiences   296
    MARGHERITA LAERA

17 Biljana Srbljanović and Ivana Sajko: Voice in the place of silence   313
    DUŠKA RADOSAVLJEVIĆ

18 debbie tucker green and Alice Birch: 'Angry feminists' on the
    European stage   334
    MARISSIA FRAGKOU

19 Peter Handke: Inhabiting the world together   352
    HANS-THIES LEHMANN

| | | *Contents* | vii |

20 Jonas Hassen Khemiri: Writing out of the binary 364
    BRYCE LEASE

21 Marie NDiaye: Eliding capture 374
    KÉLINA GOTMAN

Afterword: The constructed space 389
DAVID GREIG

Index 401

Figures

2.1 Werner Schwab's *ÜBERGEWICHT, unwichtig: UNFORM – Ein Europäisches Abendmahl (OVERWEIGHT, unimportant: MISSHAPE – A European Supper)*, directed by Johannes Lepper (2017) at Schauspiel Dortmund. Photograph © Birgit Hupfeld   53

3.1 Agnieszka Jakimiak's *Hitchcock*, directed by Weronika Szczawińska (2017), at the Mladinsko Theatre, Ljubljana, Slovenia. Photograph © Nejc Saje   72

4.1 András Visky's *Juliet*, directed by Boian Ivanov at 'Sava Ognyanov' State Drama Theatre Ruse, Bulgaria (2016). Photograph © Boian Ivanov   82

5.1 Jon Fosse's *Barnet* (*The Child*), directed by Johannes Holmen Dahl at Dramaten Stockholm (2015). Photograph © Roger Stenberg   108

6.1 Simon Stephens' *Three Kingdoms*, directed by Sebastian Nübling at the Lyric Hammersmith, London (2012). Photograph © Tristam Kenton   123

7.1 Marius von Mayenburg's production of his own *Ein Stück Plastik (Plastic)* at the Schaubühne Berlin (2015). Photograph © Arno Declair   143

8.1 Sarah Kane's *Zerbombt* (*Blasted*) at the Schaubühne Berlin (2005) directed by Thomas Ostermeier. Photograph © Arno Declair   155

9.1 Kirill Serebrennikov's 2004 production of the Presniakov Brothers' *Izobrazhaia zhertvu* (*Playing the Victim*) at the Chekhov Moscow Arts Theatre, Moscow, 2004. Photograph © Oleg Chernous   176

10.1 Grzegorz Jarzyna's production of Dorota Masłowska's *Inni ludzie* (*Other People*) at the TR Warszawa, Warsaw (2019). Photograph © Marcin Oliva Soto   197

11.1 Juan Mayorga's *El chico de la última fila* (*The Boy at the Back*), directed by Andrés Lima at the Sala Beckett, Barcelona (2019). Photograph © Kiku Piñol   217

12.1 Natalia Vorozhbyt's *Viy 2.0*, directed by Maksym Holenko (2016) at Wild Theatre in Kyiv. Photograph © Gala Lavrinets   240

List of illustrations ix

13.1 *Ballyturk* (2014) written and directed by Enda Walsh; Landmark
Productions and Galway International Arts Festival. Photograph
© Patrick Redmond   256
14.1 Miguel del Arco's production of Yasmina Reza's *'Art'* at the
Pavón Teatro Kamikaze, Madrid (2017). Photograph © Vanessa
Rabade   266
15.1 *Vitriol* by Yannis Mavritsakis, directed by Olivier Py (2013) at the
National Theatre of Greece. Photograph © Marilena Stafylidou   289
16.1 *Boala Familiei M* (*M Family Illness*) by Fausto Paravidino, directed
by Radu Afrim at the Teatrul National Timişoara (2008).
Photograph © Radu Afrim   303
17.1 *Rose is a rose is a rose is a rose*, written, directed, and performed by
Ivana Sajko (2010). Photograph © Dražen Smaranduj   319
18.1 debbie tucker green's *stoning mary*, directed by Marianne Elliott at
the Royal Court Theatre, London (2005). Photograph ©
Tristram Kenton   339
21.1 André Engel's production of Marie NDiaye's *Papa doit manger* at
the Comédie-Française, Paris (2003). Photograph © Cosimo
Mirco Magliocca   378
22.1 *The Suppliant Women* by Aeschylus, adapted by David Greig and
directed by Ramin Gray at the Royal Lyceum, Edinburgh (2016)
Photograph © Stephen Cummiskey   391

Acknowledgements

We owe a debt of thanks to the many people and institutions who worked with us in the process of researching, commissioning, and delivering this volume. First, the authors who contributed to this volume for their patience and generosity and the photographers and theatres who shared images, resources, and time, including: Oleg Chernous, Tristam Kenton, Gala Lavrinets, Stefan Okołowicz, Małgorzata Makowska, Dražen Smaranduj, Teatro de la Abadía Madrid, Pavón Teatro Kamikaze Madrid, Sala Beckett Barcelona, Galway Arts Festival, TR Warszawa, Mladinsko Theatre Ljubljana, Sava Ognyanov Drama Theatre Ruse, Dramaten Stockholm, Schaubühne Berlin, Chekhov Moscow Arts Theatre, Wild Theatre Kyiv, Royal Lyceum Theatre Edinburgh and Zagreb Youth Theatre.

Thanks also to those whose conversations with us enriched this volume: Elizabeth Angel-Perez, Lola Arias, Miguel del Arco, Matthew Cornish, Kate Dorney, Nuria Espert, Clare Finburgh Delijani, Maggie Gale, Lia Ghilardi, Lynette Goddard, Jean Graham-Jones, Ágnes Havas, Agnieszka Jakimiak, Marcin Kościelniak, Jean-Marc Lanteri, Bárbara Lluch, Katie Mitchell, Marcos Ordóñez, Jen Parker-Starbuck, Lluís Pasqual, Andrea Peghinelli, José María Pou, Mark Ravenhill, Talia Rodgers, Tiina Rosenberg, Mercè Saumell, Aleks Sierz, Joanne Tompkins, Elisabeth Wennerström, Simon Williams, and Marilena Zaroulia. Karen Jürs-Munby and Lisa Moravec co-produced an excellent translation of Hans-Thies Lehmann's portrait of Peter Handke – and particular thanks to Karen for the additional translation of Lehmann's response to Handke's Nobel Prize. Peter Boenisch offered helpful advice far beyond the bounds of his own chapter in this volume. Our thanks to Ben Piggott, Laura Soppelsa, Zoe Forbes, and Kate Edwards at Routledge for their support for the project and to James Rowson for his work on the index.

Maria Delgado would like to acknowledge the assistance of The Royal Central School of Speech and Drama, University of London's Targeted Completion Fund for their financial support of this volume. Thanks are due also to Joshua Abrams, Ross Brown, Broderick Chow, Stephen Farrier, Tony Fisher, Dan Hetherington, Kate Pitt, and colleagues in the European Theatre Research Network. She would also like to acknowledge the conversations and discussions with colleagues on the International Ibsen Award Committee: Anders Beyer, Roman Dolzhanskiy, Kilkka-Liisa Iivanainen, Ingrid Lorentzen, Thomas Oberender, and Hanne Tømta. Bryce Lease would like to thank Olga

Drygas at Nowy Teatr for her assistance with tickets to relevant performances and sourcing images. He would also like to acknowledge the many members of the Instytut Teatralny in Warsaw for their excellent and under-appreciated work in generating and caring for crucial theatre and performance archives. Changes in government and funding structures continue to put such institutions at risk across Europe. Delgado and Lease's work on the book has also been supported by the AHRC-funded project, 'Staging Difficult Pasts: Of Narratives, Objects and Public Memory' (Grant Reference: AH/R006849/1). Dan Rebellato would like to thank the Universities and Colleges Union for calling a strike that, ironically, opened up time and space to finish work on this book.

Thanks also to Henry Little, Tom Delgado-Little, Martin Schnabl, Lilla Rebellato, and Ethan Blue Rebellato.

David Bradby wrote so eloquently about playwrights in Europe. His star continues to burn bright and his memory and legacy continues to be an inspiration in troubling times.

Contributors

David Barnett is Professor of Theatre at the University of York. He has published monographs of Heiner Müller (1998), Rainer Werner Fassbinder (2005), Bertolt Brecht (2014), and The Berliner Ensemble (2015). He has written articles and essays on German, English-language, political, and postdramatic theatre.

Noah Birksted-Breen is a theatre-maker and scholar, specialising in new writing in the UK and Russia. He founded Sputnik Theatre Company – the only British company dedicated solely to bringing new Russian plays to UK stages. For Sputnik, he has directed and/or translated new Russian plays for Soho Theatre, BBC Radio 3's Drama of the Week, Southwark Playhouse, and Theatre Royal Plymouth (http://sputniktheatre.co.uk). Noah is Postdoctoral Research Associate at Oxford University, working on the AHRC-funded project Creative Multilingualism.

Peter M. Boenisch is Professor of Dramaturgy at Aarhus University, and Professor of European Theatre at The Royal Central School of Speech and Drama, University of London. His research specialisms are directing and dramaturgy in Continental European theatre, politics of theatre aesthetics, and institutional critique of theatre production. His publications include *Directing Scenes & Senses: The Thinking of Regie* (2015) and (co-authored with Thomas Ostermeier), *The Theatre of Thomas Ostermeier* (2016).

Maria M. Delgado is Professor and Director of Research at The Royal Central School of Speech and Drama, University of London, and co-editor of *Contemporary Theatre Review*. She has published widely in the area of Spanish- and Catalan-language theatres. Her books include *Federico García Lorca* (2008), *'Other' Spanish Theatres* (2003, revised Spanish-language edition 2017), and ten co-edited volumes.

Molly Flynn is a Lecturer in Theatre and Performance at Birkbeck, University of London and the author of *Witness Onstage: Documentary Theatre in Twenty-First-Century Russia* (2019). Molly's research focuses on social theatre practice in Russia and Ukraine. Her writing has appeared in *New Theatre Quarterly, RiDE: The Journal of Applied Theatre and Performance, Problems of*

Post-Communism, and *Open Democracy.* In addition to her work as a teacher and researcher, Molly is a theatre-maker and a co-founder of the US-based theatre collective the New York Neo-Futurists.

Marissia Fragkou is Senior Lecturer in Performing Arts at Canterbury Christ Church University. She has published on contemporary British and European theatre and performance as well as performance and cultural politics, ethics of responsibility, and radical democratic politics. Her monograph entitled *Ecologies of Precarity in Twenty-First Century Theatre: Affect, Politics, Responsibility* was published by Bloomsbury Methuen in 2018. She has also co-edited a special issue on contemporary Greek theatre with Dr Philip Hager for *The Journal of Greek Media and Culture* (2017).

Dominic Glynn is Assistant Professor in Translation at the City University of Hong Kong. He is currently leading research projects on transnational theatre practices and on the translation of French plays to the UK stages. Previously, he was the principal investigator of an Arts and Humanities Research Network Grant entitled 'Literature under Constraint', which investigated how different factors (mind-sets, political contexts, social environments, intermediaries) shape and constrain contemporary literary production. Publications include *(Re)Telling Old Stories* (2015) and *Lignes de fuite* (2015), as well as co-edited volumes *Littéraire. Pour Alain Viala*, volumes 1 & 2 (2018).

Kélina Gotman is Reader in Theatre and Performance Studies at King's College London, and author of *Choreomania: Dance and Disorder* (2018) and *Essays on Theatre and Change* (2018), as well as co-editor of *Foucault's Theatres* (2019). She is editor of the four-volume *Theories of Performance: Critical and Primary Sources* (2021), and translator among others of Marie NDiaye's *The Snakes* (2016) and Félix Guattari's *The Anti-Oedipus Papers* (2006), as well as various plays for production. She was Hölderlin Guest Professor in Comparative Dramaturgy at the Goethe Universität Frankfurt (2019).

David Greig's plays include *Europe, The Architect, The Cosmonaut's Last Message to the Woman He Once Loved in the Former Soviet Union, Outlying Islands, San Diego, Pyrenees, The American Pilot, Yellow Moon, Midsummer, Dunsinane, The Strange Undoing of Prudencia Hart, The Events,* as well as versions of Camus's *Caligula,* Euripides's *The Bacchae,* Strindberg's *Creditors,* Aeschylus's *The Suppliant Women,* and adaptations of *Charlie and the Chocolate Factory, The Lorax, Local Hero, Solaris,* and *Touching the Void.* He co-founded the theatre company Suspect Culture in 1990 and in 2016 was appointed Artistic Director of the Royal Lyceum Theatre in Edinburgh. His work has been widely produced across Europe and beyond.

Andrew Haydon is a freelance theatre critic based in Manchester. He has written for the *Guardian, Nachtkritik.de, Frakcija, Kultrpunkt.hr, Szinhaz.hu,* and *Exeunt,* among others. He blogs at Postcards from the Gods (http://postcardsgods.blogspot.co.uk).

xiv *List of contributors*

Rikard Hoogland is Associate Professor in Theatre Studies at Stockholm University. He received his PhD in 2005 and teaches across theatre history, contemporary theatre, and performance and cultural policy. He has published in peer-reviewed journals – including *Nordic Theatre Studies* and the *Nordic Journal of Culture Policy* – and in anthologies published by Cambridge University Press, Ohlms, Palgrave, and Rodopi et. al. In 2017, he was a visiting scholar at Freie Universität, Berlin. Between 2014 and 2017, he was part of the research project 'Turning Points and Continuity: The Changing Roles of Performance in Society 1880–1925', financed by the Swedish Research Council.

Karen Jürs-Munby is a Senior Lecturer in Theatre Studies at the University of Lancaster, UK. She translated and wrote a critical introduction for Hans-Thies Lehmann's *Postdramatic Theatre* (2006). Together with Jerome Carroll and Steve Giles, she co-edited *Postdramatic Theatre and the Political* (2013). Her publications on Elfriede Jelinek include the special issue *Jelinek in the Arena* (Austrian Studies 22, 2014), co-edited with Allyson Fiddler. She is currently completing a monograph on the innovative postdramatic stagings of Jelinek's theatre texts by major German directors. *Jelinek in Practice: German Directors' Theatre, Politics and Aesthetics* will be published by Bloomsbury Methuen Drama.

Jozefina Komporaly lectures in performance at the University of the Arts, London, and translates from Hungarian and Romanian into English. Jozefina is editor and co-translator of the critical anthologies *Matéi Visniec: How to Explain the History of Communism to Mental Patients and Other Plays* (2015) and *András Visky's Barrack Dramaturgy: Memories of the Body* (2017). She published extensively on translation and adaptation for the stage in a European and British context, such as the monographs *Staging Motherhood* (2006) and *Radical Revival as Adaptation: Theatre, Politics, Society* (2017).

Margherita Laera is a Senior Lecturer in Drama and Theatre at the University of Kent, Canterbury, and Co-Director of the European Theatre Research Network. She is the author of *Theatre & Translation* (2019) and *Reaching Athens: Community, Democracy and Other Mythologies in Adaptations of Greek Tragedy* (2013), and the editor of *Theatre and Adaptation: Return, Rewrite, Repeat* (2014). Margherita is also a theatre translator working with Italian and English. Her research on theatre translation won the Theatre and Performance Research Association's Early Career Research Prize for 2018. Margherita is the Online Editor for *Theatre Journal* and *Theatre Topics.*

Bryce Lease is Reader in Theatre and Performance Studies at Royal Holloway, University of London and co-editor of *Contemporary Theatre Review*. His publications on Polish theatre include his monograph *After '89: Polish Theatre and the Political* (2016), the forthcoming co-edited volume *The History of Polish Theatre* (2021), and numerous articles. Between 2018–21, he is

List of contributors   xv

leading the AHRC-funded project 'Staging Difficult Pasts: Of Narratives, Objects and Public Memory'.

Hans–Thies Lehmann was the University Professor for Theatre Studies at the Johann Wolfgang Goethe-University in Frankfurt am Main (1988–2010) and has been Visiting Professor to numerous Universities in Europe and the USA. His numerous publications include: *Theater und Mythos* (1991) on the constitution of the subject in ancient Greek tragedy, *Writing the Political* (2002), *Heiner Müller Handbuch* (with Patrick Primavesi, 2004), and *Postdramatic Theatre,* first published in 1999 and translated in to 26 languages.

Patrick Lonergan is Professor of Drama and Theatre Studies at National University of Ireland, Galway and a member of the Royal Irish Academy. He is the author of many books on Irish theatre, including *Theatre and Globalization* (Winner of the 2008 Theatre Book Prize) and *Irish Drama and Theatre Since 1950* (2019).

Duška Radosavljević is a dramaturg and Reader in Contemporary Theatre and Performance at The Royal Central School of Speech and Drama. She is the author of award-winning *Theatre-Making* (2013) and editor of *The Contemporary Ensemble* (2013) and *Theatre Criticism: Changing Landscapes* (2016). Her work has been funded by the AHRC, including The Mums and Babies Ensemble project in 2015 and the Aural/Oral Dramaturgies Leadership Fellowship (2020–21). She regularly writes for *The Stage, Exeunt,* and *The Theatre Times.*

Dan Rebellato is Professor of Contemporary Theatre at Royal Holloway, University of London. He has published widely on post-war British theatre, and his books include *1956 and All That* (1999), *Theatre and Globalization* (2009), *Modern British Playwriting: 2000–2009* (2013), the *Cambridge Companion to British Theatre since 1945*, and the *Cambridge Companion to Contemporary British Plays and Playwriting* (2020). He is co-editor, with Jen Harvie, of the 'Theatre &' series, which contains around 50 titles and counting. He is also a playwright whose works have been performed on stage and radio in Britain, Europe, and the USA.

Tiago Rodrigues is a director, writer, and actor. Having directed the Mundo Perfeito company for 12 years alongside Magda Bizarro, where he staged over 30 works, he is now the artistic director of Portuguese National Theatre D. Maria II, since 2015. His many productions include *By Heart, Antony and Cleopatra, Bovary* and *Sopro.* In 2018 he was awarded the XV Europe Prize Theatrical Realities for his contribution to theatre in Europe and in 2019 he became one of the youngest recipients ever of the prestigious Pessoa Prize. His work has been widely seen across Europe and beyond.

xvi *List of contributors*

Elizabeth Sakellaridou is Professor Emerita of Theatre Studies at Aristotle University of Thessaloniki, Greece. She has taught widely on contemporary theatre in Greece, elsewhere in Europe, and the USA. She has published on contemporary British and European theatre, classical and modern Greek theatre, performance theory, cultural and gender studies, and, more recently, the hybrid space of performance phenomenology. Her publications include *Pinter's Female Portraits* (1988), *Contemporary Women's Theatre* (2006), *Theatre, Aesthetics, Politics* (2012), and numerous articles and chapters published in international journals and collected volumes. She is also a critic, dramaturg, and translator of dramatic works from English and Greek.

Foreword

Tiago Rodrigues

Letter to Ikram, the student from Toulouse

Dear Ikram, you wrote me a letter ten months ago. In this letter you apologised for the fact that you and one of your friends had left the theatre during a show I was presenting at Théâtre Garonne, in Toulouse. As you might remember, I was very upset when you stood up in the audience during a very silent and vulnerable moment. From the stage, I watched you and your friend walk towards the exit. Everybody in the venue could hear your footsteps. I stopped the performance and asked: 'Why are you leaving when the show is clearly about to end?' I couldn't understand why you couldn't wait for another minute. It didn't look like there was an emergency or something of the kind that might force you to leave. You heard my question from the stage, looked at me but didn't answer. Then you proceeded to the exit, opened the door and left.

The next day you wrote me a letter and sent it to the theatre. In this letter, you explained that when you were leaving, you hadn't realised the impact of your action. It was only the following day, in theatre class in your high school, that you started to look at things differently. Your classmates probably told you how I reacted after you left. I was very frustrated. I tried to get back to the text I had to say on stage but couldn't. I was angry. I overreacted. I think that, at one point, I even told the audience that you had broken my heart. I normally don't react this strongly when spectators leave one of my shows. It's always a bit harmful, but being an actor is also about learning to deal with the fact that sometimes people don't want to look at or hear you anymore. Why was this time different? Because it was the end of the performance and also its most intimate and relevant moment. Because it felt personal.

By Heart is the title of this play that you watched for 99 per cent of its duration. As you might remember, it consists largely of me teaching Sonnet 30 by William Shakespeare to ten people that have agreed to come on stage just at the beginning of the performance. While I teach the poem, I tell several stories about the importance of learning texts by heart involving writers like George Steiner, Boris Pasternak, Osip Mandelstam, Ray Bradbury, and others. I also tell the story of my grandmother Cândida, who is the main reason why I wrote and perform this play. When she was 93 years old and about to go blind, my grandmother asked me to choose a book for her to learn by heart so that she

xviii *Foreword*

could continue reading when her eyes finally failed her. By writing this play, I wanted to talk about the infinite saving power of words and also about the invisible and universal connection that literature can reveal between a humble cook in a small village in the mountains of Portugal and a Nobel Prize winning writer in Russia. Somehow, the whole play is about which book I chose for my grandmother and if she actually learned it by heart. When you got up and left the room, dear Ikram, we had arrived at the last minute of this hour and a half show, in which I was about to reveal the answer to both these questions.

I'm not writing this to make you feel even worse than you did when you wrote to me. On the contrary. I'm just trying to explain why I reacted so strongly to your exit. At that moment, I could only think of two reasons for you leaving the show at that given moment. Reason number 1: you just weren't paying any attention to the show; hence you had no idea what was going on and you didn't realise you were disturbing the most crucial moment of my performance, equivalent to the revelation of who is the murderer in a crime story or the moment when Berenice delivers her final monologue in Racine's tragedy. Reason number 2: you *were* paying attention to the show, fully understood what was going on, but decided to state that you didn't give a damn about me, my grandmother, and the whole effort put in to that evening of theatre. The first hypothesis would mean I had failed to grab your attention for an hour and a half. The second one would mean that you were quite rude, to say the least. After I read the letter you sent me with your heartfelt apologies, I was sure it was the first one. I had failed. And for that, I'm sorry.

During the past ten months, I've been meaning to answer your letter. I've kept it in my notebook for almost a year, taking it with me to rehearsals, work meetings, performances, tours in several countries, from Spain to Uruguay, from Norway to Austria. Every time I would finish a notebook I would transfer your letter to the newly-bought still-blank notebook. I thought of writing to you several times, but I always convinced myself that I was too busy or too tired or I would come up with some other excuse. Then, something happened that impelled me to finally answer your letter. Some days ago, one of my country's greatest artists died. His name is José Mário Branco. He was a songwriter who left an enduring impression on generations of Portuguese, both for his musical and literary genius as well as for his civic and political engagement. He was involved in the recording of the song that was played on the radio as code by the young captains that propelled the Carnation Revolution in 1974, allowing Portugal to become a democracy and leading to the independence of ex-colonies such as Angola, Mozambique, Cape Vert, and Guinea-Bissau. There are many amazing stories about José Mário Branco, but one of them concerns Lisbon's National Theatre – Teatro Nacional D. Maria II – where I currently work. Nine years ago, José Mário Branco was at the theatre, collaborating on a performance, for which he had composed music. They say that, one evening, there were not that many people in the audience and the artists were obviously disappointed. José Mário Branco is told to have entered the dressing rooms and said: 'You must never count how many people are in the audience. When you go on stage you are always performing for the whole of humanity'.

I have always considered this the best and also most exaggerated motivational speech you can offer to actors when there is not a large audience in the house. However, when I heard the news of José Mário Branco's death, I remembered this story and I knew immediately that I had to write to you. This story explained to me clearly that it was my time to apologise and give some explanations. I want you to know that the reason why I considered that I'd failed you that February evening when you left Théâtre Garonne is that the audience has always been at the centre of my work. I consider the audience not only a witness but also a protagonist of any theatre performance. When I'm writing a play, I imagine that all the white space I leave on the page will be filled by the audience's reactions, laughter, silence, imagination. I believe that we're only doing theatre when we're in front of an audience. Writing, rehearsing, designing sets and costumes and lights is not theatre. It's preparing for theatre. Theatre only happens when people like you, dear Ikram, enter a space and take part in everything we prepared during the previous months. As with many other playwrights I know, I try to write stories that touch people somehow. I surround myself with other people who want to do the same and we build theatre performances that are capsules or portraits of the time we lived together, our debates and our collective imagination. And then we share it with people who are only there once and, hopefully, the effort of making the performance makes even more sense than before. So, you see, it's easy for a show to become very personal to an actor or an author.

One could say that one writes theatre to start a conversation with the whole of humanity. At least, I try to do so. But, as I write it, I realise how grand and solemn it sounds to talk about 'the whole of humanity'. What I mean is *you*. Someone like you and your friend. People one is not yet acquainted with: the others. After 20 years working in theatre, I still find it inexplicable that so many people come together and sit to watch a performance. In societies controlled by the laws of profit, where one is told that one's value is proportional to the lack of effort one had to spend in order to get something, I am puzzled that people still go to theatres. At a time where information, entertainment, groceries, and whatnot is available at the distance of a click on a screen, it's fantastic that people still leave their houses, spend time and money crossing the city, to go to a theatre where it will probably be too cold or too hot and sit rubbing elbows next to perfect strangers, having spent money on a ticket to watch something they still aren't sure they will like. If you go to a supermarket, you want to make sure that you get your money's worth and you buy the yogurt you know you like for the best price possible. At the box office you buy a ticket to a mystery and you even say to theatre artists: 'take my time, control it, my precious time, my most valued treasure, I'll pay you, do what you want with it!' If you think about it, probably never before was going to the theatre such a political and rebellious act as nowadays. The simple fact of watching a theatre show is already, somehow, going against all odds and challenging the rules.

xx   *Foreword*

Hopefully, by sharing the way I see the audience and the agnostic miracle of their presence on the theatre, you are closer to understanding why I had such a strong reaction to your exit from the venue while I was performing. But I want to reassure you that you are not alone. There are many people that feel like leaving shows before they're over. I know I have been one of those people more often than I'd like to admit. In some way, I admire your bravery. You have, like any audience member, the right to get up and leave. You were brave enough to exercise that right when no one else dared to do so. And I don't doubt there might have been more people at the Théâtre Garonne that felt like leaving that evening. And, by the way, if we are talking about 'the whole of humanity', we must not forget the huge majority of people that never leave a theatre venue because they've never entered it in the first place.

However, both in Portugal, where I live, as well as in France, where you live, there are many playwrights trying to start conversations with humanity in different ways. Actually, across Europe you have hundreds of different conversations starting. And if one single playwright can't yet address the whole of humanity, a wide range of theatre authors of our time might be close to doing it collectively. Maybe I was not the right one for you. Maybe you feel that going to the theatre is too conventional, a gesture filled with too much protocol and codes that you think you don't know enough about. If that's the case, I advise you to discover the theatre of, among others, Jon Fosse, who accuses theatre of being more convention than art and is disgusted at the stuffy mannerisms of conventional theatre. Maybe you feel like the stories being told are not for you, or about people like you, or told by people like you. I can assure you those are issues that many playwrights are dealing with for decades and I believe great progress is being made. In many of her plays, debbie tucker green addresses such questions, writing the stories of Black women and men, and searching for a theatre written for people who will feel it, for people who come out saying 'That just like my aunty' or 'That's just like me'. And she's not alone in the diverse and vibrant landscape of living European theatre writers. Maybe you feel that life is much harder than the soft way it's portrayed on stage. Then, I'd challenge you to plunge into the theatre of Elfriede Jelinek, profoundly committed to writing about abuses in public and political life, or that of Sarah Kane, savagely investigating the borders between self and other, or even Emma Dante, a master at uncovering the unease and the problems people tend to suppress. Maybe you watch theatre and you feel that actors talk like they're in a book, aloof and distant from real life. But then don't hesitate to go and watch a play by Enda Walsh, for instance, with his feverish first-take colloquial approach to dialogue that can turn your world upside down. Or Spiro Scimone, with his inventive dialect that transforms everyday situations into magical insights into human nature. Or Pascal Rambert, with his furious non-stop ranting characters that seem truer than life.

I'm sure that, somewhere in Europe, there's a playwright who will be perfect to start a conversation with you, dear Ikram. All across the continent, writers are engaged in examining the past and the present. Either confronting the narrow limits of social and religious traditions or revealing the painful stories of colonial or dictatorial roots, the past is being questioned in theatre venues. Calling out current phenomena and approaching the intimate and public human experience in all its complexity, the stage is interfering with the present. Public and independent theatres across Europe are the places where disruptive new stories are being told. And they're also the place where old stories and myths are being questioned, rewritten, and told in the language of our time. Maybe they're not the right place for you to easily find that comfortable entertainment that people look for 'just to get rid of the problems of daily life', but that kind of spectacle is almost everywhere else. And those are not conversations. They might be crowd-pleasing mainstream stories, but you can be sure they're not directed at 'the whole of humanity'. They're often directed at what one minority imposes as normality, but 'the whole of humanity' is often living in neighbourhoods that entertainment rarely visits. In public and independent theatres, there's a limit to the number of people that can fill the seats or the amount of money you can make out of it. Probably that's why, many times with public support, it's in these theatres that you'll find the stories crafted with most freedom. Where profit doesn't run the game, and where experimentation and innovation thrive. All over Europe, you can find playwrights that are writing in order to overcome the obstacles that we inherited from history or to bring down the walls that fear-mongering politicians are trying to raise. All over Europe, you can find many alternative ideas of what Europe is about. And that's why we have to protect and support these places where another way of telling stories is still possible, the places where the untold and the unseen are being imagined for you and the whole of humanity.

So, you see, dear Ikram, there's an almost endless menu of theatrical banquets at your disposal. I might have failed you, but some other author won't. Your story is out there for you to find it. And you don't have to travel the continent to do it. Translators and theatre companies are making sure that many of these stories are staged in many countries. Theatres and festivals are making sure that these stories travel, crossing borders and enlarging horizons. I'm confident that you will find your story at Théâtre Garonne or any of the other theatres of Toulouse. And if that doesn't happen, you can tell your own story. I didn't forget that you reveal in your letter that you're a theatre student. You can do what many European playwrights are also doing: when they didn't find the stories that they wanted to see in theatres, they started writing those stories themselves. If you do that, if you start writing and persuade some of your friends to stage that play in Toulouse, I promise I'll do my best to be in the audience. I will play the role of 'the whole humanity', even if just for one evening. And, most of all, I promise not to leave before it's over.

Tiago Rodrigues
18 December 2019

Introduction

Maria M. Delgado, Bryce Lease and Dan Rebellato

On 11 October 2019, Peter Handke was announced as the 116th winner of the Nobel Prize for Literature 'for an influential work', the Committee argued, 'that with linguistic ingenuity has explored the periphery and the specificity of human experience' (nobelprize.org). The award was greeted with a degree of incredulity across much of Europe, not merely because the Committee had appeared to renege on a commitment to ensure the award be 'less male' and 'Eurocentric' (Cain 2019), but because of Handke's controversial position in relation to the Serbian atrocities that followed the break-up of Yugoslavia in the 1990s. Novelist Jennifer Egan, President of PEN America, broke with convention on Handke's announcement as the 2019 recipient of the Prize: PEN 'does not generally comment on other institutions' literary awards' but, she went on to state,

> Today's announcement must be an exception … We are dumbfounded by the selection of a writer who has used his public voice to undercut historical truth and offer public succor to perpetrators of genocide, like former Serbian President Slobodan Milošević and Bosnian Serb leader Radovan Karadžić. We reject the decision that a writer who has persistently called into question thoroughly documented war crimes deserves to be celebrated for his 'linguistic ingenuity.' At a moment of rising nationalism, autocratic leadership, and widespread disinformation around the world, the literary community deserves better than this.
>
> (cited in Cain 2019)

Andrea Aguilar of Spain's *El País*, charting the disquiet of writers like Joyce Carol Oates, Salmon Rushdie, and Slavoj Žižek to the news, noted that a petition in Kosovo had garnered 30,000 names in less than 24 hours to have Handke stripped of the prize (Aguilar 2019). Elsewhere, Handke's prize was celebrated by playwright Elfriede Jelinek ('He should have won it before me'), filmmaker Wim Wenders, and theatre director Claus Peymann, as well as Austria's left-leaning President Alexander Van del Bellen. In Poland, the critic and translator Monika Muskała was explicitly critical of Handke's actions, such as his participation in Milošević's funeral; nevertheless, she wondered if underlying the media's attack on Handke there might lie 'the bad conscience of Europe' for its own failures in Bosnia and asked whether 'the furious attacks on Handke are also a kind of expiation?' (Muskała 2019).

2   *Maria Delgado et al.*

Handke's Nobel Prize is a powerful reminder of the intertwining of art and politics and theatre's public, civic role to engage in debates over – and question our complicity in – political violence, the failures of democracy, and historical injustice. The Nobel controversy raised a number of issues about the role of the playwright at the end of the second decade of the twenty-first century where 'fake truths' circulate, the 'non-European other' is demonised, and the vision of open borders is under attack once again. What responsibilities does the playwright hold in such a world and how does she exert them? What commitment does she have to the truth? Can she represent the other without misrepresenting them? How might new play forms interrogate our changing continent? And how far can she trouble the relationship between the writer and society, between stage and audience? These are central questions negotiated by the dramatists discussed in this volume.

European *playwriting*

Contemporary European Playwrights samples a range of key writers who have radically reshaped European writing and whose work is in dialogue with Europe today. These are 'generative' playwrights whose work circulates across the continent, staged in different languages and productions, whose writing has opened up dramaturgical possibilities of style, form, and subject for other writers and enabled new kinds of work in performance. Some have strong connections with a particular theatre in their home country – as in Martin Crimp's association with the Royal Court, Dorota Masłowska with Warsaw's TR Warszawa, or Marius von Mayenburg with Berlin's Schaubühne – but all have achieved a strong profile across Europe and beyond. To cover as wide a range of writers as possible and to allow for sharp and productive dialogue across the book, most chapters pair related playwrights to contrast or compare their histories, styles, aims, and attitudes. Within and between chapters, then, there are continuities and contrasts. The volume mixes many well-established and familiar names (Handke, Jelinek, Mark Ravenhill) with those whose impact is more recent (Natalia Vorozhbyt, Lena Kitsopoulou, Alice Birch).

While many of these writers have worked principally within the subsidised sector (as with the Presniakov Brothers, Marie NDiaye, Weronika Szczawińska, Fausto Paravidino), others have forged reputations often in the commercial theatre. Jordi Galceran, Martin McDonagh, Yasmina Reza, Enda Walsh, and Florian Zeller have reached audiences in their millions. Translated into 30 languages, Reza's *Art*, reworking the comedy of manners, and, a little short of two decades from its premiere, was reported to have grossed close to £200m (Day 2012). In 1997, McDonagh had four plays running in the West End simultaneously (see Lonergan 2012b) and Ravenhill, Walsh, and David Greig have all written librettos for musicals. As of 2018, there are over 60 translations of Galceran's 2003 play *El método Grönholm* (*The Grönholm Method*) (Ordóñez 2018).

Introduction 3

We have sought to offer different models of playwriting – from Marius von Mayenburg's conceptual allegories to the philosophical realism of Juan Mayorga; the 'poor theatre' of Emma Dante to the ornate Beckettian wordplay of Enda Walsh; the austere elegance of Jon Fosse to the political commentaries of Roland Schimmelpfennig; the playful paraphrases of Paweł Demirski to the 'barrack dramaturgy' of András Visky. Crucially, dramatists have been chosen that allow for a discussion of wider schools of writing (as in Kane and Ravenhill's complex allegiance to 'In Yer Face' or to the 'Blood and Sperm Generation') or to reveal chains of influence and effect (as with Ivan Vyrypaev and his wider influence on figures such as Natalia Vorozhbyt or Jelinek's impact on Werner Schwab). Furthermore, the selection allows for comparative examples to inform the discussion, such as the Presniakov Brothers' black satire in juxtaposition with Vasilii Sigarev's poetic realism.

Many of these writers (Crimp, Fosse, Kane, Mayenburg, for example) resonate with Hans-Thies Lehmann's argument that postdramatic strategies more accurately address contemporary social issues – ranging from neoliberalism to terrorism and post-identity politics – than traditional forms of drama (Lehmann 2006: 16–28). What's more, the turn towards more collaborative forms of writing in the form of director–writer partnerships (as in Paweł Demirski and Monika Strzępka, or Simon Stephens and Sebastian Nübling) or the use of improvisation and sustained rehearsal processes with particular theatre companies has offered writers alternative approaches to playwriting. Some of the playwrights regularly (Dante, Paravidino, Walsh) or occasionally (Mayorga, debbie tucker green) direct their own work.

Our selection of playwrights moves across the breadth of Europe from Ireland (Walsh) to Russia (Sigarev, the Presniakov Brothers, Vyrypaev) and the Ukraine (Vorozhbyt). There are writers here from the continent's southern nations: Spain (Mayorga and Galceran), Italy (Dante and Paravidino), Greece (Kitsopoulou and Yannis Mavritsakis). And there are also several from Europe's northern edge (Lars Norén, Fosse, Jonas Hassen Khemiri). Several of these playwrights emerged in nations still coming out from the shadow of Soviet domination: Poland (Demirski, Masłowska, Szczawińska, Agnieszka Jakimiak), the former Yugoslavia (Biljana Srbljanović and Ivana Sajko), Romania (Matéi Visniec and Visky). Several writers who have resisted Britain's notorious insularity to engage with the wider European theatre culture are represented here (Ravenhill, Greig, Kane, tucker green, Birch, Stephens, Crimp). Some of these dramatists have themselves migrated (Visniec), or are the descendants of migrants (McDonagh, NDiaye, Khemiri, Reza) and reflect the shifting boundaries of a continent that has been refashioned in the aftermath of 1989.

Indeed, the issue of migrancy runs across the volume. Jozefina Komporaly frames Visniec within a broader culture of Romanian writers based outside their country of birth: Visniec, like Alexandra Badea, is based in Paris, Ştefan Peca lives in Berlin, Alexandra Pâzgu in Giessen. Visky, like his colleague Csaba Székely, grew up as a Hungarian speaker in Romania as a result of the cultural displacements brought about the Treaty of Trianon following the First

4   *Maria Delgado et al.*

World War. Linguistic dexterity is, as Galceran (working across both Catalan and Castilian) shows, part of what it means to work across boundaries. Such border crossing results in shared concerns, such as the widespread implications of a post-2007 double-dip economic recession in Spain, Italy, and Greece which feature in the chapters on Galceran, Mayorga, Dante, Paravidino, Kitsopoulou, and Mavritsakis. Other borders are destabilised, as with the chapter on Srbljanović and Sajko where the focus is on the specific socio-historical context that has shaped contemporary Serbia and Croatia in a mode that reaches across difference rather than asserting it. Greig's afterword focuses on his new version of Aeschylus's *Hiketides* (*The Suppliant Women*) a play about refugees, Europe, and democracy from the infancy of European theatre.

While seeking geographical coverage, we have also attempted to bring together different generations of writers – from those whose trajectories were forged before 1989 to those who have emerged in the twenty-first century. Rebellato's opening chapter offers a sweep across five decades to offer a sense of the 'dramaturgical imaginary' produced by those postwar playwrights who attempted to engage and resist, interrogate and elude political authority, and left a series of templates for the post-1989 generations to adopt, adapt, or reject. All of these writers (apart from Schwab and Kane) are alive at the time of writing, but many of them, regardless of their international eminence, have been subject to little critical work in the English language.[1] This book analyses some of the most important playwrights in Europe since 1989, but, in many cases, it will almost certainly *introduce* a large number of these playwrights, because cultures select in complex and subtle ways the writers that speak to them.

European playwriting?

The book aims also to start a conversation about the contemporary European dramatic repertoire, seen in the round. It is clear from all of these chapters that there are chains of influence linking many writers across national boundaries. It is tempting to speculate that as we see the influence of Kane on Mayenburg, of Müller on Crimp, Ravenhill on Paravidino, and more that some kind of larger European dramaturgy is being developed. Such a thought would chime with the recent revival of interest in the idea of 'world literature', as famously predicted in *The Communist Manifesto*:

> In place of the old local and national seclusion and self-sufficiency, we have intercourse in every direction, universal inter-dependence of nations. And as in material, so also in intellectual production. The intellectual creations of individual nations become common property. National one-sidedness and narrow-mindedness become more and more impossible, and from the numerous national and local literatures, there arises a world literature.
>
> (Marx and Engels 2002: 223–4)

The evidence is not perhaps yet conclusive that our contact with other nations has eliminated narrow-mindedness and insularity, yet many of the *Manifesto's* other predictions have been borne out in the various manifestations of globalisation over the last 40 years.

Has a world literature begun to arise? And is it a good thing? As Aijaz Ahmad writes, it is easy to miss Marx's dialectic in the *Manifesto*, and forget that 'what he requires us to do is to view capitalism as both – *simultaneously* – the best as well as the worst thing that ever happened to history' (2000: 7). Of course, the notion of a world literature has been powerfully critiqued by postcolonial scholars who understand the expression of such a development as uneven and unequal, as another form of colonisation or domination that marginalises just as it seeks to think 'globally'. We might ask if the development of a 'European Drama' also obfuscates the power politics of influence, subsidy, accessibility across north and south, east and west. Nevertheless, the question remains whether European playwriting is something more than the aggregate of plays produced on the continent.

The idea of a transnational theatre community has had its vicissitudes over the last century. Plays have crossed national borders for over two millennia, sometimes through tours and revivals, sometimes through theft and appropriation. More formally, the Berne Convention of 1886 helped reduce the theft and encouraged free dramaturgical movement by establishing a system of mutual recognition of author's rights in their work. More grandly, in the 1920s, French actor-director Firmin Gémier proposed a 'Société Universelle du Théâtre', in the League of Nations' spirit of international cooperation and it ran, organising conferences, helping facilitate the exchange of knowledge and skills, until European conflict overshadowed such cosmopolitan efforts in the second half of the 1930s. It was, however, a forerunner of the International Theatre Institute established after the Second World War in 1948 under the wing of UNESCO, organising conferences, festivals and World Theatre Day. The founding of international theatre festivals – most famously in Edinburgh and Avignon in 1947, one month apart – may be a sign of a benign internationalisation of theatre or, as some have argued (e.g. Zaiontz 2018: 69–91), a commodification of international theatre that, rather than rising to a world theatre status, just produces the internationally inoffensive.

The topic of a world literature has been much debated. Franco Moretti's influential essays on the topic (2000, 2003) seek to restore culture to the narrowly economistic discourse around global integration. By contrast, Pascale Casanova (2007 [orig. 1999]) argues for the existence of a 'world literary space' with 'its own economy, which produces hierarchies and various forms of violence; and, above all, its own history' (11). Casanova's model seems to duplicate the economic priorities of contemporary market capitalism, and, in imagining this world literary space as a dynamic system of literary-market transactions between centre and periphery as world-literary works rise and fall in world favour, might seem to be offering a rather Eurocentric, even Parisian view of the world. David Damrosch argues that a 'world literature' does not

6   *Maria Delgado et al.*

rise *above* cultural difference, as Casanova seems to suggest, but is distinguished by its very negotiation *of* cultural difference, its ability to be sustained and enriched in cultural and linguistic translation: 'the variability of a work of literature is one of its constitutive features' (2003: 5). Sceptical of all of this is Emily Apter's *Against World Literature* (2013), which observes that even in Damrosch's celebration of translatorly difference there is an assumption of smooth continuities across linguistic and cultural faultlines that marginalise the 'untranslatable', the stubbornly resistant incommensurabilities of linguistic systems that must be appreciated in all their global melancholy.

Here we have an opportunity to observe some of the smooth and bumpy routes that several dramatic texts have taken. At times the 'fit' between a source text and a target culture seems so exact as to erase difference in the way that Casanova celebrates (e.g. Reza in Britain); at times a play can take on a vividly different meaning in its new cultural context (e.g. Ravenhill in Germany); sometimes what seems to be displayed is the play of difference, the irreducible otherness of the text, the difficulty of hospitality, the cultural exchange itself dramatised and presented (as in the Ukrainian, German, and British collaboration *Three Kingdoms*, see pp. 122–126). In the theatre, a play is never precisely exhausted by a single production or performance, so always resists hospitality, no matter how genuine the welcome, and the cross-cultural production of new plays, therefore, may be a particularly vivid site for exploring how sharply the edges of culture can cut.

Some of these chapters note the specific emergence of these playwrights within their particular theatrical cultures, as with Bryce Lease's chapter on Demirski and Masłowska and Elizabeth Sakellaridou's on Kitsopoulou and Mavritsakis. But others are concerned with considering how and why certain writers might be received or understood as distinctly 'European'. Rikard Hoogland's examination of Norén's often immediate, realistic, politically agitational plays contrasts them with Fosse's allusive, elliptical work, mapping the journeys of both through the German-language, French, and English theatre landscape. Haydon observes that Ravenhill and Kane have been encouraged to experiment formally in contact with European theatre practices, and Fragkou finds Birch and tucker green's linguistic and structural complexity better understood abroad than at home. In his consideration of the work of Crimp and Stephens, David Barnett notes the deployment of particular characteristics – as with the non-attribution of a character's name to a speech or the dismantling of plot or cause and effect – as determining traits of what critics might have seen as constituting 'Europeanness'. For Barnett, however, it is the ability of particular European theatres to 'treat their texts in ways that are appropriate' to these 'formal features' (p. 112) where this elusive label of 'European' may ultimately be located.

Cultures of playwriting

It is true that there is no European country without a tradition and current network of playwriting, but the cultures in which that playwriting appears have evolved in very different ways in the postwar world. For instance, while in

Britain, Germany, and France, playwrights often have agents who negotiate with theatres on their behalf, they are relatively rare in Italy and Spain. Similarly, while most countries have writers' guilds, associations, and collecting societies, these enforce authors' rights to varying degrees of success; broadly, writers are more comprehensively unionised in northern Europe than southern Europe. Playwrights in Mediterranean Europe tend to have to rely on individual agreements with theatres which their collecting societies enforce (in Greece and Spain, the main societies have been embroiled in scandal for failing to effectively enforce and distribute copyright and royalties), while in Britain, Ireland, Norway, and Sweden, for example, there are centrally negotiated framework agreements and fees. Under communism, writers across Central and Eastern Europe (CEE) were required to join unions, which were sometimes directly controlled by the government, though sometimes not. The Union of Polish Writers (Związek Literatów Polskich, or ZLP), for example, has a complex history of both collaborating with the communist state and supporting *wydawnictwa podziemne* (referred to in the English-speaking world by the Russian *samizdat*, meaning covertly self-published) against official censorship and getting banned work published or performed abroad. Since 1989, unionisation across CEE countries has been uneven. The playwright is likely to be heavily involved in the first production of their play in Britain, Ireland, and France, but in Germany the dramaturg will often function as their representative in the rehearsal room. In Germany and Scandinavia, plays are relatively rarely published; across Central and Eastern Europe, but especially Poland and the Czech Republic, there is a strong tradition of publishing plays in theatre journals; in France and Britain, hundreds of individual plays are published each year.

In some countries, it is usual for playwrights to work in another literary field. Handke and Jelinek are as distinguished as novelists as they are playwrights. Fosse, Jelinek, Zeller, NDiaye, and Khemiri were established novelists before they turned to playwriting. Indeed, the novel remains the paradigmatic form of writing for Khemiri and NDiaye; the play is just another mode of 'presenting' their fiction. While NDiaye rejects speaking explicitly about *mise en scène* and has never been directly involved in the staging of her work – indeed she claims that it is unnecessary to hear her words spoken aloud on a stage – Khemiri understands fundamental shifts in time and embodiment when his texts are staged that cement rather than destabilise his primary commitment to prose writing. By contrast, none of the seven major British playwrights represented here has (yet) published a novel.

There are different routes into playwriting across the continent. Kitsopoulou and Mavritsakis were both actors before moving into playwriting. Galceran, Mayorga, and Stephens enjoyed spells as secondary school teachers. Mátei Visniec was employed as a journalist for Radio France and, like Visky and Mayorga, operates as a public intellectual whose opinions on historical and cultural memory circulate across a range of media. Many of these writers can be positioned as what Hari Kunzru defines as public intellectuals 'able to make a robust defence of human rights in the face of the indifference of our political

8 *Maria Delgado et al.*

leaders' (cited in Cain 2019). In CEE countries, the role of the writer as dissident meant that, as the politics of the region shifted, some playwrights were propelled into political authority; the most notable of these was Václav Havel who became President of the Czech Republic, though Marin Sorescu also took a role as Culture Minister in Romania after the revolution, while András Sütő had been a member of the Romanian parliament in the 1960s before becoming disillusioned with communist rule. In the west, the freedom of the playwright to bitterly oppose the values of their own culture – to be, in the German phrase, a *Nestbeschmutzer* (someone who fouls their own nest), as Jelinek has been labelled – has been long established, and even cherished. Writers like Mayenburg, Kane, and Paravidino have been valued as *enfants terribles* of the theatre and in doing so they continue a noble postwar tradition. John Osborne's virulent essay 'Damn You England' is matched by Thomas Bernhard's 30-year history of contempt for Austria, culminating in a stipulation in his will banning his works from being published or performed in his homeland.

These cultures of writing can be glimpsed through the variety of institutional support for writing as art and craft. The hard slog of testing, trying out, and dealing with uncertainty (relished by Enda Walsh) is contextualised in relation to institutional cultures that have very small – or no – budgets, thus explicitly connecting funding, subsidy, and output. Shifts in economies of support and political projects have impacted theatre-making as a collaborative process, in which writing is understood as *one* aspect of broader material production. The role of the playwright thus often collapses into other roles. As Szczawińska and Jakimiak exemplify, since the early 1970s, methods of play creation have diversified and are not reliant on the model of the single author sending readymade scripts to professional theatres. Scripts have been produced through collective creation, sometimes by writers working with directors and actors; there have been moves to train writers in organisations like Denmark's Dramatic Studio, set up by the writers' union under playwright Leif Petersen in 1976, or the Royal Court Theatre's Young Writers Programme, which for 10 years was taught by Stephens. Molly Flynn observes that post-Soviet theatre-making 'notably displaced the centrality of the director-*auteur* as the primary conduit for a play's artistic vision and focused instead on the primacy of the playwright who came to stand at the centre of the creative process' (p. 226).

Relatedly, the term dramaturg today serves different analytic purposes, as well as representing various forms of labour. Schimmelpfennig and Mayenburg first emerged as dramaturgs and they continue to blur the boundaries of this role in relation to the composition and provenance of a work of art. The significant change to our understanding of authorship provokes a range of responses: NDiaye questions the very existence of the playwright in an era that privileges *Regie* or devising practices, while Duška Radosavljević celebrates the horizontal and coalitional production of an 'author' that she locates within women's work in the Balkans. This volume asks where and how such *work* occurs and what it means to understand this in relation to the proximate but not identical term *playwriting*.

Translation has also played a significant role in the establishment of new writing cultures, either through the development of new plays in international theatres and festivals or through the confrontation with texts that resist translation through their creative deformations of language and grammar, appropriations of slang, invention of neologisms, or use of puns and other linguistic tricks (Crimp, Masłowska, Walsh, and debbie tucker green come to mind here). Translations abound outside of the English language between European spaces, and this occasionally happens within linguistic groups rather than across them. Playwriting in dialect has been a significant feature of European playwriting since the war, from the Neapolitan plays of Eduardo de Filippo to the revival of the *Volksstück* tradition in the work of Martin Sperr, Franz Xaver Kroetz, and Wolfgang Bauer (see Cocalis 1981) and poses particular issues for translation within and across cultures. Some playwrights, such as Dante, resist incorporating their own cultural otherness into an accessible mode through translation, while writers such as Khemiri and NDiaye praise translators for their careful attention to linguistic difference and nuance. It is worth noting that a number of the writers covered in this volume are translators of their own work (Galceran) and the work of others (Crimp, Mayenburg, Mayorga, Ravenhill). This aids the broader circulation of a body of European writing. Stephens, for example, has rendered Fosse in English, Galceran has translated Reza, Mayenburg has translated Kane, Paravidino has translated Greig. Given their crucial role in transcultural transmission it is not, perhaps, insignificant that translators and translation figure as prominent characters in a number of plays by Mayorga, Greig, and others.

Borders and their discontents

Each chapter establishes a genealogy of writers and texts to offer a context for each playwright's work. The chapters discuss not just their plays but the plays in performance and what it is about the writing that embodies, expresses, and interrogates the nature of Europe in the twenty-first century. Thinking across borders, both in terms of transnational production histories and artistic influences, differentiates this book from a study solely focused on individual authors. The chapters build collaborations – between writers and directors, writers and theatres, writers and nations – into their very structure(s). As we write, in 2020, we are fully aware that national borders have returned as a pressing political issue in European politics. The European Union's longstanding commitment to reducing the significance of the continent's internal borders has been challenged by the rise of anti-immigration populism parties that have, at times, threatened to pull apart the EU's famous four freedoms (of goods, services, capital, and people). A new protectionism and a new xenophobia are currently on the rise in Europe (particularly the UK, Poland, Turkey, and Hungary) and beyond (the US, Brazil, India, and more). It is not innocent, then, that playwriting examines what it finds within borders, the meanings they generate, and the complex patterns of people, ideas, and things that flow across them.

10   *Maria Delgado et al.*

A significant number of chapters firmly position the dramatists within a national context that has undergone significant changes in the twenty-first century. Both Flynn and Noah Birksted-Breen frame their consideration of the post-Soviet Sigarev, the Presniakovs, Vyrypaev, and Vorozhbyt within the wider economic, political, and social changes that followed the collapse of the Soviet Union in 1991. Andrew Haydon places the emergence of Kane and Ravenhill against the comically bathetic travails of the Conservative administration of 1992–7. Sakellaridou's discussion of Kitsopoulou and Mavritsakis situates their trajectories against the climate of financial crisis, high unemployment, and sustained austerity that followed the collapse of the Greek economy in 2008. Lease assesses Demirski and Masłowska's writing against the rising tide of Polish nationalism and the wider implications that these nationalist discourses have on the construction of collective memories. Radosavljević writes about the practices of Srbljanović and Sajko within a discussion that recognises the limited knowledge – shaped by Balkanism – of (post-)Yugoslav theatre in the English-speaking world. The idea of crisis, political and historical, is key to the work of many of these dramatists.

Other writers reflect or embody the effect of open borders and migratory flows in the EU, including Jelinek, Masłowska, Mayorga, and Schimmelpfennig. Meanwhile, some of the most dynamic and significant productions of Fosse's plays – many of which are geographically ambiguous – have been produced outside of their native countries. Mayorga's works demonstrate how his writing has been transformed and enriched by his encounter with a broader European theatre culture. Komporaly goes so far as to define Romanian playwriting as a negotiation between cultures and further argues that for writers working in Hungarian the historical shifts of geographic boundaries (particularly in Transylvania) have shaped some of their most successful work. She concludes that this 'may well have to do with their exposure to more than one cultural tradition, and most importantly in this context, to the thriving Romanian theatre scene' (p. 77).

Since the war, movements in playwriting have transcended borders, even if those movements are always inflected by particular cultures. Rebellato's introductory chapter examines the interplay of realism, absurdism, and epic theatre across the continent in playwriting of the 1950s, 1960s, and 1970s. In the post-Berlin Wall era, the new movements have been less easy to define. The 'postdramatic' was announced by Hans-Thies Lehmann in his 1999 book *Postdramatic Theatre* who notes that

> when the progression of a story with its internal logic no longer forms the centre, when composition is no longer experienced as an organising quality but as an artificially imposed 'manufacture' [...] then theatre is confronted with the question of possibilities beyond drama.
>
> (2006: 26)

Lehmann's reflections have been contested, but his argument that a 'theatre of sense and synthesis has largely disappeared – and with it the possibility of synthesizing interpretation' (2006: 25) is reflected in the work of Jelinek and Handke but also in that of Crimp and Fosse, as the chapters by Barnett and Hoogland show.

Equally contested and equally influential is Aleks Sierz's description of 1990s British playwriting as 'In Yer Face' theatre, which he characterises as a 'theatre of sensation', employing violence, nudity, shock tactics to 'jolt […] both actors and spectators out of conventional responses, touching nerves and provoking alarm' (2001: 4). While Kane and Ravenhill are central to Sierz's argument, he would accept that the label describes them less well the more their work developed, yet the aggressive, explicit style is visible in work across the continent, including in plays by Mayenburg, Paravidino, Mayorga, and the Presniakov Brothers.

In part, this may be because of the influence of the Royal Court's international department, which has played an important role in exporting a particular model of writing across Europe and beyond and into other media, including film and television, but also into opera and music theatre (see Aston and O'Thomas 2015). Andrew Haydon's chapter on Kane and Ravenhill acknowledges their association with the Royal Court, where both also tutored on the international writing schools, workshops, and residencies, but also how their work now transcends this early association. Indeed, a number of the chapters present writers who formed part of these Royal Court initiatives. Mayorga has acknowledged the influence of Sarah Kane as one of the tutors he encountered at the Royal Court (Mayorga 2012: 479), while Demirski was strongly impacted by David Hare's journalistic approach during his time in the theatre's international writing programme. Birksted-Breen's treatment of Sigarev and the Presniakov Brothers recognises that the Royal Court has been the single most important factor in their reception in Europe (p. 177). Laera, Flynn, and Radosavljević note the decisive importance of particular London productions to the careers of Paravadino, Vorozhbyt, and Tena Štivičić. While the importance of the Royal Court's International department is underlined across a number of chapters, the role of Barcelona's Sala Beckett, Berlin's Schaubühne, Moscow's Teatr.doc, the Teatro della Limonaia outside Florence, and Madrid's Pavón Teatro Kamikaze also deserves highlighting as venues supporting the development and production of new writing from writers across Europe.

The role of literary agents, festivals, and showcases in supporting the theatre across borders is evident in several chapters. Sajko's works were impacted by the artists invited to Croatia as part of the EUROKAZ festival, including Forced Entertainment, DV8, Goat Island, Jan Fabre, and La Fura dels Baus. Hoogland maps the importance of Fosse and Norén's agents as gatekeepers of the playwrights' work, locating partnerships with powerful international agents and translators (p. 107). The role of Berlin's Theatertreffen proved seminal to Norén's canonisation in Germany (see pp. 103, 106, 107) and the role of the Schaubühne in launching the German-language trajectories of Ravenhill and

12   Maria Delgado et al.

Kane is recognised in Haydon's chapter on both dramatists (see p. 154). Networks of co-producers have facilitated the transnational circulation of key productions covered in the volume – as with Patrice Chéreau's staging of Simon Stephens' translation of Fosse's *I am the Wind* in 2011, Luc Bondy's staging of Crimp's *Cruel and Tender* in 2004, and Sebastian Nübling's production of Stephens' *Three Kingdoms* in 2011–12. Celebrity translators – such as Christopher Hampton's association with the work of Reza and Zeller in the UK – perhaps serve to 'endorse' plays whose foreignness might prove off-putting to more conservative audiences.

Our framing of these writers acknowledges how their work in the theatre promotes particular languages, vocabularies, or discourses that have proved generative outside their home nation. As Patrick Lonergan observes in his treatment of McDonagh's works, even the 'personal authorial protest against Irish terrorism' embedded in *The Lieutenant of Inishmore* can give rise, through the dramaturgy, to a 'more complex set of reactions to (and against) political violence' (p. 258). As such, McDonagh – like Walsh – creates spaces for meanings that 'locate Ireland firmly in European contexts while also locating Europe firmly in Irish contexts' (p. 258). This interdependence reveals why writers such as Vorozhbyt, whose plays are embedded in and motivated by her Ukrainian national culture, resonate so much more widely. Playwriting is here a way of reflecting on European history since 1989, a way of thinking through, as British writer-performer Chris Thorpe observed in 2015, how theatre functions as 'a national laboratory for thinking about how we think and how we are and what we are' (cited in Gardner 2015).

Europe in the aftermath of 1989

The overview of emerging trends in European writing that are presented in this volume respond to conflicted and contested political landscapes; these are anchored by 1989 as a reference point. Given the histories of censorship and exile in communist Europe, there was, in many cases, a dearth of playwrights in these countries immediately after 1989 – this situation also prevailed in the early years of the transition to democracy in post-fascist Spain and Portugal. While these writers negotiated mass censorship, anti-democratic bureaucratisation, systemic corruption, and the brutal disciplining of political dissidents, artists working after 1989 have negotiated the positive growth of multiculturalism and the related rise of nationalism and xenophobia in the move to democracy.

History plays a major role in interpreting the present, and, as organic memory fades, our duty to remember collectively is articulated as an ethical imperative. Cultural memory, despite being thorny, multifaceted, and contradictory, remains a fertile ground for new forms of solidarity and coalition as much as for contesting rhetorical battles. Mayorga structures a theatre of political quandaries and moral debates, of unresolved issues from twentieth-century history (the Spanish Civil War, the Holocaust) and a wider sense of Europe's broader political past. For Visky, 'the theatre of memory is predicated on audience participation and aims for a shared experience of meanings' (p. 84).

While Visniec's theatre plays an active role in refreshing collective memories of communism, Masłowska challenges the easy acceptance of neoliberalism that replaces one oppressive system with another. The partial histories of postwar Europe form the backbone of the works of writers in Poland, Hungary, and Romania. In Serbia and Croatia, the 1990s are weighted with political implication, while theatre makers in Russia and Ukraine continue to grapple with historical revisionism and basic freedom of expression and protest.

We have been careful not to elide or subsume all (writing) cultures and spaces as indistinguishably 'global' or irreducibly 'European'. In this regard, we are alert to the discussions that centralise Europe at the price of Eurocentrism. A number of the chapters critique the idea of CEE countries as 'transitioning' towards Europe. 'Within this unemancipatory process they are always condemned to an unequal relationship: having to "keep up" and be trend-followers rather than trend-setters', Radosavljević observes. Certainly, there is an uneven distribution of dominance and influence: the writers from the UK, Ireland, France, Germany, and Scandinavia tend to have the most visibility throughout the continent, judged by the number of international translations and productions of their works. Plays written in French and English dominate through their circulation and reach in modes that have not been attainable for texts written in language groups with smaller populations. Lithuanian playwright Marius Ivaškevičius is aware of the challenges globalisation presents for those countries where citizens speak marginalized languages and this resulted in his first attempt to produce a play with broad European appeal, *Artimas Miestas* (Close City, 2005), by using Sweden and Denmark as cultural markers. Jeff Johnson suggests that such strategies are the inevitable price a small nation state has to pay for integration into a larger social unit such as the EU (2007: 53–4). Positions of cultural and linguistic privilege should not remain unmarked.

Such questions of privilege are also addressed in relation to casting policies. Some playwrights here directly address issues of migration and multiculturalism, while others address it perhaps more obliquely through unmarking race in their texts. While Schimmelpfennig 'defends his preference for poetic, cross-ethnic, colour-blind *Verfremdung*' (pp. 132–3), Khemiri observes that it would simply be false to write about Sweden in an outdated 'blue-eyed' fashion that would ignore people from different backgrounds and which would prevent the inclusion of actors of colour (p. 367). NDiaye aligns herself with Bernard-Marie Koltès' view that 'a black character is unequivocally to be played by a black actor' (p. 375), which opens up space for examining difficult questions about visibility, accessibility, and representation that continue to sit at the heart of European theatre today. debbie tucker green's strategy, in *stoning mary*, as Marissia Fragkou argues, uses cross-casting in a radical way to draw attention precisely to white privilege, legacies of colonialism, and the gaps and continuities between the Global North and the Global South (pp. 337–43).

But there is much work to do, and plays and playwriting are at the heart of the theatrical struggle. The Deutsches Theater's plan to use 'blackface' in their productions of Dea Loher's *Unschuld* (*Innocence*, 2011) and Bruce Norris's *Clybourne Park* (2012), and the 'yellowface' casting in the Royal Shakespeare Company's *The Orphan*

14   *Maria Delgado et al.*

of Zhao and the Print Room's premiere of Howard Barker's *In the Depths of Dead Love* (2017) show the persistent need for serious political debate about casting practices (see Seig 2015; Thorpe 2014). The problem is not easily resolved into a gap between the literalism of realist methods and the representational critique of Brechtian techniques. Howard Barker's anti-realist defence of the casting – 'The "Chinese" nature of the play is within the setting, which is entirely artificial, and the naming of the characters. It's entirely European in its sensibilities' (cited in Snow 2017) – only compounds the misjudgement, demonstrating that non-realist techniques can redouble the exceptionalism of whiteness as the founding basis of representation on European stages that relegates other racial and ethnic subjectivities to the background. This is an urgent question for playwrights but is also, of course, a question of who has access to professional training and employment and is thereby granted recognition in the broader public sphere. Kélina Gotman notes that the first black actor did not join the Comédie-Française ensemble until 2002, and France's most renowned theatre troupe still in 2020 employs no Arabic actors (pp. 375–6).

In 1989, Francis Fukayama (in)famously declared that the collapse of the Soviet bloc meant the end of history, arguing that the long Hegelian dialectic between east and west, communism and capitalism, had been decisively won in capitalism's favour. His remarks have not aged well. Capital's victory lap lasted almost 20 years and took the form of an unleashed, turbo-capitalist appetite for the marketisation of everything and the destruction of all barriers to profit and exchange. This was, we hope, the high-water mark of neoliberalism, which has helped generate violent lurches between growth and unemployment, expansion and depression, resulting in alienation, exclusion, and inequality on a scale unprecedented in human history (Piketty 2014; Maddison 2001). The devastating economic downturn that dominoed around the world in 2008 showed the shallowness of neoliberal claims that markets were rationally self-correcting and they hit Europe very hard. However, the European Union, often the focus of anti-immigration protests, has sometimes behaved like a neoliberal agent of free markets and small states (most notably in their handling of Greece's debt crisis in the 2010s), while at other times seeming to have an appetite for expansive regulations on capital. Further, while it insists on open borders within, it can jealously guard its borders without. Concerns over human rights has meant the exclusion of some CEE countries from European Union expansion, and this liminal, semi-European status rumbles through many plays from these regions.

The effects of all of these policies unfold in these plays. In Spain, issues of nationalism shape the narratives, thematic concerns, and languages of performance (Catalan, Basque, Galician). Galceran, for example, has chosen to write in Catalan but his translations into Castilian offer useful points of discussion around issues of local reception, linguistic transfer, and dramatic register. In Scotland, using non-British theatre traditions has been a means of asserting a distinct and dissident national identity – one that has been further reinforced since the UK's 2016 Brexit referendum. Writers in Austria (Jelinek) and Germany (Mayenburg) participate in an explicit and widespread critique of nationalism, and others (Srbljanović, Mayorga) consider historical and recent ethnic conflicts that continue to define the terms of nationalistic politics today. Redressing public invisibility and exclusion from national imaginaries, in CEE countries, where nationalism was often a form of resistance to Soviet-enforced communism, playwrights like Demirski and Masłowska have been sensitive to the ways in which nationalism can reemerge under liberal democracy as a conservative force. Relatedly, those working in Russia and the Ukraine like Vorozhbyt and Vyrypaev have – and at considerable risk – made significant attempts to offer narratives counter to the chauvinistic nationalism of Putinism.

There has been a shift in concepts and themes that reflects changes in writing approaches that are in close kinship to political change and advocacy. The 1990s and early 2000s were dominated by confrontational forms of writing that exposed themes of violence – both explicit and latent – that resonated across the work of the selected playwrights, and this offered a particularly striking perspective on European culture. This has been evident in the explicit violence of the Russian state explored in the work of the Presniakov Brothers, to the implicit but undefined eruptions of political and corporeal violence and terror in the works of Kane, Jelinek, and Vyrypaev. It is further explored in the violent histories that are resurrected and enacted in order to shed light on the contestation of formerly repressed narratives connected to the Holocaust, fascism, and communism (Demirski, Mayorga, Vorozhbyt, Visniec), as well as post-1989 political events, such as Srbljanović's open resistance to and condemnation of Serbian nationalism, a position that contrasts with the views of Handke referred to at the opening of this introduction.

As this book traces the emergence of new playwrights and of new forms and methods of playmaking, we see violence begin to form part of a broader landscape of unresolved social tensions. We chart new forms of affiliation that arise from the accession of CEE countries into the EU; mass migration into Europe from Africa and the Middle East; the Eurozone crisis and the debates over Brexit. As Flynn notes, even Vyrypaev's plays have become more concerned with existential philosophy and spiritual inquiry than with inexplicable acts of violence (p. 238). Khemiri reappropriates problematic language and cultural stereotypes as tools for self-empowerment, and intimacy, affiliation, and solidarity arise as the most potent themes in his work in which the word 'brother' acts as a strategic alliance (p. 370). In a well-known letter, Khemiri asked Beatrice Ask, the then Swedish Minister of Justice, to switch bodies and memories with him. 'If I inhabited her body I would understand male privilege', he observed, 'and if she inhabited my body she would remember being followed in stores by security guards, being stopped in customs at airports, being stopped and put in the backseat of police cars, for no reason' (p. 372). This radical form of empathy is one that centres around exchange and embodiment that might complicate the assumption of shared access to the public sphere and renew political alignments. Such coalitional forms have emerged in feminist practices as well. Radosavljević asks how (rather than whether) writers have achieved a transnational feminist perspective that 'dislocates the viewer

16   *Maria Delgado et al.*

from her familiar viewing position' (p. 315) and argues that Srbljanović and Sajko's use of stage directions promotes an emancipatory practice that foregrounds their voices – which, in contradistinction to the gaze, has been central to feminist discourses – as a strategy for self-inscription and new modes of being together (p. 320). While women still remain professionally marginalised – the only play written by a woman to be produced at the Comédie Française is Marie NDiaye's *Papa doit manger* (2003) – change is visible. Szczawińska notes that when theatre academies in Poland stopped only admitting men onto their directing programmes the presence of women in positions of authority resulted in structural changes to the professional theatre system that had formerly relied on neatly gendered binaries between writers and directors (pp. 71–2).

The theatre is a site of cultural debate and struggle: as we write, Viktor Orbán, Hungary's authoritarian prime minister, has introduced a law that would give the government control over which directors are appointed to state-subsidised theatre, meaning that, in the words of Róbert Alföldi, director of the Hungarian National Theatre before 2013, 'everyone who gets a chance to make culture and create work would have to be a loyal servant of the regime' (cited in 'Editorial' 2019). In the midst of the return of fascism and rightwing populism in Europe today, these artistic and institutional transformations are trying to keep open a space for a more inclusive and substantive democracy.

Beyond

This volume cannot be exhaustive. European playwriting has been remarkably fruitful over the last 30 years; the limits of space mean there are conspicuous figures who do not feature, not because their work is not relevant or important but because we have sought to offer as panoramic a view of European playwriting as possible, to draw from right across the continent, and represent something of the range and diversity of forms and subject matter of Europe since 1989. We would nevertheless like to signal some further writers who have emerged in the subsequent three decades, who are wrestling both with Europe's political, economic, social, and existential crises and the place and position of theatre in twenty-first century society, and who deserve to be better known in the English-speaking world.

Translated into 28 languages, the German dramatist Dea Loher (who studied under Heiner Müller) creates characters that often operate on the margins of society, characters scarred by neoliberalist promises and societal injustices. Sybille Berg, born in East Germany but now based in Switzerland, offers a different point of reference – recognised first as a novelist and now also a director and columnist for *Der Spiegel* – as a prominent cultural critic with a body of work that brutally chronicles the lives of those marred by the legacy of reunification. Writers who have sought to examine the changing face of Europe in the aftermath of the fall of the Soviet Union include Lithuania's Gabrielė Labanauskaitė and Marius Ivaškevičius. Both have both challenged well-worn narratives of cultural nostalgia and collective memory. David Harrower's plays have mirrored the Europhile politics of Scottish nationalism playing of the traditions of his two

Introduction   17

overlapping home nations (Scotland and Britain) and engaging with those of Europe more widely, working with conspicuous auteur-directors like Peter Stein and Claude Régy to offer troubled explorations of Europe's heritage and future. Dennis Kelly's mischievous, fractured, logorrheic plays offer violently funny explorations of debt and death, power and poverty; his plays are translated right across Europe (and he has also returned the favour, by making English versions of plays by Kleist, Kaiser, and Péter Kárpáti).

Mariana Salzmann's 'post-migrant' theatre at Berlin's Maxim Gorki theatre has provided a complex articulation of European migrant identities that resonate across a wider body of writing concerned with an embodied past that individuals carry within them whether they acknowledge it or not. French writer-choreo-grapher-director Pascal Rambert's plays, revolving around desire and its discontents, are frequently conceived around productions that he directs in quick succession at Paris's Bouffes du Nord and Madrid's Pavón Teatro Kamikaze. Noëlle Renaude is a French writer of remarkable linguistic delicacy who increasingly uses all the typographical and visual resources of the page to create radical performance texts that make the experience of text visceral. Italian Letizia Russo is one of a number of writers that include Davide Enia, Mario Perrota, Daniele Timpano, Mimmo Sorrentino, Stefano Massini, Mimmo Borrelli, whose work has shaped both contemporary Italian dramaturgy and European understandings of what constitutes Italian playwriting.

The impact of Sergi Belbel's spare elliptical Koltèsian dramas influenced a generation of writers (Lluïsa Cunillé, Josep Maria Miró, Guillem Clua) who have gone on to provide telling commentaries on the vestiges of Spain's colo-nialist past and the legacies of its fratricidal civil war. Angélica Liddell and Rodrigo García both operate at the boundaries of performance-making and writing, creating extreme works that fragment the dominant narratives of neoliberalism, question established perceptions of artistic merit, and destabilise psychologically dominant understandings of self and other. Signa, the Copen-hagen-based artistic collective founded by Signa Sørensen and Arthur Kóstler, refashion the relationship between writing, directing, and environment in their sensory performance installations. Ida Müller and Vegard Vinge too have pulled apart the relationship between writer and director in their refashioning of the Ibsen corpus as new plays, asking profound questions about what constitutes dramatic language and how theatre operates. Tiago Rodrigues, who provides the foreword to this volume, provides a voice from Portugal, another nation too often positioned on the margins of Europe. In his intersecting roles – writer, actor, director – he operates across a number of the bound-aries identified in this volume.[2]

The playwrights represented here are emerging and established, working in national and international contexts, in alternative and mainstream theatres, writing individually and in collaboration, working in the dramatic and the postdramatic, restlessly seeking out new forms and subjects. Their practice reinvents the role of writer – and often provokes a reinvention of the role of director, designer, actor, and audience. All of these writers seem to detect and

18   *Maria Delgado et al.*

broaden the faultlines and fissures, aporias and blindspots of the culture, to become, as Milo Rau described himself in 2018, 'a moderator for things that stand outside my control' (cited in Boffey et al. 2018).[3] Our hope is that the trajectories across Europe's stages of these dramatists, those that feature in the volume and others, will inspire further consideration of how plays travel across Europe's national boundaries and what this tells us about the broader playwriting scene in and across the continent, and ultimately what we hope this book helps us to see is how these writers seize a moment, frame the world for us, challenge us with our responsibilities. Szczawińska captures this in a remark about two of her contemporaries but she could be talking about any writer represented here: the joy of this kind of work, she says, is that 'you could point at these writers and say that this is how the world is supposed to react to the contemporary moment' (p. 67).

Notes

1   The exceptions are dramatists writing in English, although the critics here tend to position their work within national traditions of playwriting, as with Angelaki (2012) and Sierz's (2013) monographs on Crimp. Saunders' (2002) study of Kane locates her work in the same transnational and interactive paradigms set out in this collection but this relates to early productions of her plays rather than twenty-first century stagings. Greig's and Stephens' work has been the subject of two special issues of *Contemporary Theatre Review* (Barnett 2016; Bolton 2016). Studies of Walsh and McDonagh's work include Caulfield and Walsh (2019) and Lonergan (2012a) respectively. Bryce Lease's *After '89: Polish Theatre and the Political* (2016), Molly Flynn's *Witness Onstage: Documentary Theatre in Twenty-First-Century Russia* (2019), and Jozefina Komporaly's books on Romanian and Hungarian writing (2015, 2017) offer a discussion of writing cultures within these respective national frameworks.
2   Some of these non-English-language writers have received English-language critical attention; see, for example, George (2010) on Belbel; Orozco (2010) on García; Friedman (2019) on Vinge/Müller; Noonan (2007, 2010, 2013, 2014) on Renaude.
3   This article is a valuable series of introductions to contemporary European playwrights, Belgium's Ismael Saïdi, Turkey's Esmeray Özatik, Greece's Marianna Calbari, Romania's Gianina Cărbunariu.

Works cited

Aguilar, Andrea (2019) 'Escritores contra Peter Handke', *El País*, 12 October, https://elpais.com/cultura/2019/10/11/actualidad/1570818371_712786.html

Ahmad, Aijaz (2000) 'The Communist Manifesto and World Literature', *Social Scientist*, 28: 3–30.

Angelaki, Vicky (2012) *The Plays of Martin Crimp: Making Theatre Strange*, Houndmills: Palgrave Macmillan.

Apter, Emily (2013) *Against World Literature: On the Politics of Untranslatability*, London: Verso.

Aston, Elaine, and Mark O'Thomas (2015) *Royal Court: International*, Houndmills: Palgrave Macmillan.

Barnett, David (ed.) (2016) *Contemporary Theatre Review*, 26(3): Simon Stephens: British Playwright in Dialogue with Europe.

Boffey, Daniel, Constanze Letsch, Philip Oltermann, Helena Smith and Kit Gillet (2018) '"I wanted to channel the anger": Europe's fearless political playwrights', *Guardian*, 12 February, https://www.theguardian.com/stage/2018/feb/12/europe-p olitical-playwrights-theatre

Bolton, Jacqueline (ed.) (2016) *Contemporary Theatre Review*, 26(1): David Greig: Dramaturgies of Encounter and Engagement.

Cain, Sian (2019) 'A troubling choice: authors criticise Peter Handke's controversial Nobel win', *Guardian*, 11 October, https://www.theguardian.com/books/2019/oct/10/troubling-choice-authors-criticise-peter-handke-controversial-nobel-win

Casanova, Pascale (2007) *The World Republic of Letters*, Cambridge, MA: Harvard University Press.

Caulfield, Mary P. and Ian R. Walsh (eds), (2019) *The Theatre of Enda Walsh*, 2nd edn, London: Peter Lang.

Cocalis, Susan (1981) 'The politics of brutality: toward a definition of the critical Volksstück', *Modern Drama*, 24: 292–313.

Damrosch, David (2003) *What is World Literature?*, Princeton, NJ: Princeton University Press.

Day, Elizabeth (2012) 'Yasmina Reza: "There's no point in writing theatre if it's not accessible"', *Guardian*, 22 January, https://www.theguardian.com/stage/2012/jan/22/yasmina-reza-interview-carnage-polanski

'Editorial: The Guardian view on Viktor Orbán's laws: controlling culture' (2019) *Guardian*, 11 December.

Flynn, Molly (2019) *Witness Onstage: Documentary Theatre in Twenty-First-Century Russia*, Manchester: Manchester University Press.

Friedman, Andrew (2019) 'Modernist afterlives in performance – inside Ibsen: avant-garde institutionality and time in Vinge/Müller's Ibsen-Saga', *Modernism/Modernity*, 4 (3), 10 October.

Fukayama, Francis (1989) 'The end of history?' *The National Interest*, 3–18.

Gardner, Lyn (2015) 'Chris Thorpe: Theatre is a "laboratory for thinking about how we think"', *Guardian*, 7 April, https://www.theguardian.com/stage/2015/apr/07/chris-thorpe-theatre-confirmation-a-nations-theatre

George, David (2010) *Sergi Belbel and Catalan Theatre: Text, Performance and Identity*, London: Tamesis.

Gotman, Kélina A. (2019) 'On the difficult work of translating translation; or, the monolingualism of translation theory. Languaging acts in (and after) Marie NDiaye's Les Serpents', *Studies in Theatre and Performance*: 1–28.

Johnson, Jeff (2007) *The New Theatre of the Baltics: From Soviet to Western Influence in Estonia, Latvia and Lithuania*, Jefferson, NC: McFarland & Co.

Komporaly, Jozefina (2015) Introduction to *Matéi Visniec: How to Explain the History of Communism to Mental Patients and Other Plays*, Kolkata: Seagull, pp. vii–xlii.

Komporaly, Jozefina (ed.) (2017) *András Visky's Barrack Dramaturgy: Memories of the Body*, Bristol: Intellect.

Lease, Bryce (2016) *After '89: Polish Theatre and the Political*, Manchester: Manchester University Press.

Lehmann, Hans-Thies (2006 [1999]) *Postdramatic Theatre*, trans. with an introduction by Karen Jürs-Munby, London: Routledge.

Lonergan, Patrick (2012a) *The Theatre and Films of Martin McDonagh*, London: Bloomsbury.

———— (2012b) 'Seven steps to Martin McDonagh', *Irish Times*, 6 November, https://www.irishtimes.com/culture/stage/seven-steps-to-martin-mcdonagh-1.548074

20 Maria Delgado et al.

Maddison, Angus (2001) *The World Economy: A Millennial perspective*, Paris: Development Centre of the Organisation for Economic Co-operation and Development.

Marx, Karl and Frederick Engels (2002) *The Communist Manifesto*, Harmondsworth: Penguin.

Mayorga, Juan (2012) 'Theatre is the art of the future', in Maria M. Delgado and David Gies (eds), *A History of Theatre in Spain*, Cambridge: Cambridge University Press, pp. 478–485.

Moretti, Franco (2003) 'More conjectures', *New Left Review*, 1: 73–81.

——— (2000) 'Conjectures on world literature', *New Left Review*, 20: 54–68.

Muskała, Monika (2019) 'Nagroda Zwymyślana', *Dwutygodnik*, 266, October, https://www.dwutygodnik.com/artykul/8516-nagroda-zwymyslana.html

Noonan, Mary (2007) '"l'Art de l'écrit s'incarnant": the theater of Noëlle Renaude', *Yale French Studies*: 116–128.

——— (2010) 'An archaeology of soundscapes: the theatre of Noëlle Renaude', *Studies in Theatre and Performance*, 30: 115–125.

——— (2013) 'Un corps vivant de symbôles: Noëlle Renaude's Staging of the Writing Self', in Gill Rye and Amaleena Damlé (eds), *Experiment and Experience: Women's Writing in France 2000–2010*. Oxford: Lang, pp. 175–90.

——— (2014) '"La mise en scène du journal crypté de l'écriture": The Theater of Noëlle Renaude', *Women in French Studies*: 232–245.

Ordóñez, Marcos (2018) 'De repente Galceran', *El País*, 30 May, https://elpais.com/cultura/2018/05/30/actualidad/1527691705_263899.html

Orozco, Lourdes (2010) 'Rodrigo García and La Carnicería Teatro: from the collective to the director', in Maria M. Delgado and Dan Rebellato (eds), *Contemporary European Theatre Directors*, Abingdon: Routledge, pp. 299–316.

Piketty, Thomas (2014) *Capital in the Twenty-First Century*, Cambridge, MA: Harvard University Press.

Saunders, Graham (2002) *Love Me or Kill Me: Sarah Kane and the Theatre of Extremes*, Manchester: Manchester University Press.

Sieg, Katrin (2015) 'Race, Guilt and innocence: facing blackfacing in contemporary German Theater', *German Studies Review*, 38: 117–134.

Sierz, Aleks (2001) *In-Yer-Face Theatre: British Drama Today*, London: Faber and Faber.

——— (2013) *The Theatre of Martin Crimp*, 2nd edn, London: Bloomsbury.

Snow, Georgia (2017) 'Howard Barker defends Print Room casting from "yellowface" criticisms', *The Stage*, 20 January, https://www.thestage.co.uk/news/2017/howard-barker-defends-print-room-casting-yellowface-criticisms

Thorpe, Ashley (2014) 'Casting matters: colour trouble in the RSC's *The Orphan of Zhao*', *Contemporary Theatre Review*, 24: 436–451.

Vulliamy, Ed (2019) 'Peter Handke's Nobel prize dishonours the victims of genocide', *Guardian*, 12 October, https://www.theguardian.com/commentisfree/2019/oct/12/a-nobel-prize-that-dishonours-the-victims-of-genocide-peter-handke

Zaiontz, Keren (2018) *Theatre & Festivals*, London: Palgrave.

1 European playwriting and politics, 1945–89

Dan Rebellato

Like its companion volume (Delgado and Rebellato 2020), this book takes as its starting point the opening up of the Berlin Wall in November 1989 and focuses largely on playwrights who have developed their European profile in the years after that momentous shift in the continent's geopolitical structure. However, crucial though that moment was, it did not wipe the dramaturgical slate clean, and all playwrights write in the shadow of the traditions, the institutional arrangements, and the playwrights that preceded them. The aim of this chapter is to outline some of the broad forms and movements of playwriting – the dramaturgical imaginary, one might say – that dominated the years before 1989 and forms a mental and cultural landscape against which more recent playwriting may be placed.

Clearly, it will not be possible to cover all plays and playwrights over five decades and across over 40 countries, so the survey will be necessarily selective and will aim to note divergences as much as commonalities between playwriting traditions. Each country's theatre history has its own character; for much of the period, as an example, Greece and Spain's theatres did little to encourage contemporary writers, while the United Kingdom and the Netherlands prized the new play almost above all else; France's great period of discovering new playwrights was in the 1940s and 1950s, Poland's was the '50s and '60s, while Germany's was in the '60s and '70s; in the UK the playwright is increasingly someone who only writes, while in Italy throughout the period a playwright will typically also be an actor or a director; in northern Europe the distinctions between popular and art theatre are typically fairly sharp, while in southern Europe these forms are more likely to blur. Even these generalisations, of course, must admit of exceptions but nonetheless they illustrate that there is not a single story of postwar European playwriting.

Nonetheless, a few convictions shape this account: first, while the emergence of directors' theatre in the 1970s is one of the most distinctive and important features of Europe's theatre in the postwar years, this should not obscure the persistent vitality and diversity of European playwriting in the same period and indeed the way that playwriting has adapted to, even contributed to, some of the director- or company-led revolutions in theatre practice; second, related, the play has been a locus of constant theatrical experimentation since the

22   Dan Rebellato

Second World War, Europe's playwrights showing an undimmed interest in finding new subjects, structures, forms, and styles in which to capture and interrogate the contemporary world; third, the play, for reasons that we will discuss, has often been at the sharp end of confrontations between the theatre and the state, between artists and governments (of all political stripes). If there is a particular focus to this investigation, it will be to note the ways in which politics and playwriting have engaged in running battles, exemplified in a number of extraordinary flashpoints, the ripples of which have been felt not just in theatre, but in the wider political culture, indeed, at times, right across Europe and beyond.

That said, it is also important to observe the importance with which theatre has been held in postwar Europe. All European countries have some form of state subsidy for the theatre, sometimes very substantial (as in Germany and Sweden), sometimes relatively modest (as in Italy and Ireland). In many countries, the theatre (and the arts more generally) have been prized by governments, sometimes as a fundamental welfare constituent of a good society, sometimes as an emblem of national prestige, sometimes as a tool of social engineering, sometimes as a means of ideological control – and in most countries, all of these things have been true at one time. Notably, after the Second World War, although playhouses were often damaged in the bombings, many countries – for example Germany, Poland, and Hungary – made reopening the theatres a priority. Jean Monnet, one of the architects of the European Union, is often quoted as reflecting, in the 1970s, 'If we were to start [the European project] all over again, we would start with culture' (cited in Shore 2001: 170). In fact, it seems that this quotation is apocryphal, yet that perhaps only confirms the widespread belief that the theatre has had a central role to play in the reconstruction of postwar European identity.

It is no exaggeration to say that, after the war, Germany sought to relearn its identity through culture. Theatre had an important role in helping the country in the project of *Bewältigung der Vergangenheit* (coming to terms with the Nazi past). Seeking non-Nazi German voices was key to helping the country understand what happened between 1933 and 1945 and, to that end, German theatres took in anti-Nazi plays written by German writers in exile like Ferdinand Bruckner's *Die Rassen* (*The Races*, 1933), Friedrich Wolf's *Professor Mamlock* (1934), and Bertolt Brecht's *Furcht und Elend des Dritten Reiches* (*Fear and Misery of the Third Reich*, 1938). These plays demanded that German audiences faced up to the horrors committed in their name. The more complicated reception of later plays showed clearly how plays could become crucibles for the painful adjustment to a post-Nazi Germany. The Berlin premiere in January 1948 of Sartre's *Les Mouches* (*The Flies*, 1943) caused great controversy. It is a reworking of the Orestes story and embodies Sartre's existentialist call for continual renewal through action and not letting who you already are limit you; when it premiered in Nazi-occupied Paris, it was widely understood as a call for resistance; in postwar Germany, it was seen by some left commentators as letting the Germans off the hook. One of the biggest hits of the period was

European playwriting and politics, 1945–89   23

Carl Zuckmayer's *Des Teufels General* (*The Devil's General*, 1946), in which a German airman, General Harras, who is critical of the Nazis despite flying for them, is tasked with finding a saboteur among the engineers. He discovers that the culprit is a friend and realises that he must sacrifice himself to protect his friend and to stop being the 'Devil's general'. Despite its success, it faced some criticisms at its German premiere in 1947 from members of the audience who thought it presented a falsely heroic vision of Germans as critical and self-sacrificing and let them off the hook by characterising Hitler as a supernatural force (The Devil) rather than a product of German society.

It was perhaps the suspicion that some parts of Germany wanted to hastily whitewash the War that led to Martin Walser writing *Eiche und Angora* (*The Rabbit Race*, 1962), whose three sections take us from 1945 to 1960 and paint a picture of a convenient German amnesia about the recent past.[1] Relatedly, in Italy, Vitaliano Brancati's play *La governante* (*The Governess*, 1952) satirised bourgeois hypocrisy in its portrait of a rigidly moralistic bourgeois family whose façade of Catholic respectability masks their own complicity with fascism and stirrings of lesbianism. The play was prohibited from performance and Brancati wrote a celebrated pamphlet *Ritorno alla Censura* (*Back to Censorship*, 1952) criticising the hypocrisies of Italian culture.

A key political development of the period was the forced abandonment of their colonial empires by France, Belgium, and Britain, and this too is reflected upon and interrogated by their writers. In France, this included plays like Martinican writer Aimé Césaire's *Et les Chiens se taisent* (*And the Dogs Were Silenced*, 1956) and the Algerian Kateb Yacine's *Le Cadavre encerclé* (*The Corpse Encircled*), published in 1954 but so controversial during the Algerian War that it could only be performed in France secretly in 1958. Genet would explore these themes too, and one can see the resonance of these early attempts to find a theatrical language for the anti-colonial struggle in a later play like *Combat de nègres et de chiens* (*Black Battles with Dogs*, 1982) by Bernard-Marie Koltès, who would go on to influence later writers like Sergi Belbel and Mark Ravenhill. In Britain, the colonial legacy is addressed throughout the period by plays like John Arden's *Serjeant Musgrave's Dance* (1959) and Howard Brenton's *The Romans in Britain* (1980), a play whose prosecution for supposed indecency was in part a conservative response to its anti-colonial politics. The dramaturgical picture was also informed by the new wave of Black British playwrights who brought the view from the former colonies, most notably the Trinidadian writer Mustapha Matura with plays like *As Time Goes By* (1971), that debates the contradictory pull of colonial home and colonial centre in Black British identity. Here and elsewhere, new playwriting has been at the heart of Europe's developing identity in the postwar world.

'Not working'

A curious thought experiment about postwar European theatre is to wonder what Samuel Beckett's *Waiting for Godot* (1953) might have looked like rewritten by Bertolt Brecht. The idea of a forced marriage between the giants

24   Dan Rebellato

of metaphysical and materialist theatre seems preposterous on the face of it, and yet it nearly happened. In the six months before his death in August 1956, Brecht annotated his personal copy of *Warten auf Godot* with a series of suggestions for how to transform the play from a drama of existential ennui to a critique of capitalist society.[2] The list of characters is annotated 'Estragon, a proletarian, Wladimir, an intellectual, Lucky, a donkey, or policeman, von Pozzo, a landowner'. The playtext itself sees various lines redistributed between the characters and sometimes rewritten, usually in a more vernacular form, identifying the two main characters as more evidently working class. Beckett's play opens with Estragon's line 'Nothing to be done' or 'Rien à faire' (Beckett 1966: 9; 1986: 11). Brecht amends this to 'Geht nicht' ('Not working'), thus replacing what may feel like a defeated declaration of human passivity into an observation that *something* requires *fixing*.

What needed fixing might well have been, in Brecht's eyes, the capitalist system but it could also be Beckett's dramaturgy, which many in Europe (not just in the East) thought deeply conservative, and the play was banned in East Germany and East Berlin until the late 1980s (see McGowan 2002: 134–5). On the other hand, while the ideological differences may have been particularly sharp to mid-century observers, at this distance we might appreciate them both as products of late modernism, and indeed Carl Weber (2002) observes some significant overlaps in their visual approach to theatre, while Hans–Thies Lehmann notes their shared fondness for parable, abstraction, and stories of failure (2002: 44–5, 47). It may be that there is a third reference point behind that 'Not working' that both men would share. Perhaps, in mid-1950s Europe, what was not working was realism.

What is so enticing about the thought of the Brecht *Godot* is that it brings together the two great European influences on playwriting of the third quarter of the twentieth century: Brechtian epic theatre and the so-called 'Theatre of the Absurd'. The emergence of these two forms was itself political, the absurd founded not merely in mid-century philosophical existentialism, but the nihi-listic violence of the Second World War, while Brecht's epic theatre was a response to the emergence of capitalist mass culture across the Europe and the ideological debates about how it might be constrained or overthrown. That there are huge differences between them should not be ignored: the absurd's preference for whimsical fantasy, parodic illogic, surreal imagery, and comic despair contrasts sharply with Brecht's profoundly social vision, his direct arousal of audience engagement, his rooting of the story and stage imagery in material human practice. Yet, more immediately, the particular flowering of interest in these opposed dramaturgical options may share a root of opposition to the dominance of various realist traditions across Europe.

The real

The importance of naturalism to European theatre cannot be ignored. Although many of its original emphases – the valorisation of scientific method, its preference for the problem play, its tendency to represent bourgeois society – may have

European playwriting and politics, 1945–89 25

become less unquestioned under the repeated assaults of modernism, psychological realism, realist stage design, and the desire to *épater le bourgeois* continued to be influential, even in theatre forms that were not thoroughgoingly naturalist. Although it is the challenges to realism that have attracted most attention in the postwar theatre, realism has continued to be a powerful force, often at moments of the most direct challenge to prevailing social values. It's there in the titles of important new theatres and companies like the Realistické divadlo in Prague (1945), Realistiko Theatro in Athens (formed in 1949 under Aimilios Veakis), and Spain's Grupo de Teatro Realista (formed in 1960 by director José María de Quinto and playwright Alfonso Sastre). The year before, de Quinto had directed a celebrated production of *Look Back in Anger* by John Osborne in Madrid, a reminder that British playwriting in the 1950s had been renewed by the angry realism of Osborne, Arnold Wesker, Shelagh Delaney, and others, whose works quickly made their way into the European repertoire on both sides of the East-West divide. Elsewhere, broadly realist playwrights included Lauro Olmo and José Martín Recuerda in Spain, Paul Koeck and Walter van den Broeck in Belgium, John Boyd and Martin Lynch in Ireland. The documentary theatre movement in 1960s Germany, which included Peter Weiss, Rolf Hochhuth, and Heinar Kipphardt, took a different theatrical form but still placed realistic engagement with society at its heart.

But by far the most important realist movement in postwar Europe – and the one that perhaps did most to discredit realism as a form – was the state-sanctioned socialist realism that dominated Eastern Europe from the late 1940s. The policy was adopted by the USSR at the Soviet Writers Congress in August 1934, and when Eastern Europe fell under Stalin's control, the policy quickly spread through the region. Between 1948 and 1949, theatres in the Soviet bloc were nationalised and socialist realism became the official style. This meant realism from a socialist perspective, revealing the social and material conditions determining human behaviour, promoting a teleological vision of history culminating in communism, denouncing bourgeois capitalism, offering rationalism rather than mysticism, political economy rather than individual psychology.

Socialist realism was stylistically quite flexible, it being principally a stipulation about content and meaning, rather than theatrical form. It included many comedies, since, as Paul Trensky observes, 'this genre corresponded to the greatest degree to the official optimism the plays were expected to convey' (1978: 6). *Dobrá píseň* (*The Good Song*, 1952), the first play by Pavel Kohout, one of the towering playwrights of postwar Czechoslovakia,[3] was a socialist realist comedy – in verse. There were also satires, agitprop plays, romances, melodramas, plays set in villages and factories, history plays depicting pioneers of socialist progress or the historic contradictions that could only be resolved under communism. Typical of socialist realism at its cruder end was Czech writer Ota Šafránek's *Ráno startují letadla* (*Morning Take-Off*, 1950), later retitled *Čest poručíka Bakera* (*The Honour of Lieutenant Baker*, 1951), a fictional account of the pilot who dropped the atomic bomb on Hiroshima, imagining his postwar life, unemployed and disillusioned with capitalism, improbably longing for the socialist dawn.

26   *Dan Rebellato*

The policy of socialist realism insistently demanded the eradication of nationalism and romanticism. These were intertwined principles for many countries of the Soviet bloc; for countries like Poland, that had long struggled for an independent political and cultural existence, romanticism had been a key means of autonomous cultural expression in the nineteenth century. Its veneration of valiant struggle, its emphasis on will, imagination, and heroism appealed to anyone seeing to find, define, and maintain a distinct national identity. The theatre had played a significant role in this and key nineteenth-century romantic dramas – like Hungarian Imre Madách's *Az ember tragédiája* (*The Tragedy of Man*, 1861), a poetic drama that begins in the Biblical creation story and follows Lucifer as he takes Adam and Eve on a tour of human history, or Polish author Adam Mickiewicz's *Dziady* (*Forefathers' Eve*, 1823–60), a poetic epic that deals with mystical spirits, the power of love and the persecution of the Polish people – becoming rallying points for the cause of national self-determination.

When many of these countries achieved independence with the break-up of the 'great powers' after the First World War, theatre and playwriting flourished. In Czechoslovakia, for example, the confidence of the interwar theatre can be measured by the emergence of outstanding playwrights like František Langer, whose *Perifirie* (*Outskirts*, 1925) was a serious exploration of crime, punishment, the city, and the human will, and Karel Čapek whose most famous plays *R.U.R.* (1921) and *Ze života hmyzu* (*The Insect Play*, cowritten with his brother Josef, 1922) use expressionist techniques to explore technology, greed, and authoritarianism. Alongside this flourished a deeply searching and productive intellectual culture around the theatre, notably in the work of the 'Prague Structuralists' one of whose leading members, Jindřich Honzl, was a leading theatre director as well as an important theorist of theatrical meaning (see Matějka and Titunik 1976).

All of this was eradicated with the imposition of socialist realism. In Hungary, productions of *The Tragedy of Man* were forbidden. Mickiewicz's *Forefathes' Eve* had a revival at the Teatr Stary (Old Theatre), Kraków in 1945, but in 1948, when Leon Schiller tried to revive his celebrated prewar production, it was banned. That a 100-year-old mystical-poetic drama could genuinely alarm the Soviet authorities is confirmed by its continued status as a rallying point for resistance. In 1967, when Kazimierz Dejmek, artistic director of the Teatr Narodowy (National Theatre) in Warsaw opened a production, the authorities closed the show mid-run, fired him from the theatre, and expelled him from the Communist Party. His case would be taken up by protesting university students, which influenced Alexander Dubček's liberalising reforms that, in turn, lead to the Warsaw Pact invasion that crushed the revolt. In 1973, Konrad Swinarski staged it right through the interior of the Teatr Stary in Kraków in a legendary production that swept the audience into the performance.

In its strictest form, socialist realism was mostly applied for a relatively short period, from the late 1940s to the mid-1950s. Even here though, there is considerable diversity: in Poland, playwriting opened up enormously after 1956, but in some countries like Hungary the official realist policy continued to be promoted into the

European playwriting and politics, 1945–89   27

1960s, while in the 1970s, when other Soviet countries were experiencing some cultural liberalisation, Romania under Ceaușescu had perhaps the most restrictive cultural policy anywhere in Europe. This is not to say that all socialist-realist plays were bad; some writers were able to find some room for complexity. Hungarian author Gyula Hay's *Az élet hídja* (*The Bridge of Life*, 1950), concerning the reconstruction of a bridge in Budapest over the Danube, represented the workers with complexity, emotional depth and force; there is some power in the work of a rare female playwright of the period, Romania's Lucia Demetrius whose *Trei generații* (*Three Generations*, 1956) showed the condition of women in the 1890s, 1920s, and 1950s, offering a relatively complex vision of how capitalism and patriarchy are intertwined (before, inevitably, women being liberated under communism). Miloslav Stehlík's *Nositelé řádu* (*The Award Winners*, 1953), placed at its heart a heroic worker, of the kind usually hymned by socialist realism, but all his awards and recognition have turned him into a monster of vanity and cruelty.

It should also be noted that the doctrine of socialist realism was applied unevenly across the bloc. The Bosnian writer Skender Kulenović was celebrated for his wartime fight against fascism and for his stirring poetry; his play *Svjetlo na drugom spratu* (*Light on the Second Floor*) was published in 1954, shortly after he and members of his circle had fallen out of favour with President Tito and contained criticisms of the Party; it would be widely performed five years later, though not in the main cities of Belgrade or Zagreb, which was perhaps the Yugoslavian Communist way of turning a blind eye. In East Germany, the major playwright Volker Braun seemed to offer increasingly bleak criticisms of Erich Honecker's state from a left perspective. This can be seen in the lengthy evolution of *Die Kipper* (*The Dump Trucks*, 1972), which began life as *Der Totale Mensch* (*The Whole Man*, written but unpublished 1962), in which a dump truck driver, Paul Bausch, tries to bring about full communism despite the shortcomings and slow progress of industrial reality; his own vitality as a character is a symbol of the 'whole man' [sic] that will be released when full socialism arrives. This was published in *Forum*, the journal of the Free German Youth, under the name *Kipper Paul Bausch* in 1966 and was already controversial, forcing the resignation of *Forum*'s editor. It was finally produced at the Deutsches Theater in 1972 and in the process of revision the emphasis of the play had moved from the vigorous cheerfulness of Bausch's optimism to a grimly detailed landscape of industrial monotony, famously describing East Germany as 'the most boring country on Earth' (Braun 1989: 126).

Even in the Soviet Union itself, writers like Aleksandr Vampilov dragged socialist realism in a Chekhovian direction with plays often focused on young people, like *Utinaya okhota* (*Duck Hunting*, 1976). He died young in a boating accident but his work was enormously popular in the 1970s and 1980s, to an extent that strongly suggests his ability to exceed the limitations of the form. A different approach is taken by Ignatii Dvoretski's *Chelovek so storoni* (*The Outsider*, 1972), which shows a young engineer successfully transforming an inefficient factory; although it adhered strictly to the Party line in showing a heroic worker's success, it, like Volker's *The Dump Trucks*, gave full expression to all the problems and inefficiencies that beleaguered the Soviet system (Marsh 1986: 121).

28   Dan Rebellato

In allowing that *The Outsider* might have a covert implication that contradicted its apparent meaning, we touch on the complex subtextual dramaturgy of much Soviet-era work. After Stalin's death in 1953, the range of playwriting styles broadened in most areas, as did the topics; indeed, in the era of Khrushchev's de-Stalinising 'thaw', plays critical of Stalinism were encouraged. Nikolai Pogodin's *Sonet Petrarki* (*A Petrarchan Sonnet*, 1957) suggested that the state should not interfere in personal relationships, a critique that could be applied beyond Stalin to the wider Soviet system. But mostly the criticisms of the system had to be mild and even a major writer like Aleksei Arbuzov, in his impeccably socialist-realist drama *Irkutskaya istoria* (*An Irkutsk Story*, 1959) about a dissolute young woman who is redeemed by her love for a worker at a Siberian hydroelectric plant, faced criticisms that the romance plot insufficiently encouraged its audience to join the revolutionary struggle (Arbuzov 1963). Part of the problem for playwrights was that socialist realism was never precisely defined. At the 1932 Writers Congress, A. I. Stetsky, the Secretary of the Department of Culture and Propaganda, rebuked writers for demanding 'a theory of socialist realism complete in all its details', before offering the circular argument that 'socialist realism can best be shown in those works of art which Soviet writers produce' (Gorky et al. 1977: 265). This gave the authorities a free hand to censor and condemn anything they wished and heightened the sense of risk for the writer. (This was not unique to the Soviet system. Under Franco's Spain, the stringent rules of theatre censorship were notorious for not being written down anywhere [Wellwarth 1972: 2–3].)

To the playwright who wanted to explore themes beyond love stories in Siberian power plants, there were a few options open. One was to write plays set in far-off locations or in apparently distant historical periods.[4] The Slovak author Ivan Bukovčan started in a socialist-realist mode, but risked censure with plays about human dilemmas in times of oppression – of which *Kým kohút nezaspieva* (*Until the Cock Crows*, 1969) is the best known – before transplanting his stories to exotic locations, the political resonance of which was clear but plausibly deniable. In Hungary in the early 1950s, *Fáklyaláng* (*Torchflame*, 1952) by Gyula Illyés, a veteran left-wing activist, was set in 1849 during the Hungarian War of Independence and centred on a debate between Lajos Kossuth and Artúr Görgei, the political and military leaders of the struggle to overthrow Habsburg rule; its pertinence to Soviet control of Hungary was widely recognised. Illyés's comrade in the wartime Hungarian underground, László Németh, wrote the still more provocative *Galilei* in 1953. The play concerned the astronomer Galileo's decision to choose between authority and his scientific principles and was initially banned, but, when it opened in Budapest on 20 October 1956, the audience immediately understood it as a protest against political oppression and it became part of the groundswell of feeling that would manifest in the Hungarian Uprising three days later.

The brutal crushing of the Uprising by the Soviet army had an effect on playwriting too. Some Hungarian writers, like Gyula Illyés, fell silent; others, like Gyula Hay, were imprisoned for their role. Some writers found ways of

European playwriting and politics, 1945–89 29

using loosely socialist-realist techniques to interrogate the country's problems, like Lajos Mesterházi's *Pesti emberek* (*People of Budapest*, 1958), given a grand production by Károly Kazimir at the Magyar Néphadsereg Színháza (Theatre of the Hungarian People's Army). Others retreated into painful expressions of personal dilemmas, like Károly Szakonyi in *Életem Zsöka* (*Sophie, My Life*, 1963) whose protagonist Köves is a wretched figure incapable of standing up to the Party, abandoned by his wife and by an old comrade who takes his own life in despair. Imre Sarkadi's late plays, written before his suicide in 1961, include *Oszlopos Simeon* (*Simeon on the Pillar*, 1967) and *Elveszett paradicsom* (*Paradise Lost*, 1961), and show dark struggles to keep hold of ideals in a world seemingly designed to strip everyone of them.

This turn inward was also characteristic of some later Romanian drama. Nicolae Ceauşescu was elected President of state council in 1965 and there followed an almost immediate liberalisation of cultural policy, but in 1971, following visits to Mao Zedong's China and Kim Il-sung's North Korea, he announced a new cultural revolution in the 'July Theses' which included a demand for all culture to take on a newly militant, propagandist character. This was so strictly enforced that the subtexts and double-meanings deployed by theatre-makers elsewhere in the East were almost impossible in Bucharest. Perhaps Romania's best-known playwright of the period, Marin Sorescu, had his breakthrough play *Iona* (*Jonah*, 1969) banned, because, in director Andrei Serban's production, this apparently philosophical monologue (about the Biblical Jonah) resonated as a story of survival even in the worst of conditions to an audience living in the belly of Romanian communism (Sorescu 1985: xi). Sorescu's later plays retreat even further, like *A treia ţeapă* (*The Third Stake*, 1978),[5] in which the fifteenth-century Dracula has ascended the throne of Wallachia through the expense of some violence and betrayal; as the play begins, he has placed two men on stakes to die. These wretches debate the times, sometimes with Vlad's involvement, until he erects a third stake and kills himself, his final words ringing in the air 'why don't we laugh any more?' (Sorescu 1987: 111). There are implied criticisms, but the play's deeply elliptical layers of history, philosophy, and fantasy serve as protective barriers against persecution. Sorescu's contemporary Dumitru Solomon spent much of the seventies writing a cryptically allegorical trilogy of plays about philosophers, *Socrate, Platon*, and *Diogene câinele* (*Socrates, Plato,* and *Diogenes the Dog*, 1974–6). In 1970s Romania, the gap between text and subtext was wider than anywhere else in postwar Europe.

Playwriting also functioned in different ways under authoritarian regimes, East and West, in the revival of classic plays. Although romanticism was banned in Poland, Shakespeare was allowed to be performed, and became a site for 'monumental' performances in which romantic motifs would be prominent. The repertoire of the Slovak theatre, Nová Scená, in Bratislava, was made up of European classics like Molière, Gogol, and Goethe, though their productions were frequently angled to generate sly criticisms of the Czech-Soviet regime. On the other hand, in fascist Spain, productions of the classics by Calderón de la

30 *Dan Rebellato*

Barca and others were angled to produce 'delirious spectacles of patriotic sacrifice and fervent Catholic sentiment that effectively announced the co-opting of the Golden Age to the ideological sentiments of the Nationalist cause' (Delgado 2012: 435). Meanwhile the more intractable classics were simply rewritten, including, in the Barcelona of 1943, a Nora who stayed with her husband and a Hedda Gabler who outlives her play (London 2012: 345). In Portugal, conversely, under military rule from 1926, Shakespeare's *Julius Caesar* was banned as dangerously provocative.

Many playwrights found their work falling foul of the censor only to have it re-emerge much later. Josef Kainar's *Ubu se vrací* (*Ubu Returns*, 1949) brought Alfred Jarry's Ubu back to comment on power and its abuses; after its short run it was banned and disappeared entirely from the Czech repertoire before being gloriously rediscovered in 1988 at the Kavárně Viola (Viola Café). Playwrights of the Second Spanish Republic, like Lorca, Valle-Inclán, and Casona were suppressed for 25 years under Franco but cautiously reintroduced into the repertoire in the early 1960s and then more enthusiastically after the restoration of democracy. In Poland, after Khrushchev's denunciation of Stalin, the prewar work of two greats was rediscovered: Stanisław Witkiewicz and Witold Gombrowicz. Both would go on to be significant influences on the playwrights of the 1960s.

Witkiewicz – or Witkacy, as he called himself to mark a difference from his celebrated father – was a painter, novelist, thinker, and enthusiastic experimenter with narcotics, as well as a playwright, and, although he was eccentrically individual to a fault, he nonetheless tacks closely to some main currents in European modernism, particularly in his advocacy of artistic autonomy in his lecture 'Czysta Forma w teatrze' (Pure Form in the Theatre) delivered at the Mały Theatre, Warsaw, in 1921. In it, he urged his audience to 'disregard the inessential period of realism' and acknowledge that art is not 'the expression of some kind of real-life content ... [...] something that has value only when compared to something else of which it is the reflection' (Gerould 1993: 148, 149–50). This perfect autonomy required a reconstruction of the relation between writer and director; the play is no longer a literary and complete object, but a 'kind of libretto' (151) that has its full realisation in the Pure Form of performance. Witkacy wrote something like 40 plays in the seven years between 1918 and 1925, around half of which have survived; he took his own life in 1939, in despair at the Nazi–Soviet invasions of Poland, so did not live to see the rediscovery of his work in the 1950s, beginning with Tadeusz Kantor's 1956 production of *Mątwa* (*The Cuttlefish*, written 1922, performed 1933), which he chose to open his new theatre, Cricot II in Krákow.

Although Witkacy advocated a theatre of Pure Form, he also acknowledged that this metaphysical conception was unlikely to be fully realised and so realism needed to be displaced by use 'of non-sense and of deformation of the world' (149). *The Cuttlefish* is a good example of this; it defies easy precis, but loosely concerns an artist, Paul Rockoffer, who we meet in some kind of afterlife or limbo, lamenting that his paintings have just been destroyed by a department of the state; he is visited by a former lover, a former Pope, and a

European playwriting and politics, 1945–89   31

former schoolfriend who has declared himself Hyrcan IV, 'king of the artificial kingdom of Hyrcania' (Witkiewicz 2004: 256). The characters exchange philosophical wisecracks about being, art, love, truth, and language. Hyrcan IV declares the secret of power to be the creation of fictions and masks to persuade people that falsehoods are true: 'But how does all this differ from theatre?' asks Rockoffer (262), a question that resonated richly in Poland under communism. Despite, or because of, their subversive deformations of reality, Witkacy's plays were enormously popular, with *Sonata Belzebuba* (*The Beelzebub Sonata*, 1925) having its world premiere in Białystock in 1966 and seeing major revivals in Łódź, Wrocław, Poznań, and Warsaw before the end of the decade (Witkiewicz 1980: 182).

Witold Gombrowicz was a generation younger than Witkacy and lived until 1969, but it was only in his last decade that his singular contribution to Polish writing was recognised. His work was banned at home and he lived abroad after 1939, first in Buenos Aries then France. His plays mix fable and satire in uncanny and undecidable ways. His best-known play internationally, *Iwona, księżniczka Burgunda* (*Princess Ivona*, written 1938, produced 1957), follows the crisis that afflicts a royal court when the Prince chooses for his bride an ungainly, unattractive, depressive young woman, Ivona, who spends the play virtually silent, allowing everyone else to project their feelings on her. In a famous scene, the Prince and his friend goad and encourage her to speak and, when they fail, they interpret and reinterpret her silence by turns as a sign of impertinence, offendedness, lethargy, sulking, fear, trauma, self-protection, arousal, and insult (Gombrowicz 1998: 28–34). Eventually, the court is so unsettled by her glum presence that they kill her, the play ending with the royal family kneeling reverentially and hypocritically in her memory. The play has echoes of Shakespeare, perhaps filtered through Jarry, and in its portrait of a preposterous bureaucracy with cruel and arbitrary authority, the play emerged as a brilliant satire of dogmatic, totalitarian systems.

Both these writers were influential on Polish playwrights by seeming to anticipate – and to offer a distinctly Polish version of – one of the most important European playwriting forms of the 1950s: the absurd.

The absurd

In 1961, Martin Esslin, a Hungarian refugee from the Nazis, published his book *The Theatre of the Absurd*, gathering a range of disparate authors under the umbrella of a single movement. The book itself became famous, its title passing into general use as an image of any preposterously illogical public event. Its first edition focuses on Samuel Beckett, Arthur Adamov, Eugène Ionesco, and Jean Genet. In subsequent editions (1968, 1980), he drew an ever-greater number of playwrights into the absurd, to a point where it threatens to lose all meaning (itself an absurdist move). This new generation of playwrights, at first mostly writing in French, had a vivacity, boldness, and confidence that enlivened a French stage that had become tired of the finicky elegance of Jean Anouilh or Henry de Montherlant or the dour and rather traditional playmaking of Jean-

32 Dan Rebellato

Paul Sartre. The newly confident theatricality of these authors – their vast (and sometimes miniature) striking images – were important in the development of a new generation of visually bold European directors and designers.

But, in fact, little is shared theatrically by Ionesco, Beckett, and Genet. The term 'absurd' has its value in picking out some features of their work – a nihilistic vision of the postwar world, a fondness for parodying philosophical or logical procedures, a distaste for naturalism – but there are profound differences between Genet's deep political anger, Beckett's bleakly austere comedy, Ionesco's philosophical playfulness, and Adamov's increasingly revolutionary satire, and emphasising the commonalities risks effacing the key differences.

In particular, Esslin seems determined to strip the plays of their politics, though in this he was not alone. In June 1958, the theatre critic Kenneth Tynan, who had championed Ionesco's work in Britain, had clearly got cold feet and he expressed his reservations in a famous *Observer* review of *Les Chaises* (*The Chairs*, 1952) at the Royal Court Theatre. In the review he denounced Ionesco as a false messiah whose bubble reputation appealed only to those who wanted to ignore reality. The plays, he suggested, deprive themselves of meaning in order to declare the world meaningless: his work is, he wrote famously, 'a self-imposed vacuum, wherein the author ominously bids us observe the absence of air' (Ionesco 1964: 92). The former aesthete Tynan was busy reinventing himself as a left-wing intellectual at the time and his argument has some affinities with socialist realism, especially in his peremptory judgment that 'Ionesco's theatre is pungent and exciting, but it remains a diversion. It is not on the main road' (92). It is true that Ionesco's dizzying verbal paradoxes have little to do with Brechtian analysis, but from this distance we can say that to see them as merely fantastical surrealism is to ignore the brutal critique of liberal democracy in *Tueur sans gages* (*Killer*, 1958), the implicit allegory of European fascism in *Rhinocéros* (*Rhinoceros*, 1959), and the satire of authoritarianism in *Le Roi se meurt* (*Exit the King*, 1962).

Genet's work is deeply engaged with class and gender politics in *Les Bonnes* (*The Maids*, 1947), the sexual politics of power in *Le Balcon* (*The Balcony*, 1956), and anti-racist and anti-colonial politics in *Les Négres* (*The Blacks*, 1959) and *Les Paravents* (*The Screens*, 1966). Similarly, Arthur Adamov's early plays like *Le Professeur Taranne* (*Professor Taranne*, 1954) seemed closer to Ionesco, but with *Le Ping Pong* (*Ping Pong*, 1955) and *Paoli Paoli* (1957), he shows the increasing influence of Brecht, both in his dramaturgy and his politics. Esslin 'promotes' Harold Pinter to the front rank of the absurdists in the 1980 edition of his book, just about the time that Pinter himself was becoming less absurd and more political. Much of his work after 1980 – such as *One for the Road* (1984), *Mountain Language* (1988), *Party Time* (1991), and *Ashes to Ashes* (1996) – was unmistakeably concerned with state violence and oppression, the complicity of the bourgeoisie, and the memory of European fascism.

Even more evidently, absurdism as it manifested in Eastern Europe had remarkable political potency. In 1954, the director Vasilije Popović persuaded the director of the Beogradsko Dramsko Pozorište (Belgrade Drama Theatre), Predrag

European playwriting and politics, 1945–89 33

Dinulović, to let him direct *Waiting for Godot*. The play was regarded as 'decadent' by the authorities and not everyone within the theatre agreed that it should be presented. So nervous was the company that the public were excluded from the first performance, which could only be watched by the theatre's staff; this caused an uproar, with protests on the street from people angry at being excluded, and some people breaking into the theatre and hiding in the auditorium to see the performance, after which it was banned. A private performance was given in an artist's studio a few months later and, in late 1956, the whole production was remounted in a new small-scale studio theatre, Atelier 212 (Bradby 2001: 162–4). A production followed at the Teatr Współczesny (Contemporary Theatre) in Warsaw, January 1957, where it seemed that waiting for Godot was like 'waiting for the fulfilment of all the vain promises in the name of which the communist rulers demanded sacrifices from society' (Kędzierski 2009: 165). Polish critic Jan Kott later declared 'When we want realism we do *Waiting for Godot*' (quoted 167). Elsewhere, Godot was slow to arrive; Czechoslovakia didn't see the play until 1964, Hungary 1965, Croatia 1966, Estonia 1977, East Germany 1987, Bulgaria 1988 (Saiu 2009; Rákóczy 2017; Sabljo 2013: 212; Bradby 2001: 240). In Bulgaria, Elizabeth Sotirova reports that *Godot* first circulated in the late 1950s, when a diplomat's daughter returned from Paris with a magazine containing the text that enthusiasts would copy out by hand in order to read it (1995: 49), a common method of exchanging dissident plays in authoritarian states.[6]

Beckett was a particular influence on playwrights in the Soviet bloc looking for a way to create a dramaturgical resistance to their authoritarian governments that might avoid the attention of the censors. Together, the work of writers like Václav Havel (Czechoslovakia), Sławomir Mrożek and Tadeusz Różewicz (Poland), István Örkény (Hungary) and others forms what is sometimes called an 'Eastern European Grotesque' (e.g. Nagy 1994: 13), marked by dark humour, allegory and allusion, ambiguity, and a profound mockery of rules and conformity. Havel's *Vyrozumění* (*The Memorandum*, 1965) is a superb example of the style: the boss of a firm is alarmed to receive a memorandum requiring all future communications to be conducted in the incomprehensible language of 'Pytdepe'; the boss's attempts to investigate the language leads him into a labyrinthine bureaucracy with bewildering rules and vicious hierarchical conflicts that are by turns comic and terrifying. Something of the same absurdist satire can be seen in the episode from Mrożek's *Vatzlav* (1968) in which General Barbaro (certainly a close relation of Witkiewicz's Hyrcan IV) orders that all camels be castrated, while reserving to himself the right to say who counts as a camel: 'First they castrate,' remarks one observer, 'then they look to see if you're a camel' (Mrożek 2004: 294). This critique of the military mind is also found in Örkény's *Tóték* (*The Tot Family*, 1967), set during the Second World War, and concerns a small-town family who are persuaded by their son, serving in the army, to take in his commanding officer, who is suffering from a nervous condition brought on by war. His condition requires comically extreme adjustments in the family which are all in vain since, unbeknownst to them, their son has been killed.

34   Dan Rebellato

It is tempting to divide the absurd into a western version that expresses comic melancholy at an absurd universe and an eastern version that expresses comic melancholy at an absurd political system, but the differences are more subtle. For one thing, Beckett's theatre emerges not merely from existential ideas but the experience of European fascism (Beckett was involved in the French Resistance) and the prospect of nuclear destruction hangs over the western absurdists. But also the absurdism of the East has some distinctive features that respond much more to local traditions and concerns than to the western European example. Tadeusz Różewicz's *Kartoteka* (*The Card Index*, 1960) is a kind of monodrama, whose anonymous central character seems to be a collection of incompatible fragments who spends the play trying to assemble his life as friends, family, colleagues, and acquaintances come and go with the fluidity of a dream. The protagonist is referred to as the 'Hero', which is plainly ironic. In his opening author's note, Różewicz declares: 'I am not offering a list of characters. The play's "Hero" is of indeterminate age, occupation and appearance. On various occasions our "hero" ceases to be the hero of our tale and is replaced by other "heroes"' (Różewicz 1969: 38). It seems indebted in part to Witkacy's *The Cuttlefish* not just in its evocation of fragmented subjective experience, but also in its attempt 'not [to] imitate or embellish life' but to create 'a self-contained reality on stage' (Filipowicz 1984: 395). It is no doubt also a deliberate rejection of the heroic protagonists of socialist realism. Simultaneously, in Czechoslovakia, there was a concerted effort to 'deheroize' new plays and plays instead focused on the 'passive hero-victim' (Trensky 1978: 18). Examples of this include Pavel Kohout's *Taková láska* (*Such a Love*, 1957), a tale of a love triangle that ended tragically, in which all the characters seem equally guilty and equally unheroic, or indeed Havel's 'Vaněk' plays, *Audience* (1975), *Vernisáž* (*Unveiling*, 1976), and *Protest* (1979), each of which feature the comic 'little man' Ferdinand Vaněk, a dissident playwright forced out of his calling, whose quiet resolve challenges everyone around him. While there are affinities between these passive characters and figures like Vladimir and Estragon, Krapp, and Winnie, Różewicz has stated firmly 'I wrote my plays in opposition to Beckett's. His dramatic work was my point of departure, not a point of arrival' (quoted, Filipowicz 1984: 407). These non-heroes are a distinctively Eastern European piece of dramaturgy.

The Card Index managed nine performances before it was banned, primarily because its experimentalism was too at odds with official policy to ignore, though the protagonist's struggle to reconcile the various demands of their social, political, and personal roles had its own significance for Polish audiences in 1960. Later, in 1971, Różewicz published a new, complete version, including scenes he had initially suppressed, which oriented the 'Hero's fragmentation explicitly with the dislocations of Soviet communism and immediately revived interest in the play (see Filipowicz 1984). Mrożek's most celebrated play *Tango* (1965) shows well how the mixture of absurdism and the anti-heroic hero served to produce allegories of communist living. The play's madcap logic disguises a play about the failure of successive generations to take responsibility for Poland leaving the way clear for the brutal thuggery of Stalinism.

European playwriting and politics, 1945–89   35

It is ambiguous whether Mrożek is arguing that a truer, more successful socialism could have been achieved or that a reduction to brutality is a permanent condition of human existence. The permissiveness towards critiques of Stalinism after 1956 combined with the allusiveness of the Grotesque style meant that even in brutally censored Romania, a play like *O pasăre dintr-o altă zi* (*A Bird from Another Day*, 1972) by Dumitru Radu Popescu, made its way onto the stage of the Romanian National Theatre and despite some self-censorship by its author received a production from the eminent director Alexa Visarion that took the play's delicate anti-Stalinist hints and gave them full political value. There are strands of the Eastern European Grotesque that seem politically focused in their commentary, while at other times there is a nihilistic quality to this work that aims, in the words of one critic, 'to make sense of nonsense by making nonsense of sense' (Goetz-Stankiewicz 1979: 8).

These absurdist experiments benefitted from being somewhat at the periphery of Soviet authority: Havel's early plays were performed at the Divadlo Na zábradlí (Theatre on the Balustrade), a small unofficial theatre, on the edge of Prague's theatre district. Radu Popescu's *A Bird from Another Day* was performed at the National Theatre building in Cluj-Napoca, not Bucharest. Closer to home, absurdism made little inroads to the Soviet Union's theatre culture. Viktor Slavkin, strongly influenced by Mrożek, wrote short plays for the 'Nash Dom' (Our Home) student company at Moscow University including *Orkestr* (*Orchestra*, 1966) and *Plokhaia kvartira* (*Bad Apartment*, 1966). In the former a musician turns up for a concert and realises he can't open his instrument case, rendering his presence meaningless; in the latter, a couple have been rehoused after their previous accommodation collapsed, but the new apartment is a shooting gallery and they spend the play going about their domestic life while dodging bullets. It's not hard to see these plays as comments, respectively, on the role of the artist and personal life under totalitarianism. In the 1970s, Slavkin would gain wide acclaim for his full-length realist plays, most famously *Vzroslaia doch' molodogo cheloveka* (*A Young Man's Grown-Up Daughter*, 1978) and leave the absurd behind (see Russell 2000). There are moments of absurdism in the plays of Grigory Gorin, such as *Zavyt' Gerostrata!* (*Forget Herostratus!*, 1972), set in the fourth century BCE, based on the actions of historical arsonist Herostratus. Though Gorin's absurdism seems to derive more from Shavian paradox than Slavkinian allegory, the historical setting and the freewheeling debates allow for some ferocious critique of the preening demagoguery of the political class.

Perhaps in response to the eastern evolution of the absurd, it started to take on an increasingly political character in the west. We've seen the drift towards more explicit political engagement from Genet and Adamov (and arguably Ionesco). Even Samuel Beckett produced a vaguely political playlet in *Catastrophe* (1982), a five-minute scene in which a Director and their assistant manipulate a passive protagonist in an ultimately unsuccessful attempt to produce a spectacle of his humiliation, though perhaps the most recognisably political words in the play are the dedication 'For Vaclav Havel' (Beckett 1986: 455). (In a similar act of solidarity, Harold Pinter played Vaněk in a BBC 1977

36   Dan Rebellato

radio production of *Audience* and *Unveiling*.) Fernando Arrabal's playful absurdism in plays like *El arquitecto y el emperador de Asiria* (*The Architect and the Emperor of Assyria*, 1967) gave way, following a period of incarceration in Spain for blasphemy, to a more politically engaged dramaturgy in plays like ...*Y pusieron esposas a las flores* (...*And They Put Handcuffs on the Flowers*, 1969), a prison drama that makes a ferociously scatological plea for infinite freedom. In Greece, Vasiles Ziogas's *Paschalina paichnidia* (*Easter Revels*, 1966) takes us through the stages of a Passion from crucifixion to resurrection in a story of a son's paradoxical redemption of his ideologically compromised father by murdering him; and *Polē* (*The City*, 1965) by Loula Anagnostaki shows a man and woman coax an elderly photographer to their apartment to arouse and then reject him, but are rejected in their turn, the cruel abstraction of the play offering a vision of nihilistic amorality. Although the absurd seemed to have run its course by the late 1970s, its plays have remained at the heart of the modern European repertoire, and the style is something that reappears in surprising places, such as Caryl Churchill's nightmarish vision of global, political and environmental war, *Far Away* (2000).

The epic

The influence of Brecht is as broad and pervasive as that of the absurd and, in many ways, is even more varied. Brecht had a long writing life and while some playwrights have been influenced by his epic history plays like *Mutter Courage und ihre Kinder* (*Mother Courage and Her Children*, 1941) or *Leben des Galilei* (*The Life of Galileo*, 1943, 1955), others have been drawn to the didactic, directly revolutionary plays like *Die Mutter* (*The Mother*, 1932); while some have admired the dialectic complexities of the late work like *Der kaukasische Kreidekreis* (*The Caucasian Chalk Circle*, 1954), others have been exhilarated by the amoral brutality of the young Brecht in *Trommeln in der Nacht* (*Drums in the Night*, 1922) or *Baal* (1923). For some, he is a profound deconstructionist of theatrical representation; for others, it is the purity of his revolutionary message that appeals. His influence is both as a voluminous theorist and a wholly practical man of the theatre. Brecht's theorising is formidable and developed restlessly from 1920s to his death in 1956, but it did not appear in isolation. One of the reasons that it can be difficult to draw out his influence is that he draws on so many other forms of performance, from Berlin Cabaret to Beijing Opera, from expressionism to puppetry, from boxers to balladeers.

One might, for example, see some influence of Brecht in the theatre of Dario Fo, in his direct engagement of the audience, his mixture of popular and art theatre, his delirious political provocations, in a play like *Morte accidentale di un anarchico* (*Accidental Death of an Anarchist*, 1970), a glorious political farce that toured during the inquest into an act of murderous police brutality in Italy that used the police's own constantly revised testimony to update the play's plot at each performance. But Fo is also drawing on long traditions of commedia, clowning, and satire, so Brecht's influence may only be in shaping the receptiveness

European playwriting and politics, 1945–89   37

of a wide European audience for this work. In Greece, Iakovos Kambanellis's *To megalo mas tsirko* (*Our Grand Circus*, 1973) was a subversive pageant of anti-authoritarian resistance and an enormous box office success; like Fo's *La Signora è da buttare* (*Throw the Lady Out*, 1967), it employs a panoply of exuberant theatrical devices that are indebted equally to Brecht and circus. Elsewhere, one might detect the imprint of Brechtian models on John McGrath's *The Cheviot, the Stag and the Black, Black Oil* (1973), but its episodic mixture of political commentary, song, and storytelling may derive directly from the ceilidh, just as similar techniques in contemporary Spanish and Greek plays may owe more to the *zarzuela* and *epitheorisi* than to Brecht.

But elsewhere his influence is clear. Luigi Squarzina's play *La Romagnola* (*The Woman from Romagna*, 1959) concerned a tragic conflict within a group of resistance fighters during the Second World War, but demonstrates a more direct Brechtian influence in the ensemble playing, the use of signs, the presentation of the artifice, and the nimble dialectic of the storytelling. France discovered Brecht in the 1950s and he had a particularly profound impact on the work of Michel Vinaver, beginning with his *Aujourd'hui, ou Les Coréens* (*Today, or The Koreans*, 1956), which explores an encounter between a French patrol and a group of Korean villagers and employs an ensemble staging to generate some complex shifts and contradictions. In Belgium, the Flemish writer Tone Brulin worked for a while in Africa, trying to find ways of using Brechtian techniques to theatrically explore the process of postcolonialisation; his anti-apartheid drama *De Honden* (*The Dogs*, 1960) was so electrifying that when it was announced in the programme of the Théâtre de Parc in Brussels, the South African Embassy lobbied furiously (and unsuccessfully) to have the play banned. In 1970, Marianne Van Kerkhoven resigned as dramaturg for the Koninklijke Nederlandse Schouwburg (Royal Dutch Theatre) in Antwerp after the management rejected her play *Het Trojaanse Paard* (*The Trojan Horse*, 1970) – with its Brechtian subtitle *of de stuitbare opkomst van Victor De Brusseleire* (or, *The Resistible Rise of Victor de Brusseleire*) – for being too political. Instead, she formed her own company, also called The Trojan Horse, and they mounted the play to great acclaim. Two years later she worked with another company to produce Dario Fo's *Mistero Buffo* (1969), which became one of the key moments in Belgian political theatre.

Brecht has had a significant impact on British playwriting, ever since the legendary visit of his Berliner Ensemble in the summer of 1956. John Arden, Edward Bond, Howard Brenton, and others have all noted (and sometimes denied) his influence. In particular, the historical sweep of epic theatre is a contributor to the development of the 'state of the nation play' in the 1970s, typically placing individual stories against a national landscape and decades of history, deploying signs, direct address, jagged juxtapositions of scenes in a Brechtian style that confront audiences with dialectics of character and context, psychology and politics. Some of the best-known of these include Howard Brenton's *The Churchill Play* (1974), David Hare's *Plenty* (1978), and David Edgar's *Maydays* (1983), anatomising respectively the possibilities and dangers of British socialism, the disappointments of liberal democracy, and the drift to the

38   *Dan Rebellato*

right of certain sixties radicals. The form spread further afield, with a play like Brian Friel's *The Freedom of the City* (1973) presenting conflicting perspectives on a shooting of civilians by the British army during a civil rights protest, the chronology disrupted, mixing realist scenes with direct address, to stimulate both understanding and anger, while also carefully dismantling the centrist liberal position.

In fascist states, Brecht was even less tolerated. In 1960, the first Brecht production to play in Portugal was a version of *Der gute Mensch von Sezuan* (*The Good Person of Setzuan*, 1943) by a touring Brazilian company, which was promptly banned after five performances. In the same year Brecht's influence could be found in José Cardoso-Pires's *O render dos heróis* (*Relief of the Heroes*, written 1960, first performed 1965), which used epic theatre techniques to retell the story of the nineteenth-century 'Maria da Fonte' popular uprising in a way that invited comparison between the Cartista government of the 1840s and the *junta* of the 1960s. In Spain, Jordi Teixidor's *El retaule del flautista* (*The Legend of the Piper*, 1970) retold the Pied Piper of Hamelin story, but now the state refuses the Piper's offer to rid the town of rats because the authorities are in the pocket of the rat-trap manufacturers. The play was a huge success in Catalan, but when a Madrid company tried to produce it in Castilian, with references to contemporary political figures, the show was banned (see London 2012: 369).

But one can see Brecht's influence also in his investigation and revelation of the politics of theatrical representation and spectatorship. Handke's *Publikumsbeschimpfung* (*Offending the Audience*, 1966) goes far beyond Brecht in its intensification of awareness of the theatrical moment. This plotless, fictionless, characterless play confronts its audience with the very experience they are now having. In a different way, Heiner Müller's *Die Hamletmaschine* (*Hamletmachine*, 1979) pushes Brechtian juxtaposition much further into thoroughgoing fragmentation, where the splintered shards of the play make synthesis of the contradictions almost impossible.

1968 and all that

The 1960s saw a reinvention of playwriting right across Europe. Many countries created new alternative networks of small, independent theatres: the German 'Freie Szene', the French 'Off' and Café Theatres, the Spanish 'teatros de cámara' and 'teatro independiente', the British 'fringe', and the networks of attics, basements, and private homes in Czechoslovakia where *samizdat* theatre was performed. The kinds of plays written for these places tended to be shorter, the style abrasive, but with a greater freedom for formal invention. One characteristic of the years around 1968 is the appearance of some shockingly violent plays, frequently in a realist style. British playwright Edward Bond's *Saved* (1965) is famous for the central scene in which a group of young men stone a baby to death in a park; from Finland, Jussi Kylätasku's *Runar ja Kyllikki* (*Runar and Kyllikki*, 1974) centres on a young couple whose relationship is warped by

European playwriting and politics, 1945–89 39

rigid values of their remote village and ends in rape and murder; Wolfgang Bauer's *Magic Afternoon* (1968) follows four young people through an afternoon of music, drugs, sex, and violence, while Franz Xaver Kroetz's *Stallerhof* (*Farmyard*, 1972) shows the emotional and sexual abuse of a teenage girl. Later, the brutal, senseless violence of György Spiró's *Csirkefej* (*Chickenhead*, 1986) suggested the blank nihilism of Hungarian communism in its dying years.

These plays reflected, in some ways, different kinds of social tensions that were building up around Europe. The invasion of Czechoslovakia sent a chill through all Eastern European states. The Colonels' coup in 1967 meant that Greece was the third western European country under fascist rule and there were fears and rumours that the pattern might be repeated elsewhere. The wars in Vietnam, Biafra and elsewhere were flashpoints for intense protest and 1968 saw uprisings of students in Paris, London, Madrid, Rome, Stockholm, Warsaw, Prague and elsewhere. Often these protests were met with violent counter-reactions. In Italy, the years around 1970, which saw disturbing allegiances between the police and the far right, are referred to darkly as 'gli anni di piombo' (The Years of Lead). These new counter-cultural theatre movements contributed to these protests; university and student theatre groups had been important sites of resistance as far apart as Poland and Spain.

In the Netherlands during the war, the theatre had been used by the Nazis as a means of legitimising their occupation, and many theatre workers had been collaborators, leaving a lingering distrust of the theatre establishment. This manifested itself in two movements in the 1960s: first, the Provo movement of the mid-1960s (see Pas 2011), whose ludic, anarchic cultural interventions included smoke-bombing the 1966 Dutch Royal Wedding; if anything this had an anti-dramatic vision of the value of 'play' (see van Lente 2013: 64–9), but the student movement turned its attention to the theatre in November 1969 with the advent of the Aktie Tomaat (Tomato Action), in which students disrupted theatre shows by throwing tomatoes, smoke bombs, and other objects at theatre they considered too compromised, elitist, and hierarchical. A symbolic moment in *les événements* of May 1968 in Paris had been the student occupation of the Odéon, though as Kate Bredeson (2008) has shown, this spectacular action was only part of a network of encounters – some hostile, some friendly – between the theatre and the students.

These actions had an effect on playwriting. In many societies, new forms of playmaking emerged; *création collective* (to use the phrase championed by Mnouchkine and the Théâtre du Soleil from 1968) started to challenge the cachet of the individual author. In 1970 the Werkteater company was founded in Amsterdam, developing its shows collectively through improvisation and discussion and becoming a major force in the theatre of the Netherlands. In Sweden, playwrights Kent Andersson and Bengt Bratt worked collaboratively with a group of actors and local communities to create forceful political plays based around particular sections of society, including *Hemmet* (*The Home*, 1967) and *Sandlådan* (*The Sandbox*, 1968), looking at contemporary Sweden in turn through the eyes of the very old and the very young. Britain's Joint Stock

40   *Dan Rebellato*

theatre company developed a collaborative system for the development of new plays, while the 1970s also saw several plays being written by groups of writers. These innovations were enormously important in this decade and helped transform performance-making across Europe. Mainstream theatre generally tended to return to the older model of individual authorship in the 1980s, though the legacy of these experiments can be felt in a beautiful play like Judith Herzberg's *Leedvermaak* (*The Wedding Party*, 1982), whose text – a subtle consideration of identity, history, and trauma – comprises over 80 scenes which the director and actors are permitted to perform in any order. This has echoes in more recent plays like Martin Crimp's *Attempts on Her Life* (1997) and Simon Stephens's *Pornography* (2007), which also withdraw from some aspects of traditional authorial control to offer new kinds of collaboration with other theatre workers. Playwriting itself in the 1980s had unrecognisably changed since the 1950s, and Della Couling's words about Dutch theatre has validity across the whole continent: 'the art of the playwright really took off when the text lost its central and previously unassailable place within the method of performance' (1997: x).

One consequence of challenging the theatre's hierarchies was the influx of women playwrights across Europe, bringing a distinct *écriture féminine* to dramatic form. Major figures who emerged in the 1970s include Caryl Churchill (UK), Hélène Cixous (France), and Elfriede Jelinek (Austria, see pp. 00–00). But even less well-known figures are worth noting, including Italy's Dacia Maraini, whose best-known play is *Dialogo di una prostituta col suo cliente* (*Dialogue Between a Prostitute and Her Client*, 1978) and who set up the influential Maddalena women's theatre collective in Rome, 1973. In the Netherlands, Matin van Veldhuizen wrote several plays about women writers examining their ability to live an authentic life, including *Jane* (1983) about Jane Bowles. The death of Franco saw a generation of Spanish and Catalan women playwrights appear, including Paloma Pedrero, Carmen Resino, Carme Riera, and Ana Diosdado.

But the political tide appeared to have turned in the 1980s. In western Europe, the move to the left post-1968 had been replaced by a move to the right. The election of Margaret Thatcher in 1979 was a decisive moment, as was the '*tournant de la rigueur*' (turn to austerity) in France, March 1983, when François Mitterand's government conceded defeat after the international financial markets turned against its socialist policy programme. The forces of globalised capitalism and neoliberalism were on the rise. These were resisted by plays as diverse as Caryl Churchill's *Serious Money* (1988), a British play about city financiers in all their brutal vulgarity, written in a loose jangling verse, and *Minderleister* (*Underachievers*, 1988) by Austrian writer Peter Turrini, a powerful vision of the brutalising effect of the free market's evisceration of European industrial production. Meanwhile, in the Soviet bloc, the advent of *glasnost* (openness) under new liberalising President Mikhail Gorbachev did mean that criticisms of the Soviet system began to appear in plays by Alexander Gelman, Mikhail Shatrov, and others. In Czechoslovakia, Stanislav Štepka's *Vygumuj a napíš* (*Delete and Write Again*, 1989), produced on the very eve of the Velvet Revolution, observed with weary despair and bitter humour the frustrations of artists battling with a dying system.

The theatre that emerged from the embers of Cold War Europe owes a considerable debt to the earlier generations that took playwriting as it was practised in 1945 and turned it into a more open, more challenging, politically engaged, and enormously flexible thing. Realism, absurdism, and Brechtianism may have lost some of their urgency for the writers discussed here, but none of them would be who they are without the transformations effected, the battles fought, on national stages and covertly copied pages, between writer and censor, play and public, in those remarkable years.

Notes

1 Walser has drifted to the right in later years, arguing that Auschwitz had become a 'moral bludgeon' with which to beat the Germans (see Kovach and Walser 2008: 100) and later still being accused of antisemitism in his *roman à clef, Tod eines Kritikers* (*Death of a Critic*, 2002), showing that the process of coming to terms with the past is still not complete many decades later.
2 These annotations can be found in Bertolt Brecht Archive (2007: 166–9). I'm grateful to David Barnett for help in exploring Brecht's project.
3 Czechoslovakia no longer exists, having split, on 1 January 1993, into two separate states: the Czech Republic and Slovakia. When referring to plays staged between 1918 and 1992, I shall refer to Czechoslovakia, though sometimes the specific ethnicity of the playwright will make it valuable to specify their Czech or Slovak origins.
4 In fascist Spain, a similar strategy was deployed by Antonio Buero-Vallejo, who located politically subversive plays like *El sueño de la razón* (The Sleep of Reason, 1970) safely in the past.
5 This play is better known in English as *Vlad Dracula the Impaler* (see Sorescu 1987).
6 See also Wellwarth (1972) for evidence of how this kind of *samizdat* functioned in Spanish theatre under Franco.

Works cited

Arbuzov, Alexis (1963) *An Irkutsk Story*, New York: Pitman.
Beckett, Samuel (1966) *En attendant Godot: Pièce en deux actes*, London: Harrap.
———— (1986) *The Complete Dramatic Works*, London: Faber & Faber.
Bertolt Brecht Archive (ed.) (2007) *Die Bibliothek Bertolt Brechts*, Frankfurt: Suhrkamp.
Bradby, David (1991) 'A theatre of the everyday: The plays of Michel Vinaver', *New Theatre Quarterly*, 7, 261–283.
———— (2001) *Beckett – Waiting for Godot*, Cambridge: Cambridge University Press.
Braun, Volker (1989) *Texte in zeitlicher Folge 1*, Halle: Mitteldeutscher Verlag.
Bredeson, Kate (2008) '"Toute ressemblance est voulue": Theatre and performance of May '68', *Modern & Contemporary France*, 16: 161–179.
Couling, Della (ed.) (1997) *Dutch and Flemish Plays*, London: Nick Hern.
Delgado, Maria M. (2012) 'Directors and the Spanish Stage, 1823–2010', in Maria Delgado and David T. Gies (eds), *A History of Theatre in Spain*, Cambridge: Cambridge University Press.

42   Dan Rebellato

Delgado, Maria M. and Dan Rebellato (eds), (2020) *Contemporary European Theatre Directors*, 2nd edition, Abingdon: Routledge.

Esslin, Martin (1961) *The Theatre of the Absurd*, New York: Doubleday.

——— (1980) *The Theatre of the Absurd*, 3rd edition, Harmondsworth: Penguin.

Filipowicz, Halina (1984) 'Tadeusz Różewicz's *The Card Index*: A new beginning for Polish drama', *Modern Drama*, 27: 395–408.

Gerould, Daniel (ed.) (1993) *The Witkiewicz Reader*, London: Quartet.

Goetz-Stankiewicz, Marketa (1979) *The Silenced Theatre: Czech Playwrights Without a Stage*, Toronto: University of Toronto Press.

Gombrowicz, Witold (1998) *Three Plays*, London: Marion Boyars.

Gorky, Maxim, Radek, Karl, Bukharin, Nikolai and Zhdanov, Andrey (1977) *Soviet Writers' Congress 1934: the debate on socialist realism and modernism in the Soviet Union*, London: Lawrence and Wishart.

Ionesco, Eugene (1964) *Notes and Counter-Notes*, London: John Calder.

Kędzierski, Marek (2009) 'Beckett's reception in Poland', in Mark Nixon and Matthew Feldman (eds), *The International Reception of Samuel Beckett*, London: Continuum.

Kovach, Thomas A and Walser, Martin (2008) *The Burden of the Past: Martin Walser on Modern German Identity: Texts, Contexts, Commentary*, Rochester, NY: Camden House.

Lehmann, Hans-Thies (2002) 'B, B, and B. Fifteen minutes to comply', in Stephen Brockmann (ed.), *Where Extremes Meet: Rereading Brecht and Beckett*, Madison, WI: International Brecht Society.

London, John (2012) 'Theatre under Franco (1939–1975): Censorship, playwriting and performance', in Maria Delgado and David T. Gies (eds), *A History of Theatre in Spain*, Cambridge: Cambridge University Press.

Marsh, Rosalind J. (1986) *Soviet Fiction since Stalin: Science, Politics and Literature*, Totowa, NJ: Barnes & Noble.

Matějka, Ladislav and Titunik, Irwin R. (1976) *Semiotics of Art: Prague School Contributions*, Cambridge, MA: MIT Press.

McGowan, Moray (2002) 'Waiting for *Waiting for Godot*: Echoes of Beckett's play in Brecht's chosen land', in Stephen Brockmann (ed.), *Where Extremes Meet: Rereading Brecht and Beckett*, Madison, WI: International Brecht Society.

Mrożek, Sławomir (2004) *The Mrożek Reader*, New York: Grove.

Nagy, Péter (1994) 'Eastern Europe' in Don Rubin (ed.), *The World Encyclopedia of Contemporary Theatre, Volume 1: Europe*. London: Routledge.

Pas, Niek (2011) 'Mediatization of the Provos: From a local movement to a European phenomenon', in Martin Klimke, Jacco Pekelder and Joachim Scharloth (eds), *Between Prague Spring and French May*, Oxford: Bergahn.

Rákóczy, Anita (2017) 'The Godots that arrived in Hungary: The first Budapest productions before and after 1989', *Samuel Beckett Today/Aujourd'hui*, 29: 283–297.

Różewicz, Tadeusz (1969) *The Card Index and Other Plays*, London: Calder and Boyars.

Russell, Robert (2000) 'Blues at forty: The plays of Viktor Slavkin', in Arnold McMillin (ed.), *Reconstructing the Canon: Russian Writing in the 1980s*, Amsterdam: Harwood Academic.

Saiu, Octavian (2009) 'Samuel Beckett behind the Iron Curtain: The reception in Eastern Europe', in Mark Nixon and Matthew Feldman (eds), *The International Reception of Samuel Becket*, London: Continuum.

Shore, Cris (2001) 'The cultural policies of the European Union and cultural diversity', in Tony Bennett (ed.), *Differing Diversities: Transversal Study on the Theme of Cultural Policy and Cultural Diversity*, Strasburg: Council of Europe.

European playwriting and politics, 1945–89 43

Sindičić Sabljo, Mirna (2013) 'The reception of Samuel Beckett in Croatia during the 1950s', *Scando-Slavica*, 59: 207–218.

Sorescu, Marin (1985) *The Thirst of the Salt Mountain: A Trilogy*, London: Forest.

——— (1987) *Vlad Dracula the Impaler*, London: Forest.

Sotirova, Elizabeth (1995) 'The absurd as a specific form of realism', *History of European Ideas*, 20: 49–52.

Trensky, Paul I. (1978) *Czech Drama Since World War II*, White Plains, NY: Sharpe.

Van Lente, Dick (2013) 'Huizinga's children: Play and technology in twentieth century Dutch cultural criticism (From the 1930s to the 1960s)', *Icon*, 19: 52–74.

Weber, Carl (2002) 'Beckett and Brecht: Comparing their "scenic writing"', in Stephen Brockmann (ed.), *Where Extremes Meet: Rereading Brecht and Beckett*, Madison, WI: International Brecht Society.

Wellwarth, George (1972) *Spanish Underground Drama*, University Park, PA: Pennsylvania State University Press.

Witkiewicz, Stanisław Ignacy (1980) *Beelzebub Sonata: Plays, Essays and Documents*, New York: Performing Arts Journal.

——— (2004) *Seven Plays*, New York: Martin E. Segal Theatre Center.

2 Elfriede Jelinek and Werner Schwab

Heimat critique and dissections of right-wing populism and xenophobia

Karen Jürs-Munby

Introduction

Any comparison between the Austrian playwrights Elfriede Jelinek and Werner Schwab is bound to be as instructive as it is asymmetrical. The 'shooting star' and self-styled *'enfant terrible'* Schwab[1] (b. 1958), who emerged from obscurity to meteoric fame in the early 1990s, became the most frequently performed living German-speaking playwright in the last decade of the twentieth century, writing 16 plays in the short time before his untimely death from alcohol poisoning at the age of 35 on New Year's Day 1994. Meanwhile, Elfriede Jelinek (b. 1946), who was for years reviled in her own country as a *'Nestbeschmutzer'* (a person who befouls her own nest), and who like Schwab has consequently often presented herself as an outsider,[2] saw her plays much less frequently performed in the early 1990s but after winning numerous prestigious prizes – including eventually the Nobel Prize for Literature in 2004 – is by now one of the most performed German-speaking play-wrights internationally with a playwriting career spanning over 40 years.

Schwab's plays have sometimes been described as postmodern punk theatre – the band Einstürzende Neubauten being an important influence – whereas Elfriede Jelinek's playwriting has often been associated primarily with her feminist, anti-fascist, and anti-capitalist political engagement.[3] However, no such 'pigeonholing' along the divide of aesthetics and politics can do justice to either author, as Schwab's formal deconstructions, flippant self-stylisations, and public denial of any political agenda often disguise the morality and social criticism embedded in his plays (Hochholdinger-Reiterer 2002), while the overtly political nature of Jelinek's plays is equally inextricable from the linguistic and formal innovations of her playwriting. Despite their real or perceived differences, there are many affinities between Schwab's and Jelinek's oeuvres, forms of writing and overlapping political concerns that speak to discussion of European theatre.

'Austria is a small world in which the great one holds its rehearsals'

Thematically Jelinek and Schwab share a basic concern with the structural violence inherent in gender relationships and the nuclear family under capitalist

Elfriede Jelinek and Werner Schwab   45

patriarchy. In Schwab's plays, 'the unmasking of the petit-bourgeois family as a hell-hole and the exposure of the family ideal as a modern form of serfdom' are two recurring themes (Hochholdinger-Reiterer 2002: 302); for example, when a phrase like 'eigene Kinder' (one's own children) is turned into 'leibeigene Kinder' (children in bondage).[4] The 'depiction of the abuse of children in the family environment [...] constitutes one of [Schwab's] most important taboo topics' (ibid.: 304). It is a topic that Jelinek, too, would turn to after the horrendous revelations about the Fritzl case in Amstetten, in her *FaustIn and out* (2011). Both Schwab and Jelinek relate violence in the domestic sphere to the power of the Catholic Church and its reinforcement of patriarchal power relationships in family and society. In Schwab's plays, 'the brutality of dominating mother figures (all of them practising Catholics) corresponds to an equally violent Catholicism' (Hochholdinger-Reiterer 2002: 303), while in Jelinek's *FaustIn and Out* the abusive Catholic father has assumed the power of an almighty god.

Furthermore, both authors repeatedly make connections between the unit of the family, the ideology of the *Volk* and the nation state that recruits the family for its purposes. Hochholdinger-Reiterer (2002: 306) cites as an example the scene in Schwab's *Antiklimax* (*Anti-Climax*) when the father catches his son masturbating and declares: 'The *Volk* does not masturbate, it impregnates'. And in Jelinek's *Sports Play* the mother is told by the Chorus to let go of her son, so that he can join sports and ultimately war: 'Your son is vital! We need people who are concerned about their bodies and unconcernedly throw away their souls' (2012 [1997]: 51). As in these plays, both authors repeatedly and vehemently address the postwar legacy of National Socialism and renewed far-right populism in their native Austria. This context became especially acute when Kurt Waldheim, who was revealed to have been a former SA officer under the Nazis, was elected president of Austria in 1986, and when the right-wing opposition party Freedom Party of Austria (FPÖ) under its charismatic leader Jörg Haider rose to prominence throughout the 1990s and eventually became part of the coalition government in the 1999 parliamentary elections. Both authors explore how the national-socialist past is sedimented in everyday language, although Jelinek puts more emphasis on how this language is mediated by discourses in television, film, and the press. Importantly she often uses current news stories as material for her texts.

While many of Schwab's and Jelinek's plays may seem concerned primarily with Austrian national issues, the shared European history of the Second World War and the Holocaust as well as the recent resurgence of right-wing populism and xenophobia across much of Europe mean that their plays are highly relevant transnationally and performed all over Europe and beyond.[5] As Jelinek puts it in the essay *The Forsaken Place* (2008), written after the revelation of the Fritzl case in Amstetten: 'Austria is a small world in which the great one holds its rehearsals' (Jelinek 2008). In the twenty-first century, Jelinek has kept her finger on the pulse of our times and has tackled increasingly epic European and global topics, such as the war in Iraq and its representation in the media (in

46   *Karen Jürs-Munby*

Bambiland, 2003, and *Babel*, 2005), the global financial crisis (*The Merchant's Contracts*, 2009), and the contemporary plight of refugees in Europe (in *Charges (The Suppliants)*, 2014).

'I don't want theatre' – postdramatic experiments

Both Jelinek and Schwab explicitly reject traditional theatre, especially psychological naturalism. Early on, Jelinek states in one of her essays: 'I don't want to bring to life strange people in front of an audience. [...] I prefer not to have anything on stage that smacks of this sacred bringing to life of something divine. I don't want theatre' (1983: 102). Similarly, Schwab programmatically declares: 'The heart as a piece of human flesh is a muscle, and force is the only rescue for the old animal theatre, which you rescue by crushingly excruciating it' (1991: 9). Each in their own way radically questions the concept of dramatic representation by turning a defamiliarising form of language into the actual protagonist. Schwab states categorically: 'first comes language, then the human'; while Jelinek declares about her playwriting: 'It gapes widen open, the chaos, and spits something out but they are never humans. It is speaking – period' (cited in Pełka 2005: 9). Similarly, in the productions of her plays, language is also the real actor, as she stipulates in another essay on acting that '[the actors] ARE the speaking. They do not speak' (Jelinek 1997: 9).

Early on, Gerda Poschmann associated Jelinek and Schwab with the new phenomenon she described as the 'no-longer-dramatic theatre text' because of the prominence they gave to language. In spite of differences with respect to the degree to which their theatre texts still displayed essential features of the dramatic form, she states, they 'have one thing in common: the central significance that language occupies, i.e. not primarily as represented speech of fictional figures but as an auto-reflexively used medium of aesthetic communication in the outer communication system' (1997: 180). Hans-Thies Lehmann subsequently identified both authors with the paradigm of postdramatic theatre, affirming that along with Reinald Goetz, Sarah Kane, and René Pollesch, Schwab and Jelinek, while 'retaining the dramatic dimension to different degrees [...] have all produced texts in which language appears not as the speech of characters – if there still are definable characters at all – but as an autonomous theatricality' (2006: 18). Nevertheless, the different degree to which Schwab and Jelinek retain, deconstruct, or abandon the dramatic dimension, is, as we shall see, a key aspect when comparing their work. Unlike Jelinek's progressive abandonment of dramatic dialogue and plot in her writing, Schwab's plays adhere to a relatively conventional dramaturgy that is ruptured through a defamiliarising language and excessive physicality.[6]

Both authors engage with the European dramatic tradition through adaptations or intertextual references to canonical plays. Thus, Schwab's later plays, which have posthumously been anthologised as *Coverdramen* (2009), are modelled on the practice in pop music of producing cover versions and represent radical 'versions' of plays such as Arthur Schnitzler's *Reigen* (*La Ronde*) or Shakespeare's *Troilus and Cressida*. Jelinek's first play, *What Happened after Nora Left Her Husband; or, Pillars of Society* (1979) already announced itself as a kind of post-drama that crosses Ibsen's *Doll's House* and his *Pillars of Society*, while her more recent 'Sekundärdramen' (secondary dramas) propose an even more radical concept of performing her own no-longer-dramatic texts together with a classic drama. These include *Abraumhalde* (2009) and *FaustIn and out* (2011), to be performed with Lessing's *Nathan the Wise* and Goethe's *Faust* respectively, in order to let the 'secondary drama' disrupt the classical drama in a parasitic way (Jürs-Munby 2013). Jelinek's postdramatic theatre also abounds with references to the predramatic tradition of ancient Greek tragedy, from the use of devices such as the chorus in *Sports Play* or the messenger report in *Rechnitz,* to specific intertextual references to ancient tragedies in a number of her plays.[7]

Language and language critique

In their shared focus on manipulating language in order to defamiliarise perception, Schwab and Jelinek stand in a strong Austrian tradition of language critique (*Sprachkritik*) associated with Ludwig Wittgenstein, Fritz Mauthner, and Karl Kraus, who all explored the inextricable connection between language, thought, and perception. Mauthner's affirmation that language is a social force that 'thinks' in us – 'not I think, [but] it thinks in me' (Mauthner 1923, Beiträge 1: 42) – captures the coercive power of language over the individual that both playwrights exhibit but also challenge. Thus, as Margarete Lamb-Faffelberger observes, Jelinek 'often deliberately challenges Wittgenstein's dictum "Whereof one cannot speak, thereof one must be silent", by finding ways of making her language speak the unsayable' (2007: 39). Karl Kraus is an especially important touchstone for both authors' creation of resistant montages of quoted and satirically manipulated linguistic material.[8] Other important inspirations came from the language experiments of the Vienna Group of postwar avant-garde writers and poets, including H.C. Artmann, Friedrich Achleitner, Konrad Bayer, Gerhard Rühm, and Oswald Wiener.

Jelinek's way of writing is marked by relentless punning, metonymy, and other forms of wordplay that shift meanings, rupture existing semantic patterns, and open up spaces for new associations. Her texts are highly intertextual and especially her later texts, whose form has been referred to as '*Sprachflächen*' or '*Textflächen*' (language or text surfaces), interweave and manipulate quotes from heterogeneous sources such as literature, philosophy, the media, and popular culture in order to defamiliarise language and through it ideology. Trained as a classical pianist, organist, and composer, Jelinek also uses compositional principles borrowed from music:

> Speaking in tongues, like the Holy Spirit hovering above the heads of the believers, is something I always use in theatre in order to break the language cadence into different language melodies and rhythms because I always work with language in a compositional way. It's like a piece of

48   *Karen Jürs-Munby*

> music with different voices that are drawn close in a *stretto* and then also occur in reverse. It is basically a contrapuntal weave of language that I try to produce.
>
> (Jelinek 1996: 90)

This quasi-musical composition means that her texts, especially since *Sports Play*, often lend themselves to choric forms of performance – whether or not they are indicated as such in the texts themselves.

By contrast, Schwab's texts retain the dialogue form and individual speech, but the impression of the characters' compulsive and defamiliarising way of speaking is often that of 'speaking machines' (*Sprechmaschinen*) (Meurer 2007: 76–81). The unique idiom Schwab progressively developed, for which the term '*Schwabisch*' has been coined, is characterised by a deconstruction and reconstruction of standard High German that break the rules of grammar, syntax, and lexical semantics through inappropriate use of modal verbs, verbs with inappropriate prefixes, and an abundance of neologisms, often in the form of absurdly long compound nouns (see Miesbacher 2003; Krawehl 2008). His figures' speech appears overly convoluted and often contains a strange mixture of registers including bureaucratic and overly formal language, dialect, children's language, and faecal and obscene language. It frequently exhibits a peculiar alienation of the figures from their own selves, marked by their inability to use the first person singular in phrasings such as 'my own inner person' – a phenomenon of I-lessness or *Ent-Ichung* (Merschmeier cited in Meurer 2007: 88) that, in different form, can also be found in plays such as *Not I* by Samuel Beckett, who was an important influence for Schwab.

While critics acknowledge that Schwab's artificial idiom may never have been possible without Jelinek's previous linguistic efforts (Pełka 2005: 9), she in turn admires Schwab's own resistant language. In her Afterword to his *Königskomödien*, she captures the physical difficulty of speaking this language:

> Muscles weep because, against their will, they are torn and stretched from inside out, as they are supposed to speak something they do not know. They haven't learnt it. However, they could not utter it if they had not learnt it at all. So, they can after all, but they do not want to.
>
> (Jelinek 2010: 417)

The essay goes on to articulate the way in which Schwab's language reassembles Austrian bureaucratic language in such a way that its subjugating power over common people can be sensed in a visceral way:

> They are formulaic phrases into which language has been assembled, and not in a cozy way, it's language that has been assembled with other language in order to gasp for air in a hysteric sort of way and expel a few words like an old steam engine that is supposed to drive something on. It's only vomit that comes out but that which has been learnt, the formulaic

phrases of Austrian bureaucratic language that have been commanded (and now strain at the leash) to keep the common people down until they bite into their own hands [...] this dumb language comes through again and again, it squirts through the fingers, which like talons hold the mouth tight, hold it shut, and the mouth already knows in speaking that many mouths have been kept shut just like it, so that nothing comes out, that nobody gets through.

(Ibid.)

As Petra Meurer (2007: 69–96) has analysed, Schwab's language, which is rich in metaphors, creates an 'image space' (*Bildraum*), in which the images evoked in the mind's eye are superimposed on the stage images: 'In the imagined staging [when reading the play] it is impossible to concretize both image structures and in the real staging they are directly juxtaposed' (ibid.: 70). By contrast, Jelinek tends to constitute the textual space as an 'audio space' (*Hörraum*) whose focus is not on the figures but on speech itself (ibid.: 115).[9] Paradoxically, this can mean that the actor's body becomes more present as the figure's (fictive) body recedes.

Corporeal discourses

Another important point of comparison between Jelinek and Schwab is the centrality of the body in their artistic discourses. As Pełka has analysed, even though the authors have different modes of representation, their figures appear as 'subversive grotesque bodies that are used as a medium to decode cultural ordering structures with a socio-critical impetus' (2005: 179). In their emphasis on grotesque and vulgar physicalities, they can be seen to repurpose an Austrian folk theatre tradition shaped by playwrights such as Ferdinand Raimund and Johann Nestroy and older popular comic figures such as Hanswurst, Bernadon, and Kasperle. Furthermore, their playwriting, especially Schwab's, is heavily influenced by Antonin Artaud's theatre of cruelty and its emphasis on corporeal materiality – including the corporeality of language.

However, the authors' shared focus on the body in their writing is also rooted in Schwab's background as a practising visual artist and Jelinek's activity as an art critic of contemporary art (Pełka 2005). During his time in the remote Styrian village of Kohlberg (1981–9), Schwab worked with perishable materials such as the meat and bones of animals, which he would arrange into decomposing sculptures. Pełka sees these experiments as a 'continuation of the tradition of body art, whose actions rebelled against the intact body of Western civilization and which culminated in Viennese Actionism a quarter of a century before Schwab' (2005: 14). Akin to Viennese Actionists such as Hermann Nitzsch, Günter Bruns, or Rudolf Schwarzkogler, who literally dissected bodies, Schwab can be seen to be 'dissecting' bodies in his writing but here it is not the flesh of the physical body but the 'social body' that is at the core of his work and which is being dissected 'through writing and image in order to

50   *Karen Jürs-Munby*

diagnose decay as a social – not biological – process' (ibid.: 15). Jelinek's writing, too, is influenced by an engagement with Viennese actionism but in the 1980s and 90s especially with contemporary female body art and Actionism of artists such as Valie Export, Cindy Sherman, or Mary Kelly, who attack and transform their own bodies in order to reveal the cultural construction of gender identity (ibid.: 15–17). Later she declares a special affinity with the installations of American artists Paul McCarthy and Mike Kelley (see Honegger 2006: 33), who use grotesque physical enlargements and reversals such as oversized papier-mâché heads worn backwards. As Teresa Kovacs (2017) has argued, in their art McCarthy and Kelley use similar artistic strategies to critique 'Americanness' as Jelinek uses in her plays to critique 'Austrianness'. Unlike the Viennese Actionists they deliberately work with cheap man-made materials such as plush soft toys or costumes, rubber or plastic, and papier-mâche dolls or body parts that are associated with kitsch – an aesthetic that resonates with many of Jelinek's stage directions and stagings of her work, and which is not unfamiliar to some of Schwab's stage directions and productions of his plays either.[10]

In what follows I will discuss selected plays by each author that focus especially on their treatment of the legacy of National Socialism, right-wing populism and xenophobia, as well as the dynamics of social marginalisation and neo-liberalism. In my selection of plays by Schwab, I have also been guided by the popularity of his plays across Europe and their availability in English translation. In Jelinek's case, feminist plays such as *What Happened after Nora Left Her Husband, Illness or Modern Women*, and the 'princess dramas' *Death and the Maiden I–V* are some of her most widely performed plays internationally, and interesting comparisons could also be drawn between her treatment of pornography in plays such as *Raststätte oder sie machens alle* (*Services: or they all do it*) and *Über Tiere* (*About Animals*) and Schwab plays such as *Pornogeographie*. Nevertheless, I have chosen to focus here on Jelinek plays that deal with the above-mentioned political issues and which will simultaneously allow me to trace the development of her no-longer-dramatic forms of playwriting and corresponding postdramatic aesthetics in performance.

Schwab's faecal dramas and comedies of kings

Schwab's most frequently performed plays are from the first of two anthologies published during his lifetime, *Fäkaliendramen* (*Faecal Dramas*),[11] two of which are discussed below. What distinguishes them is that they all take place in a petit bourgeois milieu of underprivileged characters and, as the title indicates, deal in abject bodily matter and by extension social abjection. Accessible in their seeming naturalism, they belong, however, to a new form of European 'hypernaturalism' of the late 1980s and 1990s that 'offers situations that exhibit a grotesque decay and absurdity' (Lehmann 2006: 117): 'this time the heightening occurs downward: where the toilets are, the scum, that is where we find the figure of the scapegoat, the pharmakos' (ibid.).

Elfriede Jelinek and Werner Schwab 51

Die Präsidentinnen (variously translated as *The Presidents, Holy Mothers*, or *First Ladies*) – premiered in 1990 at the Vienna Künstlerhaus after it had been deemed unplayable by the Vienna Burgtheater – is Schwab's most widely performed play internationally.[12] Pensioners Erna and Grete and the younger Mariedl gather in Erna's small kitchen, 'filled to the ceiling with junk (photos, souvenirs, a lot of religious kitsch [...])' (Schwab 1999: 2), in order to celebrate her acquisition of a second-hand colour TV by watching the pope celebrating mass. The stage directions note that the language produced by the women 'is what they are themselves. To generate (clarify) oneself is work, which means that basically everything is resistance. That should appear in the play as effort' (2). Language is thus explicitly performative for the figures' identity. Yet, in ironic contrast to the title, which suggests a matriarchy, the women's speech is dominated by references to what the Pope, the President, the Vicar etc. *said*, indicating an 'internalized phallogocentrism' (Pełka 2005: 100).[13]

The three women chat about their lives – Erna's economising and her son Hermann's drinking and refusal to procreate by having 'an intercourse' (7); Grete's daughter, who was abused by Grete's first husband and before emigrating to Australia 'had everything taken out, just like a dressed chicken, the ovaries and [...] all the things you need for grandchildren' (8); and Mariedl's passion for unblocking rich people's toilets with her bare hands as her 'sacrifice to Our Lord Jesus Christ' (12). An argument erupts when Grete suggests that Erna fancies her butcher Wottila Karl (a reference to Pope John Paul II) because 'he's a holy Joe' (22) and Erna retaliates by calling Grete a Nazi – even though 'no one was a Nazi in this country' (23). After a tussle they make up. In the second scene, the women indulge in fantasies of a better life over wine – Erna imagining Mr Wottila proposing to her at a fair, Grete imagining a fling with a tuba player, and Mariedl, in a grotesque tour de force of a monologue, imagining being invited by the priest to unblock three toilets from which she produces an unopened can of goulash, a bottle of Austrian beer, and a bottle of French perfume. The scene escalates when Mariedl introduces her friends' vengeful children into the story, while imagining herself as a saint, 'the human excrement on her body turn[ed] to gold dust' (47). Her transgression is cut short when Erna and Grete cut off her head in the most matter-of-fact manner.

In a third scene, a stage is erected on the stage with a stage audience watching *Die Präsidentinnen* performed by three pretty young actresses, 'overacting and screeching viciously' (51). Erna, Grete, and Mariedl are in the audience and after a while get up and leave, while *Die Präsidentinnen* continues for some time. Although Schwab at this point still uses the device of the play-within-in-the play in a fairly conventional way, it nevertheless suggests an 'unsettling link between what seem[s] a deformed version of reality and the world of the spectator' (Barnett 2000: 284), something that is radicalised in a more deconstructive way in the later play-within-the plays *Endlich tot Endlich keine Luft mehr* (*Dead at Last, At Last No More Air*) and *Troiluswahn und Cressidatheater* (*Troilus Delusion and Cressida Theatre*) (ibid.). Especially the final scene in *Präsidentinnen* seems designed to make the bourgeois spectator reflect on their own well-rehearsed response of voyeurism and social abjection towards the women.

52   Karen Jürs-Munby

As Schwab drives the model of a critically engaged *Volksstück* into the grotesque, any performance of his plays has to make decisions around the balance between emphasising the social drama with realistic means or the grotesque with exaggerated theatrical means (Meurer 2007: 96–7). In practice, productions demonstrate a considerable variety of gradients. Krystian Lupa's award-winning Polish production, which has been performed throughout Europe since its premiere in 1999,[14] places the action in a largely realistic setting and develops the figures' hubristic illusion of presidential control psychologically, albeit through an exaggerated form of acting. Bryce Lease rightly attributes the production's enormous success in Poland to the fact that

> the women's collective degradation represented a broader social malaise at the end of the twentieth century wherein the establishment of democracy and the liberalization of the market had not lived up to its promises but had instead created a disenfranchised class of working and unemployed women.
>
> (Lease 2016: 88)

By contrast, Abdullah Kenan Karaca opts for a radically grotesque staging at the Munich Volkstheater (2015) with male actors dressed in female body suits performing in separated cow pens, thereby rendering gender performative and heightening the abject isolation of the characters in a more existential way. Interestingly, the rupturing final scene is often omitted in performance, with directors finding other ways of introducing self-reflexivity: Lupa has the three sleeping women being prodded by three giggling children with long sticks between the first and second scene and introduces a Virgin Mary figure surveying the scene of Mariedl's murder; while Marie-Soophie Dudzic and Katharina Kreuzhage's at the Theater Paderborn (2017) cast younger actresses from the start and have a revived Mariedl join in singing the blasphemous ballad at the end.

ÜBERGEWICHT, unwichtig, UNFORM: Ein Europäisches Abendmahl (*OVERWEIGHT, unimportant, MISSHAPE: A European [Last] Supper*), which premiered at the Schauspielhaus Vienna in 1991 (dir. Hans Gratzer) and was recently staged by Johannes Lepper at the Schauspiel Dortmund (2017), is set in a nondescript local tavern where out-of-luck regulars gather (see Figure 2.1). The characters include the overweight childless couple Schweindi/Piggy and Hasi/Bunny, who are knitting blue and pink romper-suits in the vain hope for offspring (Schweindi turns out to be impotent and a paedophile); Karli, who 'often hits out at someone without warning', and his wife Herta, who 'gives the impression of having been knocked about a lot'; Jürgen, an older 'student type', spouting humanist views; Fotzi/Pussy, who has 'exhibitionist gestures, tries for erotic effects and fails miserably'; and the Bar Owner, who 'has a vacant look' (55–6).[15] In addition, on this night a 'beautiful couple' strays into the bar, 'their every look and gesture exclusively occupied with each other' (56). The group of regulars, who philosophise about the meaning of bread and sausage, insult and hit one another, get increasingly agitated by the couple's

Figure 2.1 Werner Schwab's *ÜBERGEWICHT, unwichtig: UNFORM – Ein Europäisches Abendmahl* (*OVERWEIGHT, unimportant: MISSHAPE – A European Supper*), directed by Johannes Lepper (2017) at Schauspiel Dortmund. Photograph © Birgit Hupfeld

silent demeanour. In a typical Schwabian escalation from speech act to physical violence, all (except Herta) turn on the 'dangerous, unbelonging people' (72) and eat them in a sexually charged orgy.

As its subtitle indicates, the play is referencing a violent European history. While the role of the cannibal during European colonialism was attributed to the colonised other, it 'served both as a foil for the emerging modern [European] subject and, conveniently, as a legitimization of cultural appropriation' (Peter Hulme cited in Henderson 2012: 57). As Henderson argues, Schwab's regulars 'celebrate cannibalism as a perverted religious ritual – an unholy communion indeed', striving to 'ingest all that the beautiful couple displays (and which eludes them): beauty, money, success and love' (57). In another one of Schwab's sudden reversals, however, the beautiful couple return in the third act for a rerun of the opening act; this time they talk, mocking the 'simple people' with their 'primitive manners' and 'rustic' fare as the 'best play in town this evening' (110–11). Their idea of having a film made about them can be seen as another form of 'cannibalism' in the form of cultural appropriation (56).

At the Schauspiel, Dortmund Lepper not only casts a male actor (Christian Freund) in the role of Fotzi/Pussy, marking gender and sexuality as performative, but crucially casts a black actress and a middle Eastern actor (Edith Voges Nana Tchuinang and Raafat Daboul) as the beautiful couple, who on their return converse in French and Arabic, thus figuring them as the perceived threat of immigrants by xenophobic right-wing populism. Lepper's production

54 *Karen Jürs-Munby*

implicitly suggests a connection between social marginalisation and xenophobic aggression.[16] Compared to the cosmopolitan, multi-cultural couple – here armed with mobile phones and selfie sticks – the regulars are stuck and left behind by neoliberal society.

Unlike the *Fäkaliendramen*, which start out in the intimacy of an inner or domestic space, Schwab's *Königskomödien* (Comedies of Kings) take as their locus the institutions of the societal or public realm, such as the arts industries that Jelinek had already focused on in her early work, most (in)famously in *Burgtheater* (1985). Schwab's *Endlich tot Endlich keine Luft mehr* (*Dead at Last, At Last No More Air*), labelled as a 'theatre extinction comedy' (*Theaterzernichtungslustspiel*), was staged posthumously at the Saarländisches Staatstheater, Saarbrücken in 1994 and saw its English premiere by Just a Must Theatre (dir. Vanda Butkovic) in London in 2014. The play-within-a-play follows the realisation of a play by the dramatist Mühlstein under the director Saftmann. Its rehearsal is complicated by a pervasive discourse of theatre from all participants in a comical defamiliarising Schwabisch, as when the director addresses the present playwright:

> Dear Mühlstein, please forgive us this Mühlstein-drollery-comprehension-delay in the waiting room of your patience-capacity, but the theatre rabble is unable to play an absurdist normality. Your inner writer will suffer like a progressive dog in a senseless animal experiment, but the end-game-outcome may possibly be a human-digestible elixir of life destined to warm the pulse of our dying theatre.
>
> (Schwab 2014: 39)

When the actors eventually walk out, Saftmann recruits new performers from the local home for the elderly in the hope of injecting authenticity into theatre. However, led by the theatre's cleaner Frau Haider, the disenfranchised pensioners soon stage a coup and crown Frau Haider (with a prop Richard III crown), who promptly has the director beaten to death by the pensioner Herr Adolf. As David Barnett notes, the play 'continually raises issues of theatricality and its relationship with reality' (2000: 284). As it progresses, all certainty is undermined in the name of theatre's 'playfulness', leading ultimately to the 'convergence of life and theatre' and thus the death of theatre as a discrete entity (ibid.: 288).

Just a Must, who had staged the English language premiere of Jelinek's *Sports Play* (*Ein Sportstück*) in 2012, saw this theme of the death of theatre resonating with the present neoliberal cultural austerity politics in England, as director Vanda Butkovic states: 'I feel as a theatre community we are in a situation where the very purpose of the theatre for commentary and dialogue is not only threatened but totally undermined' (Butkovic in Damian Martin 2014: 32–3). The production's kitschy scenography made out of inflatable materials (Simon Donger) was inspired by the play's central metaphor of air/airlessness. The set is gradually deflating, while in the end Frau Haider looms large in an overinflated costume. Like Erna in *Die Präsidentinnen* and Frau Wurm in *Volksvernichtung*

(*People Annihilation*, 1991) – the German production of which gave Schwab his international breakthrough – Frau Haider is a thinly veiled reference to Schwab's mother, who was a cleaner herself, but here also to FPÖ politician Jörg Haider. This 'interweaving of the political and the domestic, the personal and the public is typical of Schwab's performative strategies' (2014: 21), as Diana Damian Martin notes. It is part of a larger dramaturgy that dismantles dichotomies between inner and outer theatrical frames, individual and society, the real world and the theatrical world (ibid.). While these strategies of the play make it impossible to decipher an unambiguous 'message', it obliquely addresses an increasing theatricalisation of public and private life in the context of nationalist populism and the concomitant 'death' of theatre as an independent critical institution. In this sense, the play reads like a response to Jelinek's *Burgtheater*.

From Jelinek's *Burgtheater* to *Charges (The Suppliants)*

Jelinek was the first Austrian playwright to expose the history of Austria's complicity with National Socialism following the *Anschluss* in 1938 and its ideological continuation after the conclusion of the Second World War. In her uncompromising early play *Burgtheater*, which premiered not in Austria but in Bonn in 1985 (dir. Horst Zankl), she approached this complex via a savagely sarcastic attack on the involvement of famous Austrian stage and film actors with the propaganda machine of National Socialism. The play was based on the Attila Hörbiger–Paula Wessely acting family who colluded with the Nazis and continued to be celebrated in postwar Austria despite the fact that Wessely had been the highest-paid female star of Nazi propaganda film. Jelinek was not interested in these individuals as such but in the wider phenomenon they represented.

While the play retained a dramatic dialogue and plot, its form was already fractured. The characters spoke in an artificial Viennese dialect peppered with punning neologisms, such as '*Saubertöte*' (clean killer) instead of *Zauberflöte* (Magic Flute), which made the horrors of Austria's fascism audible through defamiliarisation. By means of language, Jelinek aimed to demonstrate

> how little the propaganda language of blood-and-soil mythology in Nazi art differed from the language of *Heimat* films of the 1950s […]. This swamp of love, patriotism, Germanomania, a fixed role of woman as servant, mother, bearer of children and valiant companion of heroes […] was my material that I composed into a kind of artificial language because in its kitschiness and mendaciousness it could not be surpassed.
>
> (Jelinek 1984: 15)

The play's form, announced in the subtitle as a 'farce with song', is based on the popular *Altwiener Volkstheater* using intertexts by Raimunds and Nestroy. Jelinek employs this cheerfully comic form to get a contrasting message across: whilst singing, dancing, and joking around the family dining table, the actors lie

56   Karen Jürs-Munby

and manipulate, kick and murder. Thus, the mythical Alpenkönig, who begs the actor family for a donation for the anti-Nazi resistance, is beaten to death and dismembered. By 'recoding' the popular genre, Jelinek can defamiliarise diverse linguistic, musical, and physical materials from different times: 'In the manner of the avant-gardes and postdramatic theatre the material is separated into individual elements and exhibited. Language, voice and physical action do not form a unity but diverge or are juxtaposed' (Deutsch-Schreiner 2018: 75–6).

Except for one experimental performance loosely inspired by the play at the Theater im Bahnhof in Graz (2005, dir. Ed Hauswirth), the play has never been performed in Austria[17] – nor for that matter internationally due to its virtually untranslatable artificial dialect. Despite this lacuna, *Burgtheater* created a scandal in Austria that earned Jelinek the reputation of a *Netzbeschmutzer*, but at the same time exerted a considerable influence on fellow Austrian artists, including Schwab. Jelinek kept on pursuing the themes of Austria's and Germany's national socialist past and its legacy, neo-fascism and right-wing populism in many of her subsequent plays, yet moved away from using the *Volkstheater* genre (including dialect) – and increasingly from the dramatic form altogether. This shift progressively opened her work to innovative directorial approaches.

In *Stecken, Stab und Stangl – eine Handarbeit* (*Rod, Staff and Crook – a Handicraft*) (1996), Jelinek's response to the murder of four Romany men by a planted bomb in Oberwart in 1995, the themes of everyday xenophobia and neo-fascist ideology as well as some of the motivic choices resonate in interesting ways with Schwab's plays: e.g. when she sets the play at a meat-counter of a supermarket (doubling as a TV location) and images of butchers and meat are associated with evocations of murder and the Holocaust in casual conversations. However, where Schwab attributes xenophobic remarks to individually defined characters, Jelinek begins to dissolve the dramatic form of distinct individual characters. This is because she is ultimately concerned with a shared discourse promulgated by the media and their complicity in hate crimes through a systematic denial of Austria's fascist part and persistent downplaying of contemporary hate crimes. The speakers of her text are largely interchangeable, indicated as 'someone, no matter who' (Jelinek 1997: 17) or as mere types. At one point, someone says 'I thought you were Herr Stab (Mr. Staff)' (a reference to the right-wing columnist of the *Kronen Zeitung*, Staberl) to which the other answers, 'we have a whole staff of Staffs here' – pointing to the proliferation of interchangeable media voices.

The image of national European landscapes that hide stories of violent crimes, which in Schwab's *Übergewicht* are summoned virtually through the characters' fantasy journeys, in Jelinek's play are evoked not only in the text but also through envisaged actions that create a visual landscape. Thus, the motif of handicraft, which in Schwab's *Übergewicht* signifies Piggy's and Bunny's repression of their personal history of abuse and paedophilia through their knitting of romper suits, here becomes a much larger metaphor when the stage directions stipulate that all actors should be busy crocheting in pink wool, occasionally hooking each other or spectators into their needlework, until finally 'an entire handicraft-landscape has been created' (17). While Thirza Brunken's staging at the

Deutsches Schauspielhaus Hamburg (1996) does not fully realise these impossible directions, the actors' activity of crocheting little blankets in parallel to their speaking creates a metaphor of a mythical landscape covering up a hidden history which continues to be discursively 'made up' by all participants and 'hooks' individual subjects like an Altusserian ideological interpellation (Jürs-Munby 2009: 49). Jens Killian's ingenious set, reminiscent of a retro TV studio with a bouncy wobbly floor under a beige carpet lets the performers stumble and sink as in mud. Together with Jelinek's 'handicraft' of the textual montage with all its hidden depths it creates the impression of a massive and uncanny (*unheimliche*) cover-up by shallow entertainment media. The four Roma victims appear only as silent, undead figures in bright coloured suits while the TV presenters linguistically sweep them under the carpet, so to speak.

Jelinek further developed the form of her playwriting in *Ein Sportstück* (*Sports Play*), which starts with the (non-)stage direction, '[t]he author doesn't give many stage directions, she has learned her lesson by now. Do what you like' (Jelinek 2012: 39).[18] Jelinek's mock-resigned attitude – versions of which are repeated in subsequent plays – challenges directors to come up with congenial staging methods for her no-longer-dramatic texts. In *Ein Sportstück* her directions do go on to stipulate, 'the only thing that has to be kept are the Greek Choruses, as individual or *en masse*' (ibid.). By resorting to this device from Greek tragedy, pitting individuals against choruses, Jelinek implicitly appeals to theatre's ancient political role in democratic societies of staging power, questioning justice, and giving a voice to the victims and the dispossessed.[19] The play deals with the relationship between sports and war and was a direct response to the war in former Yugoslavia, which started with a football match between Dinamo Zagreb and Red Star Belgrade. It is framed by the hybrid figure Elfi-Elektra, an author alter ego thematising her ostracisation from society. As in *Stecken, Stab and Stangl*, other speakers are indicated as mostly generic figures such as the Woman, Young Sportsman, Perpetrator, Victim, Another Sportsman, Another Perpetrator etc. However, the collective voice that had surfaced as a 'we' in *Stecken* as well as *Wolken.Heim.*, now becomes the Chorus, recalling its role in ancient Greek theatre of standing in for the *polis*. The Chorus exhorts the Woman/Mother to let go of her son for the greater good of sports and the state. The claustrophobic relationship between mother and son is incidentally not unlike that portrayed in some of Schwab's *Fäkalien-dramen* but Jelinek also shows the mother as dispossessed when her son runs away to join the sports-war. Both Schwab and Jelinek draw on Elias Canetti's *Masse und Macht* (1960, translated as *Crowds and Power* in 1962) but whereas Schwab explores Canetti's insights into mob violence and the underlying desire to belong through small groupings like the regulars in *Übergewicht*, Jelinek's text shifts scale from small groups to large crowds.

Einar Schleef's premiere of *Ein Sportstück* at the Vienna Burgtheater in January 1998 took up Jelinek's challenge with a radical monumental performance involving 142 performers (including a 105 strong chorus), its 'short' version lasting 5 hours, the long one 7 hours. The durational experience served to honour both the epic topic

58   Karen Jürs-Munby

of the play as well as the form of Jelinek's own 'marathon' of a text.[20] Schleef deploys choruses in multiple ways, not just for the sections designated as such in the text but also turning figures of the 'Perpetrator', 'Sportsman', and 'Diver', as well as 'Elfi Elektra' into chorus groups of various sizes. In the famous 'sportsmen scene', a condensed treatment of a long passage of interchangeable sportsmen speaking about belonging to a group, club, or nation, a large chorus in uniform sports dress keeps up a 'fight choreography' for 35 minutes to the beat of eight, transferring a palpable energy to the audience. The scene articulates the conflict between individual and group in a physicalised and ritualistic way that shifts away from the classical *agon* to a postdramatic experience of *agony* (Jürs-Munby 2014: 19). At other moments Schleef stages marginalised voices in the '*Hörraum*' of the cavernous Burgtheater, for example when the all-female Elfi Elektra chorus can only be heard singing from backstage (ibid.: 20–21). Schleef's pioneering choric approach paved the way not just for other European stagings of this play,[21] but for many other Jelinek stagings in the twenty-first century, for example by important Jelinek directors such as Nicolas Stemann and Karin Beier, who developed their own forms of choric performance.

Jelinek herself continued to employ chorus figures or the choric 'we' in her writing to address large-scale societal issues, e.g. in *Das Werk* (*The Works*), *Kontrakte des Kaufmanns* (*The Merchant's Contracts*), and, more recently, in *Die Schutzbefohlenen* (*Charges*). The latter theatre text was sparked by the plight of a group of asylum seekers from Afghanistan and Pakistan, who had occupied the Votive Church in Vienna in November 2012 but received its first staged reading in September 2013 by Thalia Theatre actors and refugees at the St Pauli Lutheran Church in Hamburg, where 80 of around 300 so-called 'Lampedusa refugees' from Africa had found accommodation. A full production of the play directed by Stemann premiered at the Theater der Welt (Theatre of the World) Festival in Mannheim in May 2014 with the involvement of local refugees, before its official premiere at the Thalia Theater Hamburg in September 2014 with the involvement of a large chorus of the 'Lampedusa refugees', in addition to the ensemble of professional actors.

Charges interweaves manipulated quotes from Aeschylus' *The Supplicants* – one of Europe's oldest extant tragedies, which features a chorus of refugees (the Danaian maidens) as protagonists – and references to Ovid's *Metamorphoses* with references to media coverage of protests by contemporary refugees, as well as quotes from the brochure 'Living together in Austria' published by the Ministry of the Interior, State Secretariat for Integration, along with 'a pinch of Heidegger' (Jelinek 2016: 82).[22] As practised with *The Merchant's Contracts* in response to the unfolding financial crisis, Jelinek also responds to the rapidly growing refugee crisis with addenda to the main text. These addenda interweave references to current media coverage of the crisis with further canonical European intertexts such as the *Odyssey* and Euripides' *Iphigenia in Aulis*. While Jelinek's writing is decidedly 'no longer dramatic', her intertextual use of ancient Greek tragedy also evokes a tradition that is 'pre-dramatic', involving a '"speaking out" more than "speaking with each other"' (Lehmann 2016: 195). The text has no designated speakers whatsoever and is written throughout in the first-person plural, a shifting 'we', addressed directly to the audience.

One of the issues that Jelinek addresses in the text is that of political representation, for example, when the voices say they would willingly tell 'the bosses in this land and the representatives of the bosses in this land and the representatives of the representatives of the bosses of this land' of their guiltless flight, 'but no one [...], not even a representative of a representative wants to hear it' (Jelinek 2016: 7). The unheard refugees find no political representation or voice. The opening of Stemann's performance adds to this concern with political representation a concern with representation in the theatre: after a pre-performance set in which actors and refugee performers are milling about on stage, with a live video feed projection onto a large disc suspended above the stage showing some of them being interviewed about their current situation and activism, the performance proper suddenly starts with the formation of a line of refugees walking towards the audience shouting in English: 'We are here! We will fight, for freedom of movement, it's everybody's right!' The line freezes and we begin to hear the Jelinek text calmly spoken in German by three actors from upstage, behind the chorus of refugees still facing us downstage, as if voicing the thoughts of the refugees who remain silent: 'We are alive. We are alive. The main thing is we live and it is hardly more than that after leaving the sacred homeland. No one looks down with mercy at our train, but everyone looks down on us' (Jelinek 2016: 1).

The involvement of actual refugees in the production can be read as an attempt to transgress the aesthetic frame, echoing ancient Greek pre-dramatic practices that were more closely related to extra-theatrical reality (see Lehmann 2016). However, this project was fraught with practical and ethical problems: Jelinek's literary *Kunstsprache* benefits from being spoken by trained actors and the refugees were still learning German; yet it seemed presumptuous for comparatively privileged actors to speak as the 'we' of the excluded refugees; moreover, even paying the refugee performers for their work proved difficult under the circumstances.[23] Stemann's directorial method is to include improvised reflections on these issues of the process in the performance itself. These include comically awkward scenes that involve the actors' performance of black, yellow, and red face, in order to expose historical and contemporary issues of racism in theatrical representation, as well as a poignant scene towards the end of the evening when refugee performers can be seen quietly approaching actors for help with accommodation until the actors burst out: 'We cannot help you, don't you see! We have to play you!'

In conclusion, while Schwab's plays still have the capacity to shock in their unexpected disruptions of dramatic forms from *within* conventional forms – perhaps even more so in the context of an increasing prevalence of postdramatic forms – Jelinek's progressive abandonment of dramatic characters, dialogue, and plot structures in favour of polyphonic *Textflächen* has allowed her to continue to address the most burning social and political issues of our times through multi-layered texts that allow for associations between a wide range of sources, including European dramatic and pre-dramatic traditions. And while Schwab addressed social abjection and its reinforcement by bourgeois naturalism through an artificial

60   Karen Jürs-Munby

idiom, hypernaturalism, and devices such as the play within a play, Jelinek's texts are especially open to postdramatic forms that address the representation of marginalised and excluded groups on the level of theatrical representation itself.

Werner Schwab – four key productions

Volksvernichtung oder Meine Leber ist sinnlos (*People Annihilation or My Liver is Senseless*). Directed by Christian Stückl. Set and Costumes by Marlene Poley and Christian Sedelmayer. Dramaturgy by Laura Oliviv. Cast: Heide von Strombeck, Michael Tregor, Peter Herzog, Jennifer Minetti, Petra Einhoff, Bettina Hauenschild, Doris Schade. Münchner Kammerspiele, Werkraum, 25 November 1991.

Prezydentki/The Presidents (*Die Präsidentinnen*). Translation by Monika Muskała. Direction, arrangement of text, arrangement of music, and set design by Krystian Lupa. Assistant direction by Halina Rasiakówna. Cast: Bożena Baranowska, Halina Rasiakówna, Ewa Skibińska, Aldona Struzik. Teatr Polski, Wrocław, Świebodzki Train Station Stage, 17 September 1999.

ÜBERGEWICHT, unwichtig, UNFORM (*OVERWEIGHT, unimportant, MISSHAPE*). Direction and set design by Johannes Lepper. Costume design by Sabine Wegmann. Lighting design by Sibylle Stuck. Sound Design by Chris Sauer. Dramaturgy by Michael Eickhoff. Cast: Uwe Rohbeck, Andreas Beck, Marlena Keil, Frank Genser, Friederike Tiefenbacher, Christian Freund, Edith Voges Nana Tchuinang / Nina Karimy, Raâfat Daboul. Schauspiel Dortmund, 17 December 2017.

Dead at Last, At Last No More Air. Translation by Meredith Oakes. Directed by Vanda Butkovic. Dramaturgy by Diana Damian Martin. Scenography by Simon Donger. Lighting Design by Ana Vilar. Produced by Berislav Juraic. Cast: Niall Murray, Drew McKenzie, Denise Heinrich-Lane, Ingrid Evans, Jeremy Hancock, Ben Hood, Delia Remy, Tom Jacobs. Camden People's Theatre, London, 6 May 2014.

Elfriede Jelinek – four key productions

Burgtheater. Directed by Horst Zankl. Dramaturgy by Karl Baratta. Set and Costumes by Ilse Träbing. Cast: Carmen-Renate Köper, Wolfgang Kraßnitzer, Robert Tillian, Ariane Gaffron, Sue Schulze, Carla Butterfield, Luise Prasser, Susanne Tremper, Harald Schrader. Bühnen der Stadt Bonn, 10 November 1985.

Stecken, Stab und Stangl. Directed by Thirza Bruncken. Set and Costume Design by Jens Kilian. Lighting Design by Rebekka Dahnke. Dramaturgy by Stefanie Carp. Choreography by Anthony Taylor. Musical Direction by Franz Wittenbrink. Cast: Monika Bleibtreu, Peter Brombacher, Marlen Diekhoff, Barbara Nüsse, Jörg Schröder, Anne Weber, Michael Wittenborn. Deutsches Schauspielhaus Hamburg, 12 April 1996.

Elfriede Jelinek and Werner Schwab 61

Ein Sportstück. Directed by Einar Schleef. Assistant Direction by Susan Todd. Dramaturgy by Rita Thiele. Costume Consultation by Annette Beaufays. Main Cast: Elisabeth Augustin, Martin Brambach, Heinz Frölich, Rudolf Melichar, Franz Morak, Hubertus Petroll, Dierk Prawdzik, Elisabeth Rath, Einar Schleef, Hermann Schmid, Julia von Sell, Bibiana Zeller. Chorus of 100, full cast list available at https://de.wikipedia.org/wiki/Ein_Sportst%C3%BCck. Burgtheater, Vienna, 23 January 1998.

Die Schutzbefohlenen. Direction, Music and Set Design by Nicolas Stemann. Costume Design by Katrin Wolfermann. Cast: Thelma Buabeng, Ernest Allan Hausmann, Felix Knopp, Isaac Lokolong, Daniel Lommatzsch, Barbara Nüsse, Dennis Roberts, Sebastian Rudolph, and a Refugee Chorus. Thalia Theater, Hamburg, 12 September 2004.

Notes

1 According to his biographer Helmut Schödel, Schwab, who was from a very deprived background, deliberately created a public persona in order to survive the intense media attention once he had been catapulted into the limelight:

> Schwab created a double for himself that suited this nightmare. He carved out the dark sides of his person and sold the shadow as the poet Werner Schwab. With long strides, aviator boots, flowing trench coat, and a blonde strand of hair, a bad city cowboy conquered our pacified theatre landscape. That was what he himself called *project Schwab* […] Like a Sid Vicious of literature he was to come across, fallen from the sky like a meteor – only to impact.
>
> (Schödel, cited in Preece 1999: 15–16)

NB: All translations of quotes in this chapter, unless otherwise indicated, are by the author.

2 Peter Clar (2013: 24) notes that Jelinek presents herself as 'urbane and elegant and as acquainted with the cultural canon as [she is] rebellious, experimental, and above all as an outsider, who repeatedly shows herself in solidarity with other outsiders'. This is also true for her Nobel lecture (via video in her absence), 'Sidelined', https://www.nobelprize.org/mediaplayer/index.php?id=721. Importantly, Clar notes that the 'author figure' must not be confused with the 'real Jelinek' and should rather be read as a 'mask' that points to its construction (25).

3 Artur Pełka (2005: 7) makes the point that Schwab is associated with nihilistic postmodernism, while Jelinek's engagement is often accorded a primary role and her work is frequently read through the 'prisms of feminism and Marxism'.

4 This pun in *Die Präsidentinnen* (15) is lost in Michael Mitchell's translation 'your own flesh and blood' (9).

5 For the European reception, translation, and production of Jelinek's theatre texts until 2008, see Clar and Schenkermayr (2008), who show that until 2008, there were 173 translations of Jelinek's theatre texts into 23 'European' languages (17 of which by US American/ South American translators) (19) and 107 (non-German) European Jelinek productions and scenic readings of her plays (with France taking the lead, followed by Poland, Italy, the Czech Republic, and Sweden) (62); the award of the Nobel Prize in 2004 clearly acted as a 'motor' for the international reception (114). No comparable study exists for the international reception of Schwab's plays but the archive of his estate lists European productions in 21 countries (see https://static.uni-graz.at/fileadmin/gewi-institute/Franz-Nabl-Institut/Dokumente/2013_Gesamtaufnahme_Schwab.pdf).

62 *Karen Jürs-Munby*

6 As Petra Meurer states, Schwab's 'contempt for theatre shows itself perhaps most clearly in the fact that he did not even bother with adaptation but uses the existing theatre apparatus as a mere vehicle' and as a 'space for experimentation for his language' (Meurer 2007: 73).

7 Thus, there are intertextual references to Aeschylus' *Oresteia* in *Sports Play* and *The Farewell*, to *The Persians* in *Bambiland* and to *The Suppliants* in *Charges*, as well as to Euripides' *Trojan Women* in *Das Werk* and to *The Bacchae* in *Rechnitz*.

8 Both Schwab and Jelinek refer to the linguistic material they manipulate in their texts as the accumulated refuse, junk, or rubble of society, with Schwab describing himself as playing with found language as with 'scrap metal in a junkyard' (Schwab quoted in Hochholdinger-Reiterer 2002: 308), while Jelinek, conscious of her work as a female European postwar author, describes herself as a '*Trümmerfrau* [rubble woman] of language' (Honegger 2006: 29).

9 Significantly, Jelinek started out by writing audio plays in the 1970s and many of her contemporary theatre texts are also staged as audio play versions. This medium is ideally suited for treating language in a musical way and focusing attention on listening without the 'distraction' of visual representation.

10 For example, both authors critique the commodification of sex and the body itself through the use of kitsch-inspired genital protheses. Thus, in one of Schwab's 'cover dramas', *Der Reizende Reigen* (*The Round of Pleasure*), based on Arthur Schnitzler's *Der Reigen* (*La Ronde*), all male figures have 'screw-off sexual organs', all female figures 'interchangeable female couplings' (Schwab 1999: 122); while Jelinek in one of her 'princess dramas', *Sleeping Beauty*, calls for the Prince to put on a 'plush costume featuring a very big penis' and for Sleeping Beauty to put on 'a white rabbit's costume made of plush, with a vulva sticking out' (Jelinek 2006: 50–51).

11 According to Daniela Bartens (2018) of the Schwab Estate, there were roughly 370 productions of Schwab's plays worldwide until 2014, ca 300 of which from the *Fäkaliendramen*.

12 According to Bartens (2018), there were around 203 productions of the play until 2014, ca 150 in German-speaking countries (115 Germany, 28 in Austria, and 7 in Switzerland) and 53 in non-German speaking countries.

13 In this respect the 'presidents' are somewhat comparable to the 'princesses' in Jelinek's series *Death and the Maiden* whose speech more knowingly articulates their dependence on the man/prince in their life to give their existence meaning.

14 Pełka highlights that Schwab was by far the most successful foreign dramatist in Poland around the millennium: 'Polish theatre makers discovered in him a subversive dramatist who "brutally reveals the order of developed, democratic societies"' (Pełka 2005: 186). Generally, *Die Präsidentinnen* seems to resonate most strongly in Catholic regions of Europe.

15 Noticeably Schwab's directions do not 'fix' the characters but allow for the realisation that their identity is 'performative' in the sense of being a result of '"stylized repetition" of violent acts that constitutes their characters' (Henderson 2012: 54).

16 Significantly, the programme notes contain an excerpt of an essay by Jens Roselt (2001) on shame, envy, and murder, where he states: 'in a society that considers liberty its brand, shame is an effective means of control and regulation. Our life has to be fit for commercials. Anybody who does not meet these expectations has to pillory themselves […]. Liberty means: if you don't meet the norm, it's your own fault' (48–9).

17 After the intense personal attacks in her home country, Jelinek has prohibited all further performances of the play in Austria (see Janke et al. 2018: 375).

18 The stage direction was most likely a response to Frank Castorf's staging of *Raststätte, oder sie machens alle* (*Services, or they're all at it*), in which he had an actress read out the stage direction that the performance should be inspired by the aesthetic of commercial porn movies in a headteacher-like manner. The production ended with

a blow-up Jelinek sex doll mumbling incomprehensible monologues – a choice that Jelinek found personally offensive but aesthetically entirely appropriate.

19 In an interview with Simon Stephens, Jelinek describes herself as 'a sort of justice fanatic' and points out that the oldest surviving tragedy, *The Persians* by Aeschylus, beats the emergence of Attic democracy by a fraction, thus showing that 'art precedes the civilization of people through democracy' (in Jelinek 2012: n.p.).

20 Many of Jelinek's theatre texts are excessively long by the standards of a 'well-made play' and deliberately strain the listening capacity of the audience. Directors regularly cut her texts for performance quite heavily, and even Schleef made severe cuts (while also inserting his own scenes, e.g. from Hoffmann's *Penthisilea*) but still found ways of doing justice to the durational, meandering experience of the text.

21 Until 2014 there had been 27 additional stagings of the *Ein Sportstück*, eight of which were in translation. For details see Janke (2014: 122–3).

22 Heidegger haunts most of Jelinek's texts. While she acknowledges him as a great thinker, she critiques his 'self-assured notion of homeland (Heimat)' and his entanglement with the Nazis that he never owned up to (Honegger 2016: 162–3).

23 Initially the authorities would not allow the Thalia Theater to pay the refugee performers, as most of them did not have work permits. After a long struggle, Hamburg's mayor granted an exception.

Works cited

Barnett, David (2000) 'Access denied: Werner Schwab, the explosion of character and the collapse of the play-within-a-play', in Arthur Williams, Stuart Parkes, and Julian Preece (eds), *German-Language Literature Today: International and Popular?*, Bern: Peter Lang, pp. 281–294.

Bartens, Daniela (Werner Schwab Nachlass (Estate), Franz-Nabl-Institut für Literaturforschung, Universität Graz) (2018), personal correspondence.

Clar, Peter (2013) 'Selbstpräsentation', in Pia Janke (ed.), *Jelinek-Handbuch*, Stuttgart: Metzler, pp. 21–26.

Clar, Peter and Christian Schenkermayr (2008) *Theatrale Grenzgänge: Jelineks Theatertexte in Europa*, Vienna: Praesens.

Damian Martin, Diana (2014) 'Werner Schwab's *Dead at Last, At Last No More Air*: The poetics of radical dramaturgy' (foreword), in Werner Schwab, *Dead at Last, At Last No More Air*, Meredith Oakes (trans.), London: Oberon Books.

Deutsch-Schreiner, Evelyn (2018) 'Ein Matsch, der nach dem Krieg nie richtig trockengelegt worden ist', in Pia Janke, Teresa Kovacs and Christian Schenkermayr (eds), *Jelineks Burgtheater – Politik und Ästhetik, Elfriede Jelineks Burgtheater – Eine Herausforderung*, Vienna: Praesens, pp. 74–84.

Henderson, Heike (2012) 'Performing cannibalism: Werner Schwab's ÜBERGEWICHT, unwichtig, UNFORM', *Journal of Austrian Studies*, 45 (1–2): 51–68.

Hochholdinger-Reiterer, Beate (2002) '"Theater as a Form of Upscale Junkyard": Werner Schwab's plays: Nonsense that defies reason or disguised morality', in Linda C. DeMeritt and Margarete Lamb-Faffelberger (eds), *Postwar Austrian Theatre*, Riverside, CA: Ariadne Press, pp. 300–327.

Honegger, Gitta (2006) '"I am a Trümmerfrau of language"' (interview with Jelinek), *Theater*, 2: 21–37.

——— (2016) 'Greifvogel: I am a bird of prey – in conversation with Elfriede Jelinek', in Elfriede Jelinek, *Charges (The Supplicants)*, Gitta Honegger (trans.), London: Seagull pp. 146–200.

64   Karen Jürs-Munby

Janke, Pia (ed.) (2013) *Jelinek-Handbuch*, Stuttgart: Metzler.

——— (2014) *Elfriede Jelinek: Werk und Rezeption*, Teil 1 und 2, Vienna: Praesens.

Janke, Pia, Teresa Kovacs, and Christian Schenkermayr (eds), (2018) *Elfriede Jelineks Burgtheater – Eine Herausforderung*, Vienna: Praesens.

Jelinek, Elfriede (1983) 'I want to be shallow' ['Ich möchte seicht sein', essay], Jorn Bramann (trans.), in *Theater Heute Jahrbuch*, p. 102, http://www.elfriedejelinek.com/fseichte.htm

——— (1984) 'Ich schlage sozusagen mit der Axt drein', *TheaterZeitSchrift*, 7: 14–16.

——— (1992) *Theaterstücke* [*Was geschah, nachdem Nora ihren Mann verlassen hatte oder Stützen der Gesellschaften; Clara S. musikalische Tragödie; Burgtheater; Krankheit oder Moderne Frauen*], with an afterword by Ute Nyssen, Reinbek bei Hamburg: Rowohlt.

——— (1996) '"Ich bin im Grunde ständig tobsüchtig über die Verharmlosung", interview with Stephanie Carp', *Theater der Zeit*, 49 (5/6): 90.

——— (1997) *Stecken, Stab und Stangl; Raststätte oder sie machens alle; Wolken.Heim;* with the essay 'Sinn egal. Körper zwecklos', Reinbeck bei Hamburg: Rowohlt.

——— (2006) 'Sleeping Beauty', Gitta Honegger (trans.), *Theater*, 2, pp. 47–51.

——— (2008) 'The forsaken place' ['Im Verlassenen', essay], Margarete Lamb-Faffelberger (trans.), http://www.elfriedejelinek.com/famstete.htm

——— (2010) 'Sprachverbau. Eine Wand, die einem spanisch vorkommt. Aber sie funktioniert (ein paar Fetzen zu Werner Schwab)', in Werner Schwab, *Königskomödien*, Werke Band 7, Graz, Vienna: Droschl, pp. 417–419.

——— (2012 [1997]) *Sports Play*, Penny Black (trans.) with translation assistance and a foreword by Karen Jürs-Munby, includes '"I am a sort of justice fanatic": An interview with Elfriede Jelinek by Simon Stephens', London: Oberon.

——— (2016) *Charges (The Supplicants)*, [translation of *Die Schutzbefohlenen*, 2013], Gitta Honegger (trans.), London: Seagull.

Jürs-Munby, Karen (2009) 'The resistant text in postdramatic theatre: Performing Elfriede Jelinek's Sprachflächen', *Performance Research* 14(1): 46–56.

——— (2013) 'Parasitic politics: Elfriede Jelinek's '"Secondary Dramas", Abraumhalde and FaustIn and out', in Karen Jürs-Munby, Jerome Carroll, and Steve Giles (eds), *Postdramatic Theatre and the Political: International Perspectives on Contemporary Performance*, London: Bloomsbury, pp. 209–231.

——— (2014) 'Agon, conflict and dissent: Elfriede Jelinek's Ein Sportstück and its Stagings by Einar Schleef and Just a Must Theatre', *Austrian Studies*, 22, special issue: 'Jelinek in the Arena: Sport, Cultural Understanding and Translation to Page and Stage', Allyson Fiddler and Karen Jürs-Munby (eds): pp. 9–25.

Kovacs, Teresa (2017) 'Criticizing "Americanness", Criticizing "Austrianness". Paul McCarthy, Mike Kelley, Elfriede Jelinek', in *JELINEK[JAHR]BUCH*, Elfriede Jelinek-Forschungszentrum 2016–2017, Vienna: Praesens, pp. 187–202.

Krawehl, Stephanie (2008) '*Die Welt abstechen wie eine Sau', Sprachgewalt und Sprachentgrenzung in den Dramen Werner Schwabs*, Oberhausen: Athena.

Lamb-Faffelberger, Margarete (2007) 'The audacious art of Elfriede Jelinek: *Tour de Force* and Irritation', in Matthias Konzett and Margarete Lamb Faffelberger (eds), *Elfriede Jelinek: Writing Woman, Nation, and Identity: A Critical Anthology*, Vancouver: Fairleigh Dickinson University Press, pp. 37–52.

Lease, Bryce (2016) *After '89: Polish Theatre and the Political*, Manchester: Manchester University Press.

Lehmann, Hans-Thies (2006 [1999]) *Postdramatic Theatre*, Karen Jürs-Munby (trans.), London: Routledge.

—— (2016) *Tragedy and Dramatic Theatre*, Erik Butler (trans.), London: Routledge.

Mauthner, Fritz (1923 [1901–1902]) *Beiträge zu einer Kritik der Sprache*, 3 volumes, Leipzig: Felix Meiner.

Meurer, Petra (2007) *Theatrale Räume: Theaterästhetische Entwürfe in Stücken von Werner Schwab, Elfriede Jelinek und Peter Handke*, Berlin: LIT Verlag.

Miesbacher, Harald (2003) *Die Anatomie des Schwabischen: Werner Schwabs Dramensprache*, Graz, Wien: Droschl.

Pełka, Artur (2005) *Körper(sub)versionen: Zum Körperdiskurs in Theatertexten von Elfriede Jelinek und Werner Schwab*, Frankfurt am Main: Peter Lang.

Poschmann, Gerda (1997) *Der nicht mehr dramatische Theatertext. Aktuelle Bühnenstücke und ihre dramaturgische Analyse*, Tübingen: Max Niemeyer (Theatron. Bd. 22).

Preece, Julian (1999) 'Form, structure and poetry in the varied plays of Werner Schwab', in Frank Finlay and Ralf Jeuter (eds), *Centre Stage: Contemporary Drama in Austria*, Amsterdam: Rodopi, pp. 15–30.

Roselt, Jens (2001) 'Die Würde des Menschen ist antastbar', in Carl Hegemann (ed.), *Erniedrigung genießen: Kapitalismus und Depression III*, Berlin: Alexander Verlag, pp. 47–59.

Schwab, Werner (1991) 'Das Grauenvollste – einfach wundervoll', *Theater Heute* 12: 9.

—— (1999) *An Anthology of Plays* [*First Ladies; OVERWEIGHT, unimportant: MIS-SHAPE; The Round of Pleasure*], Michael Mitchell (trans.), afterword by Gerlinde Ulm Sandford, Riverside, CA: Ariadne Press.

—— (2009) *Coverdramen* [*DER REIZENDE REIGEN nach dem Reigen des REIZENDEN HERRN ARTHUR SCHNITZLER; FAUST: MEIN BRUSTKORB: MEIN HELM; TROILUSWAHN UND CRESSIDATHEATER; ANTIKLIMAX*], afterword Eckhard Schumacher, Werke Band 8, Graz, Wien: Droschl.

—— (2010) *Königskomödien* [*OFENE GRUBEN OFFENE FENSTER. EIN FALL von Ersprechen; HOCHSCHWAB: Das Lebendige ist das Leblose und die Musik, eine Komödie; MESALLIANCE aber wir ficken uns prächtig. Eine Variationskomödie; ENDLICH TOT ENDLICH KEINE LUFT MEHR. Ein Theaterzernichtungslustspiel; PORNOGEOGRAPHIE Sieben Gerüchte; ESKALATION ordinär. Ein Schwitzkastenschwank in sieben Affekten*], afterword Elfriede Jelinek, Werke Band 7, Graz, Wien: Droschl.

—— (2013) *Fäkaliendramen* [*Die Präsidentinnen; ÜBERGEWICHT, unimportant: UNFORM; Volksvernichtung oder Meine Leber ist sinnlos; Mein Hundmund; Der Himmel Mein Lieb Meine sterbende Beute*], Nachwort Helmut Schödel, Werke Band 6, Graz, Wien: Droschl.

—— (2014) *Dead at Last, At Last No More Air*, Meredith Oakes (trans.), foreword by Diana Damian Martin, London: Oberon Books.

3 Weronika Szczawińska and Agnieszka Jakimiak

Dramaturg as a figure of transition

Bryce Lease

Weronika Szczawińska has created performances in theatres and art galleries across Poland as a director, dramaturge, translator, and performer. Working first with Piotr Borowski's Studium Teatralne, she later graduated from the Directing Department at the Aleksander Zelwerowicz Theatre Academy in Warsaw before completing a PhD at the Institute of Art of the Polish Academy of Sciences. Nominated for the Polityka Passport Prize for her innovations in theatre practices, she has been the Artistic Director of the Teatr im. Boguslawski in Kalisz since 2014. Szczawińska generates performances, texts, and installations in collaborative processes that extend traditional boundaries between playwright, dramaturg, director, and deviser. As both a writer and an artistic director of a major public theatre, Szczawińska offers a wide perspective on curating theatre repertoires, the creation of new audiences, activism in the theatre, and the negotiation of complex funding systems in an increasingly conservative political environment. One of the founders of the Contemporary Civic Theatre Forum, an organisation that assembles directors and playwrights born in the 1970s and 80s, her writing and cultural criticism has appeared in top Polish journals such as *Dialog, Didaskalia, Teatr*, and *Res Publica Nowa*. Szczawińska's theatre, often divisive or controversial, is politically engaged, deeply sceptical of authority, and critical of national myths. As well as Polish collective memory and history, her performances are noted for their interrogations of feminist biographies, racial and ethnic politics, queer identities, neoliberalism, and Poland's ambiguous status as a postcolonial space after the collapse of communism. Playwright and dramaturg Agnieszka Jakimiak has been one of Szczawińska's closest collaborators. Their performances have been staged at the country's most renowned mainstream theatres, including Teatr Polski Bydgoszcz and Narodowy Stary Teatr in Kraków, as well as Poland's experimental independent venues, such as Komuna Warszawa.

This interview is based on two conversations conducted in Warsaw in May and July 2017.

BRYCE LEASE: After 1989, a number of scholars have pointed out that while there was a strong tradition in Poland for directors there was a scarcity of playwrights. In part, this can be seen as a result of the history of censoring play texts under communism. How do you see writing cultures developing since the early 1990s in Poland?

WERONIKA SZCZAWIŃSKA: I am not sure about the scarcity of playwrights. The directors were just more powerful, shaping even the most iconic texts to their taste. Anyway, there was a crisis in Polish theatre after 1989. What were we supposed to do? Theatre is the most collective form of art and the collective itself had changed. The national component of drama that is so strongly embedded in our canon – particularly from the nineteenth century – was seen as insufficient. Starting from the early 1990s we had a strong desire for contemporary drama. Gustaw Holoubek, the famous actor, director, and politician, wrote an article at that time in which he argued that we needed to change. He claimed that Poles needed to adopt what the so-called 'normal' or 'civilised' part of the world was doing. This meant finishing with a national canon and looking for something more universal, which included themes such as love or the plight of the human being. There was a crisis of tradition and a need to be contemporary. This was an auto-colonising gesture. What do the big Western democracies have? They have drama. We wanted something like contemporary Shakespeare for ourselves. We envied the Austrians and Germans, such as Werner Schwab, Thomas Bernhard, Elfriede Jelinek (although with Jelinek, our interest only arose after she won the Nobel Prize). You could see how emotional we were at that time about British writing as well. The top of the list would be Sarah Kane and Mark Ravenhill. You could point at these writers and say that this is how the world is supposed to react to the contemporary moment. We needed to have the West as a counterpart, which was connected to a crisis of tradition. Polish plays finally started to bloom when writers found supporters, such as Tadeusz Słobodzianek, who started a writers' laboratory, and Roman Pawłowski, a critic who wrote about the need to have new drama and then published an important anthology of Polish plays that he called *Porno Generation.*[1] So the situation was ambiguous. On the one hand, we wanted the contemporary world to enter our theatre, and on the other hand we aspired to be someone else, a different society. Of course, I did not experience all of it myself. I was too young. But I also need to underline that I have never been a great fan of this 'new wave' of Polish plays. They seemed outdated the same moment they were created.

BL: When did these strict differences between East and West begin to break down or become more fluid?

WS: I think it started to change at the beginning of the 2000s. In the first decade, the categories of the universal and the local were undermined. Roughly speaking, in the '90s we thought that we were East but we wanted to be West. What is the West? It's universal, but it's also modern. It's brutal. We needed to search for a Polish Sarah Kane and to abandon the national classics. We also looked for examples from Shakespeare. Shakespeare was our contemporary again. Everything that was local was not interesting. Everything local felt outdated. By the early 2000s this view finally changed and we started to seek insights into what was happening in our own society. This is linked to the fact that there was a 'memory

68 *Bryce Lease*

boom'. Plays become less about universal themes and become more oriented on local problems, such as those of Polish collective memory. Things really change after the groundbreaking cultural event that was the publication of Jan Gross' *Neighbours* in 2000.[2] It really changes theatre and it really changes playwriting. We start to see plays about Polish Jewish relations. So, the first thing that became more fluid was that we no longer wanted to be 'West' anymore, because we started to see ourselves as a society. Maybe not as a nation, but as a society that has its own problems. Then there was another change that I think is still the most important development today. In Poland in the 1990s and early 2000s, we were obsessed with plays, but then plays and playwriting mutated into something we might call 'writing for theatre', that is texts, propositions, or scripts for theatre. This sparked the emergence of the role of the dramaturg. Attitudes toward text became more nonchalant and less reverential. Texts were written for particular productions that were not meant to be staged by different directors. They were written in collaboration with the entire creative team. We developed quite far from the original idea of having a canon of contemporary universal plays.

AGNIESZKA JAKIMIAK: At the beginning of the twenty-first century Polish theatre makers had many possibilities to engage with contemporary European productions, and this had a meaningful and influential impact on how theatre languages and the need for plays began to evolve. Festivals such as Festiwal Festiwali in Warsaw's Dramatic Theatre (Teatr Dramatyczny) and later Central Warsaw (Warszawa Centralna) or Reminiscencje and Dialog invited the most prominent avant-garde theatre pieces, such as works by Heiner Goebbels, The Wooster Group, and Christoph Marthaler. That enabled Polish theatre makers to gain a new perspective on how texts for the theatre can be invented, which led to the reinvention of established Polish theatre traditions in response to these new forms. When we look at the scripts of Jerzy Grzegorzewski – Weronika's and my own favourite Polish director – there can be no doubt that even before 2000 the aim was not to 'stage a play' in a traditional sense, but much more about processual writing, the deconstruction and atomisation of texts.[3]

BL: And where are the renowned modernist Polish playwrights situated in this discussion for you? I am thinking particularly about Witold Gombrowicz, Sławomir Mrożek, or Tadeusz Różewicz.

WS: I think Mrożek is a separate case from Gombrowicz and Różewicz. Mrożek was very much present in the discussion of modern theatre, because he was the ultimate figure of crisis. The more conservative or traditional oriented people would ask, 'Why don't you stage Mrożek?' More progressive theatre makers would reply that this was precisely the kind of modern playwriting that we do not want to have because it is a closed form of writing. It is so detailed that you cannot change anything. You must obey the author in everything. He is important because there were times when discussions of the modern canon would only be about

Mrożek. With Gombrowicz and Różewicz, they were also victims of this conservative narrative, but I think it is still possible to do many revolutionary things with them. Różewicz's plays are really amazing because they are written totally against theatre. This is a bit like Jelinek's strategy. She would always say, 'I hate theatre. I'll give you this text and I am sure it will give you a lot of trouble. I did my best to make it unstageable for you.' I think that was also what Różewicz was doing. The reception of his work has been oversimplified. As well as being on the national school curriculum, his play *Kartoteka* (*Card Index*, 1960) has been staged many, many times. As a result, it has become banal. And I think the same has happened to Gombrowicz. The older master directors staged these playwrights and so the younger generation of directors has not been that interested in them.

BL: You both write and direct. Traditionally, these roles were seen as distinct in Poland, but there appears to be more fluidity between them now. You are also often credited as a dramaturg rather than as a writer. Can you explain your approach to creating a text for theatre, and to what extent this is – or is *not* – a process of adaptation?

WS: The word dramaturg is a very big bag and we can put many things into it. This position, or function, or job must always be defined in relation to the other members of the creative team. Sometimes a dramaturg is a researcher who offers a context for a production. Sometimes she is the author or co-author of a text, or someone who is not the author but writes the improvisations down. It is someone who should be the guardian of the structure of the performance. Someone who helps the director and those making a production to keep some distance from it. It is very easy to lose distance when you are making work and you are no longer able to see what is happening on stage. You are too close. So, we might call the dramaturg the 'distancer'. I really love working as a dramaturg because it has all the good parts of being a director apart from the emotional distress. Because the dramaturg doesn't usually work with the actors in a way the director does. Even if you feel responsible for the actors, or even if you interfere with their job *as* a dramaturg, the stress is not on you. Rather, you really see the work in a more relaxed way so that you can be this 'distancer'. As for adaptation, I think a skilled director should be able to make an adaptation by herself. I don't need a dramaturg to write an adaptation. That is a basic directing skill. In Polish theatre, the dramaturg was a key figure of change. We not only started thinking differently about writing, but also about directing and about acting and the members of the creative team, because at the beginning we were faced with this bizarre idea of a dramaturg. I really like the concept that the performance studies expert Dorota Sajewska (who was actually one of the first Polish dramaturgs) has in her recent book *Nekroperformans* (2016).[4] As an expert in both Polish and German theatre, Sajewska considers the impact of the First World War on theatre and analyses the emergence of the figure of a

70   *Bryce Lease*

dramaturg, for example in the work of Erwin Piscator. She sees the dramaturg as a figure of crisis. This war brought the necessity to change theatre, which starts to be fragmented, critical, and political. It distances itself from the big narratives and from plays. It is at this moment that the dramaturg appears. And this is what has happened for us more recently in Poland. After decades of not having a proper discussion about political or critical theatre, we started to invent such theatre through new forms that were arriving from elsewhere. We borrowed the dramaturg from the German theatre. For me, then, this role is a convincing figure of transition, just as it was historically. And we continue to discuss the relevance of the dramaturg in public debates. Some people feel it is a big waste of money. For Tadeusz Słobodzianek, for example, he would never have a dramaturg in his rehearsals. There is only the director, the play, and the performance. This is a generational difference.

AJ: On the other hand, what we understand as the dramaturg bares little similarity to the function of this role in Germany or the Netherlands. In recent years the basic mode of work established in Polish theatre relies on creating duos or teams consisting of a director, a dramaturg, and close coworkers. Dramaturges are rarely an extension of the theatre institution itself, but members of a creative team. They usually do not only have at their disposal the 'distanced perspective', but their work starts long before rehearsals, while they are working on the context, concept, and the whole matrix environing the project.

BL: As part of this process of adopting new forms, such as the dramaturg, to what extent do you see yourself as a European or as a specifically Polish theatre maker?

WS: For me, the term European is connected to words like 'public' or at least 'state funded' or officially supported culture. Working in Slovenia for the first time this year, I would also interpret European in relation to a tradition of critical theatre. If it is German, or Polish, or Slovenian or any other of the countries of the former Yugoslavia, there is a very similar discourse and very similar strategies. In this way I see myself as a European theatre maker. The conservative backlash in my homeland makes me very distrustful towards the word 'Polish'.

BL: Looking at written histories of Polish theatre, it is clear that women have often been left out or written out. How do you see this situation today?

WS: Speaking about the past, this is still a mystery. Fortunately, there is a research group that is called 'HyPaTia. Kobieca historia polskiego teatru' (Hypatia. Women's history of Polish theatre), which is linked with the Instytut Teatralny (Theatre Institute, Warsaw). This includes Joanna Krakowska and Agata Adamiecka-Sitek, amongst others. They are working on female histories of Polish theatre and building a lexicon of plays, playwrights, directors, and set designers. One of Krakowska's ideas is that women played an important role in creating new theatrical languages and took risks (that men benefited from) without receiving proper recognition.

For example, we were speaking about Różewicz's *Card Index*, which is the most iconic Polish play of the postwar era. Yet nobody knows that it was first staged by a woman at the Teatr Dramatyczny in Warsaw, a very important institution at the time. And nobody remembers her name, which was Wanda Laskowska. She died last year. Everyone remembers the play and the theatre, but no one remembers this director, even though she was one of the women who introduced the avant-garde to the Polish stage. For example, she staged Witkacy in the years after his work had been prohibited.[5] Perhaps we could also consider another hypothesis. Theatre in Poland is very much associated with the narrative of the collective, to nation and to tradition. These terms are not seen to be connected with what femininity stands for culturally. Working in Polish theatre – before Polish theatre started to psychoanalyse itself – was a suicidal move. If you worked there as a woman, you would be excluded. It excluded every kind of queerness, I would say. We are very good at turning queer into national. Jerzy Grotowski's work is a perfect example of queerness turned into something else. Only recently there have been studies like Agata Adamiecka-Sitek's article 'Grotowski, kobiety i homoseksualiści' ('Grotowski, women and homosexuals') or Dorota Sajewska and Karol Radziszewski's video-theatre collaboration 'Książę' ('Prince') in 2014, which have touched upon this aspect of Grotowski's work.[6] The irony of it all: the highly eroticised body of Ryszard Cieślak (eroticised in the manner that surpasses usual hetero-norms) has historically been interpreted only in relation to a Christ-like figure. Of course, this interpretation was also due to Grotowski's misleading strategies. He would never present his work in this manner. But if you look at Grotowski's productions with a fresh eye, the queer aspect is striking.

BL: Your work has attended to multiple feminist and queer questions and for-mations of identity and culture. How do you see these shaping your work and those of your contemporaries?

WS: Of course, things are different now but they are far from perfect. At one point we really started having to use military terms, such as 'an offensive' of women directors. For example, when I started my studies in Warsaw Theatre Academy, it was 2003. This was the moment when the majority of the students at this institution became women. Before that, each year group would consist of men only. Sometimes there would be one woman. A similar change began in Kraków. It's not only that they started to take more women, but also that more women started to appear. There have been two waves now of women directors. Some of this is PR. It is very easy to say that our theatre is so successful because so many women are directing, which is unusual in European theatre. Some of my professors would claim this change came because the theatre professionally does not offer very much money. Where the economic value goes down, that's where women appear. On the other hand, with the second wave of women directors something is changing. It is not only about gender, it is also about the general attitude towards the structure. Our involvement in theatre making changes the professional structure. We are more interested in networks, collaboration, in flattening hierarchies. The problem in the beginning was that we had new women directors but we didn't have any feminist plays. In terms of the boom in Polish playwriting, many women have been involved. Many of them had experience in journalism, so that's where they were coming from. And now there is a visible change in the core of the structure of Polish theatre. We are feminising or queering it [see Figure 3.1]. I am really up for that. It means thinking about identity at a very different level. Again, not only about gender. This undermines every stable identity. Before it was about what was 'national', or the position of the director or the playwright. Now it is more about collaboration. AJ: What we are still lacking is an ability to make open statements, undermining the patriarchal perspective of theatre pieces and working in a theatre institution itself. This skill and courage characterises the academic work of Adamiecka-Sitek and Krakowska, but it still needs to be done in the field of professional theatre practice. The distribution of gender roles on the stage is more or less fixed and while it is being discredited or questioned, one usually comes across accusations of being too hermetic, not universal, obsessed, or insane. Performances that represent the universal value or crisis of humanity are always more highly esteemed than feminist approaches that challenge existing institutional hierarchies.

Figure 3.1 Agnieszka Jakimiak's *Hitchcock*, directed by Weronika Szczawińska (2017), at the Mladinsko Theatre, Ljubljana, Slovenia. Katarina Stegnar and Damjana Černe as Tippi Hedren and Alfred Hitchcock re-enact the British film director's oppressive audition process. Photograph © Nejc Saje

BL: Over the past few years, since a very conservative government has come to power, a number of artistic directors of major public theatres have been replaced. This has called into question the power of governments over theatre through their state funding.

WS: Fortunately, there is still a lot of public funding for theatre, but the problem is that this money is sometimes distributed in a bizarre way. Some theatres get enough and some theatres do not get enough. And we do not know why. We know that this money exists and that it is there to be spent on culture. A good example is the Teatr Dramatyczny in Wałbrzych, which is famous for producing new critical directors. Now they are struggling and we don't know why. When I was working there a few years ago they had a consistent level of funding. Suddenly, the money was cut, and this was not due to some kind of economic catastrophe in the region. Theatres depend financially upon local authorities or the Ministry of Culture. While we have money, what we lack is institutional autonomy. In this way, public funding can be a tool of censorship. Even if the money is secure, there can be some suggestions or small attempts to censor productions. I think in this underhand way more revolutionary forms of critical theatre are being cut. Let's take this very banal example of the Catholic Church. It is fair to say that Oliver Frljić's production of Stanisław Wyspiański's *Klątwa* (*The Curse*) at the Teatr Powszechny in Warsaw in 2017 is the first performance in Polish theatre that deals with the Catholic Church in such an open way. Although for years we have been so proud of our critical theatre, nobody would go for the Church in the way Oliver and his collaborators − such as Agnieszka Jakimiak, Joanna Wichowska, Goran Injac, and the acting team − have attempted. I think it was also partly because the managers of public theatres were really afraid. A few years ago, I wanted to make a production about John Paul II and his dear friend Wanda Półtawska, who advised him about things like body politics. Półtawska really influenced his view towards abortion and contraception. My boyfriend, Piotr Wawer jr, who is also an actor and a dramaturg, and I suggested this to one public theatre and the artistic director said it was impossible because they had a very strong bishop in his town. This is what happens when you speak to the manager of a public theatre in a secular state? Public funding on the one hand enables Polish theatre to experiment in the very heart of mainstream culture. Recently at the Kalisz Theatre Meetings, which I co-curated, there were a number of very experimental new dramaturgical strategies presented from theatres that all are supported through public funding. It is a big advantage that we have. On the other hand, it is a tool of censorship, and we are experiencing it as that more and more. What we lack is a third option. We have mainstream theatre, which is very rich but can suffer from censorship, and we have 'off',[7] which is very much liberated but is very poor. A good example of 'off' theatre is Komuna Warszawa, where I love working because it is independent and they never ask you what or how you are

74   *Bryce Lease*

making a production. It is really free. This has an impact on the way of making and writing for theatre. It is a nice example of a laboratory. They started by inviting dancers, who do not have their own place in Poland. We have very good dancers, but they are not funded. They invited dancers, artists, people from mainstream theatres, performers, and people like Wojtek Ziemilski, who comes from a very different multi-disciplinary tradition of making art. All these people start to mingle there. I love Komuna Warszawa because I don't have to think in institutional terms. I only work with artists who are open to every kind of shift or change, while in an institutional theatre I need to take into account the fact that the actors have not had a chance to work in a different way in ages, so I need to negotiate with them. However, I can only work in Komuna Warszawa because I work in big publicly funded theatres, where I earn my money. In Komuna, I have the freedom.

BL: Thinking about freedom of expression in Polish theatre, are there existing taboos that remain in place, which have been addressed or need to be addressed again?

WS: Referring back to Frljić's work, I think there is one even bigger taboo than the Catholic Church and that is a secular view of the world. Even now when people defend *Klątwa* they often do so in religious terms. They say: it is a performance that attacks the institution but it does not attack the faith. It is a religious tradition. So, for me, what is taboo is to be a secular person and not a religious person. It is not only about Catholicism. Our theatre is so rooted in the Romantic tradition, which is supernatural, transcendental, and spiritual, that it is difficult to keep yourself out of this sphere. I'm really looking forward to a more secular discussion, about anything.

Weronika Szczawińska – five key productions

Jackie. Śmierć i księżniczka (*Jackie. Death and the Princess*) by Elfriede Jelinek. Translated by Mateusz Borowski and Małgorzata Sugiera. Direction and dramaturgy by Weronika Szczawińska. Scenography and costume by Izabela Wądołowska. Perf. Milena Gauer. Teatr im. Stefana Jaracza Olsztyn, 7 June 2008.

Jak być kochaną (*How To Be Loved*) by Agnieszka Jakimiak. Direction by Weronika Szczawińska. Dramaturgy by Agnieszka Jakimiak. Scenography and costume by Izabela Wądołowska. Bałtycki Teatr Dramatyczny Koszalin, 8 October 2011.

Komornicka. Biografia pozorna (*Komornicka. Ostensible Biography*) by Weronika Szczawińska and Bartek Frąckowiak. Directed Bartek Frąckowiak. Dramaturgy by Weronika Szczawińska. Perf. Anita Sokołowska. Music by Krzysztof Kaliski. Scenography and costume by Anna Maria Karczmarska. Teatr Polski Bydgoszcz, Hobo Art Foundation, Scena Prapremier InVitro Lublin, 9 March 2012.

Geniusz w golfie (*Golf Genius*) by Agnieszka Jakimiak. Direction and dramaturgy by Weronika Szczawińska. Music by Krzysztof Kaliski. Choreography by Agata Maszkiewicz. Scenography and costume by Natalia Mleczak. Narodowy Stary Teatr Kraków, 11 April 2014.

Hitchcock. Text and dramaturgy by Agnieszka Jakimiak. Directed by Weronika Szczawińska. Set and costume design by Katarzyna Leks. Choreography by Agata Maszkiewicz. Dramaturgy and music selection by Piotr Wawer jr. Lighting design by David Cvelbar. Mladinsko Theatre, Ljubljana, 20 April 2017.

Notes

1 Roman Pawłowski, *Pokolenie porno i inne niesmaczne utwory teatralne. Antologia najnowszego dramatu polskiego w wyborze* (Warsaw: Zielona Sowa, 2003).
2 On 10 July 1941, in a small village in the northeast of Poland, local Jews were rounded up by their neighbours, locked inside a barn, and burned to death. Traditional Polish historiography attributed the guilt for the now infamous pogrom to the Nazis, but historian Jan T. Gross's study, *Neighbors: The Destruction of the Jewish Community in Jedwabne, Poland,* places the responsibility for the massacre firmly with the local community. The publication of Gross's monograph caused mass outrage, provoking many to identify the debate around the pogrom, and more broadly around Polish anti-Semitism, as the most important and long-standing in post-communist Poland.
3 Jerzy Grzegorzewski (1939–2005) distinguished himself as a Polish director more interested in the theatre's formalistic potentials rather than its moralising and ideological function, and the dominating themes of his work have been the condition of the artist, particularly their pursuit of excellence, struggles with moral weakness, and the limitations of the physical world. Having trained as a painter, his primary concentration was often on theatre as a visual and plastic art rather than on pictorial mimesis or psychological realism. Throughout his career, Grzegorzewski faced sharp condemnation from Polish critics due to his liberal adaptations of canonical texts, often flaunting authorial intention and stable narrative structure.
4 Dorota Sajewska, *Nekroperformans. Kulturowa rekonstrukcja teatru Wielkiej Wojny* (Warsaw: Instytut Teatralne, 2016). Sajewska uses the term 'necroperformance' to identify the cultural spectacle of Polishness that is derived from revitalising historical remnants of the 'Great War', the First World War, and – in the broader context – the reactualisation of the past that dwells upon wreckage and debris, in both psychic and material senses. Sajewska's monograph was translated into English in 2019.
5 Stanisław Ignacy Witkiewicz (also known as Witkacy) was a Polish writer, painter, philosopher, playwright, novelist, and photographer (1885–1939). He is noted for theorising the concept of 'pure form' in theatre. His plays were banned from the stage in Poland during the Stalinist period until 1956.
6 Agata Adamiecka-Sitek, 'Grotowski, kobiety i homoseksualiści', *Didaskalia* (2012), pp. 94–105.
7 This Polish term 'off' originated as a reference to 'Off Broadway', independent theatre outside of the mainstream that does not receive public funding.

4 András Visky and Matéi Visniec

Challenging boundaries of cultural specificity

Jozefina Komporaly

One of the defining features of contemporary European playwriting is that it is no longer deployed along national boundaries, and the provenance of authors and the languages in which they write do not necessarily overlap. Looking at the landscape of contemporary drama written in Romanian, it is particularly striking how few of the significant authors reside within the geographical borders of Romania: Matéi Visniec and Alexandra Badea live in Paris, Ştefan Peca is based in Berlin, Alexandra Pâzgu in Giessen. To make use of Romanian-American playwright Saviana Stănescu's terms, immigrant authors constantly live 'on the bridge of *in-betweenness:* negotiating between two cultures, […] two cities […], between the West and the East', in a world of 'hyphenate[d] identities' (in Modreanu 2019b). This complexity is paralleled by the situation of Romanian theatre directors: many of the canonical figures have achieved their international careers in exile (such as Lucian Pintilie, Liviu Ciulei, and Andrei Şerban), whilst the most innovative Romanian artists of today (the likes of Silviu Purcărete, Mihai Măniuţiu, Gianina Cărbunariu, Radu Afrim, and Radu Jude) are operating as truly transglobal artists (Modreanu 2020). It is crucial to stress, however, that irrespective whether these dramatists and theatre makers actually live in Romania at present, their work is rooted in and greatly fuelled by their experience of being brought up in Romania, and is regularly published and produced in their country of origin. Some of these playwrights continue to express themselves in the Romanian language, in addition to which many of them also write in the languages of their adopted countries (not unlike fellow Romanian-born author Eugène Ionesco); Matéi Visniec, for instance, produces multiple versions of the same text whereby he essentially engages in an act of self-translation. The work of several authors, including Alexandra Badea and Saviana Stănescu, is translated into Romanian by other important literary figures (such as Eugen Jebeleanu and Alina Nelega), thus generating synergies between authorial voices and artistic preoccupations. Furthermore, the recently founded Teatrul Dramaturgilor Români (Theatre of Romanian Playwrights) in Bucharest has already established itself as an influential creative hub in nurturing contemporary dramatists (such as Horea Gârbea, Lucia Verona, Alexander Hausvater, Sebastian Ungureanu), and in facilitating alliances between playwrights living throughout Europe.

The case of Hungarian drama, or that of dramatic works written in Hungarian, is complex for historical reasons. The category 'Hungarian literature abroad' emerged in the wake of the First World War when, after the Treaty of Trianon, significant Hungarian communities became part of neighbouring nations. The literatures written in Hungarian on these territories tend to define themselves as Hungarian with the relevant qualifier – such as Hungarian literature from Transylvania; however, their inclusion into the canon continues to constitute a sensitive matter. When it comes to high-profile authors, the sheer fact of writing in the Hungarian language prevails over geographical location, and consequently acts as a form of cultural debordering, though at times such authors may also find themselves attributed to the parallel canon in the language of their country of residence. For the purposes of this chapter, the language in which a particular playwright writes will form the basis of categorisation, nuanced by information on geographical and cultural affiliation. Looking at the landscape of contemporary Hungarian playwriting, several household names come to the fore, such as György Spiró, János Háy, János Térey, Péter Kárpáti, Zoltán Egressy, Kornél Hamvai, and Béla Pintér; yet when it comes to a predominant focus on drama in the respective authors' career and to genuinely innovative writing, it is Transylvanian dramatists that fare the best. This may well have to do with their exposure to more than one cultural tradition, and most importantly in this context, to the thriving Romanian theatre scene. The most original playwrights writing in Hungarian today, András Visky and Csaba Székely, speak and write excellent Romanian and collaborate extensively with key theatre institutions up and down the country. In this way, their work is not only influenced by concerns with visuality and movement-based practices that characterise much of Romanian theatre but is also produced in Romanian translation soon after the premiere, taking place as a rule at the Hungarian Theatre of Cluj and/or the Miklós Tompa company at the Hungarian Theatre in Târgu-Mureş.

In attempting to offer a snapshot of the current Romanian and Hungarian theatre scenes, therefore, the blurring of boundaries is key, and this chapter focuses on two renowned playwrights who started their careers in the 1980s and came to prominence after the fall of the Iron Curtain. András Visky (b. 1957) and Matéi Visniec (b. 1956) are among the most prolific authors in the Hungarian and Romanian languages, in addition to drama also writing fiction, poetry, as well as journalism. They are both respected public intellectuals whose opinions on current affairs influence large audiences, and who have been the recipients of prestigious awards and prizes. András Visky has been elected to the Széchenyi Academy of Letters and Arts in Hungary, and Matéi Visniec has a municipal theatre (in the Romanian city of Suceava) named after him that hosts an annual international festival that he co-curates. Visky and Visniec share a preoccupation with the human condition in its multiple manifestations, and invite public reflection on the role of history and its implication on the present. Actively engaged with keeping cultural memory alive, Visky and Visniec are adamant that to remember is an act of duty, and that it is imperative to configure theatre as a space that brings key concerns of our time to light.

78 *Jozefina Komporaly*

Their fascination with staging history is paramount, and they approach this with a commitment that does not shy away from braiding the tragic with the ridiculous, and the absurd with the ironic. Visniec observes: 'Here, we live the absurd, [while you, over there, you write it]' (in Komporaly 2015b: 391), whereas Visky notes that 'reality is nothing but absurd', as the theatre of the absurd does none other than 'amplify this absurd reality with mathematical precision, and make the world confront its own incongruity' (in Sipos and Visky 2009: 112). As I argue elsewhere, in adopting such an approach the playwrights embrace the postdramatic concern with 'troubling our expectations of how to interpret a text, and its rejoicing in the disruption of the hierarchical order: generic and political alike' (Komporaly 2017: 9). They both take delight in titling their plays in very unique and often striking ways that already kickstart an invitation for audience engagement. Visniec prefers relatively long titles that deploy a narrative of sorts and conjure up unforeseen juxtapositions (*How I Trained a Snail on Your Breasts, The Story of Panda Bears Told by a Saxophonist Who Has a Girlfriend in Frankfurt*), whereas Visky opts for very concise, often monosyllabic, titles that often carry internal contradictions and shock value (*I Killed My Mother, Porn*). Above all, the playwrights imagine dramatic situations that are able to capture the fragility of the individual in limit situations. They convey the essence of living under ideological oppression that can make people understand the emotional impact of the latter on a visceral level, without having had an immediate encounter with such oppression. Visky's and Visniec's plays are rooted in personal exposure to totalitarianism, yet are not 'historical plays' or 'plays about history' as such, but reflections on this limit-experience which explore the idea of captivity in multiple ways, examining the political, social, and psychological implications of confinement. Thus, prisons, forced domiciles, hospitals, mental and childcare institutions feature prominently in their work – as a code for the severe limitations to personal freedom, and this is often accentuated to absurd proportions, thus foregrounding the challenges of achieving mental freedom under any kind of ideological as well as economic pressure.

Visky and Visniec are far from being exceptions in signalling the flaws of their world; however, they tend to engage with their subject matter as authors of dramatic texts (available for others to subsequently stage), utilising a lens that zooms in on the symbolic and on universally valid human concerns that often transcend the here and now. This differentiates their approach from that of younger practitioners who often have a background in directing and are pre-occupied with scrutinising the recent past by way of verbatim theatre and/or expanded journalistic documentation, looking at issues of vital importance for Romanian society. As Romanian theatre critic Cristina Modreanu notes, such issues 'are strangely avoided by newspapers and mass-media in a general context of mass-media degradation and frequent obstructions of the freedom of expression' (2013: 385); theatre and performance thus occupies the prime position for dealing with high importance topics such as homelessness, racism, or ecological crises. Moreover, for a new wave of Romanian artists, theatre making is a collaborative art that takes place in multiple configurations and locations, often taking educational and therapeutic aims, and it is closely intertwined with the relationship between ethics and aesthetics. An emblematic figure for this strand is director-playwright Gianina Cărbunariu (b. 1977), by far the most influential voice in the generation approaching mid-career. Cărbunariu's early work *Stop the Tempo* (2003) achieved manifesto status for the 2000 generation in Romania, a peer group educated after the communist era, and 'gave a voice to a universal need of youngsters to change the world' (Modreanu 2016). In a European context, Cărbunariu is better known as a playwright; *Kebab* was staged at the Schaubühne and the Royal Court in 2007, and *Artists Talk* was included in the 2019 Brexit Stage Left Festival at the Yard Theatre in London. Csaba Székely (b. 1981) came to prominence with a play originally written in English (*Do You Like Banana, Comrades?* 2009), but has since focused on writing in Hungarian as well as Romanian. He achieved cult status with the trilogy *Minelands* (2014), highlighting the dark side of the Transylvanian psyche and examining issues such as unemployment, alcoholism, nationalism, corruption, and high suicide rates among the Hungarian population in Transylvania. His recent work includes historical comedies and political satires that deconstruct the notion of heroism and invites fresh thinking on multiculturalism, particularly in the context of Transylvania's now centennial history as part of Romania. Affiliated to the Fabulamundi network, both Székely and Cărbunariu are adamant at international co-operation in the theatre and, in common with Visky and Visniec, not only address multicultural topics but also navigate between different languages and locations, thus challenging the boundaries of cultural specificity.

Confronting communist histories

Matéi Visniec emerged on the Romanian literary scene as a poet with the volume *La noapte va ninge* (*Tonight It Will Snow*, 1980), following which he started writing drama. The political undertones of his work, however, attracted attention and censorship almost straightaway. He continued to seek public outlets for his work, but by the time a professional theatre showed interest in one of his plays – Nottara Theatre in Bucharest announced plans to stage *Caii la fereastră* (*Horses at the Window*) in 1987 – he already had an invitation to France, and once there, asked for political asylum. This meant that Visniec got well and truly blacklisted until the fall of the communist regime in December 1989, but after the political changes in 1990 his work was rediscovered almost overnight, and theatres started staging his previously censored as well as newly written plays. Within a few years, Visniec has become the most frequently staged living Romanian playwright, having multiple texts in the repertoire of professional as well as amateur theatre companies at any one time, and volumes of his dramatic output being continuously reissued by some of the most important publishing houses such as Cartea Românescă and Humanitas. His work has also become the subject of extensive critical scrutiny, generating numerous studies including an edited collection by international scholars

80   *Jozefina Komporaly*

published to mark the conferment of an honorary doctoral degree to the playwright at 'Ovidius' University in Constanța (cf. Cap-Bun and Nicolae, 2015). In parallel with this high-profile presence in Romania that has included over 20 years of productions at the prestigious Sibiu International Theatre Festival, Visniec's theatre has continued to be firmly embedded into the French theatre system where it was initially nurtured. Over the years, Visniec has developed partnerships with a number of small and medium-size companies in France such as Pli Urgent in Lyon, and established himself as one of the most popular playwrights at the Avignon OFF Festival. In the course of almost 30 years, he had hundreds of productions at the festival, directed by Christian Auger, Mustapha Aouar, Gérard Gelas, Serge Barbuscia (among others), this work also benefitting from the PR support and extraordinary enthusiasm of publisher Émile Lansman. As a result of translations into over 30 languages, Visniec's plays also appeared on the stages of some of the most prestigious theatres in Europe, including the Young Vic, Théâtre du Rond Point des Champs Elysées in Paris, Stary Theatre Krakow, Piccolo Theatre Milan, Royal Dramatic Theatre Stockholm, National Theatre Istanbul, and Maxim Gorki Theatre in Berlin.

András Visky also started his literary career with a volume of poetry – *Partraszállás* (*Debarcation*), 1984 – but turned to playwriting much later in his career, at the turn of the millennium, by which point he had already consolidated his career as a theatre critic and dramaturg. The first decade of the 2000s being a very different context from the communist dictatorship of the 1980s, his dramatic work was embraced instantly by public and critical opinion, and within just over a decade Visky had created a body of work that was staged in a variety of theatres by a range of directors, in addition to which he launched an original dramaturgical concept to underpin his approach to theatre-making and to performer–audience relationships. 'Barrack Dramaturgy' attempts to foreground deeply ingrained cultural memories, or memories that are not personal to us yet still attached to us, and reconfigure these as if they were our own. The concept departs from the premise that theatre is a place for introspection where one willingly accepts confinement to a shared intimate space, and where performer–audience communication takes place in an experiential fashion whereby all partake in the experience of one another. His ideas on Barrack Dramaturgy have been formulated alongside his playwriting practice, and offer a platform towards approaching the production process of most of his works (cf. Visky in Romanska 2015 and in Komporaly 2017). In addition to Gábor Tompa with whom Visky has been collaborating for decades, Visky credits US directors Christopher Markle and Robert Woodruff and European directors Silviu Purcărete and Yuri Kordonsky as the most influential on his career, and emphasises the defining importance of his experience as a dramaturg in developing his own distinctive voice as a playwright. In his multiple capacities as a theatre maker, Visky is concerned with exploring and expanding the boundaries of what the idea of theatre entails, and he is keen to experiment with new theatrical forms and experiences. Visky is the author of around a dozen original stage plays – including *Tanítványok* (*Disciples*) (2001), *Júlia* (*Juliet*) (2002), *A szökés* (*The Escape*) (2005), *Visszaszületés* (*Born for Never/Backborn*) (2004/2009), *Alkoholisták* (*Alcoholics*) (2009), *Megöltem az anyámat* (*I Killed My Mother*) (2010), *Pornó* (*Porn*) (2012), *Caravaggio Terminal* (2014) – and a handful of radical stage adaptations, most notably from the work of Nobel-prize winning Hungarian novelist Imre Kertész: *Hosszú péntek* (*Long Friday*) (2007). Visky's work has been presented internationally at the Avignon, Sibiu, and Edinburgh festivals, alongside productions in France, Italy, Bulgaria, Poland, Hungary, and the United States. Theatre Y in Chicago has emerged as a particularly ardent champion, and Visky has forged flourishing working relationships with actress Melissa Lorraine (formerly Hawkins) and director Karin Coonrod. Coonrod directed Lorraine in one of Visky's most iconic plays, *I Killed My Mother*, at Theatre Y and at La Mama in New York (both in 2012), which generated rave reviews in *The New York Times* for its ability to draw out 'raw and human' emotions in the audience (Brantley 2012).

Visky and Lorraine worked together most recently in May 2018 on *Stories of the Body*, a series of four short plays where the translation was created alongside the Hungarian original and the English-language premiere in Chicago preceded Hungarian stagings. This series had in fact its world premiere in London as one of the four plays, *The Unburied*. *The Saint of Darkness* (since retitled as *Teresa*) was staged by international company [Foreign Affairs] following their collaboration with the play's translator on the inaugural [Foreign Affairs] Translates! mentorship programme in 2017 (see Komporaly 2018). At the haven for experimental work that Lorraine runs in Chicago, she acted in or commissioned the majority of Visky's plays centred on strong female characters. This process started with *Juliet*, a memento for a truly exceptional woman and a deeply moving work that epitomises Visky's preoccupation with endurance, survival, and reconciliation in performance, also emblematic of his seamless intertwining of found stories with personal experience. It is thus fitting that Lorraine's image graces the cover of the first English-language anthology of Visky's work (*András Visky's Barrack Dramaturgy: Memories of the Body*, 2017), in a production directed by Coonrod, who in addition to directing Visky in the United States also created an Italian version of *Juliet* at Orvieto.

Though available in dozens of languages, it is not the existence of foreign versions that situates Visky or Visniec in a European canon but their ability to intertwine urgent existential, political, and aesthetic concerns, and the potential of their work for being incorporated into theatre traditions other than their local context. In Visky's case, for instance, Boian Ivanov's 2016 Bulgarian production of *Juliet* recalibrated the play to address the urgency of the ever-accentuating migration crisis (see Figure 4.1), while Jolanta Jarmolowicz and Cezary Studniak not only translated *Porn* into the Polish language but also conducted a transposition into Polish performance culture whereby the production by Teatr Nowy in Poznań was able to resonate with the legacy of Grotowski and Kantor at the same time as doing justice to Visky's play.

Figure 4.1 András Visky's *Juliet*, directed by Boian Ivanov at 'Sava Ognyanov' State Drama Theatre Ruse, Bulgaria (2016). Ivanov cast three actresses (Ralitsa Konstantinova, Yasena Gospodinova, Petya Venelinova) in the role of Juliet in order to explore the protagonist's complex state of the mind. Photograph © Boian Ivanov.

Underpinned by a dramaturgy that Visky calls 'fragmented' and Visniec 'modular' – one that is not linear but made up of repetitive elements, in homage to Beckett – an important distinctive feature of both playwrights' style that frames the treatment of their subject matter. Despite writing in such different languages and having appeal in different countries, the experience of communism in Romania has been foundational to both playwrights' worldview and creative practice, and also constitutes the subject matter that they have explored the most frequently and in constantly evolving ways. Visky started life as a victim of the communist regime, sent to a forced domicile at the age of two with his mother and six siblings, whilst his father was imprisoned elsewhere for supposedly anti-communist activities. He declared repeatedly that his 'true birthplace' was in the confinement of the Romanian Gulag (Huyser-Honig 2004: 5). Despite his family's release following the 'Khrushchev Thaw' of the Stalinist regime they soon found that they were only exchanging forced domicile for the larger-scale prison of communist Romania. Surveillance continued and supposed friends carried on informing on one another; Visky's play *Porn* vividly testifies to this sense of vulnerability and utter lack of privacy, whereby confidential conversations can only take place in the bathroom, to the protective soundtrack of the running tap, and couples' most intimate moments are subject to the intrusion of listening devices. Visky has written repeatedly about the act of facing his family's secret police files (after the regime change in

1990, it was possible to request such documents from the authorities), highlighting the heftiness of the material as well as the frustrations and bureaucratic complications of arranging this exchange of information.

Visniec also confronts the issue of coming to terms with an edited version of one's own life, so to speak, by way of secret police files. He even casts Eugène Ionesco as a character, and has him presented with his secret police file, as an homage upon returning to Romania after decades of absence. As an initially censored author himself, Visniec draws on the potential for and the right to free speech in various contexts. He creates a memorable alter ego of sorts in the character of blacklisted poet and journalist Sergiu Penegaru (*And Now Who's Going to Do the Dishes?*), whereas in *How to Explain the History of Communism to Mental Patients* he reworks the trope of the Shakespearean fool in order to create a space for political contestation under Stalinist conditions. The play is a virulent satire on ideological oppression, exposing the failed experiment of communism as 'the best of all possible worlds' where 'mad' people are free and 'normal' people are gradually losing their mind. Romanian critic Nicolae Manolescu noted that 'seldom has the human sub-condition been shown in such a crude, even mad light, illustrating not only a psychological degradation but also a political one' (Manolescu 1990: 1393). Like *Richard III Will Not Take Place, How to Explain the History of Communism* is a memento for the massacres committed in the name of communism, and the play is dedicated to the writer Daniil Kharms who died in socialist prisons. Visniec situates madness as a disease, and a mad social system side by side; in this way, the mental asylum chosen as setting instantly classifies ideology and becomes metonymic for the whole country, its prison-like conditions emblematic for the concentration camp universe of the Stalinist regime itself. This play was the first Visniec text to be staged in the US (by Florin Fătulescu at The Open Fist Theater Company in Hollywood in April 2000), and also led on to the English translation of *Richard III Will Not Take Place, or Scenes from the Life of Meyerhold* (2001). The latter departs from the premise of a banned theatre production, and through the character of Meyerhold, explores the fate of countless artists and intellectuals who have been fatally silenced by dictatorial regimes. Literally confronting the artist with the dictator, Visniec gets Meyerhold to expose Stalin as the representative of 'evil without ideology', and ironically invites the Generalissimo to state that the play Meyerhold is currently directing 'is more than a play, it is a trial. The trial of history.' Moreover, as Ilean Orlich argues, Visniec's play 'not only depicts trauma but also reproduces it on stage, engaging the audience to be witnesses, through theatrical performance, to the horrors of Stalin's Soviet Union' (Orlich 2017: 105).

Visniec's theatre intends to play an active role in refreshing collective memory regarding communism, which he calls an act of 'horror disguised as humanism' (Visniec 2012: 14). The volume *Procesul comunismului prin teatru* (*The Trial of Communism through Theatre*) is intended as an open invitation to relaunch reflection on the atrocities of communism, underpinned by the concern that, unless kept alive, memory will gloss over unpleasant episodes in history. According to Visniec, when

84   *Jozefina Komporaly*

democracy is in danger, it is up to theatre to raise public consciousness and challenge the threat of collective brainwashing. As Daniela Magiaru points out, Visniec shares the view of Meyerhold, the protagonist of *Richard III Will Not Take Place*:

> Today evil is cloaked in a thousand promises of a better world. Today it's not enough for evil to crush the crowd, it wants to be adored by them at the same time. The evil of today is not content to live in the palace and dominate the world, it wants to live inside the head of the people and control them from inside.
>
> (2012: 40)

Visniec aims to deal with the problem of communism by creating an emotional impact on the audience. He stresses the power of words and the importance of conveying messages through aesthetic emotions generated via plots and storylines. Thus, he addresses complex topics such as utopia, censorship, Stalinism, cultural resistance, and interethnic conflict by way of immediately engaging, perfectly crafted, and clearly manageable dramatic situations. These situations are universally accessible on a purely visceral and emotional level, seeing that, ultimately, Visniec's goal is to convey what he terms 'the essence of communism', and not to carry out an act of public denunciation. Moreover, Visniec's critique extends against any totalitarian form of governance, not just communism in post-war Romania, and in this sense has the potential to resonate with younger generations in their attempts to recover leftist progressive politics despite the troubled history of communism.

Similarly equipped with personal memories and found stories, Visky is in an ideal position to reflect on history, thus 'connecting the past with the present through the creativity of the theatre, constantly "quoting" from the past' (Rokem 2000: xiii). Visky defines the theatre of memory as an art form that operates via a 'shared, trans-individual body-based memory, in which movement precedes word, and image precedes speech' (Visky 2002: 23). He notes that while theatre dealing with history concentrates on articulating a particular message and aims to target the intellect, the theatre of memory is predicated on audience participation and aims for a shared experience of meanings (ibid.). Beate Heim Bennett elaborates on this stance in her review of the La MaMa production of *I Killed My Mother*: 'theatre is where memory and being are made manifest both in spoken language and physical stillness, but it is also where our acts of rebellion against systematic obliteration find communal attention' (2012: 97). Visky taps into personal and collective memory to evoke the past, and although inspired by local events, his plays contain a global dimension that transcends geographical and cultural boundaries. As a result, Visky's plays are human stories par excellence, and shed light on ways of being a mother, child, daughter, or lover that are ubiquitously valid. For instance, *I Killed My Mother* can be read as a contemporary rewriting of Greek mythology where the orphaned protagonist encounters her biological sister and, unaware of blood links, falls in love with her. This dimension, needless to say, charts a direct link to European cultural memory, and inscribes Visky's work into a rich continental tradition of transnational adaptations.

In another strand of his work, Visky examines the lives of extraordinary characters from the past, and indeed present, including Caravaggio, Mother Teresa, and Italian Renaissance painter Artemisisa Gentileschi, and connects his plays to various cities such as Budapest, Cluj, Kolkata, and Rome, from the seventeenth to the twenty-first centuries. The plays themselves, however, are works of fiction, rooted in the technique of open dramaturgy. Visky recommends in his stage directions that theatres experiment with a montage of theatrical images, as Robert Woodruff's production of *Caravaggio Terminal* at the Hungarian Theatre of Cluj in 2014 amply demonstrated; and they are also free to put on various combinations of the plays in *Stories of the Body*. As a result, spectators can watch different productions each time, presented in a choice of line-ups. In this way, the plays (*Teresa, Lina, Eva, Artemisia*) – and their approximately 50-minute-long stage versions – have the potential to gain meanings in each other's context: illuminating the stories of the body in the most varied refractions, as a variation of a single theatrical space and set design (Visky 2019). The possibility of manifold and cross-referential audience readings is an aspect that Visky shares with seminal Hungarian poet and playwright János Pilinszky. Prontvai (2016) argues that both write plays structured like musical scores that actors and audiences are invited to follow in order to transform content into embodied experience, and the work of both authors acquires 'meaning and life-giving force' in the light of such multiple readings.

Transnational and historical flows

As avid social commentators, Visky and Visniec have continued to keep their fingers on the pulse of times, acknowledging that the demise of communism in Eastern Europe has in no way instituted a fully democratic society. Coming to prominence precisely in the period of transition from a socialist to a market-oriented regime, both playwrights show awareness of the complexities inherent in economic as well as political and cultural change. One of Visniec's most successful early plays looks at the Yugoslav war and situates an American psychiatrist alongside a victim of genocide and rape. As an intimate two-hander confronting two women metonymic for their communities, the play offers a welcome insight into international conflict resolution, and makes an attempt at celebrating humanity even at a time of utter desperation. Faynia Williams was the first person to direct Visniec in the UK, and her production of *The Body of a Woman as a Battlefield in the Bosnian War* for the Brighton Festival in 1999 took place just as NATO bombs were falling on Belgrade during the Kosovo War. The dinner-jacketed cellist joining the original double act in Visniec's text was a character Williams invented, inspired by the famous photo of Nigel Osborne playing in the bombed out snow-covered concert hall in Sarajevo. In the production, she was on stage throughout 'like a silent nemesis, watching, waiting, and keeping culturally alive in the midst of war, rape and the discovery of mass graves' (Williams 2019). This production was the first-ever drama to be staged at the Old Market Art Centre in Hove (now known as The Old

86 Jozefina Komporaly

Market), and the play went on to be workshopped at the National Theatre Studio, this time under the direction of Alison Sinclair, and then to the Young Vic. This occasion gave Visniec his first London exposure, an event that has continued over the years with a variety of other well-received productions, including *What Shall We Do with the Cello?* directed by Vasile Nedelcu for Atelier Theatre Studio at the Vault Festival (2017).

More recently, Visniec has turned his attention to the global impact of migration, and the companion plays *Occidental Express* (2009) and *Migraaaants or There's Too Many People on This Damn Boat* (2017) shed light on the extraordinary human cost of displacement and non-belonging. Despite having been written almost a decade apart, the plays echo one another in their reflection of one of the most ardent concerns of our time, and examine assorted push-and-pull factors alongside the lure of the West. Both plays contrast the idealised image would-be migrants entertain of their target countries with the realities of the present, thus situating mythical and dystopian visions side by side. The plays respond to the dissolution of frontiers after the collapse of communism in Eastern Europe and in the first couple of decades of the twenty-first century, and highlight the drive to encounter formerly inaccessible cultures. They also prefigure Visniec's latest play that addresses the plight of children left in the care of grandparents whilst their parents are trying to make a better living abroad – *Extraterestrul care îşi dorea ca amintire o pijama* (*The Extraterrestrial that Wanted some Pyjamas as a Keepsake*) – staged in 2019 by the very theatre named after the playwright, the Matei Vişniec Theatre in Suceava. Visniec maps out the impact on different generations of the post-1989 transformations, and touches upon the fact that it is mentalities that need adjusting in order to achieve a shared European identity. The topical importance of these plays is also indicated by being published in a new Romanian edition by Humanitas as *Trilogia balcanică* (*The Balkan Trilogy*, 2018), and by being staged (in Hungarian translation at the Sándor Tomcsa Theatre in Odorheiu Secuiesc and the Szigligeti Theatre in Oradea, respectively) by Zalán Zakariás as a duology of sorts. Visniec added a number of new scenes to *Occidental Express* for this occasion, including a wedding scene that places Transylvania on the symbolic map of this Balkan itinerary and experiments with further layers of meta-theatricality; in the words of the director staging this play-within-a-play, this Dracula-myth-inspired scene is likely to 'trigger international recognition' (Hulber 2019). Appropriating a Western construct of the East in this way is really empowering, in addition to the politically important strategy of layering ethnic and cultural traditions in a transnational arena. *Occidental Express* was also put on by Visniec's most ardent US champions, the Trap Door Theatre in Chicago in 2017, directed by István Szabó K., following on from the director's previous collaboration with the company that saw the premiere of *The Word Progress on My Mother's Lips Doesn't Ring True* in 2011. Trap Door, led by artistic director Beata Pilch, have gained a reputation for championing Eastern European theatre since the company's inception, and staged and internationally toured several Visniec plays. This groundbreaking work significantly contributes to the integration of European and American traditions, facilitating bidirectional contact and arguing for the vitality and viability of European drama in a transnational context.

Some of the most memorable productions, of both Visniec and Visky's theatre in fact, have come about as a result of long-term partnerships with a handful of companies, festivals, and artistic directors. In addition to the Avignon OFF and Sibiu festivals, and repeat collaborations with Romanian director Anca Bradu and Hungarian István Szabó K. (responsible for both local and international productions), Visniec has found long-lasting creative associations with KAZE Theatre in Japan, and with director and producer Márcio Meirelles of Salvador da Bahia, who identified aspects of Visniec's work that resonated with their concerns and framed their productions with direct references to the realities of their world. This interest is testimony to the firm impact of European playwriting far beyond the geographical boundaries of the Continent, as well as to parallels between seemingly different cultural contexts. As Visniec himself notes, Brazil is the country that reminds him the most of Romania, a connection that no doubt explains the extraordinary fact that É Realizações in São Paulo has to date published over 20 volumes of his work in Portuguese translation. As Dragan Klaić observes (2009: p. xviii), 'the parabolic features' of Visniec's theatre make his work 'more accessible for foreign readers and spectators, who were most likely little informed about the everyday life under the great Conducator [Nicolae Ceaușescu]', and indeed Visniec denounces the dangers of manipulation through ideology whatever it might be, and charts a history of cultural resistance against totalitarianism of any kind. Thus, Meirelles relocates *The Body of a Woman as a Battlefield in the Bosnian War* (2014) to contemporary Brazil, and examines inter-racial relations in a postcolonial society through the play's initial juxtaposition of a Western and Eastern woman. The women are situated in mutual dependency, though it is ultimately the assessment-cum-judgement of the woman coming from a privileged background that is meant to impact on the future of the long-suffering other. A similar attempt for cultural reclamation is present in Meirelles's staging of *The Last Godot* (2014), whereby the Afro-Brazilian actor Leno Sacramento is cast as Godot, thus incorporating a canonical European character into the fabric of local ethnic categories and performance traditions in Brazil.

Visniec is fascinated by a subtle dialogue with landmark moments in theatre history, and his absurdist vein is rooted in his long-term preoccupation with the work of Cioran, Chekhov, Ionesco, and Beckett. These authors have not only influenced his style and worldview but also feature as references and actual characters in his plays (*A Paris Attic Overlooking Death; The Chekhov Machine; Nina, or the Fragility of Stuffed Seagulls*). *The Last Godot,* for instance, has at its core the two figures that are notoriously absent in *Waiting for Godot* (Godot and Beckett himself), Visniec thus transforming into characters the non-fictional person of the author and what was in Beckett's play a mere name. As Lecossois argues that 'by calling into question the status of the character and that of the author, he shakes the very foundation of theatre as a genre' (2008: 94), not in the least because the characters in Visniec's play claim that theatre has just been killed, so the play first appears a lament for the death of theatre. The trope of waiting is an underlying motif in Visniec's oeuvre, situated at the core of the popular *Pockets Full of Bread* (2004) and culminating perhaps in the waiting for Ionesco himself in *And Now Who's Going to Do the Dishes?* (2009), memorably staged in 2018 by Răzvan Mureșan at the National Theatre of Cluj.

88 *Jozefina Komporaly*

European theatre is further present in Visniec's plays in conjunction with an interest in the workings of history. Visniec has a predilection for examining the ways in which history is framed, contested, and periodically rewritten; emblematic in this sense is his theatre poem *Joan and the Fire* (2008) that discusses Joan of Arc's controversial career. Over time, his responses to communism in Eastern Europe have given way to a discussion of major conflicts in the world, and to a reflection on the impact of globalisation on our society. Despite signalling the significant differences among the various contexts, Visniec points out the totalitarian strand inherent in both socialist regimes and conspicuous consumption, claiming that whilst brainwashing was centrally imposed under the former, it has become self-inflicted in conditions of the latter: 'Disinfecting language will open up the way towards true essence' (Visniec 2016: 104). As a practising journalist (for Radio France Internationale), Visniec has first-hand insight into the workings of mass media; the drive for sensationalism at the expense of accuracy has reconfigured the ways in which people are exposed to facts, which has an impact not only on understanding the past but also on shaping the present and on charting the future.

Why Hecuba? – as an adaptation of a Greek classic – is a departure of sorts for the playwright, however, as a play dealing with the haunting of history, it is firmly embedded into long-term preoccupations. Hecuba's loss and suffering is dramatised by Visniec as an ultimate test for maternal desire, in addition to which it is also an opportunity for the exploration of the tragedy of war and for a confrontation with the forces that rule the world as we know it. As Visniec notes, *Why Hecuba?* was born out of a desire to examine matters in a different light, seeing that nobody learns from past mistakes and history is repeating itself over and over again. Indeed, Anca Bradu's production for the Radu Stanca National Theatre in Sibiu, Romania (2014) capitalised on this timeless topic to invoke the power of love as an antidote against the horrors inflicted by people on their fellow human beings. Moreover, in conversation with playwrights Saviana Stănescu and Dorota Masłowska, Domnica Radulescu (2015) also discussed Márcio Meireilles' 2014 production of this play, highlighting Visniec's geo-political and absurdist roots and emphasising a postmodern strand in much of his work.

Barrack dramaturgies

Visniec's most postmodern as well as postdramatic plays are modular texts, a selection of independent scenes that can be combined in various permutations in performance, thus allowing theatre companies full flexibility and agency towards achieving their artistic vision. Visniec takes pleasure in metatheatrical experiments and rejoices in improvisation whilst displaying a predilection for parables and writing with striking precision. He ritualises repetition and accumulation, gradually divesting words and situations of their initial meanings and connotations to the extent that they lead to a defamiliarising 'sense of apprehension' (Visniec in Komporaly 2015a: viii). *Decomposed Theater or The Human Trashcan* (1993), for instance, includes 25 disparate scenarios that illuminate psychological trauma by conjuring up an atmosphere of hopelessness and imprisonment. The play explores a gradual deployment of menace that blurs the boundaries between actual and imaginary situations, and is among Visniec's works that best transcends geographical and cultural boundaries. It is also the play that has opened up Visniec's theatrical universe towards marionette theatre, and marked the start of a collaboration with puppeteer Eric Deniaud and his company Drolatic Industry (2005). The dramaturgy of modular theatre is also present in Italian director Beppe Rosso's staging of *Attenzione alle vecchie signore corrose dalla solitudine* (*Beware of Old Ladies Gnawed by Solitude*) for A.C.T.I. Teatri Independenti Torino (2013), which aims not only for flexibility in terms of sequencing the dramatic text but also for audience integration by way of staging the play as a shared meal. The act of eating and drinking together is a well-considered dramaturgical device, and has the role of drawing attention to the dissonance between the conviviality of the shared meal and the complexity of the issues addressed. The production groups 15 short scenes around themes such as 'Borders', 'Agoraphobia', and 'Desert', and offers a poetic examination of our world through a surrealist lens. This world is perceived as simultaneously disturbing, contradictory, violent, and comical, and the aim of the production is to blend these seemingly fragmented instances into a shared ritual that charts a continuum of registers from the tragic to the ironic. Ultimately, in a manner reminiscent of Visky's 'Barrack Dramaturgy', the audience is invited to confront the above concerns in an intimate space, and engage with a range of stimuli and memories as if they had experienced them themselves.

Visky's original dramaturgical concept was initially brought to public attention in a manifesto linked to the production of *Disciples* directed by Gábor Tompa at the Hungarian Theatre of Cluj in 2005. Barrack Dramaturgy 'was born out of the need to make imprisonment a common experience', and where the audience becomes 'prisoners of [their] free will' (Visky 2015: 467). Performers and audience relinquish their freedom simultaneously, and thus are bound by a contract of sorts towards a shared experience: an enclosure into a claustrophobic space in which the performance and spectating areas are not separated. The performance commences with this joint act of being locked in, and finishes with a shared exit-cum-liberation, the latter being also symbolic of an act of doing justice. According to this approach, the aim of captivity is not simply to render actual reality but to evoke a universal experience and to suggest that 'captivity is a state of being in which we are dislocated from our bodies', and through which we are invited to explore the potential for participatory understanding (Visky 2015: 468). According to Visky, being shut in together with an aim to remember heightens the perception of the performance as an event in the present, and is predicated on unconditional involvement because its aim is to achieve a shared embodied experience. Actress Melissa Lorraine connects this shared experience with 'a celebration of the very essence of theatre: the miraculous solidarity of strangers who can suddenly see one another inside of a moment', and stresses that only 'that which actually *occurs* during the time of "incarceration" is of any value. We offer ourselves over to this mysterious communal ritual in the hope of alteration. We volunteer to

90 Jozefina Komporaly

serve the time' (Komporaly 2019). Via the concept of 'Barrack Dramaturgy', Visky also makes his preoccupation with the renewal of Hungarian theatre language explicit, and challenges the prevalence of dramatic text in performance in order to focus on the relationship between spectators and performers and the possibilities of audience engagement. Visky's works are 'texts inscribed into space' that address the question of 'captivity' on the level of content and form (Visky 2002: 8). Visky's theatre is not interested in offering an illusion of real life on stage, there is no psychological investigation of characters. Instead, he populates his plays with figures searching for their often lost identity, whose embodied retelling of stories leads to a regaining of their sense of self. In other words, Visky's plays are not representational but instances of self-conscious and self-referential theatre that calls attention to its theatricality.

Ultimately, most Visky – and indeed Visniec – plays address a recurrent central question: whether there is such a thing as a form of freedom that simply cannot be taken away and/or that cannot be renounced; and this exploration of freedom is conducted side by side with an examination of identity, in a unique braiding among performance, theatricality, and the real. Over their extensive careers, the playwrights have developed dramaturgies that illuminate contemporary concerns through the use of poetry and metaphor, and paved the way in Hungarian and Romanian drama for a quest for new artistic forms. They spot dramatic situations in an amazing variety of mundane circumstances, and have a sharp eye for detail. Visniec has an uncanny 'capacity to transform abstract ideas into characters', and his frequent intertextual references are rooted in his own rigorous practice as a most attentive reader (Ghiţulescu 2008: 518). When addressing topical social and political concerns, Visniec is motivated by an overarching sense of ethical duty, and his crusade against the atrocities of communism as well as the excesses of globalisation 'situates him as an influential public intellectual, whose legacy is bound to include a strong artistic as well as political merit' (Komporaly 2015a: xlii).

Despite authoring some of the most influential plays of the last three decades, Visniec declared that 'without a good director I haven't achieved anything' (in Boicea 2010), a view echoed by Visky who sees the dramatic text as a blueprint for further artistic experimentation on stage. It is for this reason that his plays offer a genuine opportunity for the renewal of Hungarian theatre language, and since they are originally intended for the stage and not the page, Visky's plays 'carry out the typical journey of dramatic works in Hungarian theatre culture in reverse, because they only start their quests towards literary canonization after having gone through the "purgatory" of theatrical performance' (György 2007). For Visky, play texts offer an opportunity for further exploration by other parties, and he grants them total creative freedom in terms of *mise-en-scène* and textual editing alike. Visky celebrates the exclusively live qualities of performance, and uses the term 'ephemeral' in relation to his work, thus referencing Peggy Phelan's notion that performance, whose only life is in the present, 'becomes itself through disappearance' (1993: 146). In addition to being among the most vocal commentators on the moral and existential dilemmas of our time, both European and local, Visky and Visniec occupy an essential role in contemporary European playwriting for this generosity and openness towards staging practice. Visky's and Visniec's work invite minimalism in terms of staging, and their sole requirement is an intimate space shared by performers and spectators. Systematically broadening approaches that consider the dramatic text as a fully complete entity, Visky and Visniec practice a form of theatre making that transgresses linguistic, cultural, and stylistic boundaries, and celebrates the creative potential of *mise en scène* in realising engaging and audience-centred live performances.

András Visky – four key productions

Porno (Porn). Translated into Polish by Jolanta Jarmolowicz. Directed by Cezary Studniak. Set design by Michal Hrisulidis. Costume design by Magda Hasiak. Music design by Krzysztof 'Wiki' Nowikow. Scenic movement by Ewelina Adamska-Porczyk. Video projection by Maksymilian Ławrynowicz. Cast: Edyta Łukaszewska. Teatr Nowy, Poznań, 20 September 2016.

Juliet. Translated into Bulgarian by Yulia Krumova. Directed by Boian Ivanov. Scenography by Elitsa Georgieva. Video design and 3D mapping by Todor Todorov. Sound design by S.U.S.F. Choreography by Tatyana Sokolova. Cast: Ralitsa Konstantinova, Yasena Gospodinova, Petya Venelinova. 'Sava Ognyanov' Drama Theatre, Ruse, 18 April 2016.

Caravaggio Terminál (*Caravaggio Terminal*). Directed by Robert Woodruff. Dramaturgy by András Visky. Set and costume design by Carmencita Brojboiu. Video by Bertalan Bányász. Sound design by Kata Bodoki-Halmen. Scenic movement by Ferenc Sinkó. Cast: Ervin Szűcs, Csilla Albert, Ferenc Sinkó, Csilla Varga, Balázs Bodolai, Éva Imre, Áron Dimény. Hungarian Theatre of Cluj, Cluj-Napoca, 24 June 2014.

Stories of the Body (*Artemisia, Eve, Lina, Teresa*). Translated into English by Jozefina Komporaly. Directed by Andrej Visky and Melissa Lorraine. Set Design by Péter Szabó. Costume Design by Rebecca Hinsdale. Lighting Design by Taylor Ovca. Props Design by Selma Muminovic. Cast: Kati Sherman, Matt Fleming, Nadia Pillay, Adrian Garcia, Eric K. Roberts, Katie Stimpson, Melissa Lorraine, Laurie Roberts, Kris Tori, Cody Beyer, Nicholas Barelli, Laura Jones Macknin, Zarah Pillay. Theatre Y, Chicago, 25 May 2018.

Matéi Visniec – four key productions

Body of a Woman as a Battlefield in the Bosnian War. Translated into English by Alison Sinclair. Directed by Faynia Wiliams. Set and costume design by Faynia Williams. Cast: Amanda Mealing, Liz Kettle, Sarah Sansom (cellist). The Old Market Art Centre, Hove (now known as The Old Market), Brighton Festival Fringe, May 1999.

Attenzione alle vecchie signore corrose dalla solitudine (*Beware of Old Ladies Gnawed by Solitude*). Translated into Italian by Beppe Rosso. Directed by Beppe Rosso. Set and production design by Richi Ferrero, Lucio Diana, Marco Ferrero.

92 Jozefina Komporaly

Consultants: Ornella Balestra, Monica Iannessi, Davide Bernardi, Debora Milone. Cast: Lorenzo Bartoli, Mario Pirrello, Francesca Porrini, Valentina Virando. *A.C.T.I.* Teatri Indipendenti, Turin, 1 July 2013.

De ce Hecuba? (*Why Hecuba?*). Directed by Anca Bradu. Set, video, and light design by Mihai Păcurar. Choreography by Adriana Bârză. Music and sound design by Vlaicu Golcea. Cast: Diana Văcaru Lazăr, Dana Taloş, Maria Tomoiagă, Dan Glasu, Iustinian Turcu, Arina Ioana Trif, Paul Bondane/Alexandru Malaicu, Liviu Vlad, Iulia Popa, Cendana Trifan, Vlad Robaş, Ioan Paraschiv, Gabriela Neagu, Anton Balint, Tudor Răileanu, Cristian Timbuş. National Theatre of Cluj, Cluj-Napoca, 4 October 2014.

Migránsoook — avagy túlsúlyban a bárkánk (*Migraaaants or There's Too Many People on This Damn Boat*). Translated into Hungarian by Ágota Bereczki. Directed by Zalán Zakariás. Sound design by Hunor-Lehel Boca. Lighting design by István Tóásó. Set and costume design by Csaba Csíki. Music by Csaba Csíki. Dramaturgy by Ágota Bereczki. Cast: Csaba Antal D, Árpád Barabás, Kriszta Boda-Szász, Zenkő Bekő-Fóri, Róbert Dunkler, Norbert Esti, Kata László, Eszter Márkó, Andrea Fincziski, Attila Pál, Gellért Szűcs-Olcsváry, Árpád Tóth, Márta Varga, Nóbel Kudelász. Sándor Tomcsa Theatre, Odorheiu Secuiesc, March 2017.

Works cited

Boicea, Dan (2010) 'Matei Vişniec, dramaturg: „Fără ajutorul unui regizor bun, n-am făcut nimic"' (Matéi Vişniec, Playwright: 'Without a good director I haven't achieved anything'), *Adevărul*, 12 July, http://adevarul.ro/cultura/istorie/matei-visniec-dramaturg-fa ra-ajutorul-unui-regizor-bun-n-am-facut-nimic-1_50b9f7cc7c42d5a663ad57f6/index. html

Brantley, Ben (2012) 'A Girl between a rock and a very lonely place: 'I Killed My Mother,' András Visky's play, at La MaMa', *The New York Times*, 20 February, https://www.nytim es.com/2012/02/21/theater/reviews/i-killed-my-mother-andras-viskys-play-at-la-mama. html

Cap-Bun, Marina and Nicolae, Florentina (eds), (2015) *Literatura, Teatrul si Filmul, in onoarea dramaturgului Matei Vişniec* (Literature, Theatre and Film: An Homage to Matéi Visniec), Contanţa: Ovidius University Press.

Ghiţulescu, Mircea (2008) 'Viziunile lui Matei Vişniec', in *Istoria literaturii române: Dramaturgia* (Matéi Visniec's Visions, in *The History of Romanian Literature: Theatre*), Bucharest: Editura Academiei Române.

György, Andrea (2007) 'Szavak böjtje. A kortárs magyar dráma szerepe a színházi nyelv megújításában' (Fasting words: The role of contemporary Hungarian drama in the renewal of theatrical language), *Látó*, 3: 93–102, http://epa.oszk.hu/00300/00384/ 00047/632.html

Heim Bennett, Beate (2012) 'András Visky's *I Killed My Mother*. La Mama in association with Chicago's Theatre Y, February 10–March 4, 2012', *Slavic and East European Performance*, 32(1): 93–97.

Hulber, Maria (2019) 'Itinerar teatral cu Occident Express' (Theatrical Itinerary with Occidental Express), *Observator Cultural*, no. 965, 5 April, https://www.observator cultural.ro/articol/itinerar-teatral-cu-occident-express/

Huyser-Honig, Joan (2004) Interview with Visky András, Grand Rapids: Calvin Institute of Christian Worship, http://worship.calvin.edu/resources/resource-library/interview-with-visky-Andras/

Klaić, Dragan (2009) 'Preface: Retrieved from oblivion', in Daniel Gerould (ed.), *Playwrights before the Fall: Eastern European Drama in Times of Revolution*, New York: Martin E. Segal Centre Publications, pp. xi–xxi.

Komporaly, Jozefina (2015a) 'Introduction', in *Matéi Visniec: How to Explain the History of Communism to Mental Patients and Other Plays*, Kolkata: Seagull, pp. vii–xlii.

———— (ed.) (2015b) *Matéi Visniec: How to Explain the History of Communism to Mental Patients and Other Plays*, Kolkata: Seagull Books.

———— (ed.) (2017) *András Visky's Barrack Dramaturgy: Memories of the Body*, Bristol: Intellect.

———— (2018) 'From Skopje to London via Hungarian and English: András Visky's "The Unburied"', *The Theatre Times*, 20 January, https://thetheatretimes.com/skopje-london-via-hungarian-english-andras-viskys-unburied/

———— (2019) 'Open dramaturgy and collaboration in András Visky's theatre in English translation', *Hungarian Literature Online*, https://hlo.hu/portrait/andras-visky.html

Lecossois, Hélène (2008) 'Samuel Beckett, Matéi Visniec: From one Godot to the last', in Carvalho, Paulo Eduardo and Homem, Rui Carvalho (eds), *Plural Beckett/Beckett Pluriel: Centenary Essays/Essays d'un centenaire*, Porto: University of Porto, pp. 93–104, https://ler.letras.up.pt/uploads/ficheiros/6598.pdf

Magiaru, Daniela (2012) 'Preface', in Matei Vişniec *Procesul comunismului prin teatru* (The Trial of Communism through Theatre), Bucharest: Humanitas, pp. 7–11.

Manolescu, Nicolae (1990) *Istoria critică a literaturii române* (A Critical History of Romanian Literature), Piteşti: Editura Paralela 45.

Modreanu, Cristina (2013) 'Elements of ethics and aesthetics in new Romanian theatre', *New Theatre Quarterly*, 29(4): 385–393.

———— (2016) 'Gianina Cărbunariu: Documentary theatre with political focus', *The Theatre Times*, 29 September, https://thetheatretimes.com/gianina-carbunariu-documentary-theater-with-political-focus/

———— (2019) 'Saviana Stănescu: "One could say that I am a 17-year old American playwright"', *Scena.Ro*, 20 January, http://revistascena.ro/en/interview/saviana-stanescu-one-could-say-that-i-am-a-17-year-old-american-playwright/?fbclid=IwAR2KU7ih8z6eol4g-b-pgpwltdOuxTz7HADBY1PZhgGeRprzH98rllNYvjc; also at https://thetheatretimes.com/interview-with-saviana-stanescu-one-could-say-that-i-am-a-17-year-old-american-playwright

———— (2020) *A History of Romanian Theatre from Communism to Capitalism: Children of a Restless Time*, Abingdon, Oxon: Routledge.

Orlich, Ileana Alexandra (2017) *Subversive Stages: Theatre in Pre- and Post-communist Hungary, Romania and Bulgaria*, Budapest and New York: Central European University Press.

Phelan, Peggy (1993) *Unmarked: The Politics of Performance*, New York: Routledge.

Prontvai, Vera (2016) 'Barakkból a végtelenbe: Pilinszky színházeszménye és Visky András *Caravaggio terminál* címü drámája (From the Barracks to the Infinite: Pilinszky's Ideal of Theatre and András Visky's Caravaggio Terminal'), *Vigilia* 10(81), https://vigilia.hu/content/barakkb%C3%B3l-v%C3%A9gtelenbe-pilinszky-sz%C3%ADnh%C3%A1zeszm%C3%A9nye-%C3%A9s-visky-andr%C3%A1s-caravaggio-termin%C3%A1l-c%C3%ADm%C5%B1-dr%C3%A1m

94 *Jozefina Komporaly*

Radulescu, Domnica (2015) *Theater of War and Exile: Twelve Playwrights, Directors and Performers from Eastern Europe and Israel*, Jefferson, NC: McFarland & Co.

Rokem, Freddie (2000) *Performing History: Theatrical Representations of the Past*, Iowa City: University of Iowa Press.

Romanska, Magda (ed.) (2015) *The Routledge Companion to Dramaturgy*, Abingdon, Oxon: Routledge.

Sipos, Márti and Visky, András (2009) *Mint aki látja a hangot: Visky Andrással beszélget Sipos Márti* (As If One Could See Sound: Visky András in Conversation with Márti Sipos), Budapest: Harmat.

Vișniec, Matéi (2012) *Procesul comunismului prin teatru* (The Trial of Communism through Theatre), Bucharest: Humanitas.

———— (2016) 'The Man Who Had All His Malice Removed' (excerpt), trans. Jozefina Komporaly, *Index on Censorship*, 45(2), Summer: 100–110.

Visky, András (2002) *Írni és (nem) rendezni* (To Write and (Not) to Direct), Cluj: Koinónia.

———— (2015) 'Barrack-dramaturgy and the captive audience', in Magda Romanska (ed.), *The Routledge Companion to Dramaturgy*, Abingdon, Oxon: Routledge, pp. 466–471; reprinted in Komporaly, Jozefina (ed.) *András Visky's Barrack Dramaturgy: Memories of the Body*, Bristol: Intellect, pp. 25–30.

———— (2019) 'Artemisia' (excerpt), trans. Jozefina Komporaly, *Hungarian Literature Online*, 5 April, https://hlo.hu/new-work/andras-visky-artemisia.html?fbclid= IwAR0lMyjaEQJf3Re0wPoIfEjvU9U9zcEdLwewRwww0DlHrQfoo9

Williams, Faynia (2019) Unpublished correspondence interview with Jozefina Komporaly, April.

5 Lars Norén and Jon Fosse
Nordic grey or theatre innovators?

Rikard Hoogland

Lars Norén (b.1944) and Jon Fosse (b.1959) are frequently described as the most important Scandinavian playwrights since August Strindberg and Henrik Ibsen (Westling 2014: 9; Figueiredo 2014: 457–8). What strategies have given these two Nordic authors recognition in continental Europe? Why do they appeal to an audience outside their native countries to a greater extent than the Norwegian Cecilie Løveid or the Swedish P.O. Enquist? Both have written a large number of plays; as of January 2019, Norén has written over 100 and Fosse 31. Several productions of their plays have entered into the annals of contemporary European theatre history.

In this chapter I argue that in the field of European theatre, there are theatres, festivals, magazines, directors and actors that are particularly important in achieving visibility. For this reason, I highlight what has been written about Norén and Fosse in the German publication *Theater Heute*, which has a key position when it comes to introducing new trends and playwrights in continental Europe.[1]

Two Nordic playwrights

Lars Norén's plays could not be described as having one dominant style. Several of his early plays take ancient or medieval myths as a starting point. Some of his plays explore domestic issues, and often take place in an ultramodern middle-class living room where conflict is central. For a period during the early 1990s, the 'bourgeois quartets' were Norén's hallmark. His plays started in the late 1990s to take on more political and social questions. During that period, the number of characters on stage increased, but since 2000 his plays have reduced the number of characters and words (even one without words, probably inspired by Handke's *The Hour We Knew Nothing of Each Other*) and the plays began to address existential issues such as memory and death.

Jon Fosse has not been as productive as Lars Norén, but he has had 31 full-length plays performed, as well as some minor plays and adaptions. Fosse's characters use few words and silences have the same importance as words. Often his young characters encounter a situation with relatives and unknown strangers that threaten them. His plays are often situated outside cities, often in

96   Rikard Hoogland

a rural landscape by the sea. During his most recent phase of playwriting, Fosse has given dream and memory a greater centrality. In this chapter, I not only highlight the playwrights' differences but also examine their similarities; they have even cooperated on some projects.

To begin, it is worth considering how authors known for their work in lyric poetry and fiction respectively entered the field of theatre.

Lars Norén

The first Norén play that was produced on stage was *Fursteslickare* (*The Prince's Bootlicker*), which premiered on 22 November 1973 at Dramaten (the Royal Dramatic Theatre) in Stockholm. The cast included several of Dramaten's leading actors and while the collaboration between Norén and director Donya Foyer had begun well, Norén complained to theatre manager Erland Josephson about cuts that had been made to the play (Westling 2014: 28). The production received extremely negative criticism in the daily press, with words like 'pornography' and 'amateur theatre' deployed by critics; one even demanded that the production should be cut from the repertoire (Westling 2014: 32–3).

This event has often been described as a break in the relationship between Norén and the theatre, but theatre scholar Barbro Westling has shown that he continued to maintain contact with the dramaturgs at Dramaten and Radioteatern (the Drama department at the Swedish Radio). Indeed, three of his plays were produced at Radioteatern between 1972 and 1979: the evolutionary outcome of critical reading by dramaturgs. During this period, he also had a productive relationship with Dramaten, where he also received many comments on his proposals for plays (Westling 2014: 39–42). In 1978, Norén announced that he was focusing exclusively on dramatic writing, submitting six plays to Dramaten during the course of the year. The theatre decided to produce *Orestes*, which was directed by Gunnel Lindblom in 1980 (Westling 2014: 45–7). However, this production also did not get positive reviews from the critics, and there was no breakthrough for Norén as a playwright.

Norén was forced to amend his strategy and one change involved working with the same director for several productions. Another was to work with TV drama; his 1980 play *Modet att döda* (*The Courage to Kill*) was seen by 1.7 million viewers (at the time the population of Sweden was 8 million) and established the abstruse poet as a playwright for a broad Swedish audience (Westling 2014: 56). The recurrent TV versions of his plays depicted corrosive family conflicts, demonstrating the strong influence of Strindberg, O'Neill and Albee; his dark outlook became part of the Swedish consciousness.

The Belgian literary scholar Luc Gilleman suggests that Norén's success came by turning away from the dominant impulse in dramatic writing: 'At a time when many dramatists moved away from the single-room play as an outdated bourgeois convention, Norén deliberately returned to it' (Gilleman 2010: 212). Crucially, however, by being able to control who would stage the production, he finally achieved his breakthrough as a playwright.

The radical feminist director Suzanne Osten accepted the challenge of *En fruktansvärd lycka* (*A Horrible Happiness*), which every other director at the Stockholm City Theatre had shunned because it was too dark and bourgeois (Westling 2014: 64–5). The director worked in collaboration with the author, who rewrote entire sections – especially after open rehearsals, when Norén noticed that his dialogue could be sharpened in a humorous direction. The production broke away from the naturalistic tradition both by speaking directly to the audience and by dispensing with hypernaturalistic scenes where the actors are all talking over each other. An audience sitting in the set of an ultramodern living room in a rooftop apartment had a feeling of both reality and staged reality. The premiere in 1981, combined with the TV premiere of *The Courage to Kill*, established Norén's reputation as a playwright, a process that had taken eight years since the disastrous premiere of *The Prince's Bootlicker*.

One characteristic of Norén's work that makes it difficult to translate into other languages is his use of literary word play. Literary scholar Ulf Olsson refers to the technique as 'anaclasis', in which a person's words are used in ways that change their meaning: 'such characters in Norén's semantic exchange may seem forced, but may serve as comic relief for the public: they protect us' (Olsson 2013: 43).[2] It is therefore not so surprising that the first foreign productions were staged in Denmark and Norway, since the languages and mentalities are relatively close to those of Sweden and Swedes.

Jon Fosse

Norén found the move from poetry to drama difficult, whereas Jon Fosse easily, albeit often reluctantly, transitioned from an established novelist writing in *nynorsk* to a dramatist.[3] Unlike Norén, he was not particularly interested in becoming a playwright; on the contrary, he decided that he would never write for the theatre in protest at a theatrical culture that he found to be irrelevant. His decision was strengthened after unsuccessfully attending a 10-day playwriting course in 1985 for selected authors (Seiness 2009: 132). This did not mean that all theatrical performances left him unimpressed; he mentions in an interview cited in Cecilie N. Seiness's biography that Norén's *Nattvarden* (*The Last Supper*) at Det Norske Teatret (the Norwegian Theatre in Oslo, the National theatre for *nynorsk*) was a great experience where something special took place between stage and auditorium (Seiness 2009: 131). Kai Johnsen, director at the Den Nationale Scene (DNS, The National Stage, Bergen), was convinced that Fosse could write drama, identifying a scenic potential in his prose. Fosse concludes that 'he was right, though I didn't understand it personally' (Seiness 2009: 138).

Finally, in 1994, Fosse wrote a play for DNS, *Nokon kjem til å komme* (*Somebody is Going to Come*), but the theatre was dubious and he also submitted it to Det Norske Teatret in Oslo, which purchased an option on it. The first Fosse play to be staged at DNS was *Og aldri skal vi skiljast* (*And We'll Never Part*), produced in 1994, which ran together with Botho Strauss' *Her Wedding Letter* (*Ihr Brief zur Hochzeit*). *Somebody is Going to Come* did not have its

98   *Rikard Hoogland*

premiere until 1996 and that same year *Barnet* (*The Child*) was staged during the Ibsen Festival in Oslo – the first time that it featured a contemporary Norwegian playwright. The theatre critics were divided; Norwegian historian Ivo de Figueiredo later compared the reception to that of Ibsen's *Brand*, which was not immediately accepted by the critical establishment either. 'Most critics agreed that the distinctive repetitive, monotonous and minimalist style, which was well known from Fosse's prose, was something new and different within the theatre. But was it good theatre?' (Figueiredo 2014: 428). The critics also targeted Kai Johnsen, arguing that he became far too dominant as an interpreter of Fosse's plays and that his productions made them too realistic and literal (Seiness 2009: 164). Elisabeth Rygg wrote a strong negative review of the 1996 premiere of *Somebody is Going to Come*, which she felt was 'a fabricated and naive theatrical game', but in 2001 observed that the same play was 'a type of modern classic' (quoted in Bjørneboe 2003: 101). Clearly something had happened during the seven years that had passed since Fosse's first theatrical production.

Acceptance by the theatre

Even though, unlike Norén, Fosse was at first reluctant to write for the stage, he secured a place in the Norwegian theatre somewhat faster than Norén in Sweden, and Kai Johnsen played a crucial role in this process. Where the taciturn Fosse uses words sparsely, Norén opens up the opportunity for dramaturgs and directors to fine-tune wordy scripts during the production process.

Both Fosse and Norén were recognised literary writers before they started writing for the theatre. The position of the playwright is not as independent as that of the novelist or poet, since the playwright is dependent on theatres, directors, scenographers, and actors. The two playwrights had different strategies for securing theatrical collaborators. Norén usually chooses the theatre and director that stages his plays; he has also to a greater extent personally assumed the role of director in Sweden, as well as in Germany, Belgium, and France. In contrast, Fosse has chosen to write his plays in a distinctively open style, bordering on the lyrical, which is far less textually prescriptive about how the pieces are to be staged. To achieve a recognised position in national or even the Nordic theatre is not sufficient for a breakthrough on the European stage. Finding the right stage for the performance, piquing the interest of leading directors who are prepared to develop the material for the stage, and garnering attention at major theatre festivals are all essential for a European career. Below I will review the development of Norén and Fosse as playwrights, after which I will focus on their productions and reception in Europe.

Lars Norén's dramatic writing

Norén's public breakthrough was strengthened by the two plays *Natten är dagens mor* (*Night is Mother of the Day*, 1982) and *Kaos är granne med Gud* (*Chaos is Neighbour of God*, 1983) set in Southern Sweden around 1960 in a dilapidated country hotel, with a family consisting of an alcoholic father and hotel owner, a mother who tries to hold the family together, but who is dying of cancer, and two sons, the younger of whom is homosexual. Sven Hansell has noted that the majority of Norén's plays include a character who is homosexual or bisexual and 'serves as a dramatic catalyst. The individual is often a social loser, but has also gained human insight. Through these characters the dramas expose the rigid heteronormative pattern' (Hansell 2004: 4). The plays also have a clear link to Norén's own childhood in a similar environment and he has returned to this family a number of times in his dramatic works. The two plays are heavily influenced by O'Neill's *Long Day's Journey into Night*, with similar illusions and controversies, as well as the same family constellation (including the ages of the brothers). Gilleman notes that Norén is obsessed with O'Neill's play, and that it 'is often explicitly mentioned in his plays' (Gilleman 2010: 213).

These two plays were staged at regional and municipal theatres all over Sweden, establishing the term 'Norén actors'; clearly Norén's language, and the characters emotional intensity provides room for the performers to achieve their fine performances. In 1982, Norén ended his collaboration with Osten and switched to director Björn Melander, who with actor Reine Brynolfsson in the role as the youngest son, staged the production at Gothenburg City Theatre after 18 months of rehearsals (typically, rehearsals in Sweden take six to eight weeks); the production was also filmed for Swedish television. Melander's stagings were rooted in a strong psychological realism, though the plays incorporate more dream-like elements, as suggested by the initial stage directions in the opening scene of *Night is Mother of the Day*: 'A dove walks alone across the stage and flies out through the far window' (Norén 1983: 11). Later productions of these plays emphasised these possibilities even more, such as when Tobias Theorell in 2007 combined the two plays in a five-hour performance at Stockholm's Stadsteater where the role-playing and repetitions were emphasised in a non-realistic set design. Ever since 1980, Reine Brynolfsson has partnered regularly with Norén and still is an actor in his plays, most recently in the 2015 production of *Ge oss skuggorna* (*And Grant Us the Shadows*) at the Dramaten. The plays were also staged in neighbouring Nordic countries (*Night is Mother of the Day* premiered at the National Theatre in Oslo in 1984 and in Copenhagen in 1986), but did not get as far as continental Europe. However, subsequent plays that were set in contemporary Sweden did travel further afield. Norén has described a group of these plays as 'bourgeois quartets'; they depict middle-class characters who have reached middle age, and are negotiating relationship conflicts, affairs and infidelities, controversies, and power struggles, all often fuelled by liberal consumption of alcohol. In some of the plays, we also meet the same group of relatives or friends the day after the hate-filled outbreaks, when everything has returned to 'normal' and the truths of the previous day have been repressed. The audience often encounters a stream of words that are commentaries on Swedish political events.

Norén's plays are commonly interpreted through a psychoanalytical lens; Barbro Westling notes that the scripts are often written like a diary with dates for new parts that illustrate the playwright's progress (Westling 2014: 85). One

100 Rikard Hoogland

example that is appropriate for psychoanalytical interpretation is the scene in the play *Demons* (1978), where the characters gather for a mother's funeral and place the urn with her ashes in various locations around the living room, until finally, in the heat of battle, the ashes spill out on the floor and are then vacuumed up.

Norén's decision at the end of the 1990s to devote more attention to social issues in his plays caused great surprise. He would write three plays under the theme 'Morire di Classe';[4] the first part, the monumental play *Personkrets 3:1* (*The Human Circle 3:1*) which premiered in Norén's six-hour production was realised in collaboration with Dramaten and Riksteatern (the national touring theatre) in January 1998 in the city of Umeå in northern Sweden. The audience was seated on low risers on three sides of an elongated theatre space. The actors came close to and occasionally climbed around the audience, and sometimes sat among them. The play depicts a group of people who are all social outcasts: drug addicts, minor criminals, prostitutes, individuals with mental health problems or disabilities, or those who have survived disasters that have caused them to withdraw from society. The setting is a square in a contemporary concrete city centre. Ulf Olsson concludes that the space in *The Human Circle* becomes 'unreal or surreal in all its brutality of the scenes' realism' (Olsson 2013: 67). The second in the series is the play *Skuggpojkar* (*Shadow Boys*), set in a psychiatric clinic for sexual offenders, including a number of paedophiles. We hear stories that are loathsome, told by the perpetrators as something natural or something they are fighting within themselves. Olsson wonders what attitude the audience should assume: 'are we seeing, are we witnessing – or are we monitoring?' (2013: 68).

Three prisoners contacted Norén and wondered whether he could write a play for them. They worked together with a drama teacher. The prisoners were hardened criminals; two of them turned out to be active Nazis. Norén wrote a play about their rehearsals, discussions and conflicts. The three prisoners played themselves and actor Reine Brynolfsson played the role of the playwright. The 1999 production of *Sjutre* (*Seven Three*) was widely debated; was it reasonable to let these people out on stage and allow them to express anti-Semitic and Nazi views? The day after the final performance, a bank was robbed where a police officer was shot and killed while the robbers were fleeing from the scene. Two of the actors from the performance were involved in the crime, and one of them had been part of the deadly shooting (Åsbrink 2009: 12). Riksteatern was greatly damaged by the event and a discussion began about the responsibilities of the theatre and the correctional system, especially since the bank robbery was planned during the rehearsal period and performances (Johansson et al.: 2001).

Norén was the artistic director for a section of Riksteatern (1999–2007) and staged several productions, including Chekhov's *The Seagull* (2001). He also translated Jon Fosse's *Somebody is Going to Come* that Riksteatern produced 2002 with Eirik Stubø as director. In 2007, he and Ulrika Josephson were supposed to take over leadership of Betty Nansen Teatret in Copenhagen.

Following the theatre staff's protests in favour of a Danish candidate, they did not accept the position and instead became leaders of Folkteatern (the People's Theatre) in Gothenburg from 2009 to 2012. The heavy flow of dramatic writing dwindled after *Seven Three* and the scripts that nevertheless subsequently appeared were minimalistic and fragmentary, compared with the earlier maximalist texts.

Jon Fosse's dramatic writing

On the surface, the dramatic shifts of Norén's works do not appear in Jon Fosse's plays; a superficial glance might even suggest that Fosse has continued to write the same play over the years, until he decided he would no longer create dramatic works. It is tempting to talk about his work falling into two main types: domestic plays and haunting, dreamlike plays; but even this is too simplistic. As Ivo de Figueiredo has argued, one can see Fosse's dramatic development falling into five phases (Figueiredo 2014: 431–45) – with additional work written for commission, such as the two pieces created for Robert Wilson.

Fosse's plays are most known for their pauses and silences. These intervals are to be regarded both as a rhythm in the text, but also as a marker of the unsaid – what Fosse calls 'the mute speech, filled with unknown meaning' (Fosse 2016: 53). This is where many directors make a mistake: they look for the action in the lines and treat the pauses merely as empty space. In a successful production there is a tension in the pauses and how they are perceived by the actors. Suzanne Bordermann categorises Fosse's dramatic works as follows:

> His plays lack, to varying degrees, an understandable narrative, action and cohesive meaning, recognisable characters, pace and tension. Instead he confronts the recipients with unstable time frames, cartoon figures, tendencies towards dispersed linguistic meaning and a large quantity of silence.
>
> (Bordemann 2012: 50)

The plays are not purely realistic; the mysterious dimension is central. Fosse was raised in the Quaker tradition. Dissatisfied with the teachings of the Protestant church, he later turned to Catholicism. When Swedish theatre critic Lars Ring interviewed him in the spring of 2018 he said: 'For me, [religious] belief is a position, a protest against all the commercialism, sexualisation and violence that fills our contemporary times' (Ring 2018). The plays may, on a superficial level, appear to be banal, but for Ring, they are a kind of mystery game, eluding a mystery and religiosity. Figueiredo describes Fosse's dialogue as 'a combination of the ordinary, concrete and the ritual spirit of the mass – almost like a liturgy of daily life' (Figueiredo 2014: 452).

Fosse's plays often have just a few roles, with some characters remaining nameless. The reader may not learn much about the individuals, and the past may contain experiences the characters do not wish to discuss or perhaps actively wish to hide. The past may nevertheless emerge via the questions of a

102 Rikard Hoogland

determined individual. Characters often express a desire to start over, to leave the old behind and to protect themselves against the threatening world outside. Already in *Somebody is Going to Come* someone intrudes and threatens to break up a weak relationship. In *The Child*, an observant bottle-deposit collector poses a constant threat, lurking outside the couple's flat; the church (without a priest) is a haven for them and therefore acts as a symbol of hope.

Fosse's plays assume an increasingly complicated format with parallel events and, as in *Draum om hausten* (*Dream of Autumn*, 1999), different time planes that are not in chronological order, where the living and the dead and dream and reality coexist. The final phase, according to Figueiredo, is a minimalist dream-like style, where the concrete gives way to the abstract and psychological realism to religious mystery. Several critics have pointed to Fosse's plays having a spiritual and even religious foundation. Kim Skjoldager-Nielsen has described *Sov du vesle barnet mitt* (*Sleep My Baby Sleep*, 2000) as 'existentialist meditations on knowledge, cognition, presence, and eternity' (Skjoldager-Nielsen 2018: 257).

After two decades of productive and successful playwriting, Fosse has pulled away from theatre (citing the pressures of contact with a public he shies away from) and returned to the world of fiction with the novel *Trilogy* (which has also been produced on stage by Det Norske Teatret in 2018, directed by Torkild Sandsund). However, he says that he has not definitely closed the door to dramatic work (Ring 2018), and his new adaptation of *Edda* was staged by Robert Wilson in 2017 at Det Norske teatret.

Lars Norén on European stages

In 1983 a proliferation of articles by Swedish playwrights, critics and journalists criticised the dominance of Lars Norén in Swedish drama. His drama did not reflect the political movements in society and his prominence was preventing other playwrights from having their work staged (Grafström 1983). Director Suzanne Osten stepped forward in Norén's defence and argued that 'all directors and actors should go to school to learn about the dramatic works of Lars Norén' (Osten 1983). The damage was already done, however, and in a TV interview on the daily news, Norén announced that he was withdrawing all his plays from Swedish theatres and moving the rights to his plays to Suhrkamp in Frankfurt am Main (Westling 2014: 111). In part, it was an indicator to his home country that his dramatic writing was not only aimed at the stages of Sweden and Scandinavia, but that he had ambitions to extend his influence further across Europe.

The first Norén play to be reviewed in *Theater Heute* was *Dämonen* (*Demons*), directed by Claus Peymann at Schauspielhaus Bochum in 1984. Peymann's successful productions of works by Thomas Bernhard and Peter Handke had positioned him at the centre of German theatre so he appeared a logical choice. But Peter von Becker's review in *Theater Heute* was unmerciful; under the heading 'Living Room Brawl' he summarises: 'It's a potpourri of Freud for everyone, an insane sketch from the boulevards, it's a dramatised poetry volume' and he found that the play is overly reminiscent of Edward Albee's *Who's Afraid of Virginia Woolf* (Becker 1984).

Demons was staged six months later at Burgtheater in Vienna, directed by Alfred Kirchner. The director had eliminated many of the brutal effects in the play and the production was praised in *Theater Heute* for revealing a gem of a play that could, as reviewer Sigrid Löffler noted, present 'a path that avoids the prescribed route across the boulevard' (Löffler 1985). Suhrkamp and Norén had placed the play in the hands of two of the most important theatres and directors working in the German language and the production was selected as one of the ten most distinctive German-language productions for the Theatertreffen in Berlin in 1985, a festival that is at the hub of German theatre life. Swedish newspapers, however, almost completely ignored Norén's German triumph.

Norén's plays frequently appeared on West German stages and even though *Theater Heute's* critics were not exactly dazzled, the plays were popular with audiences and, in particular, provided excellent material for the actors. In 1986 *The Last Supper* was staged in Bochum; this time Kirchner was the director and the production was once again selected for the Theatertreffen festival. Critic Michael Merschmeier was far more positive than earlier critics in *Theater Heute*, noting the balance found between the banal and the tragicomic in the production (Merschmeier 1986).

A study of the reviews over the next few years reveals a frequent use of the term 'boulevard' as a negative comment on the plays. The term operates as an umbrella term for effects the critics often felt were exaggerated, superficial and merely entertaining. During the 1990s, however, the criticism became increasingly favourable, acknowledging a broader emotional landscape in the work, with Norén increasingly being compared to Chekhov.

When theatre director Thomas Ostermeier took over the legendary Schaubühne theatre in Berlin, succeeding Andrea Breth, he chose to begin with Norén's *The Human Circle 3:1*, with Ostermeier's adaptation also published in *Theater Heute*.

Ostermeier combined two of the three main theatre spaces in Schaubühne and broke up the mass of text with choreographed sequences featuring large groups of performers. The production contains many references to Swedish politics, which the majority of the audience might not have picked up, but the archive shows that the theatre had collected several texts about the political situation in Sweden and about social legislation to offer a context for the staging. Here Ostermeier used the political Norén to criticise the German playwrights who, according to him, mainly focused on linguistic experiments. All of the major German theatre critics attended the premiere because of the Schaubühne's status in the German theatre and also because he had chosen a text from outside the German-speaking theatre for the opening. This is probably one of the reasons why the criticism was so harsh, with Norén's text described as 'a stinking flow of misery' (Diez 2000), or 'a pathetic swan song for western society' (Kümmel 2000).

It would take 10 years before Ostermeier was once again willing to stage a Norén work at the Schaubühne. This time it was the minor play *Demons* that was transformed into an intense family drama. The stage was updated

104 *Rikard Hoogland*

somewhat for the times including a flat screen television, but many of the items in Norén's prescribed set design details were included on the stage, including the Italian bike and the urn with the ashes. It has become one of the most frequently staged productions at the Schaubühne, with Lars Eidinger as Frank. One critic noted that the psychodrama that was outrageously new in the 1980s had now become something ordinary (Laudenbach 2010). Another critic argued that the misery of the housewife portrayed in the play was no longer particularly relevant. Nevertheless, she still found that this story of hopelessness was compelling to follow (Burckhardt 2010).

Norén became a prominent playwright within German theatre and directed several productions there, including at the Deutsches Theater in Berlin. He has not enjoyed such an established position in the UK. A 2003 production at the Royal Court in London of *Blood*, a work about the Chilean dictatorship, was sharply criticised. One of the most negative reviews noted that: 'The play is distasteful as well as incompetent [...] Frankly, we have enough plays of our own without needing to import them from Scandinavia' (Spencer 2003). The critic Benedict Nightingale found the play to be 'opportunistic, sensational and [...] basically melodramatic' (Nightingale 2003).

In contrast, the French-speaking theatre has increasingly produced his plays. One important reason for this success is that a theatrical agent who was extremely familiar with the needs of French theatre placed the plays at the right theatres (Petersson 2018). One of Norén's long-term collaborators, Ulrika Josephson, feels that it was the Belgian theatre manager Jean-Louis Colinet seeing Norén's production of his own play *Under* (*Below*, 1998) at a festival in Bonn in 2000 who realised that Norén could direct his own plays. And Colinet commissioned and produced the play *20th November* with the German actress Anne Tismer that premiered at the festival in Liege in 2007. This was the first step that resulted in his work being staged both at the Avignon Festival and at Paris's Festival d'Automne. Norén has also staged two productions at the Comédie Française, the most recent of which, *Poussière (Dust)*, was produced on the theatre's main stage in the spring of 2018. *Le Monde* described the production as remarkable and the staging masterful (Salino 2018). The production with 15 actors – an older group and a smaller younger group – plays across generational boundaries. The gap between life and death is another of the play's boundaries, though not one the dead seem willing to respect. His plays are performed in French translations and are frequently produced at theatres all over France. Whatever bothered the German theatre critics doesn't seem to affect the plays' reception in France, probably because of the different theatre traditions of the two countries. France's strong tradition of philosophical and existential theatre has proved more receptive than Germany's more political and materialist theatre, though the French interest in Norén's work has paradoxically stimulated renewed interest among German theatre makers, critics and audiences.

Jon Fosse on European stages

Playwright Cecilia Ölveczky at Det Norske Teatret suggested that Berit Gullberg at the Colombine theatre agency in Stockholm should deal with the rights to Fosse's plays. Gullberg failed to raise the interest of any of the major theatres in Sweden, but Stockholm's small Giljotin theatre, under director Kia Berglund was the first of many to produce Fosse outside Norway (Seiness 2009: 167–8). At the time, Giljotin was located in a small basement with about 50 seats, but it successfully created the mystical atmosphere that the play requires in a charged production of *The Child* in 1997. Colombine arranged readings at Comédie Française of *Somebody is Going to Come*, and later the French director Claude Régy produced the play (as *Quelqu'un va venir*) at Théâtre de Nanterre-Amandiers and then at the Festival d'Automne. Terje Sinding, the translator who had worked with Régy in the 1980s, had noted similarities, as with the importance of silence, between Fosse and Régy. The production in 1999 was extremely slow, almost double any previous productions' running time. The Swedish theatre critic Leif Zern saw Régy's second Fosse production, *Dødsvariasjoner* (*Death Variations*, presented in French as *Variations sur la mort*, 2003) and noted that the production occupied the sphere between sleep and wakefulness. The movements were in slow motion and the lines stretched out. According to Zern the audience alternated between intense attention and exhaustion (Zern 2005: 130). The photographs from Régy's production at the Théâtre National de la Colline in 2003 show costumes in strong colours with the actors distanced from one another.

Patrice Chéreau came late to Fosse's work, directing a very special production of *Dream about Autumn* (presented as *Rêve d'automne*) in 2010, which was first performed in the Salon Denon in the Louvre before being remounted on the stage of the Théâtre de la Ville, its décor faithfully recreating its original setting. Life is presented as a museum, where the characters age, change and die during the performance. Chéreau strengthened the dream-like atmosphere of the play, where many things happen simultaneously onstage. He later staged another of Fosse's dream-like plays, *I am the Wind*, at the Young Vic in London. It was essentially the only Fosse production in the UK that received consistently positive criticism. A 2002 staging of *Nightsongs* at the Royal Court was described by one critic, who had also disliked Norén's work, as 'this wretchedly pretentious, interminably boring drama' (Spencer 2002). In the *Independent* Paul Taylor also found that *Nightsongs* 'feels like an exercise in how to make an hour and 40 minutes feel like five hours' (Taylor 2002).

Director Katie Mitchell had wanted *Nightsongs* to be a process where she was present during each performance and the production was constantly evolving. The critic Benedict Nightingale in *The Times* seems in general to be positive about the director but noted that Mitchell, 'whose strength is filling grey locations and understated situations with dramatic tension, has come up against an immovable object: *Nightsongs*' (Nightingale, 2002). The theatre's daily reports from the performances show that the audience reactions were highly

106   Rikard Hoogland

diverse; at some performances the audience was engaged, while at others some of the audience walked out. The only critic to evaluate the play in a positive manner was Michael Billington – who would be a lone voice in support of *Blood* the following year (Billington 2003) – comparing Fosse to the English playwright Edward Bond and the German Franz Xaver Kroetz. 'What makes the play compelling is the deadly accuracy with which Fosse captures his characters' verbal and emotional inarticulacy' (Billington 2002).

In 2000, Jon Fosse was introduced on German stages, starting with a Norwegian visiting production of *A Summer's Day* at the biennial for new drama in Bonn. It was followed by Thomas Ostermeier's production of *The Name* at the Salzburger Festspiele and continued with Falk Richter's production of *Nightsongs* at Schauspielhaus Zürich and Jürgen Gosch's of *The Name* at the Düsseldorfer Schauspielhaus. Ostermeier took the production to the Schaubühne and both Norén and Fosse became part of the new artistic vision at the theatre.

The theatre magazines *Theater Heute* and *Theater der Zeit* dedicated considerable space to the Norwegian playwright. Before the premiere of *Der Name* at Schaubühne, *Theater Heute* published a play by Fosse and made a presentation of his work under the headline 'Playwrights to discover'. Fosse is described as the master of the *unheimlich* (Hammerstein 2000). Meike Matthes wrote under the headline 'Fosse fever' and compared him to Norén, noting that they had both made names for themselves as specialists depicting hellish Nordic marriages and family life (Matthes 2000). According to Suzanne Bordemann, Fosse was hailed by theatre critics who were tired of violent German-directed theatre, noting that Fosse would be 'a turning point in contemporary theatre back to the core values of the bourgeois theatre culture' (Bordemann 2012). It is quite legitimate to refer to 'Fosse fever' when the play *The Name* alone was staged on 15 German-language stages in 2000 and 2001 (Colombine 2018).

The critics found that Ostermeier's staging with its onstage realism had an old-fashioned feeling. The play depicts a nightmare in which no one can find the words they need. When the German critics emphasised the grey and almost tortuous slowness, the critic in the Norwegian newspaper *Aftenposten* noted that Ostermeier has showcased the humour in the play more 'like what we are used to. Revised like a modern Fassbinder' (Rygg 2001).

Falk Richter chose not to portray a Nordic atmosphere in his production of *Nightsongs*. Association went instead both to a barren modern suburbia and to isolation. The entrances were prolonged and we saw them first outside the elongated window at the back of the stage. Judith Engel embodied the woman who must make a choice and break away from the gruelling environment.

In 2001, Belgian/German Theatre Director Luk Perceval staged *Dream of Autumn* at Kammerspiele in Munich; the production was selected for the 2002 Theatertreffen Festival. The actors had microphones that allowed them to whisper and speak in low voices, and the scenography was primarily a stage floor filled with crunching gravel. There were sudden encounters, and Perceval chose to play the action relatively quickly and in a droll manner instead of focusing on the silence. Perceval found that the microphones caused the audience to focus more intently on the stage and that this led to a 'playing style that suggested a guilty complicity between stage and audience' (David 2015: 162–3). Franz Wille wrote in *Theater Heute* that 'after this you'll never want to see another family drama, but this one should not be missed' (Wille 2002).

Summary

Productions of both Norén's and Fosse's work outside their native countries had in the beginning often a Nordic flavour which seem to locate the plays firmly in their original national context. Humour and irony in particular, as well as double entendres, are difficult to transfer. When they each entered the European theatre field, they were used as pawns in ongoing theatre debates, such as the question about the quality of German playwrights, the importance of producing contemporary plays and the dominance of directors' theatre. Festivals such as Festival d'Avignon, Theatertreffen, and Festival d'Automne in Paris and individual directors such as Thomas Ostermeier, Claus Peymann, Falk Richter, Claude Regy and Patrice Chéreau have boosted these playwrights' recognition. Theatre critics have played the roles of discoverers, but also of gatekeepers when they find that the dramatic works do not meet their cultural expectations. For Norén the accusations were often that the plays were too exaggerated, engaged in amateur psychology and were too close to the style of other playwrights. For Fosse, many critics (and directors) found the lack of action in the plot and the many silences to be challenging.

One participant rarely mentioned in analyses of a playwright's success is the theatrical agent; in both the present cases it is obvious that agents have played an active role in locating theatres and contexts where the plays could break through into a particular national context. In an interview with Jon Fosse's agent, she mentions that they do not give performance rights to amateur theatres because the plays are much too difficult for them (Gullberg 2018). Both Fosse's and Norén's agents point to the importance of finding solid partnerships with international agents and translators. They cooperate with agents such as Suhrkamp, Rowohlt, L'Arche Editeur (Gullberg 2018; Petersson 2018). However, the Cultural Councils of Norway or Sweden do little to actively promote playwrights internationally beyond covering the cost of translations.

Now that Norén is increasingly involved in staging his own plays instead of collaborating with the leading directors and Fosse has declared that he is not going to write any more plays for the theatre, is there still a possibility for them to retain their position at the heart of the European repertoire? New generations of theatre directors will need to take an interest in the plays and interpret them in their own way. One example is Fosse's *The Child* at Dramaten, directed by Norwegian Johannes Holmen Dahl in 2015 (see Figure 5.1). The play was performed with almost no scenography in a beautiful Art Nouveau room; outside the windows are the city's street lights and distant alarms. The actors sing and play music when they are not acting in a scene. They perform directly up close to the audience, hiding nothing, searching and tentative.

Figure 5.1 Ana Gil de Melo Nascimento, Eric Stern and Hulda Lind Jóhannsdóttir in Jon Fosse's *Barnet* (*The Child*) directed by Johannes Holmen Dahl at Dramaten Stockholm (2015). Photograph © Roger Stenberg from the collection of photographs at Dramaten Stockholm

This production of the play is open to the world and allows the sounds and lights of that world to suffuse it, filling its stillness and silence. It shows, if there was any doubt, that there are spaces, corners and secrets still be found in the work of Jon Fosse and Lars Norén.

Lars Norén – four key productions

En fruktansvärd lycka (*A Horrible Happiness*). Directed by Suzanne Osten. Set design by Roland Söderberg, Cast: Agneta Ekmanner, Etienne Glaser, Liselotte Nilsson, Helge Skoog. Stockholms stadsteater, 16 April 1981.

Dämonen. (*Demons*). Directed by Dieter Giesing. Set design by Rolf Glittenberg, Costumes by Andrea Schmidt-Futterer. Cast: Gerd Böckmann, Gertraud Jesserer, Erika Pluhar, Hans Michale Rehberg. Burgtheater Wien, 19 December 1984.

Personenkreis 3.1 (*The Human Circle 3:1*). Directed by Thomas Ostermeier. Set design by Jan Pappelbaum. Costumes by Almut Eppinger. Music by Jörg Gollasch. Cast: Thomas Bading, Kay Bartholomäus Schulze, Robert Beyer, Jule Böwe, Martin Brambach, Hans Diehl, Stephanie Eidt, Marina Galic, Christine Harbort, Julika Jenkins, Adnan Maral, Falk Rockstroh, Anna Schudt, André Szymanski, Mark Waschke, Ute Werner. Schaubühne, Berlin, 24 January 2000.

20 Novembre (20th November). Directed by Lars Norén. Cast: Anne Tismer. Festival de Liège in coproduction with the Théâtre National Bryssel, 9 February 2007.

Jon Fosse – four key productions

Die Name (The Name). Directed by Thomas Ostermeier. Set design by Rufus Didwiszus, Costumes by Almut Eppinger. Cast: Jule Böwe, Stephanie Eidt, Hans Fleischmann, Jens Harzer, Anja-Mariene Korpiun, Tilo Werner. Salzburger Festspiele in coproduction with the Schaubühne Berlin, 6 August 2000.

Der Nacht singt ihrer lieder (Nightsongs). Set design by Falk Richter. Art direction by Katrin Hoffmann. Music by Malte Beckenbach. Cast: Peter Brombacher, Judith Engel, Sebastian Rudolph, Kai Scheve, Nikola Weisse. Schauspielhaus Zürich, 27 September 2000.

Variations sur la mort (Death Variations). Directed by Claude Régy. Set design by Daniel Jeanneteau and Sallahdyn Khatir. Costumes by Dominique Fabrègue. Lighting design by Dominque Bruguière. Cast: Guillaume Allardi, Axel Bogousslavsky, Olivier Bonnefoy, Valérie Dréville, Bénédicte Le Lamer, Catherine Sellers. Théâtre National de la Colline, Paris, 8 October 2003.

Rêve d'automne (Dream of Autumn). Directed by Patrice Chéreau. Set design by Richard Peduzzi. Costumes by Caroline de Vivaise. Cast: Valeria Bruni-Tedeschi, Marie Bunel, Pascal Greggory, Marina Hands, Michelle Marquais, Bulle Ogier, Alexandre Styker, Bernard Verley. Théâtre de la Ville and Musée du Louvre, Paris, 2 November 2010.

Notes

1 The author is grateful to The Royal Swedish Academy of Letters, History and Antiquities and Birgit och Gad Rausings stiftelse för humanistisk forskning for their support in facilitating this research.
2 Quotes not in English are translated into English by the author.
3 *Nynorsk* is a modern Norwegian language that was constructed during the nineteenth century as part of Norway's independence movement and is based on Norwegian dialects.
4 The book *Morire di Classe. La condizione manicomiale fotografata da Carla Cerati e Gianni Berengo Gardin*, edited by Franco Basaglia and Franca Ongaro Basaglia was first published in 1969 and has been an inspiration for Norén since the play *The Prince's Bootlicker*. The photo book reveals the brutal condition of Italy's mental hospitals.

Works cited

Åsbrink, Elisabeth (2009) *Smärtpunkten. Lars Norén, Sju tre och morden i Malexander*, Stockholm: Natur & Kultur.
Becker, Peter von (1984) 'Wohnzimmerschlacht', *Theater Heute*, 12.
Billington, Michael (2002) 'Nightsongs', *The Guardian*, 25 February.
———— (2003) 'Gripping Noren at the Royal', *The Guardian*, 26 September.

110 Rikard Hoogland

Bjørneboe, Therese (2003) 'Jon Fosse på europeiske scener', *Samtiden*, 1: 101–115.

Bordemann, Suzanne (2012) '"Man må føre menneskeheten ut av fryktens og den tålmodige sløvhetens primitive stadier…": Om den tyskspråklige resepsjonen av Jon Fosses tidlige dramatikk', *Norsk Litteraturvetenskaplig Tidsskrift*, 15(1): 46–60.

Burckhardt, Barbara (2010) 'In der Laborkrabbelkiste' *Theater Heute*, 4.

Colombine (2018) 'Jon Fosse's plays and first nights', document by Colombine Theatre agent.

David, Thomas (2015) *Nahaufnahme Luk Perceval. Gespräche mit Thomas David*, Berlin: Alexander Verlag.

Diez, Georg (2000) 'Heilige des Hasses', *Süddeutsche Zeitung*, 26 January.

Figueiredo, Ivode (2014) *Ord/kjött. Norsk scenedramatikk 1890–2000*, Oslo: Cappelen Damm AS.

Fosse, Jon (2016) *När en ängel går genom scenen: essäer*, Stockholm: 10tal Bok.

Gilleman, Luc (2010) 'Lars Norén's long journey into night', *Modern Drama*, 53(2): 211–231.

Grafström, Gottfried (1983) 'Brist att så få spelas', *Dagens Nyheter*, 13 September.

Gullberg, Berit (2018) Interview with Jon Fosse's agent, 29 January.

Hammerstein, Dorothee (2000) 'Der Meister des Unnheimlichen. Über den Norwegischen Autor Jon Fosse, der auch stücke schreibt', *Theater Heute*, 1.

Hansell, Sven (2004) *Spegeln sprack från kant till kant. Konstruktionen av maskulinitet i Lars Noréns dramatik*, Falun: Högskolan i Dalarna.

Johansson, Ola et al. (2001) '"It's the real thing': performance and murder in Sweden', *European Review*, 9(3): 319–337.

Kümmel, Peter (2000) 'Gebete in Beton', *Die Zeit*, 27 January.

Laudenbach, Peter (2010) 'Musst du so sein?', *Süddeutsche Zeitung*, 5 March.

Löffler, Sigrid (1985) 'Gegen den Strich…', *Theater Heute*, 2.

Matthes, Meike (2000) 'Kosmos der Monaden. An der Schaubühne gefeiert: Thomas Ostermeiers deutsche Erstaufführung von "Der Name"', *Tagesspiegel*, 4 October.

Merschmeier, Michael (1986) '"Ausgesetzt auf den Bergen des Herzens"', *Theater Heute*, 6.

Nightingale, Benedict (2002) 'Company loves misery', *The Times*, 1 March.

——— (2003) 'Melodrama fit only for masochists', *The Times*, 26 September.

Norén, Lars (1983) *Två skådespel*, Stockholm: Albert Bonniers förlag.

Olsson, Ulf (2013) *Språkmaskinen: om Lars Noréns författarskap*, Göteborg: Glänta produktion.

Osten, Suzanne (1983) 'Det spelas för lite Norén', *Dagens Nyheter*, 8 September.

Petersson, Margareta (2018) Interview with Lars Norén's agent, 29 January.

Ring, Lars (2018) '"Jag har valt det andliga i stället för spriten"', *Svenska Dagbladet*, 20 May.

Rygg, Elisabeth (2001) 'Samtidsfestivalen: Festival på skisseplanet', *Aftenposten*, 9 September.

Salino, Brigitte (2018) 'A la Comédie-Française, la vieillesse n'est pas un naufrage', *Le Monde*, 19 February.

Seiness, Cecilie N. (2009) *Jon Fosse. Poet på Guds ord*, Oslo: Det norske samlaget.

Skjoldager-Nielsen, Kim (2018) *Over the Threshold, Into the World. Experiences of Transcendence in the context of Staged Events*, diss. Stockholm: Stockholm University.

Spencer, Charles (2002) 'Beckett without the jokes', *The Daily Telegraph*, 1 March.

——— (2003) 'Oedipus wrecked', *The Daily Telegraph*, 27 September.

Taylor, Paul (2002) 'Null points again for Norway', *The Independent*, 1 March.
Westling, Barbro (2014) *Lars Norén. Dramatikern*, diss, Lund: Bokförlaget Arena.
Wille, Franz (2002) 'Mord aus dem augenwinkel', *Theater Heute*, 1.
Zern, Leif (2005) *Det lysande mørkret: om Jon Fosses dramatikk*, Oslo: Det norske samlaget.

6 Martin Crimp and Simon Stephens
British playwrights as European playwrights

David Barnett

Martin Crimp (b. 1956) and Simon Stephens (b. 1971) are both playwrights with international reputations. Their work is played around the world and a consideration of the number of productions in Europe's most highly subsidised theatre system, Germany, reflects their continued popularity. Crimp chalked up 63 new productions from the 2000/01 to the 2014/15 season, while Stephens achieved an impressive 120 in the same period, despite only having had his first premiere in the 2002/03 season.[1] Yet performance on the European stage is hardly evidence of being a 'European' playwright. Michael Frayn's *Noises Off*, for example, is a regular favourite on the German stage. For all its inventiveness, it is ultimately a very tightly written farce that relies on a cast of stock figures.

A quick survey of Crimp's and Stephens's work reveals some formal commonalities. Both writers challenge theatres to stage their works by deliberately failing to provide them with what might once have been considered 'the necessary information'. That is, they do not always attribute a character name to a line or a speech, as is the case in Crimp's most famous play, *Attempts on Her Life* (1997), or Stephens's *Pornography* (2007). Alternatively, it is not clear how the elements of the plot fit together or what they might mean, as can be seen in Crimp's *Fewer Emergencies* trilogy of short plays (2002) or Stephens's *Carmen Disruption* (2014). One could add that poetic and metaphorical language also helps detach their plays from a simple match between words and what they are to represent.

Vicky Angelaki notes, with respect to Crimp, that 'the term "European" becomes [in British theatre reviewers' usage] a catchphrase for that which is non-traditional and uncommon because it is typically associated to [sic] theatrical traditions that challenge the spectator and impede facile meaning making' (Angelaki 2012: 6–7). This demarcation is another instance of the British theatre system distancing itself from Europe, but it also locates the 'European' in purely formal terms. I prefer to consider the epithet in this essay as something more institutional. As already noted, the German theatre system is the most highly funded in Europe, and it is this aspect that helps understand Crimp and Stephens as 'European' playwrights. It is not so much that their plays are 'non-traditional and uncommon', but rather that European theatres are able to treat their texts in ways that are appropriate to the formal features identified above.

The way in which they write can be understood through the prism of theatre as institution. While it is usual in British theatre for new work to be 'developed' in rehearsal, for a new script to be considered provisional and subject to the rigours of the rehearsal process (see, for example, Bolton 2012), both playwrights here take a different approach to the status of the text. Stephens mused that German playwrights tend not be involved in rehearsals and so that they write 'a kind of puzzle [...]. So the whole process of writing a play becomes a consideration of the putting on of a play' (Stephens 2013: 204). Crimp has a similar sense of the autonomy of the text: 'My plan is to go into a rehearsal room with a non-negotiable document' (Crimp and Sierz 2016: 114). In both cases, the playwrights position their texts in the European context of theatre-making: the theatre is presented with a play, and it is the theatre's job to stage it in all its formal difficulty. Such an approach implies the kinds of features identified above because they provoke engagement with the unknown elements of the plays rather than seeking to illuminate enigmas and potentially blunt their effects through the process of dramaturgical 'development'.

Perhaps an indicative sense of how this distinction between text as pliable and text as 'non-negotiable' might be understood in the British theatre's response to *Pornography*, a play which is set in London and deals with the Islamist attacks of 7 July 2005. The play was premiered in Hannover, Germany, not the UK, in the summer of 2007, over a year before it was given its first British production. In 2007, Stephens told a national newspaper 'I've been told [...] that the play is far too German' (cited in Logan 2007) for mainstream British theatres. Such a response may well be surprising, when a variety of German theatres, from the great municipal stages in Berlin and Hamburg to the little-known ones in Landshut and Bruchsal, had little problem producing the play.

This institutional willingness to engage with plays considered 'odd' in Britain does not, however, imply that German and other European theatres present themselves as paradisiacal venues for experimental playwrights. Stephens, someone who has often sung the praises of the German system (see, for example, Stephens 2011), found himself on the receiving end of the less positive elements of the generous system when the Deutsches Schauspielhaus, Hamburg premiered *Carmen Disruption* in 2014. He later noted that the actors took against the play and its director, and 'destroyed' the world premiere because they were a part of a permanent ensemble while the director and the play were 'ephemeral' (cited in Barnett and Stephens 2016: 312). The production was cancelled after its first season.

The point, however, is that both playwrights set the theatre problems that are more fundamental than those encoded in more conventional plays in which characters, plot, and stage directions offer explicit suggestions for a production. British theatre is not accustomed to addressing textual uncertainty, often by dint of its straitened material circumstances. First, it tends not to employ ensembles, which can develop their actors' experiences over time. Second, it is financially pressurised and thus cannot grant actors and directors terribly lengthy periods to work through the formal challenges set by experimental scripts. And

114 *David Barnett*

even subsidised British theatres often find their repertoires fashioned by the necessity of producing work that will generate sound ticket sales.

Both playwrights position their writing in the context of a theatre which is open to provocation and, perhaps more importantly, able to rise to its challenge. It is this gesture that I am identifying as 'European' in this essay.

Martin Crimp: problematising the speaking subject

Crimp was working in the theatre, notably through a close association with the small Orange Tree Theatre, London, in the 1980s before productions of his work were staged at Royal Court in London and the West Yorkshire Playhouse in Leeds in the early 1990s. His landmark play, *Attempts on Her Life*, was first performed at the Royal Court in 1997. Its form is novel for two main reasons, which themselves engender a number of effects.

First, the play is made up of 17 scenarios, as the author designates them, which are completely unrelated to each other, except for the fact that they all refer to a figure known as 'Anne', 'Annie', 'Anya' or other variations on the names. On the one hand, this is a standard feature in episodic drama where scenes contribute different perspectives to a common theme, as in Bertolt Brecht's *Fear and Misery of the Third Reich* (1938), for example. However, Crimp's twist on this device is that 'Anne' is never seen on stage at all and is only ever mentioned throughout the play. The scenes' own forms vary widely. The opening one, 'All Messages Deleted', is a compilation of answer-phone messages. Others are clearly dialogues; there is a single monologue ('Kinda Funny'); an advert ('The New Anny'); what seems to be a broadcast that then breaks down into competing dialogues ('Pornó'); and texts that could be poems or songs ('The Camera Loves You' and 'Girl Next Door'). It is also worth noting that many of the dialogues are themselves unconventional in that they feature speakers who are creating 'Anne' and her variants through language. As Elisabeth Angel-Perez writes: 'the spectator is offered a theatre of language in which the characters constitute themselves as narrators more than as actors. [...] Words circulate between the different speakers who constantly try to appropriate the voice of the other' (Angel-Perez 2014: 353). However, each form can be recognised quite easily; it is their juxtaposition that shifts the focus so wildly and invites the audience to consider the absent Anne in such a divergent number of contexts.

Second, there is a remarkable tension between eminently recognisable language and a refusal to attribute a speaker to any of the spoken text. Again, this represents a new articulation of formal developments that very much preceded it. Peter Handke in *Offending the Audience* (1966), for example, merely presents blocks of texts that are to be divided up among the play's four speakers. Crimp's innovation here is to offer an audience a monologue, dialogues and what appear to be songs that *could have been*, but have not been allocated named speakers.[2] This feature is closely aligned with the scenes' designated status as 'scenarios'. In his introductory note to the play, which is curiously absent from the version reprinted in *Plays: 2*, Crimp states: 'Let each scenario in words – the dialogue – unfold against a distinct world – a design – which best exposes its irony' (Crimp 1997: vi). Here the playwright is pointing to his refusal to connect text to discrete individual speakers. Scenarios are freer than scenes, and Crimp proposes that the unfixed spoken texts clash with the clarity of 'a distinct world' to generate a disjunction as a provocation to the audience.

The two formal features Crimp introduces present a challenge to theatre-makers. As Aleks Sierz observes: 'Crimp provides no context for this narration. This absence raises questions: who is talking? why are they talking? what relationship do they have to the events they are talking about?' (2007: 378). He then raises the possibility that narrow readings of the scenarios could be widened to all manner of potential situations. This interpretation, in turn, points to a contradiction at the heart of both the play and other experimental work by Crimp.

Heiner Zimmermann considers the ways in which *Attempts* might be understood as both postdramatic and satirical (2002: 105). The tension between the categories is derived from their apparent mutual exclusivity. A postdramatic theatre seeks to resist the dramatic theatre's desire to represent the world. It does this by suspending denotation in favour of connotation, making material associative and thus floating over a panoply of potential meanings. Crimp's main means of achieving this is his refusal to attribute named speakers to the texts. Satire, on the other hand, always has an object of critique because it is all about exposing folly or worse, often through comic means, such as exaggeration or ridicule. It is difficult to read or watch *Attempts*, or many other of Crimp's plays, without acknowledging its satirical thrust. The question remains, however, that if we do not know who is speaking, then how can the satire effectively land?

Sierz has taken issue with the play's potentially postdramatic status by pointing to a feature of some, but not all postdramatic plays: *Sprachflächen*. This term, coined by Austrian playwright Elfriede Jelinek, may be translated as 'planes of language' or 'language surfaces'. They make a bold assertion, drawn from the position that we do not speak language, but, counterintuitively, language speaks us. That is, we *appear* to control the words we speak, but, in fact, they control us. This position is, to an extent, understandable. We as individuals rarely create language, but imitate examples we hear or read. In addition, we do not organise language; we accept grammatical and syntactical structures and are obliged to put certain words in certain inflections in certain positions in a sentence so that they may have meaning. In addition, set phrases and clichés demand particular formulations that are beyond our determination. However, language is not predictable or mechanised to the degree in which one could predict how any given person will articulate their words. This, however, is not the point of the concept. It is that language pre-exists us and even the simplest of words is laden with meanings and implications that triangulate with positions and ideas that delimit individual choice and action. Sierz writes,

116   *David Barnett*

however: 'the *Sprachflächen* so characteristic of postdramatic theatre [...] have little in common with Crimp's text, which is all dialogue, and recognizably conversational dialogue at that' (2007: 380). As such, he seeks to locate *Attempts* in the world of a dramatic theatre, one which *is* engaged in representation and can thus support the satirical aims of Crimp's writing.

I propose, however, that the contradiction between postdramatic form and satirical content can be reconciled by understanding *Sprachflächen* not as Jelinek presents them (as enormous blocks of multivalent text). Instead, it is worth returning to the question of why Crimp has refused to attribute the texts to named speakers. My conclusion is that Crimp is satirically arraigning ways of speaking that transcend the individual. That is, the apparently recognisable dialogues, exchanges, and songs, have been deliberately depersonalised in order to draw the reader's and the spectator's attention to the language's structures and ideologies. Consequently, Crimp employs a form that *can* resist representation in order to attack patterns of language that themselves make use of representation in order to disguise their own pernicious allegiances and effects. That is, by pretending that individuals speak language, rather than vice versa, the mechanisms that underpin language are left with the individual rather than with the social structures that engender them in the first place. Social structures are, of course, the product of people, but it is not the agency of individuals that is involved; the pressures that fashion meanings in language are supra-individual.

This argument regarding Crimp's form may appear to be abstract and distant from issues of theatre practice, but this is not the case at all. I will now discuss a significant production of *Attempts*, directed by Katie Mitchell at the National Theatre, London, in 2007 as a way of illuminating the point about the centrality of the national institutional context I offered in the introduction to this chapter. The production marked the 10-year anniversary of the landmark play's premiere, and Katie Mitchell, a director much fêted for her encounter with European theatre, promised much to audiences keen to see what could be done with the play a decade on.

In the production, Mitchell furthered her experiment with the live manufacture of cinematic images. This began with her ground-breaking production of Virginia Woolf's novel *The Waves* as simply *Waves* at the National in 2006. In such a production, the cast is equipped with a number of cameras and lights to capture the scenes, which are relayed seamlessly to a large screen mounted above them. Rachel Clements notes that

> the co-operative acts of co-production and labour which are involved in the making of theatre in general, and which are required in Mitchell's multi-media productions in particular, acted as a kind of ballast to moor the production; to ensure that it did not become reduced to the images it was working to create and critique.

(2014: 337)

Dan Rebellato wrote of Mitchell's particular use of the film in this production: 'the tone was cold and brutal, the images suggesting the continuous and instant mediation of experience that immediately becomes captured in digital form, processed and able to circulate around the world' (2010: 335). Yet before considering the overall effects of such an approach, one has to understand just who these people were who were creating the spectacle.

What may surprise readers, expecting an experimental approach to staging text to which no speakers are attributed, was that Mitchell created an elaborate frame for the whole production. The Education Pack[3] that accompanied the show stated that Mitchell told the actors to consider themselves participants in a live TV show, a competition to identify new talent for the BBC. Each actor had to create a fully fleshed-out biography for their character. Liz Tomlin argues that 'the experience of the spectator [...], as opposed to its reader, is of a chorus of determinate identities, however minimally sketched out' (2014: 374). Consequently, the production had the effect of fixing the flux of the text and representing consistent psychological characters. Mitchell thus collapsed a central feature of the play's dramaturgy in the name of an approach to acting that is resisted by the open texts. Of course, one of the joys of theatre is to find a director challenging a text by presenting it through unlikely means. The problem with Mitchell's approach was that she was closing down rather than opening up meanings, and consequently impoverishing the play by imposing meaning where it had previously remained ambivalent and provocative.

Crimp himself has commented: 'I suppose it depends what attracts a director most to [*Attempts*]: the discontinuity of its structure, or the continuity of technique' (cited in Sierz 2013: 102). I would suggest that the former quality marks its appeal especially in university theatre departments or theatres unused to such an experimental dramaturgy: its broad openness allows students and actors to engage with different styles and to juxtapose them throughout the production. The latter quality that Crimp mentions invites theatre-makers to do the opposite. That is, to resist the urge to follow the different forms in order to uncover the common political forces behind the play as a whole: the insidious patternings of language that time and again construct verbal images of Anne. In this reading, actors do not become characters, but 'text bearers' (Poschmann 1997: 296). Mitchell's anniversary production, however, took a Stanislavskian approach to one of the most innovative plays in British theatre's twentieth-century repertoire. It is interesting to observe, however, that this production nonetheless remains the most noted production of the text in the UK. This is perhaps a reflection on the differences between the perceptions of experimental theatres in different European contexts.

An opportunity to contrast the British theatre's limited scope for experiment with the German's tradition of adding richness to productions through non-conventional directorial means can be seen in the world premiere of Crimp's *The City* at the Schaubühne in Berlin in March 2008. It premiered in London scarcely a month later, under the direction of Mitchell. In Germany, the production was directed by Thomas Ostermeier. Yet before considering his production, it is worth understanding the dynamics of Crimp's play.

118   *David Barnett*

The playwright gives the following notes on staging *The City*: '*Time*: Blank. *Space*: Blank' (Crimp 2015: 135). Geraldine Brodie suggests that the directions can be understood in two ways: they 'may be an invitation to complete the missing information. On the other hand, such blanks may be directives to the creators of a production' (2016: 84). Again, then, there is a tension between a possibility to define contours on stage or to leave them defiantly open.

Over five scenes, we meet a translator, Clair, and her husband Chris. Chris, we learn, has lost his job and ends up as a butcher's assistant in the final scene. A nurse called Jenny also makes an appearance, and a girl of about nine also appears wearing a small version of a real nurse's uniform. As time progresses, the information offered by all the figures ties itself in knots. As Sarah Grochala writes: *The City*'s 'plot structures disrupt the story-making process to the point where there appears to be no access to the story at all' (2017: 176). For the most part, very little actually happens. Instead the figures discuss their lives and their environment in language typical of Crimp, 'both natural and stylised' (Sierz 2013: 112). That is, it has a recognisable ring to it and would not be mistaken for poetry, but it can also jar. Take the following brief exchange from the start of the second scene:

CHRIS: So, you're not ever tempted?
CLAIR: Tempted to do what?
CHRIS: To write something of your own.
CLAIR: Me? (Crimp 2015: 146)

The exchange appears to be quite conventional, although it is also odd that the husband asks his wife something rather fundamental about work she has been doing for many years. This oddness points to the play's grand revelation in the fifth scene, that everything that we have heard has been the product of Clair's inadequate writing. She has tried to imagine a city, yet has failed to make the characters live. The play ends with the young girl failing to play the piano piece she practised in the third scene beyond the fourth bar.

Angelaki makes some grand claims for the politics of the play: 'Of course, the twist in *The City*, its major finale reversal, captured the collective emotion at a time of worldwide financial distress, communicating the ideas that anything and everything can be abruptly taken away at any given time' (2012: 28). The problem with this reading is that it is highly dependent on the way it is staged. Yes, Jenny talks about how her doctor husband is away fighting a secret war, and other socio-political material is also raised, but, given the narrowness of the *dramatis personae* and the space in which so few people are encountered, there is no reason not to trace the instability of the play-world back to the limited imagination of its author, Clair. As such, politics can dissolve into psychology, and there is little in the play to posit a relationship between Clair's bad writing and the world around her, because the world we see is entirely articulated by her. It turns out to be a metatheatrical hall of mirrors. Tomlin, however, proposes a more radical reading:

the characters in *The City*, it seems, are spoken – that is, brought into existence – by the very words they believe to be subject to their authorship. Here, the quotation marks are invisible, but relentlessly present, surrounding every character's seemingly original enunciation, which, in the event, is revealed to have been drawn from the text of Clair's diary.

(2014: 376)

Here the politics is more tangible: the cherished individuality of the characters is exposed as an illusion, yet, again, performance is crucial in articulating the critique for the audience, rather than simply delivering the revelation in the text, as was the case in Mitchell's conventionally realist production of the play in London.

Ostermeier managed to pre-empt the climax through his treatment of Chris, the figure we see most on stage after Clair. Initially, he maintained a standard realism, yet from nowhere, Chris performed certain moments in slow motion, became robotic and developed tics. Suffice it to say, these went unexplained in the production itself, but became evident in hindsight at the end of the show. Jenny, too, underwent momentary stylisation, and one reviewer described the Child as 'a mixture of a little sunbeam and a monster' (Peter 2008).[4] The precision of the social setting connected Clair's scribblings with their social situation, as one reviewer noted that Ostermeier had interpreted the play 'as an existential unsettling of a middle class threatened with downward mobility' (Wahl 2008). While it would be difficult to say that the production was a great hit with the critics, who often reproached Ostermeier for not pushing his material far enough, it is still noticeable that his directorial interventions at least gestured towards the larger issues at play in the work, something that was not approached in Mitchell's more psychological production.

Simon Stephens: ceding the playwright's authority

Stephens's writing reflects different modes of representing or raising questions regarding representing reality. His early plays, which he retrospectively viewed as 'naturalistic' (Stephens 2005: xii), reflect a belief that the playwright delivered works that were to be brought to the stage by a director happy to follow the playwright's instructions. A formative moment came in March 2003 when Stephens saw a production of his play *Herons* in Stuttgart, staged by the Swiss director Sebastian Nübling. A brief glance at Stephens's notes to the play reveals specific ages, psychological characteristics, and typical behaviour – a short paragraph for each character. The stage is to recreate real locations in London, and Stephens explicitly stipulates a need for accurate age-related casting. However, his understanding of naturalism is also non-prescriptive in how meaning is to emerge from the dialogues: 'my plays tell stories about people. In that sense they are riddled with contradiction and confusion and behaviour that is odd, misguided and illogical' (ibid.). As such, he assumes the role of a reporter, writing what he sees without judgement, something that is reflected in the play's title.

120   *David Barnett*

Herons are referred to on a couple of occasions, first by Charlie, the father of the central character, 14-year-old Billy. Billy has developed a passion for fishing from Charlie, who tells of his admiration for the beauty of the bird before it swoops down, bagging itself the fish he was hoping to catch. He returns with a gun with the intention of shooting the bird, but cannot not find it again. The heron gains symbolic traction through its titular prominence, yet its meaning is wholly unclear. After all, the heron is not malign; it is simply doing what it does to survive. Yet it preys on innocent fish. In addition, the conscious party to all this, Charlie, is similarly engaged in angling, but he is not judged by the text for his desire to punish the heron. The events in the play itself resonate with this moral problem. Charlie has witnessed the murder of a schoolgirl and reported it to the police. As a result, he has made himself a target for revenge from the attackers and their families. Billy is then brutally assaulted by Scott, the brother of one of the attackers, when he challenges him over his treatment of a schoolmate with whom he has developed a bond, Adele. Billy then tries to take his own revenge on Scott with his father's gun. The moral ambiguity of the plot is already made plain in an epigraph to *Herons* in which Blake Morrison comments on the ethical categories poorly applied to child criminals, in the character sketches that call both Charlie and Scott 'damaged', and in the description Adele gives of one of the attackers himself as abused and weak. To summarise, Stephens, in his early naturalistic mode, sets the director the task of presenting characters and action without inflecting them with moral categories and packaging them for an audience. That said, it is clear from the texts themselves and the notes Stephens provides that he is offering accurate slices of life, with no invitation for directors to stylise.

What the playwright saw in Stuttgart completely surprised him (see Stephens 2011). He had been told that directors in German theatres enjoy the license to do whatever they wanted with plays, deleting scenes and adding completely foreign material. Instead, he found an aesthetic that was not suggested in the play, but that vividly brought out qualities very much in tune with the content. As one reviewer of Nubling's Basel transfer noted: 'Nübling has grippingly choreographed the spiral of violence – quite without a hint of a cynical, smug Tarantino chic. The escalation is underpinned by a psychology which primarily lets the body speak' (Schlienger 2004). This experience of another kind of theatre had a profound influence on how Stephens wrote because he was forced to reassess his role as writer in the theatrical process.

Benjamin Fowler observed that the encounter with the German theatre 'disrupts the ostensible clarity of a binary between stale tradition and vitalising innovation, simultaneously illustrating the permeability of a new generation of European sensibilities, open to the generative potential of travel and collaboration' (2016: 328). What has made Stephens 'European' is not then something that can be traced to a style, but to an understanding of professional relationships in a theatrical context. Practically, this led to a dismantling of the kinds of authorial prescription associated with *Herons* and an openness to a more collaborative set of relationships, not only with directors. Sarah Frankcom noted, with reference to her experience of directing *On the Shore of the Wide World* in 2005, how Stephens, in the rehearsal room, pushes 'actors to leave behind the comfort blanket of the psychological investigative approach that almost all British actors and directors in some way use' (2016: 389).

An example of this more open relationship can be illustrated by the British premiere of *The Trial of Ubu*, directed by Katie Mitchell. The play was originally commissioned by the German Schauspiel Essen and the Dutch Toneelgroep Amsterdam, and was directed by Nübling, who had now become Stephens's regular collaborator and a trusted friend.[5] Indeed, he was the one who asked Stephens to reimagine Ubu on a modern stage in the first place.[6] The play was inspired by the trials at the International Criminal Court (ICC) in the Hague and Stephens speculated on how the monster of modernist theatre, Alfred Jarry's Ubu, would fare there. The new play is to be performed after Jarry's play, or at least a shortened version for puppets that Stephens appended to the single-play edition (but not to the collected volume).

Mitchell's production, which opened at the Hampstead Theatre, London, in January 2012, was a radical departure from the text as printed. For the most part, the play is a courtroom drama, a genre piece that makes use of conventions already established in order to probe the qualities of monstrousness and childishness that Stephens had identified in both Ubu and the plaintiffs at the ICC. Mitchell's stroke of genius was born of a minor stage direction towards the beginning of the play: '*In the courtroom multiple translations are used.* [...] *Where appropriate we can hear the translations*' (Stephens 2015: 158). She asked Stephens whether she could effectively do away with the courtroom and stage the dialogue through two simultaneous translators who are not characters in the play. The playwright excitedly accepted the proposal, and Mitchell told me that he went on to construct the interpreters' story throughout the text.[7] This was not, then, a case of the director insisting on a reading and pressing ahead with it, as is often the case in German theatre, but a process of mutual agreement between two central members of the creative team.

The design, by Lizzie Clachan, was ingenious in that the interpreters were situated above the stage in a glass booth, but the wall that enclosed them perfectly mirrored the wood panelling of the theatre itself. Their booth was integrated into the fabric of the theatre and thus brought in the audience as an organic part of the production. Mitchell directed the two new characters very much as the characters in *Attempts*: they were psychologically coherent and respected all the conventions of the courtroom, sometimes spending long periods simply watching a witness enter or leave the dock. As the trial went on, the strain was clear to read, and one interpreter actually collapsed in the booth towards the end of the production.

Mitchell's unerring commitment to naturalism had a peculiarly Brechtian quality to it in that all the text delivered by the interpreters was reported, not authentic speech. As a result, the audience was charged with imagining what had been said and how. Just as Brecht instructed his actors to rehearse their texts in the third person and in the past (see Brecht 2015: 186) in order to gain

122   *David Barnett*

distance and clarity on what they were saying, the interpreters put the written characters' speeches through their own articulations not to offer accurate imitations, but a less inflected rendition of sometimes emotive, rhetorical speech.

Such a directorial intervention is radical. It dispenses with the text as written and completely re-presents it. While the effects of the director's idea clearly resonated through the production as a whole, the more interesting aspect to this examination of Stephens as playwright is not only his openness to a reading that was clearly not a part of his original play, but his enthusiasm to support the director not only conceptually, but by rethinking the play and actively contributing to its revision.

Stephens's relationship to the institution of theatre in Europe can be understood further in two different instances. Chronologically first is the production of Stephens's play *Three Kingdoms*, performed by three different European companies, premiering in Tallinn, Estonia in September 2011, Munich, Germany the following month, and in London in May 2012. I shall conclude this section with a mention of the Secret Theatre project, which was launched in May 2013, below.

Three Kingdoms started its life as a response to commissions from both the Traverse in Edinburgh and the Schauspielhaus in Hamburg. Stephens proposed writing the same play for each house, but as time went on, the Traverse withdrew for financial reasons and the Schauspielhaus, according to Stephens, 'lost their nerve and faith in the idea' (2015: xiii). The Lyric Theatre in London and the Kammerspiele in Munich both stepped into the breach and were joined by the NO99 theatre of Tallinn.

Just as *Ubu* explored the genre of the courtroom drama, *Three Kingdoms* plays with the detective thriller. It does this by setting up a procedural drama in the first part, in which the severed head of a trafficked prostitute is found on the banks of the Thames. The trail then leads to the port city of Hamburg, where the British detectives become more aware of the international scale and dimensions of the sex trade, and comes to a close in Tallinn, the headquarters of the smuggling gang and the murderer himself. The first two parts are, broadly speaking, quite realistic in their writing. The third part, in which detective Ignatius Stone journeys illegally to Tallinn with his dubious German colleague Steffen Dresner, becomes increasingly nightmarish, and it is difficult to fathom precisely what is happening as the text seems to move from without Stone to within. A short Epilogue, not included in the original production, concludes the play: Stone returns home to his younger wife, Caroline. He is changed, clearly unsteady and disorientated, while Caroline retains the qualities seen earlier in the play.

Stephens had Nübling in mind as director from the start of the project. Nübling noted the difficulties of rehearsing with three different national traditions, and, in an interview, he drew attentions to the limitations of British actor-training. He noted that his rehearsal process *produces* character through the work itself: 'a character is defined by what an actor does on stage' (cited in Stephens 2015: 7). What he found frustrating was the British actors' desire to construct character in advance through biography and psychology. The director does not necessarily suggest that such an approach is wrong, but that the actors are prisoners of their technique, having never had the time to explore other ones.

Nübling introduced a physicality to the performances reminiscent of the quality identified in his production of *Herons*, above. Rehearsals also developed a figure totally absent in the text, The Trickster. This figure would appear at unexpected moments in unexpected places, charged with an agility that called the ostensibly realistic writing into question – the coherence of the stage world found itself under attack. Catherine Love argues that the development of this figure unleashed forces unforeseen by the playwright, but utterly embraced by him, in the course of rehearsal (see 2016: 322). Elsewhere, other elements included a full performance of the Beatles' song 'Rocky Racoon' by Dresner, a hot and sweaty section from a pornographic film, and, most controversially, a costume decision to present the prostitutes wearing headgear representing hunters' quarries (while the male traffickers later wore wolf masks) (see Figure 6.1). Maddy Costa summed up the problem concisely: 'the violence against women in the language is appalling, so is the meticulousness with which the death of a prostitute is detailed, so is the silence of the women on stage – who are spat at, transfigured as deer (the powerless prey of hungry wolves), or reduced to blankly mopping the floor' (Costa 2012). Sophie Nield responded by attributing the problem to the production itself: 'I felt little awareness here of noir's own discomfort and unease around the representation of women' (2016: 399). She

Figure 6.1 The problems of metaphorical staging strategies. Sebastian Nübling directs Simon Stephens' *Three Kingdoms* (2012). Photograph © Tristam Kenton

124   *David Barnett*

exposes how the often dazzling effects Nübling introduced into the production merely served to amplify and fashion Stephens's male-centric perspective on gender rather than using the theatre's tools to criticise itself.

The production's reception is also something worth noting here. While it was obvious to anyone who attended the productions that the three different acting constituencies offered different kinds of performance, Fowler added that as the production toured from city to city, 'it radically complicated the idea of a homogenous "we" in the audience' (2016: 336). Warm receptions in Tallinn and Munich were remarkably cooled by mainstream reviewers in London, although a host of blogging critics both embraced the experiment while not remaining uncritical on the more troubling aspects of Nübling's production.

Stephens noted that while *Three Kingdoms* might not be his best play, 'I hadn't and maybe would never make a more significant contribution to British theatre' (2015: xiv). This contention is made slightly moot by the project that succeeded the production, The Secret Theatre. Space prevents me from discussing it in any detail,[8] but Stephens, together with the artistic director of the Lyric, Sean Holmes, decided to try importing European structures to British theatre in 2013. They employed a full-time ensemble to perform in, and to occasionally devise, productions, and sought to maintain a regular team to develop the work and the company. The lack of sustained finance and a tradition of such theatre-making led to the project's demise after six diverse productions, but it represents a concerted effort to change the way in which theatre is made in order to effect a change in the type of theatre made; something, as I have argued above, that is a trait of Stephens's approach to playwriting.

Conclusion

As stated in the introduction to this chapter, my definition of Crimp and Stephens as 'European' writers for the theatre is not so much rooted in what they write, but for whom they are writing. Until the advent of cheap and easy (air) transportation, British playwrights tended to write for British theatres, something that entailed a great deal of limitation. British playwriting was conspicuous, with some notable exceptions, by its reliance on realistic language, clear situations, and plays regulated by detailed stage directions, the legacy of George Bernard Shaw.

Both Crimp and Stephens clearly have very different views on the status of the playwright's text and the relationship with its production. However, it is worth noting two features of their work and working relationships, respectively, that locate them as 'British European' playwrights. First, their plays *are* experimental, but in what I will call a 'genteel' fashion. The radical refusal to attribute speaker to text in *Attempts* nonetheless leaves the reader with recognisable situations. Stephens tends to retain realistic language, too, but in an open manner that invites directors to 'look beneath the bonnet' and dig out all manner of latent material in performance that has delighted the playwright over the years. So, while these playwrights offer texts that actively invite collaboration and input, there is always something tangible and palpable in the scenes that can then be developed further.

Their choice of collaborators is also telling, and extends the concept of genteel experimentation to the practices of theatre-making. Crimp has had his plays staged by some notable European directors, including Luc Bondy, who commissioned and premiered his play *Cruel and Tender* in 2004. He has also often worked with Katie Mitchell, as has Stephens, although the latter's main European collaborator is Sebastian Nübling. I would suggest that this group of directors see themselves as artists, able to intervene in a playwright's work, but are not at the extreme end of the directorial spectrum, particularly in the German context. Indeed, Mitchell noted that she felt free to reframe *The Trial of Ubu* because it had already been staged once. This is a curiously conservative position that suggests that her production was in some way 'illegitimate' or at least required justification (and is a little surprising given the clownish cabaret approach Nübling took to the world premiere).

I conclude, then, by understanding Crimp and Stephens, different though their writing is, that they have accepted the European institutional gauntlet in that they conceive of their work as only one element of the theatrical process. Their writing itself and choice of collaborators, however, are moderate rather than radical. This is not to be construed as a reproach, but as an acknowledgement that their experience of the British theatre system can still function as a brake of sorts.

Martin Crimp – four key productions

Cruel and Tender. Directed by Luc Bondy. Designed by Richard Peduzzi. Cast: Georgina Ackerman, Stuart Brown, Jessica Claire, Joe Dixon, Lourdes Faberes, Toby Fisher, Kerry Fox, Michael Gould, Aleksandar Mikic, Nicola Redmond, David Sibley, Mario Viera. Wiener Festwochen, Chichester Festival Theatre, Young Vic, Théâtre des Bouffes du Nord and Ruhrfestspiele Recklinghausen: Young Vic, London, 5 May 2004.

Attempts on Her Life. Directed by Katie Mitchell. Designed by Vicki Mortimer. Cast: Claudie Blakey, Kate Duchêne, Michael Gould, Liz Kettle, Jacqueline Kington, Dina Korzun, Helena Lymbery, Paul Ready, Jonah Russel, Zubin Varla, Sandra Voe. National Theatre, London, 14 March 2007.

Die Stadt (*The City*). Directed by Thomas Ostermeier. Designed by Jan Pappelbaum. Cast: Jörg Hartmann, Bettina Hoppe, Lea Draeger, Helena Siegmund-Schultze. Schaubühne am Lehniner Platz, Berlin, 21 March 2008.

In the Republic of Happiness. Directed by Dominic Cooke. Designed by Miriam Buether. Cast: Anna Calder-Marshall, Emma Fielding, Ellie Kendrick, Stuart McQuarrie, Paul Ready, Michelle Terry, Peter Wight. Royal Court, London, 6 December 2012.

Simon Stephens – four key productions

Reiher (*Herons*). Directed by Sebastian Nübling. Designed by Muriel Gerstner. Cast: Silja Bächli, Raphael Brunner, Nico Grüninger, Julian Kestler, Sebastian

126   *David Barnett*

Röhrle, Mia Sanchez, Jonas Schmid. Württembergische Staatstheater, Stuttgart, 28 March 2003.

Pornographie (*Pornography*). Directed by Sebastian Nübling. Designed by Muriel Gerstner. Cast: Sonja Beisswenger, Christoph Franken, Peter Knaack, Angela Muethel, Jana Schulz, Monique Schwitter, Daniel Wahl, Samuel Weiss. Schauspiel Hannover and Schauspielhaus Hamburg: Schauspiel Hannover, 15 June 2007.

Three Kingdoms. Directed by Sebastian Nübling. Art direction by Ene-Liis Semper. Music design by Lars Wittershagen. Lighting design by Stephan Mariani. Cast: Risto Kübar, Rupert Simonian, Ferdy Roberts, Nick Tennant, Gert Raudsep, Jaak Prints, Cigdem Teke, Sergo Vares, Mirtel Pohla, Lasse Myhr, Steven Scharf, Rasmus Kaljujärv, Tambet Tuisk. Theatre NO99, Münchner Kammerspiele & Lyric Hammersmith London: NO99 Theatre, Talinn, 17 September 2011.

The Trial of Ubu. Directed by Katie Mitchell. Designed by Lizzie Clachan. Cast: Nikki Amuka-Bird, Josie Daxter, Kate Duchêne, Paul McCleary, Rob Ostlere, George Taylor. Hampstead Theatre, 18 January 2012.

Notes

1 All data provided by Deutscher Bühnenverein, *Wer spielte was?* (various publishers, places, and years) One reason for Stephens's statistics is that he writes and is commissioned to write more plays than Crimp.
2 Theatre scholar Steve Nicholson told me that earlier drafts did attach names to texts. The decision, then, was a deliberate one taken once the material itself had been compiled.
3 All the following information is taken from this, which is available at: http://d1wf8hd6ovssje.cloudfront.net/documents/Attempts_bkpk.pdf
4 All translations from the German are mine.
5 For a discussion of the flamboyant original production, see Ledger 2016.
6 Information here and later is taken from an unpublished interview I conducted with Stephens on 6 March 2012.
7 Mitchell replied to my questions at a Q&A at Queen Mary, University of London, on 15 May 2012. This is also the source of the information regarding *Ubu* in the conclusion.
8 See Bolton (2016) for an excellent critical discussion.

Works cited

Angel-Perez, Elisabeth (2014) 'Martin Crimp's nomadic voices', *Contemporary Theatre Review*, 24(3): 353–362.

Angelaki, Vicky (2012) *The Plays of Martin Crimp. Making Theatre Strange*, Basingstoke: Palgrave.

Barnett, David and Simon Stephens (2016) '"This is why I'm really excited by British Theatre in the next five years": David Barnett in conversation with Simon Stephens', *Contemporary Theatre Review*, 26(3): 311–318.

Bolton, Jacqueline (2012) 'Capitalizing (on) new writing: new play development in the 1990s', *Studies in Theatre and Performance*, 32(2): 209–225.

Martin Crimp and Simon Stephens 127

——— (2016) 'Changing the conversation': Simon Stephens, Sean Holmes, and secret theatre', *Contemporary Theatre Review*, 26(3): 337–344.

Brecht, Bertolt (2015). *Brecht on Theatre*, 3rd edition, edited by Marc Silberman, Steve Giles and Tom Kuhn, London: Bloomsbury.

Brodie, Geraldine (2016) 'The sweetheart factor: tracing translation in Martin Crimp's writing for theatre', *Journal of Adaptation in Film & Performance*, 9(1): 83–96.

Clements, Rachel (2014) 'Deconstructive techniques and spectral technologies in Katie Mitchell's *Attempts on Her Life*', *Contemporary Theatre Review*, 24(3): 331–341.

Costa, Maddy (2012) '*Three Kingdoms*: the shape of British theatre to come?', *The Guardian*, 16 May.

Crimp, Martin (1997) *Attempts on Her Life*, London: Faber and Faber.

——— (2015) *Plays*, vol. 3, London: Faber and Faber.

Crimp, Martin and Aleks Sierz (2016) 'UCL Guest session: Attempts on His Life – Martin Crimp – playwright, translator, translated', *Journal of Adaptation in Film & Performance*, 9(1): 101–116.

Fowler, Benjamin (2016) '"Draining the English Channel": The European revolution in *Three Kingdoms* and three keynotes (by Simon Stephens, David Lan, and Edward Bond)', *Contemporary Theatre Review*, 26(3): 328–336.

Frankcom, Sarah (2016) 'Northern spirit', *Contemporary Theatre Review*, 26(3): 387–390.

Grochala, Sarah (2017) *The Contemporary Political Play. Rethinking Dramaturgical Structure*, London: Bloomsbury.

Ledger, Adam J. (2016) '"It's not about fucking it up": *The Trial of Ubu*, the text, and the director', *Contemporary Theatre Review*, 26(3): 345–356.

Logan, Brian (2007) 'One day in July', *The Guardian*, 19 June.

Love, Catherine (2016) 'New perspectives on home: Simon Stephens and authorship in British theatre', *Contemporary Theatre Review*, 26(3): 319–327.

Nield, Sophie (2016) 'Reading *Three Kingdoms* as a woman: criticism, misogyny, and representation', *Contemporary Theatre Review*, 26(3): 396–399.

Peter, Anne (2008) 'Die Ehe im Zeitalter fortschreitender Gesellschaftsdämmerung', 21 March, https://www.nachtkritik.de/index.php?option=com_content&view=article&id=1174:die-stadt-der-schnitt-thomas-ostermeier-nimmt-wieder-kurs-auf-englische-dramatik&catid=34:schaubuehne-berlin

Poschmann, Gerda (1997) *Der nicht mehr dramatische Theatertext. Aktuelle Bühnentexte und ihre dramaturgische Analyse*, Tübingen: Niemeyer.

Rebellato, Dan (2010) 'Katie Mitchell: Learning from Europe', in Maria M. Delgado and Dan Rebellato (eds), *Contemporary European Theatre Directors*, Abingdon: Routledge, pp. 317–338.

Schlienger, Alfred (2004) 'Süsser Vogel Jugend?', *Neue Zürcher Zeitung*, 22 March.

Sierz, Aleks (2007) '"Form follows function": meaning and politics in Martin Crimp's *Fewer Emergencies*', *Modern Drama*, 50(3): 375–393.

——— (2013) *The Theatre of Martin Crimp*, 2nd edition, London: Bloomsbury.

Stephens, Simon (2005) *Plays*, vol. 1, London: Bloomsbury.

——— (2011) 'Skydiving blindfolded. Or five things I learned from Sebastian Nübling', 9 May, https://theatertreffen-blog.de/tt11/2011/05/09/skydiving-blindfolded

——— (2013) 'Interview', in Duška Radosavljević, *Theatre-Making. Interplay Between Text and Performance in the 21st Century*, Basingstoke: Palgrave, pp. 197–210.

——— (2015) *Plays*, vol. 4. London: Bloomsbury.

128   *David Barnett*

Tomlin, Liz (2014) 'Citational theory in practice: a performance analysis of character-isation and identity in Katie Mitchell's staging of Martin Crimp's texts', *Contemporary Theatre Review*, 24(3): 373–377.

Wahl, Christine (2008) 'Diktaturfolklore und Abstiegsängste', 22 March, http://www.spiegel.de/kultur/gesellschaft/doppel-premiere-an-der-berliner-schaubuehne-diktatur folklore-und-abstiegsaengste-a-542929.html

Zimmermann, Heiner (2002) 'Martin Crimp, *Attempts on Her Life*: Postdramatic, post-modern, satiric?', in Margarete Rubik and Elke Mettinger-Schartmann (eds), *(Dis) Continuities: Trends and Traditions in Contemporary Theatre and Drama in English*, XIX, Trier: Wissenschaftlicher Verlag, pp. 105–124.

7 Marius von Mayenburg and Roland Schimmelpfennig

Dissecting European lives under global capitalism

Peter M. Boenisch

Roland Schimmelpfennig (b. 1967) and Marius von Mayenburg (b. 1972) represent a new generation of playwrights to emerge in the German-speaking countries in the late 1990s; other prominent protagonists include Falk Richter (b. 1969), Lukas Bärfuss (b. 1971) and Kathrin Röggla (b. 1971), as well as Dea Loher (b. 1964) and Sibylle Berg (b. 1962).[1] Many of them, like Mayenburg himself, came out of play-writing courses that were either founded or relaunched at the time at a number of arts schools and universities. Meanwhile, several theatres began to offer in-house residencies, and new festivals emerged, such as the Bonn Biennale, founded in 1992 by Mayenburg's teacher Tankred Dorst, which were specifically dedicated to new playwriting. By the turn of the millennium, two German theatres stood out in particular in their focus on contemporary authors; Schimmelpfennig and Mayenburg were associated with both of them. In Berlin, Thomas Ostermeier (b. 1967) moved from the Baracke studio at Deutsches Theater to the prestigious Schaubühne, made famous in the 1970s by director Peter Stein and his dramaturg-playwright Botho Strauss (see Boenisch 2010). Schimmelpfennig and Mayenburg were, alongside Maja Zade, the Schaubühne's dramaturgs during the inaugural seasons of Ostermeier's tenure, with Mayenburg and his English translator Zade remaining at the Schaubühne to the present day as some of the director's closest associates. Elsewhere, the work of director-playwrights Tom Kühnel (b. 1971) and Robert Schuster (b. 1970), who had studied at Berlin's Ernst Busch Theatre Academy in the same year-group as Ostermeier and who collaborate as playwrights under the joint pen name Soeren Voima, had established their reputation at the studio of Berlin's Maxim-Gorki-Theatre. As Ostermeier took over the Schaubühne, Kühnel and Schuster were brought in to the Frankfurt Theater am Turm (TAT), once a key incubator of the 1960s new writing scene, where some of the notorious work by Peter Handke (such as his *Publikumsbeschimpfung/Offending the Audience*) and Rainer Werner Fassbinder had been premiered. For the opening of their TAT direction, they commissioned Schimmelpfennig and Mayenburg to launch *Welttheater* (*World Theatre*), a stage 'serial' that was then to be continued by other playwrights.

Schimmelpfennig and Mayenburg had also both been associated with the Royal Court's writers programme in the late 1990s and early 2000s, which produced and premiered English translations of several of their plays (see Aston and O'Thomas 2015). As for a number of other emerging German writers, the

130   *Peter M. Boenisch*

1990s British 'in-yer-face'-generation of playwrights had offered them much inspiration. Following their British peers, Schimmelpfennig and Mayenburg rediscovered playwriting as a potent art form to express their generation's urgent concerns. Schimmelpfennig exemplarily articulated their commitment to the contemporary in his 2014 lectures on playwriting:

> Writers must have the ability to listen
> if they want to write about the world they live in:
> they listen, and then they respond.
> Their response is the playtext.
>
> (Schimmelpfennig 2014a, 49)[2]

Prior to the emergence of these new voices in the 1990s, Peter Handke and Botho Strauss in West Germany, Heiner Müller and Volker Braun in the GDR, and Thomas Bernhard and Elfriede Jelinek in Austria had been the foremost chroniclers on German-speaking stages of contemporary sensibilities. Their themes had included the stagnation, and then the end, of the communist utopia; feminism; the saturated complacency of the affluent middle-classes; and, a continuing concern with the disavowed atrocities and the guilt of the Nazi-parent generation, as well as the re-emerging revanchist and right-wing politics. Yet those like Mayenburg and Schimmelpfennig, who had entered their adult lives mainly in a post-1989, reunified Germany, related to different problems; for them, these playwrights represented a previous generation, and were thus unable to address them with their writing.

The 1990s also witnessed a fundamental cultural shift, not only in German society. After the end of the Soviet Union and the communist bloc, some had proclaimed, following US-political economist Francis Fukuyama, the 'end of history' (Fukuyama 1992). Following the decades marked by the Cold War competition with the communist East, capitalism now globally took hold of every aspect of society with its all-encompassing neoliberal ideology. These new times no longer seemed to allow for alternatives, let alone the political utopia of a better, fairer world. Even politicians of the moderate left, such as chancellor Gerhard Schröder's social democrats in Germany, embraced the purely economically focussed neoliberal mind-set. Traditional political orientations – not least those on the left – dissolved; for others, only a return to overt nationalism seemed the answer. Meanwhile, the world of employment shifted towards so-called 'post-industrial capitalism' and its 'immaterial labour', characterised by the significant expansion of the creative as well as the financial industries on the one hand, and the spread of 'un-creative', low-paid jobs in the service industries on the other (see Lazzarato 1996; Boltanski and Chiapello 2005). A new 'precariat' emerged that, in contrast to the traditional working class, also included many well-educated, middle-class professionals working on zero-hour contracts or in fragile self-employment. Furthermore, emerging media technologies disseminated new ways of looking at, watching, and engaging with the world. The then new, private cable-TV networks allowed

Marius von Mayenburg and Roland Schimmelpfennig 131

zapping between dozens of channels, popularised new formats of soap operas and reality-TV, and offered a new 24-hour live news coverage with global, instant reporting. In tandem with the narrative strategies and predominantly affective ways of engagement proffered by new video-gaming consoles and a first-generation of internet technology, these changing media environments not only broadened the reservoir of cultural references, but also expanded the range of formal and dramaturgic strategies young playwrights had at their disposal, far beyond actually employing video or computer technologies in their work. These shifting cultural contexts eventually invited a self-reflexive exploration of the possibilities, and limits, of dramatic representation. While a truism for all dramatic literature, Mayenburg's and Schimmelpfennig's playwriting can even less be considered detached neither from the historical context of its creation nor from its concrete realisation on the theatre stage.

Roland Schimmelpfennig: poetic concentration in a 'theatre of the imagination'

Imagine a play that consists of 48 scenic fragments; truncated, often after just a few sentences, by the (spoken) word 'pause', they rapidly cut into each other. The actors – remaining on stage throughout, just coming to the front when it's their turn – simply grab a different shirt, or pick up some prop, and swiftly change between a variety of characters each of them presents; 15, to be precise, which the play's *dramatis personae* distributes onto five actors in such a way that age, gender, ethnicity, and, in fact, life form not even remotely correspond. Conflated in one of these five roles, we find, for example, 'the young man, the grandfather, the Asian, the waitress, the cricket [sic!]'. Another reads, 'the young woman, The Man with the striped shirt, the Asian with toothache, the Barbiefucker', with the latter transpiring to be a globe-trotting airplane pilot. The corresponding air hostess, meanwhile, then surfaces in a third compound with, amongst others, 'the man over 60'. This play is Roland Schimmelpfennig's *The Golden Dragon*, premiered at Akademietheater Wien in 2009 in the playwright's own *mise en scène*. It poses, to directors, performers and audiences alike, challenges that are characteristic of Schimmelpfennig's highly composed, metatheatrical dramaturgy.

Among the playwright's internationally most successful plays, performed in London, New York, and elsewhere, *The Golden Dragon* confronts the plight of *sans papiers* immigrants working in the kitchen of a 'China-Thai-Vietnam-Restaurant' in an unnamed global city. In constant fear of being discovered, and also without medical insurance, they are unable to properly attend to a painfully aching tooth. Its butchered extraction in the restaurant's kitchen, resulting in the man bleeding to death, sets the play's chain of events in motion. As we saw above, *The Golden Dragon* uses a dramaturgic strategy very different from documentary realism. The play's short scenes appear as montage jumping between various plot-strands, which are subtly connected, beyond the consistent presence of the five performers, mainly through recurring objects

132   *Peter M. Boenisch*

and metaphors, such as travelling and eating. The extracted and discarded tooth will (with the unknowing assistance of the airplane crew) travel across the world, and eventually, deep in the sea, be reunited with the skeletal remains of its former human owner. Meanwhile, the parabolic animal characters of the cricket and the ant relate the sad fate of a Vietnamese prostitute, that chef's sister.

While this elaborate poetic metaphor about globalisation, constructed around the various floors (and floorboards) of the Golden Dragon restaurant, ends in tragedy, this, at times, absurd spectacle is also hilariously funny. The author himself describes this signature approach as *Verdichtung*, or 'poetic concentration':[3]

> I have never been after documentation. The screen can do this much better. I am after *Verdichtung*. *The Golden Dragon* uses the simple means of straight-out telling, of overt pretence, and of 'demonstrating' – but the play's purpose is not at all distanciation, but the opposite: close proximity, and identification. It is about bringing the audience as close as possible to these characters. [...] One can do a lot of research about the lives of illegal immigrants, the information is all out there and available – but what good is it if I am still unable to connect to it, not even for the duration of an evening in the theatre.
>
> (Schimmelpfennig 2011: 717)

Schimmelpfennig's *Golden Dragon* can thus be seen as a European playwright's attempt to devise a suitable form to relate a theatre audience with the migrants' plight, going beyond the exhausted form of a direct, mimetic representation. His 'concentrated' drama 'demonstrates' rather complex fictional psychologies and life-stories purely through a more lyrical than, in a Brechtian sense, epic language. Characters and action are expressed in the performers' words alone; they never 'act out' these characters, as their spoken text (also including narrative transitions, stage directions, and epic descriptions of the characters) only rarely takes the form of a conventional dramatic dialogue addressed to another character, yet all the while they are also more than just distanced narrators. Schimmelpfennig goes on to explain:

> I fear that to represent a completely foreign culture will very quickly result in something that is condescending, exoticising and, most likely, very embarrassing. It won't help at all, but, as a matter of fact, it would frustrate my aim of having the audience empathise and identify with these characters. In *The Golden Dragon*, not imitation, but pure verbal declaration puts this Chinese person right in front of our eyes.
>
> (Ibid.)

Such an approach presents a number of difficulties. In the UK, both the Actors Touring Company's 2011 production of *The Golden Dragon*, and the Hackney Empire's 2017 production of Hungarian composer Peter Eötvös's opera adaptation of the play, were accused by the Equity union of using white actors to perform Asian characters. While the German theatre certainly has a problematic relationship with its largely unchallenged white 'colourblindness' and a disturbing nonchalance about black- and yellow-facing on stage (see Sieg 2002, 2015), I do not see Schimmelpfennig's writing as part of this unreflected tradition of stage representation. His non–illusionistic 'condensation' seeks to articulate and equally challenge the split, contradictory, ambiguous (European, middle-class) attitude towards the blessings but also the immense disturbances and destructions caused by today's entirely globalised way of living. It is an attempt to credibly relate privileged theatre spectators to something that must remain foreign and unimaginable for them, above all thereby going beyond empty, affirmative gestures of criticality about our bad conscience towards the poor victims, something every audience member would easily accept, yet without consequence.

Resorting to his purely poetic 'verbal declaration' of characters and events in a notably composed and highly structured form of dramatic condensation allows Schimmelpfennig to draw on stereotypes, misperceptions, clichés and images. To function, the 'declaration' of the 'Asian migrant' must be no more nor less 'real' than that of the middle-class characters, nor of the speaking animal characters here and in other of his plays. The play's not only cross-ethnic, but also cross-gender and even cross-life-form multi-roling seeks to express in its formal over-layering and poetic condensation the very state of present globalisation; each of the compound roles is globalised precisely as an almost random conglomerate of a global multitude. Just as the 'China-Thai-Viet-nam-Restaurant' is a typical phenomenon of globalisation in its indiscriminate conflation of non-specific clichés into a recognisable brand, which we nowadays may encounter anywhere in the world, suggesting global cosmopolitan familiarity, the characters are not merely reduced to recognisable types, but they blend into each other beyond boundaries of gender and ethnicity, even life form. Rather than just talking about effects of globalisation, *The Golden Dragon* shows globalisation in the very difference of its dramatic form compared to our expectations.

At the same time, Schimmelpfennig constructs an imbalance of class, with global resonances; this is why his plays function just as much in German theatre as in Latin America and elsewhere. Again, this does not only concern the fictional story and its characters. The play is conscious in its address of an implied audience that has a privileged status, inevitable for a theatre audience able to attend a performance of Schimmelpfennig's plays. This status resonates with some of the middle-class characters in the play, as it sets them apart clearly from the global precariat. Again, already in its very form the play relates the spectators to their complicity as privileged cultured audience in the exploitative global power imbalances of the present, which play out both on a global level but as much within the local microcosm of the 'Golden Dragon' restaurant. Subsequently, the spectators are thrown back on their own (futile and largely helpless) attempts to come to terms with 'what we do' to the 'other' as an effect of globalisation.

134   *Peter M. Boenisch*

In this sense, I read Schimmelpfennig's plays as a response to the impossibility of writing, in German theatre, with straightforward, unambiguous clarity about the globalised present. His strategies of condensation and declaration are means to build effective theatral images[4] in the audience's mind that may make it possible to affectively connect to such urgent concerns, as a first step towards some form of comprehension:

> In our lives, images play an ever more central role. [...] Words evoke images. Stories are sequences of images in the mind of the spectators or readers. [...] As long as something can be described, we can imagine it. And only what we are able to imagine, we can – perhaps – comprehend.
> (Schimmelpfennig 2014a: 53, 55, 59)

Elsewhere, Schimmelpfennig has described his approach as a 'theatre of the imagination' (Schimmelpfennig 2009: 36). His characters, therefore, may switch race and gender, they may be transformed – quite regularly – into animals of various sorts, even into trees; they may equally morph and multiply, or shrink to end up in a bottle that falls from the edge of the balcony of an apartment block, with the character continuing to report on what he sees going on inside the building as he falls towards the ground. Just as Schimmelpfennig's 'condensed' characters no longer 'add up' to a singular identity, neither do the represented times and places in his plays add up to a coherent dramatic totality. In addition to the mentioned scenic rhythm of a plethora of short-cut scenes, his plays also tend to extend linear time, to suspend, or loop it. In several plays, key dramatic moments are repeated; the spectators are thus presented with various perspectives on one and the same central event as it keeps recurring, without any clear resolution, however. The scenes piece together like a jigsaw – yet the perspective does not get any clearer, let alone complete, but instead ever more complex.

Schimmelpfennig notes, 'As a writer I have never made compromises. On the contrary. The theatre needs challenges. Excessive demands. [...] The theatre I love asks a few questions of itself and of its audience.' (Schimmelpfennig 2014b: 4). The late German theatre director Jürgen Gosch (1943–2009) eventually became the playwright's congenial partner in realising this 'theatre of imagination'.[5] He had initially produced, at Deutsches Schauspielhaus Hamburg, Schimmelpfennig's 2002 plays *Push Up* and *Vorher/Nachher* (*Before/ After*); both productions were invited to Mühlheimer Theatertage, the annual playwriting showcase-equivalent of the director-focused Berlin Theatertreffen.[6] Gosch famously responded to Schimmelpfennig's scenic challenges, 'One can play anything on stage, as long as it occurs in the text' (cited in Schimmelpfennig 2009: 36). Their final collaboration, at a time the director already struggled with his terminal cancer, was *Idomeneus* at Deutsches Theater Berlin (2009), a play Schimmelpfennig had originally written for his mentor Dieter Dorn (b. 1935), the director who influenced his pronouncedly theatral vision early in his career.[7] Training originally as a theatre director at Munich's Otto-Falckenberg-Theatre

Marius von Mayenburg and Roland Schimmelpfennig 135

School, which is affiliated to the city's renowned Kammerspiele, Schimmelpfennig, instead of finishing the course, became assistant to its *Intendant*-director Dorn, who was renowned for his grand-scale, highly stylised and theatrical *mise en scène* of classical plays and opera. It was during this time that Schimmelpfennig took to playwriting. His *Die Ewige Maria (The Eternal Mary)* – the first of his plays to get a professional production, in January 1996 at Theater Oberhausen – told the story of Karl and Maria the night before their wedding, which, however, never takes place as Karl mysteriously disappears, leaving behind a ring that Maria cannot get off her finger. *Die Zwiefachen*,[8] one of two of his plays staged at Kammerspiele Munich in 1996 and 1997, featured a magical box that bestowed eternal youth to the villagers gathering for a folk dance evening. A similarly uncanny bucolic setting – echoing well-known mythical motifs from *Midsummer Night's Dream* to *Hansel and Gretel*, and featuring two characters designated in the *dramatis personae* as 'ghosts' – then returned in Schimmelpfennig's breakthrough-play, *Aus den Städten in die Wälder, Aus den Wäldern in die Städte (From the Cities into the Forests, from the Forests into the Cities)*, which opened in April 1998 at Mainz. Here, several city-couples head into the forest looking for the perfect wood to build a theatre stage, yet they get lost and, one after the other, mutate into trees.

Schimmelpfennig's early work of the late 1990s thus notably distinguished itself from his contemporaries, including Mayenburg, by its rural settings, fairy-tale plots, and magical mythology. These rather idiosyncratic parameters not only resonate with Dorn's *mise en scène*, but they may also reflect the author's upbringing in the historic medieval city of Göttingen, known for its university, amongst whose many celebrated alumni can be counted the Brothers Grimm. It is surrounded by forests, which in Schimmelpfennig's youth still led to the no-go area of the heavily fortified 'wall', the border to socialist East Germany. Having spent a year working as a translator in the USA, Schimmelpfennig moved to Berlin to take up his one-year residence at the Schaubühne. His plays became more urban, too, as in *Push Up 1–3*, his second Schaubühne play, which premiered in November 2001. In Maja Zade's translation, it was Schimmelpfennig's first work to be staged at the Royal Court, directed by Ramin Gray, in February 2002, followed within a few months by *Die arabische Nacht (Arabian Night)*, translated by David Tushingham and directed by Gordon Anderson for ATC, at Soho Theatre, after having opened first in February 2001 in Stuttgart. With these two plays, in particular, Schimmelpfennig had offered a full exposition of his 'theatre of imagination'. He pushed further his signature manipulation of plot-time, while moving ever further away from conventional dramatic dialogue (that would only consist of an exchange of meaningless, formulaic phrases) towards his characteristic commentary-speech. Rather than expressing a psychological character, it reveals a transindividual psychological state that is 'being spoken', in the first instance to the audience, as German literary scholar Johannes Birgfeld noted about *Push Up*'s long mono-logic passages, in which the characters still seemed to step out of an otherwise conventional dramatic scene: 'The spectators, in these moments, become the communicative partners of the characters' speech. Their speech is now

136   *Peter M. Boenisch*

addressed to them, and therefore the words are meaningful for them, and not for the other characters on stage' (Birgfeld 2014: 107).

While *Push Up* was set in a realistic office environment, *Arabian Night* linked – as the title indicated – the fairy-tale motifs of Schimmelpfennig's earlier plays with the complex and diverse life stories whose paths cross in a contemporary, globalised metropolis – the dominant theme of most of the author's work since. Here, the lives of five inhabitants of an apartment block (standing in, as the restaurant in *The Golden Dragon*, as a microcosm for our globalised society) intertwine in ever more bizarre ways. As the play unfolds, the realistic city-setting blends more and more into the characters' dreams, their desire and blurred memories: one of the neighbours ends up shrunk in the already mentioned bottle falling down from the seventh-floor balcony, while Fatima kills her lover Kalil, whom she erroneously believed to be having an affair with her flatmate, the insomniac Franziska, whom the widow caretaker Lohmeier, actually in charge of repairing the defunct lift and dealing with a supposed failure of the water supply, takes for the reincarnation of his former wife. *Arabian Night* was the first of Schimmelpfennig's panoramic portraits of contemporary society. His *Vorher/Nachher (Before/After)*, the first play he wrote specifically to be premiered by Jürgen Gosch (in November 2002 at Schauspielhaus Hamburg), was an even more ambitious kaleidoscope that introduced 36 characters in 51 short scenes, followed by *Auf der Greifswalder Strasse (On Greifswalder Street)*, premiered by Gosch in January 2006 at Deutsches Theater Berlin. Its 63 scenes, introducing 50 characters, were set within a period of 24 hours on and around this long central street that crosses the bohemian Berlin Prenzlauer Berg neighbourhood. The narrative motifs brought together fragments of history (the liberation of Berlin by the Soviet Red Army, which in 1945 fought its way into the city along this street, taking block by block in a bitter battle that cost many lives on both sides), mythical motifs (a werewolf, an old puppet player, an undead zombie supermarket checkout girl), everyday characters (shopkeepers; young Russian expats), symbols and metaphors (death and dying, in various manifestations; a silver spoon that connects the different times and people; a chorus of three women speaking the scene directions). Once more, a lover gets murdered. Yet it is impossible to identify a 'plot' in this somewhat bleak atmospheric portrait of globalised city life. Urban anonymity, myths and superstition are some of the major threads reverberating through the scenes. An interviewer compared the large-scale portrait of contemporary German society to earlier works by Botho Strauss, such as *Paare, Passanten (Couples, Passersby,* 1981), and Peter Handke, not least his *Die Stunde da wir nichts voneinander wussten (The Hour We Knew Nothing of Each Other,* 1992). In his response, Schimmelpfennig associated these writers, however, with a pre-1989 'semi-academic middle-class society', a generation that is no longer up to date with global life in the twenty-first century:

Berlin has changed, the country has changed. Europe has changed. This semi-academic middle-class society no longer exists in this form – at least not for me. I have lived in Turkey, I have worked in America, my wife has a Mexican passport, our children's friends have Indian, Cuban, Peruvian, Vietnamese roots […] The play does not portray the intellectuals in their galleries, but the grocer and the checkout girls, the tired, bleary-eyed girls on the tram in the early hours of the morning. This is no semi-academic society, this is a very different Berlin. An open city, an international metropolis.

(Schimmelpfennig 2011: 723f.)

It is this same magic microcosm of recognisable types (rather than unique individuals) one would meet in any globalised European city that eventually returned in *The Golden Dragon*.

Similar issues and topics also echo through a somewhat different, second strand of Schimmelpfennig's writing: his more intimate, seemingly more conventional 'living room plays', populated mostly by couples and thirty-somethings approaching their mid-life crisis – Schimmelpfennig's own generation, yet also far more of a 'semi-academic middle-class society' that would in fact still dominate Berlin theatre audiences, despite changes in the city. This strand of his work includes *Die Frau von früher* (*The Woman Before*, 2004), *Peggy Pickit sieht das Gesicht Gottes* (*Peggy Pickit Sees the Face of God*, 2010), a commission for Toronto's Volcano Theatre, and *Wintersonnenwende* (*Winter Solstice*, 2015), the latter commissioned by the Stockholm Royal Dramaten. *Peggy Pickit* replays, in this more intimate 'chamber-piece' setting, the metaphoric dramatisation of contemporary globalisation and its European repercussions encountered in *The Golden Dragon*. Two couples – former work colleagues at a hospital – celebrate their reunion over dinner, after Karen (Carol in the English translation) and Martin's return from spending six years working in Africa, 'to do something'. The experience has alienated them from the affluent, yet superficial life their friends Liz and Frank are living. Once again aided by jump cuts and a serial loop of certain repeated moments as well as his monologic commentary style, which prevents empathy and identification, Schimmelpfennig reflects on the complexity of the contemporary relationship between Europe and Africa. The corruption effected by the continent's neo-colonial exploitation eventually turns the German doctors' impulse to help into an utter disaster that will result in both couples ending at each other's throats over the dinner table. The same dramaturgic ploy – the 'return of the repressed' over a communal dinner – is used in *Winter Solstice*, as Schimmelpfennig turns to rising racism and nationalism that make a personified entry into the bourgeois living-room, not at all accidentally on Christmas Eve, in the guise of a certain Rudolf Mayer, a doctor returned from exile in Paraguay. This spontaneous guest at the Christmas dinner begins to spread his fascist ideology in a charming and seductive manner.

Schimmelpfennig remains a prolific artist, who has written more than 40 plays to date. Since 2016, he has also published two novels, while also exhibiting his paintings. He notes that he usually works on several plays at once, and thinks of them rather in terms of blocks or chunks of work, instead of individually:

138   *Peter M. Boenisch*

> As I am writing one play, I already think about the next, and a third one. That's how these blocks emerge, which to me appear like a coherent process of work. Perhaps, eventually, one thread becomes more urgent and prominent – and demands to be written up there and then. *Calypso, Idomeneus, Here and Now* and *The Golden Dragon* have emerged from such a process – very close together, within a single year. The plays are very different, however they have been conceived and devised in parallel. I have written 27 plays [at the time of the interview in 2010], but in my mind they have emerged from six or seven larger creative blocks. Currently, I am once more writing three plays simultaneously, and I know that, when I get stuck on one play, this impasse will help me with one of the other plays.
>
> (Schimmelpfennig 2011: 720)

His chilling dramatic analyses of the faultlines of globalisation are *Auseinandersetzungen* with these problems in the literal sense of the German word: they confront the privileged theatre spectators by setting not only the issues apart, but also picking apart the spectators' own attitudes towards repressed sides of present European life, as they appear in a highly symbolic 'global' space, such as The Golden Dragon restaurant, or even in the bohemian living rooms, to haunt not only the characters in the plays, but most of all the liberal theatre audiences of Schimmelpfennig's plays. He has become the most performed contemporary author in German-language theatre, while his work has become popular, in translation, not only across Europe and especially in the Nordic countries, where some of his work was premiered (*Frygt og Bæve*, Kopenhagen 2013, a commissioned play about the philosopher Søren Kierkegaard; *Winter Solstice*, Stockholm 2015; *100 Songs*, Örebro 2019), but equally in Japan (*On and Off*, 2013), and in particular in Latin America (*El Camino de las Hormigas*, Havana 2014, Buenos Aires 2017; *As quatro direções do céu*, Porto Alegre, 2015).

Marius von Mayenburg: grotesque allegories of neoliberal absurdities

One day, geeky engineer Lette is not allowed to present his technical invention at a trade fair; his boss reveals to him that he is just too ugly for the job, which Lette's own wife confirms on request. The duteous employee undergoes facial surgery, performed by a Dr Scheffler, who happens to share the name of his boss. Lette ends up looking so good that not only Fanny, an elderly investor, who has the same first name as his wife, but equally the surgeon's assistant (called, as to be expected: Fanny), as well as the rich investor's son Karlmann, sharing his name with Lette's colleague from work, all are after him. His boss and the two Karlmanns meanwhile are so impressed by the new looks that they get exactly the same new face, too. In *Der Hässliche* (*The Ugly One*), premiered at Schaubühne Berlin in January 2007, Marius von Mayenburg plays a scathing game with postmodern ideas of the 'performativity' of subjectivity and the

Marius von Mayenburg and Roland Schimmelpfennig 139

contingency of identity. These academic ideas, in the context of neoliberal capitalism, contribute to an all-encompassing commodification of individuality. Subjectivity becomes just one more thing available for order from a catalogue, making us, eventually, all faceless and interchangeable. Mayenburg makes clear in his stage directions that four actors should play the eight roles, and that no change must be made to the face of the actor playing Lette, nor the other characters undergoing surgery. Typically for his work, the playwright offers a tightly devised and economically crafted plot that leaves little space for subtle undertones, let alone depth of psychology. He does not stage private conflicts, but uses his characters, and the ploy of *The Ugly One*, as a tool to articulate some of the fundamental societal aporias of present-day, pan-European and potentially global, late-capitalist, neoliberal consumer lives.

Mayenburg's dramaturgic toolkit, here and elsewhere, includes well-made realism as well as scenic montage, multiple roles for actors, and odd plot-loops, as in his earlier *Turista* (2005), his most 'Schimmelpfennig-like' play, where the boy Oli is murdered six times by various members of the microcosmic society that has assembled on a camping ground, only to remain the only one still alive at the end of the play. The two authors discussed in this chapter clearly share some of their approaches, as both revisit and reinvent key conventional dramatic mechanisms, yet from a postdramatic horizon. Where Schimmelpfennig came to experiment in his elaborate dramaturgic constructions with poetic transformation, Mayenburg found his own way in grossly exaggerated allegory. His writing appears, formally, more immediately accessible; yet one should not overlook the layers of symbolic depth that – in a less overt manner than in Schimmelpfennig's complex plays – open up behind, underneath and all around his seemingly straightforward representations of contemporary reality. In fact, all of Mayenburg's plays transcend the hyper-realities of his scenarios into grotesque exposures of the absurdities of middle-class life under global capitalism. As critic Rüdiger Schaper noted in 2002, comparing Mayenburg to his then Schaubühne colleague, 'Schimmelpfennig is the poet, von Mayenburg the surgeon' (Schaper 2002).

The explicit theatrality of Mayenburg's writing[9] will not surprise, as throughout his career he has been directly involved in theatre-making beyond his own writing. Mayenburg began his career – again like Schimmelpfennig – as an intern at the Kammerspiele in his hometown of Munich. He later successfully applied to the 'Scenic Writing'-class of playwright Tankred Dorst (1925–2017) at Berlin's University of the Arts, and soon became involved in Thomas Ostermeier's ventures at the Baracke and later the Schaubühne; for the director, he also began translating plays, initially not least the work of Sarah Kane. While, echoing Ostermeier, Mayenburg at first had proposed that 'the classics and their eighty-fifth interpretation ought to be buried, at least for some time to come' (cited in Burckhardt 1998: 56), their joint work at the Schaubühne then led them to eventually embrace Ibsen and Shakespeare together, in Mayenburg's contemporary German translations and Ostermeier's congenial modern *mises en scène*. As with Schimmelpfennig, Mayenburg also eventually took to directing,

140   *Peter M. Boenisch*

now regularly premiering his own plays, while also producing works of other playwrights, engaging, in particular, with the distinctly Anglophone tradition of comedy, from Shakespeare (*Much Ado about Nothing*, Schaubühne 2013; *Twelfth Night*, Hannover 2015) to Oscar Wilde (*The Importance of Being Earnest*, Munich 2013) and Alan Ayckbourn (*Family Business*, Bochum 2016). Hence, an Anglophone air of puns, wordplays and punchlines, and at times outright farcical stage business, as in *The Ugly One*, has become – in addition to the stimulus of Kane and other British writers of the 1990s – a second, and in recent German playwriting rather unique, influence on Mayenburg's writerly voice.

His work as a director, as dramaturg at the Schaubühne, and as translator of canonical classics all go hand-in-glove with his own writing, bearing fruit in his plays, which he now usually writes with specific actors from the theatre's ensemble in mind. In 2008, he noted:

> I react to the traditions we are working with in the theatre, I react to the actors. And in my work, I am reading all the time. I'm always looking for what's 'missing', for what isn't being addressed in the plays around me, and then I try to write those plays myself.
>
> (Mayenburg, cited in Croggon 2008)

As critic Peter Michalzik suggested, some formal elements of other playwrights' work – from Shakespeare to Ibsen, Ayckbourn and Kane – find their echo in his plays, yet not as direct quotations, but as mere 'layers one may perceive or not, which however are not needed to understand the surface: the layers add to and enrich the play, but they do not constitute it exclusively' (Michalzik 2008: 35). Michalzik compares this unobtrusive intertextuality to the digital technique of sampling.

Mayenburg's international breakthrough came with *Feuergesicht* (*Fireface*, 1998), which was awarded the Kleist-prize for new writing and became one of the most frequently staged plays of the 1998/99-season in German theatre.[10] First premiered by newcomer director Jan Bosse at Kammerspiele Munich in October 1998, Mayenburg met his congenial interpreter, as then shooting-star Ostermeier produced the play the following year in the studio space of Deutsches Schauspielhaus Hamburg. This production was invited to the Edinburgh Festival 1999; in May 2000, Dominic Cooke premiered Maja Zade's English translation at London's Royal Court; later the same year, Oskaras Koršunovas directed a version that was invited to the Avignon Festival, the first of again numerous, internationally successful productions of Mayenburg's plays by the Lithuanian director. To date, *Fireface* has been staged in more than 40 countries. Kurt, the play's teenage protagonist, filled with adolescent anger against the world, and his parents in particular, builds bombs and sets fire to birds, rubbish bins, clothes, a factory, the church, and to his school from which he had been expelled; eventually, he even kills his well-intentioned, somehow caring, yet entirely non-understanding parents. His sister Olga, with whom Kurt engages in a bizarre incestuous relationship that wavers between fascination and

Marius von Mayenburg and Roland Schimmelpfennig 141

repulsion, at last also decides to break out of their destructive transgression of norms and society, instead returning to her conformist, motorcycle-loving boyfriend Paul, the foil, even nemesis, of pale, geeky Kurt. Paul cannot wait to become a 'proper' adult; he drinks, drives his bike, uses adult language and is much liked by Kurt and Olga's parents – although it also turns out that, at home, he is violently abused by his father. Kurt finds his like-minded spirit in the classical Greek philosopher Heraclitus, whose writings he devours (and which become one of Mayenburg's multiple textual layers beyond the plot surface); in the final moment of the play, Kurt sets himself on fire.

For Ostermeier, as for Mayenburg, life seemed a choice between breaking down in depression over one's utter contempt of the shallow, conformist society all around, becoming an arsonist or even a terrorist, eventually committing suicide, like Kurt – or blending into the superficial life-style, copying the behaviours and adopting the values, like Paul, and eventually Olga. There appeared few other options for their generation born around 1970 into a liberal, mildly affluent middle-class that meant well, and only wanted the best for their children, but at the same time stifled any change or rebellion – as if the parent's generation itself, who would have been active in the 1968 protests, monopolised the right to political action. Almut Eppinger's costumes for Ostermeier's production clearly evoked the 1970s, thereby visually linking the generation of those revolting in the 1990s, like Kurt, with their peers two decades earlier, not least the terrorists of the Baader-Meinhoff group. The production also alluded to the teenage high-school shooters who had begun to shock the US at the time, and soon appeared at German schools, too. *Fireface* thus introduced Mayenburg as a dystopian, 'German in-yer-face' playwright in the wake of Ravenhill, Crimp and Walsh. Yet looking at the play from today's vantage point, one detects core ingredients characteristic of his writing: a sober and prosaic, unemotional and matter-of-fact style of language, spiced with aphoristic (catch-)phrases that transcend the colloquial surface; an unpsychological, type-based, even schematic construction of characters. It is as if Mayenburg's writing, to follow Schaper's metaphor of the surgeon cited earlier, was taking a scalpel that dissected fundamental conflicts of contemporary society, offering a microcosmic sample for observation – to then, ultimately, take the underlying existential conflict to its most extreme conclusion within this laboratory-like set-up of his plays.

Without clear separations in the continuous text, *Fireface* consisted of 94 short scenes, sometimes no longer than a single sentence. Rendering a loose chronology of events, much remained merely evoked and implied, and was not shown on stage – the arson, incest and murder in *Fireface*, or the facial surgery in *The Ugly One*: everything only comes into existence mediatised in language. Even the hardcore realism of *Fireface* had thus been framed, from the outset, by Mayenburg's typical expressive symbolism that veered towards allegory. Ostermeier's production sustained a tempo that corresponded to the play's internal pace and its rhythm of alternating acceleration and slow motion, while never having to revert to actors emoting and shouting to express the urgency of their

142　*Peter M. Boenisch*

characters' feelings. With no blackouts, the actors were always on stage, watching from the side when they were not in the scene, to then quickly step into the next scene, and right out again. The director's 'cool' realism in a Brechtian sense never disavowed the reality of performing either, demonstrating Ostermeier's characteristic blend of a recognisable, tangible scenic realism, shot through by self-conscious theatricality. This approach resonated well with the implicit formal theatricality that already lurked behind the surface of *Fireface*, and which would come ever more to the foreground in Mayenburg's later work, where the plot may be interrupted by musical numbers, while actors address themselves by their real first-names, fall out of character and offer meta-theatrical asides to the audience.

Fireface, above all, mapped out key themes as well as the (European middle-class) universe that keeps appearing in Mayenburg's work in a variety of permutations. We usually meet settled middle-class couples, their offspring, their parents, a number of friends, bosses or colleagues. Against the conservative ideology of the family as the heart of society, Mayenburg exposes contemporary private lives as anything but comforting retreats, but as no less permeated by the individuation of society effected by neoliberal demands that disincentivise community and collective support in both the professional world as well as in personal lives.[11] More or less violently, everyone competes with, or even fights against, everyone else; meaningful communication, let alone any sense of mutual care, is no longer possible in this cold, narcissistic society of individualists, where everyone remains trapped in their own expectations imposed by the neoliberal capitalist system.

Taking his audience further to the limits of an ultimate, hardly bearable catastrophe in *Parasiten* (*Parasites*), premiered by Ostermeier at Hamburg in 2000, Mayenburg's strategy of evoking some form of cathartic cleansing then changed, from *Das kalte Kind* (*The Cold Child*, 2002) onwards, towards an intensifying finale that instead relied on absurdist exaggeration and grotesque farce, leaving behind ever further the confines of realism and believability. He notes that, 'Comedy is the back-door through which I can try to enter the minds of the audience with some unpleasant thoughts, when the front door is locked' (cited in Pearson 2017). I suggest that Mayenburg's encounters with a number of directors who staged his plays at Schaubühne contributed to this refinement of his allegoric approach. While continuing to work with Ostermeier (only once more on his own work, the 2004 *Eldorado*, thereafter as dramaturg and translator), Mayenburg's plays were premiered by directors whose aesthetics could not have been more different. Flemish Luk Perceval (b. 1957), at the time resident director at the Schaubühne, approached *The Cold Child* and *Turista* with visceral, stylised physicality in abstract, metaphorical stage worlds (see Mayenburg 2005). In 2006, Australian director Benedict Andrews (b. 1972) brought *Eldorado* to Melbourne, before premiering, at the Schaubühne itself, *The Ugly One*. Instead of having their performers act out the play's vaguely realistic scenario, Mayenburg, also contributing as production dramaturg, and Andrews invented some elaborate challenges. They kept the actors busy pumping air into apples until they exploded, tying up wires, or being suspended in mid-air on bungee-style, flexible ropes. Mayenburg hence arrived at a more nuanced understanding of the relationship between playtext and stage production, discovering the potential of more abstract and playful *mises en scène* to convey performatively, on a theatrical level, the play's thematic concerns, instead of just illustrating the spoken word.

In this spirit, Mayenburg eventually began directing his own work, such as his 2012 *Märtyrer* (*Martyr*). This play, in particular, appeared like an updated variation on *Fireface*. Where Kurt had taken literally Greek philosopher Heraclitus's suggestion that only those who burn are alive, his counterpart Benjamin, in *Martyr*, builds his half-digested teenage pseudo-philosophy on The Bible.[12] Similarly, the earlier, 2008 *Freie Sicht* (*Moving Target*), commissioned by Andrews for a production at the Adelaide Festival, addressed the fear (or, paranoia) of the parent generation about their pubescent offspring. Throughout his oeuvre, Mayenburg rehearsed a variety of teenage responses to their parents' corrupted world and values; in the 2015 *Stück Plastik* (*Plastic*), the son Vincent revolts by changing his gender, while the final act of cathartic cleansing was then acted out by the maid Jessica Schmitt, who turned into an avenging angel of the neoliberal precariat, poisoning the entire family over dinner, thus echoing the ending of *Turista* (see Figure 7.1). Yet, with the 2017 *Peng* (*Bang*), this motif seems to have come full cycle: the offspring no longer stood for

Figure 7.1 Robert Beyer and Marie Burchard as urbanite city couple, Jenny König as their cleaner, and Sebastian Schwarz as spaghetti-crowned hipster artist (clockwise, from top) deal with the mess of contemporary European middle-class lives in Marius von Mayenburg's own production of his farce *Ein Stück Plastik* (*Plastic*; Schaubühne Berlin, 2015). © Schaubühne Berlin / Arno Declair

144 *Peter M. Boenisch*

revolt and resistance; monstrous baby Ralf 'Bang' embodied the conservative roll-back of the present. In the guise of being a child, he is racist, misogynist and totally selfish, stating, 'I grapple at every woman's blouse or between their legs because: I am still a child. I do it "innocently as a baby". Purely out of "curiosity and joyful exploration"' (Mayenburg 2017). In his characteristic parabolic approach, Mayenburg thus stages the mindset of the time of Trump, Erdoğan, Brexit and the emergence of right-wing, populist leaders across Europe within the setting of a local elite kindergarten, where parents bring up their spoilt brats in the belief that anything is permitted, there are no limits, and they can never possibly be wrong. Mayenburg himself, for the premiere, set *Bang* in a full greenroom environment created by designer Nina Wetzel, which both helped with his usual, quick scene changes, and metaphorically reduced reality to a mere image composed on the screen above the stage.

The socio-political context had significantly changed from 20 years earlier, the time of *Fireface*. Discussing the common threat in the plays, Mayenburg commented in an interview:

> It feels strange to talk about *Fireface* now. Twenty years is a very long time. It almost feels like somebody else wrote the play. I can only say that I was very angry when I wrote it and that I was also very angry when I wrote *Peng*. [...] I do not like the speed with which political situations now change. I am not a fan of revolution. I believe in evolution and would always prefer this to revolution. I want spectacular sporting events, spectacular theatre, and a spectacular life, but I don't want spectacular politics. Politics become spectacular when people get killed. I prefer boring and slow politics.
>
> (Mayenburg, cited in Pearson 2017)

Over the decades, Mayenburg has remained constant in not taking sides, nor suggesting resolutions in his dramatic parodies of the narratives his urban Western middle-class characters live by. From *Fireface* to *Martyr* and on to *Bang*, he juxtaposes perspectives, making the spectator understand both sides, or, perhaps: neither. He refuses to explain, avoiding tangible 'motivations' and clear positions the audience is ostensibly meant to adapt. There are no ready-made 'take-away' messages. Instead, the spectators need to come to terms with what Mayenburg lays out in front of them, in his hyperbolic, and still clinical surgical style:

> I make an attempt to go back a step, and not to give an answer, but to offer a model like situation. [...] I aim with my work for analysis, and I hope that well-put questions will make any exact answer superfluous. If the spectators are made to think and reflect, one may indeed effect change, even improvement. While not finding any answer, the clear insight into the question may lead the audience to say, it's useless to keep treating symptoms, we have to confront the actual cause.
>
> (Mayenburg, cited in Frei 2006: 100)

Theatre as shared dialogue and critical encounter

The works of Marius von Mayenburg and Roland Schimmelpfennig thus reflect a search for, and an exploration of, identity and place in the drastically shifting European cultural formation of the present – which, since 1989, and even more so since the financial crisis of 2008 and its manifold political and socio-cultural repercussions, has been characterised by an encompassing dislocation and disorientation, and the questioning, or outright abolition, of traditional values and established positions that had previously been considered as cornerstone of the humanist tradition of European enlightenment. Following the postmodern deconstruction of the notion of fixed and stable identity and the challenge even to the idea of multilayered, psychoanalytical subjectivity, their generation of German playwrights returned to notions of dramatic characters that were able to resonate with the complex, and not necessarily self-determined psychologies of contemporary 'globalised European' societies. As Schimmelpfennig noted, in an interview conducted by his English translator, 'For me the focal point of the theatre is always people, and people are what make theatre interesting for me, not "text"' (Schimmelpfennig 2014b, 5). Yet, at the same time, their 'post-postdramatic' narrations are characterised by what Peter Michalzik termed 'split drama' (Michalzik 2008: 34): On the surface, there is a layer of realism, yet both playwrights then heighten, transgress, and ultimately bring to its implosion the conventions of mimetic representation of familiar everyday reality, as they attempt to render the experience of globalisation in the form of their plays: Schimmelpfennig primarily in the form of his writing, Mayenburg in particular in his own *mises en scène* of his work. Refusing a unifying central perspective, their dramaturgies remain fragmented, and yet they are highly complex and multi-layered – like reality, which has long stopped being 'well-made' (if it ever was). As a result, their work is characterised by an epic, presentational gesture of parabolic storytelling. It refuses to be observed from a calm, critical distance, let alone to be consumed. Instead, their work addresses the audience, and 'takes apart' their own ambivalent and unstable positions in a globalised Europe. Yet, while thereby confronting the audience, the work of both writers also discloses some form of coming together, as Schimmelpfennig has emphasised in his lectures:

> Dialogue is the core of theatre, and dialogue is the core of any civilised, peaceful society. [...] Let us remind ourselves of the basic premise of theatre: One person speaks, and hundreds listen. The theatre always brings with it such an encounter of I and THE OTHERS. One person speaks, and hundreds listen. This is no one-way street, however, but a vital process [...] Theatre is automatically always about THE WE, the 'common', and the 'common speaking with each other'.
>
> (Schimmelpfennig 2014a: 48, 60)

146   *Peter M. Boenisch*

While neither resolving the problems in the world nor suggesting an aesthetic utopia, their plays thus aim at bringing their audience out of their singularised isolation through stimulating such an encounter in discussing and debate.

Roland Schimmelpfennig – four key productions

Vorher/Nachher (Before/After). Directed by Jürgen Gosch. Designed by Johannes Schütz. Cast: Christiane von Poelnitz, Myriam Schröder, Joachim Meyerhoff, Alexander Simon, Wiebke Puls, Ilse Ritter, Anne Weber, Thomas Dannemann, Ben Daniel Jöhnk, Bernd Moss, Jörg Ratjen, Nicolas Rosa. Deutsches Schauspielhaus Hamburg, 22 November 2002.

Der goldene Drache (The Golden Dragon). Directed by Ed Sylvanus Iskandar. Design: Mimi Lien. Sound design by Katie Down. Cast: Noah Galvin, Peter Kim, K.K. Moggie, Stephen Duff Webber, Welker White. Play Company at New Ohio Theatre, New York, 8 May 2013.

Die vier Himmelsrichtungen / As Quatro Direções do Céu (The Four Points of the Compass). Directed by Camilo de Lélis. Cast: Diogo Cardoso, Maira Holzbach, Renata de Lélis, Tiago Contte. Teatro do Instituto Goethe Porto Alegre, Brazil, 17 April 2015.

Wintersonnenwende / Vintersolstånd (Winter Solstice). Directed by Staffan Valdemar Holm. Design by Bente Lykke Møller. Cast: Johan Holmberg, Anna Wallander, Irene Lindh, Magnus Ehrner, Mattias Silvell. Kungliga Dramatiska Teatern, Stockholm, 17 January 2015.

Marius von Mayenburg – four key productions

Feuergesicht (Fireface). Directed by Thomas Ostermeier. Designed by Rufus Didwiszus. Costumes: Almut Eppinger. Cast: Wolf Aniol, Gundi Ellert, Judith Engel, Robert Beyer, Mark Waschke. Deutsches Schauspielhaus Hamburg, 15 April 1999.

Der Hässliche (The Ugly One). Directed by Benedict Andrews. Designed by Magda Willi. Costumes: Almut Eppinger. Cast: André Szymanski, Bibiana Beglau, Lars Eidinger, Rafael Stachowiak. Schaubühne Berlin, 5 January 2007.

Märtyrer / Muchenik (Martyr). Directed and designed by Kirill Serebrennikov and Vera Martynova. Translated by Alexander Filippov-Chekhov. Cast: Nikita Kukushkin, Yulia Aug, Aleksandra Revenko/Anastasia Pronina, Anton Vasyliev, Victoria Isakova, Svetlana Bragarnik, Irina Rudnitskaya, Aleksandr Gorchilin, Andrey Rebenkov. Gogol Center Moscow, 13 June 2014.

Stück Plastik / Wat nu / Quoi Maintenant (Plastic). Devised and performed by tg STAN (Jolente De Keersmaeker, Sara De Roo/Els Dottermans, Damiaan De Schrijver and Frank Vercruyssen), with an additional prologue by Jon Fosse. Monty, Antwerp, 24 February 2016 (Dutch version), Théâtre Saint Gervais, Genève, 11 January 2018 (French version).

Notes

1 On contemporary German writing, see also Haas 2003; Frei 2006; Gilcher-Holthey et al. 2006; Tigges 2008.
2 All translations from German sources are my own.
3 The German word evokes both a technical compression of a substance, as well as evoking *Dichtung* (poetry), the prefix suggesting an 'over-'condensation – as in 'overcooking' that boils things down to their essence.
4 Following the German approach of theatrality studies (*Theatralitätsforschung*) as pioneered by the late Rudolf Münz and Helmar Schramm, I here and throughout maintain the terminological distinction between fake and deceptive 'theatricality', and the 'theatrality' generated by the dynamics of kinetic movement, semiotic meaning, and aesthetic affection (see Boenisch 2015, Ch. 2).
5 On Gosch's playful directorial approach, see Boenisch 2015: 97–107.
6 To date, Schimmelpfennig has been nominated with nine of his plays. He won the competition in 2010 with *The Golden Dragon*, and again in 2017, in the youth theatre category, with his play *Die Biene im Kopf* (*The Bee in the Head*), written for audience of 8 years and above.
7 On Dorn, see Poppek 2006. Schimmelpfennig wrote *Idomeneus* for Dorn's reopening of Munich's baroque Cuvilliés-Theater following renovation, where it was performed in tandem with Dorn's production (with Kent Nagano as conductor) of Mozart's opera *Idomeneo*, which in 1781 had premiered at this historic Munich venue.
8 The *Zwiefacher* (lit., 'two times') is a traditional Bavarian folk dance, alternating 2/4 and 3/4 beats, believed to be one of the oldest folk dances performed by a closely intertwined couple, rather than as a group dance.
9 See note 4 above.
10 *Fireface* was Mayenburg's examination piece at the University of the Arts. He had already become noted previously for a number of short and full-length plays, such as his 1995 debut *Haarmann* about the notorious murderer of gay men in the 1920s Weimar Germany; *Fräulein Danzer* (1996, prem. 2003, about a social worker brought in to unite a dysfunctional family, which eventually comes together plotting to kill her) had received a rehearsed reading at Berliner Ensemble, and *Monsterdämmerung* (1997) was presented at the Prater-stage of Frank Castorf's Volksbühne.
11 The writings of sociologist Eva Illouz, such as *Cold Intimacies: The Making of Emotional Capitalism* (2007) and *Why Love Hurts: A Sociological Explanation* (2012) have been widely received and referenced by the Schaubühne team, and Illouz has repeatedly given talks at the theatre.
12 The Schaubühne production featured Robert Beyer, the original 'Kurt', as the school director, and 'Olga' Judith Engel, now as the teenager's mother. Translated into more than 25 languages, amongst the non-German productions, Kirill Serebrennikov's staging at the Moscow Gogol Center was particularly successful. He exploited the Russian wordplay of the similarity of 'martyr' (*muchenik*) and 'student' (*uchenik*); the controversial Russian director subsequently turned it into a feature film (2016).

Works cited

Aston, Elaine, and Mark O'Thomas (2015) 'Conversation with Marius von Mayenburg', in Elaine Aston and Mark O'Thomas (eds), *Royal Court International*, Basingstoke and New York: Palgrave Macmillan, pp. 69–76.
Birgfeld, Johannes (2014) 'Nachwort', in Schimmelpfennig (2014a), pp. 94–107.

148 *Peter M. Boenisch*

Boenisch, Peter M. (2010) 'Mission neo(n)realism and a theatre of actors and authors', in Maria M. Delgado and Dan Rebellato (eds), *Contemporary European Theatre Directors*, Abingdon and New York: Routledge, pp. 339–359.

———— (2015) *Directing scenes and senses: The thinking of Regie*, Manchester: Manchester University Press.

Boltanski, Luc, and Eve Chiapello (2005) *The New Spirit of Capitalism*, London and New York: Verso.

Burckhardt, Barbara (1998) 'Lieber tot sein oder besoffen: Marius von Mayenburg und seine Monsterkinder', *Theater Heute*, 5: 53–64.

Croggon, Alison (2008) 'Interview: Marius von Mayenburg', http://theatrenotes.blogsp ot.com/2008/02/interview-marius-von-mayenburg.html

Dreyer, Melanie (2005) 'Roland Schimmelpfennig: Experiments in Dramatic Structure', *TheatreForum*, 27: 16–18.

Frei, Nikolaus (2006) *Die Rückkehr der Helden: Deutsches Drama der Jahrhundertwende, 1994–2001*, Tübingen: Narr.

Fukuyama, Francis (1992) *The End of History and the Last Man*, New York: Simon & Schuster.

Gilcher-Holthey, Ingrid, Dorothea Kraus, Franziska Schößler, (eds) (2006) *Politisches Theater nach 1968: Regie, Dramatik und Organisation*, Frankfurt and New York: Campus.

Haas, Birgit (2003) *Modern German Political Drama, 1980–2000*, Rochester, NY: Camden House.

Illouz, Eva (2007) *Cold Intimacies: The Making of Emotional Capitalism*, Cambridge: Polity Press.

Illouz, Eva (2012) *Why Love Hurts: A Sociological Explanation*, Cambridge: Polity Press.

Lazzarato, Maurizio (1996) 'Immaterial Labour', in Paolo Virno and Michael Hardt (eds), *Radical Thought in Italy: A Potential Politics*, Minneapolis: University of Minnesota Press, pp. 133–148.

Mayenburg, Marius von (2004) 'Desdemonas Taschentuch: Gespräch mit Marius von Mayenburg', *Theater Heute*, 12: 44–56.

———— (2005) 'Schwarzer Humor', in Thomas Irmer (ed.), *Luk Perceval: Theater und Ritual*, Berlin: Alexander, pp. 223–234.

———— (2007) 'Die japanische Lösung: Marius von Mayenburg über sein neues Stück "Der Häßliche"', *Theater Heute*, 4: 46–57.

———— (2017) *Peng*, Berlin: Henschel. (Kindle edn, n.p.)

Michalzik, Peter (2008) 'Dramen für ein Theater ohne Drama: Traditionelle neue Dramatik bei Rinke, von Mayenburg, Schimmelpfennig und Bärfuss', in Tigges, (ed.) (2008), pp. 31–42.

Pearson, Joseph (2017) 'Theatre Shouldn't Make You Feel Safe: Marius von Mayenburg's *Peng*', https://www.schaubuehne.de/en/blog/theatre-shouldnt-make-you-feel-safe-br-marius-von-mayenburgs-peng.html

Poppek, Yvonne (2006) *Was ist ein Dorn? Die Shakespeare-Inszenierungen des Theaterregisseurs Dieter Dorn*, Munich: Utz.

Schaper, Rüdiger (2002) 'Wie eisig ist dies Ländchen: Luk Perceval seziert *Das kalte Kind* von Marius von Mayenburg', *Der Tagesspiegel*, 9 December, https://www.ta gesspiegel.de/kultur/wie-eisig-ist-dies-laendchen/371240.html

Schimmelpfennig, Roland (2009) 'Ein Schwarm Vögel', *Theater Heute*, 6: 36–39.

———— (2011) 'Eine aufregende Zeit, um über das Theater zu schreiben', in *Der Goldene Drache: Stücke 2004–2011*, Frankfurt: Fischer, pp. 713–725.

—— (2014a) *Ja und Nein: Vorlesungen über Dramatik*, Berlin: Theater der Zeit.

—— (2014b) 'The Theatre needs challenges: An interview with Roland Schimmelpfennig', in *Schimmelpfennig: Plays One*, trans. David Tushingham, London: Oberon, pp. 3–6.

Sieg, Katrin (2002) *Ethnic Drag: Performing Race, Nation, Sexuality in West Germany*, Ann Arbor: University of Michigan Press.

—— (2015) 'Race, Guilt and Innocence: Facing Blackfacing in Contemporary German Theater', *German Studies Review*, 38(1): 117–134.

Tigges, Stefan (ed.) (2008) *Dramatische Transformationen: Zu gegenwärtigen Schreib- und Aufführungsstrategien im deutschsprachigen Theater*, Bielefeld: Transcript.

8 Sarah Kane and Mark Ravenhill
The 'blood and sperm' generation

Andrew Haydon

There is a strange, ironic shape to the story of Kane and Ravenhill in Europe.[1] The premières of their respective main stage debuts, *Blasted* and *Shopping and Fucking*, in England are already the stuff of domestic theatrical legend: *Blasted* opens on 12 January 1995, at the Royal Court Theatre Upstairs to near-universal condemnation. *The Daily Mail* runs a review decrying 'This disgusting feast of filth' (Tinker 1995). Nearly two years later, *Shopping and Fucking* opens (26 September 1996) at the New Ambassadors Theatre in London's West End, which has been temporarily redesignated the Royal Court Theatre Upstairs.[2] *The Daily Mail* hails 'a compelling new voice' (Tinker 1996) and the production transfers to the West End proper for a sell-out run, touring nationally for two years including appearances on the Edinburgh Fringe. Kane and Ravenhill are soon grouped together with other writers as members of a distinctive new generation of playwrights.

Superficially, there are similarities between the two plays: primarily violence, swearing, and sexual content. More in-depth study might discover what could be taken to be underlying kindred tendernesses and perhaps even similar stark, left-wing moralities; perhaps even, despite their differing theatrical modes, a similar overall approach to using the stage to generate a wider social metaphor.

However, looking at the subsequent works by each author, the most common theme to each career is a restive formal creativity and, as such, the divergence between their later work is substantial. Where Kane went from shattered naturalism of *Blasted*, through the anarchic punk classicism of *Phaedra's Love* (1996) and the haunted horror show of *Cleansed* (1998), to the modernist, postdramatic emotional landscapes of *Crave* (1998) and *4.48 Psychosis* (2000), Ravenhill's playwriting ranges from the social commentary of *Shopping and Fucking* (1996) and *Some Explicit Polaroids* (1999); Queer historical epic *Mother Clap's Molly House* (2000); plays for young people including *Education* (2004) and *Citizenship* (2005); science fiction plays such as *The Cut* (2006) and *Show 6* (2014); verbatim theatre in *North Greenwich* (2004); adaptations of the classics such as *Totally Over You* (after Moliere, 2003) and opera in *The Coronation of Poppea* (after Monteverdi, 2011); translations of Brecht in *The Mother* (2011) and *Life of Galileo* (2013); experimental pieces like *Shoot/Get Treasure/Repeat* (2008) and *Over There* (2009); and a musical, *The Boy in the*

Dress (2019). Nevertheless, it is interesting to watch the way that these two contemporaries were adopted as something like twin totems for a new European theatre in the late nineties, and what became of that theatre, and indeed that Europe.

While this chapter is concerned less with the plays' reputations at home than with their influence in Europe, it is nonetheless important to note that both *Blasted* and *Shopping and Fucking* were products of their time and place. England in 1995 was about to enter her sixteenth year of Conservative rule, following John Major's surprise election victory against Neil Kinnock's Labour Party in 1992. These latter years of Tory government differed – in tone, if not in policy – from the Thatcherism that dominated the last decade of the Cold War. While Margaret Thatcher's 'Iron Lady' leadership lasted only a year beyond the fall of the Berlin Wall, mere mention of her name still provokes strong reactions in Britain to this day. Her successor rarely succeeded in provoking much more than derision, portrayed as entirely grey by the satirical TV puppet show *Spitting Image* and wearing his Y-fronts outside his trousers like a disappointing superhero by the *Guardian*'s cartoonist Steve Bell. Prior to the airy Blairite branding triumph of 'Cool Britannia' (to which both plays were later subordinated in the popular imagination), the birthplace of these plays – and perhaps a prime factor behind their worldview – was 'Crap Britannia': a country typified by the 'Back to Basics' morality campaign, led by a party so mired in corruption and sexual impropriety that it appeared to haemorrhage ministers on a weekly basis;[3] by a Criminal Justice Act with provisions for stopping young people dancing harmlessly in fields to 'sounds wholly or predominantly characterised by the emission of a succession of repetitive beats';[4] and by a government that lost any reputation it may have had for economic competence when it crashed out of the European Exchange Rate Mechanism (a forerunner to the euro), while Britain held the Presidency of the Council of the EEC.

This farcical state of affairs contrasted with events of historic seriousness on the continent. 1989–91 saw the end of the Cold War, the fall of European communism, the start of the break-up of the Soviet Union, the reunification of Germany and the disintegration of Yugoslavia, during which Europe was suddenly home to a brutal civil war as Yugoslavia's constituent nations were drawn into in a series of wars, ethnic purges, and attempted genocides. Indeed, half of the genesis of *Blasted* is the collision of this disparity between Crap Britannia and the seriousness of civil war in the former Yugoslavia, perhaps also reflecting the UK's fraught and ambivalent relationship with the EU and European identity.

Shoppen & Ficken

At roughly the same time as Kane and Ravenhill were emerging in Britain, in Berlin a young director called Thomas Ostermeier had just graduated from the Ernst Busch academy with an acclaimed theatre piece investigating Artaudian and Meyerholdian techniques. He was quickly recruited by the Deutsches Theater (DT) in Berlin to run their new Baracke venture: 'a tiny little shoebox

152   *Andrew Haydon*

attached to the Deutsches Theater' (Ostermeier 2017). On discovering the plays of Sarah Kane and Mark Ravenhill, Ostermeier recalls:

> There was one dramaturg at DT who was in contact with the Royal Court and Elyse Dodgson [of the Royal Court's International Department] and she introduced him to this new writing, which was Mark Ravenhill and Sarah Kane. Until I turned up, this guy – Michael Ebert he was called – had these plays in his drawer. And he introduced me to this. And it struck me very much. Because I didn't have this experience of reading contemporary writing like a page-turner before. When I first read *Blasted* it was like in one go. Because I was so fascinated by her writing. Ja. That's how I got introduced.
>
> (Ostermeier 2017)

Ravenhill remembers it slightly differently:

> What happened first was – probably as early as '97 – there was a week of English plays – in translation – organised by Elyse. We hadn't heard of them [Ostermeier and his team] before. They had only just started and it was a very young team. And they'd been given this space in the DT, and they wanted to do a week of play readings. So, I would guess Elyse had given them a pile of plays and we all went out there: me and Sarah, Phyllis [Nagy] and Rebecca [Pritchard], and maybe Enda Walsh?
>
> I'm pretty sure Thomas directed the reading [of *Shopping and Fucking*], but then he said he wasn't interested; he wasn't going to do it – they also didn't do *Blasted* for ages either. But then he was in Edinburgh, I think he'd directed a Jon Fosse play for the International Festival,[5] and by that stage we were doing *Shopping and Fucking* in the Assembly Rooms, and I thought, if I just get him to see the production he'll be so infuriated by it – director's pride – that he'll say he knows how to do it. It's a director's nature: if you see someone else's production, you'll be so incensed that they didn't get it right that he'll do it. And it worked like a dream. And because [Ostermeier's production of *S&F*] worked well – like, really, *really* well. I think that tipped them into going back and looking at *Blasted*.
>
> (Ravenhill 2017)

However, it happened – and with 20 years now elapsed, and memories forever mixed into self-mythologising, it is impossible to be certain – Ostermeier's production of *Shoppen & Ficken (Shopping and Fucking)* opened at the Baracke on 17 January 1998.

Ironically, given the typical characterisations of English and German theatre, while Max Stafford-Clark's world première production of *Shopping and Fucking* was played on a highly stylised set, designed by Ultz, with neon sign backdrops and what looked like office-carpeted stage blocks as furniture, Ostermeier's production was more akin to the close-up realism associated with the Theatre

Sarah Kane and Mark Ravenhill 153

Upstairs at the Royal Court. Perhaps the most arresting aspect of Ostermeier's production, though, was this:

> The decision I made in *Shopping and Fucking* was to show the moment where [Gary] is killed with the knife up the ass. I decided you have to show it. And it lasted ten minutes until he was dead. The most disturbing thing was that Gary, he enjoys it. That was the most disturbing thing: he enjoys his death, and you can see the process of him enjoying.
>
> (Ostermeier 2017)

Ostermeier describes how this violent intervention transformed the play as a whole:

> What happened in the play was: the audience was so well entertained up to this moment; the comedy functioned in the most brilliant way … They were laughing their heads off. After this entertainment, I wanted to smash the murder in their faces in order to then prepare for the speech by this asshole [Brian] where he defends the idea of hardcore capitalism: all about money, profit, bam, bam, bam. If you underwent this performance … laughing for one and a half hours, then the big shock of the murder and people go vomiting and fainting, then: house lights on – no more illusions – this speech by Brian had a political impact.
>
> (Ibid.)

Crucially, though, this was a product of Ostermeier responding to the rhythm of the play itself – seeking to make the play more effective *as itself* – rather than imposing an external political narrative onto it (much less 'shock for shock's sake'). Despite his strong personal political convictions, Ostermeier describes himself as a sociological theatre maker, rather than a political one, concerned more with what one can gather from the way people sit, talk, and express themselves, than spelling out an ideological message of his own. In this respect, his style of theatre could be seen to be at odds with the dominant *Regietheater* (literally: director's theatre) tendency in German-language theatre, which requires that a director imposes a strong reading of the text on their production. Ostermeier's productions (certainly of Kane and Ravenhill), in fact, offer their 'directorial interventions' quite lightly. Despite this, Ostermeier's *Shoppen & Ficken* was selected for inclusion in the 1998 Theatertreffen – the most prestigious annual honour for the ten best theatre productions made in the German-speaking world that year. In 1998, Ostermeier had two productions selected, the other being David Harrower's *Messer in Hennen* (*Knives in Hens*).

In hindsight, it is tempting to conclude that these early, cramped, visceral productions cemented the reputations of Ostermeier, Ravenhill, and Kane in Berlin, in Germany, and, from there in Europe. But it would be a fallacy to chalk the success of Kane and Ravenhill entirely up to Thomas Ostermeier and the Baracke. Indeed, while Ostermeier also programmed *Blasted* at the Baracke, he did not direct it himself – the Baracke production was by directed by

154 *Andrew Haydon*

Rüdiger Burbach. Veteran director Peter Zadek opened the German-language première of *Gesäubert* (*Cleansed*) in 1998 at the Hamburger Kammerspiele, with Tinker played by Ulrich Mühe, who would go on to give an acclaimed performance as the Stasi surveillance agent in Donnersmarck's film *The Lives of Others* (2006); Zadek's production was also selected for the 1999 Theatertreffen, while elsewhere *Faust ist tod* (*Faust is Dead*) and *Gestochen scharfe Polaroids* (*Some Explicit Polaroids*) were performed on main stages in Dresden (1998) and Zurich (2000) respectively.

Gier, Gesäubert, and Zerbombt

Nonetheless, when Ostermeier was given the artistic directorship of the Berlin Schaubühne in the year 2000 he put every single one of Sarah Kane's plays into the theatre's repertoire, at the rate of one a season until, in 2005, it was possible to see all her plays there. Indeed, Ostermeier also directed the Schaubühne's first Kane première, *Gier* (*Crave*), in March 2000, and two days later, opened the Schaubühne transfer of the Baracke production of *Shopping and Fucking*. *4.48 Psychosis*, directed by Falk Richter, opened on 3 December 2001 (in a co-production with Schauspielhaus Zürich); *Phaidras Liebe* (*Phaedra's Love*) opened on 8 March 2003, directed by Christina Paulhofer. In 2004, Schaubühne associate Benedict Andrews directed *Gesäubert* (*Cleansed*), and in 2005, Ostermeier himself directed *Zerbombt* (*Blasted*).

Reviewing Ostermeier's *Blasted* at The Barbican, where it ran briefly in 2006, I wrote that it 'is, in many ways, about as far from how one imagines the play as it is possible to get without actually cutting anything' (Haydon 2006). Revisiting this almost a decade and a half later, with more experience of German theatre, I would conversely note the extent to which Ostermeier's production is 'faithful' to Kane's original script. Hopefully, in unpacking my initial surprise, we can also establish a language with which to talk about being 'faithful' to a script, about playwrights' 'intentions', about *Regietheater*, 'directorial intervention', 'off-the-peg' productions and about letting a script 'speak for itself'. My surprise in 2006 came largely from Ulrich Mühe's performance as the shouty, sweary, racist tabloid journalist, Ian. Mühe performed his entire part quietly, well dressed in a pale suit (not the leather bomber jacket of the script), and came across, as I wrote at the time, like 'a slightly depressed German designer' (Figure 8.1). There is always a sense that watching a foreign-language production with surtitles also creates a certain divorce between the words and meaning, but at the time I still found this complete re-imagination of Ian's 'character' bewildering.

Discussing this with Ostermeier years later, he seemed surprised that I'd had such a reaction to it, asking 'What? You don't think middle-class people can also be like that?', which is perhaps key to understanding the most significant change that Ostermeier made to Kane's original dynamic. Ian's class, and his class position within UK society – the working-class tabloid journalist – felt key to my English understanding of Kane's text; Ostermeier's production offers instead a more unsettling and perhaps prophetic take. Rather than presenting a

Sarah Kane and Mark Ravenhill 155

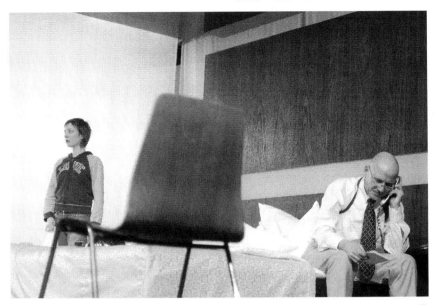

Figure 8.1 Katharina Schüttler (Cate) and Ulrich Mühe (Ian) in Sarah Kane's *Zerbombt* (*Blasted*, Schaubühne Berlin, 2005) directed by Thomas Ostermeier. © Schaubühne Berlin / Arno Declair

working-class racist rapist as in the first British productions, he creates a respectable middle-class man who hides his violence and sexual abuse behind a polite, cold demeanour, a nice suit, and designer glasses. If anything, Ostermeier's production challenges the class comforts that the original production of *Blasted* may have created, in allowing the predominantly middle-class Royal Court audience to displace the sexual abuse and genocidal racism onto a violent working-class man; Ostermeier's Ian was a member of the audience.

Beyond this, Ostermeier's production itself was far more 'beautiful' than James Macdonald's original. The hotel room at last *did* look 'so expensive that it could be anywhere', and the aftermath of the explosion consisted of snow-like ash falling onto the entire stage for minutes, recalling footage of lower Manhattan on 9/11. The running time was much longer, there was more space between everything, and the whole pace was slower, more considered. After the explosion, the realist hotel set was replaced by a bed on a revolve, turning in front of a row of neon strip lights, suggesting that not just the hotel had been destroyed but all the realist conventions of the production's first half.

Oczyszczeni

In 2007, I met some 20 or so fellow young critics from around Europe in Munich at the first of a series of ten international criticism workshops. We were each asked to introduce ourselves and name our all-time favourite piece

156 *Andrew Haydon*

of theatre. My memory is that roughly half the critics in the room named Krzysztof Warlikowski's *Oczyszczeni* (*Cleansed*). I remember being staggered at how widespread and heartfelt this acclaim was for a production of which I'd never heard. It was perhaps a defining moment in my career as a critic: realising just how isolated Britain was from productions (even of *our own plays*) that had achieved such enormous international success on the mainland.

Warlikowski's *Cleansed* opened on 15 December 2001 at the Współczesny Theatre in Wrocław, quickly transferring to production partners the Polski Theatre in Poznań on 9 January 2002 and the Rozmaitości Theatre in Warsaw on 18 January 2002 (continuing in repertoire and on tour thereafter). The production could be described as an unadorned, 'straight' – albeit intercut with excerpts from *4.48 Psychosis* – 'poor theatre' reading. Performed on an almost bare stage – a black floor painted with the basketball lines to suggest a school gym, a black vaulting horse stood to one side – it is really the acting that drives the force of the thing. The stage direction that much of the torture is performed by invisible hands is strictly observed, with actors simply arching in agony at the blows of unseen assailants. The cutting out of Carl's tongue is simply a matter of one actor opening his mouth, the actor playing Tinker making a rapid downward slashing movement with his hand, and the first screaming in pain.

Of Sarah Kane and his production of *Cleansed*, Warlikowski makes a startling comparison:

> What happened to Sarah Kane was something along the lines of what happened with Anne Frank after the war: suddenly, her diaries were found. One might have suspected that in 1946 no one would be interested in what a little girl wrote while hiding out in Amsterdam during World War II. The text was nevertheless published and spoke to many people. In *Cleansed*, viewers have the opportunity to observe something equally personal, equally intimate. They are likely to get the impression that Kane started writing in preschool. If the testimony of Anne Frank was and is so shocking to us – barring literary terms, of course – it was and is because of the directness of that record, a very important directness. I invite viewers to see *Cleansed*, to hear the heroine tell her most hidden and personal things to them. Her confession is very deep and taps into her childhood. In spite of an abundance of fiction, *Cleansed* has the strength of a deep and individual confession.
>
> ('Sarah Kane's Cleansed Directed by Krzysztof Warlikowski' n.d.)

It is fascinating that this is the take of the most celebrated European interpreter of Sarah Kane's *Cleansed* and it perhaps sheds light on the thinking behind his interpolation of sections from *4.48 Psychosis*. It certainly runs contrary to currently prevailing orthodoxy in Britain on how mental illness should be talked about, but clearly something about his interpretation went further than being merely patronising. Indeed, perhaps it is precisely this directness that makes the production so moving, juxtaposing both the metaphor for the agonies of love that Kane saw in *Cleansed*, and what Warlikowski describes as 'diaries' of *4.48 Psychosis*. Arguably, by bringing them together, despite reducing some of the metaphoric ambiguity of each, something new, more stark, and maybe even more forceful is created: a fusion of the public world of *Cleansed* and the private world of *4.48 Psychosis*. Not a 'pure' reading of either play, but instead – as is not unusual in Europe – an auteur's new work, saying what the auteur himself wants to say about love, and perhaps about the author.

Bringing it all back home – Part 1

Given that it was the conflicts between Balkan nations that seemed to provide the genesis of her only two original dramatic plays, *Blasted* and *Cleansed*, it is valuable to consider the early performance history of Sarah Kane's plays in the former Yugoslavia. In fact, as British-based Serbian academic, Duška Radosavljević, notes, 'it took a while before Kane's plays received successful productions [in the former Yugoslavia]' (2012: 507) Not least, one supposes, because many of those countries were still at war when *Blasted* premièred in the UK. Indeed, if one includes the final conflict in Kosovo, and the NATO bombing of Belgrade that ultimately brought the Milošević regime to an end, the wars in ex-Yugoslavia carried on past Kane's death in February 1999.

According to Radosavljević's account, it is Serbian Nebojša Romčević who claims to have been the first Yugoslavian to have read Sarah Kane's work

> when *Blasted* arrived at his desk at the National Theatre in Belgrade in 1996, but he also confesses that despite commissioning a translation and a director, his attempt at putting the play on failed due to the team's fears that they would not be able to find actors prepared to engage in such 'drastic' actions, or the audience prepared to watch them.
>
> (Radosavljević 2012: 508–9)

In fact, it was Warlikowski's *Cleansed* that introduced Kane's work to Serbia almost a decade later at the BITEF festival in 2004. Serbian critic Ana Tasić recalls, '[It was] a wonderful production which definitely made an impact here. Only after that did we have the first domestic production of Kane's work in Serbia: *Blasted*. This was neither good, nor successful' (Tasić 2017). Radosavljević vividly describes this first production at the Belgrade Drama Theatre in 2005, directed by Djurdja Tešić:

> the young director staged the first three scenes realistically and rendered the remaining two as a recitative with the actors standing at microphones […] The act of speaking parts of the text into the microphones and other parts directly to the audience was intended as an analogy of selective media reporting. The play did not come across to [the actors] as 'in-yer-face' but as a piece of realism … [although] they understood that Kane's intention was to bring the war closer to a UK audience.
>
> (509)

158 *Andrew Haydon*

Despite the power of this production, the cast found the piece ultimately 'elitist' and it did not find a broad audience (509). This theme of the 'difficulty' of Kane's work resurfaces time and again in discussion of its production history in the region. Indeed, ironically, given that the plays draw some of their most brutal imagery from the Balkan wars, there were concerns in the Balkans that the plays may upset audiences' and even the actors' sensibilities. Reviewing Bosnia's first production of *Blasted* in 2001, Vedrana Seksan remarked:

> [T]he extent to which Bosnia is a liberal country after all can be gleaned through the fact that this same play has had three unsuccessful attempts at production in Croatia. The reason for this, every time, was the refusal of the actors to be in a play featuring rape, cannibalism and eye-gouging.
>
> (Quoted in Radosavljević 2012: 509)

There was a successful production of *4:48 Psychosis* by Mario Kovač, staged by an independent Croatian fringe theatre company in 2003, but resistance to Kane's work persisted. Two years later, Croatian critic Sanja Nikčević wrote an article denouncing 'New European Drama – the kernel of which is "British Brutalism"' warning that the plays' popularity derived from an apolitical vacuousness that was merely an invitation to directorial intervention. Nikčević likened the plays to horror films that only 'increase an audience's tolerance towards [...] evil' (quoted in Radosavljević 2012: 510). Similarly, in 2008 the Yugoslavian-American scholar Naum Panovski, writing on theatre in the former Yugoslavia, offered the following scathing analysis of the Kane effect:

> Many of the works of these new playwrights and directors, this lost generation, as some call themselves, have been created under the influence of Sarah Kane and Quentin Tarantino ... [they] embraced and adopted Kane and Tarantino's views in their own work, resulting in a blend of gruesome fragmentary dramaturgy mixed with 'pulp' images of the brutal Yugoslav reality.
>
> (2008: 163)

It seems significant that these disparaging views are shored up primarily by misleading comparison with movies, perhaps reflecting legitimate concern about the rapid expansionism of Western culture into Eastern Europe following the fall of the Berlin Wall more than a particularly nuanced critique of Kane's theatrical dramaturgy.

At the same time, both Tasić and Radosavljević note that aside from these sporadic actual productions of plays by either Kane or Ravenhill, their influence was such that part of the reason their own plays received fewer productions was that – as suggested by Nikčević above – the plays themselves had been read and digested by playwrights in the region as inspirations, and rather than pursuing new productions of pre-existing works by these two foreign authors, they began writing their own Kane- and Ravenhill-inspired dramas which spoke even more directly to their local experience and local audiences.

Der Schnitt and Der Stadt

We have noted already the habitual pairing of Mark Ravenhill with Sarah Kane (and their insertion into wider groupings: one of the early German anthologies of new British and Irish work was called *Playspotting*, implying a kinship between Kane, Ravenhill, Martin Crimp, Marina Carr and Danny Boyle's 1996 film about Scottish heroin addicts [see Tabert 1998]). The most decisive break in their work, of course, takes place in February 1999 with Kane's death. While Kane's small, finished oeuvre continues to be picked over and over and reinvented for contemporary audiences, Ravenhill has had the unenviable task of having to come up with new plays which speak directly to them.

Two years after Kane's suicide a further schism takes place, this time between British and German political cultures. Following the 9/11 terrorist attacks on the United States, while Germany committed a small number of troops to the NATO forces fighting the Taliban in Afghanistan (as they had during the civil wars in the former Yugoslavia), in 2003 the country flatly refused to take part in the invasion of Iraq. As such, a major political perspective and experience in British new writing for much of the 2000s was quite alien to Germany or perhaps was of largely anthropological interest, rather than reflecting a shared reality (unlike, for example, *Shopping and Fucking*'s critique of Western capitalism or the dark psychological landscapes of Kane's work). While Britain was right at the heart of the decision to start an illegal war, Germany was on the outside looking in.

In 2008, Thomas Ostermeier created a double-bill staging of Mark Ravenhill's 2006 play *The Cut* (*Der Schnitt*) and Martin Crimp's new play *The City* (*Der Stadt*). Viewed in England, the plays seemed clearly to take place in the shadow of state torture, reflecting Britain's complicity in the 'enhanced interrogation' of her own citizens after 'extraordinary rendition' to 'CIA Black Sites' and was also secretly participating in the torture of foreign nationals, soldiers, and civilians in Iraq. If plays like *Blasted* and *Shopping and Fucking* had sprung partly from the compounded sense of hopelessness that many felt at the end of 16–17 years of Conservative government and the collapse of communism, then – in England, at least – plays such as *The Cut* and *The City* could be read as reflections of the stunned incredulity that (contrary to the adopted Labour anthem of 1997) things could actually get much, much worse. To the Germans, however, this unifying cultural energy appears to have been lost, with many reviews perceiving the marital relationships in each play as the clearest through-line for the evening, were any perceived at all.

A number of reviews called Ostermeier's direction of the plays themselves 'off the shelf' – the German critical go-to term for 'without significant directorial intervention', a disparagement in German theatre-thinking – and it is certainly true that the production of *The Cut* seemed straightforward. The action took place on a grey office-like platform; the characters were dressed naturalistically, in contemporary dress. The actors spoke the lines of the play as if they were inhabiting the characters. If there was any surprise to this

160 *Andrew Haydon*

production of *The Cut* it was in the pairing of it with *The City*, and in the unexpected conceptual framework which Ostermeier placed around it. For the productions – both shown together in one long night of theatre – Ostermeier used the whole of the Schaubühne's long, barn-like space, with all the usual divisions between the spaces removed, so that one play was played on a platform at one end of the space and the other on another platform at the other end. In between the two platforms, there was both an art exhibition and some inter-show contemporary dance performed. Despite this, this artistic framing seemed ultimately presentational, offering the plays up for inspection in a relatively unadorned form – almost, as British directors sometimes say, 'letting the plays speak for themselves'. Ostermeier himself remembers the production fondly and noted that they garnered some excellent reviews, but notes that, for whatever reason, the long evening failed to become a commercial success, and fell out of the repertoire relatively quickly.

Freedom and Democracy, I Hate You

German alienation from the primary concerns of British politics in the 2000s probably also constitutes one major factor in the lukewarm reception of Ravenhill's 2007 play-cycle *Shoot/Get Treasure/Repeat*, retitled *Freedom and Democracy, I Hate You* for its German-language premiere at the Berliner Ensemble in 2010. Directed by former *enfant terrible* of German theatre, Claus Peymann, the production's perceived failure might be ascribed to the widespread perception of Peymann's failing powers as a director. Summarised at the end of a chapter detailing Peymann's otherwise long and controversial career, Marvin Carlson suggested:

> Today Peyman occupies a curiously paradoxical position. His Berliner Ensemble is by some standards the most successful theatre in the capital, with a faithful public that consistently fills it to over 95 percent of capacity. It is an aging public, however, and younger theatregoers as well as Berlin's cultural taste-makers ignore this theatre almost entirely.
>
> (Carlson 2009: 70)

Peyman's production took 11 of the 17 playlets (originally run, one each morning, as *Ravenhill for Breakfast* at the Traverse Theatre during the Edinburgh Fringe, 2007; then staged across London as *Shoot/Get Treasure/Repeat* by the National Theatre, Royal Court, Gate Theatre, Out of Joint, and Paines Plough, and a final epilogue added at the Royal Court later that year). The Berliner Ensemble's *Freedom and Democracy...* was, therefore, the most concentrated form yet taken by the plays. But, strangely, despite having had a far longer amount of preparatory time than any of the English productions – all staged with an ad hoc aesthetic and minimal rehearsal times, often on the sets of other productions – Peymann's staging, such as it was, hardly improved on these impromptu versions at all. *Freedom and Democracy, I Hate You* was played on a large white tiered stage, traditionally associated with German productions of Greek tragedies (indeed, this production also looked like it could well be being played on the set of another), and, generally, it was costumed literally with soldiers in modern military fatigues, housewives dressed as housewives may dress, and so on. It was not an approach that did the plays any favours. Given the licence enjoyed by German directors, taking such an 'off-the-peg' approach to a series of plays not even particularly intended to be played as back-to-back scenes appears almost an act of wilful perversity, and as such, perhaps the most excitingly confrontational gesture of the evening beyond the title.

Andreas Schäfer in *Der Tagesspiegel* complained:

> Subtlety is not Ravenhill's thing, but Claus Peymann misunderstands gross rudeness as realistic flatness. While Ravenhill creates comic scenes, on one hand Peymann takes the characters far too seriously, painting their drama realistically and in slow motion, while on the other hand, incessantly betraying them with meticulous punchlines and silly exaggeration.
>
> (quoted in Behrens 2010)[6]

Meanwhile, in the *Berliner Zeitung*, Ulrich Seidler was

> startled at the applause of the audience in response to the sentence 'Democracy – I hate you!' Is the audience thrilled with the radicalism with which British playwright Mark Ravenhill imbues the scene, or the aesthetic and didactic fearlessness of B[erliner] E[nsemble] director Claus Peymann's stunt production? Or is it anger at the failure of democracy?
>
> (Quoted in Behrens 2010)

Perhaps inevitably, given the piece's British origins and its linguistic pre-occupations, the most positive review overall comes from Ian Shuttleworth in the *Financial Times*, arguing

> we can clearly see characters recurring, and sometimes even an organic flow from play to play, as well as the verbal and thematic motifs. The most obvious of these last are the words 'freedom and democracy' themselves. They serve as an encapsulation of values and lifestyles that are variously imposed, defended, enjoyed, undermined, hymned and excoriated; we see the ways in which these officially sanctioned totems both inform and deform all our lives, through military or police agencies or simply via cultural hegemony. [...] It is no accident that by the end of the evening, the words 'freedom and democracy' sound utterly hollow.
>
> (Shuttleworth 2010)

It seems a pity that what read to British audiences as dense and playful allegories, at once both opaque and almost too transparent in intent, were received so poorly in their German première. It is difficult not to blame Peymann for this. As noted above, his is a style that had fallen from favour. At the time, it was still

162 Andrew Haydon

possible to see, at the Burgtheater in Vienna, some of his much-fêted productions of Thomas Bernhard in repertory, almost identical in style to *Freedom and Democracy*..., with perhaps only the passage of years marking the difference between *succès de scandale* and *l'indifférence complète*. It is also depressing to note that a contemporary German critic could fall into the trap of criticising Ravenhill as lacking subtlety, perhaps thinking of the extended knife-rape of Ostermeier's *Shoppen & Ficken* while doing so. That the scene is wordless, wholly Ostermeier's, and intended anyway as an (admittedly blunt) metaphor, is almost beside the point. But perhaps again, what counts as metaphorical and allusive in English may not always translate into another tongue where the patterned iterations and subtle deformations of language that characterise these playlets may simply seem repetitive. Or perhaps, as with English critics of Kane (versus her often foreign admirers), 'lacking in subtlety' is an indicator of how far any given critic wishes to extend to the writer their credulity, sympathy, or perhaps intelligence.

As such, it is ironic to note that Ravenhill, along with Kane, besides having written some of the most influential plays of the late nineties – plays which beyond their productions, both in Britain and beyond, continued to inspire a generation of playwrights across Europe – quickly outgrew pretty much every label with which he was initially landed; wrongly lauded and deprecated for spearheading a 'movement' – variously 'in yer face', 'blood and sperm', 'Trainspotting/Tarantino' or 'British Brutalism' – he immediately outpaced these labels and left them behind.

There is, however, a fascinating coda to the performance history of *Shoot/ Get Treasure/Repeat* in Germany. In 2015 it was revived again, this time under the title *Wir sind die Guten* [literally: 'We are the good'] at Schauspiel Essen. According to Sarah Heppekausen, '[director Hermann Schmidt-Rahmer] has a clear concern. The decision to stage *We Are the Good* was a response to the attack on Charlie Hebdo. The urgency is palpable, every scene becomes a statement' (Heppekausen, 2015). From the tone of her review, the implication is that the German-language première of the plays came too soon. Several events in the 2010s intensified debates about Germany's immigration policy: Thilo Sarrazin's anti-immigration polemic *Deutschland schafft sich ab* (*Germany is abolishing itself*) was a widely condemned best-seller in 2011; the far-right party Alternative für Deutschland was formed in 2013 and within four years had become the third largest party in the German Parliament; across the decade Angela Merkel executed a *volte face* on immigration, declaring that 'Multiculturalism has failed' in 2010 but opening Germany's borders to Syrian refugees in 2015; these alongside the much-disputed New Year's Eve 2015 assaults in Cologne, the 2016 Berlin Christmas Market truck attack, and other Islamist attacks, meant that many of the questions and paradoxes raised by Ravenhill's text suddenly became much more urgent. Since 2015 there have been other revivals, each set of reviews more accepting than the last. Just as Kane's aesthetics took time to find acceptance in her homeland, so the landscape of Ravenhill's politics in this harshly searching play cycle took time to be appreciated in Europe.

Bringing it all back home – Part 2

Given that this chapter has been concerned with productions of, and the influence of, plays by Mark Ravenhill and Sarah Kane outside the UK, and has bypassed many of the key productions in their country of origin, it may seem perverse to end the chapter by looking at a British production of Sarah Kane's *Cleansed* by a UK director. However, there are several compelling reasons to do so. Throughout this chapter, I have tried to use exemplary productions of plays by Mark Ravenhill and Sarah Kane created using typically European production styles and methods to illustrate their status as distinctively European playwrights, and the way that their plays spread across the continent. In closing, then, I would like to look at Katie Mitchell's production of Sarah Kane's *Cleansed*, which opened at the National Theatre, London, on 23 February 2017.

The production could be seen as both a validation for Kane and a homecoming for Mitchell. Twenty years after its première, a revival by the National Theatre of Great Britain should be understood as an accolade for both play and playwright. Moreover, the fact of its being directed by Mitchell is not insignificant. From 2007, at the invitation of her friend Karin Beier, who was then the artistic director of Schauspiel Köln, Mitchell had begun making work in Germany in parallel to her work in England. Mitchell's work, which British critics had found increasingly alien to their tastes, was acclaimed in the German-speaking world, which recognised the deep seriousness and artistic and political explorations that animated her engagement with theatrical (and non-theatrical) texts. For five years from 2012, Mitchell pretty much only made work in the German-speaking world and her work developed accordingly in an increasingly European mode, engaging with the play text as an artistic equal. For this reason, it could be argued that this *Cleansed* can also be considered a 'European' production as much as a British one. And there was a curious sense of bringing both Mitchell and Kane 'back from Europe' (where Mitchell has also created a version of *4.48 Psychosis* at the Deutsches Schauspielhaus in Hamburg) about the event.

In fact, Mitchell's production itself could be seen as offering the best of both 'British' and 'European' approaches to Kane's work (or, naturalistic and non-naturalistic, respectively). Mitchell herself is a director best known for her meticulous use of naturalism. Indeed, for much of her work in Germany, while being enormously respected, she is seen as something of an eccentric for such stringent adherence to this form, hardly ever used by other 'star' German directors; whereas, in England, prior to her period of 'exile' in Germany, she had been increasingly viewed by older critics as almost wilfully, or perversely avant-garde.

The production took place within one very detailed set – a section of corridor in what appeared to be an institution like a university (as Kane's text suggests). Tinker's encounters with the girl in the peep show took the form of a glass booth being wheeled on and off by the 'unseen hands' (here taking the corporeal form of figures clad from head to toe in black, like *bunraku* puppeteers).

164   *Andrew Haydon*

Press attention during the previews was quickly drawn to accounts of audience members fainting, nightly, in response to the apparently unbearable levels of graphic violence within the piece. In the event, there was very little graphic violence, but the meticulous, unflinchingly realised *preparations* for brutal acts of surgical torture evoked horrific images in the mind, supported by a near-constant nightmarish score and soundscape devised by Paul Clark and Melanie Wilson that provoked remarkable dread and tension.

Mitchell's main invention within the staging, however, was to have the actress playing Grace (Michelle Terry) onstage pretty much throughout the performance, watching from the sidelines when not directly involved herself, turning the entire piece into something like one woman's nightmarish hallucination. This invention – certainly in line with Mitchell's own feminism, and maybe also Kane's – served to centralise Grace's longing for her brother. Mitchell's naturalism here found a reason for all of the play's unreal images, grounding the poetic structure of action in a fully realised portrait of suffering and experiential horror.

Sarah Kane and Mark Ravenhill were quickly identified as radical new voices in British playwriting, but it was their work in Europe that marks their true influence. Their deployment of new violent intensities in their early work offered an experiential picture of a culture out of balance that resonated across the continent, though, as we have seen, in different ways in different cultures. Perhaps their experience of European production encouraged a move in their work towards more open texts that encourage collaboration and mark a move in British playwriting towards what Lehmann (2006) has called the postdramatic. Kane and Ravenhill may have been two early tribunes taking British playwriting out into Europe, but in their practice and influence they have brought Europe back into British theatre.

Mark Ravenhill – four key productions

Shoppen & Ficken (*Shopping and Fucking*). Directed by Thomas Ostermeier. Translated by Robin Detje. Set design by Rufus Didwiszus. Costumes by Marion Münch. Music by Jorg Gollasch. Dramaturgy by Jens Hillje. Cast: Thomas Bading, Jule Böwe, Bruno Cathomas, André Szymanski, Bernd Stempel. Deutsches Theater, Berlin: Baracke, 17 January 1998.

Der Schnitt (*The Cut*). Directed by Thomas Ostermeier. Translated by Nils Talbert. Dramaturgy by Marius von Mayenburg. Set design by Jan Pappelbaum and Magda Willi. Costumes by Almut Eppinger. Music by Alex Nowitz. Video by Julian Rosefeldt. Lighting by Erich Schneider. Cast: Thomas Bading, Judith Rosmair, David Ruland, Sebastian Schwarz, Judith Straussreuter. Schaubühne am Lehniner Platz, Berlin, 21 March 2008.

Freedom and Democracy, I Hate You (*Shoot/Get Treasure/Repeat*). Directed by Claus Peymann. Translated by John Birch. Dramaturgy by Jutta Ferber. Set design by Johannes Schütz. Costumes by Wiebke Naujoks and Johannes Schütz. Lighting by Ulrich Eh. Cast: Larissa Fuchs, Anna Graenzer, Ursula Höpfner-Tabori, Friederike Kammer, Corinna Kirchhoff, Swetlana Schönfeld, Katharina Susewind, Christian Grashof, Boris Jacoby, Veit Schubert, Martin Seifert, Felix Tittel, Georgios Tsivanoglu, Harald Windisch, Thomas Wittmann, Manfred Karge (voice). Theater am Schiffbauerdamm, 29 September 2010.

Wir Sind Die Guten (lit. *We Are the Good*) (*Shoot /Get Treasure/Repeat*). Directed by Hermann Schmidt-Rahmer. Translated by John Birch. Dramaturgy by Carola Hannusch. Set design and Videography by Adrian Ganea. Costumes by Michael Sieberock-Serafimowitsch. Cast: Thomas Büchel, Daniel Christensen, Ingrid Domann, Stephanie Schönfeld, Sven Seeburg, Johann David Talinksi, Silvia Weiskopf. Schauspiel, Essen, 26 April 2015.

Sarah Kane – four key productions

Gesäubert (*Cleansed*). Directed by Peter Zadek. Translated by Elisabeth Plessen, Nils Tabert and Peter Zadek. Design by Peter Pabst. Lighting by Andrè Diot. Choreography by Verena Weiss. Cast: Ulrich Mühe, Susanne Lothar, Uwe Bohm, Knut Koch, Philipp Hochmair, August Diehl, Gabi Herz. Hamburg Kammerspiele, 12 December 1998.

Oczyszczeni (*Cleansed*). Directed by Krzysztof Warlikowski. Translation by Krzysztof Warlikowski and Jacek Poniedziałek. Set design by Małgorzata Szczęśniak. Music by Paweł Mykietyn. Lighting design by Felice Ross. Cast: Tomasz Tyndyk, Stanisława Celińska, Ewa Dałkowska, Małgorzata Hajewska-Krzysztofik, Renate Jett, Mariusz Bonaszewski, Redbad Klijnstra, Jacek Poniedziałek, Thomas Schweiberer, Tomasz Wygoda. Teatr Współczesny, Wrocław, 15 December 2001.

Zerbombt (*Blasted*). Directed by Thomas Ostermeier. Translated by Nils Tabert. Dramaturgy by Marius von Mayenburg. Set design by Jan Pappelbaum. Costumes by Almut Eppinger. Music by Malte Beckenbach. Lighting by Urs Schönebaum. Cast: Ulrich Mühe, Katharina Schüttler, Thomas Thieme. Schaubühne am Lehniner Platz, Berlin, 16 March 2005.

Cleansed. Directed by Katie Mitchell. Design by Alex Eales. Costume by Sussie Juhlin-Wallén. Movement director Joseph Alford. Music by Paul Clark. Sound design by Melanie Wilson. Lighting design by Jack Knowles. Cast: Graham Butler, Peter Hobday, Natalie Klamar, Tom Mothersdale, George Taylor, Matthew Tennyson, Michelle Terry. National Theatre: Dorfman Theatre, 23 February 2017.

Notes

1 In this essay, the name 'Europe', unless otherwise indicated, refers to mainland Europe. This is, of course, a problematic use of the term that risks reinforcing the

166 *Andrew Haydon*

politically fraught British cultural imaginary being both and neither inside and outside Europe and the European project. Nonetheless, perhaps Britain's place at the edge of the continent, but being awkwardly embraced by it, and the complexities of that cultural transformation, is part of the narrative of this chapter.

2 This move was due to refurbishment closing their Sloane Square home; 'Downstairs' was located in the Duke of York's Theatre around the corner.

3 At least, sexual scandals engulfed David Mellor, Steven Norris, Tim Yeo, Stephen Milligan and others, while Jonathan Aitken, Neil Hamilton, David Tredinnick and Graham Riddick were accused of financial misconduct, all of them Conservative Members of Parliament.

4 Wording from the *Criminal Justice and Public Order Act* 1994: http://www.legislation. gov.uk/ukpga/1994/33/part/V/crossheading/powers-in-relation-to-raves/enacted

5 In fact, Ostermeier's first Edinburgh International Festival production was in 1999, well after his production of *Shoppen & Ficken* opened at the Baracke. Perhaps Ostermeier was simply in town for meetings and to see some shows. (Ostermeier was first included in the Edinburgh International Festival in 1999 with a production of Marius von Mayenburg's play, *Fireface*, then again in 2002 with David Harrower's English-language version of Norwegian writer Jon Fosse's play, *The Girl on the Sofa*.)

6 This and the next quotation, as well as the quotation from Heppekausen later, are translated by the author.

Works cited

Behrens, Wolfgang (2010) '*Hoho, keine Angst!* – Kritikenrundschau', *Nachtkritik*, 29 September, https://www.nachtkritik.de/index.php?option=com_content&view=a rticle&id=4727&catid=50&Itemid=100476

Carlson, Marvin (2009) *Theatre is More Beautiful Than War*, Iowa City: University of Iowa Press.

Haydon, Andrew (2006) 'Zerbombt (Blasted) – Barbican', 9 November, https://a ndrewhaydon.wordpress.com/2006/11/09/zerbombt-blasted-barbican

Heppekausen, Sarah (2015) 'Hauptkriegsschauplatz Magen' *Nachkritik*, 26 April, https:// www.nachtkritik.de/index.php?option=com_content&view=article&id=10892&ca tid=97&Itemid=100190

Kane, Sarah (2001) *Complete Plays*, London: Methuen.

Lehmann, Hans-Thies (2006) *Postdramatic Theatre*, Abingdon: Routledge.

Ostermeier, Thomas (2017) Personal interview, 10 July, HOME, Manchester.

Panovski, Naum (2008) 'Old new times: a search for cultural identity in the countries of the Former Yugoslavia', in Dennis Barnett and Arthur Skelton (eds), *Theatre and Performance in Eastern Europe*, Plymouth: Scarecrow, pp. 157–168.

Radosavljević, Duška (2012) 'Sarah Kane's Illyria as the land of violent love: a Balkan reading of Blasted', *Contemporary Theatre Review*, 22(4): 499–511.

Ravenhill, Mark (2001) *Plays 1*, London: Methuen.

———— (2008) *Plays 2*, London: Methuen.

———— (2013) *Plays 3*, London: Methuen.

———— (2017) Personal interview, 18 July, London.

'Sarah Kane's *Cleansed* Directed by Krzysztof Warlikowski' (n.d.) *Culture.pl*, https://cul ture.pl/en/work/sarah-kanes-cleansed-directed-by-krzysztof-warlikowski

Shuttleworth, Ian (2010) 'Review: *Freedom and Democracy, I Hate You*', *Financial Times*, 1 October, https://www.ft.com/content/9164f574-cd82-11df-9c82-00144feab49a

Tabert, Nils (ed.) (1998) *Playspotting: Die Londoner Theaterszene der 90er*, Reinbek: Rowohlt.

Tasić, Ana (2017) Email to author, 24 January.

Tinker, Jack (1995) 'This disgusting feast of filth', *Daily Mail*, 19 January.

———— (1996) 'Review: *Shopping & Fucking*', *Daily Mail*, 4 October.

9 Vasilii Sigarev and the Presniakov Brothers

Staging the new Russia

Noah Birksted-Breen

After the collapse of the Soviet Union in 1991, Russian theatre experienced a decade of stagnation. The transition to a market economy brought economic collapse, cuts to theatre budgets, and political turmoil – as a new elite of former communists stripped the state of most of its assets within a decade. The radical economic reforms of the 1990s led to 'gangster' capitalism and Russia underwent the 'greatest economic collapse in peacetime of any country in history' (Sakwa 2008: ix). This post-communist decade ushered in freedom of speech and press, to a degree which was unprecedented in Russian history. Russia's cultural market was awash with western films, video games, and mass popular culture from abroad. A liberalisation of culture occurred in cinema and fiction but not in theatre. Most artistic directors remained in post beyond 1991 and their tastes were culturally conservative, so they filled their repertoires with conventionally staged classics and commercial entertainment, in a futile bid to navigate the 50 per cent decline in attendance at most theatres.[1] The critic Alena Zlobina characterised the driving ethos of programming in this period an 'attempt […] to leave behind topical relevance' (1998). This post-1991 tendency towards 'escapism' erased the sense of moral purpose, which prevailed as the fundamental ethos of Soviet theatre (among propagandist and dissident theatre-makers alike).[2] Psychological realism – an ossified variation of Stanislavsky's teachings, propagated by the Soviet regime – remained dominant on most stages. With reduced budgets and no agenda for theatrical experimentation, contemporary playwriting was pushed to the margins. Most Soviet-era playwrights were unable to respond – in form or content – to Russia's precipitous transformation into a new 'wild east'. Established playwrights 'either wrote less, stopped writing altogether, or were produced significantly less than in the 1980s' (Freedman 2010: 390). Yet, disillusioned with the 'bourgeois' turn in Russian theatre, a small number of Soviet-era dramatists founded playwriting journals, festivals, competitions, and studio theatres, dedicated to contemporary dramaturgy.[3] This 'alternative' theatrical infrastructure – which I have argued elsewhere was unprecedented in Russian theatre history[4] – offered unparalleled artistic and intellectual freedom to a post-Soviet generation of playwrights. Emerging in the late 1990s, this 'fringe' was a counter-cultural movement which allowed younger dramatists to side-step centuries of Russian dramatic tradition, drawing upon a diverse range of cultural sources including western art-house films and mass culture.

Vasilii Sigarev and the Presniakov Brothers 169

By the beginning of the twenty-first century, a younger generation of playwrights working in this 'fringe' started coming to the attention of critics, artistic directors and, over the course of the decade, even reaching mainstream audiences. Among the pioneers of a post-Soviet aesthetic were the playwrights Vasilii Sigarev (b. 1977) and the Presniakov Brothers (Oleg b. 1969, Vladimir b. 1974). Sigarev developed a distinctive form of realist playwriting, based on the conventions of the late Soviet period, while the Presniakovs were creating post-modern dramas which spoke to European dramatic traditions. In spite of their strikingly different aesthetics, the aims of Sigarev and the Presniakovs were similar: to refashion Russian dramaturgy in a way which would invest it with socio-political relevance; and to offer new modes of communication with audiences. With Russia's decisive turn towards authoritarianism with the election of Vladimir Putin to the presidency in 2000, Sigarev and the Presniakovs were creating expressions of cultural resistance to the establishment's bankrupt ideology. The main aims of this chapter are, firstly, to analyse the key dramaturgical interventions offered by these writers within Russian theatre and, secondly, to assess their contribution to European theatre. Ultimately, I consider how the *oeuvre* of these dramatists speaks to the conflicted relationship between Russian cultural thought and a broader European cultural practice.

1000 miles east of Moscow

Both Sigarev and the Presniakov Brothers were born and lived their formative years in the Urals region, approximately 1000 miles east of Moscow. Ekaterinburg, the regional capital of the Urals, is an industrial city of historical significance – the last Tsar of Russia, Nikolai II, and his family, were executed by the Bolsheviks there in 1918 – with a counter-cultural legacy from the Soviet era (Vedernikov 2003). Although the emergent 'fringe' in post-Soviet theatre played a pivotal role in the aesthetic evolution of Sigarev and the Presniakovs, their trajectories into theatre were significantly different – revealing a fundamental distinction in their approaches to playwriting. Sigarev's route into stage writing came fortuitously. He grew up in Verkhnaia Salda, a mid-sized town (without a theatre) in the Urals, to working-class parents: his father was an electrician in a factory and his mother worked on a poultry farm. From the outset, Sigarev's dramas were largely inspired by the people and stories of his hometown. He has stated that 20 years of living in Salda 'might even be enough for a whole lifetime of creativity' ('Vasilii Sigarev' 2003). This personal knowledge of provincial Russian life runs through his dramas. Crucially, he empathises with Russia's working class, stating provocatively in one interview about himself and the actor Iana Troianova, his regular collaborator and wife: 'we are the *bydlo* [lit. plebs, masses, trash]' (Shakina 2009). As a teenager, Sigarev dreamed of being a prose writer (Raikina 2002), but the prestigious Gorky Literary Institute in Moscow – Russia's only vocational course for prose writers after 1991 – was 'too far away' (ibid.). After completing two years of tertiary study on a chemistry and biology degree, Sigarev applied to join the Ekaterinburg Theatre Institute's

170   *Noah Birksted-Breen*

newly instituted playwriting course, founded by Nikolai Koliada. As one of the pioneers of grotesque social realism (*chernukha*), Koliada enjoyed a huge critical success and became one of Russia's most famous playwrights during *perestroika*.[5] Sigarev wrote the majority of his *oeuvre*, including his most acclaimed dramas *Plasticine* and *Black Milk*, while he was a student on Koliada's course.[6] This Soviet-era *provocateur* had a formative influence on the younger playwright, as Sigarev has himself acknowledged (Shkola zlosloviia 2010).

The Presniakov Brothers also found a spirit of opposition in their Urals upbringing, noting the importance of not being from Moscow, while rejoicing in the regional character of 'unpolished energy [and] brazen impudence' (Presniakov Brothers 2018). Like Sigarev, the Presniakovs cultivated oppositionality towards the Moscow establishment as well as the dominant culture of psychological realism in their *oeuvre*. However, the Presniakovs chose an academic route, both studying as undergraduates and postgraduates at the Urals State University. By the mid-1990s, Oleg and Vladimir were teaching at the university, literature and sociology, respectively, and they both intended to pursue academic careers (ibid.). Referring to the large quantity of international art-house and popular culture entering the Russian entertainment market, Oleg has described how, prior to 2000, 'the students were fascinated by everything [...] but there was nothing interesting going on [in local cultural circles]' (ibid.). Both brothers had a predilection for theatre, so in 1994, they provided the students with an outlet for their creativity, by founding the theatre named after Christina Orbakaite at the university. The choice of a figure drawn from the sphere of popular culture – Orbakaite is a Moscow-born Lithuanian pop-singer (b. 1971) – reveals the Brothers' intention to disrupt the distinction between *high* and *popular* art. Their amateur company played occasional productions in the Urals' State University's assembly hall (seating around 300 people). This makeshift theatrical venue was poorly equipped. Nevertheless, it was 'a cult place, at one point Gorbachev and Yeltsin had given a speech there [in the *perestroika* era]' (ibid.), so it offered an ambience of intellectual excitement. In a society which was experiencing economic freefall and social dis-integration, theatre was an 'instrument [...] to unite people' (ibid.), in order to create individual and collective meaning through shared counter-cultural activity. The Brothers' aesthetic was forged at this student theatre. They began by staging revivals of the classics but, by their own account:

> We gradually began to understand that, [in order] to speak to the auditorium truthfully, bluntly, without insincerity, then there was nothing to offer them, so we began to write [our own plays].
>
> (Dmitriev and Pozdniakova 2009)

Their phrase 'there was nothing' refers both to the outmoded naturalism across Russian theatre as well as the outdated aesthetics of playwriting by most of the Soviet-era generation of dramatists. While the Brothers drew upon contemporary speech patterns and referenced popular fashions, such as the sushi bars appearing in Moscow at the turn of the millennium,[7] their approach was conceptual. They have defined

Vasilii Sigarev and the Presniakov Brothers   171

their writing style as being 'founded on irony, word-play and inter-textuality' (Presniakov Brothers 2018). This approach distanced them both from Sigarev's grotesque realism but also verbatim playwriting, which became the dominant form among the post-Soviet generation of dramatists after 1999.[8] The Brothers stated pointedly: 'we never walked around with a notepad or dictaphone' (ibid.). They have even emphasised that the central conceit in *Playing the Victim* – in which the protagonist aids police investigations by re-enacting the role of murder victims – is entirely fictitious (Dmitriev and Pozdniakova 2009). This playwriting duo aspired to formal experimentation in playwriting, based on alternative, non-realist traditions:

> Remixes of melodies are widely accepted but there's no tradition of that in playwriting. [...] We are creating the precedent of play-remixes.
> (Dmitriev and Pozdniakova 2009)

While Sigarev has also worked in different media, primarily recreating his own plays as films, he has – in practice – treated his texts as 'finished' works with stable meanings. By way of contrast, the Brothers undermine the notion of fixed meanings through multiple iterations of their plays: *Playing the Victim* exists in two significantly different stage versions (2003, 2004), which I explore below, as well as incarnations as a film (2006) and as a novel (2007). With a particular interest in European and western art-house culture, such as the film *Trainspotting,*[9] the Presniakovs forged a postmodern dramaturgy which altered the Russian theatre landscape.

Sigarev: A pioneer of 'impossible' realism

In 2001, a Moscow 'fringe' production of Sigarev's most stylistically daring play, *Plasticine*, at the Centre for Playwriting and Dramaturgy (founded in 1998) came to be seen by many theatre-makers as a watershed moment in Russian playwriting. The critic Pavel Rudnev characterised it as 'one of the manifestos' (2018: 338) of a new Russian dramaturgy because of its experimental approach to realism as a genre, as well as its smashing of socio-cultural taboos. There was significant resistance to *Plasticine*, even among theatre-makers. Directors and programmers objected to its fragmented structure, more than its graphic content. Objections appeared to contradict each other, but were in fact capturing two aspects of the play's multifaceted composition. The critic Grigorii Zaslavskii has recalled the jury deliberations (of which he himself was a part) at the Anti-Booker Award[10] in 2000:

> [The director] Joseph Raikhel'gauz[11] was saying that this isn't a play, it's a film script, and how can we award it the prize? And [the artistic director and actor] Oleg Tabakov[12] [...] said: 'I also don't how it can be staged but I think that whoever stages it [to critical acclaim] will have discovered a new type of theatre'.
> (Khochesh' 2015)[13]

172   *Noah Birksted-Breen*

Conversely, some theatre-makers perceived *Plasticine* as old-fashioned. Vladimir Pankov, the composer and sound designer of the Moscow production, has reflected on his initial reaction to this play:

> I said to [the director Kirill] Serebrennikov: are you crazy or what? This is a typical *perestroika* text, how could it be interesting to stage it today? It's pure *chernukha*.

(Moguilevskaia 2006: 29)

These apparently contradictory perspectives – a play being both experimental and conventional – can be reconciled when considering Sigarev's aesthetic evolution. Inspired by his playwriting pedagogue, Koliada,[14] the younger dramatist developed precisely observed realistic portraits of post-Soviet Russia's emergent 'underclass'. He constructed dialogues which evoked 'a 1990s Urals' idiom' (Rudnev 2018: 354), while mostly adopting two-act structures – the form favoured by his playwriting teacher.[15] Sigarev used two-act narratives to depict routines, based on self-delusion (act one), from which the protagonists attempt to escape but cannot (act two). Sigarev's dramas were grittier and more transgressive than his mentor's *oeuvre*. While Koliada composed carnivalesque and cathartic 'melodramas' (Shcherbakova 2015), the younger playwright depicted 'down-and-out' provincials suffering humiliation and abuse, while offering no comforting resolutions.

Another influence between pedagogue and student, entirely overlooked by scholars and critics to date, may be observed in Sigarev's conceptualisation of the relationship between play text and live performance.[16] In most of his seminal plays, Sigarev intersperses dialogue with lengthy lyrical stage directions. As Sigarev's own production of *Black Milk* in Ekaterinburg in 2004 demonstrates, this dramatist perceives these lyrical passages as an invitation to directors to create non-naturalist, gestural sequences. The perverse love between two itinerant con-artists from Moscow, Levchik and his oppressed wife Shura, in *Black Milk*, is evoked with a visual leitmotif. In the first act, the stage grows dark and a spotlight isolates the hands of the actors, Oleg Iagodin and Troianova (playing Levchik and Shura), holding Chupa-Chups lollipops, which knock into each other rhythmically, associative of a romantic and sexual encounter. This sequence is underscored by *I Know What You Want* (2002) by American rap singer Busta Rhymes, creating a vivid atmosphere, akin to a pop concert. Sigarev's multi-layered realism invites audiences to experience affectively – more than cerebrally or didactically – the traumatic experience of Russia's 'underclass', and allegorically the plight of a traumatised post-Soviet generation. *Black Milk* offers at least a glimmer of hope for spiritual redemption, albeit one which is swiftly extinguished. Levchik and Shura's itinerant journey of petty crime, selling overpriced toasters to gullible locals, is interrupted when the pregnant Shura goes into labour. With no local hospital in the village, Shura is forced to give birth at a local woman's home. An emotional bond develops between Shura with this older villager, Auntie Pasha, who is presented as naive but

Vasilii Sigarev and the Presniakov Brothers   173

spiritually enlightened. The tenderness in this relationship, as if between a mother and daughter, leads to a religious awakening in Shura – which she is unable to fully realise. When Levchik abducts their baby, his wife is forced to recommence their life of fraud. Sigarev creates the image of rural Russia as a place of potential spiritual rebirth, too often crushed by metropolitan cynicism and amorality.

While continuing to draw on real prototypes from the Urals, *Plasticine* evidences a new departure in Sigarev's aesthetic evolution, moving yet further from his mentor's influence towards a bleaker aesthetic as well as drawing upon non-theatrical inspirations. The fragmented form of *Plasticine* suggests that, like many post-Soviet playwrights,[17] this dramatic writer was drawing stylistically on Hollywood's art-house films. However, Sigarev has acknowledged the influence of Stephen King's 1982 novella *The Body*, particularly its suspenseful plotting and atmosphere, which he was imitating in *Plasticine* (Shkola zlosl*o*viia 2010). Like King's novella, *Plasticine* is a peripatetic and tragic 'coming-of-age' story, narrating the final days in the life of the protagonist, Maksim, a school-boy in an unnamed small town in Russia. When a female teacher punishes the boys for smoking in the school toilets, Maksim resolves to take a juvenile act of revenge. The protagonist fashions a plasticine phallus and, when the teacher next enters the boys' toilets, he exposes his (real-looking) plasticine penis to her.[18] Maksim is expelled – and the majority of the narrative is a peripatetic tale as he explores his town, only to receive cruel and abusive treatment at the hands of the disenfranchised and passers-by. With an unsparing descent into a nightmarish vision of rural Russia, Maksim and his best friend Lyokha are raped by escaped convicts. Unlike King's optimistic ending in *The Body*, where the narrator-protagonist channels his traumatic experiences into creative writing, *Plasticine* proposes death as the sole escape from society's brutalising violence. This play ends with Maksim returning to take revenge on his rapists, only to be pushed from a high window, presumably to his death. Departing from his favoured two-act structures, Sigarev wrote *Plasticine* in 33 short scenes, some consisting mainly of visual storytelling. By fragmenting the narrative, this play-wright provides the impression of a subjective (hence cinematic) viewpoint. The artistic achievement in *Plasticine* was recognised by Elena Koval'skaia – a theatre critic advocating new, unconventional dramas – who praised Sigarev for having written 'an impossible play' (2003). Her use of the term 'impossible' recognises the extent to which the playwright had advanced forms of realist dramatic writing. By marrying *chernukha* with western mainstream and art-house cultures, Sigarev forged a distinctive post-Soviet 'voice' which – more significantly than any other since 1991 – popularised Russian dramaturgy in Russia and Europe.

Serebrennikov's ability to unlock this play's multifaceted genre was a significant factor in *Plasticine*'s critical success – and the subsequent shift in cultural discourse among Russian programmers and theatre-goers who incrementally accepted the aesthetics of post-Soviet dramaturgies. In his first Moscow production, this experienced director provided a visually rich and physically-stylised interpretation. In her review of *Plasticine*, Koval'skaia points out that Serebrennikov created 'a new text, a scenic one' (2003), which overlays the author's play 'without hitting a

174   *Noah Birksted-Breen*

false note against it' (ibid.). In other words, this director added visual leitmotifs, not included in the stage directions, to augment the themes of the play. This director's theatrical text, his visual storytelling, is woven from the different genres, combined within the play. Particularly notable – and unexpected for those who overemphasise this play's genre as a 'gritty' realist drama – are the farcical sequences and highly stylised choreography. When Maksim reveals his replica penis to the teacher, the text ends with the stage directions: 'A silent scene' (Sigarev n.d.). Sigarev does not specify what his 'silent scene' should consist of. The scholar Tania Moguilevskaia (2006) has made an insightful comparison to the canonical silent scene in Russian theatre: the dramatic coda to Nikolai Gogol's play, *The Government Inspector* (1835). This resonance is not coincidental: Sigarev has cited Gogol as the only canonical Russian author whose work he re-reads (Shkola zloslovija 2010). Sigarev's admiration of Gogol is a useful reminder that his plays, however much they resemble European social realism, are also related to Russian traditions of the grotesque, which often combines the tragic and comic. Perceiving this direct lineage, Serebrennikov staged the silent scene in *Plasticine* as stylised farce. Confronted by the phallic model, the teacher, played in drag by actor Vitalii Khaev, stumbles wildly around the stage in shock, crashing against the furniture and even fainting twice – over the course of almost 90 seconds (Spektakl' "Plastilin" 2013). By evoking this grotesque tradition, the director foregrounds the theme of existential and psychological trauma in Sigarev's text, rather than overemphasising its *implicit* social critique.

The predominantly conservative gender politics woven into the texture of Sigarev's plays become even more evident in Serebrennikov's production of *Plasticine*. It is important to note that Sigarev was defying the arch-conservative sexual politics of post-Soviet Russia, particularly in his ability to create narratives which challenge brutish masculinity. In *Plasticine*, the playwright even fleetingly portrays gay desire (Sigarev 2002: 12–13) – rarely represented in Russian theatre. Yet, the playwright's gender politics are not progressive by European cultural standards. The female characters in *Plasticine* – as well as throughout his *oeuvre* – are usually depicted as either sexually exploitative or as victims. While no doubt contributing to a broader European canon by expanding the conception of what might constitute realist dramatic writing, any consideration of Sigarev's 'impossible' realism nevertheless needs to take account of the male heterosexual bias of the writing.

The Presniakov Brothers: Creators of postmodern 'remixes'

When *Terrorism* premiered at the Chekhov Moscow Arts in 2002, the theatre programme referenced the national, and even international, significance of this cultural intervention with two photographs on the same page. An iconic image of Chekhov, Stanislavsky, and the Moscow Arts' actors was juxtaposed with a contemporary photograph of the Presniakov Brothers, Serebrennikov, the director, and the acting ensemble. The creative team of *Terrorism* were all imitating exactly the same postures as Chekhov and his contemporaries. With this provocation, this theatre symbolically, albeit with ironic bravado, notified the mainstream theatre-going public of its embrace of a postmodern dramaturgy. In their debut Moscow production and in *Playing the Victim*, staged at the same venue in 2004, the Brothers were depicting post-Soviet Russia as a spiritual vacuum. This collective existential crisis creates the conditions for a horrifying type of violence in their plays, which is frequently disproportionate, unmotivated or irrational. In *Terrorism*, this playwriting duo reposition this endemic violence as a global phenomenon. Divided into six scenes, this play is set in disparate locations around an unspecified Russian city, most likely Moscow. There is a circularity to the structure since the play begins with Passenger,[19] who is delayed by a bomb alert at an airport; in the final scene, he is on board a plane, a few hours later. Each scene provides clues for its narrative connection to the overriding storyline: the 'bomb scare' prompts Passenger to return home, where he discovers his wife being unfaithful, after which he orchestrates a gas explosion to kill her. The other scenes depict unwitting participants in his act of revenge or those with a tangential relationship to the main narrative. This drama seeks to reframe the public discourse around 'terrorism', by depicting cultures of violence embedded into the daily routines of nominally 'developed' societies.

Where Sigarev uses the adolescent consciousness to evoke a traumatised society, the Brothers write philosophical dramas, portraying the post-Soviet generation as the cypher for the postmodern condition. In *Playing the Victim*, the Brothers interweave alternating scenes from Valia's personal and professional life. So unstable is this 30-year-old's sense of self that, in the first version produced in 2003 at the Royal Court, the Brothers do not provide him with a character name (except when he is at work with a defined role to perform). Valia's existential dread affords him an ironic detachment, through which he perceives that life in the postmodern era is 'one long, forensic experiment … the real crime is to give birth, to bear a person' (Presniakov Brothers n.d. [2004]: 42). Both versions of *Playing the Victim* revolve around a depiction of Valia, while also providing the Soviet generation's perspective of this protagonist. In both versions, *Playing the Victim* contains one of the most famous scenes in Russian theatre history. During one forensic reconstruction, the Captain (Valia's boss) expresses his exasperation at the senseless murders, committed by the younger generation, which he investigates. In response to Verkhushkin's admission that he 'popped' a bullet into his victim, the Captain responds:

> You popped him! *Popped* him. You think it was a toy gun? The bullets were real! … Like fucking children! They buy themselves all sorts of shit, the pederasts! And then we gotta clean up the whole mess! You fucking idiot! How did you even get a gun? How do you people even get any of your shit?! What fucking planet do you come from?! […] We studied at the same schools, we had the same teachers, your parents are pretty much my contemporaries, for fucks' sake! How did you turn out like this?!
> (Presniakov Brothers n.d. [2004]: 36)

The Captain's outburst perfectly encapsulated the confusion of the Soviet generation towards the apparently consumerist and apathetic post-Soviet generation. Simultaneously, the Captain's extended monologue transgressed a long-standing socio-cultural taboo in Russia of swearing on stage, by using manifold profanities – mentioned in six reviews by national critics[20] – on a sacrosanct stage at Russia's 'high arts' theatre.

What differs between the two versions of *Playing the Victim* is primarily the intended form of spectatorship. The earlier version offers a metatheatrical 'coda' which deconstructs the fictional on-stage world. Two new characters are introduced in its final scene. An unnamed director proposes an idea for a new play, to an unnamed writer:

> Other Man: A bloke [has] an unusual job, he pretends to be a victim [...] during forensic experiments.
>
> (Presniakov Brothers n.d. [2003]: 49)

In other words, this scene purports to portray the 'real-life' genesis of *Playing the Victim,* destabilising any sense of narrative resolution. By the 2004 version, produced at the Chekhov Moscow Arts, the Brothers had rewritten this drama within a canonical frame of reference. With clear overtones of Shakespeare's *Hamlet,* Valia's dead father appears to the protagonist at the start of the play, speaking in verse, to inform his son that he was poisoned by his wife and brother (see Figure 9.1).

Figure 9.1 Petr Kislov's Valia sees a nightmarish vision of his late father, played by Vitalii Khaev, in Kirill Serebrennikov's production of the Presniakov Brothers' *Izobrazhaia zhertvu (Playing the Victim)* (Chekhov Moscow Arts Theatre, Moscow, 2004). Photograph © Oleg Chernous

Vasilii Sigarev and the Presniakov Brothers   177

Resonating with *Hamlet*, Valia murders his mother and uncle – by serving them poisoned sushi. It is striking that the ghost in this new version of *Playing the Victim* never demands revenge, instead only demanding that Valia should 'bear a child' (Presniakov Brothers n.d. [2004]: 3). Allegorically, there will be no rebirth for Russia with Valia's generation, either literal or spiritual. In the spirit of postmodernism, the Brothers provide both versions of *Playing the Victim* to potential producers, without privileging one over the other (Presniakov Brothers 2018). This approach further undermines the notion of a definitive literary original. Furthermore, the Presniakovs expect directors to make textual changes to serve their directorial vision, which contrasts with Sigarev's embedding of a performative language into his dramas. Each work has the potential to become a dramatic remix – a new iteration of their play with its own distinctive form and meaning. In Serebrennikov's productions of *Terrorism* and *Playing the Victim*, he forged an ironically detached directorial tone which, as one reviewer suggested, 'did not amplify the tragedy in the slightest' (Solomonov 2002). This director established the Brothers as the *fathers* of a postmodern dramatic tradition in post-Soviet Russia, while signalling their relevance – aesthetically, thematically – to a broader European and western cultural discourse.

Sigarev and the Presniakovs in the UK and continental Europe

More than any other single factor, the Royal Court in London has influenced the reception of Sigarev and the Presniakovs in Europe. Globally renowned for its advocacy of contemporary playwrights, this company became actively engaged in Russia from 1999, running seminars about 'new writing' (Aston and O'Thomas 2015: 32–5). This cross-cultural relationship led to five premieres in Europe: Sigarev's *Plasticine* (2002), *Black Milk* (2003) and *Ladybird* (2004), as well as the Presniakov Brothers' *Terrorism* (2002) and *Playing the Victim* (2003 – a world premiere). Although presented in the Upstairs Studio, these productions created an awareness of the post-Soviet generation of playwrights beyond Russia, particularly after Sigarev became the first-ever non-British recipient of an Evening Standard Most Promising Playwright Award for *Plasticine*. A range of approaches was used by directors towards these writers, although what emerges is a dominant tendency towards naturalist conventions, especially in relation to performance style. In the interpretations of Sigarev's dramas, the primary cultural translation which occurred was the use of an expressive scenography, in order to evoke the non-naturalist properties of this writer's texts. The boldest example of this approach was Dominic Cooke's visually inventive production of *Plasticine*. Surprisingly, given the Court's tradition of 'new writing', Cooke has recalled objections to this play, which echoes the Russian theatre industry's reservations:

> At a script meeting, where [*Plasticine*] was discussed, there was a feeling that it was really a film script and shouldn't be produced at the Court. However, the [rehearsed] reading [at the Court in 2001] revealed that it took the

178 *Noah Birksted-Breen*

audience into a subjective experience rather than a literal one and in that way was very theatrical.

(Aston and O'Thomas 2015: 94)

Understanding that he had to 'do something radical spatially' (ibid.) in his production to respond to the play's fragmented form, Cooke – and designer Ian McNeil – created a promenade production in the studio space. In order to depict rape, the actors stood on a platform, several metres high, which moved across the auditorium, reducing the available standing space for the audience – evoking the protagonist's feeling of suffocation and trauma. Interpreting Sigarev's stage directions in a literal manner, Cooke staged the representation of rape off-stage, hidden by the platform, but audible to the spectators. This approach disrupted a passive spectatorship, while continuing to speak to the conventions of televisual naturalism familiar to most British audiences.

The playfully parodic tone of the Presniakovs' dramas encouraged the Court's directors to depart further from naturalism. The most striking disruption was taken by the director Richard Wilson who staged *Playing the Victim* 'almost as a piece of stand-up comedy' (Presniakov Brothers 2018) – a response to Valia's monologues in the earlier version. Wilson's production began with an extended silence by the actor Andrew Scott (playing Valia), who made eye-contact with the audience, to provoke discomfort and ultimately laughter from the audience (ibid.). What unifies these diverse approaches to Sigarev and the Presniakovs was the overarching practice by British directors of working within an Anglo-American text-centric and broadly naturalist paradigm. Their aesthetic minimalism privileged the socio-political effect of these plays, in order to portray a nightmarish vision of a distant foreign culture. This tendency towards naturalism – and Russia as a cultural *other* – was consolidated by the translator of all five plays, Sasha Dugdale. Elsewhere, Dugdale has reflected upon her decision to make Sigarev's grotesque and highly stylised obscenities more natural-sounding in English (Beumers and Lipovetsky 2009: 21). The significance of this becomes evident in her rendition of Sigarev's stage direction 'a silent scene' in *Plasticine* into 'There is silence' (Sigarev 2002: 18). Her translation implies a passive resolution, rather than non-verbal storytelling. Under the well-documented pressures on the play translator to 'tone down' cultural difference (O'Thomas 2014: 127), Dugdale's translations of Sigarev offered a greater cultural approximation to Anglo-American naturalism, most likely augmenting the misperception of this dramatist's work across Europe solely as a 'political' playwright, rather than also as a dramatic innovator. Conversely, her minimalist aesthetic as translator accentuated the mordant irony of the Presniakovs. By rendering *Izobrazhaia zhertvu* (lit. *Depicting the Victim*) into *Playing the Victim*, she provided an ironic label, which resonates with the philosophical dimension of this play. Her writing style may also have helped reviewers to observe the cross-cultural traditions embedded into the Presniakovs' texts, including parallels with continental European playwrights such as Arthur Schnitzler (Billington 2003).

After the Court's premieres, the work of Sigarev and the Presniakov Brothers had a sporadic and uneven pattern of production across Europe. For example, in France, there has yet to be a single production of Sigarev's plays at the time of writing, and only one by the Presniakovs, *Playing the Victim*, in a Lithuanian production which toured to Paris in 2007. Similarly, in Norway, these writers have received one production apiece: *Black Milk* at the Den Norske Theatre in Oslo in 2005 and *Terrorism* at the Trøndelag Teater in Trondheim in 2004. The relative lack of interest in these writers by French and Norwegian theatres appears to relate to a greater focus on domestic playwrights because of engrained cultural preferences, further accentuated by material realities and state-funded institutional systems. The association between Sigarev, and perhaps to a lesser extent the Presniakovs, with the Royal Court is likely to have played a further role in creating a misperception about the genre of their work, as belonging to a naturalist tradition of political playwriting in the vein of 'British new writing'. Most European programmers encountered these writers' plays in Dugdale's translations,[21] with their emphasis on naturalistic dialogue, at least in Sigarev's dramas. Since the Court produced the more radical, and artistically disparate, version of *Playing the Victim*, continental European theatres may have encountered that version and overlooked it for their programme, based on its eclectic and metatheatrical structure.

In contrast to British naturalism, a widespread director-led practice in continental Europe tended to manifest itself in gestural performative languages. In a review of *Terrorism* directed by Carlos Aladro at the Teatro de La Abadía in Madrid (2004), the scholar Simon Breden characterises the choreography, caricatured performances and drag costumes as forms of communication through body-language: 'this is Brechtian theatre at its most powerful, where grotesque gesture becomes an alienating device' (ibid.). A non-naturalist performative language was also employed in Norway. The director Lars Erik Holter planned an abstract scenography for his production of *Black Milk* in Oslo. During rehearsals, he reverted to a naturalistic set design, depicting a derelict train station (Holter 2018). He has described working with the performers in this way:

> We used a lot of time [in rehearsals] to improvise, especially between the two [actors playing Levchik and Shura, Axel Hennie and Ingrid Bolsø Berdal], we worked a lot with rhythm. We [had long sections] where there was no talk. [...] [With] these improvisations [the actors] made their own staging.
>
> (Ibid.)

The continental European productions tended to explore gestural performative traditions as a means of unlocking these writers' dramaturgy. By deriving meaning from non-naturalist aesthetics, continental European practice perceived these writers' dramaturgies as offering narratives about inherited psychological trauma, with traces remaining in the body even when forgotten by the conscious mind. This perspective conceptualised Russia as a *near abroad*, defined not so much by its own specific set of socio-political conditions, but instead as part of a broader European cultural space with shared historical traumas.

180   *Noah Birksted-Breen*

Conclusion

After 1991, it appeared as if Russia would rejoin a European cultural space, to which it had arguably belonged prior to the Soviet era.[22] After 2000, the Russian government's rhetoric became increasingly hostile to the West, culminating in Putin's re-election as president in 2012 – after which he explicitly demonised Europe and the West as Russia's enemy. During the Putin era, Sigarev and the Presniakov Brothers were investigating an unstable Russian identity. Sigarev's plays reverberate with the nineteenth-century 'Slavophile' tradition of perceiving Russia as having a 'distinctive civilisation of its own, midway between Europe and Asia' (Davies 1996: 11). He envisages Russians – particularly the provincial, 'common folk' – as a potential source of a spiritual rebirth. Furthermore, the playwright subtly reiterates a male heterosexual bias widespread in Russian cultural thought, while nevertheless challenging the most entrenched stereotypes of brutish masculinity. All in all, Sigarev's unconventional realism draws upon both Russian traditions and dramatic forms as well as western popular and art-house culture, offering a distinctively Russian voice to European dramaturgy. The Presniakovs' satirise European social customs in several works, most notably in *Sexual/floor covering* (2000). Yet, beneath their parodic mockery, the Brothers' texts speak to European and western literary postmodernism.[23] Even so, their dramas also possess pronounced Russian characteristics, particularly the foregrounding of philosophical questions over political ones, as well as a bleakly absurdist humour. Putin's political project after 2000, characterised by an increasingly repressive authoritarianism, has left the dramas of Sigarev and the Presniakov Brothers as testament to Russia's ambivalent desire to belong to a European cultural space.

Vasilii Sigarev – four key productions

Plastilin (Plasticine) by Vasilii Sigarev. Directed by Kirill Serebrennikov. Scenography by Nikolai Simonov. Cast: Marina Golub, Vitalii Khaev, Aleksandra Konnikova, Andrei Kuzichev, Sergei Mukhin, Natasha Shvets, Viktoriia Tolstoganova, Ol'ga Khokhlova, Dmitrii Ul'ianov, Egor Kholodkov. Centre for Dramaturgy and Direction, Moscow, opening night unknown, 2001.

Plasticine by Vasilii Sigarev, trans. by Sasha Dugdale. Directed by Dominic Cooke. Scenography by Ian MacNeil. Cast: Daniel Cerqueira, Bryan Dick, Matthew Dunster, Molly Innes, Liz Kettle, Michael Legge, Mary Macloed, John Rogan, Russell Tovey, Myfanwy Waring, Liz White. Royal Court Upstairs Theatre, London, 15 March 2002.

Chernoe moloko (Black Milk) by Vasilii Sigarev, directed and scenography by Vasilii Sigarev. With: Alla Antipova, Irina Belova, Evgenii Chistiakov, Aleksandr Efimov, Sergei Fedorov, Natal'ia Garanina, A. Gerasimov, Oleg Iagodin, Sergei Kolesov, Svetlana Kolesova, Galina Morozova, Vera Tsvitkis, Sergei Tushov, Iana Troianova, M. Udintsev, Tamara Zimina. Puppet Theatre (transferring to Koliada-Theatre), Ekaterinburg, April 2004.

Black Milk by Vasilii Sigarev, trans. by Sasha Dugdale. Directed by Simon Usher. Scenography by Delia Peel. Lighting by Simon Bennison. Cast: Sarah Cattle, Paul Ready, Suzan Sylvester, Gary Oliver, Di Botcher, Sheila Reid, Alan Williams. Royal Court Theatre Upstairs, London, 31 January 2003.

Oleg and Vladimir Presniakov – four key productions

Terrorizm (*Terrorism*) by Oleg and Vladimir Presniakov. Directed by Kirill Serebrennikov. Scenography by Nikolai Simonov. Choreography by Al'bert Al'berts. Cast: Kristina Babushkina, Anatolii Belyi, Natal'ia Bochkareva, Iuliia Chebakova, Eduard Chekmazov, Aleksandr Fisenko, Marina Golub, Vitalii Khaev, Sergei Medvedev, Grigorii Ryzhakov, Vladimir Timofeev. Chekhov Moscow Arts, Small Stage, Moscow, 8 November 2002.

Izobrazhaia zhertvu (*Playing the Victim*) by Oleg and Vladimir Presniakov. Directed by Kirill Serebrennikov. Scenography by Nikolai Simonov. Cast: Maksim Blinov, Iulia Chebakova, Eduard Chekmazov, Marina Golub, Vitalii Khaev, Oleg Mazurov, Sergei Medvedev, Dar'ia Moroz, Nikita Panfilov, Tat'iana Pavlova, Alla Pokrovskaia, Tat'iana Pavlova/Natal'ia Turiianskaia (shared role), Igor' Zolotovitskii. Chekhov Moscow Arts, Moscow, 18 September 2004.

Terrorism by Oleg and Vladimir Presniakov, trans. by Sasha Dugdale. Directed by Ramin Gray. Scenography by Hildegard Bechtler. Cast: Di Botcher, Sarah Cattle, Ian Dunn, Paul Hilton, Gary Oliver, Paul Ready, Sheila Reid, Suzan Sylvester, Alan Williams. Royal Court Theatre Upstairs, London, 10 March 2003.

Playing the Victim by Oleg and Vladimir Presniakov, trans. by Sasha Dugdale. Directed by Richard Wilson. Scenography by Nicolai Hart Hansen. Cast: Hayley Carmichael, Paul Hunter, Amanda Lawrence, Michael Glenn Murphy, Ferdy Roberts, Andrew Scott. Traverse Theatre, Edinburgh, 12 August 2003.

Notes

1 Anecdotally, on a number of research field trips in Russia between 2012–16, I heard from Russian theatre-makers that auditoria in most large and medium-scale venues were filled to under a 50 per cent capacity, more or less across the board in the 1990s, in contrast to the full or near-capacity houses which were the norm at the most popular venues during the Soviet era.

2 The Soviet tradition of socialist realism obliged playwrights and directors to replicate contemporary socio-political themes, albeit in a way which glorified the authorities. Conversely, dissident directors tended to use allegory to criticise the state, turning theatres into 'shrines for some people [and] for most people – a free press and parliament' (Davydova 2005: 14, 15, 16): not literally but in their evocation of a higher spiritual or moral purpose.

3 The critic John Freedman has written extensively about this period (2010).

4 Elsewhere (Birksted-Breen 2017), I have described these new institutions as the birth of a 'fringe', distinctive from the culture of 'studio theatres' (fostered as a concept in the early twentieth century at the Moscow Arts Theatre), because they

182 *Noah Birksted-Breen*

appeared mostly as independent institutions, unrelated institutionally or materially to the state-run repertory theatres (which constitute the majority of the theatre sector in Russia, even at the time of writing, June 2018).

5 *Perestroika* (lit. 'restructuring' or 'rebuilding') is the term given to the final political period in the Soviet Union, from 1987 to 1991, when Gorbachev initiated significant political and economic reforms, designed to liberalise Soviet society.

6 By 2002, while still studying with Koliada, Sigarev had written 15 plays (Raikina 2002) including the majority of his most acclaimed works. At the time of writing, he has written 22 texts. Sources: vsigarev.ru; https://yeltsin.ru/affair/yana-troyanova-i-vasilij-sigarev

7 From the unpublished play text of *Playing the Victim* (as used in the 2004 production), pp. 33–44.

8 Birksted-Breen (2017: 88–94) and Flynn (2019).

9 The Brothers have recalled their fascination in the 1990s with cultural works with multiple iterations in different media; one of their inspirations during that period *Trainspotting,* a novel by Scottish novelist Irvine Welsh (1993) turned into a film by director Danny Boyle (1996) (Interview with the Presniakov Brothers 2018).

10 The Anti-Booker (1995–2001) was arguably the most prestigious literary and dramatic award in Russia in the 1990s.

11 Founding Artistic Director of the School of the Contemporary Play (1989–ongoing).

12 Artistic Director of the Chekhov Moscow Arts Theatre from 2000 until his death in 2018.

13 All citations in Russian in this chapter are translated by this author.

14 I have written at length about Koliada's practice as director and artistic director of the Koliada-Theatre (2001–ongoing) in Birksted-Breen (2017: 177–203).

15 A list of Koliada's plays between 1986 and 2010 in Shcherbakova (2013: 210–16) shows that slightly over half were written as two-act dramas, notably it was the form of his most critically acclaimed and most frequently produced works, such as *The Slingshot* (1986) and *Murlin Murlo* (1989).

16 From 1994 onwards, Koliada-as-director developed a non-mimetic aesthetic to stage his own plays, using stylised choreographic sequences, scenography created from 'found' objects and musical underscoring with pop music (Shcherbakova 2013: 73–121).

17 In their article on post-Soviet dramatic writing in Russia, including a section on politicised rap in Russia in the beginning of the twenty-first century, the critics Vladimir Zabaluev and Aleksei Zenzinov posited that 'rappers and playwrights share a teacher – the contemporary cinematographers Scorsese and Tarantino, Danny Boyle and David Fincher' (2008).

18 In numerous interviews (Raikina 2002; 'Vasilii Sigarev' 2003), he has specified which storylines in *Plasticine* were drawn from real-life. For instance, his brother brought a plasticine model of a penis into school to flash at his literature teacher, at Sigarev's suggestion (Raikina 2002), as occurs in *Plasticine* (Sigarev 2002: 17–18).

19 All characters in this play are given only generic names, 'Passenger', 'Man', or 'Colleague'. This lack of a proper name further contributes to the sense of individuals being stripped of their individual identity. The Brothers use this technique in many of their other plays including *Europe-Asia.*

20 Source: *Teatral'nyi smotritel'*, http://www.smotr.ru/2004/2004_mhat_zhertva.htm

21 Holter read the English translation of *Black Milk* before commissioning a Norwegian-language one (ibid.). Another common practice is 're-translation' from the English, where there is a lack of qualified Russian translators. Antonio Fernández Lera translated *Terrorism* from English into Spanish for its premiere in Spain (Breden 2005: 55).

22 Prior to 1917, Russia aspired to join a European cultural space, emblematised by Catherine the Great, who declared in 1767: 'Russia is a European state' (Davies 1996: 11).
23 The term literary postmodernism reflects the textual experiments of the Brothers. I have avoided the term postdramatic since their work does not alter a conventional 'fourth wall' mode of spectatorship. In the early 1990s, Russian auteur-directors, rather than playwrights, were forging postdramatic theatrical forms, for example Kama Ginkas in his 1994 production of *K.I. from Crime* (Lehmann 2006: 150). The term postdramatic entered Russian critical discourse in 2013 when Lehmann's seminal volume on the postdramatic was published in translation in Russia (Lehmann 2013).

Works cited

Aston, Elaine, and O'Thomas, Mark (2015) *Royal Court: International*, Basingstoke: Palgrave Macmillan.

Beumers, Birgit, and Lipovetsky, Mark (2009) *Performing Violence, Literary and Theatrical Experiments of New Russian Drama*, Bristol: Intellect.

Billington, Michael (2003) 'Terrorism', *Guardian*, 15 March, p. 18.

Birksted-Breen, Noah (2017) *Alternative Voices in an Acquiescent Society: Translating the New Wave of Russian Playwrights (2000–2014)*. Unpublished PhD thesis. Queen Mary University of London.

Breden, Simon (2005) 'Madrid gets physical: Six productions in Spain's capital city', *Western European Stages*, 17(2): 55–62.

Davies, Norman (1996) *A History of Europe*, Oxford and New York: Oxford University Press.

Davydova, Marina (2005) *Konets teatral'noi epokhi*, Moscow: Zolotaia Maska.

Dmitriev, Mikhail, and Pozdniakova, Galina (2009) 'Brat'ia Presniakovy: "V Portugalii my chuvstovali, chto mir do sikh por ne otkryt"', *Konkurent*, http://www.konkurent-krsk.ru/index.php?id=2192

Flynn, Molly (2019) *Witness Onstage: Documentary Theatre in Twenty-First Century Russia*, Manchester: Manchester University Press.

Freedman, John (2010) 'Contemporary Russian drama: The journey from stagnation to a golden age', *Theatre Journal*, 62(3): 389–420.

Holter, Lars Erik (2018) Interview with the author, Oslo, 30 May.

Khochesh' ponimat' segodniashnii den' – chitai p'esy (2015) Radio Vesti-FM. 13 September.

Koval'skaia, Elena (2003) 'Plastilin', *Afisha*, https://www.afisha.ru/performance/65367/review/145353

Lehmann, Hans-Thies (2006) *Postdramatic theatre*, trans. Karen Jürs-Munby, London and New York: Routledge.

——— (2013) *Postdramaticheskii teatr*, trans. Natal'ia Isaeva, Moscow: ABCdesign.

Moguilevskaia, Tania (2006) 'Le comique "avorté" de Vassilii Sigariov', *Recherche & Travaux*, 69: 63–75.

O'Thomas, Mark (2014) 'Stages of the loss, translation as contamination: How the ritual made it to the Royal National Theatre, London', *Theatre Research International*, 39(2): 120–132.

Presniakov, Vladimir and Oleg (2001) *Evropa-Aziia* [*Europe-Asia*] (unpublished play text).

184   *Noah Birksted-Breen*

———— (n.d.) *Polovoe pokrytie* [*Sexual/floor covering*]. Russian play text sent by email to this author.

———— (n.d.) *Terrorizm* [*Terrorism*]. Russian play text sent by email to this author.

———— (n.d. [2003]) *Izobrazhaia zhertvu* [*Playing the Victim*]. Russian play text sent by email to this author, version used in the 2003 Royal Court production.

———— (n.d. [2004]) *Izobrazhaia zhertvu* [*Playing the Victim*]. Russian play text sent by email to this author, version used in the 2004 Chekhov Moscow Arts production.

———— (2018) Moscow, 12 March.

Raikina, Marina (2002) 'Neofit iz plastilina [Interview s Vasiliem Sigarevym]', *Moskovskii komsomolets*, http://www.newdrama.ru/archive/event/plasticine/art_1663

Rudnev, Pavel (2018) *Drama pamiati: ocherki istorii rossiiskoi dramaturgii. 1950–2010-e*, Moscow: Novoe literaturnoe obozrenie.

Sakwa, Richard (2008) *Russian Politics and Society*. London: Routledge.

Shakina, Ol'ga (2009) 'Vasilii Sigarev, Iana Troianova: "Bydlo – eto my"', *Colta.ru*, http://os.colta.ru/cinema/names/details/12581/page3

Shcherbakova, Natal'ia (2013) *Teatral'nyi fenomen Nikolaia Koliady*. Unpublished doctoral thesis. St. Petersburg State University.

Shcherbakova, Natal'ia (2015) Ekaterinburg, 11 November.

Shkola zlosloviia: Vasilii Sigarev i Iana Troianova (2010) NTV, 31 March.

Sigarev, Vasilii (n.d.) *Chernoe moloko* [*Black Milk*], http://vsigarev.ru/text.html

———— (n.d.) *Plastilin* [Plasticine], http://vsigarev.ru/text.html

———— (n.d.) *Chernoe moloko* [*Black Milk*]; *Plasticine* (2002), trans. Sasha Dugdale, London: Nick Hern Books.

Solomonov, Artur (2002) 'Vo MXATe poigrali v terroristov', *Gazeta*, http://www.smotr.ru/2002/2002_mhat_ter.htm

Spektakl' "Plastilin" (2013) Directed by Kirill Serebrennikov, [Film], https://www.youtube.com/watch?v=U-PIHOVNMbQ&t=1931s

'Vasilii Sigarev: Ia prosto rasskazyvaiu o strastiakh i bedakh chelovecheskikh' (2003) *Teatral'naia afisha*, http://www.teatr.ru/docs/tpl/doc.asp?id=605

Vedernikov, Vladimir (2003) 'Rok kul'tura na Urale', *UralRock*, https://uralrock.ru/content/view/107

Zabaluev, Vladimir, and Zenzinov, Aleksei (2008) 'Novaia drama: praktika svobody', *Novyi Mir*, 4, http://magazines.russ.ru/novyi_mi/2008/4/za14.html

Zaslavskii, Grigorii (2004) 'Na polputi mezhdu zhizn'iu i stsenoi', *Oktiabr'*, 7, http://magazines.russ.ru/october/2004/7/zasl10-pr.html

Zlobina, Alena (1998) 'Drama dramaturgii. V piati iavleniiakh, s prologom, intermediei i epilogom', *Novyi mir*, 3, http://magazines.russ.ru/novyi_mi/1998/3/zlobin.html

10 Paweł Demirski and Dorota Masłowska

Painful pasts, transformative presents[1]

Bryce Lease

In the first decade of the new millennium, after the disorientation and pessimism of the 1990s, it appeared that theatre could cultivate new forms of engagement and activism in Poland. A renewed emphasis on theatre as a locus of political commitment and as an instrument for social change prompted substantial public debates and moved performances out of theatres into local public spheres. As a consequence, the working vocabularies and artistic economies of theatre makers changed as a necessary component of emerging philosophies and creative practices. Although in the late 1990s and the early 2000s the so-called Western brutalists that were most popular to stage amongst younger directors were largely Anglophone, including Mark Ravenhill and Sarah Kane, Joanna Derkaczew (2011) was right to point out that Polish artists also learned from assisting and directing in theatres in Hamburg, Berlin, and Munich, and purloined strategies from Frank Castorf, René Pollesch, Falk Richter, Armin Petras, Thomas Ostermeier, and Einar Schleef. They dealt in the aesthetics of shock and the criticism of an emerging bourgeoisie, took up strategies from postdramatic theatre, and changed literary directors into dramatists. At the same time, Derkaczew observes, Polish theatre was both decentralised – many of the most interesting performances were taking place outside of Warsaw and Kraków – and internationalised through global tours and participation in international festivals.

After 2000, performance writing developed through competitions on playwriting and dramaturgy, workshops in theatres such as TR Warszawa, the briefly lived openings of performance spaces that championed new writing such as Teatr Powszechny's Garaż and the creation of the Teatr Wytwórnia in an old vodka factory in the Praga district of Warsaw, and the publication of plays in the journal *Dialog*. In 2007, Paweł Demirski wrote a seminal article called 'The Theatre of the Playwright', which was published by *Krytyka Polityczna* (*Political Critique*) (reprinted in Demirski 2015), a movement and publication house of politically progressive Polish intellectuals, artists, and activists founded in 2002 by Sławomir Sierakowski. In the essay, Demirski explains that Polish theatre remains, despite the influx of interest in new dramaturgy, the realm of the director. In order to submit themselves to the required tests and public scrutiny of their genius, directors require canonical plays, whose historical stagings form the basis of a transgenerational comparison (such as *Hamlet* or

186 *Bryce Lease*

Stanisław Wyspiański's *Wesele* [*The Wedding*]). Staging a contemporary drama is a small test in comparison, and, ultimately, Demirski argued, young writers are not offered an appropriately nurturing environment to develop their work. They are quickly and poorly staged, and then placed at the forefront of national debates that eclipse their artistic outputs. Thrust into the limelight by the press as provocateurs and attacked by conservative critics for their treatment of social taboos, lack of depth, existential insight, or stage metaphors, they are not able to take time to develop their craft, to fail and to try again.

More than a decade later, the scene has changed. Experiments in devising practices in venues such as Komuna Warszawa are rejecting any neat separations between writer, director, performer, and choreographer. As Marcin Kościelniak (2021) has argued, contemporary Polish playwriting does not repeat modernism's glorification of the autonomous artwork; new writing cannot be fully distinguished from either its stage realisations or the writer's institutional affiliations. In line with Kościelniak's observation, then, I will demonstrate how Paweł Demirski and Dorota Masłowska's texts are embedded in the work of the directors who develop their aesthetic vocabularies and generate solutions for the theatrical problems they propose (Monika Strzępka and Grzegorz Jarzyna, respectively) as well as the theatres that support their artistic production. Even if the forms in which these writers are working differs – Demirski writes exclusively for theatre and television, while Masłowska is primarily a novelist – it is within these contexts that one can accurately chart and interpret two of the most significant contemporary writers for theatre to emerge in Poland over the past two decades. On the whole, these writers have critiqued neoliberalism, reanimated political engagement, and encouraged new modes of historical encounter as resistance to the promotion of collective memory for nationalistic goals. However, I will argue that while Masłowska's writing has retained its critical bite, a growing conservatism and fidelity to a Christian status quo can be detected in Demirski's later plays. My concern in this chapter then is additionally to advocate caution in reducing a playwright's oeuvre to a singular critique.

Fragments and paraphrases

Paweł Demirski worked as literary manager under Maciej Nowak at Gdańsk's Teatr Wybrzeże where he composed plays with sociopolitical resonance that broadcast his radically leftist position as a staunch member of Krytyka Polityczna. Nowak produced a number of Demirski's early plays, whose widely varied topics included a biopic of the Solidarity leader Lech Wałęsa, a caustic depiction of Polish migration on a mass scale, and a scathing attack on the violation of the country's labour rights, based on a real-life case in Łódź where a factory worker was decapitated due to lax health and safety controls. Demirski joined forces with the director Monika Strzępka in 2007 and the pair have worked together on nearly every production since. Breaking away from a classical model in which the playwright prepares a text for a director to stage, Demirski and Strzępka co-create their texts for theatres in an open-ended model of research and experimentation. Demirski usually starts out with about ten pages of writing and the subsequent process of development relies upon a 'range of crises'. 'The whole struggle is that we invent the show during production', Demirski explains, 'and we don't know how it will all end up. And the first general rehearsals always end up badly, these rehearsals are awful, hideous, so we do another montage of scenes' (2015: 4).

Pawłowski noted that the Szybki Teatr Miejski (Fast City Theatre) project Demirski curated at the Teatr Wybrzeże was strongly influenced by Moscow's Teatr.doc, who visited Gdańsk as part of the Saison Russe festival of Russian drama in 2003 (Pawłowski 2016: 6–7), where they presented verbatim works by Galina Sinkina, Ruslan Malikov, and Aleksandr Vartanov. Demirski was also influenced by British playwright David Hare's tackling of contemporary social problems in his dramatic texts. This influence sees its origins in Demirski's participation in workshops at the Royal Court Theatre in London where Hare introduced him to writing forms that had links to journalism, verbatim practices, deep archival research, and social engagement. Kościelniak (2021) claims that this artistic strategy is less about art as intervention than about theatre as social diagnosis, which is a critique that could very well be reflected back at Hare.

Using postdramatic, ludic, or parodic forms, Strzępka and Demirski also cultivated a number of international influences from European political theatre, including German director René Pollesch and German-speaking playwrights such as Thomas Bernhard, Heiner Müller, Werner Schwab, and Peter Turrini. In 2007, the same year Demirski wrote his influential article, Pollesch made his first professional visit to Poland, collaborating with Grzegorz Jarzyna at the TR Warszawa. Renowned for his fairground aesthetics, destabilisation of character, direct audience address, lyrical monologues, chaotic stage action, and carefully articulated expressionist stage design there are certainly a number of indicative overlaps with Demirski's writing and Strzępka's direction, particularly with what Demirski has coined his 'political tabloid' theatre, constructed from political incorrectness, circus athleticism, and ready-made propaganda. As Rafał Węgrzyniak (2010) observed, at least some of the ideas, themes, and solutions appearing in Strzępka and Demirski's productions were adapted from modern theatre practices commonly associated with the historical prewar radical left in Poland, and not only from British and German-speaking theatre traditions. At the same time, the pair have used Polish romantic texts as a springboard for blazing critiques of Polish society and politics. In their early work, Strzępka and Demirski the theatre is not a spiritual or ritualistic space in which to honour culture through convenient and celebrated modes of describing the world, but a dissecting table where the audience must face ugly truths frequently ignored or disavowed. This critical strategy, as I will show, changed in the 2010s, a decade when mixed genres were becoming increasingly prevalent as playwrights eschewed classical principles of dramatic form such as linearity, compositional unity, coherent personae, mimesis, and narrative closure, and reorganised theatrical space and temporality through postdramatic strategies. The role of the playwright also became more amorphous and less autonomous with the rise of the dramaturg/

188   *Bryce Lease*

director relationship (see Szczawińska and Jakimiak, Chapter 3 this volume). These emerging experiments in theatre-making have no doubt been influenced by Demirski and his rejection of the well-made play, which entails the elimination of plot as a dramatic device. Demirski claims,

> Characters governed by plot are not only its tools but, primarily, they are slaves of principals of the order of reality from which that plot was derived. For plot is nothing other than a reconstruction of a cultural narration so universal as to be imperceptible, organizing all elements of the world and thus also determining the possibility of movement within it.
>
> (2015: 4)

This makes Demirski difficult to categorise. As Anna R. Burzyńska has argued, Demirski has created 'plays unlike anything previously identified with political theatre in Poland' (2015: 1). Igor Stokfiszewski has observed that after writing *Kiedy przyjdą podpalić dom, to się nie zdziw* (*Don't Be Surprised When They Burn Your House Down*) in 2006, Demirski began a second stage in his career (2011a: 8). Abandoning the strict technical principles of conventional playwriting, Demirski would rework a large number of significant texts, from Jean Racine to Anton Chekhov and Bertolt Brecht. These experiments were dubbed *parafrazy* (paraphrases) in a collection of his plays published under that name. Burzyńska aligns this stage of Demirski's writing with the French situationists and redeploys the concept of 'found footage' to define not only the recycled material Demirski uses as his sources (images, words, sounds, ideas) but also to highlight the ways in which such sources are deformed and distorted through a (false) collective unconscious that 'feeds on mediated experience' (2015: 4). Burzyńska astutely interprets Demirski's 'paraphrases' as, on the one hand, a form of Debordian plagiarism, which 'served to dissect dead works of the past and connect them to a living being to allow them to return to reality', and, on the other, as a refusal to compose an artwork as a cohesive whole. Instead, Demirski produces a diffusion of fragments 'subservient only to their own anarchic dynamic', thus 'shifting their meanings, subverting sense and causing countless transgressions against good middle-class taste and traditional notions of logic' (2015: 3).

Emphasising their uncertain literary and theatrical status, theatre historian Joanna Krakowska has playfully named these 'demi(d)ramas' (2011: 477). The use of the parentheses in Polish allows for a double meaning, invoking demi as partiality both in reference to the drama and to its frame (*rama*). Krakowska formulates the paraphrase as a modification, freely and creatively developing the ideas of an original while bearing the mark of secondariness (2011: 476). To her mind, Demirski's reference points from one source (quotations, character names, motifs, scenes) are subordinated to a new structure, style, and autonomous message. Any leftover relations to reference texts are backward or upside down. Demirski himself claims that classical plays are a single 'element among common intellectual resources' rather than material to be produced on stage (2015: 6). Kościelniak (2021) contends that Demirski's 'critical and polemic dialogue with the broadly understood classic' – which the playwright considers to be an inadequate tool for the diagnosis of mechanisms that govern contemporary individual and social life – 'is one of the most characteristic phenomena of contemporary landscape of theatre and texts for the theatre'. For Krakowska, demi(d)ramas are both funny and depressing, and, like Enlightenment drama, this genre combines pathos and seriousness with foolishness and triviality in which even the most tragic characters are ridiculed. Politically devoid of utopian delusions, Krakowska concludes, 'their leftist sensitivities are not accompanied by left-wing optimism' (2011: 478). What makes this artistic gesture a political one is the way Demirski forces audiences to resign from fabricated impartiality, disingenuous subversive rhetoric, and noble universalisation (2011: 479).

The first example of Demirski's 'paraphrase' is his most significant engagement with Polish romanticism, *Dziady. Ekshumacja* (*Forefathers' Eve. Exhumation*), which Strzępka directed at Wrocław's Teatr Polski in 2007. The play was intended as a structural and aesthetic reform of the age-old reverence for Adam Mickiewicz's canonical text and could be read as a series of small skirmishes with romantic philosophy, cultural reverence for metaphysics, and legendary twentieth-century productions of the play. Strzępka maintained that this was not an adaptation of Mickiewicz but an original reinterpretation. Demirski's reworking of found material, activating the legible legacies of spectators' cultural memory, turned out to be his greatest skill; it is also what makes his plays difficult to tour outside of their cultural specificity. Demirski, treating *Dziady* as raw material for the formation of a political text that has contemporary relevance, asked to what extent Polish cultural life continues to be determined by the philosophical premises espoused by Mickiewicz. Such a treatment requires the opposite of veneration for a canonical play and Demirski's use of stock characters (Konrad, Father Piotr, Mrs. Rollinson) and scraps of dialogue not only fail to conform to the parameters of a 'faithful' performance, they actively resist and argue with the source text. The exhumation referred to in the title gestures towards those topics that continue to be contentious, including Polish Catholicism and disavowed historical transgressions, such as lustration, the communist past, antisemitism, and unacknowledged war crimes. Digging up the corpse of Polish romanticism, insincere or hypocritical patriotism is presented in contrast to the interrogation of the assumptions that found national identity.

Later the same year, Demirski wrote *Był sobie POLAK POLAK POLAK i diabeł* (*There was a Pole, Pole, Pole and the Devil*), which can be seen as a continuation of the exhumation project, the all-out confrontation with Polish romanticism propelled by frustrations with public hypocrisy and political turpitude. Rather than working with biography or adaptation to directly assail a venerated leader or source text, Demirski wrote an original play using the critical conventions of positivist philosophy and romantic poetry to comment on 'Polish provincialism, vulgarity, greed, historical hypocrisy, empty martyrdom and stale holiness' (Wysocki 2007). Set on half a football pitch with the audience seated on bleachers, Demirski maintained that the sublime status of the sport in Poland made it the

190   Bryce Lease

ideal location for any discussion of national values (quoted in Kyzioł 2007). At the beginning of the performance, body bags are dug up which contain the carcasses of deceased characters caught in a temporary purgatory. Unlike the metaphorical practice of disinterring of a canonical text in the previous performance, these exhumations were framed by slapstick humour, visual gags, and cabaret that produced a powerful satire on contemporary themes ranging from postwar German resentment over lost territory, antisocial behaviour and hooliganism, paedophilia in the Catholic Church, Poland's participation in globalisation, and Holocaust memorials. Neither completely dead nor entirely stripped of life, the actors inhabit an undefined space where national themes are argued in juvenile fits of rage, depression, and hyperactivity. This style offered a response to the director Michał Zadara's petition to Polish theatre-makers to 'find new, lightweight communicative forms for important topics' (cited in Kyzioł 2007).

Neoliberalism's losers

Demirski and Strzępka widened the remit of their socio-political critique. While many of their peers focused on PiS, Catholicism, and conservative political elites, Demirski and Strzepka were equally critical of liberals, progressives, former dissidents, and spokespersons for moral freedom. Examples of such critiques range from *Diamenty to węgiel który wziął się do roboty* (*Diamonds Are Coal That Got Down to Business*, 2008), to *W imię Jakub S.* (*In the Name of Jakub S.*, 2011), which uses Jakub Szela, the leader of a peasants' riot in 1846 'to draw a very harsh parallel between the nineteenth century's serfdom and today's indebtedness to banks' (Popovici 2014). Although this has drawn significant attention to inequalities of class politics and the mode in which neoliberalism has marginalised sectors of society in contemporary Poland, I would like to examine two examples that are more problematic in their attention to the structures of social economies that universalise other forms of oppression and exclusion, before turning to Dorota Masłowska's critique of neoliberalism in her first text written specifically for theatre, *Dwoje biednych Rumunów mówiących po polsku* (*A Couple of Poor, Polish-Speaking Romanians*, 2006).

Demirski once again turned to Polish romanticism in his adaptation of Zygmunt Krasiński's *Nie-Boska komedia* (*Un-divine Comedy*), adding the subtitle *WSZYSTKO POWIEM BOGU!* (*I WILL TELL GOD EVERYTHING!*, 2014). Strzępka included a scenographic element that called up painful historical connections. In the corner of the stage the director placed a carousel, an explicit reference to the carousels that stood on Krasiński Square and remained operational just outside the walls of the Warsaw Ghetto during the German occupation. Czesław Miłosz describes the carousel in his poem 'Campo dei Fiori' (1943) as a metaphor for ethnic Poles' indifference to the suffering of Polish Jews. Krasiński's play revolves around political upheaval and a social revolution that gives rise to anxieties over class inequality and the historical process. Demirski kept one scene intact from the source play in his 'paraphrase' that contains the central argument between Count Henry, an aristocrat who believes in the individual and sees revolutionary social change as destructive, and Pancras, a revolutionary leader who personifies human reason and a belief in mass movements. Rather than looking to the Messianic future envisaged by Mickiewicz, Henry feels one must look to the past, the great era of pre-partition Poland, for the proper direction, while Pancras' focus is on the future. This dramaturgical choice prompts two important critiques of this play that I will now briefly outline.

In her critical analysis of the production, Monika Kwaśniewska observes an emerging trend in Demirski's work that frames fear of radical social change as the bastion of Catholic faith. Rather than offering a diagnostic appraisal of the consequences of melding Church, state, and social and political life, this frame eschews any institutional critique. Treating the Church as a metonym for faith – rather than as institution – allows Demirski and Strzępka to turn a blind eye to systemic problems such as sexual violence, the construction of an ethno-nationalistic Polish mythical and symbolic imaginarium, the status of women in the Church, and its attitude towards identity and non-normative sexuality (Kwaśniewska 2018: 117). Kwaśniewska expresses her deep scepticism when she asks to what extent these problems are opened up to real criticism, and how much their evocation is 'subject to the paradoxical mechanism of justification and legitimization of the [existing] order' (2018: 118).

If this play signals a return to the very Christian values that support hierarchical social structures, there is another important concern that arises for me. While many critics drew attention to the stubbornly persistent focus on the past and future as intractable binaries in the playwright's thinking about social change, a few reviews also mentioned the ambiguous status of anti-Semitism in Demirski's writing. In Krasiński's source text, Jews join Pancras' revolution, but they secretly plot to overthrow the Christian infidels as soon as the fighting is finished for their own ends. Krasiński's warning follows standard conventions of anti-Semitism: if the Jews are forgiven their betrayal of Christ then Christians will in effect become the victims of their own obtuseness. This logic suggests that the sons of Christians would, in due course, become servants to the sons of Caiaphas. What we see in Count Henry's anti-Semitism is none other than a symptom that revolves around a previous disavowal: that society is *not* inherently split by class antagonism but is capable of functioning as a corporate whole. In *Un-divine Comedy*, Pancras, the revolutionary leader, is not constructed as a villain. He may be misguided, but it is clear that society has fallen apart to the point to which revolution appears as the only logical answer to the deadlock of partitioned Poland. So not only do the converted Jews follow Pancras' leadership, they are at the same time the object-cause of the revolution, the positive entity of an 'organic' feudal society's meltdown.

While Demirski clearly critiques Krasiński's paranoia about a Jewish plot, he chose to write in a new character, Rotschild, a Jewish industrialist that is complicit in Henry's individualistic, capitalist-driven worldview. Rotschild suggests that he has the financial means to immigrate, thus escaping the horrors of the Holocaust. This problematically suggests that Jewish families' ability to survive the Holocaust was directly related to their class privilege, which is not

192   *Bryce Lease*

only factually inaccurate it also negates recent scholarship that shows how some Poles financially benefited from the Jewish extermination (see Leder 2014). What's more, Rotschild's wealth aligns him with the Krasiński family and the Polish aristocracy. While the subject of anti-Semitism is explicitly expressed through both dialogue and scenic elements, the point is here that Demirski chooses to foreground mass moral panic over forms of persecution related to ethnicity and faith. And, what's more, this critique is formed with the stark absence of the Church itself as a culpable historical institution.

In *Trybuna tęczowa 2012* (*Rainbow Tribunal 2012*, 2011) Demirski focuses on gay rights as a means of interrogating class politics and democratic systems. In the same year this production premiered a media frenzy grew around the Euro2012 football tournament set to take place across Poland. As in most countries, football and nationalism are strongly linked – and often gender bound – as is hooliganism and binge drinking. As a result of the aggressive male bonding enacted at most matches, it was reported that a coalition of football supporters decided to start a campaign for stadiums to establish separate stands for gay fans who might otherwise be verbally abused or physically threatened by homophobic supporters. Strzępka claimed that she and Demirksi had been in contact with the gay men who had created the coalition while developing their new play. However, Demirski and Strzępka eventually revealed that they had fabricated the gay-rights project and the group's host website. Their ostensible goal in creating the 'Rainbow stand' was an attempt to test the ability of a grassroots organisation to find a platform from which it could actively intervene in Polish politics and public space initiatives, such as the building of the new national stadium in Warsaw.

Stokfiszewski (2011b) staunchly defended *Rainbow Tribunal 2012*, arguing that the production was an attempt to initiate a social movement by artists that is part of a broader trend to transform the political imagination in both the social field and in legislative processes. Questioning the homogenous nature of Polish collective identity, manifested in such mass spectacles as the European football championships, and breaking with the standard social passivity of audiences, Stokfiszewski suggested that the production tested the ability of cultural institutions to adequately operate at the level of civil society. Stokfiszewski also argued that the production and its concomitant activist platform exposed a fundamental weakness in Polish theatre criticism – most reviews carefully omitted analysis of the relationship between civil actions and performance – concluding that reviewers were insufficiently able to deal with real political acts. Even if Strzępka and Demirski's movement did not achieve the desired social effects, Stokfiszewski reasoned, it developed specific knowledge about the mechanisms of the functioning of democracy and paved the road for future initiatives.

Rainbow Tribunal 2012's focus on Euro 2012 demonstrated the flawed structural dynamics of power in Polish democracy, and further established how these inadequate structures interpenetrate cultural and sexual identity, economic status, citizenship, and nationality. Taking the construction of the football stadium in Warsaw for the Euro 2012 – the total investment in infrastructural change was 20 billion euros – as an example testifies to the indelible link between capitalist accumulation and expressions of national fervour. The homophobic rhetoric in the Polish public sphere worked across economic stratifications, indeed this rhetoric was primarily concerned with cultural identification that impart what Pierre Bourdieu calls 'common symbolic forms of thought' and 'social frames of perception' (2003: 175) that cast homosexuality as antithetical to Polishness. Although one might attribute the significance of *Rainbow Tribunal 2012* to its ability to test the boundaries of healthy democratic systems, if one fails to see sexuality as a key interpretive focal point for this performance then gay rights simply stands a synecdoche for a whole range of identity politics that is founded on opposition to discrimination on the basis of race, gender, or creed.[2] Such easy shifts between disparate categories of revolt, opposition, and activism undermine the individual historical and political trajectories that frame activists' platforms. Given this open-ended focus on democracy and its faults, I argue that this results in two fundamental problems in Demirski's approach to political critique. In *Rainbow Tribunal 2012*, Demirski is more concerned with a universalising tendency that privileges class over particular and local understandings of lesbian and gay identity that are played down 'into just one of many "lifestyles"' (Freeman 2010: xv).[3] In *Un-divine Comedy, I WILL TELL GOD EVERYTHING!,* class difference is eschewed in an implicit defence of a traditional (and even aristocratic) Christian social order founded both on clearly defined class hierarchies and widespread panic about social transformation.

While Demirski tests the elasticity of democratic systems, Dorota Masłowska drills down into the affective qualities of lived experience under neoliberalism. Both playwrights are interested in the ways historical discourses shape the present and fail to offer alternative modes for the future. Masłowska's *A Couple of Poor, Polish-Speaking Romanians* addressed contemporary national complexes around economic migrants. The play was the first drama written by the then 24-year-old Masłowska, whose first two novels won Poland's most prestigious literary prizes. Controversial for her direct style and use of street vernacular, Masłowska was commissioned to write the play as part of the 2006 TR/PL festival at the TR Warszawa designed to diagnose new social, political, and moral challenges for Poland in the wake of EU accession. The action follows two young Poles (Parcha, a television actor, and Dżina, an unemployed single mother) pretending to be Romanian migrants on an all-night drug-fuelled road trip.[4] In Warsaw, the play was initially given a staged reading, starring Masłowska herself as the teenage mother, and directed by Przemysław Wojcieszek, who saw the text as a manifesto for the dispossessed generation born in the 1980s. Pawłowski (2006), a strong proponent of Masłowska, saluted the inexhaustible deposits of humour in her work, which allows an audience 'to look deep into the psyche of an average Pole, shaped by television, the Church and the Catholic family'. The young novelist's celebrity attracted a large and enthusiastic crowd at the reading, and the play was formally produced at the TR later that year. It subsequently received a number of stagings around the country, the most significant of which was Agnieszka Glińska's production at the Teatr Studio in Warsaw in 2013.

194   *Bryce Lease*

Lisa Goldman (2008), who produced the play at London's Soho Theatre, was drawn to the dark humour of the play, which, despite certain provocative overlaps with in-yer-face aesthetics, went far to reinterpret the political at the level of the personal in opposition to the prototypical British tendency to make political theatre that is 'sociological', 'issue-based', and concerned with newspaper headlines, and produced it in the UK in 2008. Masłowska is known for her dismantling of the Polish language through the deliberate misuse of grammatical structures, the appropriation of slang, club culture, and television jargon, as well as the invention of neologisms, puns, and other linguistic tricks, all of which makes her writing notoriously difficult to translate. The perspective of the narration changes rapidly and somewhat inexpertly, and what begins as a dark comedy turns abruptly to a brutal tragedy. Polish critics did not agree over the heterogeneity of the structure, some seeing it as a comedic art grappling with a serious tone (Pawłowski 2006) and others as a structural defect (Miłkowski 2006).

At many turns in the play, the plausibility of the existence of 'Polish-speaking Romanians' is called into question. Rather than remarking on a scarcity of economic migrants in Poland, the 'Polish-speaking Romanian' functions as a structural social fantasy through which Masłowska critiques a deeply embedded intolerance towards heterogeneity. 'Romanian' thus stands in for an imaginary figure that is the opposite of a refined or middle-class Pole: unconcerned with social etiquette, obsessed with material wealth, and defined by an ability to live by one's wits. Later, when Parcha grumbles that 'We're Polish-speaking Romanians, we're lesbians, queers, Jews, we work in an advertising agency' (Masłowska 2008: 47), the Romanian is positioned as a metonym for prejudice and misplaced social anxiety. These conglomerations of exclusion would return with force in Masłowska's novel *Inni ludzie* (*Other People*, 2019), which was adapted for TR Warszawa in a production directed by Jarzyna. In *Other People*, Warsaw residents bemoan the presence of 'others' in a cityscape made up of ethnic and religious others, sexual minorities, migrants, foreign students, and tourists. Despite the rampant nostalgia for a Warsaw that no one visited and an aggressive dismissal of visible diversity, it is the white ethnically Polish city residents themselves that drive each other crazy.

Similar to her award-winning novel *Wojna polsko-ruska pod flagą biało-czerwoną* (translated as *White and Red,* 2002), Pawłowski (2006) delights in the way Polish insecurity complexes are compensated for by stereotypes in Masłowska's writing. Embracing the theme of the fancy-dress party ('dirt, stench and disease'), Parcha dresses in a filthy shell suit and blackens his teeth with a marker, while Dżina disguises herself as a pregnant teenager. When referring to their lives back in Romania a number of ridiculous and farfetched details are invented, from living in huts and gathering grain from the fields to working in a dog and monkey factory and surviving solely on scraps of meat. The pair leaves the party early, ending up stranded on a rural highway without a means to travel back to Warsaw, the ultimate point of geographical identification. After unsuccessfully begging for a lift at a petrol station, Parcha breaks down and takes a man hostage. The drive that ensues is punctuated by sudden outbursts of violence. (Another strong connection between this play and *Other People* is the depiction of cars as sites of luxury, wealth, and independence that ultimately produce angst around traffic, overcrowding, poor driving, and air pollution. Thus, middle-class privilege results in middle-class anxiety.) Under the influence of narcotics, Parcha and Dżina fully assume the identity of the mythical 'Romanians', a murderer and a thief (she tries to steal the driver's air freshener), temporarily capable of committing transgressions that are precluded in their normal, law-abiding lives. The scene oscillates between pleas for help and threats of aggression and brutality, drawing attention to the various configurations of victimhood the West places on the subaltern, epitomised here by the Romanian. This is matched by a temporary loss of linguistic ability through flawed, repetitive syntax, indicating that socialisation and politeness values are entrenched in the Polish language. Rather than soliciting empathy with the protagonists that absolves them of responsibility, Masłowska challenges spectators to consider how emerging trends in cosmopolitan Polish life have produced a generation, generous and violent in turns, that is self-centred, materially driven, and immature. By the conclusion of the play, Parcha admits that his imagined Romania is indeed a paradise in contrast with the new Poland. Perhaps this very fixed focus on the complexities and instabilities of Polish culture led the production to receive mixed reviews from the British media, many of whom expressed anxiety that the play probably held greater significance for home audiences,[5] suggesting that the British public knows very little about the cultures of the largest foreign-born community currently living in the United Kingdom.

Painful pasts, haunting presents

Having considered the different modes in which these playwrights construct political critique, in this section I outline a significant connection between Demirski and Masłowska through their preoccupation with painful pasts and difficult histories that elude historicist grasp and classical dramaturgy. Both writers draw attention to the struggle over memory as opposed to memory's simple invocation, and the ways in which memorialising practices have been in ideological sympathy with advertising industries, neoliberal consumerism, and imagined urban utopias. While Poland's complex historical past is a common interest, there is no formal contiguity between the writers' artistic strategies. Demirski dealt with Polish memory and history in plays such as *Niech żyje wojna!* (*Long Live the War!*, 2009), 'a deconstruction of historical imagination shaped by infantile and propagandist images of war' (Krakowska 2011: 480), and *Bitwa Warszawska 1920* (*Battle of Warsaw 1920*, 2013), an 'anti-history' which uses an historical event, the so-called 'Miracle on the Vistula' battle, as a frame for the collision of prominent historical personages such as Józef Piłsudski and Rosa Luxemburg with ordinary figures to deconstruct mythologised Polish narratives. If Demirski uses fragments as a way of addressing our inability to suture memory together into a self-consistent whole, where the 'past is always

196   *Bryce Lease*

subject to revision' (Burzyńska 2015: 6), Masłowska focuses on what Dominick LaCapra (2014: 215) has called the 'unsettling after effects' and 'haunting presences' of the past in the present.

In 2009, as part of the 'International Author's Festival on Identity and History – Digging deep and getting dirty' at Berlin's Schaubühne, which commissioned writers to interrogate how the past shapes national consciousness and collective, individual, and political identities, Masłowska wrote *Między nami dobrze jest* (translated as *No Matter How Hard We Tried*), which was co-produced with TR Warszawa. The play offers a critical and humorous multigenerational perspective on Polish identity with a particular focus on lives marginalised under neoliberalism.

No Matter How Hard We Tried circulates around three generations (grandmother, mother, daughter) left behind in the postcommunist upward redistributions of wealth. Stuffed into the same apartment, their enforced physical proximity under the socio-economic conditions of the free market offers indifference and loneliness rather than intimacy and economic security. Everything is cheap, greasy, unhealthy, out of date, run down, toxic. The mother's job at Tesco is not tiring, but it is demanding and unrewarding. Babcia (grandmother in Polish) is a wheelchair-user but lives in a building without a lift. Her physical isolation is matched by her emotional alienation from her daughter, who works until 11pm, and her granddaughter, who ignores her to watch television after school. The Second World War haunts the play both as a theme and a character. 'I remember the war', Babcia says. 'The what?' Little Metal Girl responds. Defying expectation of stories of victimhood and survival, Babcia then recounts pleasant memories of walking by the Vistula, a time when her legs still worked and she was mobile, the time of her youth. Each of these romantic images is undermined and parodied by her granddaughter: the Vistula is a shit stream, filled with disease and gasoline fumes where one can fish for used condoms.

As in *Polish-Speaking Romanians*, Masłowska hedges between satire and parody that invites the audience to laugh both at and with the characters of the Mother and her neighbour, and the morbid banalities of lived realities under neoliberalism make way for memories of painful pasts.[6] In a cheap outfit from Tesco that is covered in grease and sweat stains and costs 28 PLN (£5), the Mother has time to save her plastic yoghurt pots and to wait for WWII to knock on the door. The neighbour asks why she should be entitled to a mobile phone when she is a *fat pig*, thus literalising the neoliberal rhetoric that intertwines youth, beauty, health, economic achievement, and entitlement. The family's lives are ultimately realised through negation: the holidays they will not take; the products they will not consume; the future they will not have. 'Nowhere, good old nowhere – all the memories it brings back!' the Mother declares while a virtual, projected Babcia drives in circles on the wall – 'nowhere' is familiar, intimate, whimsical. Masłowska suggests that this radical negativity that co-constructs contemporary Poland does not only mask an emotional purpose-lessness, it produces its own sources of pleasure and its own assurances around subjectivity. In Jarzyna's production, many critics stressed the contrast between the worn-out aesthetics of the text and the supermodern style of the set. Smooth white walls became screens for digital images of the impoverished household in the tenement block. Domestic objects appear (and disappear) in the style of children's drawings. This divergence between textual and staged worlds is a productive technique that renders visible otherwise less perceptible social processes. Between the grimy and grim apartment and the slick, supermodern set, there is no nourishment, nothing sticks, and nothing lasts.

In *Other People*, this environment is updated through three vertical screens that mimic the world-making space of mobile phones (see Figure 10.1). As in *No Matter How Hard We Tried*, both domestic and public space also surrender to digital surface, reliant on green screens and pixels for its construction and reconstruction. Characters, who emerge from across the socio-economic strata of Warsaw, are filmed behind the screens so that actors' bodies are hidden even from the audience. Although we can hear actors speaking, their voices are mediated through microphones, which produces an encounter more akin to the cinematic close-up than the declamatory voice of a stage actor. If everyday moments of live, situated interpersonal communication remain mediated through the technologies of phones, sex is one of the rare occasions when bodies (clumsily) come together on stage. Inadequate and unsatisfying, sex never legitimates intimacy or affection but rather propels people further apart – making them into 'other people'.

Figure 10.1 Maria Maj and Yacine Zmit singing on vertical screens in Grzegorz Jarzyna's production of Dorota Masłowska's *Inni ludzie* (*Other People*, 2019), courtesy of the TR Warszawa Archive. Photograph © Marcin Oliva Soto

198   *Bryce Lease*

The trope of the screen also moves from the domestic to the cinematic. In *No Matter How Hard We Tried* a film director (Man) speaks about and simultaneously constructs the historical biopic *The Horse Rode Horseback*, a parody of both Hollywood narrative on the one side and the dismal tragic endings of the classic Polish cinema on the other. In both cinema cultures, history is constructed through representational narratives that play a hegemonising function. The end of the play disrupts and places at risk everything that has come before. The Man, who commands the enunciative structure of his imagined film and Masłowska's play, declares that Babcia was killed when her building was bombed during the war, which means in turn that her descendants do not exist. Little Metal Girl is a ghost of someone who has not died because she was never born. Jarzyna framed this revelation with archival footage, a bird's eye perspective of Warsaw's bombed-out streets. The footage is played across the set (another screen) in reverse, so destroyed buildings are made whole again, a filmic strategy that refuses cinema's claims to untroubled access to visual archives. The projection then moves to the present day in which the former buildings form a large construction site. This technology mirrors that of human memory, which seeks to reconstruct what has been lost, abandoned, or destroyed, but which instead only succeeds in constructing something new. Babcia fails to recognise the street she was walking down the day the war broke out. The conflation of Babcia's memory, her lack of recognition, and the archival footage require spectators to also look differently at the cityscape. Although Babcia's memory has not been erased – she is neither senile nor suffering from amnesia – it does not help her to recognise the (transformed) street. This is comparable to a scene in *Other People* in which one character plays 'Warsaw 2020', a video game set in a city in ruins. In the former play, the authenticity of the technologies of the archive are themselves called into question through the reversal of a standard cinematic flashback, while in the latter Masłowska and Jarzyna construct the anxiety of Warsaw being destroyed a second time through a desire to play this destruction as a game. In both productions, the visual space breaks up and becomes pixelated, a site of spatial exclusion, through the destruction of the war and the reconstruction of capitalist wealth, and social prejudice based on class and ethnic difference. Jarzyna's staging of screens thus develops an idiom for Masłowska's social critique.

Babcia's death in the war makes Mother and Little Metal Girl spectral, not as traces of a lost past but rather as imagined projections of an unlived future past. This again is playing with and subverting cinematic temporality. We are back in the world of the filmmaker who is a shadow on the back of the stage. This shadow announces: 'And this is when we realise that the grandmother died in the air raid'. While we might at first be tempted to interpret this ending as a disruptive alternative to the imagined film, Masłowska defies audience expectation by circulating back within the film's diegesis itself. As spectators, we are not looking with a critical gaze from the outside of the film of great Polish patriotism, victimhood, and heroic exceptionalism, we are already trapped inside its narrative form and framework. Any empathetic pull the audience is tempted to feel at the realisation of the grandmother's death and the granddaughter's inexistence is conditioned by the very structure of the mainstream film we are invited to laugh at. I would argue that this sudden change of context – the horrifying discovery that we are complicitly *within* rather than critically *without* – is one of the most powerful strategies in Masłowska's playwriting.

Demirski and Masłowska's interrogation of Polish pasts sits uneasily alongside the now voracious appetite for historical museums in Poland and the impulse to pass punitive laws that regulate collective memory – a trend that is discernible across Central and Eastern Europe, but the model for which was established in Poland (see Koposov 2018: 300–10). I am reminded of Andreas Huyssen's prescient argument at the turn of this century that what is at stake in the 'history/memory debate is not only a disturbance of our notions of the past, but a fundamental crisis in our imagination of alternative futures' (2003: 2), which draws together these playwrights' critiques of nationalist historical narration and the enforcement of neoliberal capitalism as the only possible future after communism. During the preparation for this chapter, the PiS-led government approved a new law that criminalises accusations of Polish participation in the Holocaust and war crimes committed while Poland was occupied by Germany between 1939–45. Historian Marci Shore (2018) argued that 'the rejection of the universal – the insistence upon Polish exceptionalism – is at the heart of Poland's "historical policy", which aims to control the narrative of the twentieth century in such a way as to glorify and exonerate Poles'.[7] In the politically charged atmosphere in which historical policy and the development of extreme nationalism in Poland are serving as 'an evasion of responsibility, an attempt at psychic consolation through the exporting of guilt', Demirski and Masłowska's exposures of the struggles over national memory – as opposed to the representation of the struggles to remember – are crucial as theatrical forms of civic enfranchisement. What is particularly noteworthy is that both playwrights yoke their critiques of an overdetermined and rapidly transforming politics of memory to neoliberalism and the development of class inequalities. Such experiments in stage writing evoke Joanna Krakowska's (2011: 480) prescient reminder that in order to change our reality we must first change our imagination.

Paweł Demirski – four key productions

Dziady. Ekshumacja. Directed by Monika Strzępka. Cast: Adam Cywka, Wojciech Mecwaldowski, Marian Czerski, Rafał Kronenberger, Jolanta Zalewska, Agata Skowrońska, Alicja Kwiatkowska, Marcin Czarnik, Jakub Giel, Michał Kusztal, Andrzej Mrozek, Cezary Kussyk. Teatr Polski Wrocław, January 2007.

Był sobie Andrzej Andrzej Andrzej i Andrzej. Directed by Monika Strzępka. Cast: Małgorzata Białek, Agnieszka Kwietniewska, Sabina Tumidalska, Mirosława Żak, Daniel Chryc, Włodzimierz Dyła, Jerzy Gronowski, Rafał Kosowski, Sebastian Stankiewicz, Ryszard Węgrzyn. Teatr Dramatyczny im. Jerzego Szaniawskiego, Wałbrzych, May 2010.

200   *Bryce Lease*

Trybuna tęczowa 2012. Directed by Monika Strzępka. Cast: Michał Majnicz, Marcin Pempuś, Adam Cywka, Katarzyna Strączek, Jolanta Zalewska, Agata Skowrońska, Mariusz Kiljan, Jakub Giel, Michał Chorosiński, Michał Opaliński, Michał Mrozek, Igor Kujawski. Teatr Polski Wrocław, March 2011.

nie-boska komedia. WSZYSTKO POWIEM BOGU! Directed by Monika Strzępka. Cast: Szymon Czacki, Marcin Czarnik, Juliusz Chrząstowski, Małgorzata Hajewska-Krzysztofik, Michał Majnicz, Adam Nawojczyk, Marta Nieradkiewicz, Marta Ojrzyńska, Dorota Pomykała, Anna Radwan-Gancarczyk, Radomir Rospondek, Dorota Segda, Małgorzata Zawadzka. Narodowy Stary Teatr, Krakow, December 2014.

Dorota Masłowska – four key productions

Między nami dobrze jest. Directed by Grzegorz Jarzyna. Cast: Roma Gąsiorowska, Magdalena Kuta, Lech Łotocki, Rafał Maćkowiak, Maria Maj, Agnieszka Podsiadlik, Danuta Szaflarska, Katarzyna Warnke, Adam Woronowicz. Schaubühne am Lehniner Platz, Berlin, March 2009.

Dwoje biednych Rumunów mówiących po polsku. Directed by Agnieszka Glińska. Cast: Marcin Januszkiewicz, Monika Krzywkowska, Dorota Landowska, Agnieszka Pawełkiewicz, Modest Ruciński. Teatr Studio, Warsaw, September 2013.

Wojna polsko-ruska pod flagą biało-czerwoną. Directed by Paweł Świątek. Cast: Karolina Kazoń, Anna Paruszyńska, Merta Konarska, Natalia Strzelecka, Marta Waldera, Katarzyna Zawiślak-Dolny. Teatr im. Juliusza Słowackiego, Krakow, January 2019.

Inni ludzie. Directed by Grzegorz Jarzyna. Cast: Marcin Czarnik, Cezary Kosiński, Natalia Kalita, Magdalena Kuta, Rafał Maćkowiak, Maria Maj, Agnieszka Podsiadlik, Aleksandra Popławska, Tomasz Tyndyk, Adam Woronowicz, Yacine Zmit, Agnieszka Żulewska, Michał DJ B Olszański. TR Warszawa, Warsaw, March 2019.

Notes

1 This chapter is supported by the AHRC-funded project, 'Staging Difficult Pasts: Of Narratives, Objects and Public Memory' (Grant Reference: AH/R006849/1). My thanks to Marcin Kościelniak for his insightful comments on a draft of this chapter.
2 Relatedly, Kościelniak (2011) questioned the omission of the Catholic Church from this discussion of social discrimination against homosexuality.
3 While Demirski and Strzępka briefly flirted with optimism in *Triumf Woli* (*Triumph of the Will*, 2016), which catalogued examples of hope and its emancipatory capacities for overcoming serious obstacles, they have since returned to their pessimistic conclusion that moral panic continues to dominate politics.
4 Masłowska is calling attention to the particular and deeply problematic use of the term 'Romanian' in Polish as a pejorative reference to poverty, backwardness, provincialism, and shame.
5 See Gardner (2008) and Hopkins (2008)

6 One of the public debates that erupted from the play centred around whether Masłowska was siding with or empathetic to the Catholic or neoconservative right. When the play was first published, critics of her novels that had previously dismissed her as a recalcitrant and unsophisticated youth lacking in good taste and floundering in moral turpitude stood up in defence of this play. This unexpected advocacy from the right resulted from Masłowska's parody of pro-feminist or gay perspectives and depiction of anti-social and economic liberal views, which was mistakenly read in a literal valence and compared to the prose of Jarosław Marek Rymkiewicz, a staunch supporter of the Law and Justice Party. What commentators who defended this position missed was the playwright's equally critical stance across the political spectrum. If Demirski critiqued the left for its moral panic, Masłowska placed pressure on the disingenuousness of liberal political correctness and tested accepted discourses of tolerance that mask intolerance. Therefore, her condemnation of nationalistic rhetoric should not be mistaken for empathy or unity with PiS or its supporters. Far from literalism, Masłowska shines a critical light on forms of language that have lost meaning through their discursive circulation.

7 This is hauntingly reinforced by one of Vladimir Putin's political technologists, Gleb Pavlovsky, who observed that in a 'commemorative era' in which memory becomes the instrument of European politicians 'the politics of history will become the standard of politics as such' (cited in Kopsov 2018: 59).

Works cited

Bourdieu, Pierre (2003) *Pascalian Meditations*, Cambridge: Polity Press.

Burzyńska, Anna R. (2015) 'From documentarist to situationist: The plays of Paweł Demirski', *Polish Theatre Journal*: 1–7.

Demirski, Paweł (2015) 'Theatre of the playwright', *Polish Theatre Journal*: 1–7.

Derkaczew, Joanna (2011) 'Dekada teatru', *Gazeta Wyborcza*, 1 January.

Freeman, Elizabeth (2010) *Time Binds: Queer Temporalities, Queer Histories*, Durham, NC: Duke University Press.

Gardner, Lyn (2008) 'A Couple of Poor, Polish-Speaking Romanians' [review], *The Guardian*, 7 March.

Goldman, Lisa (2008) 'Interview with Alex Fleming', Soho Theatre, London, 28 February, http://sohotheatre.jellycast.com/node/3.

Hopkins, James (2008) 'Biedni Anglicy nic nie pojmują', trans. Grzegorz Sowula, *Rzeczpospolita*, 20 March.

Huyssen, Andreas (2003) *Present Pasts: Urban Palimpsests and the Politics of Memory*, Palo Alto, CA: Stanford University Press.

Koposov, Nikolay (2018) *Memory Laws, Memory Wars: The Politics of the Past in Europe and Russia*, Cambridge: Cambridge University Press.

Kościelniak, Marcin (2011) 'Cukierek z nadzieniem', *Tygodnik Powszechny*, 4 July, http s://www.tygodnikpowszechny.pl/cukierek-z-nadzieniem-140054.

——— (2021) 'Teatr (bez) dramatopisarzy', in Katarzyna Fazan, Michal Kobialka and Bryce Lease (eds), *A History of Polish Theatre*, Cambridge: Cambridge University Press.

Krakowska, Joanna (2011) 'Demi(d)ramy', in Paweł Demirski, *Parafrazy*, Warsaw: Krytyka Polityczna.

Kwaśniewska, Monika (2018) 'Krytyczna przeciwskuteczność i utajony konserwatyzm. Wiara, Kościół i społeczeństwo w wybranych spektaklach Moniki Strzępki i Pawła Demirskiego', in Agata Adamiecka-Sitek, Marcin Kościelniak and Grzegorz Niziołek (eds), *Teatr a Kościół*, Warsaw: Instytut Teatralny im. Zbigniewa Raszewskiego.

202 Bryce Lease

Kizioł, Aneta (2007) 'Trupa wyciąga trupy', *Polityka* 17/18, 29 March.

LaCapra, Dominick (2014) *Writing History, Writing Trauma*, Baltimore, MD: Johns Hopkins University Press.

Leder, Andrzej (2014) *Prześniona rewolucja. Ćwiczenia z logiki historycznej*, Warsaw: Krytyka Polityczna.

Masłowska, Dorota (2008) *A Couple of Poor, Polish-Speaking Romanians*, trans. Lisa Goldman and Paul Sirett, London: Oberon.

Miłkowski, Tomasz (2006) 'Sztuka zapowiada mocny spektakl', *Przegląd*, 13 June.

Pawłowski, Roman (2006) 'Królowa w rumuńskim przebraniu', *Gazeta Wyborcza*, 24 May.

——— (2016) 'Towards the Private: Notes on Contemporary Non-Fiction Theatre', *Polish Theatre Journal:* 1–13.

Popovici, Iulia (2014) 'Monika Strzępka and Paweł Demirski: The Theater of Social Anarchy', *Howlround Theatre Commons*, 16 December.

Shore, Marci (2018) 'Poland digs itself a memory hole', *New York Times*, 4 February.

Stokfiszewski, Igor (2011a) 'Demirski. Synteza', in Paweł Demirski, *Parafrazy*, Warsaw: Krytyka Polityczna.

——— (2011b) 'W stronę akcji bezpośredniej', *Krytyka Polityczna*, 31 December.

Węgrzyniak, Rafał (2010) '"Ale dramaturg, kim on jest?" Dramaturdzy i ich protoplaści w historii', *Notatnik Teatralny*, nr 58–59.

Wysocki, Tomasz (2007) 'Polak ogląda w lustrze swoje czarne podniebienie', *Gazeta Wyborcza*, 17 April.

11 Jordi Galceran and Juan Mayorga
Unravelling the present, narrativising the past[1]

Maria M. Delgado

At first glance there appears to be little in common between the works of Juan Mayorga (b. 1965) and Jordi Galceran[2] (b. 1964), although they can lay claim, with the exception of Fernando Arrabal, to being Spain's most internationally staged living playwrights. Mayorga is only one of two theatre-makers – the other is actor-director José Luis Gómez – to currently hold seats in Spain's Royal Academy (Real Academia Española or RAE), the body founded in 1713 to safeguard the 'correct' and 'proper' use of the Spanish language - *castellano* or Castilian. There are only a handful of dramatists born in the twentieth century – José López Rubio (1903–96), Antonio Buero Vallejo (1916–2000), and Fernando Fernán Gómez (1921–2007) — who have served as *académicos* before him. Born in Madrid, where he currently resides, he has written over 40 plays, translated into over 30 languages that explore historical accountability, narrative silences, and the faultlines of language. Mayorga writes on a large canvas, engaging with key events in modern Europe – from the Dreyfus Affair of 1894 in *La tortuga de Darwin* (*Darwin's Tortoise*, 2008) to Jewish resistance in the Warsaw Ghetto in *El cartógrafo (Varsovia 1:400.000)* (*The Cartographer. Warsaw 1:400,000*, written 2010, first presented in French in 2012).[3] These are plays that embrace different formal conventions – from first-person narrative that frames the first scene of *Himmelweg (Camino al cielo)* (*Way to Heaven*, 2003) to intersecting time periods (the early 1940s, 1981, 1995, and 2008) in *The Cartographer*. Moving across space and time, they prise apart the identification of actor and role; two performers, for example, took on all 12 roles in Mayorga's 2016 staging of *The Cartographer* and four male actors are called on to play canines in *La paz perpetua* (*Perpetual Peace*, 2008).

Galceran, born in Barcelona but currently Madrid-based, writes in Catalan, although he has also produced translations of his work into Castilian-Spanish.[4] Galceran's plays tend to observe a unity of time, place, and action. Evolving in pressured contexts and habitually deploying a ticking-clock scenario, they tend to avoid easy placement within a specific geographical context – *Burundanga* (2011), which evolves in a present-day Barcelona, is an exception. Galceran scored a significant commercial success with an early work, *El mètode Grönholm* (*The Grönholm Method*, 2003), which gave him, in the words of Sharon G. Feldman and Anxo Abuín González, 'a level of commercial success unsurpassed

204   *Maria M. Delgado*

by any Catalan playwright of his generation' (2012: 408). While Mayorga has worked primarily within the subsidised sector, Galceran's career in Spain is now predominantly within the commercial theatre, where he has enjoyed extensive runs: *Burundanga*, for example, has played for eight seasons in Madrid, first at the Lara and then the Maravillas theatre, with a tour that has taken in 40 cities, as well as a Barcelona run at the Villaroel; it has been seen by over a million spectators in Spain (Ferrer 2018). Galceran writes also for television and film;[5] Mayorga has never written for television, and while he has worked on a prior film script with Juan Cavestany, at the time of writing (August 2019), he is collaborating with director Paula Ortiz on screenplays for two of his plays, *El arte de la entrevista* (*The Art of the Interview*, 2013) and *La lengua en pedazos* (*Language in Pieces*, 2012).

In addition, while Mayorga frequently deploys irony and absurdist comedy within a dramatic register, Galceran writes comedies that have made him, in the words of his press team, the 'Rey Midas del teatro español' (King Midas of the Spanish theatre) (cited in Morales 2014). Mayorga has adapted works from the Spanish canon (by Valle-Inclán, Lope de Vega, and Calderón), international classics including Dürrenmatt's *The Visit* (2000), and Ibsen's *An Enemy of the People* (2007), in a staging by Gerardo Vera which acquired particular resonance during the early years of Spain's economic crisis. Galceran's 20-plus translations include an adaptation of Gogol's *The Government Inspector* (2009) and contemporary comedies (reworked into Castilian or Catalan) that have been tried and tested in domestic markets, as with Matthieu Delaporte and Alexandre de la Patellière's contemporary farce, *El nom* (*The Name*, 2012), Yasmina Reza's *God of Carnage* (2016), and Claudio Tolcachir's *La omisión de la Familia Coleman* (*The Coleman Family's Omission*, 2018). Galceran's work has been compared to Reza for its witty, polished dialogue.[6] Like Tolcachir, he too creates works marked by mechanical plots and terse, witty dialogue. Galceran and Mayorga both acknowledge a mutual influence.[7]

Galceran: refashioning genre from a nation's woes

Jordi Galceran turned to writing professionally in 1995 when his early work *Dakota*, centring on a dentist who suffers an accident and begins to dream of characters who predict the future, won the Ignasi Iglesias prize and was subsequently staged at Barcelona's Poliorama theatre.[8] Describing it as a 'surrealistic work, perhaps the strangest piece I have written' (cited in Yuste 2015) and 'the play that changed my life' (cited in Bravo 2015), he followed it with *Palabras encadenadas* (*Killing Words*, 1995) the piece that first demonstrated what was to become Galceran's trademark characteristic: a small number of characters trapped in a tense dramatic context where a cat-and-mouse situation ensues, resolved in part through linguistic games. The tense two-hander, a basement-set psychological thriller, sees Ramón take his ex-wife, Laura, hostage. He dangles the prospect of release if she can outwit him in a game where he gives her a word and she subsequently responds with a word where the first syllable rhymes with the final syllable of Ramón's word. If she loses, he will pluck out her eye. The play's opening production at Barcelona's Romea theatre in 1998 initiated a working relationship with British-born director Tamzin Townsend – who directed both the Catalan- and the Castilian Spanish-language productions of *Killing Words*, the latter also enjoying a Buenos Aires run in 2001 – and has gone on to direct the Castilian Spanish-language openings of *The Grönholm Method* (2004), *Carnaval* (*Carnival*, 2008), and *Fuga* (*Escape*, 2011), as well as Galceran's adaptation of Reza's *God of Carnage* (2016). Galcaran sees the director's role in text-based theatre as one of articulating the clarity of a scene, and his views on the rise of directors' theatre indicate that the model of the director as lead creative artist is not one that he would like to see for his own theatre (cited in Redacción 2008).

Killing Words' rhyming wordplay presents particular demands on translators and this may be one reason why despite enjoying runs in Buenos Aires, Caracas, Medellín, and Mexico City, it has been translated less widely than Galceran's later plays. *Killing Words* was adapted by Fernando de Filipe into a film directed in 2003 by Laura Maña with Argentine actor Dario Grandinetti in the role of Ramón and Goya Toledo as Laura. The adaptation opened the narrative out from the single location to present a veteran policeman Espinosa (Fernando Guillén) and his rookie sidekick Sánchez (Eric Bonicatto), who question Ramón about Laura's disappearance – adding a second layer of cat-and-mouse pursuit to the narrative. Here it is Ramón on the back foot, engaging in careful wordplay when Espinosa tries to catch him out. Ramón's profession was altered from civil servant at the Ministry of Agriculture to university lecturer in the Philosophy of Aesthetics – the shift here pointing to 'writing' as a profession. The play's topicality – 91 women were murdered by abusive partners in 1997 – provides early evidence of Galceran's ability to engage with key issues tarnishing the surface of Spain's democratic success story.[9]

His subsequent play, *The Grönholm Method,* was developed under the auspices of the T6 programme of the Catalan National Theatre to encourage and promote Catalan playwriting. *The Grönholm Method* marks a shift of direction towards what he terms 'more realist comedies. I like comedy to have a point of credibility' (cited in Bravo 2015). Working with dramatist-director Sergi Belbel – who has gone on to direct other Galceran Catalan-language premieres, including *El Crèdit* (*Credit,* 2013) and *Carnival* (2006) – the compact 90-minute play uses the premise of four candidates turning up for the final stages of a job interview for a senior position at a multinational company, to explore the cut-throat politics of corporate capitalism. As they wait to be called in for interview, it dawns on all four that this is not a 'normal' recruitment process. Rather, they are obliged to literally fight it out in a series of exercises devised to test their ability to work under pressure. The winner takes the gilded prize of the much-coveted job. The other three are destined to go away demoralised and empty-handed. Belbel's staging, which opened at the TNC's Salla Tallers, went on to enjoy a three-year run at the Poliorama theatre. Characterisation was precise and accentuated, with four different personality 'types' contrasted: audacious go-getter Ferran (Jordi Boixaderas), ready able to manoeuvre any situation to his advantage; the

206 *Maria M. Delgado*

awkwardly jovial Enric (Lluís Soler) who has fallen on difficult times and is seeking new challenges in a corporate world where compassion has no place; the casual Carles (Jordi Diaz) looking for a career change; and the ambitious Mercè (Roser Batalla), icy, professional, and cautious.

Belbel's staging, featuring a lobby set designed by Paco Azorín with Le Corbusier imitation chairs and a scattering of corporate mineral-water bottles, boasted a strong visual reference to Reza's *Art* in the production's imposing painting, a twinkling surrealist eye staring wickedly down at the anonymous space where the 'guinea pigs' enact this experiment. The origins of the play lie in a story that reached Galceran of documents found in a bin from the Human Resources department of a well-known supermarket chain where an employee was found to have written a list of negative comments about interviewees for a cashier's job.[10] The dehumanised climate of nascent corporate capitalism functions both as the play's target and propeller. *Art* may be the play's most evident sibling, but there are echoes of Sartre's *Huis Clos* (*No Exit*, 1944) in the suffocating claustrophobia generated by the four trapped characters. This contemporary purgatory may dehumanise them, but it also proves an adrenalin-fuelled competitive drug that they find it hard to walk away from. If any of the four don't feel up to the assignment they have the option of leaving the room but cannot then re-enter. The moment they leave, they are, in effect, disqualified. As the four 'contestants' are slipped notes of instruction by the mysterious personnel department, resourcefulness coupled with deceit increasingly proves the key weapon. For the company that is seeking to hire them, Dekia, has set them a number of unusual tasks that call each one of their 'roles' into question. It is not clear if one is a mole planted by the organisation, or as in *Killing Words*, revelations are further layers of fiction.

Galceran's Castilian-language version reset the play in Madrid, shifted a few jokes and gave the characters Spanish versions of their names. Gabriel Carrascal's design offered a grimmer space of anonymous beige plaster, orange sofas, red chairs, and supermarket music that seeped ghostlike from the enclosing walls. Whereas Belbel chose to provide a dynamic pace, with Jordi Boixaderas's Ferran entering on a high and remaining dangerously wired for the whole evening, Townsend's production had a Pinteresque inflexion. Carlos Hipólito appeared a less volatile Fernando but one whose poisoned tongue became more apparent as the action progressed, moving from affability to menace in the blink of an eye. From the drab surroundings to the menace of the ordinary, her reading confirmed the personal as political, with a form of emotional torture located very firmly within the workplace rather than the home of Pinter's *The Homecoming* (1965).

The domestic success of both of these productions served as the launch pad for further international runs. Belbel's production had a three-season record-breaking run at the Poliorama (2004–7) before returning in 2010 with the original cast but a modified set and costume design. Townsend's staging had four seasons at Madrid's Marquina theatre as well as a tour of Spain undertaken by the second cast that took over in January 2007. Daniel Veronese's Buenos Aires production opened at

Teatro la Plaza in 2006. The play's Argentine success over three seasons – 600 performances seen by 250,000 spectators (Ferrer Hammerlindl 2012: 226) – was a factor in Marcelo Pineyro's decision to direct a film adaptation in 2005, *El método* (*The Method*). Galceran was unhappy with the version (adapted by Piñeyro with Mateo Gil), which expanded the initial four into seven candidates with a company employee watching over them. The three company moles of the original were here two moles, and the rewritten ending saw Mercedes (here renamed Nieves) leaving the Dekia headquarters building having triumphed over Fernando,[11] with an anti-IMF demonstration raging outside. Galceran judged that his 'black comedy' had been turned into an 'anticapitalist' drama (cited in Pejenaute 2012). Subsequently, Galceran threatened to withdraw rights for a German-language staging when a request was made to change the ending (Ferrer Hammerlindl 2012: 226), although he did allow a different ending for both the US and the UK productions, perhaps because it avoided the feelgood ending of classic comedy.

By 2015, the play had been seen translated into over 30 languages and seen by over two million spectators in 200 productions in 60 countries (Bravo 2015; see also Redacción 2010). Galceran identifies its success in its presentation of a situation – a job interview – that audiences can easily identify with (Pejenaute 2012). A four-year run in Germany included simultaneous performances in 25 cities, with Galceran claiming it was 'the fifth most represented work in the German theatre' (Graell 2010). Javor Gardev's 2010 Russian production juxtaposed the realistic and the metaphorical: Nikola Toromanov's slick corporate office was offset by a life-size shark suspended above the set – a reference to Damian Hirst's artwork *The Physical Impossibility of Death in the Mind of Someone Living*, now owned by millionaire hedge fund manager Steven A. Cohen.[12] Thierry Lavat's 2011 adaptation at Paris's Théâtre Tristan Bernard drew out links with Sartre and Reza while keeping a strong farcical dimension to the action, best evidenced in a role play set piece when the cast don the outfits of a bishop, a clown, a bullfighter, and policeman to try and argue their way to be given the only lifejacket in a plane that is about to crash.

The English-language premiere took place at Melbourne's Red Stitch Actors' Theatre in 2010 and the translation presented in London in 2018 (by Anne García Romero and Mark St. Germain) was previously premiered at Los Angeles' Falcon Theatre, both directed by BT McNicholl.[13] The London production, opening at the Menier Chocolate Factory in 2018, was set in the slick upper floor suite of New York Fortune 500's skyscraper offices, designed by Tim Hatley. And while the slick, pacey production and deft writing was admired, critics wondered whether the text might appear 'overfamiliar' (Billington 2018), and have benefited from revision to 'reflect, perhaps, the new Trump-era brutality, whereby animosity is worn as a badge of manliness' (Wolf 2018). The play may have reached London a decade too late. The analogies with Mike Bartlett's *Bull* (2013), alongside a recognition that the play predates *Bull* by a decade (Shuttleworth 2018), the recognition of the shadow of *The Apprentice* on the piece (Billington 2018), the echoes of Neil LaBute and Agatha Christie's *And Then There Were None* (Wolf 2018) and Paul Taylor's

208   *Maria M. Delgado*

description of the play as 'a twisted cross between *Survivor* and Pinter's *The Dumb Waiter* or *Glengarry Glen Ross* reimagined by Sartre' (2018) may have ultimately rendered Galceran's play less assertive than it appeared when first seen in pre-recession Spain.[14]

Galceran's admiration for David Mamet and Arthur Miller has been noted by critic Jesús Ruiz Mantilla, who also sees him as an heir to Antonio Buero Vallejo – one of Spain's most respected anti-Francoist dramatists (Ruiz Mantilla 2015). Galceran's dramatic construction, however, is tighter than that of Buero, his language less verbose. Buero wrote earnest allegories about the state of the nation; Galceran writes dry comedies and, in this respect, Alan Ayckbourn is a clearer point of contact.[15] Galceran has acknowledged admiration for Martin McDonagh's acerbic dialogue and Mamet's feral fables.[16] Both *Killing Words* and *Carnival* show a debt to Anthony Schaffer's *Sleuth* (1970). The latter also deploys a thriller format as the police investigate the disappearance of a child with a 30-minute ultimatum played out in real time. Esteve Soler identifies the 2001 TV series *24* as the clearest influence on *Carnival* (Soler 2008), but traces of Mamet are present both in the noir-thriller scenarios of *Killing Words* and *Carnival* and the tense wordplay and verbal violence that underpins both plays. Mamet's influence on *The Grönholm Method* is evidenced in the lying, deception, impersonation, and unethical gameplay that the characters embark on in the name of winning.

For Galceran, plot always trumps character (cited in Yuste 2015). He eschews experimentation, opting instead for a simplicity in the premise and structure of a play – often adopting a conflict-based narrative where one character tries to secure something from his or her opponent. 'If I can narrate in a single space, in a single act and in real time, I'll do that' he has stated (cited in Bravo 2015). Even *Cancún* (2008), a 'what if' comedy where two holidaying couples are transported back, 25 years earlier, in a husband-swap where their lives take different directions, observes a unity of place in its single setting: the holiday bungalow in Cancún. Galceran writes when he realises he has a good idea and in between he undertakes commissions – translations, television screenplays, musicals.[17] He no longer pressures himself to write an original work, recognising the writing block experienced between *Killing Words* and *The Grönholm Method*: 'I'd like to be Woody Allen who makes a film a year but lamentably that's not me' (cited in Yuste 2015). He has spoken of writing quickly and then rewriting over a longer period of time and he doesn't usually attend rehearsals, preferring to hand over the text to a creative team,[18] hence the importance of the select number of directors (Belbel and Townsend, but also Josep Maria Mestres and Gabriel Oliveras[19]) to which he has entrusted the majority of the Castilian Spanish- and Catalan-language premieres of his work.

Galceran's resonance as a dramatist is also partly due to his ability to theatricalise a high-stakes performative situation that resonates with an audience. This was the case both in *The Grönholm Method* and *Credit*, a two-hander, where a smug bank manager is visited by a client, Antoni Vicens, who hopes to secure a much-needed loan. The audience never find out why he is in this predicament, but the situation needed little explanation in the climate of recession-hit Spain, where unemployment stood at a record high of 27 per cent in early 2013.[20] Refused a €3,000 loan, Antoni throws a spanner in the works by threatening to sleep with the bank manager's wife. Something becomes unhinged in the tightly wound bureaucrat, and the tables turn as Antoni begins to predict a falling on hard times that comes to pass later in the play. The bank manager has been thrown out by his wife and he wants to win her back. He is recklessly throwing credit at Antoni for his advice – €12,000 instead of the €3,000 Antoni initially requested – a reference to the reckless spending that brought Spain to its economic knees in 2007.

Credit proffers a variation on the odd couple pairing; two contrasting alpha males in conflict in a restrictive space where they run and tumble like mice in a cage. Marcos Ordóñez assessed Sergi Belbel's Catalan-language production as manic farce, with Francophone influences – Georges Feydeau, Claude Magnier, and Francis Veber (Ordóñez 2013); Max Glaenzel's revolving set presented a merry-go-round where Jordi Bosch's bank manager and Jordi Boixaderas' client moved in a high-energy waltz of collapsing capitalism. Bosch's slapstick clowning – his legs kicking up and down like John Cleese's Basil Fawlty – allowed Boixaderas to slip around him opportunistically. In Act 2, discarded coffee cups littered his once immaculate table, his fevered caffeine-drenched eyes telling a story of hysteria and overstimulation. At the production's end, it was as if the two men were animated toys that had been put to sleep in a pod as the nation remained in a spiral of debt and borrowing that showed no signs of abating. Gerardo Vera's Madrid production opted for a less effusive tone, with Ordóñez viewing it as an Italian tragicomedy, with echoes of Luigi Pirandello, early Eduardo di Filippo, and Ettore Scola (Ordóñez 2013), Ordóñez's referencing of these writers evidently inscribing Galceran within a European canon. Carlos Hipólito – an actor who also premiered *The Grönholm Method* and *Dakota* in Madrid – presented a more affable bank manager, one whose fall felt more gradated, while Luis Merlo's client, here given the Castilian version of his name, Antonio Vicente, looked less poised than Boixaderas' arch antagonist. The contrast between the characters has often been played out in costuming that has juxtaposed the suited bank manager with a more streetwise client in hoodie and flat cap (dir. Hendrick Toompere, Draamateater Estonia, 2016), or accentuated generational differences (dir. Mihai Constantin, National Theatre of Bucharest, 2016), or placed a focus on class differences (dir. Bina Haralampieva, Plovdiv Drama Theatre, Bulgaria, 2016). Eric Civanyan's staging at Paris's Théâtre de la Gaîté Montparnasse (2019) had two world-weary middle-aged men tussling for ascendancy. All these stagings nevertheless demonstrate how neoliberalism's values contaminate all aspects of domestic life.

'All my plays', Galceran stated in 2011, 'are about people who want to be one thing and end up becoming another' (cited in EFE 2011). *Burundanga* evidences the end of the Basque armed separatist organisation, Euskadi Ta Askatasuna (ETA), through a frothy romantic comedy which Galceran conceived as 'an episode of *Friends* where some terrorists arrive' (cited in Pejenaute 2012).

210   *Maria M. Delgado*

Drugging her boyfriend Manel with the truth drug burundanga, pregnant Berta gets more than she bargained for when Manel admits that he loves her but also that he is a member of ETA. The Basque friend he is planning to bring round for drinks, Gorka, is a fellow member of the same cell and together they are plotting a kidnapping to raise funds for the organisation. Only the kidnap victim, Jaime, turns out to have been part of a revolutionary cell in the 1970s, and he relishes the opportunity to advise the two hapless ETA activists on underground tactics. I have written elsewhere of the play's layered references, from Alexander MacKendrick's Ealing comedy *The Ladykillers* (1955) to Marc Camoletti's *Boeing-Boeing* (1960) with nods also to McDonagh's *The Lieutenant of Inishmore* (2001) and Sean O'Casey's *Juno and the Paycock* (1924).[21] Multiple comings and goings imbue the action with a comical frenzy. Anna Tusell's bright, pop-influenced set for Gabriel Olivares' Madrid production pointed to a space of regression and playfulness. Sebastià Brosa and Eli Pérez's mustard-coloured living-room for Jordi Casanovas' 2012 Barcelona production had a retro-Almodóvaresque feel. Subsequent productions have also opted for a colourful aesthetic either in the characters' costumes (dir. Corina Fiorillo, Multitabarís Comafi, Buenos Aires, 2019), set, as with Albert Alpár's bouncy aqua and red beanbags for Csábi Anna's Hungarian production (Thalia's Arizona Studio, Budapest, 2019), or both, as in the vibrant colour clashes of Ondřej Zajíc's staging for Prague's Rokoko Theatre (2014).

If *The Grönholm Method* and *Credit* exposed capitalism's contamination of all aspects of life into a culture of bartering and selling, *Burundanga* showed the desperation of a society grappling for a sense of purpose – references to austerity and institutional fraud position the play *c*. 2011, the year of its opening. Throwaway comments by the unemployed Gorka suggest he may have turned to ETA for camaraderie when he was no longer able to earn his living as a cook. Manel also points to a generation that has lost its bearings – youth unemployment ran at 46 per cent in the second quarter of 2011 (García 2011). Jaime, once a rampant revolutionary working to dislodge the Franco regime, has jettisoned his egalitarian ideals in favour of economic wealth, with offshore investments that align him with Spain's corruption scandals. Jaime offers the men the possibility of employment in Honduras – only by leaving Spain can they hope to find a future for themselves, and it is a future that may not be entirely legal. Seen by over a million spectators in its seven-year run at Madrid's Maravillas theatre, *Burundanga* shows the appetite of Spanish audiences for a play 'that creates humour from its [a nation's] tragedies' (Vallejo 2011). Indeed, Galceran's deployment of topical motifs as the narrative pretexts for tense thrillers and black comedies has made him Spain's most commercially successful dramatist of the twenty-first century.

Mayorga: towards a theatre of memory

If Galceran's plays deal with 'little people' caught in situations that spiral dangerously out of control, Mayorga's works occupy a more expansive canvas with characters caught in epic historical moments where they are called upon to act in ways where the implications of their actions are not always clear. Mayorga took a double degree in Philosophy (from the National University of Distance Education) and Mathematics (from the Autonomous University of Madrid). Mayorga obtained his doctorate (published in 2003) on Walter Benjamin, supervised by the eminent philosopher Reyes Mate, to whom he dedicated his 2010 play *The Cartographer*. His playwriting is accompanied by work as an essayist – a collection of his essays was published in 2016. While Galceran studied Catalan Philology at the University of Barcelona, Mayorga attributes his pursuit of an 'essential language, without any padding' to his training as a mathematician and his attraction to 'questions that have no answers' to his philosophical background (Mayorga 2012: 479). Like Galceran, Mayorga taught in a secondary school, experiences that informed his 2006 play, *El chico de la última fila* (*The Boy at the Back*). His pedagogical experience also involves a position with specialisms in dramaturgy and philosophy between 1998 and 2006 at the RESAD, Madrid's theatre conservatoire. He currently has an affiliation with Carlos III University. He has acknowledged the importance of workshops he attended with Sala Beckett founder José Sanchis Sinisterra – a key figure in the development of a new playwriting scene in Spain – and Chilean Marco Antonio de la Parra, as well as the experience of having formed part of the Royal Court's Summer School in 1998, where Sarah Kane featured among the tutors (ibid.).

Mayorga's works have always been concerned with the ways in which the past is narrativised. *Más ceniza* (*More Ash*, 1994) explored the behind-the-scenes machinations before a coup d'état. In *El jardín quemado* (*The Scorched Garden*, 1997), a young researcher enters a psychiatric hospital during the transition to democracy where Republican prisoners are alleged to have been killed during Spain's Civil War. Confronting the institution's head doctor, Garay, Benet is able to both expose the mechanisms of erasure that 'disappeared' the prisoners and construct an alternative history that questions the 'official' version promoted by Garay. In *Siete hombres buenos* (*Seven Good Men*, written in 1989, first staged in 2020), the Spanish Civil War is repositioned by members of the Republican Government in exile. The mechanics of power – most specifically consolidation and execution – are key to his plays whether they occur within the domestic sphere, as with the Pinteresque *Animales nocturnos* (*Nocturnal*, 2003), or in a more overtly political arena – *Cartas de amor a Stalin* (*Love Letters to Stalin*, 1999). In the latter, a culture of surveillance comes to haunt the psyche of banned writer Mikhail Bulgakov. His letters to Stalin request permission to be expelled from Soviet Union, but as he waits in vain for a reply – a Godot that will never appear – he becomes ever more paranoid about his wife's loyalty, craving the approval of an omniscient dictator who has rendered him a shadow of his former self. It is one of four of his plays to have premiered or had runs at Madrid's María Guerrero theatre – part of the Centro Dramático Nacional (CDN) – a *de facto* national theatre for which he has declared a special affinity (Mayorga 2012: 481–2).

212   *Maria M. Delgado*

Mayorga's debates are often articulated across key moments in twentieth-century European history that have shaped nation formation: Stalinism in *Love Letters to Stalin*, the persecution of the Jews in Warsaw during the Second World War in *The Cartographer,* the Holocaust in *Way to Heaven*, the spread of fascist ideology across national boundaries in *Blumemberg's Translator*, and Spain's Civil War in *The Scorched Garden* and *Seven Good Men*. His is a theatre that brings to the stage both 'Europe's dreams but also its nightmares' (Mayorga 2016a: 193) and he positions the Spanish Civil War (1936–9) as one of the latter. *The Scorched Garden* is one of the first theatrical works to tackle Spain's transition to democracy, its failure to dismantle the structures of sociological Francoism, and its responsibility to the more than 120,000 disappeared of the Civil War and its aftermath.

The idea of Europe – as a concept, as a body, as a set of ideas – is central to many of his plays, a number of which feature the names of European cities, writers, politicians, or peoples in their titles. *Darwin's Tortoise* positions a humble tortoise, Harriet, transported by Charles Darwin from the Galapagos Islands to England in 1835, as a witness to the atrocities of twentieth-century Europe: two World Wars; Stalin's purges; the Spanish Civil War; the Holocaust; totalitarian regimes. She questions the narratives authored by an academic historian (known as the professor) who challenges her right to intervene. 'I was there', she replies. 'That's what gives me the right' (Mayorga 2017: 479; *Darwin's Tortoise* 3) and she proceeds to give a version of what she has seen and heard, arguing for memory as a resource that can defy those who have 'a stake in forgetting' (ibid.: 481; 4). Her vision of history 'from below' (ibid.: 482; 6) takes on board the plurality of embodied experience, embodying Benjamin's dictum that 'to articulate the past historically does not mean to recognise "the way it really was" (Ranke)' but rather it means to 'seize hold of a memory as it flashes up at a moment of danger' (Benjamin 1968: 255). The professor sees history as an 'objective' science and refuses to acknowledge the relationship between history and literature (Mayorga 2017: 485–6; 8). Harriet celebrates the insignificant details that the professor disdains: brushing against Marx in a crowded Soho; the face of a private in the First World War as he reads a letter from his fiancée; standing at the feet of the guards in Red Square in the aftermath of the Russian revolution; the collective hysteria of burning books in 1930s Berlin; escaping from being burned alive during the bombing of Guernica in 1937; hiding a little boy in her shell in the Warsaw ghetto in 1942. She embodies the Benjaminian need to empathise with the vanquished (Benjamin 1968: 255, 256); this was eloquently realised in Ernesto Caballero's 2008 Teatro de la Abadía production where Carmen Machi's tortoise was often at eye level with the audience but (literally) looked down on by José Luis Alcobendas' Professor.

In Mayorga's theatre, language is the tool of narration, a means for communication and the possible exchange of ideas, but it is always bound up with coercion and intimidation, seduction and exploitation. Words have the power to kill, Harriet reminds the professor in *Darwin's Tortoise* (ibid.: 497; 18). She herself is exploited by

Jordi Galceran and Juan Mayorga   213

the doctor, the professor, and the latter's wife, Beti, who wants a slice of the gains, planning to make a 'star' of Harriet in a stage musical. The professor may accuse Beti of turning Harriet into 'a fairground freak' but he too sees her as a means to an end (Mayorga 2017: 504; 25). He wants her to provide him with exclusive testimony that he will use to provide a new historical tome, and when she can no longer furnish him with information, he proposes shooting her. The doctor views her as a way of rebooting his waning career at a time when he finds himself a discredited figure in the profession. He has no qualms about submitting her to a range of invasive medical tests. Harriet has survived 200 years of tumultuous European history and when she faces extinction at the hands of the professor, his wife, and the doctor, she shows how her evolution has been grounded in an instinct for survival.[22]

Mayorga's humanisation of animals – a feature also of *Perpetual Peace, Palabra de perro* (*A Dog's Word*, 2009) and *Últimas palabras de Copito de Nieve* (*Snowflake's Last Words*, 2004) – may be a further strategy in his wish to present histories from the perspectives of those who are usually positioned at its margins. These fables offer a mode of theatricalising power dynamics and illustrate Mayorga's understanding of theatre as an act of imagination where a complicit audience is engaged in an encounter where they participate in a process of transformation. Snowflake, the world's only known albino gorilla, was a Barcelona icon, euthanised in November 2003, whose cancer and subsequent death inspired a collective mourning that became a global news story. Mayorga's 'brush[ing] history against the grain' (Benjamin 1968: 257) allows for an interrogation of the politics of exhibition: Snowflake addresses those who would see him as existing only as an exotic object of display; he returns the gaze, with a speech reflecting on Montaigne's 1580 essay 'That to philosophize is to learn to die', which demonstrates his capacity for reason and reflection.

Mayorga's animals are not merely human metaphors, as in George Orwell's *Animal Farm*.[23] Carmen Machi's reptilian characterisation of the elderly tortoise, swathed in woollen garments that cover her shell, in Ernesto Caballero's 2008 production of *Darwin's Tortoise*, reminds the viewer that theatre is the art of transformation, 'the disappearance of the actor' bringing 'the reality of the character into light' (Mayorga 2016b: 2). In *Snowflake's Last Words*, the zoo has indoctrinated Snowball's black gorilla companion into eating bananas using techniques that have been lifted from the Guantanamo Bible – one of a number of references in the play to modes of torture perpetrated by the US in the name of anti-terrorism.[24] Mayorga's theatre is centrally concerned with the operation of power and the dynamics of coercion – an interrogation of the politics of violence as understood to be 'the domination of one human being or reality by another' (Mayorga, cited in Gabriele 2000: 11). Mayorga practices a theatre of intervention – of giving voice to the marginalised, of making visible abuses which are normalised, of exposing the workings of a social order that functions on intimidation and exploitation, of giving significance to that which has been rendered of no importance. Mayorga's intervention is a Benjaminian insistence on 'the *now* in history' (Benjamin 1968: 261, my emphasis) and one which needs to make the invisible visible because, as Mayorga revealed in a 2008 interview, 'reality is not always visible' (Mateo and Ladra 2008: 71).

214   Maria M. Delgado

There is often a revisiting of contemporary icons in his work: Snowflake in *Snowflake's Last Words*, Laurel and Hardy in *El gordo y el flaco* (*Stan and Olly*, 2000), ex-Prime Minister José María Aznar's daughter Ana in *Alejandro and Ana. Lo que España no pudo ver del banquete de la boda de la hija del presidente* (*Alejandro and Ana. What Spain couldn't see in the wedding banquet of the President's Daughter*, co-authored with Juan Cavestany, 2003), Margaret Thatcher and Augusto Pinochet in his scene for the multi-authored *Shock* (2019). The need to 'protect' a particular party line – as with the Guardian's insistence that Snowflake tow the zoo line on the conditions in which the animals are kept – is often the narrative impulse unravelled and exposed as the action progresses. There are ideological stakes to be protected in Mayorga's theatrical worlds and conflict comes in the ways through which these stakes are dismantled.

Mayorga's is a theatre of memory which recognises the importance of remembering in a country where institutionalised amnesia promoted by the 1977 Amnesty Act – which forbids any investigation of crimes related to the Franco regime – has led to a pact of silence about so much of its recent past. 'Theatre', he articulated in a 2003 lecture, 'is a political act' and 'probably the first ever form of doing history' (Mayorga 2016b: 1). Writing is always a practice of 'making visible the wounds of the past that the present has not been able to heal' so that 'the silences of the vanquished resonate' (ibid.: 10). 'The best historical theatre', he goes on to argue, 'opens the past. And in opening the past, it opens the present' (ibid.: 11). Historical characters are thus always his contemporaries (Bravo 2014) – something that is literally realised in *The Cartographer* as characters from different time periods share the stage. 'Theatre gives shape to the self-understanding of an era and thus pushes in a certain direction the future of that era' (Mayorga 2016b: 8).

For Mayorga it is in that which is not immediately translatable that he locates his own sense of purpose. 'Europe needs a theatre', he wrote in 2013, 'which allows you to see that which nobody wants to see; which allows you to hear that which nobody wants to hear; which allows you to remember that which almost all have forgotten' (2016a: 192). In addressing history's gaps, he also deconstructs processes of historicisation. In *The Cartographer*, struck by the absences he witnessed in trying to trace the buildings and people seen in photos of the Warsaw ghetto, he provides an analogy, through the character of an ageing mapmaker, for his own practice 'To see, to select, to represent: these are the secrets of the cartographer' (2017: 611). 'Maps', the Old Man goes on to state, 'make memory' (ibid.). When Blanca, the wife of Raúl, a Spanish diplomat in Warsaw, speaks of 'a cartography of disappearance' (ibid.: 646), she is articulating Mayorga's vision of theatre as the art of challenging that which history has put to one side (Mayorga 2016a: 192–3). His own staging of the play with a striking red costume design, three red chairs and small tables, and a contrasting jet-black floor, provided an empty space where the audience were invited to put together the different pieces of history – like a jigsaw. The play's Polish outings include a reading directed in Marta Jordan's Polish translation by actor Andrzej Seweryn (known for his work with Peter Brook and Andrzej

Wajda as well as for the Comédie-Française) in 2013 and a subsequent performance of Mayorga's staging in 2019 at Teatr Kwadrat. Laura Yusem's 2019 staging at Buenos Aires' Teatro San Martín, realised on Graciela Galán's layered set of fragmented maps, resonated in a country marked by extensive Polish migration to escape political persecution.[25]

In *Way to Heaven* too, the act of making theatre is bound up with ideological messages that have a particular resonance in Spain. Here, a concentration camp – based on the Czech 'model' internment camp of Theresienstadt – is reframed as a 'Jewish re-plantation-zone' (Mayorga 2005: 27; Mayorga 2017: 304) in order to be shown off to a visiting Red Cross representative. This narrator buys into the performance charade crafted by the Commandant with a Jewish prisoner charged to be a translator-interlocutor in the role of the town Mayor – a figure whose name is tellingly Germanised by the Commandant from Gershom to Gerhard. Crafting a script to be enacted on a set that includes a park, a synagogue, a school, and a football pitch, the Commandant prepares an illusion using Aristotle's *Poetics* as a framework. While the Red Cross representative acknowledges the mechanised nature of the scenarios enacted before him, he does not intervene, he accepts the performance. As the play progresses, the Commandant's intricate (and obscene) preparations are exposed. The image of civility he seeks to present – an erudite man of letters caught in a conflict not of his making – masks a barbarism that sees all those not deemed fit to perform refused the role of extras and dispensed to the infirmary; his irritation at the little girl, who refuses to deliver the lines he had scripted, is menacing. The claustrophobia rendered in Ramin Gray's 2005 staging at the Royal Court Upstairs theatre sought to implicate the audience in the coercion (of Jewish prisoners) and censoring of activities – most conspicuously the arrival of trains transporting prisoners to their deaths – perpetrated by the Commandant. The audience were all given a volume from the Commandant's library as we entered the auditorium – Calderón, Corneille, Shakespeare – which we carried in with us as we followed the action through the camp. Theatre is co-opted to promote genocide. While Gray's reading promoted a claustrophobic atmosphere where the audience jostled with the performers in ways that could never allow for the slick performance that the Commandant craved, Jorge Lavelli's 2007 production at Théâtre de la Tempête opted for an empty stage, one where the gaps in the narrative were clearly physicalised. The grey stage presented a world that Pierre-Alain Chapuis' imposing, immaculately groomed Commandant could not animate with his fictions; the designated performers retained an automated quality that proved disarming. For Lavelli, the play offers a means of discussing twentieth-century atrocities organised on an industrial European scale (cited in Sadowska Guillon 2007: 45). Jorge Eines' 2007 Buenos Aires staging made direct references to Argentina's 1976–83 military dictatorship. Translated into 16 languages and produced, at the time of writing, in 19 countries, it is one of his most internationally renowned works.[26]

Mayorga acknowledges the multiple points of origin for his plays. *The Cartographer* was inspired by his 2008 visit to a synagogue in Warsaw where he saw an exhibition of photographs of the Warsaw Ghetto in the early 1940s. A 2006

216   *Maria M. Delgado*

newspaper article on the death at the age of 175 of one of the tortoises thought to have been taken from the Galapagos Islands in 1835 on the HMS Beagle by the author of *The Origin of the Species* was the inspiration for *Darwin's Tortoise*. A newspaper article on the records at a psychiatric hospital during the Civil War was the genesis for *The Scorched Garden*. *Intensamente azules* (*Intensely Blue*, 2018) was inspired by the breakage of his glasses over a bank holiday weekend that obliged him to wear his swimming goggles and experience the world anew.[27] *El buen vecino* (*The Good Neighbour*, 2002), commissioned by the Royal Court, was a response to Prime Minister José María Aznar's reactionary 2000 *Ley de Extranjería* (Spanish Aliens' Law). *Perpetual Peace* takes its title from a 1795 essay by Immanuel Kant, and looks at the tests that four personified dogs are put through in their wish to form part of an elite anti-terrorist squad, a plot device that recalls *The Grönholm Method*. Benjamin's pervasive influence, commented on earlier in this chapter, also extends to an overt discussion of his ideas in *Intensely Blue*,[28] and more generally a way of engaging with translation, ideology, and dialectics as active acts of critical engagement and meaning-making across all his work – both plays and essays.[29] Mayorga's theatrical influences are far-reaching – from the Greeks to Tadeusz Kantor, Harold Pinter to Sarah Kane, Lope de Vega to Lorca. His contemporaries – including Belbel, Cavestany, Luïsa Cunillé, and Rodrigo García – are also acknowledged as an influence (Mayorga 2012, 2016).

He refuses to say that he has a method for writing (Bravo 2014), recognising that different works require different approaches and he admits to consistently rewriting pieces even after publication.[30] When rehearsing *The Cartographer* in 2016, Mayorga reordered scenes, reshaping a sequence to keep the focus firmly on Blanca's journey. Changes were further introduced for its Barcelona opening in 2019 because 'it's a play that speaks about time and time rewrites it' (Mayorga, cited in EFE 2019). Mayorga views writing as a process, with reflection and research before the crafting begins and rewriting that takes place before production or publication (Mayorga 2012: 482), which means a work is never complete (cited in Alvarado 2014), not even post-production. 'The text knows things that the author does not know', Mayorga reflected in 2014 (cited in Bravo 2014).

Processes of meaning-making are also foregrounded in his work: translation and interpretation in *Blumemberg's Translator*,[31] spatial politics in *Stan and Olly,* scriptwriting and performance in *Way to Heaven*, the alchemy of magic in *El mago* (*The Magician*, 2018), the mechanics of theatre in the Brechtian *Hamelin* (2005), and playwriting in *The Boy at the Back*. The latter is perhaps his most influential work, presented as a BBC Radio 3 drama (translated by David Johnston) in 2014 and adapted by François Ozon – who saw Lavelli's staging at the Théâtre de la Tempête – into an award-winning film, *Dans la maison*, in 2012. *The Boy at the Back* concerns the relationship between a secondary-school language and literature teacher, Germán, and a teenage boy who habitually sits at the back of his class, Claudio. The latter delivers a homework assignment on what he did at the weekend that intrigues Germán in its voyeuristic precision. Germán's wife Juana, who runs an art gallery, is unnerved by the boy's forensic dissection of his classmate

Rafa's home and parents. Germán, however, decides to mentor Claudio with advice on creative writing and feedback on subsequent instalments chronicling Rafa's home life with mother Ester and father Rafa (see Figure 11.1).

Mayorga structures the play as a single continuous act with scenes that flow into each other without demarcated breaks. Moving between the classroom, Germán's home, and Rafa's home, the three spaces bleed into each other in the writing. Ozon's film, moving the action to an unnamed town in France, proffers a spatial specificity, concretising the places where the narrative evolves – Germán's apartment, the classroom at the tellingly named Lycée Gustave Flaubert, Rafa's home, the park, Juana's art gallery. Names are amended to their French equivalents (Germain, Claude, Rapha, Jean, Esther). For his 2019 staging, Andrés Lima chose a deceptively simple design by Beatriz San Juan which deployed a single desk and chair, a moveable sofa (which converts into a bed), and a thin wide white curtain that camouflages and hides as the key scenographic elements.[32] Jacopo Gassmann's open production for the Piccolo Milan in the same year presented a more exposed stage set where visibility presented its own dangers through the open embodiment of a voyeurism that proves both dangerous and destructive.

The Boy at the Back provides a playful contemplation of dramatic tropes, tricks, and techniques. Germán, once an aspiring writer, sees it as his mission to advise Claudio on purpose ('who am I writing for?, Mayorga 2017: 437; *Boy at*

Figure 11.1 A book exchanged between Guillem Barbosa's Claudio and Sergi López's Germán behind the back of Arnau Comas's Rafa in Juan Mayorga's *El chico de la última fila* (*The Boy at the Back*), directed by Andrés Lima (Sala Beckett, Barcelona, 2019). Photograph © Kiku Piñol / Sala Beckett

the Back 13), storytelling ('people need stories', ibid.: 446; 22), narrative ('show not tell', ibid.: 451; 27), realism ('if it's not realistic, it's no good, even if it's real', ibid.: 464; 38), titles ('The title commits. The title establishes a pact with the reader', ibid.: 452; 27), and endings ('the hallmark of a good ending. Necessary and unforeseeable', ibid.: 469; 43).

Ozon strips these reflections on narrative (as well as dialogues on philosophy and mathematics between the two students) but maintains the line 'to be continued', used by Claude to keep the reader engaged in his storyline. The shift of title is a way of acknowledging the home both as the subject of the fiction and also as a house of fiction – as the different narrative fictions intersect, the question emerges as to whether the entire piece is being authored by Claude (as alter-ego for Mayorga). Rewrites to Claude's narratives are enacted in Rapha's house where windows and mirrors – spaces of reflection, visibility, and voyeurism – abound. 'You don't love me, you love an image', Esther says to Claude at one point. Ozon rewrites Mayorga's ending to keep the complicity between the former student and his pupil: Germain loses his job and his wife, but Claude remains at his side as the two construct lurid stories from their voyeuristic gaze at the windows of the apartments opposite the bench where they sit. Mayorga has Germán ask Claudio to stay away from his house while the teenager closes the narrative, trumping his past mentor as he shifts the story's focus from Ester to Juana.

The focus on the spectator's complicity in meaning-making that Ozon foregrounds is indeed a central motif in all of Mayorga's plays. Representation can never be disentangled from the real because it structures how we view the world. In asking questions of the ethics of crafting fictions from the lives of others, Mayorga's *The Boy at the Back* functions as emblematic of his oeuvre – a body of work engaging with the ethics and responsibilities involved in artistic creation.

Conclusion

There has been a topicality to Galceran's writing, plays that have been able to capture the zeitgeist of Spain's changing times. *Escape* was inspired by political corruption – an institutional epidemic that brought down Prime Minister Mariano Rajoy in 2018. *Burundanga* envisaged the end of ETA as a farcical case of mistaken identities and visual gags. During one Madrid performance, an audience member stood up declaring 'You can't make comedy with this' (Allwebber 2013) but for Galceran there are few topics that aren't suitable for comedy, 'it's all a question of tone' (cited in Allwebber 2013). *Burundanga* struggled to find a Catalan producer – the play was staged in Barcelona five months after its Madrid premiere because it was felt 'people didn't want to laugh with ETA' (cited in Pejenaute 2012) but the Basque performances suggested otherwise (Pejenaute 2012). Galceran's reference point of Quentin Tarantino's *Inglorious Bastards* (2009) may have found a suitably satirical register for the play.

Mayorga's theatre is underpinned by a belief that theatre contributes to 'those images of the past that nourish and foster what we call "collective memories"' (Mayorga 2016b: 1). It is a theatre rooted in the need to bring the past into the present (ibid.: 2) and one which has proved particularly resonant in a country still coming to terms with the legacy of a 36-year dictatorship. His plays engage with large philosophical questions around responsibility, censorship, and account-ability – it is perhaps no surprise that *The Scorched Garden* was pulled from the CDN programme in 2007 when a new right-wing government appointed a new artistic director to the theatre for whom a piece about exploring Spain's post-Civil War past was clearly not a priority.[33] *Perpetual Peace* examines at the boundaries of what can be justified in the name of tackling terrorism in the aftermath of 9/11 – it is one of Mayorga's most staged works, translated into Bulgarian, English, French, Galician, Greek, Korean, Polish, Portuguese, Rumanian, and Turkish. *Way to Heaven* explores how censorship can be nor-malised. Mayorga's plays scratch beneath the surface – of stories, of language. *Hamelin* deconstructs a sensationalist news story on a paedophile ring as a means of examining the slippery nature of language and the possibility of a poetics of ethical narration. Language is here not a means for understanding but for coercion. It is perhaps no surprise that Mayorga's inaugural lecture on entering the RAE in 2019,[34] addressed the issue of silence – that which cannot be uttered, a means of locating the other, a means towards listening in a society which has forgotten how to listen.

Mayorga's protagonists are those caught in the making of history who have to take difficult ethical decisions with far reaching implications. Galceran's characters function on the borders of legality: tricksters and con artists who have a slick answer for everything. The power of his plays lies in the fact that it is the audience who are frequently put into the position of the conned protagonists. For Mayorga the audi-ence is always an active participant in a theatre of dialectics 'where you can defend to death people or positions that you don't agree with' (cited in Mateo and Ladra 2008: 68). Ultimately, both ask questions of a society where nothing is ever quite as it first appears and language operates as a means for evasion – whether that be civic responsibility or the sense of an environment where values have been corrupted in pursuit of a model of capitalist endeavour that knows no limits.

Jordi Galceran – four key productions

El mètode Grönholm (*The Grönholm Method*). Directed by Sergi Belbel. Set by Paco Azorín. Costumes by M. Rafa Serra. Sound by Xavi Oró and Pep Solórzano. Lighting by Kiko Planas. Cast: Roser Batalla, Jordi Boixaderas, Jordi Diaz, Lluís Soler. Teatre Nacional de Catalunya, Barcelona, 29 April 2003.

The Grönholm Method. Trans. by Anne Garcia-Romero and Mark St. Ger-main. Directed by BT McNicholl. Set by Brian Webb. Costumes by Ann Closs-Farley. Lighting by Jennifer Schriever. Sound by Cricket S. Myers. Cast: Jonathan Cake, Graham Hamilton, Lesli Margherita. Stephen Spinella. Falcon Theatre, Los Angeles, 7 August 2012.

220 *Maria M. Delgado*

Burundanga. Directed by Gabriel Olivares. Design by Anna Tusell. Lighting and costumes by Felype R. De Lima. Sound and musical adaptation by Tuti Fernández. Cast: Mar Abascal, Eloy Arenas, César Camino, Antonio Hortelano, Marta Poveda. Teatro Maravillas, Madrid, 29 June 2011.

Le Crédit. Adapted and directed by Eric Civanyan, assisted by Sylvie Paupardin. Design by Pauline Gallot and Capucine Grou-Radenez. Lighting by Yann Varicci. Music by François Peyrony. Cast: Daniel Russo and Didier Bénureau. Théâtre de la Gaîté-Montparnasse, Paris, 15 January 2019.

Juan Mayorga – four key productions

El traductor de Blumemberg (*Blumemberg's Translator*). Directed by Guillermo Heras. Set by Héctor Becerra. Music by Ciro Cabaloti. Cast: Joaquín Bonet, Rubén Szuchmacher. Teatro Nacional Cervantes, Buenos Aires, 16 August 2000.

Way to Heaven. Trans. by David Johnston. Directed by Ramin Gray. Design: Miriam Büther. Lighting: Johanna Town; Sound design. Ian Dickinson. Cast (includes): Vanessa Ackerman, Daniel Hart, Richard Katz, Claire Lichie, Emma Pinto, Jeff Rawle, Dominic Rowan. Royal Court Theatre, London, 16 June 2005.

Lettres d'amour à Staline (*Love Letters to Stalin*). Trans by Jorge Lavelli and Dominique Poulange. Directed by Jorge Lavelli. Set and costumes by Graciela Galán. Cast: Gérard Lartigau, Luc-Antoine Diquero, Marie-Christine Letort, Théâtre de la Tempête, Paris, 29 April 2011.

El chico de la última fila (*The Boy at the Back*). Directed by Andrés Lima. Set by Beatriz San Juan. Lighting by Marc Salicrú. Costume design by Míriam Compte. Sound design by Jaume Manresa. Cast: David Bagés, Guillem Barbosa, Arnau Comas, Míriam Iscla, Sergi López, Anna Ycobalzeta. Sala Beckett, Barcelona, 23 January 2019.

Notes

1 My thanks to Juan Mayorga for sharing materials about his work, to Anne García Romero for discussing her translations of Galceran's plays, to Marcos Ordóñez, Juan Matabosch, Anxo Abuín, Emilio Peral Vega, Ventura Pons, Mercè Saumell, and Duncan Wheeler for conversations over the years on Galceran and Mayorga's work, and to Andrés Lima, Jorge de Juan, and Paula Paz for discussing their stagings of Mayorga's work with me. This chapter is supported by the AHRC-funded project, 'Staging Difficult Pasts: Of Narratives, Objects and Public Memory' (Grant Reference: AH/R006849/1) and dedicated to the memory of Narcis Fernández Nogales.

2 I have opted to use the Catalan spelling of Galceran (as opposed to the Castilian Galcerán) although both are used by critics and I have respected the Castilian-language spelling where citing from another source.

3 Dates in brackets are of first productions or public readings unless otherwise stated. When citing from plays by Mayorga translated into English, I have referenced both the Castilian-language version and the English-language translation where possible. In all other cases of translation from the Castilian Spanish or the Catalan, the translation is mine.

4 My use of Castilian recognises that Catalan, Basque, and Galician are also official languages of Spain.

Jordi Galceran and Juan Mayorga   221

5 Galceran's extensive (co)screenwriting credits include: for television – *Nit i dia/Night and Day* (2016–) and *Sin identidad/No Identity* (2014–16); for film – Jaume Balagueros' *Frágiles/Fragile* (2005), Ventura Pons' *Carícies/Caresses* (1998), and Lluís Miñarro's *Stella Cadente* (2014).

6 See Ordóñez (2018); Delgado (2005).

7 See Ferrer Hammerlindl (2012: 228); Mayorga (2012: 484).

8 I will not be focusing in this chapter on pieces written prior to 1995 while Galceran was working with an amateur theatre group and teaching in a secondary school: *Alta fidelitat* (*High Fidelity*, 1991), *Fauna* (1993) and *Vigílies* (*Days Before*, 1995). For the post 1995 plays, I have consulted the published editions of the plays published in Catalan (see Galceran 2010) but am also drawing on having seen his works in performance in Barcelona and/or Madrid.

9 For statistics on domestic violence in Spain, see Medina-Ariza and Barberet (2003). For further information on domestic violence in Spain and how artists have responded to it, see Wheeler (2008).

10 See Vallejo (2004).

11 A version filmed by the Catalan-language TV3 with the original cast was first broadcast in 2012.

12 See Freedman (2010).

13 Anne García Romero mentions that the ending was changed to give Ferran (here renamed Frank) the final word at Mike Nichols' suggestion in both the Los Angeles and London productions (García Romero 2019). Nichols had worked in an advisory capacity throughout the US process – BT McNicholl had worked as Nichols' assistant director on numerous occasions – and was planning a New York production that stalled after his death in 2014 (see Ordóñez 2018).

14 Plans for a West End staging directed by Laurence Boswell were noted in the Spanish press as early as 2006 (see Hevia 2006).

15 Galceran is also a huge fan of musicals – he admits to having travelled regularly to London to see new work before his children were born (Allwebber 2013). Galceran is responsible for adaptations of *The Lion King* and *They're Playing our Song*, as well as Catalan-language collaborations with Albert Guinovart (*Gaudi* and *Paradis*).

16 See Ferrer Hammerlindl (2012: 228).

17 See Yuste (2015); Bassas (2017).

18 See Allwebber (2013).

19 *Cancún* (2008), *Dakota* (2006), and Galceran's adaptation of Santiago Carlos Oves's screenplay *Converses amb la mama* (*Conversations with Mother*, 2008) were directed by Mestres in Catalan-language productions; Gabriel Olivares directed the Madrid premieres of *Burundanga* (2011) and *Cancún* (2014).

20 See Tremlett (2013).

21 See Delgado (2016).

22 On the play's Madrid premiere in 2008, Mayorga noted that he didn't want to provide a history lesson or lecture with *Darwin's Tortoise*, but rather to look at how histories are constructed (Anon 2008). The play's trajectory in Europe – with productions in London (dir. Paula Paz, Cervantes Theatre 2017), Fribourg (dir. Phillipe Adrien, Centre Dramátique Fribourgeois, 2011), Lyon (dir. Florence Mallet, Théâtre Le Fou, 2009), Athens (dir. Maria Ksanzopulídu, Vafio Theatre, 2012), and Rome (dir. Stefano Messina, Vittoria Theatre, 2010) – as well as further afield (in Seoul and São Paulo), demonstrates the ways in which its articulation of Benjamin's view that '[n]othing that has ever happened should be regarded as lost for history' (1968: 254) has resonated in a twenty-first century that is still grappling with the spectres of the century that preceded it.

23 Mayorga reflects on his deployment of animals, including the relationship with Kafka, in an interview with Mateo and Ladra (2008: 65).

24 See also Materna (2017).

222   *Maria M. Delgado*

25 See Zubrzycki (2012).
26 For a reading of Katarzyna Kalwat's 2011 staging at the Juliusz Slowacki Theatre in Krakow, see Sawicka (2011).
27 See Delgado (2019a).
28 See Delgado (2019a).
29 Emilio Peral Vega's introduction to *Hamelín* and *La tortuga de Darwin* offers an excellent reflection on the philosophical underpinnings of Mayorga's work (2015: 9–91).
30 See Mateo and Ladra (2008: 66).
31 For a discussion of Mayorga in relation to translation, see Brodie (2018): 135–7, 146–50).
32 See Delgado (2019b).
33 See Gabriele (2000: 12).
34 Now available as a publication (see Mayorga 2019).

Works cited

Allwebber (2013) 'Jordi Galcerán', Love4Musicals.com, 8 October, https://www.love4musicals.com/2013/10/08/entrevista-a-jordi-galceran/
Alvarado, Esther (2014) 'El texto teatral ha de ganarse su autoridad frente a director y actores', *El Mundo*, 21 May, https://www.elmundo.es/cultura/2014/05/21/537c59a1268e3e8d0c8b456b.html
Anon. (2008) 'Harriet la tortuga con la que Mayorga revisa la Historia', *La Razón*, 8 February, https://www.larazon.es/historico/harriet-la-tortuga-con-la-que-mayorga-revisa-la-historia-RJLA_RAZON_43149
Bassas, Antoni (2017) 'Jordi Galceran: "Depens del talent, el treball i la sort. I només pots controlar el treball"', *Ara*, 23 September, https://www.ara.cat/societat/JORDIGALCERAN-Depens-talent-treball-controlar_0_1875412467.html
Benjamin, Walter (1968) *Illuminations*, trans. Harry Zohn, ed. Hannah Arendt, New York: Schocken Books.
Billington, Michael (2018) 'The Grönholm Method review – apprentice-style contest keeps you guessing', *Guardian*, 23 May, https://www.theguardian.com/stage/2018/may/23/the-gronholm-method-review-menier-chocolate-factory
Bravo, Julio (2014) 'Juan Mayorga: "No hay nada más parecido a la vida que el teatro"', *ABC*, 28 May, https://www.abc.es/cultura/teatros/20140527/abci-entrevista-juan-mayorga-201405271359.html
——— (2015) 'La política cultural catalana debe favorecer la calidad, no el idioma', *ABC*, 4 April, https://www.abc.es/cultura/teatros/20150403/abci-entrevista-jordi-galceran-dakota-201504011847.html
Brodie, Geraldine (2018) *The Translator on Stage*, London: Methuen.
Delgado, Maria (2005) 'Barcelona via Madrid: revisiting the past and prophesying the future', *Western European Stages*, 17(1) (Winter): 116–123.
——— (2016) 'Spain: runaway hits and ephemeral memorabilia', *European Stages*, 8(1) (Fall), https://europeanstages.org/2016/10/19/spain-runaway-hits-and-ephemeral-memorabilia/
——— (2019a) 'Juan Mayorga's "Intensely Blue": Spain's Premier Dramatist Seeing The World Anew', *The Theatre Times*, 16 March, https://thetheatretimes.com/juan-mayorgas-intensely-blue-spains-premier-dramatist-seeing-the-world-anew/
——— (2019b) 'Sergi López Heads an Impressive Cast in Andrés Lima's Staging of Juan Mayorga's "The Boy at the Back"', *The Theatre Times*, 27 April, https://thetheatretim

es.com/sergi-lopez-heads-an-impressive-cast-in-andres-limas-staging-of-juan-ma
yorgas-the-boy-at-the-back/

EFE (2011) 'Jordi Galcerán llega al Teatro Alcázar de Madrid con "Fuga"', *EcoDiaro.Es*, 13 January, https://ecodiario.eleconomista.es/cultura/noticias/2740018/01/11/Jor di-Galceran-llega-al-Teatro-Alcazar-de-Madrid-con-Fuga.html

EFE (2019) 'Blanca Portillo y Juan Mayorga defienden la memoria en "El cartógrafo"', *EFE*, 2 July, https://www.efe.com/efe/espana/cultura/blanca-portillo-y-juan-ma yorga-defienden-la-memoria-en-el-cartografo/10005-4014235

Feldman, Sharon G. and Anxo Abuín González (2012) 'Nationalism, identity and the theatre across the Spanish state in the democratic era, 1975–2010', in Maria M. Delgado and David Gies (eds), *A History of Theatre in Spain*, Cambridge: Cambridge University Press, pp. 391–425.

Ferrer, Clara (2018) 'Eloy Arenas: «El humor no tiene límites o filtros, es la gente quien los tiene»', *Última Hora*, 27 December, https://www.ultimahora.es/noticias/cultura/2018/12/27/1047507/eloy-arenas-humor-tiene-limites-filtros-gente-quien-tiene.html

Ferrer Hammerlindl, Carlos (2012) 'El teatro en el cine: el caso de Jordi Galcerán', in Rafael Alemany Ferrer and Francisco Chico Rico (eds), XVIII Simposio de la SELGYC (Alicante 9–11 de septiembre 2010) [XVIII Simposi de la SELGYC (Alacant 9–11 setembre de 2010)], Literatura i espectacle [Literatura y espectáculo], Alacant: Universitat d'Alacant, SELGYC [Sociedad Española de Literatura General y Comparada], pp. 225–234.

Freedman, John (2010) 'Corporate chic becomes drama of sleek surprises', *Moscow Times*, 8 April, https://www.themoscowtimes.com/archive/corporate-chic-becom es-drama-of-slick-surprises

Gabriele, John P. (2000) 'Juan Mayorga: una voz del teatro español actual', *Estreno*, 26: 8–11

Galceran, Jordi (2010) *Sis comedies*, Barcelona: Edicions 62.

García, Juan Ramón (2011) 'Youth unemployment in Spain: causes and solutions', Working papers 1131, BBVA Bank, economic Research department, https://www.bbvaresea rch.com/en/publicaciones/youth-unemployment-in-spain-causes-and-solutions/

García Romero, Anne (2019) Correspondence with the author, 19 August, 10 September.

Graell, Vanessa (2010) 'Grönholm, el fenómeno del teatro español', *El Mundo*, 29 August, https://www.elmundo.es/elmundo/2010/08/27/cultura/1282910570.html

Hevia, Elena (2006) 'El metodo Grönholm pasa a ser un fenómeno mundial', *El Periódico*, 12 March, https://www.elperiodicoextremadura.com/noticias/cultura/el-meto do-gronholm-pasa-ser-fenomeno-mundial_226428.html

Mateo, Nieves and David Ladra (2008) 'A propósito de La paz perpetua. Conversación con Juan Mayorga', *Primer Acto*, 326: 63–71.

Materna, Linda (2017) '"I've never loved you": Juan Mayorga's Últimas palabras de Copito de Nieve and the Politics of Animal Captivity', *Ovejas Muertas*, 28 September, https://ovejasmuertas.wordpress.com/2017/09/28/ive-never-loved-you-juan-ma yorgas-ultimas-palabras-de-copito-de-nieve-por-linda-materna/

Mayorga, Juan (2003) *Revolución conservadora y conservación revolucionaria. Política y memoria en Walter Benjamin*, Barcelona: Anthropos.

———— (2005) *Way to Heaven*, trans. David Johnston, London: Oberon.

———— (2009) *Nocturnal*, trans. David Johnston, London: Oberon.

———— (2012) 'Theatre is the art of the future', in Maria M. Delgado and David Gies (eds), *A History of Theatre in Spain*, Cambridge: Cambridge University Press, pp. 478–485.

224   Maria M. Delgado

—— (2016a) *Elipses*, Segovia: La UÑa RoTa.

—— (2016b) *The Playwright as Historian*, trans. Claire Montgomery, Madrid: Postmetropolis.

—— (2017) *Teatro 1989–2014*, La uÑa RoTa: Segovia, 3rd edn.

—— (2019) *Silencio*, Madrid: Real Academic Española.

—— (n.d.) *The Boy at the Back*, trans. David Johnston. Unpublished.

—— (n.d.) *Darwin's Tortoise*, trans. David Johnston. Unpublished.

Medina-Ariza, Juango and Rosemary Barberet (2003) 'Intimate partner violence in Spain: findings from a national survey', *Violence Against Women*, 9(3): 302–322. doi:10.1177/1077801202250073

Morales, Clara (2014) 'Malditas vacaciones en el Caribe', *El País*, 7 October, https://elpais.com/ccaa/2014/10/06/madrid/1412616248_952613.html

Ordóñez, Marcos (2013) 'Galceran/Koltès: nuevas miradas', *El País*, 5 November, https://elpais.com/cultura/2013/11/05/actualidad/1383654470_721294.html

—— (2018) 'De repente Galceran', *El País*, 30 May, https://elpais.com/cultura/2018/05/30/actualidad/1527691705_263899.html

Pejenaute, Leyre (2012) 'Intento dar donde más duele', *El País*, 30 November, https://elpais.com/ccaa/2012/11/29/madrid/1354223574_789191.html

Peral Vega, Emilio (2015) 'Introducción', in Juan Mayorga, *Hamelin. La tortuga de Darwin*, ed. Emilio Peral Vega, Madrid: Cátedra: 1–91.

Redacción (2008) 'Carnaval, el regreso de Jordi Galcerán tras 'el método Grönholm', *La Vanguardia*, 24 March, https://www.lavanguardia.com/cultura/20080324/53448334545/carnaval-el-regreso-de-jordi-galceran-tras-el-metodo-gronholm.html

—— (2010) '"El mètode Grönholm" vuelve intacto a Barcelona tras su éxito mundial' *La Vanguardia*, 23 September, https://www.lavanguardia.com/cultura/20100923/54010384961/el-metode-gronholm-vuelve-intacto-a-barcelona-tras-su-exito-mundial.html

Ruiz Mantilla, Jesús (2015) 'O me presta 3.000 euros o me acuesto con su mujer', *El País*, 10 August, https://elpais.com/cultura/2015/08/09/actualidad/1439150510_311622.html

Sadowska Guillon, Iréne (2007) 'Entrevista con Jorge Lavelli. "Himmelweg": el teatro de lo irrepresentable', *Primer Acto*, 320: 44–48.

Sawicka, Anna (2011) 'No dirás falso testimonio contra tu prójimo. Himmelweg de Juan Mayorga en Cracovia', *Studia Iberystyczne*, 10: 295–315.

Shuttleworth, Ian (2018) 'The Grönholm Method, Menier Chocolate Factory, London – a portrait of corporate brutality', *Financial Times*, 23 May, https://www.ft.com/content/a287c5b8-6003-11e8-9334-2218e7146b04

Soler, Esteve (2008) 'Jordi Galceran, comediògraf', *Pausa: Quadern de teatre contemporani*, 29: http://www.revistapausa.cat/jordi-galceran-comediograf/

Taylor, Paul (2018) 'The Grönholm Method, Menier Chocolate Factory, review', *Independent*, 23 May, https://www.independent.co.uk/arts-entertainment/theatre-dance/reviews/the-gronholm-method-review-menier-chocolate-factory-theatre-a8364981.html

Tremlett, Giles (2013) 'Spain unemployment soars to record high', *Guardian*, 25 April, https://www.theguardian.com/world/2013/apr/25/spain-unemployment-soars-record-high

Vallejo, Javier (2004) 'Por el ojo de una aguja' *El País*, 7 August, https://elpais.com/diario/2004/08/07/babelia/1091833569_850215.html

——— (2011) 'Melocotón en almíbar con cuajada', *El País*, 2 July, https://elpais.com/diario/2011/07/02/madrid/1309605866_850215.html

Wheeler, Duncan (2008) 'Intimate partner violence in Spain (1975–2006)', *Cuestiones de Género*, 3: 173–204.

Wolf, Matt (2018) 'The Grönholm Method, Menier Chocolate Factory – sleek and short but in no way deep', *The Arts Desk*, 25 May, https://theartsdesk.com/theatre/grönholm-method-menier-chocolate-factory-sleek-and-short-no-way-deep

Yuste, Javier (2015) 'Jordi Galcerán', *El Cultural*, 2 April, https://elcultural.com/Jordi-Galceran

Zubrzycki, Bernarda (2012) 'Polish immigrants in Argentina', *Polish American Studies*, 69 (1) (Spring): 75–98.

12 Ivan Vyrypaev and Natalia Vorozhbyt

Language, memory, and cultural mythology in Russian and Ukrainian new drama

Molly Flynn

The foundation myth of Soviet socialism's historical inevitability came crumbling down at approximately the same time as the Berlin Wall. The state-sponsored mechanisms at the centre of the Soviet narrative had been rusting internally for decades and were quick to give way to the criminality of unregulated capitalism in the region in the 1990s. During these years, several key figures paved the way for a new kind of theatre in Russia. The new post-Soviet approach to theatre-making notably displaced the centrality of the director-*auteur* as the primary conduit for a play's artistic vision and focused instead on the primacy of the playwright who came to stand at the centre of the creative process. The opening of alternative theatre venues, the founding of theatre festivals, and the publication of journals dedicated to playwriting made for a remarkably generative new writing movement in Russia at the turn of the twenty-first century.

By the year 2000, writers from across the former Eastern Bloc had begun to survey the destruction of the Soviet years and sort through the chaos of those that came after. It was in the late-1990s and early-2000s that artists from across the region began to pick up the pieces of the Soviet Union's splintered cultural narratives as they set to work composing the origin stories for a new era. At the forefront of this effort were playwrights. To describe emerging forms of drama-turgy 'New Russian Drama' was coined as an umbrella term that encompasses any new play written since the mid-1990s that uses contemporary Russian language to portray the experience of everyday life in the late-twentieth and early twenty-first century. As Birgit Beumers and Mark Lipovetsky argue in their groundbreaking study of the form, one of the hallmarks of the genre, particularly in its early years, was the use of physical, psychological, and verbal violence as a way to explore and expose the historical and cultural trauma of the region's twentieth-century past (Beumers and Lipovetsky 2009: 36).

The development of New Russian Drama was also shaped, in large part, by the introduction of the verbatim playwriting technique to Moscow's theatre artists in 1999 and 2000 via a series of writing workshops led by delegates from London's Royal Court Theatre including Stephen Daldry, Elyse Dodgson, Ramin Gray, and James Macdonald. Supported by the British Council in collaboration with the Liubimovka New Play Festival, these workshops were an inspiration to Moscow's prolific community of young playwrights. The documentary approach to theatre-making swiftly became one of the most innovative and socially engaged forms of the era. The Royal Court workshops were a galvanising force in a creative movement that had already captured the imaginations of theatre artists from across the post-Soviet space. They led directly to Russia's first documentary theatre festival in 2000 and the founding of Teatr.doc in 2002, Russia's first theatre venue exclusively dedicated to the production of new plays.

Teatr.doc was created by playwright Elena Gremina and director Mikhail Ugarov in collaboration with a small collective of international theatre artists that included playwrights and directors from Russia, Ukraine, and Germany. Together these artists worked to renovate their dishevelled rented basement into a vibrant underground performance space. The plays they produced there used the spoken word as a mechanism with which to enact a new kind of cultural history and a revised vision of civil society. Through the barebones presentation of documentary and dramatic texts in performance, these revolutionary theatre-makers sought out alternative ways to represent and interpret the Soviet past and its continued resonance in the present. In this way, the playwrights of New Russian Drama became the chroniclers of their time and the creators of new cultural narratives at a pivotal moment in the region's history.

The documentary approach to playwriting proved an important influence across dramatic works of both fiction and non-fiction. Never before had quotidian and contemporary language so dominated the country's stages, a realm previously perceived to be reserved for the most sophisticated and refined forms of artistic expression. By collecting and composing everyday language for performance, Russia's new dramatists began writing plays explicitly built to explore the generative nature of speaking and listening to texts in performance. By staging their seemingly simple stories of everyday life, playwrights of the era created a singular space for the collective renegotiation of cultural narratives and the reimaging of the region's foundation myths. Among the artists at the centre of this project are the two writers whose works are analysed in this chapter, Ivan Vyrypaev and Natalia Vorozhbyt.

Ivan Vyrypaev is a Russian playwright who writes in Russian and lives in Warsaw. Married to Polish actress Karolina Grushka, Vyrypaev immigrated together with his family in 2016. Natalia Vorozhbyt is a Ukrainian playwright who writes in Ukrainian and Russian and lives in Kyiv. After ten years in Moscow, the writer returned to her home city of Kyiv where she has played a key role in the development of New Ukrainian Drama. Both writers have shaped the trajectory of Russian language playwriting since the early-2000s. Vorozhbyt and Vyrypaev have also proven particularly relevant to a broader European audience as evidenced by their productions and commissions from stages across the continent including London's Royal Court Theatre, the Düsseldorf Schauspielhaus, the Royal Shakespeare Company, National Theatre of Warsaw, Berlin's Gorki Theatre, and Madrid's Teatro Kamikaze, to name a few. Although this chapter is primarily focused on the resonance of the two writers' works within their local contexts in Russia and Ukraine, it is also important to note the extensive circulation of their plays across Europe and beyond.

228 *Molly Flynn*

By comparing the works of these two writers, this chapter treads a fine line as it aims to acknowledge points of shared cultural history between the first generation of post-Soviet playwrights while avoiding the common pitfall of eliding the history and significance of Ukrainian art and culture with Russia's. To this end, it is important to emphasise that Ukraine is a bilingual country and that, until the war in the Donbas region of eastern Ukraine began in April 2014, collaborations and exchanges between Russian and Ukrainian theatre artists were common. Vorozhbyt spent close to a decade studying and working in Moscow which is one reason why her work is commonly included in the category of New *Russian* Drama despite the fact that almost all of her plays are set in Ukraine and are rooted in a specifically Ukrainian cultural context. These are among the complexities this chapter seeks to highlight in its analysis of the two writers' works.

Additionally, this chapter explores how the historically specific set of circumstances in Russia and Ukraine at the start of the twenty-first century positioned playwrights of this era uniquely to rewrite the cultural narratives of their epoch. It reveals a common interest in the mechanics of language in Vyrypaev's and Vorozhbyt's plays and compares the various styles both writers apply in pursuit of a parallel set of questions regarding the role cultural mythology plays in a society's path to self-definition. Through comparison of these two highly distinctive writers, this chapter considers the extent to which Vorozhbyt and Vyrypaev can be said to share a generational and/or cultural investment in the power of the spoken word and in theatre's capacity to re-inscribe the origin stories of two countries on the edge of change.

Symbols of a generation

Ivan Vyrypaev and Natalia Vorozhbyt both moved to Moscow in the late 1990s as students. Originally from Irkutsk and Kyiv respectively, the two writers were among the many young artists from across the former-Soviet space who relocated to the capital to study and join the bourgeoning underground arts scene. Both writers had seen several of their early works staged in their home cities and were quick to find critical recognition in Moscow as well. Having shown his work as a playwright, actor, and director in Irkutsk, Magadan, and Kamchatka, Vyrypaev's breakout success was his 2002 play *Kislorod* (*Oxygen*) which premiered as part of the opening season at Teatr.doc in Moscow.

Reframing the Ten Commandments for contemporary audiences, *Oxygen* is a rap-inspired decalogue, a musical mash-up of hip-hop culture and biblical theology. Two actors speak the text to the accompaniment of a DJ whose electronic music provides the rhythm for the performance. Together they narrate the story of a man named Sasha from the suburban city of Serpukhov. The two performers are identified in the text as HE and SHE and, in the original production, were played by Vyrypaev and actress Arina Marakulina. Spoken primarily in the past tense and in the third person, the text narrates how Sasha failed to hear the directive 'thou shalt not kill' over the music playing through his headphones and for this reason, the speaker imagines, Sasha coldly murdered his wife with a shovel to the chest. Before killing his wife, the audience soon learns, Sasha had fallen in love with a beautiful woman from Moscow, also named Sasha. '[W]hen he realized that his wife wasn't oxygen but that Sasha was', HE informs the audience, 'and when he realized that you can't live without oxygen, he took a spade and cut the legs off the dancers dancing in his wife's breast' (Vyrypaev 2005a: 50).[1]

In the play, oxygen becomes a metaphor for life, for freedom, and for religious belief. The protagonists appear gasping for air in a city sick with cynicism and corruption. The recurring leitmotif of asphyxiation in Vyrypaev's work expresses a common theme of suffocation and an attempt to breathe life back into the act of speaking. Colleen Lucey argues that it is through the articulation of the spoken word that Vyrypaev's actors search for meaning. For Vyrypaev, Lucey writes, 'the ultimate question of each drama is existential in nature: how does one live and breathe, let alone speak, when the air is poisoned?' (Lucey 2011: 6). This question and its variants prove enduring in Vyrypaev's diverse works. Though each of his plays approaches this question from a different aesthetic angle, they are all fixated to some extent on the search for meaning in everyday life and the capacity of language to express, explore, and explicate that meaning in the act of performance.

Through its unusual mixture of club culture and religious scripture, *Oxygen* found unique resonance with audiences of the era as it came to represent, according to anthropologist Sergei Oushakine, both a 'symbol and a symptom of a generation' (Oushakine 2009: 1). Born in 1974, Vyrypaev was 17 years old when news broke of the dissolution of the Soviet Union. He came of age in a period of time when the historical narratives of his generation were under rapid revision. As the influence of Western capitalism came rushing into the region and the pre-existing corruption of the Soviet system was repurposed for a new regime, Vyrypaev and his generation of post-Soviet theatre artists found themselves tasked with interpreting the drastic changes unfolding around them. These are among the historically and culturally specific circumstances Vyrypaev refers to in the play and are also among the topics his early plays share with those of Vorozhbyt.

The year following the premiere of *Oxygen*, Vorozhbyt gained her fame in Moscow when her semi-autobiographical play *Galka Motalko* was awarded the Eureka Prize in 2003.[2] Lauded for the way it captures the naïve and enduring hope of adolescence, the play follows a teenage girl through her early days as a student at a boarding school for young athletes. In her opening monologue, Galka (short for Galina) informs her audiences, 'I'm starting a new life now, because in my old life I was often a silly cow' (Vorozhbyt 2002: 1). Surrounded by young Olympic hopefuls, Galka finds that her new classmates seem a higher species of student in comparison to her old schoolmates, and she is quickly seduced into their world of drinking, smoking, and less than consensual sexual encounters. Eventually and inevitably, Galka is inspired by her newfound experience of female friendship to participate in a prank against one of her teachers that leads to her expulsion from the school.

230   *Molly Flynn*

In one sense, the play tells a familiar coming-of-age story complete with the follies of youthful comradery. In another sense, *Galka Motalko* mirrors broader cultural and political trends in Russia and Ukraine in the early 2000s, two countries that were, at the time, searching for new narratives with which to build a revised sense of identity following the collapse of the Soviet Union. Through its pairing of youthful hope and self-destruction, *Galka Motalko* reflected a crucial time of transition in the region. The crass language of teenage slang blends with specialised, athletic jargon that bumps up against the lyricism of Vorozhbyt's self-reflective prose in the play. The linguistic and stylistic bricolage of *Galka Motalko* serves to draw audiences' attention to the mechanism of the spoken word. It asks spectators to consider how the act of both speaking and hearing stories in performance can come to shape our perceptions of and relationships to the world around us.

Dedicated interest in the complexities of text in performance is one of the central characteristics Vorozhbyt's writing shares with Vyrypaev's, although the two writers have markedly different approaches to narrative composition and dramatic structure. Vyrypaev's plays are often abstract and always existential in nature. They offer paths towards the exploration of philosophy and religious scripture. Vorozhbyt's plays, on the other hand, are rooted in the intimacy that comes from portraying relatable characters who face familiar challenges. They offer insight into the ways in which history and politics come to impact interpersonal relationships. Alongside these differences, however, Vorozhbyt and Vyrypaev use the process of composition and performance to investigate the extent to which the spoken word has the capacity to reflect and refract the experience of everyday life. Both writers work the space between fact and fiction, reality and representation, as they seek to gain a greater understanding of how language makes meaning in performance.

Pavel Rudnev describes precisely this dynamic when he writes that, 'Ivan Vyrypaev's theatre is interested, above all else, in the life of language, the life of words, the conflict of language, the critique of language, and language as such' (Rudnev 2018: 376). Vyrypaev and Vorozhbyt share a singular interest in the generative nature of language in performance. The primary substance of their plays is not located within the plot, the narrative, or the action that takes place onstage. It is rather the act of articulating their texts that becomes the most resonant element of performance. To quote Rudnev on Vyrypaev again, 'The actor does not play the text, the text plays the actor and thereby becomes the dominant element of the show' (2018: 379). Although Rudnev is writing specifically about Vyrypaev's plays in this passage, I suggest that the same can be said of Vorozhbyt's plays and her instrumental approach to the pronunciation of texts onstage.

These two writers' focus on the generative nature of language in performance is, I argue, connected to certain discursive shifts that were taking place in the region when Vyrypaev and Vorozhbyt were beginning their careers as playwrights. Less than one year apart in age, both writers grew up in a nation that ceased to exist at the precise moment they reached adulthood. Although the significance of Soviet

Ivan Vyrypaev and Natalia Vorozhbyt   231

historical narratives had diminished for many citizens well before *perestroika*, the collapse of communism in the region left people searching for a new set of foundation myths with which to interpret the changes unfolding around them. According to Beumers and Lipovetsky, 'New Drama undoubtedly represents the most distinct reaction to the identity crisis that characterizes the post-Soviet era' (Beumers and Lipovetsky 2009: 34).

The plays composed by Vyrypaev, Vorozhbyt, and their new dramatist colleagues in the first decade of the new millennium challenged both artists and audiences to reconsider their relationships to the Soviet past and acknowledge the unreliable nature of historical narratives in the twenty-first-century present. As the region's history was being rewritten yet again, the first generation of post-Soviet writers sought new ways to articulate their experiences and the challenges they faced. Both Vyrypaev and Vorozhbyt used their early works to consider the extent to which text in performance could express the complexities of their era. They sought out a new way of writing, one that reflected the world they saw before them and the language that it produced. In this way, Vorozhbyt and Vyrypaev were at the forefront of a creative movement that was built to speak directly to the cultural concerns and anxieties of everyday life in the post-Soviet space.

Acts of estrangement

One of the hallmarks of New Russian Drama in performance was a style of acting that necessitates the purposeful distancing of actor from character. This style can be observed most clearly in Vyrypaev's productions, particularly those directed by his long-time collaborator Viktor Ryzhakov. Perhaps the most striking example of this dynamic, which Natalia Yakubova describes as the 'radical estrangement' of actor from character, appears in Vyrypaev's 2006 play *Iul'* (*July*) (Yakubova 2010: 40). The text consists of a monologue spoken in the first person and in the past tense from the point of view of a mentally deranged murderer and cannibal. Speaking inexplicably from beyond the grave, the character Piotr reveals himself to the audience as a man in his sixties. He begins by describing with chillingly detached detail how he murdered his neighbour and his neighbour's dog before setting off on a journey to check himself into a mental hospital in nearby Smolensk. Along the way, Piotr murders a homeless man and another dog, which he unremorsefully eats under a bridge before lying silently in the resulting streams of blood for the rest of the afternoon. Next, the narrator befriends a priest whom he also murders and dismembers before finally landing in a psychiatric ward where he attempts to cannibalise a nurse and is subsequently beaten to death by hospital attendants. The impact of the play's content is powerful but, as Boris Wolfson suggests,

> *July's* force in production derives from an even more radical disjunction between the idea of a fictional character's interiority and the conventional means for signifying that interiority in the theatrical practice. The

232   *Molly Flynn*

confession of a 62-year-old male serial murderer is, the stage directions inform us, to be delivered by a woman.

(Wolfson 2015: 275)

In *July*'s premiere (2006) the role of Piotr was played by actress Polina Agureyeva, who performed the text in a style reminiscent of a classical music recital. She articulated the words with elegance and refined formality, a near-virtuosic feat given the repulsive nature of the narrative she recounts. In her performance, the revolting details recalled onstage are shaped by the beauty of the prose so exquisitely composed and embodied by Agureyeva with the clarity and composure of a skilled and practiced artist. The play is built, according to Rudnev, on precisely this 'hideous and flagrant imbalance, the disparity between beauty and disgust'. In this way, Rudnev suggests, 'Vyrypaev takes on the philosophy and ideology of art in our epoch, in which form is forever separate from content. Picasso's *Guernica*, Dali's *Soft Construction with Boiled Beans* – what is beautiful in art is ugly, indeed revolting in life' (Rudnev 2006). By persistently playing the proximity between beauty and horror or, as Beumers and Lipovetsky describe, the sacred and the abject, Vyrypaev's early works come together to form an extended inquiry. The distance between actor and character calls audiences' attention to precisely the space in between the two. In this way, Vyrypaev's plays bring into view a familiar emptiness, a void at the sight of which audiences are invited to take a leap of faith and imagine what alternative might be accessible on the other side.

Following the success of *July*, Vyrypaev gained international recognition as a filmmaker. His film debut *Eiforiia* (*Euphoria*, 2006) won the Grand Prix at the Warsaw International Film Festival and the Little Golden Lion award at the Venice Film Festival in 2007. In 2009, he wrote and directed a film adaptation of *Oxygen* that won best director at the Sochi Open Russia Film Festival. More recent films, *Tanets deli* (*Delhi Dance*, 2012) and *Spasenie* (*Salvation*, 2015), have also proven popular on the Russian and European festival circuits. Additionally, before relocating to Warsaw in 2016, Vyrypaev served as artistic director of Teatr Praktika for three years. This fashionable state-funded studio space just down the street from the original Teatr.doc had become a creative home for the playwright well before he took over the reins from producer and director of the Golden Mask Festival Eduard Boiakov in 2013. It was directly preceding these years as artistic director at Teatr Praktika that Vyrpaev's writing took a noticeable shift towards a quieter and more introspective tone. Before analysing this later phase of the writer's work, however, I will first address how the themes of violence and estrangement have proven important to Vorozhbyt's oeuvre as well.

After making her mark in the Moscow theatre scene in 2003, Vorozhbyt returned to her hometown of Kyiv in the wake of the Orange Revolution in 2004. Having left many of her closest colleagues behind in Russia, the Ukrainian playwright began a concerted effort to establish initiatives explicitly built to foster a community of young playwrights in Ukraine, something Vorozhbyt

Ivan Vyrypaev and Natalia Vorozhbyt   233

recalls was conspicuously lacking in Kyiv at that time. In 2005, Vorozhbyt was selected to attend a residency at the Royal Court Theatre in London, during which time she wrote *Khroniky sim'i Khomenko* (*The Khomenko Family Chronicles*) a one-act play that marked the start of the playwright's ongoing relationship with several of the UK's major-theatre institutions (Vorozhbyt 2007). Since that time, Vorozhbyt has premiered numerous new works on British stages including *Shchodennyky Maidanu* (*Maidan Diaries*, 2014), and *Pohani dorohy* (*Bad Roads*, 2017) at the Royal Court, *Zernoskhovyshche* (*The Grain Store*, 2009) at the RSC, *Zavtra* (*Tomorrow*, 2015) at the Traverse, and *Sasha, vynesy smittia* (*Take the Rubbish Out, Sasha*, 2015) at the National Theatre of Scotland.[3] In fact, before 2014, Vorozhbyt's writing had received significantly more attention in the UK and Russia than it had in Ukraine. Prior to the Maidan Revolution in 2014, Vorozhbyt was best known locally for her work as a writer on the television series *Shkola* (*School*, 2010), a gritty portrayal of teenage life which was directed by Valeria Gai Germanka and ran for one controversial season on Russia's Channel One. It was, in large part, her pioneering work in reaction to the revolution and the war in Donbas that made Vorozhbyt a particularly well-known and highly respected public figure in Ukrainian circles.

Despite the widespread appeal of her plays among international audiences, Vorozhbyt has always maintained that she writes with local audiences in mind. Her plays are firmly rooted in Ukrainian culture and Ukrainian history and have frequently served to represent Ukraine's publics, politics, and histories to both Russian and European audiences. In her play *The Grain Store*, which premiered in Stratford-Upon-Avon in 2009, for example, Vorozhbyt applies the darkest of satire to depict the devastating reality of Holodomor, Stalin's man-made famine that killed approximately 3.9 million Ukrainians between 1932–33.[4] *The Grain Store* was commissioned by the Royal Shakespeare Company as part of artistic director Michael Boyd's *Revolutions* season, which also included *The Drunks* by Russian playwrights Mikhail and Vyacheslav Durnenkov. Originally staged at the RSC's Courtyard Theatre and directed by Boyd, *The Grain Store* weaves a story of star-crossed lovers together with the slow starvation of almost everyone who surrounds them.

At the start of the play, a shock brigade of agit-prop activists descends on the village in the guise of an amateur theatre troupe sent to 'educate' the locals about the 'virtues' of collectivisation. The agit-prop actors become increasingly cruel and violent towards the villagers as the play continues. Some local residents are recruited to join their ranks while the rest of the village is overcome by the famine. Notably, *The Grain Store* also includes reference to cannibalism, although, unlike in Vyrypaev's *July*, Vorozhbyt's audiences are left with the unsettling knowledge that the events represented and referenced in the play did in fact take place.

In one of the most disquieting scenes from the play, the agit-prop activists are shown preparing for a visit from a delegation of filmmakers who have been sent to the village from Moscow to shoot a film about the success of Stalin's Five-Year-Plan and the fictional abundance of Soviet collectivisation. Red flags

234   *Molly Flynn*

are hung around the town square and the sign for the local reading room is changed to 'Canteen'. The village residents are lured by the shock workers – or *udarnyky*, members of a shock brigade in the early Soviet Union – into participating in the charade with the promise of food which they are assured will be provided during filming. The plentiful spread has already been laid out on a table that 'groans under the weight of the feast', a temptation that lures the villagers into participating in the degrading and deceptive charade (Vorozhbyt 2009: 5).

The townspeople are costumed and made up to look as though they were not starving to death. At one point a shock worker approaches an old woman to inform her that she is not suitable for the film, meaning she will not be granted access to the food on the table. What do you mean, not 'suitable'? she replies, 'Why ever not? I can sing, I can dance'.

IVAN IVANYCH: Old lady, you can hardly stand up. Don't make us laugh. We need young people and cheerful songs.
OLD WOMAN: I'm still young. And I can sing such cheerful songs that you'll wet yourself laughing.(Vorozhbyt 2009: 65)

The Old Woman proceeds to sing a satirical song that draws the attention of everyone around her. She even manages to execute a few unusual dance steps at the end before she finishes the song and drops down dead. The dark absurdity of the starving villagers attempting to represent abundance in hopes of eating a single meal comes to a crescendo when they eventually rush towards the table of food and are shot dead by the cruellest of the shock workers.

The dialogue in the play is contemporary and conversational. It maintains its satirical edge even in the most atrocious and disturbing sequences. By drawing on the real-life stories she heard from her grandparents about the famine, Vorozhbyt blends personal narratives with the history of her country and in doing so presents an image of the famine that had never before been seen onstage. *The Grain Store* is a family history set within a national tragedy. It incorporates themes, images, and structural elements from both early-Soviet agitation materials and 1950s Socialist Realist cinema. Vorozhbyt's play calls attention to its own constructed nature and, in this way, questions the relationship between the experience of everyday life and its artistic representation. In addition to writing the history of Holodomor onto international stages, *The Grain Store* raises important questions about how narratives of the past can shape our experiences of the present.

The Grain Store was the first play ever written about Holodomor, a defining event in Ukraine's twentieth-century history. Even more surprising is that the play was not staged in Ukraine until 2015. In my interview with Vorozhbyt in 2014, she attributed the fact the play had not yet been performed in Ukraine to three specific reasons. First, she explained that there had been a production in rehearsal in the western Ukrainian city of Kolomyia before Viktor Yanukovych was elected President in 2010.

When the regime changed, and Yanukovych took office the play was banned a week before its premiere. The topic of Holodomor became immediately irrelevant. Also, *The Grain Store* is an expensive production, it was written on a grand scale for the Royal Shakespeare Company and our theatre is a poor theatre. Lastly, our audiences don't like to suffer. Or, more accurately, our directors believe they don't like to suffer and therefore choose not to stage plays about the most important topics for Ukraine, such as Holodomor.

(Vorozhbyt 2014)

Here Vorozhbyt echoes an earlier claim that Ukrainian theatres had not yet learned how to stage new plays and were too reliant on the staging of classics. 'Audiences need to be educated', the playwright asserted. 'And to do so they need to suffer. Theatre should make you think and feel empathy – that is its primary purpose [...] I'd like to see a theatre of hooligans', she goes on, 'a theatre of provocation, wicked productions of new plays that react to our contemporary reality' (Vorozhbyt 2011).

In 2011, Vorozhbyt could not have foreseen the seismic shift on the horizon of Ukraine's social and political landscape. However, her call for a theatre of provocation, a theatre of hooligans responding to the world around them has, in some ways, come to the fore in recent years. As Ukraine's artists respond to the legacy of the Maidan Revolution and the ongoing war with Russian-backed separatists in the east of the country, new theatre venues, collectives, and artists such as Post-Play and Wild Theatre in Kyiv as well as the works of director Roza Sarkisian are challenging cultural assumptions about theatre's role in society. Since 2014, Ukraine has witnessed a relative boom in new, independent, and socially oriented theatre making. One of the most impactful projects of this kind has been Vorozhbyt's documentary theatre company, the Theatre of Displaced People, which she created in 2015 together with fellow Teatr.doc co-founder, German director Georg Genoux. Since that time, the two theatre-makers have initiated dozens of projects that feature children, soldiers, journalists, activists, and internal refugees speaking their own stories onstage.

The war in Donbas has called many of Ukraine's most accomplished artists into action as they seek to create spaces for the collective renegotiation of cultural narratives and to facilitate dialogue across cultural divisions. This has been the main focus of Vorozhbyt's work since 2014. Between 2016-18, Vorozhbyt also led an annual collaborative playwriting programme for teenagers from across the country. Modelled on a programme created at the Traverse Theatre in Edinburgh in the 1990s, Ukraine's *Class Act – East/West* brought groups of teenagers from east and west Ukraine to Kyiv for two weeks of playwriting workshops every summer. While participating in the workshops, the students wrote 10-minute plays in pairs and their plays were subsequently staged by professional directors at a gala performance at the end of the two weeks. Since Vorozhbyt first ran *Class Act* in the summer of 2016, the initiative has became known across the country and included performances by several of Ukraine's most famous actors from theatre, film, and television. Projects such as

236 *Molly Flynn*

Class Act and the Theatre of Displaced People are evidence of Vorozhbyt's dedication to theatre as a space for dialogue and reconciliation.

In addition to these explicitly social projects, Vorozhbyt also wrote the award-winning screenplay for the Ukrainian film *Kiborhy* (*Cyborgs*, 2017) which depicts the Battle of Donetsk Airport, one of the bloodiest episodes from the first year of the war. In November 2017, she premiered a new play, *Bad Roads*, at the Royal Court. In the play, Vorozhbyt fuses fact and fiction into an unsettling montage of loosely connected scenes about women in wartime. *Bad Roads* features stories from girls and women whose lives have been touched by war. Many of the narratives included in the play are based on those Vorozhbyt heard during her work with the Theatre of Displaced People and throughout her research for *Cyborgs*. A journalist is detained in the occupied territories and held in captivity for days, suffering physical, psychological, and sexual abuse. A group of local teenage girls linger outside an army checkpoint. They boast about the gifts that were given to them by the Ukrainian soldiers before they are summoned, one by one, into the woods by soldiers who are stationed in their town for the supposed purpose of protecting them. One of the most harrowing scenes from the play depicts a female Ukrainian soldier driving away from the front line with her lover's headless corpse stashed in a freezer in the back of the vehicle. Already in a state of panicked grief, the woman is pushed to her limits when she begins receiving text messages from her dead lover's phone number. 'They've got his phone, they're playing games' (Vorozhbyt 2017: 40), a second soldier tells her and instructs her to block the number. 'Block Vitya? I can't', she eventually responds, 'It's like him continuing in some way...' (43).

Most memorable is the play's opening sequence, a 20-minute monologue written in the second person and spoken from the point of view of a woman who shares her name, appearance, and biography with Vorozhbyt. The speaker recalls how she was conducting research for a screenplay she was writing about the Battle of Donetsk Airport, just as the playwright did. In connection to this work, one of the soldiers she interviews invites her to join him on the front line to witness the world she seeks to depict in her screenplay. Surrounded by weapons and warfare, the speaker who calls herself Natalia describes how she is overcome with desire for the soldier who brought her there.

The uncomfortable irony of her romantic yearning set against the backdrop of death and devastation is emphasised when she frequently calls up the imagery of heroic soldiers from war films as she struggles to come to terms with the actual destruction that surrounds her. A sophisticated narrator with a shrewd sense of sarcasm, Natalia recalls her deepening desire with self-deprecatory wit. She describes lying in bed awake in a hotel room:

> You lie down on the bed on the right, lay your machine gun and handgun tenderly by the pillow [...] I lie on hot coals all night. And not because I see before my eyes the photographs from the commander who forgot that you shouldn't show civilians pictures of bodies ripped to pieces by

explosions. And not because you are snoring. I lie on hot coals for one reason only. I want you.

(Vorozhbyt 2017: 6)

When Natalia's fantasies finally come to fruition, they take the form of a kiss set against the backdrop of explosions across the bay from Ukrainian-controlled Mariupol. 'Over there is the village of Shirokino and the front line. Over there right now, men are blowing each other to bits with rocket launchers. The March sun is so bright'. The bright rays of the sun and the image of exploding rocket launchers are linked in these lines in such a way as to highlight the awkward alliance of love and war in our culture. What could be more romantic than love in times of war, the monologue asks. And what could be more horrific?

You kiss me for the first time. You decide when and how to do it. I decide nothing. My legs go weak. I can't stand. It feels like, this is fucking it, here it is, that very scene from the film about love, I have seen it and heard about it so many times, and felt it for others, but never for myself. Here you are, love. In your honour bombs are falling on the far shore. In your honour someone has just got their leg ripped off.

(Vorozhbyt 2017: 6)

The sick brutality of war grates against the romance of heroic narratives in this sequence. In this way, Vorozhbyt's text reveals the ways our interpretations of both personal and historical events are inevitably intertwined with the representation of those events in art and culture.

In the act of articulating the porous boundaries between the experience of everyday life and its artistic representation, Vorozhbyt's play calls attention to the role that creative and cultural narratives play in the construction of both individual and national identity. In her able hands, text is not only an instrument with which to tell a story. It is the substance of the story itself. Her characters speak themselves into existence and simultaneously use the practice of speaking and listening as a path to self-reflection. Her plays give voice to those who are not often given the space to speak in national media or on international stages and they offer audiences insight into private spaces that are frequently hidden from public view. *The Grain Store* depicts the stories of the famine Vorozhbyt heard from her grandmother and grandfather as a child. *Bad Roads* reveals the inner-lives of women in wartime. *Take Out the Rubbish, Sasha* explores the intimacy of the family home and the process of mourning a loved one. In one way or another, each of Vorozhbyt's works invites its audiences into private spaces inhabited by speakers who are navigating their way in the world through the act of speaking and the self-definition it inspires.

238   *Molly Flynn*

The tragedy of meaning

Beginning with his play *Delhi Dance* (2009), Vyrypaev has also turned his attention towards the intimacy of private spaces and the resonance of interpersonal communication. Gone are the inexplicable acts of violence described in *Oxygen* and *July* and, in their place, Vyrypaev has created a more exacting and refined approach to the enduring themes of existential philosophy and spiritual inquiry that run throughout his opus. For example, in his play *Illuzii* (*Illusions*, 2011), four speakers recount the stories of two elderly, married couples who have shared decades of friendship. As the play's tragicomic narrative of confession and betrayal unfolds, the text continually calls into question the notion of belief. When one of the protagonists takes her own life, the letter she leaves for her husband contains a resonant phrase that speaks to the heart of the struggle each of the play's protagonists is shown to face. 'Dear Albert', she writes,

> I have decided to do this because I have entirely ceased to understand how everything functions here. I don't understand how everything fits together here, what follows what. I can't see the grounds by which everything moves forward, develops. I can't find order, I can't find permanence. There's got to be some kind of permanence, right, Albert? There has got to be at least some kind of permanence in this enormous, shifting universe, Albert? There's got to be some kind of permanence in this shifting universe, Albert?
>
> (Vyrypaev 2011: 41)

The rest of the page, on both sides, is inscribed with this single phrase: 'There's got to be some kind of permanence in this shifting universe, Albert?'

This precise question about the transient nature of love, life, and an individual's search for meaning is located, in one form or another, at the centre of each of Vyrypaev's later plays. The overt references to religious scripture so often seen in his earlier work have been overtaken by more subjective and self-referential questions about faith, belief, and the presence of a higher power. Like *Illusions*, the play *Nevynosimo dolgie ob'iat'ia* (*Unbearably Long Embrace*, 2015) approaches the topic of impermanence through the lens of romance and betrayal. In *UFO* (2016) the unknowable qualities of the world are brought partially into view through the stories of individuals recalling their encounters with the extra-terrestrial. In *P'ianye* (*Drunks*, 2013), the inebriated protagonists stumble into moments of unusual lucidity, although the clarity they encounter turns out to be as ephemeral as their altered state of mind. In his most recent play, *Iranskaia konferentsiia* (*Iran Conference*, 2017), Vyrypaev draws each of these narrative threads into a text that weaves together many of the most vexing developments in contemporary European culture with satirical self-reflexivity.

These are among the qualities, I suggest, that have drawn directors and actors across Europe to Vyrypaev's texts leading to productions that speak to a variety of both local and global cultural concerns in the twenty-first century. For example, in the 2018 production of *Illusions* directed by Miguel del Arco at Madrid's Teatro

Kamikaze, the play's questions about self-determination, fate, and the relationship between an individual and collective found resonance in the aftermath of Spain's financial crisis as audiences grappled with a new understanding of democracy in their country. Since the play's premiere at Teatr Praktika in Moscow in 2011, *Illusions* has been produced on over a dozen stages from London to Warsaw, from Toronto to Beirut. The popularity of Vyrypaev's work internationally testifies to the universality of the existential questions his plays seek to excavate.

Although Vyrypaev's plays written after 2010 undoubtedly mark a clear shift in his writing style, there are certain elements of his earlier texts that remain. In *Bytie No. 2* (*Genesis No. 2*, 2004) for example, Vyrypaev appears onstage as himself explaining that the play's text has been sent to him by a patient in a mental hospital named Antonina Velikanova. He goes on to read aloud some of his correspondence with Velikanova in which he aims to guide her in her comprehension of dramatic structure. 'You wrote that my play is in need of more of a plot', Velikanova is said to have written to Vyrypaev.

> But why does it need a plot, so the spectator can understand what's going on? The spectator doesn't even understand what's going on in his everyday life. Why should anyone feel empathy for the person standing onstage? It would be better for each person in the audience to feel empathy for themselves. Ivan, a plot only gives the illusion of meaning, when it is meaning itself that is tragic.
>
> (Vyrypaev 2005b: 222)

Though this passage of text is attributed to a fictional character in 2004, it resonates across Vyrypaev's oeuvre and presages the shifts in the playwright's aesthetic approach to the composition and articulation of text in performance. Moreover, the illusory nature of dramatic structure and the tragic connotations it contains is made apparent in each of Vorozhbyt's most recent works which serve to explore and expose the inscrutability of life, love, and loss during wartime. While the style and structure of the two playwrights' works are immensely varied, this chapter has sought to illustrate their common investment in the exploration of language and its capacity to facilitate the comprehension of the ever-shifting universe their protagonists inhabit.

Conclusion

For Vyrypaev, language in performance becomes an instrument with which to illuminate the paradoxes of modern life and to confront the inherent frailty of human desire. His protagonists commit acts of cruelty towards one another, sometimes intentionally, other times unknowingly. And yet, the overarching theme in each of his plays is love – love as an expression of belief, love as that which gives meaning to life, love in the face of spiritual, psychological, and physical violence. He places the text at the centre of each of his plays and thereby asks his audiences to consider the extent to which the reciprocal act of speaking and listening has the capacity to bring us closer to ourselves, to those around us, and to the idea and/or absence of a higher power that consistently haunts the playwright's works either explicitly or implicitly. While the abject nihilism of Vyrypaev's earlier writing has since focused into a softer, more nuanced process of inquiry, his post-2010 plays present a picture of the world that is no less distressing than the murderous and cannibalistic themes of his earlier works.

Vorozhbyt's plays take a more familiar approach to dramatic structure than Vyrypaev's. Her protagonists inhabit concrete times and spaces. The dialogue she provides may not be stylised in the sense that Vyrypaev's is, but its style is no less integral to its communicative method. Whereas Vyrypaev often turns to the abstract in his portrayal of an individual's search for meaning, the exceptionally incisive quality of Vorozhbyt's writing is rooted in its realistic, indeed documentary-like dialogue. Her plays explore the way history, culture, and politics come to shape the private and the personal. As a writer, Vorozhbyt most often deals in the domestic with a focus on interpersonal relationships (see Figure 12.1). Running throughout her texts however, is a strand of self-reflexivity, a wry irony

Figure 12.1 Natalia Vorozhbyt's *Viy 2.0*, directed by Maksym Holenko (2016) at Wild Theatre in Kyiv. Ivan (Oleksiy Dorichevksy), one of several millennials from the rural village portrayed in the play, drinks homemade vodka (*horilka*) and laments the lack of job prospects for young people in the region. Photograph © Gala Lavrinets

that creates a sense of distance between the story and its speakers. In this way, her plays express a simultaneous sincere investment in the people and topics they seek to represent, in combination with an ironic detachment that invites audiences to acknowledge the absurdities of the familiar practices portrayed onstage.

The two writers approach their work from very different aesthetic angles. Over the course of his career, Vyrypaev's plays have moved towards the global. His characters hail from all over the world and the geographical settings of his plays are more metaphorical than literal. This is one reason why Vyrypaev's work has found such international appeal. Vorozhbyt conversely lends each of her plays a concrete time and space, often specifying in which Ukrainian city or region the play is meant to be set. Even when produced abroad, Vorozhbyt's work is still closely connected to its Ukrainian origins. Alongside these differences, the two playwrights share an unusual investment in the transformative capacity of language in performance. Their texts are indicative of how written and spoken language has been used in the region in a conscious effort to re-inscribe the narratives of the present and thereby bring greater lucidity to cultural perceptions of the past. Their works often tread a fine line between fiction and non-fiction. They juxtapose the sacred and the profane. In one way or another, their works each question the veracity of language as an instrument with which to depict the absurdities of everyday life.

Their early plays raised important questions about what it means to be Russian and what it means to be Ukrainian in the early twenty-first century. Since that time, Vorozhbyt and Vyrypaev have begun asking their audiences to consider broader questions about how perceptions of contemporary culture are shaped by historical narratives both local and global. To speak and to listen to their texts is to embark upon a process of discovery. Their works are built to enact a ritual encounter with words. They cast their texts as the leading role in each of their plays and seek to call audiences' attention to the generative nature of language as a primary factor in the construction of both individual and cultural identity. By staging the distance between the speaker and that which is spoken, Vyrypaev and Vorozhbyt create the space for a process of inquiry. It is directly through the articulation of language that a play's meaning is made in these two writers' works, and it is precisely that same meaning which is constantly called into question.

Ivan Vyrypaev – four key productions

Kislorod (*Oxygen*). Directed by Viktor Ryzhakov. Cast: Arina Marakulina, Irina Rodionova, Ivan Vyrypaev. Teatr.doc, Moscow, 29 September 2002.

Bytie No. 2 (*Genesis No. 2*). Directed by Viktor Ryzhakov. Design by Dmitrii Razumov. Lighting by Anton Magula. Sound by Igor Khaidarov. Cast: Aleksander Bargman, Ainar Gainullin, Svetlana Ivanova-Sergeeva, Ivan Vyrypaev. Theatre Praktika, Moscow, 25 February 2006.

242 *Molly Flynn*

Iiul' (*July*). Directed by Viktor Ryzhakov. Design by Margarita Ablaeva. Sound by Kirill Vasilenko. Cast: Polina Argueeva. Theatre Praktika, Moscow, 24 October 2006.

P'ianye (*Drunks*). Directed by Andrei Moguchii. Design by Aleksandr Shishkin. Lighting by Stas Svistunovich. Costumes by Zhanna Serdiuk. Sound by Aleksei Titov. Video by Dmitrii Fedorov. Movement by Roman Kaganovich and Maksim Pakhamov. Cast: Karina Razumovskaia, Velerii Degtiar', Varvara Pavlova, Alena Kuchkova, Vasilii Reutov, Dmitrii Vorob'ev, Marina Ignatova, Anatolii Petrov, Elena Popva, Rustan Nasyrov, Viktor Barabanov, Evgenii Savskii, Iulia Deinega, Uliana Fomicheva. Bolshoi Drama Theatre, St Petersburg, 5 March 2015.

Natalia Vorozhbyt – four key productions

Galka Motalko. Directed by Elena Novikova. Cast: Daria Drozdovskaia, Anna Ukolova, Iurii Kviatkovskii, Dmitrii Mukhamadeev, Konstantin Pokhmelov, Viktoria Isakova. Centre for Playwrights and Directors, Moscow, September 2005.

Zernoskhovyshche (*The Grain Store*). Directed by Michael Boyd. Design by Tom Piper. Lighting by Oliver Fenwick. Music by John Woolf. Movement by Anna Morrissey. Fight choreography by Terry King. Translation by Sasha Dugdale. Cast: Joseph Arkley, Noma Dumezweni, Geoffrey Freshwater, Maria Gale, Guffudd Glyn, Greg Hicks, Kathryn Hunter, Kelly Hunter, Ansu Kabia, Tunji Kasim, Debbie Korley, John Mackay, Forbes Masson, Dharmesh Patel, Patrick Romer, David Rubin, Oliver Ryan, Simone Saunders, Peter Shorey, Katy Stephens, Sam Troughton, James Tucker, Larrington Walker, Kirsty Woodward, Samantha Young. Royal Shakespeare Company, Stratford-Upon-Avon, 24 September 2009.

Viy: 2.0. Directed by Maksym Holenko. Design by Fedir Aleksandrovych. Music by Dmytro Danov. Cast: Dmytro Hubanov, Andrii Kronglevskyi, Oleksii Zhmurko, Ievhen Koval'chuk, Dmytro Vovchuk, Liudmyla Ruslanova, Anastasiia Koval'chuk, Volodymyr Kravchuk, Kateryna Vyshneva, Volodymyr Lisko, Olena Iavors'ka, Oleksii Dorychev'skyi. Wild Theatre, Kyiv, February 2016.

Pohani dorohy (*Bad Roads*). Directed by Vicky Featherstone. Design by Camilla Clarke. Lighting by Natasha Chivers. Sound by Nick Powell. Translation by Sasha Dugdale. Cast: Anne Lacey, Katie Dickie, Mike Noble, Ria Zmitrowicz, Ronke Adekoluejo, Tadhg Murphy, Vincent Ebrahim. Royal Court Theatre, London, 15 November 2017.

Notes

1 Where possible I have quoted from published translations of play texts as indicated in the bibliography. In all other cases translations are my own. Names, cities, and play titles are transliterated from either Russian or Ukrainian as dictated by the playwrights' country of origin.
2 Here the title of Vorozhbyt's play has been transliterated from Russian as I am referring to the original production which took place in Moscow.

3 Translated by Sasha Dugdale, the play originally titled *Zavtra* (*Tomorrow*) in Ukrainian premiered with the English language title *This Elephant Speaks Ukrainian.*
4 For more on the history of Holodomor and the calculation of the famine's casualties see Applebaum (2018, p. 285).

Works cited

Applebaum, Anne (2018) *Red Famine: Stalin's War on Ukraine*, Milton Keynes: Allen Lane.

Beumers, Birgit and Mark Lipovetsky (2009) *Performing Violence: Literary and Theatrical Experiments in New Russian Drama*, London and New York: Routledge.

Lucey, Colleen (2011) 'Violence and asphyxia in Vyrypaev's plays', *Slavic Forum*, https://lucian.uchicago.edu/blogs/theslavicforum/files/2011/12/SLAVICFORUM_2011_LUCEY_PUBLICATION.pdf

Oushakine, Sergei (2009) 'Ivan Vyrypaev Oxygen: Kislorod 2009', *KinoKultura*, 26, http://www.kinokultura.com/2009/26r-kislorod.shtml

Rudnev, Pavel (2006) 'Lektsiia kannibala', *Vzgliad: delovaia gazeta*, 15 December, https://vz.ru/columns/2006/12/15/60800.print.html

——— (2018) *Drama pamiati: ocherki istorii rossiiskoi dramaturgii 1950–2010-e*, Moscow: Novoe literaturnoe obozrenie.

Vorozhbyt, Natalia (2002) *Galka Motalko*, trans. Sasha Dugdale, unpublished script.

——— (2007) *The Khomenko Family Chronicles*, trans. Sasha Dugdale, London: Oberon Books.

——— (2009) *The Grain Store*, trans. Sasha Dugdale, London: Nick Hern Books.

——— (2011) 'Natalia Vorozhbyt: Zriteliu nuzhno delat' bol'no', *Ukrains'ka pravda*, interview with Aksin'ia Kurina, https://life.pravda.com.ua/society/2011/05/13/78523/

——— (2014) 'Maidan: voices from the uprising', interview with the author, http://ceel.org.uk/culture/film-theatre/maidan-voices-from-the-uprising-molly-flynn-interviews-Natalia-Vorozhbyt-on-her-new-play/

——— (2017) *Bad Roads*, trans. Sasha Dugdale, London: Nick Hern Books.

Vyrypaev, Ivan (2005a) 'Oxygen', trans. Sasha Dugdale, *Theater* 36(1): 48–69.

——— (2005b) 'Byitie No. 2', in *13 tekstov, napisannykx osen'iu*, Moscow: Vremia.

——— (2006) *Iul'*, trans. Cazimir Liske, unpublished script.

——— (2011) *Illusions*, trans. Cazimir Liske, London: Faber & Faber.

Wolfson, Boris (2015) 'New drama', in Evgeny Dobrenko and Mark Lipovetsky (eds), *Russian Literature Since 1991*, Cambridge: Cambridge University Press.

Yakubova, Natalia (2010) 'Ivan Vyrypaev: a cultural cannibal', *Slavic and East European Performance: Drama, Theatre and Film*, 30(1): 33–41.

13 Enda Walsh and Martin McDonagh
Reimagining Irish theatre

Patrick Lonergan

On 1 February 1996, Galway city marked the opening of a new municipal theatre by premiering *The Beauty Queen of Leenane*, the first play by a then-unknown writer called Martin McDonagh. In the local press, he had described growing up in London as the son of Irish immigrants and had spoken eloquently about his literary influences – figures such as Borges and Nabokov (McBride 1996: 23). He also seemed grateful: his play had been pulled from a pile of unsolicited scripts in the local company Druid Theatre, having previously been rejected elsewhere. His was a story that seemed very familiar: that of the young writer, hopeful and humble, dreaming of a breakthrough.

While *Beauty Queen* was opening in Galway, in Cork another young playwright was about to begin writing a new play. The writer was Enda Walsh, and the play was *Disco Pigs*; it would premiere in September of that year in a production directed by Pat Kiernan for his company Corcadorca. Where McDonagh had worked alone, sending his scripts to theatres in the hope of being discovered, Walsh had been learning about stagecraft by collaborating with Kiernan on devised and improvised works-in-progress that were performed in small venues around Cork city. 'It was an incredibly productive time, and we made a lot of work', he later told Jesse Weaver:

> It was all bad – really bad – but we knew it was bad. We just got up and did it, and then asked the audience why it was bad: 'Let's try and learn together what the work is,' we said. What happened then was that the audience got to know us, they became like our mates. We built an audience over a year by just asking after each [performance], 'Ok. That was a little bit better than the last time. Why do you think it was better? Can you see what we're getting at?'
>
> (Weaver 2012: 132–3)

That collaborative ethos had been evident in the plays that Walsh had written before *Disco Pigs*. There was *Fishy Tales* (1993), for example: a play for children for the Cork-based theatre-in-education company Graffiti, the production credits for which show that Walsh had not just provided the script but had built the set and operated puppets too (Irish Playography 2018). Where McDonagh

Enda Walsh and Martin McDonagh   245

had seen playwriting primarily in literary terms – using his first interviews to emphasise his autonomy as the creator of his work – Walsh from the beginning displayed a fascination with theatre-making as a collaborative artform.

That distinction between the two playwrights forms the starting point for this chapter. Walsh and McDonagh have much in common – including the fact that they have significantly enhanced, and in some ways transformed, the international reputation of contemporary Irish drama. McDonagh's most dominant interest, however, is in the process of storytelling, in how the creation of the meaning of a narrative is a shared enterprise between an author and an audience. Walsh certainty shares that interest: most of his plays focus on characters who obsessively narrate stories (albeit that Walsh tends to devote more attention to the obsession than the story *per se*). But Walsh's preoccupation is with theatricality, with the collaborative use of a stage space to evoke emotion and thought, and to generate meaning. To describe McDonagh primarily as a storyteller and Walsh primarily as a theatre-maker is not to denigrate the theatrical knowledge of the former or the formidable literary accomplishments of the latter, but to provide a point of comparison that enables a clearer understanding of the different pathways taken by the two playwrights as their careers have developed.

A useful starting point for that comparison, however, is with something Walsh and McDonagh have in common, which is that both of their careers began with an attempt to reimagine Irish theatre. On that opening night of *Beauty Queen* in 1996, McDonagh's play had initially seemed like a story the audience had seen many times before. It was set in an Irish country cottage, and explored such well-worn themes as the challenges of emigration, the persistence of intergenerational conflict, and the stifling nature of rural Irish life. That first audience would instantly have been reminded of other Irish plays, many of them previously staged by Druid. *Beauty Queen* featured Druid's co-founder Marie Mullen as Maureen, a young woman who has been trapped into caring for an elderly female relative – a role Galway audiences had seen her perform in Tom Murphy's *Bailegangaire* (1985), a play with an almost identical setting that used a similar (though more realistic) west-of-Ireland dialect. With its presentation of characters who yearn for escape from Ireland, *Beauty Queen* was also reminiscent of Brian Friel's *Philadelphia, Here I Come!* (1964) and the many other plays that had explored the impact of emigration on Irish life. And in portraying a character whose chance of forming a loving relationship is thwarted when a letter to her is deliberately destroyed, McDonagh seemed to be drawing on the melodramas of John B. Keane, whose play *Sive* (1959) turns on that plot-twist (Keane 2009: 84).

It soon became apparent, however, that McDonagh was using those over-familiar Irish tropes to lull audiences into a false sense of security: one that would make his play's subsequent events feel all the more shocking. Druid's Artistic Director Garry Hynes explained that this was a deliberate strategy. 'For the first few moments [of the action of *Beauty Queen*] the audience will feel *oh lovely, this is a Druid play, we know where we are.* And then…' (quoted in Woodworth 1996: 10).

246   *Patrick Lonergan*

That ellipsis was Hynes's way of alluding to (without revealing) the many surprises contained in the play. Its sensationalistic use of violence might have had its roots in melodrama but seemed to audiences at the time to be more directly indebted to the films of Quentin Tarantino, which were then a source of controversy in Ireland (*Natural Born Killers*, directed by Oliver Stone from a script by Tarantino, had been banned there in 1994). McDonagh's jokes about how 'it's usually only the older priests go punching you in the head' displayed a willingness to address openly the reports that had been circulating since the beginning of the 1990s about Irish priests and nuns abusing people in their care (McDonagh 2009: 14). And then there was the play's tone: its strange combination of tastelessness, sentimentality, kitsch, and iconoclasm – which was accompanied by a sincere authorial sympathy for the heroine and her would-be lover. Audiences at *Beauty Queen* found themselves caring for characters who were also caricatures, and laughing at jokes that upon reflection they decided they probably shouldn't find funny. Confronted by such confusion, some audience members chose to blame McDonagh for their negative responses: he was accused of being exploitative, unoriginal, and disrespectful (see Waters 2001: 32). But for others, his was a thrilling new voice, doing for Irish drama what Shane McGowan and the Pogues had done for Irish music – which is to bring the punk sensibility of the second-generation immigrant to bear on traditional material, simultaneously celebrating, desecrating, and revitalising it (as discussed in O'Toole 2006).

Disco Pigs also seemed initially to be retracing territory that had been well charted in the Irish dramatic tradition. Walsh's play features two characters who directly address the audience, a style of performance that had become common in Ireland in the early 1990s as a result of the revivals of Beckett at Dublin's Gate Theatre; *Disco Pigs* bears a resemblance to his *Play* (1963) and *Not I* (1972) in featuring characters whose lines are delivered so quickly as to be barely comprehensible. Also, an apparent influence was Brian Friel, whose monologue play *Faith Healer* (1979) had finally been acknowledged as a masterpiece during its revivals at the Abbey Theatre from 1991 to 1994. Walsh's use of language also seemed to draw on the earlier dramatic tradition, presenting an exaggerated and poeticised version of an Irish idiom, rather like John Millington Synge and Sean O'Casey had done in such works as *The Playboy of the Western World* (1907) and *Juno and the Paycock* (1924) respectively.

What was different about *Disco Pigs* was the quality of speech delivered by the two characters, a young man called Pig and his girlfriend Runt. Their language had a kinetic physicality that had been worked out in the imagination of the author but perfected in the rehearsal room; it had also been sensitively enhanced by a soundscape composed by Cormac O'Connor. Playing Runt was Eileen Walsh, for whom Enda had written the play (the two share a surname but are not related to each other). In the role of Pig, Corcadorca cast Cillian Murphy in his first professional role; he went on to become one of the most famous Irish performers of his generation, appearing in the BBC TV show *Peaky Blinders* and in films by such directors as Luc Besson and Christopher Nolan. He also became a regular collaborator with Walsh, especially during the 2010s.

Enda Walsh and Martin McDonagh   247

On the page, the script of *Disco Pigs* seems lyrical, dense, and surreal. But in its first performances, what was striking was how the actors used Walsh's words not only to convey mood but also to recreate the landscape of Cork and its surroundings. Speaking of a fight in a Cork pub, for example, Eileen Walsh as Runt delivered language that not only reveals the meaning of her words but also uses sound to convey the violence that her character is carrying out:

> I face dis ugly puss an holdin a fist full a scampi fry I mash it inta her gob! When SHLAP!! She pack a punch dis doll! SSMACKKK!! Opens up da nose an blood all drip drip drop from da Runt! She hold hold a my hair an spit da scampi mush back inta my face an onta da fancy top I do wear. Dat stain won' shif too easy, I tink! FUCKKKKK!!! Where Pig? Where ya now Mister Kissy!? Mister Kissy! Mister Kissy! Mister kissy! Mister Kissy!!
>
> (Walsh 1997: 23).

The phonetic representation of speech intensified audiences' understanding of the violence, the repeated 'd' sounds operating not only as an accurate representation of the character's working class Cork accent (which involve 'th' and 't' sounds being rendered with 'd' sounds), but also in creating a repetitive rhythm that matches the punches that Runt is throwing. The delivery of these lines in the present tense also intensified their physicality and immediacy: the audience were not hearing a story being remembered (as happens in most Irish monologue plays) but witnessing its recreation in real time. Walsh's ability to understand the relationship between words on a page and bodies in space was grounded in his trust in Kiernan, O'Connor, the two actors – and of course his audiences. So as with *Beauty Queen, Disco Pigs* is a play that deployed Irish stage conventions only to reinterpret them – even if the reinterpretation being carried out by Walsh was as much to do with how plays are made as their content.

It is this shared strategy of revision that explains why Walsh and McDonagh were soon being credited with having inaugurated a new era for Irish drama. Joining other key productions such as Marina Carr's *Portia Coughlan* (1996) and Conor McPherson's *The Weir* (1997), *Beauty Queen* and *Disco Pigs* signalled the arrival of a new generation of Irish playwrights, a group that would go on to have so major an impact that Fintan O'Toole would propose that their plays should be seen as part of a 'third renaissance' that matched the Irish dramatic revival (of roughly 1899–1928) and a second revival that began in the early 1960s with the international success of Brian Friel and Tom Murphy (O'Toole 2000: loc 1800).

In defining those plays as having inaugurated a new era, O'Toole and others were influenced by the fact that *Beauty Queen* and *Disco Pigs* premiered outside Dublin, providing evidence of the development of Irish theatre beyond the nation's capital. But the impact of those plays also lay in their success internationally. The Corcadorca production of *Disco Pigs* toured to Australia, Canada, Denmark, Germany, Hungary, and the UK from 1997 to 1999, winning awards in all of those places. It also became a major presence in the German theatre,

248   *Patrick Lonergan*

where it was given 42 different productions between 1999 and 2001 alone (see Huber 2012: 84). Walsh's work there was championed by the dramaturg and director Tilman Raabke so that – most unusually for an Irish writer – Walsh began to premiere his plays in translation in Germany before staging them in Ireland: *New Electric Ballroom* was first staged at the Kammerspiel Theatre in Munich in 2004, and (as discussed below) *Penelope* premiered at Theater Oberhausen in 2010. Walsh also premiered the short plays *How These Desperate Men Talk* in Zurich in 2004 and *Lynndie's Gotta Gun* in Lisbon in 2005. His reputation began to grow in Ireland itself during this period: his play *bedbound* was the surprise hit of the 2000 Dublin Theatre Festival, which had also included work by such prominent figures as Romeo Castellucci, Calixto Bieito, and Simon McBurney, not to mention Simon Russell Beale's *Hamlet* and a play for children that featured Geoffrey Rush (Grene and Lonergan 2008: 336–7).

McDonagh's successes were even more emphatic. Within two years of the premiere of his first play, he had moved from the Druid Theatre slush pile to a Broadway run for *Beauty Queen*, which won four Tony Awards in 1998, including one for McDonagh himself and another for Hynes, who became the first woman to win a Tony for Directing. *Beauty Queen* was joined in 1997 by *A Skull in Connemara* and *The Lonesome West* to become *The Leenane Trilogy*; all three premiered in Galway before transferring to the West End in London. Also appearing in the West End in the summer of 1997 was *The Cripple of Inishmaan*, which has premiered at the National Theatre earlier that year and was the first of another projected (and as yet incomplete) trilogy set on the Aran Islands.[1] As *Time* magazine pointed out at the time, McDonagh was the only writer other than Shakespeare to have four of his plays running on the London stage simultaneously during that season (Kramer 1997: 71). Further successes soon followed, with a second Aran Islands play called *The Lieutenant of Inishmore* appearing in 2001, followed by *The Pillowman* (2003), the first McDonagh play not set in Ireland.

He too would become a major presence in Europe, where his work was seen not so much as Irish as a typical example of the In Yer Face genre of British plays that had emerged in the late 1990s: he was more likely to be compared to Sarah Kane than John Millington Synge (see Huber 2012: 89; Raab 2002: 49). The ongoing importance of his work to the European tradition was marked by the establishment of an International Martin McDonagh Theatre Festival in Perm, Russia, in 2014, which has hosted productions of McDonagh's plays by companies from Poland, Austria, Montenegro, Lithuania, Serbia, Scotland, Ireland, and of course Russia itself.

Notwithstanding the popularity of his plays, McDonagh's international reputation has become increasingly associated with his work for cinema. He confirmed his knack for unprecedented success when his first short film *Six Shooter* won an Academy Award in 2004; he went on to write and direct the features *In Bruges* (2008), *Seven Psychopaths* (2012), and *Three Billboards Outside Ebbing, Missouri* (2017), the first and third of which have won many awards.

Walsh too had some success in cinema. *Disco Pigs* was filmed by Kirsten Sheridan in 2001 from a script by Walsh, but perhaps his most successful work in that medium is his co-written screenplay for Steve McQueen's *Hunger*, a film about the Irish Hunger Striker Bobby Sands that premiered at the 2008 Cannes Film Festival. That feature integrated Walsh's theatrical style by featuring a 17-minute monologue that was delivered in a single take by Michael Fassbender, who played the lead role. But unlike McDonagh, Walsh has tended to show a preference for live performance over film, even as his interests have broadened into opera (such as his 2017 *Second Violinist*) and live art installations (his *Rooms* series, begun in 2011). Indeed, his international fame is based mainly on stage musicals: his 2011 Tony Award–winning adaptation of the Irish film *Once*; his script for *Lazarus* (2015), the collaboration with Ivo Van Hove and David Bowie that premiered in New York only weeks before Bowie's death; and *Sing Street*, another adaptation of a John Carney movie, which opened at New York Theatre Workshop in 2019.

If McDonagh's work is seen as more accessible than Walsh's, this is perhaps attributable to his interest in plot – or, to use the different but related term with which I began this chapter, with *storytelling*. *The Pillowman*, *Seven Psychopaths*, and his play *A Very Very Very Dark Matter* (2018) all feature writers as their main characters, and in different ways consider storytelling in ethical terms.[2] In *The Pillowman*, for example, writing is seen as inherently political, even when the play's protagonist Katurian claims to act from a position of neutral disinterest:

> I say if you've got a political axe to grind, if you've got a political what-do-ya-call-it, go write a fucking essay, I will know where I stand. I say keep your left-wing this, keep your right-wing that and tell me a fucking story! You know? A great man once said, 'The first duty of a storyteller is to tell a story,' and I believe in that wholeheartedly … [T]hat's what I do, I tell stories. No axe to grind, no anything to grind. No social anything whatsoever.
>
> (McDonagh 2003: 7)

Katurian even offers to engage in self-censorship, telling the two policemen who are interrogating him that if they can find a political subtext in his work, they should 'show me where the bastard is. I'll take it straight out. Fucking burn it' (2003: 8). But the play shows that Katurian is behaving politically simply by writing in a country that is described by one of the characters as a 'totalitarian fucking dictatorship' (23). All governments seek to retain a monopoly on violence; a defining characteristic of the totalitarian state is that it also seeks to acquire a monopoly over the creation of meaning. Although ostensibly written as fairytales, all of Katurian's stories celebrate individuals who refuse to conform, whether that is a little girl who acts like Jesus, or a little pig who loves being coloured bright green. It's no surprise, then, that his captors choose to execute Katurian, locking his stories away so as to ensure that they will remain forever unpublished and unread – though the fact that the play itself allows several of those stories to be read demonstrates the subversive power of theatre and other forms of art.

250   *Patrick Lonergan*

The Pillowman considers the relationship between power and authorship from the perspective of a relatively helpless writer. *A Very Very Very Dark Matter* flips that dynamic by developing a satirical portrait of Charles Dickens and Hans Christian Andersen, who are presented as active instruments of colonial authority and patriarchal oppression. In a surreal plot involving time travel, McDonagh relates the careers of those authors to the colonisation of the Congo by Belgium from 1885 onwards – suggesting that the stories attributed to them were not written by the men themselves, but by women from Africa who have travelled back in time and are now imprisoned in each author's attic, where they are subjected to physical violence and sexual exploitation.

In suggesting that a woman locked in an attic can be an emblem for the place of patriarchy and colonialism in the British unconscious, McDonagh is repeating a strategy that is at least as old as Charlotte Bronte's *Jane Eyre* (1847) – but his entire play challenges the notion of authorial originality anyway, not least in the fact that *A Very Very Very Dark Matter* can itself be described as a self-plagiarising expansion of a story called 'the Shakespeare Room' from *The Pillowman* (2003: 42). McDonagh appears to be inviting audiences to consider how apparent symbols of civilisation (such as great literature) can be used to mask or suppress histories of violence and exploitation. In negotiating the relationship between appearance and reality, McDonagh implies, writers will always wield power, and must be held accountable for doing so.

McDonagh's consideration of the relationship between storytelling and power explains the characterisation of several of his plays' most memorable figures. The impetus for much of the plot of *Hangmen* (2015) is that one of the executioners named in the title (a barman called Harry) speaks indiscreetly with a journalist, demonstrating how he derives his sense of identity and self-respect through the narration of stories from his former career as 'a servant of the Crown in the capacity of hangman' (McDonagh 2015: 18). Many of the jokes in *A Behanding in Spokane* arise from the characters' attempts to piece together Carmichael's improbable tale about how he lost his hand. And in *The Cripple of Inishmaan*, the town gossip Johnnypateenmike literally views storytelling as a matter of life and death – first in the sense that he delivers 'news' to his fellow islanders in return for food and other forms of sustenance; and secondly when he invents a story about the parents of Billy (the play's protagonist), the apparent aim of which is to give Billy a sufficient sense of dignity to encourage him to go on living. These examples demonstrate that, as McDonagh's plays have shifted from Ireland to other settings, his treatment of the importance of storytelling has remained relatively consistent.

The stories in Walsh's plays function differently. Almost without exception, his characters engage in storytelling obsessively, not as a means of advancing plot but rather to come to terms with some trauma. In repeatedly enunciating a story about suffering, the actions of many of Walsh's characters seem explicable in relation to Irish Catholicism, one of the important features of which was an emphasis on the penitential repetition of prayers as a means of expiating sin. That cultural context might help audiences to understand why Catholicism is so dominant a presence in the play *The New Electric Ballroom*, in which three sisters recount their past through the use of a language of martyrdom and bodily shame. The youngest sister Clara, for example, sees the Virgin Mary as a kind of role model, while also recounting how her mother compared her to Christ: she 'said I had a gift for coffee cake the way Jesus had a gift for sacrifice', Clara recalls (Walsh 2008: 8).

The central moment in *Ballroom* is a re-staging of part of the biblical story of Mary, Martha and Lazarus (as outlined in John 12: 1–8). In *Ballroom*, that story is reimagined through the sisters' stripping bare and washing of a local fishmonger called Patsy, in apparently unconscious imitation of Mary's anointing of Christ. Clara starts 'vigorously scrubbing him' once his clothes have been removed, explaining how her action will free Patsy from the tyranny of being part of a story:

> Off with them words and all those stories pasted together and stuck on your back. Wipe away all them lazy images that others pin on us, Patsy … Strip away letter by letter and them terrible words will surely fall, won't they?
>
> (2008: 36)

Lest we miss the religious undertones, the next word spoken by Clara is 'Christ' – albeit that it is spat out in disgust at the smell of fish from Patsy's body.

A sense of bodily disgust and shame is also derived from a distorted understanding of religion in *Misterman*, originally presented in 1999 with Walsh himself in the lead role and then revised for a Galway production that starred Cillian Murphy in 2011. The play is set in a disused warehouse in which the only onstage character – a young man called Thomas – acts out the events of an (at first) apparently typical day in an Irish town called Inishfree (its name drawn from the famous Yeats poem 'The Lake Isle of Inishfree' rather than any real place). Thomas takes us through a bewildering series of interactions with local villagers, ranging from the surreal to the hilarious, but culminating in Thomas's murder of a local girl called Edel. Using tape recordings of some of the villagers but acting out the words of others, Thomas attempts to explain and justify his violence against Edel. Unable to do so according to ordinary legal or ethical precepts, he engages in a transvaluation of values, characterising himself as an instrument of God's will:

> And God said to me, 'Come back up to Heaven, Thomas! Your good work has been ignored, as was my son's good work! Join your daddy! … Leave Inishfree, Thomas! Leave them to die!' And we will go up to Heaven and sit with the Lord God and we will make a new house up there… and I will forget you and that girl you sent to trick me! I will start each new day and night with my soul clean, my heart light, this town forgotten! … I am stronger than the lot of you and I will watch you die… because you are not God's friends – you are the Devil's friends! SO… HEAR… THIS… NOW!
>
> (Walsh 2012: 50–1)

252   *Patrick Lonergan*

Thomas's deity is a God of vengeance rather than forgiveness, a God who allows Thomas to see himself as righteous and to think of his victims as sinners – but also a God who makes Thomas feel that he is not just being heard but listened to.

Walsh ensures, however, that his audience will realise that Thomas is acting out this story not because he genuinely believes his own version of events but, on the contrary, because he knows it is a fabrication and is trying desperately to make it feel true, if only to himself. Almost paradoxically, Thomas's credibility is undermined by how convincing he is, since we must understand that the virtuosity of his performance – the speed with which he moves from one part of the set to another, his familiarity with the carefully timed sound cues, and his ability to enact the lives of the entire town of Inishfree – can only have developed through acting this story out many times. Like a Beckettian tramp who must fail better next time, Thomas is trapped in a cycle of endless repetition: we realise that what we are seeing is one of a series of performances that will continue indefinitely. Walsh thus shows that Thomas's attempts to justify himself in religious terms have been futile, with the play's final stage directions stating that '[f]or all his trying to escape his past... in the moment [Thomas] knows the fight is lost. His hand slowly holds the microphone out from his body. He drops it. It smashes against the ground' (Walsh 2012: 53).

It is both possible and desirable to see Walsh's development of that theme in the context of Irish culture. In the period between the premiere of *New Electric Ballroom* and the revised version of *Misterman* the Irish government published a document known informally as the *Ryan Report* (2009), which was the outcome of an Irish statutory inquiry into the abuse of children in institutions run by the Catholic Church. That inquiry found that tens of thousands of people had been subjected to physical, emotional, and sexual abuse by Irish priests and nuns from the 1930s to the 1990s, demonstrating how Thomas in *Misterman* was far from unusual in seeking to use religion to explain and justify his violence. Somewhat similarly, the incarceration of the three sisters in *The New Electric Ballroom* can be seen in the context of the revelations from the late 1990s onwards of the mistreatment of thousands of Irish women in Magdalene Laundries, institutions that were *de facto* prisons for women who were judged to have transgressed sexually in some way. And even in his adaptation of *Sing Street*, Walsh draws on the script's exploration of how the resistance to Catholic power motivates the protagonist's development as a musician – showing that Walsh's perspective on this theme is shared by other Irish artists. This is not to propose that *Misterman, Ballroom*, and *Sing Street* are 'about' the Catholic church in any journalistic sense, but rather to show how Walsh's work mirrors events in Irish culture. But of course, as the German origins of *Ballroom* and the American premiere of *Sing Street* demonstrate, his plays also function meaningfully in non-Irish contexts.[3]

Walsh's ability to speak simultaneously to Irish concerns while addressing a broader European audience is most clearly manifested in *Penelope* (2010), a reimagining of the Homeric story of Odysseus's wife and her suitors in which four Irish men gather each day in a drained-out swimming pool to compete to win the love of the eponymous character. The play was commissioned by Tilman Raabke as one of six plays by European writers, all inspired by *The Odyssey*, and was staged at the Theater Oberhausen as part of the Ruhr Valley's year as European Capital of Culture in 2010. (The other contributors were Grzegorz Jarzyna, Peter Nadas, Emine Sevgi Ozdamar, Christoph Ransmayr, and Roland Schimmelpfennig – see Pilny 2016: 90.)

Walsh stated in a public interview that his composition of *Penelope* was informed by a sense that the theatre he was writing for was based in a part of the city that he considered relatively isolated and impoverished; he therefore believed that its German audience might identify with the suitors (Walsh 2013). But he also wrote the play with an Irish production in view, giving most of his characters names that were reminiscent of the prominent businessmen who had partly been responsible for the economic crisis that had afflicted Ireland from 2008 onwards (see Lonergan 2015). As *Penelope* begins, the suitors have just become aware that Penelope's husband – who is never named but whom we may safely call Odysseus – is going to arrive home later that day. The four men have to overcome their rivalries with each other to ensure that one of them seduces Penelope before her husband returns, thereby forestalling or even preventing the violence that he will undoubtedly want to inflict upon them. The play dramatises a situation in which an era of excess is about to be brought to a violent conclusion, and thus can be seen as an allegory of the status of Ireland before and after 2008, when the Celtic Tiger period of economic success (from roughly 1995 to 2008) gave way to an economic crash that saw the unemployment rate in that country jump from 3 per cent to 15 per cent in a matter of months, and which culminated in a bailout from the International Monetary Fund and the EU.

Yet *Penelope* is also speaking directly to the European tradition of Homeric storytelling – and indeed to the broader economic crisis that was afflicting the EU at that time. Walsh's decision to blend Irish characters with Greek myth in 2010 had subtle contemporary resonances: both Ireland and Greece had, after all, been lumped together in media reports as one Europe's 'PIIGS', an acronym for Portugal, Ireland, Italy, Greece, and Spain, the indebted nations whose financial indiscipline was seen as threatening the European project generally – but which also obscured the responsibility of larger countries such as Germany in insisting upon economic policies that made such problems possible. *Penelope* – like most of Walsh's plays – uses a heightened, allusive language and adopts a style of stage realism that is at once coherent and unfamiliar. That style allowed audiences to interpret the action according to the conditions of their own geographical spaces, their own historical era.

McDonagh's popularity in Europe also relates to the extent to which his work is produced in ways that transcend narrowly Irish contexts. This can be illustrated by the varying responses to productions of *The Lieutenant of Inishmore*, McDonagh's savage satire about Irish terrorism. Although it premiered at the Royal Shakespeare Company in 2001, *The Lieutenant* might be seen as a play

254 *Patrick Lonergan*

that is deeply embedded in Irish culture. Some of its humour, for example, depends upon audiences' knowledge of the differences between the IRA (Irish Republican Army) and the INLA (the Irish National Liberation Army), an awareness that might be assumed in Ireland and amongst older audiences in Britain, but which is unlikely to be general in other countries. Other jokes are similarly dependent upon knowledge of the significance of such real British and Irish historical figures as Roger Casement, Airey Neave, Oliver Cromwell, or the Guildford Four. Furthermore, McDonagh has spoken in interviews of how the composition of the play arose from his own passionately personal rejection of the rhetoric of Irish terrorism: 'hang on,' he thought, 'this is being done in my name [and] I just feel like exploding in rage' (Spencer 2002: 2). For these and other reasons, *The Lieutenant* might be seen as McDonagh's most explicitly Irish play. How then to explain the fact that it is also one of his most popular plays in continental Europe?

One way to answer that question is to consider a production that was not well received. In its Viennese premiere at Akademietheater in January 2002, *The Lieutenant* met with some hostility – precisely because of an excessive level of awareness of its Irish contexts. 'This version', writes Werner Huber, 'was seen by the majority of critics as a kind of "Reservoir Cats" and "trash comedy" that dealt with the issue of terrorism in an irresponsible manner' (2012: 86). Huber's suggestion is that critics were uneasy with the play on ethical grounds, expressing discomfort with McDonagh's willingness to turn a 'bitter tragedy of a troubled country into a farce' and to make a 'grotesque comedy' about 'old-style terrorism' (87).

In most other European productions, however, the play has been popular when its Irish contexts have been set aside or transcended. For example, in December 2003, Mehmet Ergen directed his own translation of the play in Istanbul only weeks after terrorist bombings of synagogues and the British consulate in that city had killed almost 60 people. As Susannah Clapp explains, 'some of the cast thought they should cancel [the production]. They had all heard about people picking up body parts in the streets; the play ends with body parts strewn over the stage' (2003). But the production did go ahead, and by providing audiences with the opportunity to laugh at the hypocrisy of terrorism, the play's appearance in Turkey was seen as cathartic rather than disrespectful, according to Clapp.

Other productions have ignored the political elements of the script, emphasising its farcical elements instead. Debora Biancheri (2008) has explored an Italian staging of *Il tenente di Inishmore* by Teatro della Corte di Genova in 2003 which, she states, cut many of the references to Ireland, but did briefly play U2's Troubles anthem *Sunday, Bloody Sunday* (though McDonagh's script does not actually refer to that song). Its director Marco Sciaccaluga used circus, puppetry, and film to explore the way in which the play undermines the distinction between reality and fiction; the production was, in other words, an attempt to explore theatricality itself, and was well received on that basis.

We also find McDonagh's work being used by audiences to think about national identity. For example, in 2003, *The Lieutenant* was produced in Estonia's Draamateater in a production directed by Tiit Ojasoo. As Kersti Tarien Powell writes,

> McDonagh's success in Estonia does not owe so much to soap operas or to Tarantino's movies as it does to the rather confusing "realism" of his plays. For Estonians, the realism [...] resides in their engagement with such thematic focal points as lost love, emigration, and life in a newly rich capitalist environment.
>
> (2011: 138)

That production might also be seen, however, in the context of Estonia's accession to the EU, with Ireland's status within that bloc being presented as something that Estonia might both aspire to and learn from. 'Estonia shares many similarities with Ireland and the Irish experience', writes Powell:

> Each has historically been a country controlled and absorbed by a powerful neighbor; more recently, each exemplifies a successful "tiger economy" that must now grapple with the effects of global recession and its repercussions [...] If McDonagh subverts stereotypical modern Irish reality, then it is life itself that is frighteningly similar both in Leenane and Estonia.
>
> (2011: 138–9)

The Irish origins of McDonagh's work were important in Estonia, but only emblematically: the popularity of *The Lieutenant* arose not from any direct engagement with the realities of Irish history but rather from a sense that the country's economic success exemplified a possible future for Estonia.

McDonagh has sometimes reacted negatively to productions that have adopted an experimental approach to his scripts. Indeed, he places an unashamedly anachronistic joke about that practice in the mouth of Andersen in *A Very Very Very Dark Matter*: when asked about how his stories are really composed by his African prisoner, Andersen explains that: 'We co-write [the stories]. I just don't do any of the writing. I change the bits I don't like and then erase all the rest from history. I'm more like a German theatre director. Or, y'know, a German generally' (McDonagh 2018: 27). We might question the appropriateness of such a joke in a play being staged in post-Brexit England – but leaving that aside (when has McDonagh ever been 'appropriate'?), the line is another example of McDonagh's assertion of authorial autonomy, of his belief that a writer's words should be treated as the primary source of a play's meaning. A mild irony here, of course, is that the evidence points to the conclusion that his popularity in Europe can be attributed at least partly to the willingness of directors to 'change the bits they don't like and erase the rest'.

Contrastingly, Walsh has been more comfortable with experimental processes, and has encouraged – or, more correctly, has been less inclined to discourage – productions that depart from his original intentions. Since 2008, he has directed the premiere of all of his new plays, a decision that he explained in 2013 as coming from a desire to ensure that his work is as fully developed as possible, so that it can then be handed on to other directors and theatre-makers in future productions (Walsh 2013). And as he has directed more of his own work, it has taken on an ever-more metatheatrical quality: plays such as *The Walworth Farce* (2006), *Misterman*, and *Ballyturk* (2013) all feature plays within the play, for example, showing how Walsh understands that the theatrical process involves recurrent improvisations, improvements, and revisions – some of which may have been unintended by the original creator. In *The Walworth Farce*, for instance, the authorial centrality of Dinny breaks down due to the unexpected arrival to his London flat of a young shop assistant. And in *Ballyturk* the story being acted out by the two main characters (see Figure 13.1) is disrupted when the box-set is literally deconstructed, allowing a god-like figure to arrive through a collapsed wall in order to take one of the actors away with him. Walsh's plays show that authors do not usually have much control over how their work will be staged once the play goes out into the world.

That growing use of metatheatricality has also allowed Walsh to locate his stage spaces in what could be termed a string of metonymic associations. His characters are trapped in rooms that stand metaphorically for the theatre itself – and those rooms/performance spaces in turn operate metaphorically as encapsulations of the lives of the characters. Those metonymic rooms have been present in Walsh's work since *bedbound*; they also feature in work he has adapted (such as his stage version of Max Porter's novel *Grief is the Thing with Feathers* in 2018) and even in

Figure 13.1 Cillian Murphy and Mikel Murfi in *Ballyturk* (2014) written and directed by Enda Walsh; Landmark Productions and Galway International Arts Festival. Photograph © Patrick Redmond

his work as a director of others, such as his production of Bartok's *Bluebeard's Castle* (2018) for Irish National Opera. It would be banal to describe that approach as representing the idea that 'all the world's a stage' but it is nevertheless apparent in plays such as *Arlington* (2016) and *Medicine* (2020) that Walsh's rooms are intended to be understood as metaphors for human existence very broadly. In the opening scene of the former play, for example, we find a man interrogating Isla, a young woman who is trapped in a mostly empty room; between the two of them they work to imagine an existence outside that space:

> To be chosen and grown and cared and fed and envied – to be at the centre and honoured and blessed to be kept in this place. To be the sun and built about you this other universe – a world outside being made from your dreams, Isla – a city of people building your hopes – and to be called then and to walk out into those dreams … to be inside here and cared and allowed to dream a life … to be at the centre and honoured and blessed.
>
> (Walsh 2016: 25)

Walsh is suggesting that using a stage space to engage in acts of authorship rehearses a form of invention that can be applied to the outside world, and thus might make the outside world a better place. Given the centrality of collaboration to Walsh's work, it is noteworthy that this act of imagination arises from the interplay between two characters.

This observation returns us to the distinction between McDonagh and Walsh that was proposed at the start of this chapter. In order to be fully understood, Walsh's plays must be seen in a theatre – perhaps the best example of which is the stage direction for the second scene of *Arlington,* which states only that the character in the scene must dance for 20 minutes and then jump from a window – an instruction that does little to capture for readers what the experience of watching this scene was like, or might be like when it is performed live (Walsh 2016: 29). His plays also reward close and repeated reading, of course – but a work such as *Arlington* positions Walsh less as a playwright/director than as the curator of a multidisciplinary art installation that combines the work of other artists: digital projections, a musical score, the fully choreographed 20-minute dance mentioned in those stage directions, and much more. McDonagh, in contrast, has never directed one of his plays; his scripts tend not to provide extensive instructions in relation to set, costume, lighting, or music – and while he always speaks with great respect for the actors who have worked with him, there is no evidence that he has altered his scripts during rehearsal in response to their suggestions. This observation, however, is not intended to neglect the theatricality of his plays, many of which evoke viscerally emotional reactions from their audiences through the use of on-stage violence, gunshots, or other forms of melodramatic sensationalism that can only be fully effective when performed live.

Yet despite these differences, the careers of McDonagh and Walsh share a trajectory away from the specificity of Irish stage conventions. Walsh's plays often *perform* Ireland – but are they actually set there? The characters who re-enact the Walworth Farce do so from a flat in London; *bedbound, Misterman,* and *Ballyturk* feature Irish

258   *Patrick Lonergan*

people playing out stories that have an Irish setting, but the rooms in which they carry out that work could literally be anywhere; there are no concrete geographical markers that require these plays' versions of the 'outside world' to be Ireland, although audiences might still assume that they are set in that country. For example, in its premiere production, *Arlington* featured Irish actors but was otherwise free of any geographical markers: the play's name conjures associations with American's national cemetery, but the English-speaking world is full of housing estates with names like Arlington Heights, Arlington Lawns, and so on. And like Walsh, McDonagh seems to have moved towards greater levels of geographical imprecision. His first four plays were set in Ireland; the subsequent four were set elsewhere: in a police-station somewhere in central Europe in *The Pillowman*, a hotel room somewhere in middle America in *A Behanding in Spokane*, a pub somewhere in the middle of England in *Hangmen*, and an attic somewhere in an imagined version of Copenhagen in *A Very Very Very Dark Matter*.

Walsh also demonstrates that the stereotypical division between continental and Anglo-American modes of playwriting need not hold true: his work displays the linguistic virtuosity that is a characteristic feature of the Irish literary tradition but also demonstrates a willingness to accord authorial power to others involved in the theatre-making process. McDonagh has been less willing to allow his plays to become the subject of directorial experimentation, but he understands that the live theatrical performance involves an act of collaboration with the audience, that the meaning of plays such as *The Lieutenant of Inishmore* can shift from the specificity of a personal authorial protest against Irish terrorism to a broader and more complex set of reactions to (and against) political violence.

Perhaps, then, we might then see Irishness as a kind of anchor for these plays, a fixed point that allows them to be reimagined and reinterpreted in different local and national contexts. In suggesting that Walsh and McDonagh must be seen not just as important playwrights but as important European dramatists, my intention is to call attention to the way in which both create space for their works to find and generate new meanings, to locate Ireland firmly in European contexts while also locating Europe firmly in Irish contexts.

Enda Walsh – four key productions

Disco Pigs. Directed by Pat Kiernan. Designed by Aedin Cosgrove. Sound design by Cormac O'Connor. With Eileen Walsh and Cillian Murphy. Corcadorca Theatre Company, Triskel Arts Centre, Cork, September 1996.

Penelope. Directed by Tilman Knabe. Design by Kaspar Zwimpfer. Costumes by Gabriele Rupprecht. Dramaturgy by Tilman Raabke. With Manja Kuhl, Peter Waros, Michael Witte, Torsten Bauer, Hartmut Stanke. Theater Oberhausen, January 2010

Once: A New Musical. Directed by John Tiffany. Music and lyrics by Glen Hansard and Markéta Irglová. Designed by Bob Crowley. Bernard B. Jacobs Theatre, New York, 2012.

Ballyturk. Directed by Enda Walsh. Designed by Jamie Vartan. Lighting by Adam Silverman. Sound by Helen Atkinson. Music by Teho Teardo. With Cillian Murphy, Mikel Murfi, Stephen Rea. Landmark Productions and Galway International Arts Festival, July 2014.

Martin McDonagh – four key productions

The Beauty Queen of Leenane. Directed by Garry Hynes. Designed by Francis O'Connor. Lighting by Ben Ormerod. With Marie Mullen, Anna Manahan, Tom Murphy, Brian F O'Byrne. Druid Theatre and Royal Court Theatre, Town Hall, Galway, February 1996.

The Pillowman. Directed by John Crowley. Designed by Scott Pask. Lighting by Hugh Vanstone. Sound by Paul Arditti. With David Tennant, Jim Broadbent, Nigel Lindsay, Adam Godley. National Theatre, London, November 2003.

The Cripple of Inishmaan. Revival production. Directed by Michael Grandage. Set and costumes by Christopher Oram. Lighting by Paule Constable. With Daniel Radcliffe, Pat Shortt, Sarah Greene. Michael Grandage company at the Noel Coward Theatre, London, June 2013.

A Very Very Very Dark Matter. Directed by Matthew Dunster. Designed by Anna Fleischle. Lighting by Philip Gladwell. With Jim Broadbent, Johnetta Eula'Mae Ackles, Phil Daniels. Bridge Theatre, London, November 2018.

Notes

1 *The Aran Island* plays are generally considered to be similar to the *Leenane* plays in terms of language, tone, and theme, though there are some minor differences. Perhaps because they were premiered by well-resourced British companies, the two *Aran Islands* plays produced to date have multiple settings and require large casts. In contrast, the *Leenane Trilogy* plays are set almost entirely in a country cottage settings and none requires more than four actors. The *Aran* plays are unified only by setting; they take place in different historical periods and have different themes – but the *Leenane* plays are all set in the mid-1990s and share characters and some plot threads. The final *Aran* play, *the Banshees of Inisheer*, has never been produced.
2 It is also worth observing here how deeply embedded *The Pillowman* and *Dark Matter* are in the European fairytale tradition, especially in its northern European manifestations such as in the works of the Grimm Brothers or Hans Christian Andersen.
3 This is not to ignore the fact that Walsh's plays are sometimes successful because of cultural references that are shared between Ireland and other countries: for example, the place of Catholicism in Spain can to some extent account for the popularity of Walsh's works in that country. That topic is addressed more broadly in relation to the place of Irish theatre in Galicia in Serra Porteiro (2015).

Works cited

Biancheri, Debora (2008) 'McDonagh's exportation to Italy: the blurred line between laughter and tragedy in The Lieutenant of Inishmore', unpublished conference paper, Irish Society for Theatre Research annual conference, Dublin, June.

260   *Patrick Lonergan*

Clapp, Susannah (2003) 'Pack up your troubles', *The Observer*, 30 November, http://www.guardian.co.uk/stage/2003/nov/30/theatre.turkey

Grene, Nicholas and Patrick Lonergan (2008) *Interactions: The Dublin Theatre Festival 1957–2007*, Dublin: Carysfort Press.

Huber, Werner (2012) 'Contemporary Irish theatre in German-speaking countries', in Nicholas Grene and Patrick Lonergan (eds), *Irish Drama: Local and Global Perspectives*, Dublin: Carysfort Press, pp . 81–92.

Irish Playography (2018) 'Fishy tales', http://www.irishplayography.com/play.aspx?playid=30250

Keane, John B. (2009) *Sive*, Cork: Mercier Press.

Kramer, Mimi (1997) 'Three for the show', *Time Magazine*, 4 August: 71.

Lonergan, Patrick (2015) 'The lost and the lonely: crisis in three plays by Enda Walsh', *Etudes Irlandaises*, 40(2): 137–154.

McBride, Charlie (1996) 'New Druid playwright is a "natural"', *Galway Advertiser*, 11 January: 23.

McDonagh, Martin (2003) *The Pillowman*, London: Faber.

——— (2009) *The Beauty Queen of Leenane*, London: Methuen.

——— (2015) *Hangmen*, London: Faber.

——— (2018) *A Very Very Very Dark Matter*, London: Faber.

O'Toole, Fintan (2000) 'Irish theatre: state of the art', in Eamonn Jordan (ed.), *Theatre Stuff*, Dublin: Carysfort. Ebook.

——— (2006) 'A mind in Connemara: the savage world of Martin McDonagh', *The New Yorker*, 6 March: 40–47.

Pilny, Ondrej (2016) *The Grotesque in Contemporary Anglophone Drama*, Basingstoke: Palgrave.

Powell, K. (2011) '"Life just is like that": Martin McDonagh's Estonian enigma', *New Hibernia Review*, 15(3): 138–150.

Raab, Michael (2002) 'The end of a wave: new British and Irish plays in the German-speaking theatre', in Margerete Rubik and Elke Mettinger-Schartmann (eds), *Contemporary Theatre and Drama in English*, Trier: WVT, pp. 39–46.

Serra Porteiro, E. (2015) *Performing Irishness: translations of Irish drama for the Galician stage (1921–2011)*, PhD Thesis, University College Cork. Cork Open Research Archive, http://hdl.handle.net/10468/2887

Spencer, Charles (2002) 'Devastating masterpiece of black comedy', *Daily Telegraph*, 28 June: 13.

Walsh, Enda (1997) *Disco Pigs*, London: Nick Hern.

——— (2008) *New Electric Ballroom*, London: Nick Hern.

——— (2012) *Misterman*, London: Nick Hern.

——— (2013) Public interview with Patrick Lonergan, Synge Summer School, Rathdrum, Ireland, 29 June.

——— (2016) *Arlington*, London: Nick Hern.

Waters, John (2001) 'The Irish mummy: the plays and purpose of Martin McDonagh', in Dermot Bolger (ed.), *Druids, Dudes and Beauty Queens: The Changing Face of Irish Theatre*, Dublin: New Island, pp. 30–54.

Weaver, Jesse (2012) '"The words look after themselves": the practice of Enda Walsh', in Nicholas Grene and Patrick Lonergan (eds), *Irish Theatre Local and Global Perspectives*, Dublin: Carysfort, pp. 129–139.

Woodworth, Paddy (1996) 'Druid – celebrating in the present tense', *Irish Times*, 24 January, p. 10.

14 Yasmina Reza and Florian Zeller
The art of success

Dominic Glynn

Yasmina Reza (b. 1959) and Florian Zeller (b. 1979) are among the most successful French theatrical exports of the early twenty-first century. Reza's *"Art"* (*Art*)[1] has been translated in 35 languages (Cénac 2017), while in 2015, Zeller was the most performed living French playwright (Philibert 2015). Productions of their plays have won prestigious prizes, including awards at the Molière, Laurence Olivier, Tony, and WELT ceremonies. They have featured a host of famous stage and screen actors (Daniel Auteuil, Laetitia Casta, Kenneth Cranham, Fabrice Luchini, to name but a few), enjoyed long runs in theatres across Europe and further afield. Yet, in spite of their success, both playwrights have been the subject of mockery at the hands of theatre professionals and media critics. Dominic Dromgoole's entry 'Yasmina Reza' in *The Full Room* is disparagingly short: 'Yasmina Reza is very rich. *Yasmina Reza est très riche'* (Dromgoole 2001: 239). Christophe Ayad's profile of Florian Zeller in French newspaper *Libération* is filled with sardonic comments: 'In real life, Florian Zeller is a writer. The proof being that he lives on the boulevard Saint-Germain in a boho–chic apartment, which shares its address with the national union of publishers'[2] (Ayad 2006). Such disdain has been followed by a general lack of scholarly interest. Academics who do look at their (primarily Reza's) plays adopt a defensive if not hagiographic tone, as studies by Hussein (2009), Giguere (2010), and Jaccomard (2016) attest.

With this in mind, there are at least three ways of reading the title of Denis Guénoun's (2005) *Avez-vous lu Reza?* (*Have You Read Reza?*). The first is to interpret the question as an open invitation to discover an author whose work is implicitly accessible to a wide readership. The second is as a mocking criticism of those who comment on Reza without having read anything she has written. Such is Reza's status as a successful author that judgement is passed on her by people who have not actually engaged with her writing. Third, and in contradiction with the first interpretation, it is implied that Reza's work demands close interpretative rather than cursory, superficial reading. To date, no one has written a similar companion to Florian Zeller, but Olivier Ceilik's preface (2012) to the seven plays assembled under *Théâtre I* (*Theatre I*) puts forward similar arguments about his plays being both entertaining – they work in the theatre – and artistically demanding.

262   *Dominic Glynn*

The premise of this chapter is to reflect on Reza and Zeller's contribution to contemporary European dramaturgy. I shall do so by underlining the distinctiveness of their playwriting while taking into account criticism that has been labelled at them. I will begin by anchoring the writing careers of Reza and Zeller within French theatre history and discourse. Examining how by being French they are European will be key to justifying their fit in this volume. I will analyse how their work has been appraised in literary and theatrical terms, since both playwrights have also written novels. I will then draw out the specific features of their writing in order to investigate their significance on the European stage.

There are many reasons for looking at Reza and Zeller comparatively. Their plays are built along similar lines. They explore relationships at breaking point with humour that is savage and devastating. The domestic environment, in particular, becomes a truly antagonistic space where hidden truths are revealed, certainties made uncertain. Making use of small casts, their dramaturgies are chamber orchestra scores in which secrets play out variations on the theme of deception. They do so with a lightness of touch, using comic reprieve to undercut what would otherwise be pervasive melancholy or despair. There are, however, pitfalls in presenting their work side by side. Their plays, for all their similarities, present a considerable number of differences. Reza foregrounds how violence simmers under the fragile surface of social conventions. Zeller, on the other hand, explores how shifts in perception undermine steadfast illusions about the fixed nature of feelings or relationships.

There is also a tendency, by virtue of the fact that both writers are commercially successful, to forget that they have charted their own distinctive course. Reza is twenty years Zeller's senior and started her (play)writing career well before he did. The opportunities available to a playwright (or play-write) in the 1980s were not those of the early 2000s. To understand what unites and separates Reza and Zeller as writers, it is necessary to consider their careers in relation to changes in the theatrical landscape in the late twentieth and early twenty-first centuries. This means uncovering how Reza and Zeller became actors in the theatrical field – to use Pierre Bourdieu's terminology (1992) – developing their craft with respect to openings available to them and to contemporary discourse about practice.

Struggles on the French scene

In France, the creation of a network of state-funded theatres in the aftermath of the Second World War facilitated the rise of a 'director's theatre' (Bradby and Williams 1988). With the need to fill large auditoria, and the prestige attached to 'classics', directors developed ambitious 'sum-total' stage projects (Biet and Triau 2006: 726). As a result, it became difficult for living playwrights to see their work performed, a complaint voiced by leading dramatists of the 1980s.[3] The situation has not improved much in the twenty-first century. As José Valverde puts it bluntly:

if you want to make a name for yourself as a director in France you have to direct Shakespeare or Molière in a novel fashion, but in so doing you're killing the theatre. Living writers need to be at the heart of what is performed.

(cited in Fondu 2016: 83)

One of the problems lies in the fact that playwrights lack decisional power to remedy this situation since few are the helm of a major subsidised theatre. In 2018, Pauline Sales's co-direction of the Préau in Normandie was something of an exception.

To say that nothing has been done to remedy the situation would, however, be misleading. From the 1970s onwards, there have been initiatives to give new writing more stage space and visibility. Robert Abirached, in charge of theatre affairs in the Ministry of Culture in the 1980s, set up a writer's commission with the aim of stimulating new writing for the theatre, ensuring the publication and performance of plays. In 1984, it was stipulated that at least two new works by living dramatists writing in French had to be staged by a Centre Dramatique National (National Drama Centre) during the term of office of each artistic director. And in 1988, Théâtre Ouvert (Open Theatre) became the first National Drama Centre whose mission was exclusively to promote work by living writers. Following in its footsteps, the Théâtre du Rond-Point, with Jean-Michel Ribes at the helm since 2002, has also devoted itself to staging living playwrights. What is more, a wave of 'texto-centric' directors (Vossier 2013: 378) with a keen interest in new writing began to emerge in the 1990s. Chief among these was Stanislas Nordey who became artistic director of the Théâtre Gérard-Philipe in 1998,[4] and nearly brought about its financial ruin by staging a large number of productions, many of which were of works by contemporary and living writers (Glynn 2015: 66).

Changes in the subsidised theatre sector are only part of the story. One of the specificities of the French theatrical field is an entrenched division between the subsidised and commercial sectors, the so-called '*théâtre public*' (public theatre) and '*théâtre privé*' (private theatre). These two 'families' operate according to different logics (Marchand 2015). The commercial theatres have to make money through the productions that they stage. Success is judged in terms of box office returns and sell-out runs. Historically, new writing for the private theatres dwindled at approximately the same time as it decreased in the public theatres. This was not because of a marked increase in the power of directors, but rather that new writing was deemed risky business. Gone was the vitality of the post-war era when Marcel Aymé, Jean Anouilh, and Sacha Guitry infused the private theatre with 'dreamscapes, playful self-reference, and often polemical treatments of the slippery line between truth and fiction in the modern world' (Turk 2011: 135). It was only in the late 1980s and early 1990s that things started to look up when a new generation of writers, which included Reza, married commercial success with subtle changes to formal conventionalism.

264   *Dominic Glynn*

Writing for the private theatre scene has been a significant feature of Reza and Zeller's careers. Dramaturgies of private theatre are characterised by their small casts and relatively simple sets. These specific constraints have certainly helped them transfer to commercial stages across Europe. However, in France, productions in the private and public theatre networks rarely cross over since plays produced in the former are considered by artistic directors of the latter to be lacking in artistic audacity. This has meant that Reza, who started her career writing in subsidised theatre, was only let back in thanks to the intervention of foreign companies, while Zeller's work is conspicuously absent from the public theatre stages.

The other major change in contemporary French-language theatre occurred when the business of publishing plays began to pick up also. Playwriting had disappeared as a literary practice at roughly the same time as it was being pushed off the stage in the late 1950s and early 1960s. This was due to the decline in publishing outlets added to a lack of interest in reviewing plays in the literary pages of the generalist press. However, in the course of the 1980s and 1990s, a handful of small French and Belgian publishing houses and specialised collections emerged (Les Solitaires intempestifs, Éditions Lansman, Actes Sud-Papiers). According to figures provided by Pierre Banos-Ruf (2008: 108), during the 1980s, the number of plays published every year varied between 75 to 125. This figure includes new editions of classics, which shows quite how marginal theatre publishing was. Twenty years later, in 2004, 405 new plays – not including reprints of classics – were published. There was therefore an upturn in the demand in publication that meant playwrights could be given extra visibility even when their productions were not on stage.

Nevertheless, the separation of the literary field and the theatrical field is evident in the disassociation of the publication and stage destinies of the play-texts. Publishing does little to increase the likelihood of being performed (Fondu 2016: 94). To become a playwright – a maker of plays for performance – thus implies getting actively involved in the collaborative art world of the theatre producing scene. Both Reza and Zeller are known and recognised in France for their dramatic and non-dramatic literary production, but it is significant that they place considerable value on seeing their plays performed. As Reza revealed, she thought for a long time that the act of reading a play was not enough to take account of its full measure, and this was why she refused to have her dramatic work published before it was performed (Garcin 2014) – a position she has since softened. Zeller has spoken about learning his craft as a playwright from watching the microvariations in performance from one night to another (Barbier 2014). As their plays have travelled round Europe, and the rest of the world, this opportunity has been experienced by both dramatists on multiple occasions.

Yasmina Reza's dramatic art

Reza started her writing career when Zeller was just about learning to write. Born in Paris to a Hungarian violinist mother and a Russian-Iranian engineer father, she grew up with exposure to various languages and cultures, regularly spending vacations in Switzerland and Austria. These experiences directly fed into her writing, more specifically into her early play *La Traversée de l'hiver* (*Winter Crossing*), which features melancholic holiday-dwellers in a Swiss mountain resort. At university, she read theatre and sociology before completing her theatre training at the Jacques Lecoq theatre school and working as an actress. She then turned her hand to writing, developing stage and film scripts quickly off the back of each other. The beginning of Reza's writing career occurred precisely at a time when small changes in both the public and private theatre networks had opened up opportunities for living playwrights to see their works performed. It was just becoming possible to make a name as writer on the French stage, and this is precisely what Reza achieved.

Her first play *Conversations après un enterrement* (*Conversations After a Burial*) was staged at the Théâtre Paris-Villette in a production directed by Patrice Kerbrat in 1987. A sign of things to come, it received three awards: the Molière for the best play, the SACD prize for new talent, and the Johnston foundation prize. *Conversations After a Burial* is set in the rural family home of brothers and sister Nathan, Alex, and Édith. Their uncle Pierre, his wife Julienne, and Élisa, Alex's former mistress now in love with Nathan, have been invited for the burial of Simon Weinberg, the siblings' father. Family tension is at the heart of this dramatic comedy, and there is an ebb and flow of verbal violence as the illicit relationship between Élisa and Nathan threatens to tear the brothers apart. This comes to a head when Nathan and Élisa have sex at the father's burial site, and Alex notices. To Julienne's innocent question in the following scene, 'where is Élisa?', Alex coarsely replies: 'She's fucking my brother' (158). The scenes alternate between interior and exterior settings, but the stills of Kerbrat's original production (Cande 1987) reveal how the internal turmoil of each character, particularly the hypersensitive Alex, is manifest on stage. A curtain was drawn across the length of the back of the stage throughout the production. This created the impression of a house withdrawn on itself in mourning. Even during scenes that were set in the garden, the curtain was present, suggesting an intimate connection between outer and inner spaces.

In 1989, Kerbrat directed Reza's next play *Winter Crossing* at the Théâtre d'Orléans. It has a Chekhovian quality to it, as each character expresses her or his melancholy: 'I'm not looking to please you' Avner says to the young Ariane who responds with much pathos: 'No… And yet you have managed to do so to such an extent that even these words don't hurt me' (171). These early plays, staged in subsidised venues, both dwell more on pain and suffering than her later ones do: 'let me be your pain' says Élisa poignantly to Nathan in *Conversations After a Burial* (157), just before they have sex. A key collaborator of Reza in France, from these early productions onwards has been Patrice Kerbrat, a renowned actor who had often worked with Antoine Vitez. Kerbrat was progressively to start crossing over more to the private theatre scene in order to direct plays – one of the few to straddle both sides of the divide. It was he who directed Reza's breakaway success in 1994: *Art*. Reza's became a household name with *Art*, after it was staged at the Théâtre des Champs-

Elysées. The production featured famous actors of the stage and screen, Pierre Vaneck, Pierre Arditi, and Fabrice Luchini, who played Marc, Yvan, and Serge respectively.

As with many of Reza's works, the play revolves around a simple plot idea: three long-standing friends tear each other apart following the decision of one of them to buy a (nearly) blank canvas for a large sum of money. On one level, the play is a satire of the modern art market – a precursor in this respect to Michel Houellebecq's *La Carte et le Territoire* (*The Map and the Territory*, 2010). Reza has argued though that the white painting is merely a pretence to explore the trials and tribulations of friendship: 'You paid two hundred francs for this shit?' asks an incredulous Marc to his friend Serge, who, hurt by what he considers to be the arrogance of an enemy of modernism, responds incredulously, 'What do you mean, "this shit"?' (9). In the initial production, Luchini took particular care to detach the words 'this shit' as he got on his moral high-horse about the value of art.[5] In the ensuing battles, Reza's comedy really takes off when alliances between the three friends, Marc, Yvan, and Serge are made and undone. In Miguel del Arco's 2017 production of *Art* in Madrid, the actors danced around each other with the dexterity of kick-boxers (see Figure 14.1). The shifting configurations gave 'the production the air of agile *danzteater*' (Delgado 2017).

Figure 14.1 Jorge Usón's Iván and Cristóbal Suárez's Sergio confront Roberto Enrique's Marcos in Miguel del Arco's production of Yasmina Reza's '*Art*' (Pavón Teatro Kamikaze, Madrid, 2017). Photograph © Vanessa Rabade / Teatro Kamikaze

Art was a game-changer for Reza in more ways than one. It brought her fame in France, which was then followed up by even greater renown internationally. Following the French premiere, the play was quickly performed in other European cities, such as Berlin (1995), London (1996), Porto (1998), and Madrid (1998), to name but a few. According to figures quoted by Marta Mateo (2006: 175), the play had already grossed £157 million by the year 2000. It was to prove the catalyst for further successes on European and North American stages. One of these, *Trois versions de la vie* (*Life × 3*) had productions opening within a few days of each other in Vienna, 29 October, directed by Luc Bondy; Paris, 7 November, directed by Patrice Kerbrat; Athens, 10 November, directed by Georges Remoyndos; London, 2 December, directed by Matthew Warchus.

Life × 3 revolves around the (lack of) career progression of Henry, a scientist at France's leading scientific research centre, the CNRS. It hinges on a simple dramatic concept: the same scene is played out three times with slightly different outcomes. Henry and Sonia unexpectedly receive a home visit from Hubert (Henry's boss) and Inez, his wife, after they realise that they've mixed up the dates. Meanwhile their young son refuses to let them alone, providing an unwelcome distraction as they try to keep face. Hubert relishes his position of power and releases a bombshell: a publication has just appeared in a leading journal that completely defeats all the hard work Henry has put in over the last few years. 'Thank you, Hubert. Sincerely thank you' says a desperate Henry without a hint of irony, to which his wife responds sarcastically 'For what? For ruining your weekend?' (2013: 220). *Life × 3* plays out the theme of the loser at the end of his tether. Henry follows in the footsteps of Yvan in *Art*, who experiences 'a crisis, an insoluble problem, major crisis' because 'both stepmothers want their names on the wedding invitation' (2005: 34). The crazed atmosphere was brought out in the original production by Luc Bondy, in which the design of the living room furniture, white low back sofas with steel frames, turned the home into something more of a mad house, thereby providing a literal interpretation of Hubert's patronising line: 'I didn't expect this leap into the irrational' (2013: 220).

Another of Reza's major successes in Paris, London, and later adapted to film by Roman Polanski, was *Le Dieu du carnage* (*God of Carnage*), first performed in German, like *Life × 3*, but in Zurich this time, in 2007. The Vallons and the Reilles meet following the unprovoked attack of one boy on the others' son. 'The prevailing mood is serious, friendly and tolerant' (2008: 3) as both sets of parents work on a joint statement. However, the atmosphere degenerates as Alain quibbles over word choices (he is a lawyer), and each parent defends their family unit, before turning on each other: 'you keep vacillating, trying to play both ends against the middle' (30), Véronique complains to her husband Michel. For Hélène Jaccomard, the eruption of violence in *God of Carnage* is particularly traumatic and scandalous as it takes place in a realistic domestic setting (2016: 435). There is nothing of the savagery of Dennis Kelly or a playwright in the in-yer-face tradition, nor does the verbal jousting show any

268 *Dominic Glynn*

signs of the technical prowess of Bernard-Marie Koltès's or Jean-Luc Lagarce's work. But the play provides enough meat for actors well-versed in film or television dramas to sink their teeth into the snarling dialogue. Ralph Fiennes, for instance, as Alain in the UK production 'radiate[d] contempt', while Ken Stott was 'genial, raging and disappointed' (Clapp 2008). Indeed, Reza's writing since *Art* has quite a lot in common with film or television script-writing, perhaps as a result of her forays into the cinema.

In France, *Art* signalled a move away from the state-subsidised sector into the private theatre, with future productions in France staged at the Théâtre Hébertot and the Théâtre Antoine. It was only in the 2010s that Reza was again staged in the public theatre. Even then it took productions by the highly revered German director Thomas Ostermeier (*Bella Figura*, 2015), to re-open the stage door that had been locked resolutely shut. This did not necessarily equate with a reconciliation with theatre critics who were quick to praise the companies and the director, but not the playwright. For instance, the critic for *Libération* wrote about *Bella Figura*: 'Yasmina Reza is Machiavellian, by putting on the most obviously one-dimensional comedy in front of the gratin of the Parisian intelligentsia who watched the show because it was directed by Ostermeier' (Diatkine: 2015). Where Yasmina Reza has gained some more credit, even though again reviews in the press have been mixed, is in her non-dramatic work. Her short story *Hammerklavier* (1997) won the Académie française's prize for the novella. To date, her most important literary work outside the theatre is *Babylone* (2016), which was awarded one of the most prestigious literary prizes in France, the Renaudot. It is certainly true, as Sylvie Ducas (2013) has argued, that literary prizes are somewhat discredited today. Yet, the novel is still invested with considerable symbolic capital as the pre-eminent form of literature in France. The fact that Reza has increasingly written other literary genres signals her wish to be considered as a writer as well as a maker of plays. It is clearly within literature that Reza is looking for symbolic recognition in France by means of making up for her lack of it on the national stage. A lack, which is already compensated in part, of course, not only by her success in terms of box office returns, but also in terms of generating interest from directors hailing from other European countries.

Florian Zeller's family dramas

Zeller is another writer whose work crosses fictional boundaries, and who is no stranger to literary prizes. Born in Paris, he grew up in Brittany before going to study at the famous Institut des études politiques de Paris, more commonly known as Sciences Po. He published his first novel, *Neiges artificielles* (*Artificial Snow*) in 2002 when he was just 22. It was awarded the Fondation Hachette prize. His second novel *Les Amants du n'importe quoi* (*The Lovers of Anything Goes*), published one year later, received the Pierre-Prince de Monaco literary prize. And his third, *La Fascination du pire* (*The Fascination of Evil*), won the Interallié prize in 2004. In his mid-twenties, Florian Zeller was therefore a

Yasmina Reza and Florian Zeller 269

prolific, multi-prize-winning novelist. When he turned his hand to theatre, he was equally successful in obtaining prizes as *Si tu mourais* (*If You Died*) in 2006 won the Young Author's prize of the Académie française, *La Mère* (*The Mother*) won the award for best actress at the 2010 Molière, and *Le Père* (*The Father*) has won multiple awards. Even more so than with Reza, it can be tempting to list Zeller's prize-winning achievements in lieu of a summary of his career. However, such information only reveals part of the picture. Zeller's literary career has been forged through perseverance, luck, and especially through the contacts that he has managed to establish, for instance with Bernard Murat, one of the stalwarts of the private theatre scene, who directed a production of *Le Mensonge* (*The Lie*) in 2015.

Florian Zeller's first experience of writing for the stage was to adapt *Hary Janos* by Zoltan Kodaly for a production staged as part of the Montpellier festival in 2002 that featured the celebrated film actor Gérard Depardieu. Following on from this, he was invited to write a series of scenes whose evocative titles evoke motifs in eighteenth-century portraiture ('Erring shadows', Taciturn jealousy'), as part of the Festival Couperin in 2003. This gave an initial version of *L'Autre* (*The Other*), which was staged at the Théâtre des Mathurins one year later. Featuring characters named Her, Him, and The Other, the play revolves around the affair of Her and The Other, and how this reconfigures the relationship between Her and Him. In his great work, À *la recherche du temps perdu* (*In Search of Lost Time*), Marcel Proust used the trope of the kaleidoscope to describe how one's perception of an event or a situation can shift at any given moment. The plays of Florian Zeller feature moments when the kaleidoscope is shaken, revealing a different picture. In *The Other*, this occurs when there is an imagined scene of jealous murder by Him of Her, which is recounted to The Other, which ends with a gunshot and Her falling to the floor. In the next scene, The Other and Her are united again, and it is the start of their affair, which 'must stay a secret' (2004b: 48). In Annick Blancheteau's original production, the three actors wore white clothing that simultaneously evoked their ethereal nature of 'erring shadows' and the bedsheets in which the intrigue was knotted. In similar fashion, the image chosen for the cover of *Theatre I*, Magritte's painting *Les Amants* (*The Lovers*) is a good illustration of the games at play in Zeller's writing for the stage. The two figures kiss each other, one sporting a suit and tie, the other in what appears to be a dress. However, they are both wearing sheets on their head. As a result, they are not identifiable except by type: these are two characters who hide their love, but who are interchangeable with (each) other(s).

With both Reza and Zeller, couples are often at the heart of the plays. These couples, as in *The Other*, are most often not couples exactly but love triangles or even more complicated arrangements. Such relationships can be inter-generation: mother–son and father–daughter relationships are also portrayed on stage. What is more, they are almost invariably shown in various states of crisis, whether it is the 'crisis of the couple starting out or of the couple on its way out' (Ceilik 2012: 12). For instance, the very title of Zeller's first-written (but second-performed) play, *Le Manège* (*The Merry-Go-Round*), provides an apt description of the giddy games of love that will take place in the piece, as characters exchange places, becoming the actors in each other's love affairs. 'Manège' is close to 'ménage' (couple/home), as the magic roundabout turns, couples morph into each other. The plot is relatively simple: Nicolas overstays his welcome at his ex's house from which he refuses to leave, inviting his new partner over, getting in the way of her burgeoning new relationship also.

Zeller stages power battles. He looks at how, within couples, there is a thirst for knowledge, but that secrecy helps pin things together. As Kate Kellaway noted in her review of *La Vérité* (*The Truth*): 'Lying and its multiple uses interest him, and pretended ignorance emerges here as the most devious tool: hidden knowledge is power' (2016). The key difference between him and Reza is that for the most part Reza's characters tear each other apart revealing the savagery beneath, whereas for Zeller it is taken as a given that all truth is shifting, and that each persona is a masque. This was brought out in Lindsay Posner's production of *The Truth* at the Menier Chocolate Factory in London in which Robert Portal's portrayal of cheated best friend Paul as a 'blockish bloke with an aggressive stare and a trump card up his sleeve' (Kellaway 2016) exemplified the social games played with a poker face. Zeller draws his influences and references from his training at Sciences Po. Thus, it is with Goffman's theory of social performance and of keeping face. These references are awkwardly thrust into the mouths of the protagonists in his early work, such as in *Elle t'attend* (*She's Waiting for You*) which features a heavy-handed recreation of the scene at the beginning of Jean-Luc Godard's *Le Mépris* (*Contempt*, 1963) with Brigitte Bardot and Michel Piccoli, as Elle (Laetitia Casta) enumerates the parts of her body asking Lui (Bruno Todeschini) if he likes them.

Zeller's work certainly gains in maturity in his later plays as in *The Mother*, which director Andrés Lima describes as being about one of those vertiginous moments in life when everything is called into question (Antón 2017). In Lima's production in Barcelona (2017), Emma Vilarasau brought out the dark suffering of the character of the mother, haunted by figures of her husband's lovers, her son's girlfriend and her daughter. *The Mother*, in addressing suffering and mental affliction paved the way for what is undoubtedly Zeller's masterpiece, *The Father*. This play was to prove to be the launchpad for Zeller's international career, in much the same way that *Art* was for Reza. First performed in 2012 at the Théâtre Hébertot with veteran Comédie-Française actor Robert Hirsch in the title role, *The Father* is a play with a 'Pinteresque edge' (Gardner 2014). André, the father, shows signs of dementia. As his illness progresses boundaries are blurred, the reader/spectator loses their points of reference. André's relationships with his family become strained since it is never clear what is actually happening: we do not know for sure whether his daughter Anne lives in Paris with André or has moved to London, whether she is married or in a new relationship. André's confusion is mirrored by that of the audience unable to work out for sure how each character relates to the others.

In *The Father*, dementia is an affliction that raises all kinds of questions. Thematically, it makes the play a play for our times, but also a meta-commentary on the theatre, an art form that relies so much on memory. In addition, the failings of the patriarch can be exploited to thread a narrative about the voluntary amnesia that occurs after historical events. In this sense, the productions in France but also in Spain, where Héctor Alterio performed the ageing patriarch in Barcelona (2016), were particularly powerful as the countries' dark pasts are rewritten by revisionist historical narratives. Zeller's play in production makes the point that history is being rewritten, and it is not simply personal but collective memory that mutates. Alzheimer's functions as a powerful metaphor for the challenges facing contemporary societies in face of cultural memory. What is more, the actors playing the parts of André were very aged. In France, by having Hirsch perform on stage, the production tested the neat boundaries of fiction. In light of his great age – Hirsch was 88 for the original production in 2012 and played the same part three years later in 2015 – pulling off the performance was a feat in itself.

Theatre in translation

Reza and Zeller have both had their plays staged in a number of European countries. Sometimes, as in Reza's *Life × 3*, these have even taken place quasi simultaneously. Not least among their contributions to shaping the landscape of contemporary European playwriting has been their ability to make a very big name for themselves on the notoriously insular UK stage. In the 1990s and 2000s, the new writing scene was vibrant and there was no perceived need to look elsewhere for new material. With such a closed system, it is more important than ever for theatre-writing imports to fit into pre-conceived ideas about what makes a good play for British audiences. As Clare Finburgh has convincingly argued, 'performativity' is a culturally specific notion. In the UK, 'plays that are more or less naturalist, narrative-driven and issue-based are considered to guarantee a British audience' (2010: 233). This explains why twenty-first century French playwriting is very little present on British stages because it 'tends to foreground form' (Finburgh 2017: 10).

Reza and Zeller's works have been deemed (and proven to be) performable on the British stages because of their broadly naturalist traits and their focus on pan-European issues (couples in crisis, interpreting art, memory, and domestic politics). Moreover, it is certainly the case that success breeds success. Christopher Hampton, translator of both Reza and Zeller, makes this clear with respect to the former, in an interview conducted by Roger Baines and Manuela Perteghella. Hampton explains that his agent, Peggy Ramsey, brought Reza's work to his attention by providing him with a script of *Conversations After a Burial* (2010: 182–3). However, producing a young virtually unknown writer would have been unfeasible. It was only when he attended the sold-out production of *Art* in Paris that he decided that he wanted to translate her. Hampton felt a strong affinity with Reza's work, but it was its success during its Paris run that opened the

272   *Dominic Glynn*

door to its translation to the London stage. Indeed, Hampton then found out that the actor Sean Connery had already bought the rights and put himself forward to translate the play (183).

The situation was a little different with regard to *The Father*, though it too had enjoyed a popular run in Paris. The Cross-Channel Theatre group, which is composed of theatre professionals in the UK (agents, producers, directors, actors) who have an affinity with France, selected the play. They choose plays that they believe would work on the UK stage, based on a set of shared assumptions relating to what is performable. The group reads ten plays, and each member comes up with his or her ranking. The top play (or plays) in the list are translated and given a reading at the Soho Theatre to a group of professionals, including producers. In 2015, the then French ambassador to the UK held a reception in Florian Zeller's honour, in which the members of the group received thanks for their vital role in granting Zeller a passage across the Channel (French Embassy 2015).

However, neither Reza nor Zeller's plays are devoid of what Javier Franco Aixelá has termed 'culture-specific items' (1996: 52). Specifically concerning *Art*, Ángela Magdalena Romera Pintor has analysed in detail the translation procedures used by Josep Maria Flotats – who was also actor and director of the play at the Teatro Marquina in 1998 – to substitute items in his Spanish translation, such as meeting times which are delayed by two hours, as 7.00 to 7.30 pm is changed to 9.00 to 9.30 pm, on account of differing eating habits (2012: 248). Indeed, Flotats' translation even moves the location of the play from Paris to Madrid (Mateo 2006: 77). Christopher Hampton in his English translation adopts an ethos of sticking close to the texts of Reza and Zeller. There are name changes, such as in *God of Carnage*, where the Houllié family becomes the Vallons; however, locations are kept in Paris. However, given that the plays of Reza and Zeller have been frequently performed on stages throughout Europe and thus translated into many languages, it is not as if such culture-specific items pose insurmountable barriers to their border crossings. Indeed, both playwrights have arguably enjoyed greater success and renown outside of their own countries; translators, directors, and casts from around Europe have been the mediators of this achievement.

Conclusion

It is perhaps unfair that in the cases of Reza and Zeller, they are most often accused of not doing things. Theirs is not an overtly political theatre; they do not write issue-driven plays in which the fate of society is at stake. Neither does their work grapple with philosophy in the way that Eric-Emmanuel Schmitt does in his rewriting of the Don Juan myth, *La Nuit de Valognes* (*Don Juan on Trial*, 1991) (Schmitt 2004). Nor do they play with the conventions of language or drama in the manner of such authors as Philippe Minyana or Noëlle Renaude. What they do offer is drama that stages tensions in families, in friendships, and in amorous relationships. These tensions come to the fore at particular points when characters drop their masks and their gloves. In their plays, the domestic environment is especially highly charged as it is where tensions fuelled by jealousy, suspicion, or resentment constantly simmer and occasionally come to the boil. Friends, relationships, and families are put to the test with tears and laughter ensuing.

In France, both playwrights are clearly identified as belonging to the private theatre scene. This is not necessarily a label they would choose to stick with. Reza, for one, has suggested that she would like to see her plays performed in the subsidised theatres again, but that this has become complicated after *Art* (Garcin 2014). Zeller has not clearly expressed such a desire. Nevertheless, on the domestic front, his lack of exposure on the public theatre scene has prevented his work from being appreciated by vast sways of the press, or indeed acknowledged in academic publications. It is certainly the case that translation to other European stages has helped grant both authors symbolic credit. Directors not caught in the schism between French private and public theatre have been able to forge other opinions of the attributes of Reza and Zeller's dramas. This breaking of barriers is without question something to be celebrated.

Yasmina Reza – four key productions

"Art". Directed by Patrice Kerbrat. Sets by Edouard Laugh. Costumes by Pascale Fournier. Lighting by Laurent Béal. Cast: Pierre Vaneck, Fabrice Luchini, Pierre Arditi. Comédie des Champs Elysées, Paris, 28 October 1994. Videorecording available at: https://www.dailymotion.com/video/x66105

Bella Figura. Translated by Thomas Ostermeier and Florian Borchmeyer. Directed by Thomas Ostermeier. Dramaturgy by Florian Borchmeyer. Sets by Jan Pappelbaüm. Costumes by Florence von Gerkan. Music by Malte Beckenback. Video by Guillaume Cailleau and Benjamin Krieg. Lighting by Marie-Christine Soman and Erich Schneider. Cast: Nina Hoss, Mark Waschke, Stephanie Eidt, Renato Schuch, Lore Stefanek. Schaubühne, Berlin, 16 May 2016.

Drei mal leben (*Trois versions de la vie; Life × 3*). Translated by Eugène Hemlé. Directed by Luc Bondy. Dramaturgy by Stephan Müller. Sets by Wilfried Minks. Costumes by Rudy Sabounghi. Music by André Serre. Lighting by Dominique Brughière. Cast: Susanne Lothar, Ulrich Mühe, Andrea Clausen, Sven-Eric Bechtolf. Wiener Akademietheater, Vienna, 29 October 2000.

God of Carnage (*Le Dieu du carnage*). Translated by Christopher Hampton. Directed by Matthew Warchus. Sets and costumes by Mark Thompson. Music by Gary Yershon. Sound by Simon Baker/Christpher Cronin. Lighting design by Hugh Vanstone. Cast: Ralph Fiennes, Tamsin Greig, Janet McTeer, Ken Stott. Gielgud Theatre, London, 25 March 2008.

Florian Zeller – four key productions

L'Autre (*The Other*). Directed by Annick Blancheteau. Set by Pace. Costumes by Pascale Bordet. Lighting by Laurent Beal. Cast: Nicholas Vaude, Chloé Lambert, Clément Sibony. Théâtre des Mathurins, Paris, 14 September 2004.

274 *Dominic Glynn*

La Mare (*La Mère; The Mother*). Translated by Ernest Riera. Directed by Andrés Lima. Cast: Emma Vilarasau, Pep Pla, Oscar Castellví y Ester Cort. La Villaroel, Barcelona, 19 February 2017.

Le Père (*The Father*). Directed by Ladislas Chollat. Sets by Emmanuelle Roy. Costumes by Jean-Daniel Vuillermoz. Music by Frédéric Norel. Lighting design by Alban Sauvé. Cast: Eric Boucher, Elise Diamant, Isabelle Gélinas, Robert Hirsch, Marie Parouty, Bernard Yerlès. Théâtre Hébertot, 20 September 2012.

The Truth (*La Vérité*). Translated by Christopher Hampton. Directed by Lindsay Posner. Sets and costumes by Lizzie Clachan. Lighting by Howard Harrison. Sound by Gregory Clarke. Cast: Tanya Franks, Alexander Hanson, Frances O'Connor, Robert Portal. Menier Chocolate Factory, London, March 2016.

Notes

1 The speech marks are part of the French and English titles but will be dropped for convenience of reading.
2 Unless otherwise stated, all translations are my own.
3 See Vinaver (1982) and Koltès (1999).
4 Nordey directed the Théâtre Gérard-Philipe between 1998 and 2001. Since 2014, he has been the director of the Théâtre national de Strasbourg.
5 A video recording of the initial production is available here: https://www.dailym otion.com/video/x66105

Works cited

Antón, Jacinto (2017) 'Madre hay más que una', *El País*, 29 January, https://elpais.com/ccaa/2017/01/28/catalunya/1485635647_879652.html

Ayad, Christophe (2006) 'Les Illusions perdurent', *Libération*, 6 September, http://www.liberation.fr/portrait/2006/09/06/les-illusions-perdurent_50383

Baines, Roger and Manuela Perteghella (2010) 'Interview with Christopher Hampton', in Roger Baines, Cristina Marinetti and Manuela Perteghella (eds), *Staging and Performing Translation: Text and Theatre Practice*, Basingstoke: Palgrave Macmillan, pp. 173–186.

Banos-Ruf, Pierre (2008) *L'Édition théâtrale aujourd'hui: enjeux artistiques, économiques et politiques: l'exemple des Éditions Théâtrales*, PhD Thesis, Université Paris-Nanterre.

Barbier, Christophe (2014) 'Florian Zeller: "Le publi a toujours raisons"', *L'Express*, 8 November, https://www.lexpress.fr/culture/scene/florian-zeller-le-public-a-toujours-raison_1619047.html

Biet, Christian and Christophe Triau (2006) *Qu'est-ce que le théâtre?*, Paris: Gallimard.

Bourdieu, Pierre (1992) *Les Règles de l'art. Genèse et structure du champ littéraire*, Paris: Seuil.

Bradby, David and David Williams (1988) *Director's Theatre*, London: Palgrave Macmillan.

Cande, Daniel (1987) 'Conversations après un enterrement, texte de Yasmina Reza: photographies / Daniel Cande', Bibliothèque nationale de France, département Arts du spectacle, DIA-PHO-6(431), https://gallica.bnf.fr/ark:/12148/btv1b9002184z/f5

Yasmina Reza and Florian Zeller 275

Ceilik, Olivier (2012) 'Préface. Les illusions perdues in Florian Zeller', in *Théâtre I*, Paris: Quatre-vents/L'Avant-scène théâtre, pp. 7–13.

Cénac, Laetitia (2017) 'Yasmina Reza: Ma façon d'écrire provient de mes origines', *Le Figaro*, 20 November, http://madame.lefigaro.fr/celebrites/yasmina-reza-ma-facon-decrire-provient-de-mes-origines-201117-145625

Clapp, Susannah (2008) 'Are you sitting uncomfortably?' *Guardian*, 30 March, https://www.theguardian.com/stage/2008/mar/30/theatre3

Delgado, Maria (2017) 'Madrid's theatre takes inspiration from the Greeks', *European Stages*, 10, https://europeanstages.org/2017/10/28/madrids-theatre-takes-inspiration-from-the-greeks/

Diatkine, Anne (2015) '"Bella Figura" Gâche ta joie', *Libération*, https://next.liberation.fr/theatre/2015/11/26/bella-figura-gache-ta-joie_1416403

Dromgoole, Dominic (2001) *The Full Room*, London: Methuen.

Ducas, Sylvie (2013) *La Littérature à quel(s) prix? Histoire des prix littéraires*, Paris: La Découverte.

Finburgh, Clare (2010) 'The politics of translating contemporary French theatre: how "linguistic translation" becomes "stage translation"', in Roger Baines, Cristina Marinetti and Manuela Perteghella (eds), *Staging and Performing Translation: Text and Theatre Practice*, Basingstoke: Palgrave Macmillan, pp. 230–248.

Finburgh, Clare (2017) 'Introduction', in Chris Campbell, *The Oberon Anthology of Contemporary French Plays*, London: Oberon Books, pp. 10–14.

Fondu, Quentin (2016) 'L'Auteur.e dramatique: entre reconnaissance professionnelle et précarité économique', in G. Sapiro and C. Rabot (eds), *Profession? Écrivain*. Paris: Le Motif, pp. 83–103, https://www.enssib.fr/bibliotheque-numerique/documents/66460-profession-ecrivain.pdf

Franco Aixelá, Javier (1996) 'Culture-specific items in translation', in Román Álvarez and M. Carmen-África Vidal (eds), *Translation, Power, Subversion*, Clevedon: Multilingual Matters, pp. 52–78.

French Embassy (2015) 'Réception donnée en l'honneur de Florian Zeller à l'occasion de la présentation de The Father au Wyndham Theatre', 5 November, https://www.google.com/url?sa=t&rct=j&q=&esrc=s&source=web&cd=2&ved=2ahUKEwirnqHN6obgAhXS7mEKHdFkAiMQFjABegQICRAC&url=https%3A%2F%2Fuk.ambafrance.org%2F5-November-Reception-for-Florian-Zeller&usg=AOvVaw0RoSjz1vFakxmsr7Huqp-w

Garcin, Jérôme (2014) 'Yasmina Reza "J'écris avec mes phobies"', *Le Nouvel Observateur*, 24 November, https://bibliobs.nouvelobs.com/theatre/20141124.OBS5989/yasmina-reza-j-ecris-avec-mes-phobies.html

Gardner, Lyn (2014) *The Father* five-star review – a savagely honest study of dementia', *Guardian*, 23 October, https://www.theguardian.com/stage/2014/oct/23/the-father-review-ustinov-theatre-royal-bath-florian-zeller

Giguere, Amanda (2010) *The Plays of Yasmina Reza on the English and American Stage*, Jefferson, NC: McFarland.

Glynn, Dominic (2015) *(Re)telling Old Stories. Peter Brook's Mahabharata and Ariane Mnouchkine's Les Atrides*, Brussels: Peter Lang.

Guénoun, Denis (2005) *Avez-vous lu Réza?* Paris: Albin Michel.

Houellebecq, Michel (2010) *La Carte et le Territoire*, Paris: Flammarion.

Hussein, T.M. (2009) *La Quête identitaire dans le théâtre de Yasmina Reza*. PhD Thesis, Université Lumière – Lyon II, https://tel.archives-ouvertes.fr/tel-01540262/document

276 *Dominic Glynn*

Jaccomard, Hélène (2016) 'L'humour comme arme: Le cas du *Dieu du carnage* de Yasmina Reza', *French Cultural Studies*, 27(2): 190–198.

Kellaway, Kate (2016) '*The Truth* review – a devious must see', *Observer*, 20 March, https://www.theguardian.com/stage/2016/mar/20/the-truth-florian-zeller-menier-observer-review

Koltès, Bernard-Marie. (1999) *Une part de ma vie – Entretiens*, Paris: Minuit.

Marchand, J. (2015) *Mission théâtre public, théâtre privé*, Paris: Ministère de la culture et de la communication, http://www.culture.gouv.fr/Espace-documentation/Rapports/Mission-Theatre-public-theatre-prive

Mateo, Marta (2006) 'Successful strategies in drama translation: Yasmina Reza's "*Art*"', *Meta*, 51(1): 175–183, http://www.lestroiscoups.com/article-22991087.html

Mépris, Le (2000) [DVD]. Directed by Jean-Luc Godard (1963). France: G.C.T.H.V.

Philibert, Anne Elizabeth (2015) 'Florian Zeller, actuellement l'auteur le plus joué à l'étranger', *France Info*, 6 December, https://culturebox.francetvinfo.fr/theatre/theatre-contemporain/florian-zeller-actuellement-l-auteur-francais-le-plus-joue-a-l-etranger-232833

Proust, Marcel (1999) *À la recherche du temps perdu*, Paris: Gallimard.

Reza, Yasmina (1997) *Hammerklavier*, Paris: Albin Michel.

——— (1998) *Théâtre*, Paris: Albin Michel.

——— (2005) *Plays*, trans. Christopher Hampton, London: Faber.

——— (2007) *Le Dieu du carnage*, Paris: Albin Michel.

——— (2008) *God of Carnage*, trans. Christopher Hampton, London: Faber.

——— (2013) *Life × 3*, trans. Christopher Hampton, London: Bloomsbury.

——— (2016) *Babylone*, Paris: Flammarion.

Romera Pintor, Ángela Magdalena (2012) 'El arte de traducir a Yasmina Reza: Los retos del francés', in Pilar Martino Alba (ed.), *Actas del IULMYT, XIII Encuentros (II): La traducción en las artes escénicas*: 245–256, https://cvc.cervantes.es/lengua/iulmyt/traduccion_artes.htm

Schmitt, Éric-Emmanuel (2004) *La Nuit de Valognes*, Paris: Magnard.

Turk, Edward Baron (2011) *French Theatre Today: The View from New York, Paris, Avignon*, Iowa: University of Iowa University Press.

Vinaver, Michel (1982) *Écrits sur le théâtre I-II*, Lausanne: Éditions de l'Aire.

Vossier, Frédéric (2013) *Stanislas Nordey. Locataire de la parole*, Besançon: Les Solitaires intempestifs.

Zeller, Florian (2002) *Neiges artificielles*, Paris: Flammarion.

——— (2003) *Les Amants du n'importe quoi*, Paris: Flammarion.

——— (2004a) *La Fascination du pire*, Paris: Flammarion.

——— (2004b) *L'Autre*, Paris: L'avant-scène théâtre.

——— (2012) *Théâtre I*, Paris: L'avant-scène théâtre / Collection des quatre-vents.

15 Lena Kitsopoulou and Yannis Mavritsakis

Greek theatre at the antipodes of crisis

Elizabeth Sakellaridou

The turn of the millennium found Greece in an elated spirit of high expectations. Its admission to the Schengen Agreement in 1992 had already made the country feel a more central part of the European Union and its subsequent entry to the Eurozone in 2001 consolidated further its feeling of sharing the stability and prosperity of the big European family of member states. For a small country like Greece, the fall of national borders and the European monetary union provided a historic upgrading of the national image. The ensuing Olympic Games in Athens in 2004 fuelled further aspirations for regaining the nation's lost pride after an endless series of war traumas and national tragedies that were its legacy of the long twentieth century.

The few years that elapsed between the splendour of the Olympic grand spectacle and the economic crisis of 2008, historically speaking, were no more than a prolonged hangover, during which a hazy memory of illusory triumph and complacent satisfaction prevented the country from any effective exploitation of whatever gain (spiritual or material) was achieved by the Games. When the financial bubble burst, the awakening to the new harsh reality was shocking and devastating. The country entered a long period of austerity and went through an endless series of repressive policies, which strangled its vitality in many respects with job cuts and salary and pension reductions that caused some of the best-qualified young people to seek work abroad. The political climate, which had always been animated by factional disputes, added new tensions to civic life with the rise of the ultra-right and the legal admittance of the Golden Dawn Party to the Greek Parliament, despite its fascist ideology and criminal involvement in organised violence. High unemployment and social insecurity, the serious demographic problem arising from a steady drop in the birth rate, political confusion, and the complexities of a new global system of governance all impacted Greek citizens.

Contemporary Greek theatre, as the most public of arts, has been most susceptible to the sea changes that an unprepared, fairly resistant (though actually grudgingly adaptable) Greek society has been forced to adjust to. The more persistent the symptoms of financial crisis and social disintegration, the more constant and resilient the Greek stage seems to be. Reviewing the phenomenon of theatrical proliferation for the 2017–18 season, critic Matina Kaltaki estimates the total number of performances in Athens to be just less

278   *Elizabeth Sakellaridou*

than 1200 (Kaltaki 2018). Has the theatre become the survival kit not only for ailing artists but also for anguished audiences? Are we seeing a dynamic theatre revival, where troubling public affairs find a bold expression as in ancient times? As Philip Hager notes, the sharing of the Documenta exhibition between Kassel and Athens in 2016 was symbolically seen as the transformation of the crisis-stricken Greek capital to a global arts centre (Hager and Fragkou 2017) – a hypothesis which is variously supported by the multiplying numbers of foreign artists and international art projects finding a hub of artistic inspiration and activity in Greece. In terms of the pivotal role that theatre, in particular, can play in the present moment of crisis, critic Dimitra Kondylaki assumes a strong militant tone, urging Greek playwrights to see beyond the 'toxic ego' of contemporary society, which is simply 'punitive and vindictive', and to turn the theatre into a 'therapeutic mirror', a more constructive social role (Kondylaki 2014: 70, 61). This may be an extreme and rather prescriptive view but it clearly reflects the dynamism of the country's theatrical production beyond the plethora of foreign translated plays and invited productions from abroad. The Greek Play Project (founded in 2014), an open platform for the promotion of new Greek dramatic writing, lists about 60 practising playwrights, including writers of three generations: the 1970s–80s, the 1990s, and the new millennium.

The foundations of a new theatrical climate in Greece roughly go back to the last two decades of the twentieth century (the so-called *metapolitefsi* era, that is, the post-junta years), through the strengthening of the theatre establishment (the two already-existing National Theatres in Athens and Thessaloniki and the Karolos Koun Art Theatre), its further expansion (the founding of Municipal Theatres in all major cities of Greece), the renewal of theatre policies (including state subsidies for the arts), the reorganisation and upgrading of the Greek Festival (in Athens and Epidaurus), and the founding of three new major cultural institutions (the Onassis, the Kakoyannis, and, more recently, the Niarchos Centres for the Arts). One more private theatre institution, the Analogio Festival, has been playing a pivotal role since its foundation in 2003 in promoting the writing and production of new Greek plays by organising annual stage readings of new plays, commissioning new writing, and promoting Greek plays for the international theatre market. Greek theatre has indeed started travelling abroad, with plays being translated into foreign languages and productions participating in international festivals and projects.

As Lina Rosi remarks, many new playwrights are actively involved in theatre production (Rosi 2014: 23, 24). They re-emerge as hybrid artists, combining the art of playwriting with that of actor and/or director, occasionally also practising dancing and singing. The two twenty-first-century playwrights I have chosen to discuss as representative writers of the new trends in contemporary Greek dramaturgy both belong to this exciting category of hybrid artists. Yannis Mavritsakis (b. 1964) made his artistic debut as an actor and he then turned to playwriting and, more recently, to prose writing. Lena Kitsopoulou (b. 1971) is an even more multi-faceted artist. Making her first public appearance as an award-winning film actress, she has continued acting on the stage, while also writing prose and drama, gradually adding theatre directing and singing to her professional artistic engagement. Both developed an international profile, with their plays being translated and performed outside the Greek national borders. At first, Mavritsakis's oeuvre appeared to have a stronger appeal in France, whereas Kitsopoulou has had institutional support within German theatre culture. They both draw on a very complex thematic reservoir (social, mythical, psychic, and emotional) and experiment with various forms of linguistic and visual representation, where dissonance and contradiction are in constant interplay. Their art functions as work-in-progress, conversing with the flow and contradictions of the current global realities.

Under closer scrutiny, these two writers seem to follow opposite routes in their process of writing. Kitsopoulou is turning more and more extroverted, loud, and aggressive – sometimes almost verging on insolence – as she becomes more directly involved with live performance (as director, performer, and singer). She emerges as the representative of a Greek 'in-yer-face-theatre'; her writing has traits of Sarah Kane though is perhaps closer to the savage, ironic subversiveness of Martin McDonagh. Mavritsakis, on the other hand, seems to gradually move from the blended realism of his earlier work to greater introversion in tone and address. It is a retreat into a private universe, where echoes of a traumatic reality are filtered into a mythical or metaphysical quest of the self and the world in many ways reminiscent of Kafka, Beckett, Pinter, and Barker. In this respect, Mavritsakis's writing brings him closer to a trend that Chris Megson has explored in contemporary British theatre – that of 'postsecularism' and the 're-enchantment of the world' (Megson 2013, 2016).

The heretical Lena Kitsopoulou

Multi-talented, angry, provocative, aggressive, subversive, irreverent, transgressive, blasphemous, iconoclastic are all epithets consistently used to characterise Kitsopoulou's art. A graduate from the prestigious Drama School of Koun's Art Theatre, she received the best actress award at the Thessaloniki Film Festival in 1996 but she refused a promising career as a screen actress because it was the theatre that most excited her. She was drawn to writing, music, and performance from her school days at the German School of Athens. Here she also formed an early link with German culture, developed later through her artistic activities and collaborations.

Kitsopoulou first appeared on the literary scene in 2006 with Νυχτερίδες (*Bats*), a short-story collection, which drew immediate critical attention and was awarded the emerging writer's prize for that year. Her actual entry to the theatrical scene came three years later with the monologue M.A.I.P.O.Y.Λ.A (*M.A.I.R.O.U.L.A.*), which she directed for the National Theatre and which became an immediate success. Two earlier short plays, the one-acter *Μνήσθητι την ημέραν του Σαββάτου αγιάζειν αυτήν* (*Remember the Sabbath Day and Keep It Holy*) and the monologue *Το πράσινό μου το φουστανάκι* (*My Green Dress*), were staged in 2007 and 2008 respectively by director Vicky Georgiadou, and these already marked her as a significant new voice in Greek theatre. The

280   *Elizabeth Sakellaridou*

former in particular, presented on the experimental stage of the National Theatre, served as her entrance ticket for what has proved a relatively stable collaboration with the country's top establishment theatre.

From the start, Kitsopoulou developed a strong anti-establishment critical stance, militant but anarchic, aggressive, and contradictory, which gained her an enthusiastic cult following. She thus became the *enfant terrible* of the Greek stage, occupying a similar position to the young Sarah Kane in the UK in the 1990s. Kitsopoulou was seized by Greece's theatrical establishment, which turned her into the more controversial image of an *enfant gâté*, proving the power of postmodern mainstream culture to naturalise all expressions of heterodoxy and revolt. In addition to the National Theatre, Koun's Art Theatre, the Greek Festival, and the Onassis Cultural Centre Stegi opened their gates to admit Kitsopoulou both as dramatist and stage director. A recent commission in 2019 came from the Niarchos Foundation for Culture for an opera libretto in collaboration with composer Nikos Kypourgos.

The artist herself insists on projecting an eccentric persona, a fringe personality snubbing all aspects of mainstream hierarchies and institutions both in Greece and abroad. In her interviews she renounces ideological labels and refuses to see herself as writing from the perspective of feminism or post-feminism (see Bekri 2014: 120), rather positioning herself instead as 'a woman, possessing all the traits of a woman [...] I write as a woman [...] all naturally, according to what I have experienced or thought. Not as a woman-who-is-the enemy of men or who belongs to a certain camp' (Bekri 2014: 120).

In a 2017 interview, she makes a similar disclaimer about the connection of her writing with the current Greek or global crisis:

> For me personally, there's no actual change. I'm constantly in a personal crisis. One way or another, one has to be in crisis to do this job; it's our existential crisis and the one we encounter as humans who know they are born and die. In terms of the context, I think it has always been difficult. Wasn't it difficult in other periods like the junta? It is the work of the artist to resist the establishment, to reject such a life, such a politics. I believe that crises give birth to both good and bad.
>
> (Kangelari 2017: 254)

Her works, her interviews, and her bio-politics converge into the image of the artist as a person in a constant state of emergency; a migrant (or fugitive) subject, always 'packed for nowhere'. It is this image of the artist in an interminable transit state between artistic commissions in Germany, Switzerland and Greece, between life in the cacophony of Athens and the serenity of the islands, between turbulent nightlife and solitary writing that has turned her into the epitome of the anguished, schizophrenic Greek citizen living in a fluid and uncertain political climate. It is this feeling of perpetual *emergency* that fuels Kitsopoulou's theatre, reflecting the country's fatigue, anger, and despair.

Her 'anger', even if she disavows a systematic political engagement, has strong political edges, addressing the perennial pathologies of modern Greek society. Here she converges with contemporaries, including detective-fiction writer Petros Markaris and sociologist Constantinos Tsoukalas in her indictment of the fixation of the Greeks with the 'ghosts' of the past.[1] By comparison, however, Kitsopoulou's writing is more somatic and existential, partly because of her migrant and impulsive idiosyncrasy and partly because of her double engagement with live theatre as director and performer.

It is hard to list and categorise the works of a writer like Kitsipoulou when there is no definitive published text. So far, *M.A.I.R.O.U.L.A.* is the only play, a monologue, that has seen an official Greek edition (Kitsipoulou 2009), followed by an English translation, which was included in the recent Oberon Anthology of Contemporary Greek Plays (2017). Even in this unique case of a dual publication there are major differences between the Greek and the English versions, so that one can hardly talk of a definitive text.[2] The rest of Kitso-poulou's oeuvre on the whole circulates in a provisional form, which leaves the door open for further changes or elaboration.

As a director and performer, Kitsopoulou is in constant conversation with her other persona as a writer, a condition that makes her work flexible and adaptable to different cultural, institutional, and spectatorial situations. For instance, her recent play *Αντιγόνη – Lonely Planet* (*Antigone – Lonely Planet*, 2016/17), initially written for presentation at the Onassis Cultural Center in New York, opens with a bold satire of the lavishness of the Onassis Founda-tion, which stands in vivid contrast to 'the difficult times we live in and experience' (*Antigone*: 1–2). The same tactic of specifically targeted institutional/cultural abuse is applied again in a recent play, *Cry*, which premiered at Geneva's Saint Gervais theatre in February 2018.[3] It starts as an innocuous welcome and vote of thanks to the theatre which later evolves into more uncomfortable insults directed at the audience, including ambiguous intercultural comments with a strong political edge:

> We are happy about this evening […] It's so nice tonight. What a wonderful opportunity is offered us by this theatre; we sit here and you sit there; all in one group really, one large group which can say in the end, how nice it was. Do you remember that evening at the Saint Gervais theatre, how nice it was? […] We thank you first of all for not being bored and for being in such a good mood. It is really moving. You have such a Swiss politeness – really remarkable […]

The cross-cultural satire also includes self-mockery, which is typical of Kitsipou-lou's performance tactics:

M. (MAN): I think you have a problem with the Swiss. You shouldn't be in Switzerland. Are you in Switzerland?
L. (LENA): Yes. I am in Switzerland.

282 *Elizabeth Sakellaridou*

M.: You *live* in Switzerland, right?

L.: Yes, I live in Switzerland.

M.: Fine. Then say thank you to Switzerland.

L.: Say thank you for what?

M.: Say thank you to Switzerland for allowing you to stay in Switzerland. This is what you must say. Aren't you Greek?

L.: Yes, I am.

M.: Fine. So, thank Switzerland because you live in Switzerland and not in Greece.

L.: Thank you Switzerland.

M.: Wonderful. Now you are bringing out something very beautiful, indeed. And most generous.(*Cry*: 2–4)

These two quotes are indicative of Kitsopoulou's sharp satire which goes to extremes both in terms of menacing imagery and linguistic violence.

Αθανάσιος Διάκος – Η επιστροφή (*Athanasios Diakos – The Return*, 2012a) savagely lacerated the Greek neurosis around the three pillars of modern Greek identity: the family, the nation, and the church. Choosing as her main character one of the most emblematic figures of the Greek Revolution,[4] Kitsopoulou offers a provocative depiction of contemporary Athens, combining aspects of crisis and decadence: materialism, sex, ethics, misogyny, and racism. Looking through the same critical sociological lens as Tsoukalas in his publication, *Greece of Oblivion and Truth*, Kitsopoulou attempts precisely to 'crash land the dreaming nation down on the surface of reality', pointing to the wounds of both an 'imaginary surplus' and a 'pragmatic deficit' through the course of history (2012: 39). Making such honest but painful historical disclosures in the theatre – especially when this is voiced from the official stage of the International Greek Festival – creates more seismic public reaction than any sociological study meant for private reading. The production of *Athanasios Diakos* ignited a fierce controversy in the press and a public commotion, with the Golden Dawn threatening to violently disrupt performances of the piece. It was the first time that Kitsopoulou's provocation stretched public tolerance, splitting the audience into devoted followers and bitter enemies of her work. Ironically, the play won the International Playwright's Award at the Heidelberg Stückemarkt in 2013, thus consolidating the Greek writer's European profile.

Exposing the persistent pathogenies of Greek society permeates the whole of her work in both an overt or a more cryptic manner. In *Άουστρας ή Η Αγριάδα* (*Austras or The Weed*, 2012b), in a sense a twin play with *Athanasios Diakos* (since it was written at the same time and in the same critical vein), she makes xenophobia the centre of her relentless attack against the Greek fantasy of national superiority and difference. What makes her attack even more apoc-alyptic is that the characters' racism is not simply targeted at the powerless category of economic migrants and refugees from the East but also against Western tourists, who are normally received with the courtesy of the mythic Greek *philoxenia* (hospitality to strangers). This tradition is violently torn apart as the three young Greek characters, degraded by contemporary material and moral boredom and decay, assault their foreign guest with verbal violence, which gradually escalates to Dionysian butchery and murder. Thus, xenophobia becomes savage animalism – aesthetically and stylistically close to Martin McDonagh's dark brutality. Like McDonagh on stage (or Tarantino on the screen), Kitsopoulou uses an overdose of the splatter aesthetic, with guns and sharp instruments (such as knives and poles) and an overflow of blood, in order to question the very efficacy of visual horror techniques on contemporary audiences. Extreme shock tactics become the means of their own subversion through the use of a very black and twisted form of humour which often borders on paranoia.

Her early monologue, *My Green Dress* (2008), reveals this puzzling, double-edged sarcasm that has become the trademark of all her art. This totally anarchic play script in fact rehearses all the major themes which keep returning in her later work: the debunking of Greek and European narratives of ethnic and cultural homogeneity and their destabilising effect on individual lives in search of new hybrid identities. Her heroine is the embodiment of various neuroses and phobias (of uncertain social or private origin) which she can hardly identify or cope with. The play opens with the appearance of 'a woman all covered in a long burka' (*My Green Dress*: 1). After the first visual shock of doubt for the audience, the voice under the cover identifies herself as 'a female greek national, spelling "greek" with the "g" in the lower case', who has bought the burka in the flea market to test her own shaken identity. When she takes off the burka a second shock awaits the audience as she exposes the badly bruised face of an apparently savagely abused woman. In her state of confusion her emotions fluctuate between complete rejection of violence and atrocity in the contemporary global situation on the one hand and extreme self-victimisation on the other. In the most dramatic paragraph of the play, which blends the verbal cruelty of Crimp's *Attempts on Her Life* (1997) with the discourse of self-denial in Beckett's *Not I* (1972), she tries to cast off any kind of perceptual and ethical involvement in the 'evils' of the world. In the end, however, all the collective guilt of western hypocrisy inscribed on herself comes out in a shocking confession of a literal self-bashing, which brings the protagonist only one step away from the suicidal heroine of *M.A.I.R.O.U.L.A.*:

> I inflicted all this on myself, this morning, all by myself [...] I hit myself with my own hands, with whatever I found in front of me, heavy objects, sharp instruments, the fireplace pincers, even the cat's empty tins. I'm in no way an Albanian, no way a slut, no connection with all that – quite the opposite [...] *I bashed myself on my own*, just like that, for no reason at all, this morning, in my own home.
> *Well, not quite without some kind of reason –*
> (*My Green Dress*: 15, emphasis added)

284   *Elizabeth Sakellaridou*

Surprisingly, between the lines of harsh language and nihilistic views verging on cynicism,[5] the two monologues hide a deep melancholy for the frustrations of love; they strike a tender chord, voicing a longing for lost emotion, in the same way that Sarah Kane's extreme atrocities in *Blasted* (1995) and *Cleansed* (1998) are, for her, a desperate cry for love.[6] The two monologues are the closest that Kitsopoulou has come to female experience and sensibility. The theme of the physical and sexual abuse of women and children is actually the bitterest point of her critique. Two other one-act plays of hers, *N-Euro-se* and *The Price*, which participated in two international theatre festivals in Berlin and London respectively (2012c, d), tackle child abuse in a nightmarish fashion. In the former, a family dinner scene exposes the parents' growing social neurosis that finally drives the adolescent daughter (or son) to take their own life with father and mother left as callous, clinical observers of the gruesome result. The picture is greatly reminiscent of the unbearably cruel irony of *American Beauty* (dir. Sam Mendes, 1999). *The Price* takes place in a supermarket, reminding us of the respective scene in Ravenhill's *Shopping and Fucking* (1996). Kitsopoulou's love for excess pushes even further the situation of absolute consumerism by turning the child into a commodity, over which a strong bargain is struck between husband and wife and then between husband and cashier. The play closes in a rather sloppy, farcical manner with the purchase of a dead child (that was the cheapest they could get) in a capacious shopping bag, in which the man also thrusts his arguing wife while also desperately offering to check out his own sterile penis, furious at what he takes as the cashier's lack of professional courtesy to the customers.

Kitsopoulou's dramatic representations of other themes do follow the same aesthetic of provocative and harsh satire but they do not reach the unspeakable brutality described above. They are more like performance tricks and games played with the audience. Whether deconstructing traditional children's tales (as in *Κοκκινοσκουφίτσα – Το πρώτο αίμα* [*Red Riding Hood or The First Blood*, 2014]), or demystifying Greek tragedy and satirising the Greek skiing trend of the 1980s and after (as in *Antigone – Lonely Planet*), her written text has a loose, sketchy form, which apparently allows for actor improvisation and audience participation but actually critiques the lack of expertise, authority, and control in contemporary performance. For example, in her most Pirandellian play, *Cry*, she rips open the mechanics of performance, creating a metatheatrical frame in which the actors cannot distinguish between their personal lives and their theatrical role while an amateur pianist is ridiculed for volunteering to play in the performance under fake musical credentials. The cultural industries come under attack (with specific venom reserved for theatre management and theatre critics) but it is the audience that forms her constant target with *Red Riding Hood* including the most extensive audience abuse in the style of Peter Handke's *Offending the Audience* (1966).

An incessant, multifarious creative process

Kitsopoulou has never given up her acting career. Although her appearance in other people's productions is now more limited, she continues to appear in productions of her own plays, reserving for herself a lesser part since her major responsibility is the role of the director. As a performer, she expends most of her bodily and vocal energy in singing *rebetiko* songs at various venues in Athens and the islands. Apart from directing her own work, she has also been offered work directing other plays at major Greek institutions such as the Art Theatre (an adaptation of Grigorios Xenopoulos's *Χαίρε Νύμφη* (*Hail, Bride*, 2012) and the National Theatre (an adaptation of Lorca's *Blood Wedding*, 2014) and also the Apo Michanis theatre (an adaptation of Giorgos Chronas's *Η γυναίκα της Πάτρας* [The *Woman from Patras*, 2010]). In 2016 she was also invited to direct Ibsen's *Hedda Gabler* for a German state theatre near Düsseldorf. Several of her own productions have also transferred abroad.

Kitsopoulou has so far published three collections of short stories: the award-winning *Νυχτερίδες* (*Bats*, 2006), *Μεγάλοι δρόμοι* (*Big Roads*, 2010) and *Το μάτι του ψαριού* (*The Fish's Eye*, 2015b). As their production runs almost parallel to her dramatic writing, they can be viewed as a useful backdrop to her plays, on the one hand reflecting most of her thematic preoccupations and, on the other, indicating her concern for craftsmanship and formal experimentation. The pain of loss (either as physical death or frustrated love), the pressures of conformity in the familial and social environment, repressed drives, violence against women and children, intolerance of the racial or sexual other are some of the themes expressed in her prose narratives, which are initially placed in a suffocating, backward provincial location and gradually move – especially in her third collection – to an urban environment, occasionally identified as the decaying landscape of contemporary Athens, a city in crisis. However, she continues to be attracted by the 'closed provincial communities of deep Greece' (Ioannidis n.d.) where she looks for the key to the enigmatic origins of the Greek folk and pop tradition: its ugliness and its fascination. 'My heart always beats in the provinces; I feel something familiar in the Greek folk landscape, the paper tablecloths, the *tsipouro* drinks and the *bouzouki* sound; I feel I belong to them', she is reported to say in one of the controversial reviews of the production of *Athanasios Diakos*, the play which transfers most graphically to the stage all the pathogenies of 'deep Greece'[7] that are extensively analysed in her narrative prose ('Review of Athanasios Diakos' 2012).

Some of her stories have such a strong grip through the imaginative power and linguistic skill of the narrative that, beyond inspiring the writing of plays on the same lines by Kitsopoulou herself, they have also been adapted for the stage by other directors who have recognised their dramatic appeal. Two stories from her second collection, 'Ο μουνής' ('The Male Cunt') and 'Μεγάλοι δρόμοι' ('Big Roads'), and another two from her third collection, 'Ο καραφλομπέκατσος' ('The Bald Woodcock') and 'Η Σπυριδούλα' ('Spyridoula') have been dramatised for stage presentation.[8]

286   *Elizabeth Sakellaridou*

In 'The Male Cunt', Kitsopoulou keeps repeating the refrain 'what a train that man was'. The image of a puffing train, a full-steam, non-stop train, is the most apt self-reflective comment she could have made about herself; an artist who lives and creates phenomenologically and who declares:

> I think there is something anarchic and automated that is close to me, because that's how I write myself, in flux, without coordinated thinking, more physical. I lose myself in it. Of course afterwards I edit and change things, but there are many things I leave as they were written.
>
> (Kangelari 2017: 257)

It is with such statements that Kitsopoulou provokes the enmity of a number of critics who take her artistic carelessness at face value and her deliberate use of four-letter words as misusing the writer/actor's privilege to stretch the performative dynamic of language dangerously off limits. But it is precisely her incessantly inventive, if irreverent, audacity that has gained her a large group of supporters for carrying the can of artistic iconoclasm and social revolt on behalf of them all.

The hermetic Yannis Mavritsakis

There is something austere in Yannis Mavritsakis's structural form. His mind digs into abyssal depths or soars to vertiginous heights, seeking to break the limitations of human possibilities, struggling to uncover and disturb the universal laws of biophysics and the sociopolitical order that mimics the cosmic order. His imagery, rebellious and chaotic, unleashes uncontrolled powers. However, as an artist he has full control over his material. His own verdict that he *constructs a mechanism that creates life* (Georgiou 2016) is suggestive of his dominant authorial position at the top of his own parallel, mythical universe. His plays have been translated in many languages, have participated in international festivals, including Athens and Avignon, and have been presented as stage readings or as full productions in the US, France, Germany, Italy, Romania, Slovakia, Cyprus, and Turkey. Two of his plays, *Blind Spot* and *Wolfgang*, have won prizes for best play in Greece. *Wolfgang* has also received the French award 'Palmares' in 2010.

The 'lonely wolf' of contemporary Greek theatre is a characteristic label that has been attached to Mavritsakis (Loverdou 2013). As he avoids making a public persona for himself and seldom – if ever – gives interviews, his portrait can only be peripherally drawn, best elucidated by the accounts of the people who have collaborated with him. Born in Montreal, Canada, in 1964, he has lived in Athens since 1970. He is a graduate of the National Theatre Drama School and he pursued an acting career for 18 years (1986–2004). During that time he collaborated with distinguished and innovative stage directors (among them Yannis Kakleas and Stathis Livathinos) and had the opportunity, through a variety of roles, to become familiar with a great number of canonic works (both classic and contemporary) by Euripides, Shakespeare, Ford, Wedekind, Brecht, Bulgakov, Koltès, and others. According to testimony, he had always been writing but not bringing anything to public attention (Kakleas, cited in Loverdou 2013). The year 2004 was a turning point in his artistic career: he suddenly gave up acting in order to devote himself solely to playwriting.

Behind this sketchy portrait there emerges an intriguing personality, seemingly withdrawn but vigilant, observant, and creative. His dramatic work reflects an enigmatic, dark vision of the world: an interest in dreamy situations mixed with extreme nightmares and terror. Tracing the themes of all his plays, it is hard to miss his persistent search for the hidden, the unspeakable, and the unseen, the very vortex of existence in and of the world. In a rare interview on the occasion of the Cypriot production of *Wolfgang* (the play that made his fame as a new playwright), he gave some useful clues concerning the making of his work: 'To live is always an extreme condition [...] I do not narrate. I construct a mechanism that produces life'. To the reviewer's question on his thematic preoccupations he answered enigmatically: 'Of course they are there but I'd rather keep them a secret'. He was equally laconic and evasive to another question concerning his motivation for writing: 'It is a way for me to exist' (Georgiou 2016).

His personal preference for reticence and obscurity is to some extent illuminated by the testimony of his artistic collaborators – mainly directors who have directed him as an actor or his plays for the stage. Olivier Py (former director of the Odéon Theatre in Paris and subsequently director of the Avignon Festival), who directed *Vitrioli* (*Vitriol*, 2013) both in Greece and in France, says of him that 'he is a great contemporary poet' (Loverdou 2013). Katerina Evangelatou (one of the most promising young directors of the Greek stage), who directed *Wolfgang* (2008), draws attention to his linguistic idiolect: elaborate, precise, and very personal. She also recalls his personality as that of 'a secluded and [...] lonely man who kept his distance from the performance' (Loverdou 2013). Earlier collaborators, who had directed him as an actor, focus on his impenetrable personality. Kakleas recalls: 'He has depth. It is as if he crawled into dark holes; as if he wanted to discover something that tormented him' (Loverdou 2013). Livathinos, on the other hand, also recalls his more human side as a 'tender, special, creative, vulnerable and interesting' person (Loverdou 2013). Theatre reviewer Myrto Loverdou, who has collected all the above interviews to make the collage of his portrait, sheds some more positive light to this profile: 'He is strongly politicised and has sensitivities – something that becomes so obvious in his themes: his interest in the injustices of the world, even though his work cannot classify as theatrical realism' (Loverdou 2013).

2017 marked a new turn in Mavritsakis's artistic career. As he disclosed in a conversation with the present writer (2017), after the completion of his as yet unstaged play *Quasar* (2015b), he decided to take time off from writing for the theatre, turning instead to prose writing: to the greater privacy of the room and to the more liberating form of narrative, addressed directly to solitary readers. As a parallel activity to his playwriting, this new phase of experimentation with language (also one of greater retreat from the public eye) does not come as a

288   *Elizabeth Sakellaridou*

surprise from a solitary artist like Mavritsakis, who, even in his early days as an actor, was always poring over the analysis of theatre scripts, always writing something – according to Kakleas's testimony (Loverdou 2013). The very process of his dramatic writing from one play on to the next reveals, apart from the undeniable thematic links, a tendency towards greater depths, a persistent excavation of darker holes into the earth (as in *Vitriol*) or vertiginous flights into the black holes of the universe (as in *Quasar*).

A dramaturgy of darkness

Starting from real-life episodes and situations – the mourning of a beloved husband by a young female bank employee in *Το τυφλό σημείο* (*Blind Spot*, 2008); or the real story of the abduction and underground imprisonment for 10 years of a young Austrian girl in *Wolfgang*; or working under the revolting, behind-the-scenes conditions of a fast-food company in *Κωλοδουλειά* (*Fucking Job*, 2015a) – Mavritsakis gradually moves to greater territorial and temporal abstraction and a greater archetypal shaping for his characters.

Indeed, *Blind Spot* is very much the humane, almost tender story of Niki (the name in Greek means victory), who, being unable to let her deceased love go, lives for a while in a spectral condition (with constant visitations from her dead husband's ghost) – something which destroys her professional and personal life (she is fired from her post at the bank and she cannot enjoy a sexual relationship with a new partner) and ultimately leads her to a willed death (she is run over by a van at a street crossing). The play consists of 21 episodes in which Niki is either juxtaposed to other, realistic characters, all traceable figures in the social conundrum of contemporary city life (a butcher's assistant, a travelling salesman, a female street vendor who might be an immigrant, three violent youths, a young girl – also an immigrant – trapped in the trafficking of women), or made the object of their externalised thoughts. The form chosen is that of a 'panopticon', where the central character becomes in passing the object of all secondary characters' gazes as their existence and different stories brush past hers. From this point of view it can be said that the dramatist develops a psychosocial perspective, which is firmly grounded in epistemological data: either sociological or psychological or a mixture of both. However, Mavritsakis's enquiry goes to deeper, darker corners of life, ethics, and philosophy: the will to death, the desire to kill, and the voyeuristic pleasure of a 'splatter' spectacle (accidental or planned). Among other violent thoughts or acts in the play, Niki herself kills (or may have killed) three men she seduced before letting herself be run over by the van. At this point, the idea of evil starts growing into something beyond the firm grasp of psychosocial explication; it points towards the ungraspable realm of the metaphysical.

The next two plays, *Wolfgang* and *Fucking Job* more or less move in a similar territory, at the border of the psychosocially explicable and the underground realm of suppressed desire and impermissible thought. The guilt of the girl's male abductor in *Wolfgang* is reassessed in the light of his troubled relationship with his parents and the issue of evil is seen as part of contemporary social banality, potentially affecting other characters in his environment, including his own victim, Fabienne, whose feelings fluctuate between submissive love and murderous hate for her kidnapper and seducer. In *Fucking Job* the darkness within gains a more iconic representation. The image used in the previous play, that of digging a hole in the ground to create a hiding place, now becomes the high-tech underground compartment of a fast-food company, where all disgusting elements of meat processing are kept out of sight. Yet this dungeon of animal torture and non-hygienic food processing becomes an aphrodisiac for the robotised employees of the company. Throughout the play, the solitary protagonist, a female second kitchen-assistant, is seen to respond to the off-stage commands of an invisible, mechanised superintendent so that the interaction between the two is carried only on the vocal/aural level. As critic Giorgos Pefanis suggests, *Fucking Job* is built on the Foucauldian technologies of power and surveillance, where individuals are pressed to conform to a dehumanising system of hierarchies, illustrating a dystopia which also bears some more terrifying, Kafkaesque features (Pefanis 2015: 9–10). It is this more alarming aspect of the play that I want to stress because it is this theme of a substratum of darkness (whether a physical terra incognita or the instinctual or phantasmal side of the human) that is further explored in his subsequent plays, taking on almost demonic dimensions.

This becomes obvious in *Vitriol* (Figure 15.1), firstly because the play opens with a discomforting incantation of exorcising evil, an impressive verbal ritual which runs – with several variations – for four consecutive pages:

Figure 15.1 Haris Georgeakis in *Vitriol* by Yannis Mavritsakis directed by Olivier Py (2013). Photograph: Marilena Stafylidou © National Theatre of Greece

290   *Elizabeth Sakellaridou*

In deep sleep,
in sickness,
in laughter or tears of lust,
lecherous,
with desire,
debauchery and poison,
either by chance or sent by someone,
known or unknown,
from an unthinking territory,
get out of him,
now
                    (*Vitriol*: 13, emphasis added)

What is more, an enigmatic Latin epigram before the beginning of the play turns its rather innocuous title into an acronym (V.I.T.R.I.O.L.) of a cryptic invitation to the occult: 'Visita Interiora Terrae Rectificando Invenies Occultum Lapidem' (visit the interior of the earth and rectifying you will find the hidden stone).[9] The more abstract concept of the characters also assists with the creation of a surrealistic atmosphere – half science fiction, half metaphysics. In this, most Faustian of his plays, Mavritsakis makes his central character the ambiguous host of a virus lethal to existing humanity; a dubious visionary who seeks to break human limitations through his own death.

The next three plays, *Μετατόπιση προς το ερυθρό* (*Redshift*, 2014), *Η επίκληση της γοητείας* (*The Invocation of Enchantment*, 2014), and *Quasar* become even more enigmatic in their cosmic wanderings. Moving between biophysics and astrophysics, mixing fantasy and desire, technology and science fiction, they still carry echoes of the pressures, fears, and frustrations of a social reality in crisis. All these elements are transformed into a new vision of chaos and eternity. The very titles of the plays suggest a cosmic awe, a terror of, and a fascination with the unknown secrets of the universe. Also present are the modes of resistance to the indomitable laws that govern our social and biological existence: disruption of the canonising conformity of life; disturbance of the technologies of harmony with the irregularity of desire and the alchemy of love. The most impenetrable of the three plays, *Quasar*, brims with invocations to the dead:

Rise
Your dispersed molecules must recompose the form
Tie your eyes on me
And I'll struggle to pull you up
No drop of spirit must be wasted
Until the powers find their way
Remember the beautiful days
The light by which we were admitted to knighthood
No gods nor demons

Put on the armour I wear
Grasp the sword I hold
Cut off any head that blocks your way
Do not spare it
At the end you will meet me

(Quasar: 18)

The play concludes with a defiance of God and an assertion of the power of love (*Quasar*: 22), an unprecedented lyrical and romantic turn, fairly atypical of his usual style which includes sharp and cynical observation, extreme surrealistic images, strong (sometimes even offensive) language, violence and atrocity, and dark humour. *The Invocation of Enchantment* is, in my view, much more representative of the progress of his thematic and aesthetic experimentation and it is with this that I want to conclude.

The play focuses on the nature of evil and the tendency of humanity to either hush the unpleasant or demonise evil rather than engaging with them in a pragmatic encounter. Although the issue is placed in a narrow domestic situation in a suburban setting (a nuclear family consisting of father, mother, daughter, and faithful dog), it gradually gains cosmic proportions, with each member of the family being separately persecuted by a seductive but menacing figure of a different form (a Passer-by for the Mother, a Man for the Daughter, a Trainer for the Father, a Flying Beast for the Dog). As the play unfolds, we witness a process of what Megson describes as 're-enchantment of the world' (2013). Combining Megson's philosophical argument with the sociological stance of Frank Furedi in *Culture of Fear* and the more specifically Greek-oriented analysis of Tsoukalas in *Greece of Oblivion and Truth*, I would like to argue that Mavritsakis creates a two-fold perspective on this recent phenomenon. On the one hand, he renders a poetic version of the irrational fascination of the unknown (the fear of which leads to zoomorphism and demonisation), and on the other, he uncovers the technologies of power behind the insidious methods of charm and oblique terrorisation.

At the crossroads of culture and crisis

In this discussion of Kitsipoulou's and Mavritsakis's theatrical work, I have deliberately refrained from direct comparisons between the two and rather opted to give my parallel study of their work a more global perspective since both writers are in conversation with other cultures and wider issues and concerns that are both topical and diachronic, but traverse the limited space of Greek locality. If I were to attempt a final comparative statement on two diametrically opposite artistic idiosyncrasies, I would venture to say that they both respond to the multiple crises of our age and to perennial human experience in a very particular way, which, in a sense, interestingly corresponds to the eccentric patterns set by contemporary Greek 'weird wave' cinema.[10] Kitsopoulou performs all the neuroses of social and personal crisis in an existential

292 *Elizabeth Sakellaridou*

way, interacting with the audience in a raw, affective manner. Mavritsakis chooses a more meditative approach – one which distils social anger and existential despair into a more contained and restrained artistic form. His method of looking at the world is poetically laid out through his shadowy mouthpiece in *Quasar*: 'Then I might have the opportunity to change my abode, to move to the next stage, the less gross, the more refined, the one that [only] the insightful and the inspired talk about' (2015b: 11). Kitsopoulou is the vibrant body and the loud voice, the provocative physical presence who places herself centre stage; Mavritsakis is the persisting, haunting shadow behind the backdrop and in the wings.

Lena Kitsopolou – four key productions

M.A.I.R.O.U.L.A. Co-directed by Lena Kitsopoulou and Maria Protopappa. Set and costume design by Elli Papageorgakopoulou. Music design by Lena Kitsopoulou and Maria Protopappa. Performer: Maria Protopappa. National Theatre production, Synchrono Theatre, Athens, 27 March 2009.

Athanasios Diakos – The Return. Directed by Lena Kitsopoulou. Set and costume design by M. Avgerinou. Cast: Nikos Karathanos, Yannis Kotsifas, Yannos Perlengas, Emily Koliandri, Ioanna Mavrea, Lena Kitsopoulou. Greek Festival, Venue: Peiraios 260, Athens, 14 July 2012.

Little Red Riding Hood or The First Blood. Directed by Lena Kitsopoulou. Set and costume design by Elli Papageorgakopoulou. Lighting design by Nikos Vlassopoulos. Music by Nikos Kypourgos. Production management: Polyplanity Productions/Yolanta Markopoulou. Cast: Yannis Kotsifas, Ioanna Mavrea, Yannos Perlengas, Emily Koliandri, Nefeli Maistrali, Lena Kitsopoulou. Onassis Cultural Centre Stegi, Athens, 14 May 2014.

Antigone – Lonely Planet. Directed by Lena Kitsopoulou. Set and costume design by Elli Papageorgakopoulou. Lighting design by Nikos Vlassopoulos. Video: Angelos Papadopoulos. Sound design: Kostas Bokos. Assistant director: Marilena Moschou. Cast: Lena Kitsopoulou, Sofia Kokkali, Andreas Kontopoulos, Yannis Tsortekis, Petros Georgopalos, Nikoleta Grimeki, Vasilis Safos. Production management: Polyplanity Productions/Yolanta Markopoulou and Vicky Strataki. Onassis Cultural Centre Stegi, Athens, 14 December 2017.

Yannis Mavritsakis – four key productions

Wolfgang. Directed by Katerina Evangelatou. Set and costume design by Konstantinos Zamanis. Music design by Stavros Gasparatos. Lighting by Melina Mascha. Cast: Vasilis Andreou, Loukia Michalakopoulou, Sotiris Tsakomidis, Nikolaos Angelis, Maria Zorba, Manos Vakousis, Serafita Grigoriadou. National Theatre, Athens, 7 November 2008.

Vitriol. Directed by Olivier Py. Set and costume design by Pierre-Andre Weitz. Lighting by Bertrand Killy. Cast: Maria Kehagioglou, Haris Georgeakis,

Periklis Moustakis, Kitty Paitazolgou, Yannos Perlengas, Dimitris Lalos, Minas Hatzisavvas, Nikos Hatzopoulos. National Theatre, Athens, 20 March 2013.

Blind Spot. Romanian translation by Elena Iazar. Directed by Radu Afrim. Set design by Adrian Damian. Costume design by Claudia Castrase. Cast: Ada Simionica, Ioan Coman, Clara Flores, Christian Popa, Bogdan Farcas, Mihaela Popa, Karl Baker, Ionut Visan, Andrei Ciopec, Robert Oprea, Ioana Farcas, Andrei Radu, Razvan Baltaretu, Ionut Manea, and the dog Freyja. Toma Caragiu Theatre, Ploesti, Romania, 28 February 2016.

The Invocation of Enchantment. Directed by Roula Pateraki. Set and costume design by Angelos Mentis. Lighting by Roula Peteraki. Assistant director: Evanthia Kourmouli. Cast: Maria Zorba, Nikos Mavrakis, Kostas Serifis, Eleftheria Konstantopoulou, Alexis Diamantis, Spyros Varelis, Thanasis Dovris, Tsimaras Tzanatos, Marina Saini. Small wind ensemble: Thanos Hatzopoulos, Poly Thanou, Savvas Athanasiadis. Roes Theatre, Athens, 30 May 2018.

Notes

1 Markaris talks about the 'vampires' of the Greek political unconscious (Matsiori 2018). More dramatically, Tsoukalas refers to the 'perennial ghosts which continue to persecute us' (2012: 32).

2 The published Greek text is in the form of an almost non-stop, breathless prose monologue. The stage script has been enriched with very few stage directions and was used only for the specific National Theatre production of March 2009. The published English translation was the initiative of actress Aliki Chapple for her own performance of the monologue with the Lancaster-based theatre company Sturgeon's Law in 2013. In her translation note she explains that she has edited and occasionally rewritten the original text for the sake of greater orality and cultural clarity in the English language.

3 The play was performed in Greek with French surtitles.

4 My reference is to the 1821–30 Greek War of Independence from a 400-year Ottoman occupation, in which Athanasios Diakos played a crucial role first as a heroic fighter and subsequently as a national martyr, as a result of his execution by impalement after his arrest by the Ottoman army.

5 Critic Lina Rosi aptly describes Kitsopoulou's work as 'replete with visual, aural and physical *cacophony*' (Rosi, 2017, p. 189, emphasis added).

6 The concept/image of a 'cry' is repeatedly attached to Kitsopoulou's work. Apart from her conscious use of the term as a title for her recent play *Cry*, it is also to be found in the criticism written about her. For instance, Yannis Moschos concludes his review of the production of her *Μια μέρα όπως κάθε άλλη μέρα…* (*One Day as Any Other Day…*, 2015a) with an interesting comment on the play's affective impact on the audience as 'a constructive burden deriving from the unbearable lightness [of being]', which he identifies as a 'cry' (Moschos 2015). Another reviewer gives a very apt summary of Kitsopoulou's artistic personality as 'a *cry* that can be contained in a poem' (Harami 2018, emphasis added).

7 This expression hints at the parochial, insular attitudes of a certain section of Greek society which stubbornly sticks to the past, denies cultural hybridity, and refuses its own modernisation.

8 *The Male Cunt* was staged at the Neos Kosmos theatre in October 2013. *Big Roads* was staged at the same theatre in January 2015. *The Bald Woodcock* and *Spyridoula* were presented in a double bill at the Stathmos theatre in February 2018.

294 *Elizabeth Sakellaridou*

9 The motto originates in *L' Azoth des Philosophes* by the fifteenth-century alchemist Basilius Valentinus.
10 This is a branch of the 'new wave' Greek cinema. It took its nickname 'weird' because of its unusual narrative and characters, both reflecting the current state of chaos and instability of the country under the stress of a prolonged socio-economic crisis. The best internationally known name in this group of directors is Yorgos Lanthimos.

Works cited

Beckett, Samuel (1984) *Not I*, in *Collected Shorter Plays*, London and Boston: Faber, pp. 213–223.

Bekri, Magdalini (2014) 'Interview with Lena Kitsopoulou', in *Γυναικείος λόγος, μονολογικά κείμενα: Το παράδειγμα της Μαργαρίτας Καραπάνου* (Female Discourse, Monological Texts: The Case of Margarita Karapanou). MA thesis submitted to the University of West Macedonia, Department of Paedagogics, 1 June, pp. 120–125.

Crimp, Martin (1997) *Attempts on Her Life*, London and Boston: Faber.

Furedi, Frank (2006) *Culture of Fear Revisited*, 2nd edition, London: Bloomsbury.

Georgiou, Antonis (2016) 'Interview with Yannis Mavritsakis', *Dialogos*, 13 November, https://dialogos.com.cy/giannis-mavritsakis-to-na-zis-ine-pantote-mia-akrea -sinthiki/

Hager, Philip and Marissia Fragkou (eds), (2017) *Journal of Greek Media and Culture*, 3(2), Special Issue: Dramaturgies of Change: Greek Theatre Now.

Handke, Peter (1971) *Offending the Audience*, in *Offending the Audience and Self-Accusation*, trans. Michael Roloff, London: Methuen, pp. 8–39.

Harami, Stella (2018) Interview with Lena Kitsopoulou, *Monopoli.gr*. 12 December, https:// www.monopoli.gr/2018/12/12/people/288441/lena-kitsopoulou-den-niotho-ksexor isti-niotho-fysiologiki%C2%B7-aplos-to-fysiologiko-isos-na-einai-telika-ksexoristo/

Ioannidis, Grigoris (n.d.) 'Lena Kitsopoulou's dramaturgy', *The Greek Play Project*, http:// www.greek-theatre.gr/public.gr/greekplay/index/reviewview/6

Kaltaki, Matina (2018) 'The art of theatre (a review: Part One)', *Kathimerini on Sunday*, Arts Section, 20 May, 10.

Kane, Sarah (1996) *Blasted*, in *Blasted and Phaedra's Love*, London: Methuen, pp. 1–58.
——— (1998) *Cleansed*. London: Methuen.

Kangelari, Dio (2017) 'A conversation between Lena Kitsopoulou and Dio Kangelari', *Journal of Greek Media and Culture*, 3(2): 253–258.

Kitsopoulou, Lena (2006) *Bats*, Athens: Kedros.
——— (2007). *Remember the Sabbath Day and Keep It Holy*, Typescript held by the author.
——— (2008) *My Green Dress*, Typescript held by the author.
——— (2009). *M.A.I.R.O.U.L.A*, Athens: Kedros.
——— (2010) *Big Roads*, Athens: Metaichmio.
——— (2012a) *Athanasios Diakos or The Return*, Typescript held by the author.
——— (2012b) *Austras or The Weed*, Typescript held by the author.
——— (2012c). *N-EURO-SE*, Typescript held by the author.
——— (2012d) *The Price*, Typescript held by the author
——— (2014) *Red Riding Hood or The First Blood*, Typescript held by the author.
——— (2015a). *A Day Like Any Other Day...*, Typescript held by the author.
——— (2015b). *The Fish's Eye*, Athens: Metaichmio.

—— (2016) *Antigone – Lonely Planet*, Typescript held by the author.

—— (2017) *Tyrannosaurus Rex*, Typescript held by the author.

—— (2018). *Cry*, Typescript held by the author.

Kondylaki, Dimitra (2014) 'The "Polis" and the "Political" in contemporary Greek drama since the eruption of the Greek crisis: a first appraisal (2009–2015)', *Gramma* 22(2): 61–72.

Loverdou, Myrto (2013) 'Yannis Mavritsakis: The "lonely wolf" of the theatre', *To Vima online*, 10 February, http://www.tovima.gr/culture/article/?aid=497216

Matsiori, Lena (2018) 'We live with our ghosts', Interview with Petros Markaris. *Kathimerini on Sunday*, Arts Section, 18 March: 4.

Mavritsakis, Yannis (2008, 2014) *Blind Spot*, Athens: Nefeli (2008); Odos Panos (2014).

—— (2008, 2016) *Wolfgang*, Athens: Nefeli (2008); Sokoli (2016).

—— (2013) *Vitriol*, Athens: Odos Panos.

—— (2014) *Redshift*, Athens: Odos Panos.

—— (2015a) *Fucking Job*, Athens: Mov Skiouros.

—— (2015b) *Quasar*, Manuscript held by the author.

—— (2018) *The Invocation of Enchantment*, Athens: Mov Skiouros.

Megson, Chris (2013) '"And I was struck still by time": Contemporary British theatre and the metaphysical imagination', in Vicky Angelaki (ed.), *Contemporary British Theatre: Breaking New Ground*. Basingstoke: Palgrave/Macmillan, pp. 32–56.

—— (2016) 'Beyond belief: British theatre and the re-enchantment of the world', Siân Adiseshiah and Louise LePage (eds), *Twenty-First Century Drama: What Happens Now?* London: Palgrave/Macmillan, pp. 37–57.

Moschos, Yannis (2015) 'Review of Kitsopoulou's One Day As Any Other Day…', https://www.clickatlife.gr/theatro/story/50518

The Oberon Anthology of Contemporary Greek Plays (2017) London: Oberon.

Patsalidis, Savas and Anna Stavrakopoulou (eds), (2014) *Gramma*, 22(2), Special Issue: The Geographies of Contemporary Greek Theatre: About Utopias, Dystopias and Heterotopias.

Pefanis, Yiorgos (2015) Introduction to Yannis Mavritsakis, *Fucking Job*, Athens: Mov Skiouros, pp. 7–16.

Ravenhill, Mark (1996) *Shopping and Fucking*, London: Methuen.

'Review of Athanasios Diakos and interview with Lena Kitsopoulou' (2012) *Proto Thema* 4 September, http://www.protothema.gr/culture/theater/article/220730/ebgalan-soyblatzh_-kerata-syzygoktono-ton-athanasio-diako/

Rosi, Lina (2014) 'The diverse landscape of contemporary Greek playwriting'. *Gramma*, Special Issue on Contemporary Greek Theatre, 22(2): 19–36.

—— (2017) 'Cartographies of gender in contemporary Greek theatre: a work in progress?' *Journal of Greek Media and Culture*, 3(2): 177–193.

Sakellaridou, Elizabeth (2017) Conversation with Yannis Mavritsakis, Ianos Bookstore, Athens, 14 November.

Tsoukalas, Constantinos (2012) *Greece of Oblivion and Truth: From a Prolonged Adolescence to a Violent Maturation*, Athens: Themelio.

16 Emma Dante and Fausto Paravidino

Families, national identity, and international audiences

Margherita Laera

This chapter investigates the work of two Italian dramatists, actors and directors, Emma Dante and Fausto Paravidino. Since the early 2000s, when their careers began, Dante and Paravidino have both enjoyed considerable national and international acclaim, but the mode in which spectators have experienced their work abroad has been significantly different: while Paravidino's plays have been translated into foreign languages and staged with local casts, Dante's productions have toured untranslated, with their original Italian performers, mostly accompanied by surtitles. Both authors also routinely direct, and sometimes perform, their own scripts, following that distinctively Italian tradition that has more often produced actor-authors than 'pure' playwrights (Fischer 2013; Barsotti in Valentini 2015: 249–89).[1] Paravidino is one of very few living Italian dramatists to be known in Britain, thanks to his work with London's National and Royal Court Theatres. His plays have been seen throughout Europe and beyond and have been translated into 12 languages. Dante, on the other hand, has only rarely toured to the UK, but her theatre productions have travelled extensively to continental Europe, North and South America, and Asia.

Both theatre-makers dissect aspects of contemporary Italian culture in their writing, often focusing on dysfunctional family relations, the pervasiveness of sexism and other forms of discrimination, and the intimate effects of politics and economies. These similarities might suggest that Dante and Paravidino depict similar characters and stories, but nothing could be further from the truth. The world of Paravidino is that of the urban and suburban Europe-facing North of Italy where people speak current standard Italian, and his stories could be easily relocated anywhere in Europe or in the western world; on the contrary, Dante's characters are inspired by the marginalised inhabitants of the rural, desolate, and destitute areas of the South, especially Sicily, where only or mostly local dialects are spoken. The rest of Italy, let alone the European continent, is framed as a distant, unknown land that has forgotten them. There is a certain cosmopolitanism in the writing of Paravidino, and a marked localism in Dante's work, albeit one that aspires to 'universality'. Paravidino's characters are citizens of the world, while Dante's characters are citizens of a metaphorical Palermo, seen as the city by antonomasia, a metonymy for every other city in the world. In what follows, I assess some of their most significant plays and

The theatres of Emma Dante and Fausto Paravidino

Emma Dante was born in Palermo in 1967 but spent much of her early life in Catania. In the mid-1980s she moved to Rome to attend the Accademia d'Arte Drammatica Silvio D'Amico, graduating in 1990. In 1999 she founded the Compagnia Sud Costa Occidentale, with which she came to national and international attention, winning the prestigious Premio Scenario (2001) and Premio Ubu (2002) for her production *mPalermu* (*In Palermo*), which toured internationally across Europe. The two following productions – *Carnezzeria* (*Butchery*, 2002), which also won a Premio Ubu, and *Vita mia* (*My Life*, 2004) – focus on family matters, and together with *In Palermo* became known as the *Trilogia della famiglia siciliana* (*Trilogy of the Sicilian family*). Written in a Palermitan dialect interspersed with standard Italian, the trilogy explores three local family situations that weave the comic with the tragic and the grotesque. The productions travelled extensively as separate performances in Italy and abroad, reaching about 20 countries between 2001 and 2009.

Dante's work came to the attention of Cardinal Bertone, the Vatican's Secretary of State, who threatened to excommunicate spectators of Dante's production *La scimia* (*The Monkey*, 2004) because he had read that, amongst other blasphemous actions, an actor in the show would repeatedly scratch his testicles with a crucifix. Dante has denied any intention to desecrate the cross, preferring instead for her work to be labelled 'old-fashioned, universal, timeless' (2017a). While *The Monkey* saw an abrupt end to its tour as no venue dared to host it, Dante's subsequent productions, such as *Cani di Bancata* (*Parasite Dogs*, 2006), about the religion-infused rituals of the mafia and its family-inspired system of kinship and belonging, and *Le Pulle* (*The Whores*, 2009), about the dreams of five prostitutes, have continued to tour throughout Italy, France, Switzerland, Belgium, and Germany. In 2009, Dante inaugurated the opera season at Milan's La Scala with her version of Bizet's *Carmen*, conducted by Daniel Barenboim, and has subsequently staged numerous other operas, such as Auber's *La muette de Portici* (*The Mute Girl of Portici*) at the Opéra Comique (2012) and Verdi's *Macbeth* in Turin's Teatro Regio (2017), which also toured to the Edinburgh International Festival.

After turning to Greek tragedy with an adaptation of Euripides, *Verso Medea* (*Towards Medea*, 2014), presented at the Teatro Olimpico in Vicenza, in 2014 Dante was appointed Artistic Director of Palermo's Teatro Biondo and its drama academy, while her production *Le sorelle Macaluso* (*The Macaluso Sisters*) was co-produced by Naples' Teatro Mercadante, the Festival d'Avignon, Volktheatern Göteborg, and Brussels' Théâtre National, touring to 17 countries (and still touring in 2020 at the time of writing). Dante is also the author of a novel, *Via Castellana Bandiera* (*Castellana Bandiera Street*, 2008), and of several

298   *Margherita Laera*

children's books, such as *Gli alti e bassi di Biancaneve* (*The Highs and Lows of Snow White*, 2012). Although Dante is best known for her directorial and playwriting work, she still often performs, for instance in her recent production inspired by the *Odyssey*, entitled *Io, Nessuno e Polifemo* (*I, No-one and Polyphemus*, 2014) and in *White Rabbit Red Rabbit* by Nassim Soleimanpour, which she staged at the Teatro Biondo in Palermo in 2017.

Dante is notorious for being extremely demanding and meticulous and for her heated manner in rehearsals; her unsparing training method has prompted many to leave the company over the years. Through her ensemble work with a group of trusted actors, she explores the misery, foolishness, and dignity of human beings through the lens of Sicily, without ever talking about Sicily in an explicit way. Her stories – performed through spoken word, choreographed movement, and crossing genre boundaries – feature a hallucinating blend of the living and the dead, reality and desires, exploring themes that Dante sees as common to all. Her brand of 'poor theatre', anchored on the movement and symbolism of actors' bodies, has often been compared to the *tanztheater* of Pina Bausch and Tadeusz Kantor's theatre of death (Porcheddu 2010: 107, 124, 128–9; Dante 2016: 16, 20). Her dramaturgy is primarily one of the body and its articulations, and only secondly one of text.

Fausto Paravidino was born in Genoa in 1976 but grew up in a small provincial town, Rocca Grimalda, near Alessandria, in the north of Italy. He attended the Academy of Dramatic Art in Genoa but dropped out to move to Rome and establish his own company with some classmates. At the age of 23, Paravidino won the prestigious Tondelli award for Best Play with *Due fratelli – tragedia da camera in 53 giorni* (*Two Brothers – Chamber Tragedy in 53 Days*, 1999) and in 2001 his production of the play won a Premio Ubu. In the same year, Paravidino wrote one of his most successful plays, *Natura morta in un fosso* (*Still Life in a Ditch*), about the murder of a young woman, which had its debut in Milan, then went on to be staged in Catalan, French, German, and Portuguese; it is often revived.

Paravidino was selected to take part in an international residency at the Royal Court Theatre with *La malattia della famiglia M* (*The M Family Illness*, 2001), which is about incommunicability among family members. The play was then translated for productions in French, German, Polish, and Romanian (in the latter it was directed by Radu Afrim at the Timişoara National Theatre in 2008, then toured to Paris). Paravidino's London experience resulted in two commissions: the first from the National Theatre Connections festival, for which he wrote *Noccioline* (*Peanuts*, 2002), a metaphorical investigation of socio-political issues through the interactions of a group of youngsters; and the second from the Royal Court itself, for which he wrote *Genova 01* (*Genoa 01*), a text made of interlocking voices about the death of Carlo Giuliani and the treatment of anti-globalisation protesters at the 2001 G8 Summit in Genoa, directed by Simon McBurney.[2]

Il diario di Mariapia (*Mariapia's Journal*), a play staging Paravidino's mother's last days before she died of cancer, premiered as a reading at Stockholm's Dramaten Theatre in 2010, and then was translated for productions in German and French. Meanwhile, in Rome, the Teatro Valle, one of the oldest modern

Emma Dante and Fausto Paravidino   299

theatres in the city, was closed down by the Italian authorities and later occupied by some of its former employees in 2011, who objected to the plans for its privatisation. Paravidino was invited to lead playwriting workshops as part of the occupied theatre's activities to re-imagine a new, bottom-up type of cultural institution serving the people. Out of this experience came *Il macello di Giobbe* (*Giobbe's Butchery*, 2014), an allegorical play with Biblical resonances about the private consequences of the financial crisis on an Italian butcher and his family, produced by Rome's Teatro Valle Occupato and directed by Paravidino himself, which opened at Brussels' Bozar Theatre. He has continued to stage his own texts and to work internationally in the US, UK, and France. In 2018, unusually for Italy, Paravidino was appointed Resident Dramaturg by the Turin Teatro Stabile. Paravidino's vision for this role is to make the venue a writers' theatre, almost an Italian Royal Court (Paravidino 2018).

In Paravidino's plays, the private is explored for its political dimensions, and the political is exposed for its reverberations in the private sphere. A son of two physicians, Paravidino is a keen observer of human illness and psychology. His characters are often afflicted by hypochondria or actual diseases – curable or incurable, congenital, acquired or psychosomatic – whose causes Paravidino traces back to urgent political issues in our society, such as the material conditions in which personal interactions take place in late capitalism and during the financial crisis.

Dante's families: love, death, and tragedy

Despite not originally being conceived as a three-part work, the *Trilogy of the Sicilian Family* was retrospectively labelled as such by Dante when it became apparent that the first three nationally and internationally successful productions presented by the Compagnia Sud Costa Occidentale were all about relationships between Palermitan-speaking mothers, fathers, children, siblings, and other relatives. Despite the title mentioning a 'Sicilian family', Dante insists we should understand the word 'Siciliana' as if it were a surname, much like Paravidino's 'famiglia M'. The problematic gender politics in the *Trilogy* denounces, yet is fully embedded in, the abusive and casual sexism plaguing what was then Berlusconi's Italy.

The first episode, *mPalermu*, sees five members of an extended, destitute family, the Carollos, trying to leave the house to go for a Sunday stroll in the city centre, and failing to do so. Each member of the family – from the elderly granny, nonna Citta, to the authoritarian grandson, Mimmo – is preparing to walk out, each holding a freshly baked Sicilian *pasticcino* (pastry) wrapped up in patisserie paper and bow, but one reason or another makes it impossible for them to leave the apartment. Firstly, Rosalia, wife of Alfonso – who is not in the play because he works 'up North' – is still wearing her slippers and the others would not allow her to go out looking so scruffy. The family also protest that Mimmo's trousers are too short and tight, causing a minor argument between Mimmo and Giammarco, a distant relative. Nonna Citta further delays the stroll by insisting that the Church in the little-known town of Pollena Trocchia is bigger than the Palermo Cathedral – a statement that Mimmo cannot tolerate. At one point the relatives find themselves

300 *Margherita Laera*

playing football while leaving their *pasticcini* on the floor, but another quarrel breaks out between Mimmo and Giammarco about whose pastry this or that parcel contains, and whether the profiterole is filled with chocolate- or coffee-flavoured custard cream. The conversation casually moves from banter to insult, from tender remark to sexist commentary, but then the Garollos quickly gather all in line again and start unwrapping their *pasticcini* – two profiteroles, a cassata, a cannolo, and a croissant – only for the parasite Giammarco (played by Sabino Civilleri) to devour everyone else's pastry in a matter of seconds, concluding his exploit with the words: 'I'm thirsty'. Despite the extreme drought and water-rationing measures in place in Palermo, the characters start playing with water, spitting it and throwing it in each other's face. The most memorable moment in the production – which I attended in Milan in 2002 at the height of Berlusconi's second time in office – is when, as if in a miracle, the water supply becomes endless and the characters get entirely soaked. Still determined to leave, Mimmo, Giammarco, Rosalia, and Zia Lucia line up by the door, but Granny Citta is missing. She collapses on the floor and breathes her last breath there and then, preventing everyone from leaving the house once and for all.

In this piece, each character is inextricable from his or her own way of speaking and gesticulating, and their gestural and linguistic mannerisms provoke much of the laughter. The production was created in Palermo over a year's worth of workshops and improvisations with the Sicilian cast – including long-term fellow-Sicilian collaborators Manuela Lo Sicco, Sabino Civilleri, and Gaetano Bruno – distilled by Dante after rehearsals into a script. The distinctive combination of the Palermitan dialect, supplemented by the actors' body language and gesticulation, roots the piece to Dante's home city, which she conceptualises as a metaphor of immobility. In an interview with critic Andrea Porcheddu, Dante referred to *In Palermo*'s first foray into continental Italy as a trip 'to see what foreigners would make of this language' (2010: 56). This piece exposes Palermitan tropes, distortions, and injustices in the manner of dream-like, grotesque sequences through a distillation of the city's local parlance. Dante's Palermitan is a rather distinctive language, as she puts it, 'adapted and reinvented for theatrical writing: not a simple verbal instrument, but an element that loyally represents the actors' physicality' and developed in collaboration with her ensemble (2017b).[3] The group paralysis, almost a kind of imprisonment, is only too symbolic of the geographical and cultural confinement of Sicily, which is both removed from the seats of power in continental Italy and Northern Europe and deprived of opportunity. It is also an acute metaphor of Italy's political situation, of a country stuck – even as I write, nearly 20 years after the play's premiere – in the quicksand of corruption and collusion with organised crime. To me, the play's characters – vainly concerned with their appearance, purposelessly passing time and seeking moments of subversive celebration while failing to 'get out' – symbolised the generation of young Italians – of which I was part – who had grown up in a stagnant economy while dreaming to go elsewhere. But it was also a powerful parable of the human condition and theatre itself – a liminal state between life and death, where characters wait for something to happen that never does, with echoes of Beckett's *Waiting for Godot*.

In the second episode, *Butchery* – written in standard Italian with strong dialect inflections – the relationship between three brothers and their sister is manipulative, vicious, and abusive – almost unbearable to watch. It is Nina's wedding day: she is nine months pregnant and single, and her three brothers, Paride, Toruccio, and Ignazio, have organised her marriage to a man she has never met – and who will never turn up – in order to remove the stain of dishonour from the family. Nina is only partly aware of her fate, day-dreaming of a handsome man who will love her and take care of her child. Towards the end of the play, resulting from the abuse of her brothers, Nina becomes delirious and eventually kills herself on the altar. This is a tragedy with all its most topical components – family, love, incest, and suicide – with the addition of brutality, sexism, and homophobia. *Butchery* arguably condenses, distils, and denounces some of the horrors of what Dante calls a 'Mafia-like' manner of conducting oneself – a moral code that breeds and supports the flourishing of Mafia in her native region. The final episode, *Vita Mia*, then concludes with a mother preparing for the funeral wake of one of her three sons.

Although the three productions oscillate between the ridiculous and the regretful, between the entertaining and the traumatic, behind every laugh there is a Pirandellian twist that uncovers an inescapable catastrophe. A tragic death concludes each episode: in *In Palermo*, the matriarch's passing inexorably condemns the family to its paralysis; in *Butchery*, suicide is the only way out for Nina; and in *My Life*, a mother can only defer the tragic, accidental death of her son for the time that she is on stage – the end of the play coincides with the end of her life, and that of her other two children. The *Trilogy* still remains a defining moment in Dante's career, with the episodes traveling to at least 32 cities in Europe and internationally, not counting the Italian tour.

Hailed by some critics as the fourth instalment of the *Trilogy, The Macaluso Sisters* focuses on a reunion of seven sisters and their parents, blending past and present, in which long-buried tragedies and resentments flare up, leading up to the final revelation that the family reunion is actually the funeral of one of the sisters. The plotless dramaturgy of this play hinges on the rhythmic exchanges in Palermitan and Apulian dialects from Bari (spoken by one of the sisters, Katia), rather than on well-rounded characters, and is interspersed with group choreographic movements and exaggerated facial expressions. Subtitled *Una liturgia familiare: Balletto della vita e della morte* (*A Family Liturgy: Ballet of Life and Death*) in its published book form, *The Macaluso Sisters* is both a ritual lamentation and the realisation of Dante's most cherished desire to meet her dead mother and brother again. Co-produced by Italian, Belgian, French, and German venues, the show has so far travelled to 17 countries in Europe and beyond – including Spain, Portugal, Romania, Sweden, Serbia, Belarus, Russia, Mexico, US, and Brazil – and is soon to be turned into a film.

Dante's Palermitan-speaking families may rely on their encounters with 'foreigners' in order to come to life, but she insists she could never imagine giving away the translation and performing rights to other international directors. Therefore, surtitles have become the precondition of her international career's

302 *Margherita Laera*

existence, and yet there is so much that surtitles cannot convey in a different language. It is in the allure of the mysterious, inaccessible world of the 'Sicilian family' that the key to Dante's success can be found.

Paravidino's families: between illness and delusion

Paravidino's early play on family relationships, *Two Brothers*, encapsulates the themes of much of his later work. *Two Brothers* is a dark comedy about siblings Lev and Boris, who share a flat with an outgoing, flirtatious girl called Erika. She is supposedly going out with Lev, who is madly in love with her, but she soon makes it clear that she does not love him. This prompts Lev to leave town, and Boris, who suffers from obsessive-compulsive disorder, to fantasise about a relationship with Erika. Meanwhile, Lev and Boris exchange letters with their parents who live in a different city, making up an illusory life for their benefit. Miscommunication between the brothers motivates Lev to come back and kill Erika in order to 'protect' himself and his mentally ill brother. The play ends with the two brothers writing to their parents, promising to drive home in their shiny new car accompanied by their girlfriends. The gap between reality and delusion grows too large and becomes a vortex of psychological malaise. In the first staging of the play, directed by Filippo Dini in Bolzano, the action took place in a green kitchen, designed by Laura Benzi, and Paravidino played Lev. The production won major Italian accolades, and critics hailed it as an accomplished Pinteresque comedy, hinging on a few concise sentences and much unspoken content. *Two Brothers* was subsequently staged in German at the Cologne Schauspiel in 2003, and in Portuguese by the contemporary playwriting company Artistas Unidos in 2004.

The M Family Illness stages another family unit – an elderly Father with Alzheimer's, his three children Maria, Marta, and Gianni, and Maria's boyfriends Fulvio and Fabrizio – falling apart because of a shared disease, namely the inability to communicate with one another. Doctor Cristofolini, the local physician, is the narrator of the play. The central, comical scene – a perfectly constructed vaudevillian situation in the manner of Georges Feydeau or Eugène Labiche – revolves around a case of mistaken identity during a Sunday lunch at the family house, when Luigi and Marta have extended the invitation to Fulvio for the first time, not knowing that they have in fact invited Fabrizio. However, the play quickly shifts genre when Gianni dies of a brain injury following a car accident. This sudden bereavement, along with years of unspoken resentment, persuades the two sisters to leave their home town. Heading in different directions, they abandon their father in an elderly care home.

Paravidino's depiction of dysfunctional family relations is a powerful commentary on what philosopher and sociologist Zygmunt Bauman (2000) has called 'liquid modernity' – whereby under the condition of uncertainty in late capitalism, subjects are fragmentary and fluid, unable to take full responsibility for their actions, drifting instead into constant anxiety and dissatisfaction. This is also a nod to Chekhov's characters' desire to always be elsewhere. Paravidino explained that the play is concerned with the 'extended suburbs of the West', namely those provincial towns, once connected to farming and nature, where half of Europe's populations now live, mostly wishing they lived in larger, more exciting capital cities (2011). *The M Family Illness* is about people who do not feel they belong in the urbanised countryside and who no longer have any connection with nature, having grown up shopping at local supermarkets, watching *Star Wars* and Disney films. This rift between provincial and mainstream culture causes unease when suburban dwellers feel no sense of belonging and, consequently, no longer fully engage with those around them.

In 2008, the play was translated into Romanian for a production directed by Radu Afrim at the Timişoara National Theatre (Figure 16.1), which toured to Paris's Odéon Theatre. The Romanian version took place in a non-conventional space, a large disused royal manège in the city centre, with very high ceilings and large windows, which gave the production a site-specific feel. Velica Panduru's set design imagined the action to take place in a surreal location, interweaving the woods – short, leafless trees scattered around the stage area and red leaves and moss covering much of the floor – with the interior of a house, a dining table with chairs, a bed, and a bath tub. The Romanian production filled the intentional gaps and silences in Paravidino's writing, featuring a rich visual and sound landscape

Figure 16.1 The *M Family Illness* (*Boala Familiei M*), by Fausto Paravidino, directed by Radu Afrim. Claudia Ieremia as Marta and Malina Manovici as Maria. Teatrul National Timişoara, 2008. © Radu Afrim

304   *Margherita Laera*

with extended use of colours, movements across the large stage, change of lights, and a selection of pop songs played at key moments. The actors displayed a marked physicality, often adding symbolic actions, like having a bath, smoking, riding a bike across the woods, and singing (notably a group performance of the famous 1960s Italian song 'Una lacrima sul viso' by Bobby Solo) where the script had not specified any. The production by Afrim transposed a bare, sometimes austere script into a vivid, sumptuous performance tapping into the tradition of physical acting reminiscent of Jerzy Grotowski. Paravidino, who attended the performance, commented: 'This was an excellent show, but a terrible staging of my play'. Specifically, Paravidino objected to the ease, naturalness, and even 'joy' with which the Romanian actors seemed to communicate with one another: 'In watching it, I didn't see what "illness" we were actually talking about' (Paravidino 2018).

Paravidino's 2011 staging for the Comédie Française was, by comparison, restrained and unadorned. Laura Benzi's small circular set for the Vieux Colombier also merged the interior of the M family house with the rural exterior, covering the floor with fallen autumn leaves and planting a tree trunk next to the living/dining room. Through an open door at the back of the set, spectators could see a long corridor 'leading to the family mystery, a place both tender and horrible' (Paravidino 2011: 5), symbolising the unspoken rift between the characters, but also the repressed suicide of the mother. The French actors in the production were instructed by Paravidino that the beats between lines were almost as important as the lines themselves, as the silences were a primary symptom of the eponymous illness. The result was a less flamboyant, less visually pleasing production, but more consonant with the main theme of incommunicability.

The third family play where incommunicability ultimately leads to a tragic ending is *Still Life in a Ditch* (2001). Its first staging in a small theatre in Milan was directed by Serena Sinigaglia and performed by the young virtuoso Fausto Russo Alesi, who played all the characters. Subsequently, Paravidino directed it in Bolzano in 2003 with a cast of six. The play is structured as a whodunit and written in a fast-paced comic rhythm. Character names are originally in English – Boy, Mother, Father, Pusher, Cop, Bitch, and Boyfriend – signalling a reference to the American small-screen detective fiction genre. The play starts with Boy finding the naked dead body of a young woman off a provincial road where he has just crashed his car. Interlocking monologues and testimonies from all other characters follow, creating a mosaic of voices that are never in dialogue with one another. Fragments of stories and clues gradually paint a bleak picture of what has happened: the woman, Elisa, had been pushed to prostitute herself by her Boyfriend in order to pay off his drug-related debt. Picked up by a man that ironically turns out to be her Father, Elisa ends up being killed by him, out of shame for both his actions and hers.

Lack of communication between family members is again what enables the final tragedy: neither parent was aware that Elisa's friends were drug dealers; the Mother did not know that the Father had been frequenting prostitutes; and the Father

Emma Dante and Fausto Paravidino   305

initially attempted to cover up his actions. The Mother's gradual realisation of what has happened, of how estranged she has become from the members of her own family, is the most touching aspect of the play. Quick-witted and elegantly structured, *Still Life* is by far Paravidino's most often revived script, with over 30 productions in France, Spain, Germany, Brazil, Belgium, and Luxemburg between 2005 and 2018. *Still Life* captured European and international audiences with its entertaining humour and parody of the police fiction genre. It was also presented as a reading at the Italian Cultural Institute in London in 2009, but according to Paravidino, 'nobody found it funny there' (Paravidino 2018).

Judging from these three early plays, one could argue that Paravidino's vision of the modern family is one of individuals that barely know each other and can hardly care for one another. But two later plays, *Mariapia's Journal* and *Giobbe's Butchery*, paint a slightly different picture. In the former, an autobiographical text, a tender and thoughtful relationship is explored between Fausto, his sister Marta, and their Mother, Mariapia, as she approaches her passing in hospital. The latter is a tragicomic family parable where Father and Son clash over their approach to money. This is one of Paravidino's most ambitious directorial projects to date, based on a collective approach to creation, in which he worked with stage artists, musicians, technicians, and performers to investigate a new, democratic approach to theatre-making. With long mimed sequences interspersed throughout the narrative, extended use of masks, props, original music, choreography, and lighting effects, the two-and-a-half-hour production is broadly speaking an interrogation of the causes of evil. As well as the family, the script also features two threatening clownish characters representing the farcical and nefarious aspects of capitalism, initially presenting slapstick interludes, and then gradually being integrated into the narrative as faceless agents of neoliberalism.

Giobbe, Father of Son and Daughter (the latter has a congenital degenerative disease), is the owner of a butcher's shop. As the consequence of the crisis, the shop is losing business. Son, who has studied management and lives abroad, comes back to help his Father, but Giobbe is opposed to his Son's capitalist approach, and instead would have opted for heroic bankruptcy. The rift between the two, the illness of Daughter and sudden death of Mother cause Giobbe to become homeless and estranged, bringing Daughter down with him. The play closes with Son finding Father and Daughter in a hospital after a long time and asking them for forgiveness. Inspired by the Biblical character of Job – the just who is made to suffer unjustly by the will of God – Paravidino's Father also symbolises those who are oppressed by the neoliberal rule. In this play, incommunicability takes on a different form: rather than being investigated as the consequence of modernity, the lack of dialogue between Father and Son is due to their opposing ideologies. 'Through evil, you cannot obtain good', Giobbe says to his Son. Like tragic characters, they are unable to mediate between their two absolute, opposite positions.

Afrim's and Loichemol's stagings largely approached the play with the same sensory flamboyance that characterised Paravidino's version. But while Loichemol worked closely with Paravidino, Afrim brought his own vision of

306   *Margherita Laera*

the play to the second largest city in Romania, Iași, where according to the director, 'people have a special bond with the Church', in order to raise debate about 'the dialogue with God' (2018); Paravidino's clowns became cross-dressers in a provocative move against widespread homophobia in the Romanian public sphere; and when it came to performing the act of butchering cattle, Afrim nodded to animal rights issues, a theme that is not explored in the play. According to Afrim, however, *Giobbe's Butchery* carries a main tragic message: 'that if you try to set yourself free from the reign of capital, you are dead' (2018). Paravidino's family is here a metaphor of society at large, a society subjugated by capital and its tentacles.

How do you translate 'family'?

Family relations – seldom of the affectionate, nurturing, and respectful kind – are the great protagonists of Dante's and Paravidino's work. Families are deployed as microcosms that communicate both literally – that is, that speak about blood relationships in their respective cultural and aesthetic framework – and metaphorically, as pretexts to explore society itself or wider issues and topics such as power, fear, war, the tragic, and theatre itself. In Paravidino, family often signifies a place where people who love each other are incapable of communicating with one another, while for Dante it is the primary frame of reference for an individual, and a site where society's power relations can be explored. The introverted, inexpressive characters of Paravidino's plot-driven scripts end up severing their ties with family members, either by killing, abandoning, seriously mistreating, or betraying them; in Dante's plotless plays, family rituals such as meals, weddings, and funerals, and themes such as violence, incest, gender, and sex are dissected as elemental building blocks of human society.

Family and its cultural associations in Italy, especially in the South, are not immediately communicable across Europe or elsewhere. The set of social structures, moral attitudes, and behavioural conventions that surround how one deals with blood relationships and acquired relatives in the Mezzogiorno are partly shared with some European countries, such as Greece and Spain, but can come across as quite distant from customs in Northern Europe. In the words of Sabino Civilleri, co-founder with Dante of the Compagnia Sud Costa Occidentale, 'In Sicily, family is something that one never really leaves. Not even when, as an adult, you leave home' (2018). Sociological studies stress how conceptions of family have shifted and 'modernised' in Southern Italy in recent decades, especially since the second half of the twentieth century (De Spirito 2005: 33–4). However, compared to family ties in Northern European cultures, blood relationships in Southern Italy can still often be engulfing, so much so that individuals can remain stuck in the ties of tradition and loyalty, unable to conceive of themselves outside of their family home. The kinship-driven manner of constructing identity found in Sicily (and hence in mafioso culture), where the individual is next to nothing if not a member of a pack or tribe, exudes from each of Dante's productions and has driven the way her company – her theatrical family – is organised as an ensemble whose membership rests on loyalty, total dedication, and an exclusive relationship.[4] Such a notion of family and its rootedness in local culture has driven all of Dante's aesthetic choices – language, themes, performers, rehearsal spaces – and made her theatre so distinctive in terms of visual language and actorial work. And yet, Dante rejects the idea that her dialect-speaking characters may be geographically specific:

> They may express themselves in Palermitan, but they represent humankind. The families I portray are not local families, they are universal families. They do operate within codes that are linked to Southern Italian traditions, but their stories are about love, hate, power, sex – things that we all share.
>
> (2018)

Dante conceptualises both continental Italians and non-Italians as 'foreigners' but has always aspired to address both constituencies as her primary audiences. Despite the consciousness of her Sicilian identity and of its 'otherness' vis-à-vis broader notions of European culture, Dante does not see Sicilians as the ideal beneficiaries of her theatre. Any reference to local culture and language is 'trivialised', in her view, when received by someone who is embedded in the same context, because her theatre relies on distancing mechanisms to spur the imagination. What she asks of her 'foreign' audiences, instead, is that they may recognise the 'universal' in the particular, the familiar in the unfamiliar, and that they may see themselves reflected in the otherness they experience at the theatre. This mechanism fundamentally relies on what she sees as the impossibility of translation:

> I could never translate my texts into other languages because I could never change performers. Either they are polyglots, which they are not, or it would be impossible [...] My plays are full of codes, notions and words that are untranslatable, but at the same time these are our biggest resource. Everything that is comprehensible at a local level is not necessarily conducive to the artistic encounter between audiences and theatre makers. That which we can comprehend is not necessarily always good. There are some Palermitan expressions that I use in my theatre that, as soon as they are understood by Palermitans, lose their exotic beauty, their secret – they are diminished. If these concepts remain imprisoned in the context that has generated them, there is little that can be seen as rich and beautiful in them
>
> (2018).

Dante's faith in the strength and ability of theatre to cross linguistic and cultural borders is demonstrated by her initial choice not to use surtitles for the international tour of *In Palermo* in 2002. Dante thought that if continental Italians could appreciate the production performed in Palermitan dialect – a language so distant from standard parlance across the peninsula – then other 'foreigners'

308 *Margherita Laera*

could do so too. However, after some 30 performances abroad, Dante was persuaded to use surtitles by venue managers and has argued that as a consequence of surtitles, 'when we work abroad, people understand us, but in Italy we don't use surtitles and audiences don't understand what we're saying' (2018). The risk of Dante's approach to intra- and intercultural communication, with her emphasis on cultural alterity as a key experience, is that her work might be perceived and enjoyed as exotic, and that the pleasure of experiencing the 'foreign' comes at the expense of mounting stereotypes over notions of 'Sicilianness'. While she insists her use of Palermitan language and culture is not literal, but an aesthetic distancing strategy to stimulate the imagination, readings of her work as an expression and representation of 'Sicilianness' or 'Italianness' are not uncommon. Yet elsewhere, Dante states that hers is a 'theatre of identity' and that 'Sicily is what I am', hence 'it is natural to link my theatre to my land' (2017b). She explains that she is interested in classical drama and myths because they 'are the roots of the culture I belong to' (2017b). Europe does not feature prominently in Dante's thinking, but through her engagement with classical mythology and with the legacies of embodied dramaturgies, such as those of Kantor and Bausch, her theatre is firmly placed within a European lineage.

If Dante uses Sicily as metonymy to communicate across linguistic and cultural borders, Paravidino's relationship with his territory is admittedly less overt. He identifies primarily as a citizen of the world, not as a European or an Italian (Paravidino 2018). Consequently, his plays do not display much in terms of 'Italian' cultural attributes. He states:

> Sometimes I use Italy as a metaphor, or in my latest production, *The Meaning of Emma's Life*, I explore the history of Italy through the history of a family. But in general, the families I portray are not Italian [...] In theory they could have been written in any other place – but maybe that is not the case. Particularly if I am writing on commission from a foreign theatre, I try to be the least Italian I can be.
>
> (Ibid.)

The culture in which Paravidino's plays are situated is an Italian-speaking version of the western world's global village, where people drink Coke and talk like characters in a US TV series. But this does not mean that Paravidino is an uncritical consumer and supporter of cultural and economic globalisation: on the contrary, as it is apparent from *Genoa 01*, his political sympathies are with the anti-globalisation movement that manifested peacefully against the injustices of the global order, represented in Genoa by the G8 summit leaders. In his work, there is a playful exploitation of the potentialities that a global culture affords to theatre-makers wishing to communicate across national languages, as a common frame of reference to support the work of critical irony and parody.

Paravidino began to write on commission for non-Italian audiences early on in his career through his experiences in the UK in the early 2000s and adopted this cultural abstraction strategy from the beginning:

I don't like to do tourist theatre. I ask myself, how can I talk to a non-Italian audience? How can I write about something that concerns them too? I want there to be as little cultural distance as possible between my play and the performer.

(Paravidino 2018)

Paravidino plays with American film and TV genres, such as murder mystery (*Still Life*) and sitcom (*Peanuts*); his fast-paced dialogues mimic Hollywood exchanges and none of his characters – except all his Royal Court commissions and *The Meaning of Emma's Life* – ever mention any historical, geographical, or cultural facts that could be traced back to Italy, which of course makes his plays easily exportable. While Mark Ravenhill deliberately stripped any historical references from *Shopping and Fucking* to communicate that his characters live in a bubble and have no sense of history – and as a consequence created a very 'translatable' play – Paravidino creates stories devoid of local references precisely to overcome the problems of translation. However, it is impossible for Paravidino to remove himself from the socially constructed historicity of his own worldview. Traces of Italian culture can be detected through a microscope in Paravidino's plays: for instance, in *The M Family Illness*, when Maria's boyfriend is invited to a Sunday lunch to be introduced to the family, the first thing Luigi, her father, wants to know about him is: 'Is he left-wing?' (2002: 131). In the highly politicised environment that is family life in left-wing Italian culture – and Paravidino was evidently raised in such a cultural context – this sort of political vetting is extremely common, and although the question easily translates literally into other languages, it may come across as a very peculiar thing to ask, for instance, in an English-speaking context. In fact, in a British middle-class family, the question, 'Where did he go to school?' would have been a more common equivalent, inquiring instead about the boyfriend's family's financial or class status rather than political credentials.

Despite Paravidino's efforts to dispense with his cultural situatedness on a national level and his endeavour instead to play with and critically expose the transnational languages of cultural globalisation, he has not been able to displace the ideology of the nation-state in his international reception. It is indicative of the misperceptions of national thinking that Paravidino's writing style is often branded as 'British' in Italy – because of his plot-driven approach and rhythmic dialogues – while, for instance, according to the British director Ramin Gray, Paravidino's writing comes across as 'very Italian' (Paravidino and Gray 2018). Arguably, the Royal Court's commissioning and marketing strategy has turned Paravidino into an 'Italian' writer, specifically requesting plays on Italian current affairs and issues (the killing of Carlo Giuliani in *Genoa 01*; the financial crisis in *They Were in My Field*; and the so-called migration 'crisis' in *Three Migrants*). Paravidino acknowledged the intercultural negotiation mechanism that often reduces cultural products to representatives of their national identity, pigeonholing them within simplistic understandings of heritage:

310   *Margherita Laera*

When my plays are staged abroad, directors cannot resist performing Italian stereotypes. It happened at the Schaubühne too – in their staging of *Genoa 01*, they sang Adriano Celentano songs, they ate pasta on stage, and so on. But that's got nothing to do with my scripts. At the Royal Court, with *Genoa 01*, I spoke about an international tragedy, and we played with the notion of Italy, when the character of Berlusconi appeared. He is obviously a clownish character, with strong roots in the Commedia dell'Arte, so that brought along a notion of 'Italianness' within this English production, and that was fine. But generally, often people outside of Italy think that Italians do Commedia dell'Arte even if they bring to the table an imitation of Pinter. They read Commedia dell'Arte in our work even if it's evidently not there.

(Paravidino 2018)

Paravidino's remarks are a powerful reminder of the dangers of exoticisation and cultural stereotyping. The question of how a theatre-maker might engage international audiences, either through translation or subtitling, has preoccupied both Paravidino and Dante enough to greatly influence their approach to theatre writing. In order to escape the oppressive, simplistic understanding of 'Italian culture' abroad, Dante has embraced localism as metonymy, while Paravidino has established a critical dialogue with global Anglo-American culture.

Conclusion

In this chapter I have investigated how the plays of two dramatists writing in Italian and Palermitan contain at their core two distinct theories of intercultural communication through translation that try to overcome the pitfalls of national stereotyping when confronted with the need to communicate with non-Italian audiences. On the one hand, approaching the microcosm of family relations as a metaphor of society, Paravidino positions his work within the dominant global culture of Anglo-American derivation in order to exploit the common frame of reference he and his spectators share. On the other hand, dissecting blood relationships as primary location of the tragic, Dante opts for extreme particularity – by using Palermitan dialect and playfully exploring local Sicilian tropes – as an expedient to tap into her audiences' imagination through distancing. Paravidino envisages and tries to facilitate the work of the stage translator as he writes by reducing the cultural gap between the play and its international performers and audiences, while Dante relies on the supposed untranslatability of much of the content of her surtitled productions as an aesthetic device to increase the separation between her plays and her spectators. This, in her view, facilitates intercultural communication through the work of imagination. In Dante's paradoxical vision, cultural remove and inaccessibility – boundaries only partially taken down by surtitles – drive the communication potential of her theatre, but exoticisation may be a by-product of her strategy. Paravidino's approach is much the opposite, arguing that cultural distance

Emma Dante and Fausto Paravidino 311

hinders dialogue between cultures, leading to 'tourist-like' understandings of others. Whether playing with the local or with the global, Dante's and Paravidino's theatres engage audiences in a critical dialogue with ideas of cultural belonging and urge us to reconsider the role of interpretation and translation for the stage as complex ethical, political, and ideological acts with far-reaching consequences.

Emma Dante – four key productions

mPalermu. Directed by Emma Dante. Cast: Monica Anglisani, Gaetano Bruno, Sabino Civilleri, Tania Garribba, Manuela Lo Sicco. Compagnia Sud Costa Occidentale. Teatro delle Briciole – Teatro al Parco, Parma, November 2001.

   Carnezzeria. Directed by Emma Dante. Designed by Fabrizio Lupo. Cast: Gaetano Bruno, Sabino Civilleri, Enzo di Michele, Manuela Lo Sicco. CRT – Teatro dell'Arte, Milan, November 2002.

   Vita Mia. Directed by Emma Dante. Lighting design by Cristian Zucaro. Cast: Ersilia Lombardo, Enzo di Michele, Giacomo Guarnieri, Alessio Piazza. Compagnia Sud Costa Occidentale. Villa Medici, Rome, October 2004.

   Le Sorelle Macaluso. Directed by Emma Dante. Lighting design by Cristian Zucaro. Cast: Serena Barone, Elena Borgogni, Sandro Maria Campagna, Italia Carroccio, Davide Celona, Marcella Colaianni, Alessandra Fazzino, Daniela Macaluso, Leonarda Saffi, Stephanie Taillandier. Compagnia Sud Costa Occidentale. Teatro Mercadante, Naples, 22 January 2014.

Fausto Paravidino – four key productions

Due fratelli – Tragedia da camera. Directed by Filippo Dini. Set and costume design by Laura Benzi. Cast: Fausto Paravidino, Giampiero Rappa, Antonia Ruppo. Teatro Stabile, Bolzano, 6 November 2000.

   La maladie de la famille M. Directed by Fausto Paravidino. Translated by Caroline Michel. Designed by Laura Benzi. Costumes by Anne Autran. Cast: Christian Blanc, Pierre Louis-Calixte, Marie-Sophie Ferdane, Benjamin Jungers, Suliane Brahim, Nâzim Boudjenah, Félicien Juttner. Comédie Française – Théâtre du Vieux Colombier, Paris, 11 January 2011.

   Boala familiei M. Directed by Radu Afrim. Set design by Velica Panduru. Lighting design by Lucian Moga. Sound design by Radu Afrim. Cast: Ion Rizea, Claudia Ieremia, Călin Stanciu Jr., Cătălin Ursu, Victor Manovici, Mălina Manovici. Teatrul National Timişoara, Timişoara, 17 April 2008.

   Il macello di Giobbe. Directed by Fausto Paravidino. Designed by Guido Bertorelli, Marco Guarrera. Lighting design by Pasquale Mari. Music by Enrico Melozzi. Costumes by Sandra Cardini. Choreography by Giovanna Velardi. Cast: Emmanuele Aita, Ippolita Baldini, Federico Brugnone, Filippo Dini, Iris Fusetti, Aram Kian, Monica Samassa, Vito Saccinto. BOZAR, Brussels, 15 October 2014.

312 *Margherita Laera*

Notes

1 See for instance Raffaele Viviani, Eduardo De Filippo, Carmelo Bene, and Dario Fo, to name a few.
2 Both plays were also staged in other languages: in Germany, *Peanuts* was staged at Munich's Haus der Kunst Theatre in 2003, directed by Tina Lanik, and was named best foreign play in the 2002/03 season by the magazine *Theater Heute*, going on to be staged more than 15 times in Germany. *Genoa 01* was presented at Berlin's Schaubühne, also in 2003, directed by Wulf Twiehaus. In France, Stanislas Nordey directed both plays at Rennes' Théâtre National de Bretagne and at Paris' Théâtre Ouvert in 2006, and Victor Gauther-Martin directed *Genoa 01* at Paris' Théâtre de la Colline in 2008. *Genoa 01* was also staged in Catalan at Barcelona's Grec Festival in 2004, with a mise en scène by Carme Portaceli.
3 All translations from Italian are mine.
4 According to a 1981 article by Basilio Randazzo, the main value that characterises Palermitan families is cohesion (50), but this can easily deviate into defensiveness and 'Mafia'.

Works cited

Afrim, Radu (2018) Interviewed by Margherita Laera, 2 April. Unpublished.
Bauman, Zygmunt (2000) *Liquid Modernity*, Cambridge: Polity.
Civilleri, Sabino (2018) Interviewed by Margherita Laera, 13 March. Unpublished.
Dante, Emma (2007) *Carnezzeria*, Rome: Fazi.
——— (2016) *Le sorelle Macaluso. Liturgia familiare: Balletto della vita e della morte*, Palermo: Glifo.
——— (2017a) Interviewed by Raffaella Grassi. 'Emma Dante: "Il mio teatro è all'antica"', *Il Secolo XIX*, 4 July, http://www.ilsecoloxix.it/p/cultura/2017/07/04/AS5ehGDI-antica_dante_teatro.shtml
——— (2017b) Interviewed by Teresa Fiore. 'Emma Dante: Corpi e silenzi con un accento siciliano', *VNY*, 18 November, https://www.lavocedinewyork.com/arts/spettacolo/2017/11/18/emma-dante-corpi-e-silenzi-con-un-accento-siciliano/
——— (2018) Interviewed by Margherita Laera, 21 March. Unpublished.
De Spirito, Angelomichele (2005) *Sud e famiglia*, Soveria Mannelli: Rubettino.
Fischer, Donatella (ed.) (2013) *The Tradition of the Actor-Author in Italian Theatre*, London: Legenda.
Paravidino, Fausto (2002) *Teatro*, Milan: Ubulibri.
——— (2011) 'La balieue élargie de l'Occident'. In *Dossier de Presse*, pp. 3–5, Paris: Comédie Française, https://www.comedie-francaise.fr/www/comedie/media/document/presse-maladie1011.pdf
——— (2014) *Il macello di Giobbe*. Unpublished. Courtesy of the author.
——— (2018) Interviewed by Margherita Laera, 15 March. Unpublished.
Paravidino, Fausto and Ramin Gray (2018) Interviewed by Monica Capuani at the Italian Cultural Institute in London, 23 February. Unpublished.
Porcheddu, Andrea (ed.) (2010) *Emma Dante: Palermo dentro*, 2nd Edn, Civitella di Val Chiana: Zona.
Randazzo, Basilio (1981) 'La famiglia in Sicilia', *Esperienze Sociali*, Issue 2, 49–70.
Valentini, Valentina (ed.) (2015) *Nuovo teatro made in Italy: 1963–2013*, Biblioteca Teatrale 13. Rome: Bulzoni.

17 Biljana Srbljanović and Ivana Sajko

Voice in the place of silence

Duška Radosavljević

Medulin. A village on the Croatian coast, 8 km south-east of the historic city of Pula. During the Yugoslav years, Pula's Roman amphitheatre was host to an annual national film festival. In the shadow of Pula's glamour, Medulin's quiet anonymity – sleepy boats and sandy beach whose shallow end stretches all the way to the horizon – makes it seem shy and surprisingly delightful.

In March 1995, nearly four years after the start of the Yugoslav war, Medulin was the site of a largely forgotten, but historically significant, meeting of 17 women from Serbia and Croatia. One-time pioneers of feminism in Eastern Europe, Yugoslav feminists had by this time splintered into various, sometimes fluid, affiliations around their positions on nationalism.[1] As academics or activists, most of these women had personally known each other and shared a political common ground; however, the intervening war period had severed their links, and their respective 'situated knowledges' of the war developed in very different ways, inevitably shaped by their local information dissemination systems in the pre-internet age.

Those wishing to co-operate (mostly anti-nationalists on both sides) had no opportunities to compare and exchange experiences. When a 1994 peace declaration consultation in Geneva collapsed due to the former Yugoslav women activists' fundamental disagreements around the moral responsibilities of various parties in the conflict, the women instigated a closed meeting without a formal agenda.

Funded by a US donor, the Medulin meeting included a conflict resolution trainer, but the women decided that the presence of the trainer and their translator hampered the proceedings – so they dismissed both. Instead, they kissed, hugged, held hands, and wept.

Writing about the meeting at the time, the Croatian feminist Vesna Kesić and the Serbian feminist Lepa Mladjenović emphasised the notion of 'active listening' as its key component. In a short rousing article entitled 'Laughter, Tears and Politics-Dialogue: How Women Do It', they proposed a redefinition:

> Women's dialogue starts from personal stories and arrives at the political level. Women's dialogue starts from tears and laughter, from five hours of

314 *Duška Radosavljević*

> singing in an Istrian tavern, from the level of "mother/father/I," from
> childhood and our grandmother's story. Women's dialogue begins and
> returns to our own experience of war, genocide, home, land, nation...
>
> (2000: 41)

The historically unique position of Yugoslav feminism – like that of non-aligned, liberal Yugoslavia with its own economic system of self-management – is a phenomenon until recently marred in academic ignorance and misconceptions.[2] Some important remedial work is emerging from a new generation of scholars such as the Amsterdam-based Macedonian Ana Miškovska-Kajevska whose qualitative study of Yugoslav feminism during the war also focuses on the Medulin meeting.

A previously unrecorded incident that emerged during Miškovska-Kajevska's interviews was a somewhat traumatic discovery of shared personal history between two of the women – the partisan father of a Belgrade participant having been involved in a summary 1945 killing in Bleiburg of the Ustasha prisoners of war which included the father of a Zagreb participant: 'The realisation and the ensuing discussion exposed the existence of silenced places in the Yugoslav historiography which still vibrated in the family histories of individuals' (Miškovska-Kajevska 2017: 119).

The 'equalising character of Yugoslav communism' and the prerogatives of feminism had never before allowed for discussions of difference in personal experiences. The obscurity and tranquillity of Medulin, behind the scenes of war, unexpectedly created a safe space for a 'more profound understanding' to emerge.

This usually overlooked episode is recorded by Miškovska-Kajevska precisely for the significance of silence around it. 'This silence not only manifested in the scarcity of analyses, but also in the fact that the meeting format has not been repeated' (2017: 119).

Context(s): the gaze

This chapter is about the authorial voice in contemporary playwriting of the post-Yugoslav region. Troubled by the enduring grip of the Balkanist perspective formed and augmented in the 1990s by journalists (Glenny, Ignatieff, Judah), theorists (Bakić-Hayden, Todorova, Goldsworthy), as well as artists (Kusturica, Bregović), and disinclined from recycling earlier arguments,[3] I am keen to find a different way of framing the cultural output of this region. In the section above I chose to set the scene by disrupting the Western gaze and immersing the reader inside the region's lesser known landscape and history.[4]

First, it is necessary to acknowledge the ongoing scarcity of knowledge of (post)-Yugoslav theatre in the English-speaking world. This endemic obscurity confounds and is confounded by Balkanism. Despite limited literature on local theatre traditions, mentions of the region might bring about vague and isolated recollections of the alternative scene(s) – the bold experiments of Ljubljana-based NSK, physical theatre company DAH from Belgrade, or Zagreb-based BADco.[5] More recently, a European theatre-goer might have encountered the works of the Slovenian/Croatian collective Janez Janša, Bosnian/Croatian director Oliver Frljić, or Serbian director Miloš Lolić. In the UK, Croatian playwright Tena Štivičić has reached the mainstream with the production of *3 Winters* in 2014 at the National Theatre, directed by Howard Davis. Over the last two decades, post-Yugoslav playwrights' names most frequently encountered outside their original contexts include Serbia's Biljana Srbljanović, Milena Marković, and Uglješa Šajtinac, and Croatia's Ivana Sajko, Ivor Martinić, and Nina Mitrović. Despite some discernible trends, however, there is still no paradigmatic or comprehensive understanding of the theatre production coming out of the region.

In this chapter, I will advance an argument that the local context(s) can be seen to have shaped a very specific type of dramaturgy that is well exemplified by the respective authorial idioms of playwrights Biljana Srbljanović (b. 1970) and Ivana Sajko (b. 1975). I will propose that this work demands to be seen in new ways, rather than by reference to existing taxonomies and discourses.

It should be noted that, in addition to Serbia and Croatia, the post-Yugoslav region also includes Bosnia, Montenegro, Slovenia, Macedonia, and Kosovo. Whereas the similarities between Serbian and Croatian are so strong that they once formed a single language called Serbo-Croatian (also spoken in Bosnia and Montenegro), the latter three political entities coming out of the Yugoslav federation have distinct official languages. Montenegro and Bosnia form anomalous points of reference here: Montenegro is a relatively small country (600,000 inhabitants) whose cultural production was closely intertwined with that of Serbia until its independence in 2006, while the Bosnian model of training and cultural production has, following the end of the war, resulted in a more internationally noted emergence of film directors.

As part of this contextualisation, especially vis-à-vis the international gaze, I will briefly acknowledge the work of contemporary Bosnian filmmakers – which are, since the year 2000, predominantly represented by women such as Jasmila Žbanić, Aida Begić, and Marina Andree Škop. Defining the work of these artists as representative of a post-realist, post-feminist epistemological shift within world cinema – away from geo-political localism and towards conceptual issues of globalisation – American/Slovenian scholar Meta Mazaj perceives the main achievement of the Balkan women filmmakers as being a creation of a 'transnational imaginary' which supplants the self-exoticising, macho trope of 1990s Balkanism.[6] Crucially, this kind of transnationalism is not only a mode of representation but 'a viewing space, a visual territory that dislocates the viewer from her familiar viewing position and introduces a new foreign territory that has to be contended with from within its "foreignness", rather than from the outside looking in' (Mazaj 2013: 215).

Rather than analysing their cultural significance, I want to focus on the distinctiveness of the playwriting idioms manifested in the works of the two selected authors. What we can usefully take from Mazaj and the Balkan women filmmakers then is the cue to look beyond Balkanism and to the space of transnational feminism, which does not function merely as an 'alternative voice', but as a uniquely appropriate and 'necessary framework' for understanding global processes in the twenty-first century (2013: 204).

The two playwrights examined in this chapter were selected on the grounds of their local and European significance, rather than their gender identification.[7] However, the authors' gender inevitably brings into focus the heritage and relevance of feminism in the region. Recent years have seen a considerable weakening of the momentum of Yugoslav feminist activism and cessation of a once thriving culture of Yugoslav *écriture féminine* (exemplified internationally by Dubravka Ugrešić and Slavenka Drakulić). Writing in 2012, Jagna Pogačnik announces the end of this tradition as far as Croatian domestic prose is concerned, only making an allowance for theoreticians Nataša Govedić and Lada Čale Feldman, and feminist NGOs. The situation in Serbia is even worse, being characterised by a 'dominant sophisticated neoconservatism' (Rosić 2013) where notably prolific female authorship is associated with showbiz – a trend traceable back to the conscious 'destruction of alternatives' (Gordy 1999) under Slobodan Milošević. Nevertheless, one must not neglect continued resilience of the distinct liberal counterpublic of 'Other Serbia' (Russell-Omaljev 2016) that provided resistance towards nationalist conservative consensus in the 1990s.

The regional theatre scene, traditionally dominated by an osmotic model of dramatic/director's theatre,[8] represents a relevant contextual framework – specifically, the challenges and opportunities the work of Srbljanović and Sajko posed to local theatre-makers and critics. Initially these authors' works will have been described in the local critical discourse as 'fragmentary dramaturgy' (*'fragmentarna dramaturgija'*) – a syntagm used at the end of the twentieth century to denote an open, episodic, non-linear, non-Aristotelian, or postmodern dramatic structure.[9] In Croatia, the term 'postdramatic' has in recent decades gradually replaced the use of fragmentary dramaturgy, specifically in relation to devised work.[10] Simultaneously, a phenomenon perceived as trans-European and referred to as 'New Drama' has, in my view, been misapplied to the plays of Srbljanović and Sajko. Focusing on the otherwise overlooked but nevertheless distinctive use of stage directions in these playwrights' works, I will examine the available critical literature and demonstrate the need for a new perspective. Some of my underlying questions here are: to what extent are the available discourses useful and appropriate in helping these works transcend the confines of alterity? How might Srbljanović and Sajko's writing offer transnational potential hitherto eclipsed by the constraints placed on it? And, more specifically, what is the significance of the idiomatic choice, present in the work of both writers, to deploy stage directions for personal expression?

Prompted by Mazaj's showing how the female post-Yugoslav filmmakers dislocate the outside viewer from their familiar postcolonial position, I wish to curate a story about the playwriting culture in the region as a fully emancipated European practice. This practice is, for the moment, still trapped within the as yet unemancipated political context of post-socialist 'transition', but at least the notion of transition carries the promise of change.[11]

I use the term 'emancipation', not in a classical Marxist or even feminist sense, but in a more implicit, Rancièrian one – as the opposite of 'stultification', and as denoting a 'blurring of the boundary between those who act and those who look' (Rancière 2009: 19). If we metaphorically ascribe the emancipatory spectatorial gaze to the European reader over the Balkan subject, according to Rancière, the described relationship between the two parties presupposes the existence of 'the third thing', 'whose meaning is owned by no one, but which subsists between them' (2009: 15). Here the notion of 'the third thing' will apply to the works of Srbljanović and Sajko, and the focus will be on the playwrights' agency as manifested in their work.

The playwrights: journeys, themes, intersections

Srbljanović and Sajko's careers feature some similarities and significant differences. The five-year age gap sets the writers up as belonging to different generations as well as different networks of formative influences. Srbljanović began her career within the cultural isolation of mid-1990s Serbia, riven by war, corruption, anti-dictatorship protests, and political and economic crises. In an interview with Erika Munk, Srbljanović intimated that Serbia felt like a 'double prison' consisting of a dictatorship on the inside and hostility from the outside (2001: 31). Croatia, meanwhile, during Sajko's formative years, was commencing a cultural transition and opening itself up to Europe. In a TV interview in 2018, Sajko listed among her formative influences Forced Entertainment, DV8, Goat Island, Jan Fabre, La Fura del Baus – all of whom were regular guests in Zagreb as part of EUROKAZ festival in the 1990s. Although the famous Belgrade International Theatre Festival (BITEF) continued to host international work throughout the crises, the focus of the programming was on institutional theatre and the personal disposition of the selector (Jovan Ćirilov), rather than keeping up with changing trends.[12]

Reluctantly conforming to the traditional institutional theatre-making structures, Srbljanović started her career within a privileged position of the Belgrade mainstream: 'In Yugoslavia you always have to have this compromise with realism' (2001: 33). Her very early works included the cult TV series *Otvorena vrata* (*Open Door*, 1994) that ran for two seasons on state television, and her first theatre play *Beogradska trilogija* (*The Belgrade Trilogy*) was directed by renowned film director Goran Marković at the Yugoslav Drama Theatre in 1997. An international breakthrough followed immediately with multiple productions of *The Belgrade Trilogy* and, subsequently, of *Porodične priče* (*Family Tales*) (1998), which also received the Sterija Award and the Ernst Toller Prize, given exceptionally to a writer outside of Germany. Qualifying Srbljanović's international popularity, the *New York Times* stated in 2000 that by the end of the year 'some 40 theaters will have staged one of her plays' in Germany (McQueeney 2000). And in 2001, Thomas Ostermeier commissioned and directed Srbljanović's play *Supermarket – soap opera* at the Wiener Festwochen.

Ivana Sajko began her career as a theatre critic for TV and radio and as part of the editorial board of Croatian theatre magazine *Frakcija*. She was a founder member of BADco theatre company in 2000, which allowed her time and

318 *Duška Radosavljević*

space to search for her voice and to experiment with ways of working. Her early career is marred by a relative lack of local interest and opportunities for productions. Her first successful play *Naranča u oblacima* (*An Orange in the Clouds*) was written in 1997 but it received its premiere four years later in 2001 in ZKM, Zagreb, and simultaneously at Theater der Stadt, Heidelberg.[13] In 1998 she received the Marin Držić award for this text, and in 2000 for *Rebro kao zeleni zidovi* (*RibCage*). Three years later, *RibCage* was produced by BADco as an ensemble piece featuring dancer Pravdan Devlahović, philosopher Tomislav Medak, dramaturg/director Goran Sergej Pristaš, director Oliver Frljić, urban activist Marko Sančanin, and choreographer Nikolina Pristaš. The performance sampled an earlier radio version of *RibCage* and featured a DJ, and live improvisations.

A significant difference between the two authors relates to the extent of experimentation in their work. Although favouring fragmentary dramaturgy, Srbljanović writes relatively conventional dramas with absurdist elements and deals with local cultural issues. Except for *Supermarket* (2001) and *Amerika, drugi deo* (*America, Part Two*, 2003), which are fully set in Austria and New York respectively, most of Srbljanović's other plays are set in the post-Yugoslav region or they feature local protagonists. Ivana Sajko, however, sets her texts in abstract spaces and gives her characters generic denominations. A good example is the trilogy of monologues *Arhetip: Medeja/Žena bomba/Europa* (*Archetype: Medea/Woman-Bomb/Europa*),[14] featuring a variety of archetypal characters from Medea and da Vinci's Mona Lisa to Bertolt Brecht's Mother Courage. Under Sajko's direction, the experimentation in her works begins to extend to production choices too and therefore, her Croatian production in 2010 of *Rose is a rose is a rose is a rose* takes on the form of a rock concert in collaboration with musicians Alen and Nenad Sinkauz – in which the author also takes on the role of the performer of the text (see Figure 17.1).

A similarity between the two authors is an interest in intertextuality; for example, Srbljanović's *America, Part Two*, with protagonist named Karl, is an allusion to Kafka's novel *America*, whereas Sajko has repeatedly acknowledged Gertrude Stein as the source of her title *Rose is a rose is a rose is a rose*. Linked to this is a shared interest in deconstruction of myths, such as Srbljanović's *Pad* (*The Fall*) tackling Serbian mythology and folkloric tradition or Sajko's revisiting of the Greeks in *Archetype: Medea* and the Bible in *Prizori s jabukom* (*Scenes with an Apple*, 2009). Also striking is an interest in the lyrical and metaphorical value of stage imagery in both authors' texts. Sajko's work has been explicitly inspired by painters such as da Vinci (*Woman-Bomb*) and Bruegel (*Krajolik s padom* [*Landscape with a Fall*, 2012]).

It is significant that both authors' works have created resonance across the post-Yugoslav region and led to transregional collaborations. Srbljanović's play about the start of the First World War *Mali mi je ovaj grob* (*This Grave is Too Small for Me*), initially commissioned by Schauspielhaus Vienna, also received a 2014 premiere in Serbo-Croatian in a regional co-production between Hartefakt (Belgrade), Bitef Teatar (Belgrade), Kamerni Teatar 55 (Sarajevo), and Kazaliste

Figure 17.1 Rose is a rose is a rose is a rose, written, directed, and performed by Ivana Sajko (2010). Rehearsing the last scene, Sajko observed by her musicians: Alen Sinkauz, Vedran Peternel, Nenad Sinkauz, and Krešimir Pauk. Photograph © Dražen Smaranduj

Ulysses (Zagreb), staged by Sarajevo director Dino Mustafić. Srbljanović collaborated with Mustafić again in 2016 on a trans-regional production of *Tudje srce, ili pozorišni traktat o granici* (*Someone Else's Heart: Or a theatrical tract about borders*), based on documentary and verbatim materials. Sajko's text about the financial crisis *To nismo mi, to je samo staklo* (*It's Not Us, It's Just Glass*) was first staged by Bojan Djordjev and Siniša Ilić in Belgrade in 2011 as a site-specific installation in the commercial high rise building Beogradjanka.

In terms of subject matter, both authors have frequently tackled the politics of female experience. Sajko's *Archetype: Medea/Woman-Bomb/Europa* interrogates the political position of woman throughout Western history and mythology. Srbljanović's most explicit examples of this trend include examinations of family relationships in *Skakavci* (*Locusts*, 2005), *Barbelo: O psima i deci* (*Barbelo: On Dogs and Children*, 2007), and *Vrat od stakla* (*Neck Made of Glass*, 2018). The latter was a complex 'state of the nation play' named after an Albanian pop song from 1968, and rendered allegorically as a family drama about a loss of home, featuring three generations of women.[15]

In this respect, it is important to briefly consider the two writers' respective positions on feminism. Srbljanović – though also at times perceived as reactionary in her politics – has as a representative of the Other Serbia repeatedly reiterated her allegiance to feminism, criticising the younger generations' resistance and attributing it to a general ignorance of the emancipatory work from the 1970s and 1980s:

320 *Duška Radosavljević*

> What the new generations of mostly women who criticize feminism don't
> understand is that their mothers used to be feminists without having to
> prove it.
>
> (in Cvetković 2015)[16]

Sajko, on the other hand, has been more philosophical – and more precise – in her response to this question:

> Feminism no longer signifies a singular concept as it has developed in
> many different directions and is present in many different theoretical dis-
> ciplines. A theoretical framework can be applied to any work of art,
> including my work. Do I write from a particular theoretical and ideologi-
> cal position – I would not say so.
>
> (in Medelić 2010)

In the same interview Sajko further explained that her work is more concerned with 'what remains after the illusion has been broken'.

To what extent do the two playwrights achieve the transnational feminist perspective that 'dislocates the viewer from her familiar viewing position'? I propose that, given the distinct ideological and dramaturgical approaches which contribute to the pluralist transnational perspective, the more interesting question to be addressed is *how* they do it. This concerns a seemingly incidental formal characteristic – the authors' use of stage directions, which I characterise as emancipatory.

(Emancipatory) stage directions

There are very few ways in which stage directions have been given attention in academic writing, ranging from their potential reconstructive value for theatre historians to their conceptual deployment in the work of specific playwrights such as Samuel Beckett or Bertolt Brecht.

Martin Puchner (2011) notes that the late nineteenth-century professionalisation of playwrights, aided by the developing publication industry and copyright law, created an adversarial relationship between the authors of texts and the disadvantaged authors of the *mise en scène* (designers, directors, actors). This in turn led to an inherently strained relationship of co-dependence between play-text and performance, and to perpetually inferior conceptions of performance texts as either 'instructions' or as 'unfinished artworks', opposed to the creative integrity of both literature and theatre. Puchner has argued that this tension can only be diffused through a process of emancipation – modelled by the Wooster Group's 1999 adaptation of Gertrude Stein's *Faust Lights the Lights* (1938) – whereby theatre becomes art in its own right and, contrary to expectation, plays continue to exist as 'complete, finished objects', as pieces of literature.

Transcending these histories, the works of Srbljanović and Sajko introduce a new dimension of the use of stage directions – and of personal authority – without relinquishing their stake in the theatre-making process.

On the cover pages of *Barbelo* (2007), Srbljanović states that she does not expect any adherence to her stage directions,[17] and the performance text opens as follows:

> *A young woman is sitting on a low wall. Smoking and crying. (So what? I cry all the time too).*
>
> *I think she is smoking a joint. No one knows how sad she is.*
>
> *Another young woman is walking her dog. She is crying too, without knowing why. One has nothing to do with the other. I think.*
>
> (2007: n.p.)[18]

The author uses the stage directions to determine her position in relation to the text as a dispassionate observer, closer to the audience rather than the all-knowing autonomous creator; and, in the afterthought 'I think', she positions herself as a potentially unreliable/ unauthoritative narrator. Thus, she relinquishes the traditional role of the instructive playwright who aims to control the reader/ spectator's reception. The author's attitude is Brechtian in privileging diegesis over mimesis,[19] and non-Brechtian in its rejection of didacticism.

Similarly, Sajko uses the stage directions to establish an explicit rhetorical stance and to foreground the performativity (and playfulness) of her own writing. *It's Not Us, It's Just Glass* (2011) opens:

> LET'S PRAY FOR THE FUTURE OF THIS COUNTRY.
> THE SALVATION OF ITS CHILDREN AND THE CONSCIENCE OF ITS PARENTS.
>
> *Everything's gone to fuck, and it cannot be explained any other way. Sleepless parents and their children in a bad mood enter the stage. They murmur a prayer and move to the edge of the stage as if approaching the edge of an abyss, or a railing of a bridge, or the tracks of a metro. As if they will jump. The text they speak cannot be heard, the prayer is just a melody, the rest of it is useless. Their potential death would also be invisible and without any significance. Tragedies are all around, they are banal and they no longer belong to them. That's what it is all about.*
>
> (2011: 50)

The invitation to pray is immediately juxtaposed with a deployment of irreverent urban slang. The playwright uses the stage directions to construct 'the edge of an abyss' not dissimilar in its potential metaphorical value from Srbljanović's 'low wall'; however, she is not prescriptive either, offering other interpretive options. Rendering the text to be spoken by her characters as initially inaudible, or audible only as music, she inverts the conventional meaning-making priority of the dialogue over the stage

322   *Duška Radosavljević*

directions, and establishes one of the defining aspects of her performance-making idiom which favours the musicality of text. By the end of the opening paragraph, she also states explicitly – Brecht-like – the main subject of her piece.

Both authors use extensive stage directions throughout their work, into which, unusually, they inscribe themselves. It is important to note that idiosyncratic use of stage directions is not entirely exclusive to these two playwrights in the local dramaturgical tradition(s); similar practices are discernible in the metatheatrical works of Croatian Slobodan Šnajder (b. 1948) and Serbian Dušan Kovačević (b. 1948).[20] Srbljanović and Sajko have, each in her way, taken this convention to new extremes, and created an idiom influential for later generations of playwrights.[21]

From the examples above we can extrapolate a tendency in both authors to relinquish omniscience and the 'text as instructions' model of authority. However, they by no means relinquish their own agency in the performance text. Here it is useful to distinguish between two increasingly divergent meanings of the word authority – one implying a hierarchical, often political, decision-making power and the other applying to the function and agency of artistic authorship. The latter can still be political without taking on the hierarchical approach, resulting in a dramaturgy we might denote as post-Brechtian.[22]

Srbljanović and Sajko's post-Brechtain authorial voice abolishes the traditional hierarchies while deploying a more relational form of self-inscription. They make themselves audible within the stage directions to engender a metadialogue with the text and engage the reader/audience in a relationship. This is evident through a frequent use of first person and direct address which can gradually lead to a use of autobiography.

Srbljanović's play *Barbelo*, thematically concerned with motherhood, ends with a tableau of a number of characters sitting on each other's lap, and the eventual breaking of the fourth wall:

MILENA
You understand, of course,
that all this terribly long,
all this terribly long time,
I'm actually talking about myself?

They're looking at us. So ridiculous, sitting in each other's lap. And you're looking at them.
Only I am going somewhere.
Even if I don't know where.

darkness
the end

(2007: n.p.)

The formatting replicating the original layout shows a blurring of the boundaries between the text intended to be spoken by the character (aligned to the left), the author's voice (centred, italicised, orthographically complete), and the routine end-of-scene stage directions (italicised, lower case, unpunctuated). The direct address at the very end of the play both explicitly and ambiguously reveals autobiographical connection, and, through the deliberate blurring of the dialogue and stage directions, potentially positions the author as a fictionalised protagonist.

Sajko goes further in *Woman-Bomb* (2003), where, from the first page, she writes her own autobiographical voice into the text (verifiable through a reference to *RibCage*). She also dispenses with any attempt to separate the stage directions from intended speech or to delineate the distinct speaking voices for performance:[23]

> It's 10:30. February. I'm reading my agent's notice that a theatre has cancelled a production of my play RibCage since the text and the imminent war in the Middle East resonate in an undesirable way, through, I quote: 'individual resistance to superior violence'. I'll probably cry later in the day.
>
> (2010: 108)

The incidental resonance between Sajko and Srbljanović both explicitly framing themselves as vulnerable subjects who habitually cry further supports my thesis of the authors' deliberate relinquishing of authority and assertion of the private relational self (for reasons beyond narcissism). Further on the next page, in a Brechtian gesture repeated in *It's Not Us*, Sajko foregrounds the content of the piece, and then critically reflects on her own writing within the performance text, thus potentially reinforcing the authenticity of personal voice:

> The plot is simple: a woman-suicide will blow herself up as the crowd hails some important, unnamed politician. The radius of the explosion will be eighteen meters.
>
> My own sentences scare me sometimes. I imagine people reading the text that has not yet been written. I don't want to create a heroine. I'm in convulsions, but she speaks
>
> (2010: 109)

In both Serbian and Croatian the term for stage directions is *didaskalia* – the ancient Greek word which means 'teaching' or 'instruction'.[24] This notion suggests an analogy between a playwright and a teacher, and although both playwrights have also worked as teachers – Srbljanović is still a Professor of Dramaturgy at the Faculty of Dramatic Arts in Belgrade – the relevant aspect of this analogy is not literal, but the one pertaining to Rancière's 'ignorant schoolmaster' (1991) and associated ideas leading to his concept of emancipation. For Rancière the emancipation of the spectator is located in their individual 'power of associating and dissociating' (2009: 17) and their processes of interpretation and translation, on condition that we refuse 'radical distance', the 'distribution of roles', and the 'boundaries between territories' (2009: 17). Instead of establishing herself as the

324   *Duška Radosavljević*

source of knowledge, each playwright can be seen to be positioning the text, in a Rancièrian manner, between her clearly delineated self and the audience as an object 'alien to both' (2009: 15). By deploying this kind of fragmentary dramaturgy, the playwright removes the radical distance, the stultifying distribution of roles, and the boundaries between herself and the audience, thus creating gaps which are to be resolved by the audience's own intelligence.

Whether or not Srbljanović and Sajko consciously aim for any kind of emancipation for their audience, their authorial choices of staging personal deliberations within their stage directions and engaging the audience in an imaginary dialogue have this effect. It is equivalent to creating a territory that 'has to be contended with from within' (Mazaj 2013) and also to 'women's dialogue' which 'starts from the personal [...] and arrives at the political' (Kesić and Mladjenović 2000).

While not subscribing to the notion of 'text as instructions', Srbljanović's and Sajko's performative assertion of personal agency via the stage directions also precludes the possibility of the texts being seen as 'complete works of literature' (Puchner 2011). Belonging to their local genealogies of political dramaturgies as much as the transnational networks of literary and visual art influence, they transcend the text–performance binary by fostering a shared experience.

Problems of reception

In the post-Yugoslav region, the formal peculiarities of Srbljanović and Sajko's works have presented problems for both theatre-makers and critics operating within pre-existing discourses and hermeneutic paradigms. Local theatre directors, schooled in the Russian and German traditions of director's theatre, have grappled with these writers' unconventional idioms. In his 2003 production of *America, Part Two*, Serbia's oldest living auteur director Dejan Mijač resolved the problem of the persistent presence of Srbljanović's personal voice in the stage directions by succumbing to it – the playwright was recorded reading her stage directions and the recording was included in the production. Due to an initial lack of interest, Sajko has even been forced to develop her own directorial and performance practice, which she has described as 'auto-referential reading'.[25]

Critical analysis has mostly focused on the content of Srbljanović and Sajko's work, especially in Croatia, where the topic of continuity of *écriture féminine* and, more specifically, the theme of motherhood within the neoconservative postsocialist societies of Serbia and Croatia are explored. Notable examples include Leo Rafolt's (2011) feminist reading of Sajko's *Woman-Bomb* and Suzana Marjanić's (2009) political reading of the Zagreb production of Srbljanović's *Barbelo*. Lada Čale Feldman (2005) integrates formal considerations into her reading of Sajko's *Medea* which, being set in the uterus of a theatre, is seen to invert the Stanislavskian male–female/director–actor theatre-making hierarchy.[26] While eminently informative and fascinating in their insightfulness, these analyses largely maintain the embeddedness of these works in their local contexts.

In a rare comparative reading of the two authors' work, Nataša Govedić proposes the notion of 'ethical trauma' as a dramaturgical concept encapsulating the problem of apathy endemic to the present historical moment, both locally and globally. She defines 'ethical trauma' with reference to Sarah Kane and the theoretical writing of Cathy Caruth, Norman Geras, Robert Jay Lifton, and Kai Erikson, in order to analyse Srbljanović and Sajko's work through this lens. Concluding that in a context defined by ethical trauma, drama should function as a 'new institution of radical democracy' (2005: 103; 2006: 214), the critic dismisses the playwrights' notable use of 'subjective stage directions' as 'technical experiments' which do not form part of the main 'transformative potential' of the authors' work (2005: 104; 2006: 215).

Srbljanović and Sajko's use of stage directions is subjected to a narratological analysis by Paris-based academic Sava Andjelković (2008a, b) which, however, does little to challenge Govedić's view of their relative political inefficacy.[27] Andjelković's examination becomes particularly interesting when he arrives at the 'exceptions' no longer amenable to his chosen apparatus. Here he discovers modes that transcend the merely 'literary' experimentations present in the works of the previous generations of playwrights and notes instead a 'struggle for the authors' own audibility over the text of the dialogue' (2008a: 5). Despite the fact that he resorts to a very useful direct quotation of Sajko on the potential of stage directions as a place 'where you can create a subversion of your own discourse' (Sajko in Andjelković 2008a: 5),[28] Andjelković classifies this innovative recalibration of the two text registers as merely characteristic of postmodern distancing from the text, of postdramatic theatre or 'New Drama' – a categorisation that many post-Yugoslav critics unquestioningly resort to as a stylistic hold-all.

'New Drama' as a term is most commonly encountered in the Anglophone context as a translation of the Russian trend 'Novaya drama' (Beumers and Lipovetsky 2009). Confusingly, several critical texts in the Balkans have adopted the equivalent 'Nova drama' to refer to a trans-European trend, perceived as prompted by the British 'In-Yer-Face' theatre and further developed in Germany. Both Sanja Nikčević (2005) and Jasen Boko (2002) refer to the Bonner Biennale Festival 'Neue Stücke aus Europa' (1992–2015) and to the work of Thomas Ostermeier as important factors in integrating these influences together and providing a shared ground for the works of Sarah Kane, Mark Ravenhill, and Srbljanović, amongst others. While Boko (2002) is systematic in his study of the circulation of influences, and optimistic about the paradigmatic opportunities of 'Nova drama', Nikčević (2005) is more critical of what she sees as the trend's various threats, including most significantly a threat to 'writer's theatre' via a perceived servicing of director's theatre.

The currency of this term was renewed in 2005 through a conference co-organised in Croatia by Sava Andjelković and Boris Senker and a subsequent 2007 edited volume, which raised useful questions around the challenges of 'Nova drama' to existing theatre-making expertise in the region. Five years later, using a definition drawn from Miloš Lazin's contribution to this conference and influenced by Aleks

326   *Duška Radosavljević*

Sierz, Serbian theorist Ana Vujanović (2010) cautiously applied the term to the periodisation of recent Serbian dramaturgy. While rightly lamenting not only the lack of theatre-making expertise but also a noticeable absence of relevant scholarship in Serbia, compared to Croatia, Vujanović argues that the notion of 'Nova drama' only applies to the 'postpolitical' work of the Serbian playwrights who entered the professional scene in 2000, at the start of Serbia's transition to neoliberal capitalism. Vujanović thus classifies Srbljanović's work not as 'New Drama' but rather as a 'postsocialist' precursor to this phenomenon.[29]

I see several problems with the taxonomisation that promotes the label 'New Drama' in relation to the European corpus of plays that includes British playwrights (Kane, Ravenhill, McDonagh) as well as German (Mayenburg, Zade), Russian (Kolyada, Sigarev, Peresnyakov, Vyrypaev), Serbian (Srbljanović, Šajtinac, Marković), and Croatian (Sajko, Mitrović). 'New Drama' is a confusing misnomer. Its usage within the Balkan contexts clearly presupposes – or at least aspires towards – local participation in a wider European theatre context, but ends up circulating as such only in Eastern Europe. The word 'drama' is long gone from Western European discourses of theatre and performance, remaining active only in TV and radio. The term 'New Drama' does not exist in Anglophone theatre criticism, especially not in relation to the playwrights Sierz (2001) designates as 'In-Yer-Face'. Finally, the limitations of Sierz's own designation have been problematised elsewhere.[30]

The British term clumsily translated into Russian and other Slavic languages as 'New Drama' might in fact have been 'new writing', but the full meaning of 'new writing' as a curatorial writer-based workshop methodology developed in the UK does not have an easy direct equivalent in these languages, despite the methodology being actively imported into these cultural contexts via the Royal Court in the late 1990s and early 2000s. Similarly, the German *Neue Stücke aus Europa* found its semantic equivalent in a seemingly more elegant – though inexact and misleading – *Nova evropska drama* (New European Drama).

My objection is not a matter of linguistic pedantry, but a cautioning against the perpetuation of conservative modes of working through a stultifying process of translation which reaches for the closest equivalents while omitting opportunities to contemplate innovation. One problematic effect of the act of translation that produced the high circulation term 'New Drama' has been an entrenchment of the dramatic/Aristotelian heritage that might have contributed to the slow revision of local theatre-making processes. The current situation is also a symptom of a bigger problem that these countries have in 'transitioning' towards Europe. Within this unemancipatory process they are always condemned to an unequal relationship: having to 'keep up' and be trend-followers rather than trend-setters.

A crucial contribution in the Andjelković and Senker volume addressing the gap between the so-called 'Nova drama' and the available means of production in the region is by Bosnian scholar Tanja Miletić-Oručević.[31] Significantly, she chooses the paradigmatic focus on post-Yugoslav writing rather than 'Nova drama' per se. Like Govedić, Miletić-Oručević sees trauma and the predominance of women writers as the defining characteristics of contemporary writing in the region. In identifying fragmentary dramaturgy as another shared characteristic,

Miletić-Oručević, more interestingly, emphasises that this fragmentarity is not arbitrary but carefully constructed in order to contain the main concept, idea, and meaning of the text *within its gaps* (2007: 27). The related openness to interpretation and plurality of perspectives is seen by Miletić-Oručević as crucial in 'dethroning' the director, who often benefits from a dogmatically privileged position in local theatres. By extension, Miletić-Oručević argues that this kind of dramaturgy presents a necessity to overcome traditional modes of working and bestows a 'semantic mission' on the actor:

> A typical perspective of the contemporary dramaturgy is that, despite its fragmentarity and plurality, it is always characterized by an individualistic, courageous and clear voice. And it demands such an actor – an actor prepared to take responsibility for their own and the author's voice [even at the expense of the audience's affection and approval].
>
> (2007: 30)

From gaze to voice

At Biljana Srbljanović's reception of the New Theatrical Realities European Prize in 2007, Thomas Ostermeier reportedly said:

> Biljana has been the voice of the Other Serbia, against her own will, and out of necessity. [...] Today, however, she has outgrown her place of origin, and become the voice of Other Europe, the continent which is increasingly wrestling with its own identity following the wars of the new millennium. She is an important voice of my generation in that struggle.
>
> (cited in Medenica 2007)[32]

This chapter departs from the most frequently available cultural position to Serbia and Croatia – the position of the Balkanist other, also detectable in Ostermeier's inclusionary statement above. Focusing on the commonly overlooked distinctiveness of the chosen authors' playwriting idioms, I proposed to replace the postcolonial gaze mechanism within the context of post-socialist transition with a more egalitarian, potentially emancipatory one. The intervening examination of the works of Biljana Srbljanović and Ivana Sajko provides a new approach. A set of interrelated terms that recur – unnoticed – in the commentaries and critical writing around these authors' work include the terms 'voice', 'speech', and 'audibility'. Srbljanović is quoted by Ostermeier as yearning for 'freedom of speech', while Sajko has made an interesting equation between the act of speaking and politics:

> For me the stage has been – as I see it now – a place from which to speak. So, not so much the place of illusion as the place of politics. The place where you can come and speak about something that troubles you.
>
> (2018)

328 Duška Radosavljević

Voice has been as integral to the feminist discourses as *écriture féminine*, although Lipton and Mackinlay (2017) note that the advent of neoliberalism has complicated this agenda and opened up the potential of silence. The story of Yugoslav feminism at the outset of this chapter highlights the value of women's dialogue and the political potential of interpersonal relationality instead. We have seen that despite its notable early beginnings, the power of feminist ideologies has dwindled in the post-Yugoslav region. Nevertheless, the most significant post-socialist, post-Yugoslav dramaturgy is predominantly produced by female writers – and it is writers, rather than other theatre-makers, who are at the forefront of innovation.

The most distinctive aspect of the post-Yugoslav playwrights' innovation, I argue, is the deployment of their personal authorial voice within the stage directions as a means of engendering a 'territory that has to be contended with from within [...], rather than from the outside looking in' (Mazaj 2013: 215). This inherently political and potentially emancipatory technique supplants the traditional, hierarchical, ocular-centric modes of representation characteristic of 1990s Balkanism. 'Unlike the gaze, the voice is', according to philosopher Adriana Cavarero, 'always, irremediably relational' (2005: 177). Voice precludes possible hierarchies between the subject and the object which are characteristic of the gaze, because 'properly speaking, [voice] has no object' (2005: 177–8).

This chapter, therefore, opens up avenues for further research at the intersection of voice studies, feminism, trauma, politics, and the Balkans, with a view to properly understanding the specific dramaturgical trends emerging in this part of Europe.

As for the distinctive significance of Srbljanović and Sajko's playwriting, I believe that this is ultimately rooted in an understanding of theatre and live performance as a communal experience in which the authors see themselves as participants. Their work constitutes a revision of the pre-existing forms of theatre authorship in the contexts characterised by the predominance of male writers and directors as well as some outdated pedagogies of theatre-making. In this respect, the playwrights deliberately inhabit a Rancièrean emancipatory position in the very place where they should be providing instruction (*didaskalia*). At the same time, moving from the personal towards the political, they mobilise this parenthetical space – usually overlooked as silent – as a site of their authorial agency.[33]

Biljana Srbljanović – four key productions

Porodične priče (*Family Tales*). Directed by Jagoš Marković. Designed by Božana Jovanović (costume). Cast: Isidora Minić, Sergej Trifunović, Branka Šelić, Anita Mančić, Goran Šušljik, Nebojša Milovanović. Atelje 212, Belgrade, 7 April 1998.

Supermarket – soap opera. Directed by Thomas Ostermeier. Designed by Jan Pappelbaum. Cast: Falk Rockstroh, Linda Oslansky, Mark Waschke, Gerd Wameling, Jörg Hartmann, Cristin König. Wiener Festwochen, Vienna, 15 June 2001.

Barbelo, o psima i deci (*Barbelo: On Dogs and Children*). Directed by Dejan Mijač. Designed by Juraj Fabri. Cast: Ana Sofrenović, Jasmina Avramović, Nikola Rakočević, Toni Laurenčić, Goran Šušljik, Jelena Djokić, Nikola Djuričko, Mirjana Karanović, Nebojša Glogovac. Yugoslav Drama Theatre, Belgrade, 4 December 2007.

Princip (Dieses Grab ist mir zu klein) (*Princip: This Grave is Too Small for Me*). Directed and designed by Michał Zadara. Cast: Nicola Kirsch, Florian von Manteuffel, Gideon Maoz, Martin Vischer, Simon Zagermann. Schauspielhaus Wien, 16 October 2013.

Ivana Sajko – four key productions

Rebro kao zeleni zidovi (*RibCage*). Director not credited. Designed by Goran Petercol. Music by Moon's Trip. Authors and cast: Pravdan Devlahović, Oliver Frljić, Tomislav Medak, Goran Sergej Pristaš, Nikolina Pristaš, Ivana Sajko, Marko Sančanin. Company: BADco. Centar za kulturu Novi Zagreb, 27 February 2003. (The performance featured extracts from the radio-play *RibCage* (Croatian Radio's production), performed by Marko Makovičić, Borna Baletić, and Ivana Sajko, directed by Goran Sergej Pristaš.)

Rose is a rose is a rose is a rose. Directed by Ivana Sajko. Dramaturgy by Sandro Siljan. Music by Krešimir Pauk, Vedran Peternel, Alen Sinkauz, Nenad Sinkauz. Moving images by Simon Bogojević Narath. Lighting by Alekasandar Čavlek. Graphics by Mauricio Ferlin. Performed by Ivana Sajko and the musicians. Zagreb Youth Theatre, 2010.

Žena bomba (*Woman Bomb*). Directed by Maja Milatović-Ovadia and Vanda Butković. Designed by Vanda Butković. Video design by Mafalda Cruz and Dan Oki. Cast: Laura Harling, Laura Pradelska, Nikki Squire. Tristan Bates Theatre, London, 2 May 2011.

To nismo mi, to je samo staklo (*It's Not Us, It's Just Glass*). Directed by Bojan Đorđev and Siniša Ilić. Performed by Anka Aćimović, Pavle Čemerikić, Andrijana Đorđević, Andrej Kovačić, Vasilije Krstić, Nađa Marjanović, Ivana Marković, Nina Mrđa, Aleksandra Pavić, Pavle Simović, Luka Zorić, Čarni Đerić, Dragica Đorđev, Siniša Ilić, Dragana Jovović. Audio design by Nebojša Vukelić. Produced by TkH (Teorija koja Hoda). Site-specific performance at commercial centre Beogradjanka, Belgrade, 30 November 2012.

Notes

1 See Lóránd (2018) for the history of feminism in Yugoslavia.
2 See Jakovljević (2016) for Yugoslav self-management and cultural policy.
3 See Radosavljević (2009) and Radosavljević (2012).
4 Jelena Batinić (2001) has shown how even the Western feminist discourses were steeped in Balkanism during the Yugoslav war.
5 See Blažević (2006).
6 Mazaj's essay focuses on Bosnian directors Žbanić and Begić and Slovenian director Maja Weiss.

330 Duška Radosavljević

7 The notable predominance of female playwrights in both Serbia and Croatia is best measured by the gender balance represented in the two countries' respective annual awards for playwriting – Sterija Festival Award, founded in 1956 as a Yugoslav award, but now given out to the best Serbian plays in production, and the Marin Držić Award founded in 1991 and given out to the best Croatian playscripts. In the period 2000–19, the ratio between female and male recipients of the Sterija Award has been 14 to 4 (the award was not given in 2011 and 2017). In Croatia, of the 92 ranked Držić prizes given since 2000, 39 were given to female playwrights.

8 The nineteenth-century European state theatre tradition of dramatic theatre developed in conjunction with the German/Russian tradition of *regie*-theatre.

9 I have been unable to locate the original definition of this term in critical literature, although one source informed me that the play studied at the Faculty of Dramatic Arts in Belgrade as the prime example of 'fragmentary dramaturgy' is Georg Büchner's *Woyzeck*. It is interesting that this play's fragmentarity is incidental, resulting from the author's death preventing its completion. Another strongly influential theoretical text in the local dramaturgical pedagogies has been Volker Klotz's 1960 title *Open and Closed Dramatic Form*, which qualifies 'fragmentary dramaturgy' as an open form.

10 Thanks to Andrej Mirčev for pointing out that Lehmann's book, translated as a joint publishing project by Zagreb and Belgrade in 2004, exerted influence across the region.

11 'Transition' in the post-Yugoslav region has been more realistically defined by Srećko Horvat and Igor Štiks as 'an ideological construct based on the narrative of integration', which in fact conceals 'a monumental neo-colonial transformation of this region into a dependent semi-periphery' (2015: 16). According to Horvat and Štiks, despite the entry of their country Croatia into the EU in 2013, the so-called 'Western Balkans' still represents a 'sort of "ghetto"', around which 'the Schengen ring' has been enforced by the surrounding EU members (2015: 9). It is worth noting that this Euro-scepticism predates Brexit and is distinct from it.

12 According to Ana Vujanović, Bitef's neo-avant-garde theatre events were 'regarded locally as examples of Western experimentation, which had little relevance to the local scene' (2008: 204).

13 At this point Sajko also began her co-operation with Verlag der Autoren from Frankfurt.

14 The trilogy received its Zagreb premiere at ZKM theatre in 2007. Sajko directed *Archetype: Medea* (a shortened title for *Notes from a Performance Archetype: Medea – a monologue for a woman who sometimes speaks*, originally written in 2000), while the other two pieces were directed by Dora Ruždjak-Podolski and Franka Perković, respectively.

15 This particular dramaturgical trope of multiple generations of women around a home under threat evokes several other plays from the region – most famously Tena Štivičić's *3 Winters* (2014), but also Olga Dimitrijević's *It's so good seeing you again* (2016) and Lada Kaštelan's *The Last Link* (1994).

16 Unless otherwise stated, all translations from Serbian and Croatian are by the author.

17 She also 'demands a humane treatment of animals in staging the play' although 'she does not insist on the same principle in relation to humans'.

18 Unless otherwise stated, all quotations from play-texts refer to their manuscript versions. Srbljanović's manuscript in pdf was published on her Facebook page on 28 January 2013. Sajko has kindly provided me with her manuscripts. Original formatting is retained in all translations.

19 The subversive deployment of Elin Diamond's (1997) gestic feminist mimesis is thus also superseded as a potential technique.

20 See Radosavljević (2005) and Radosavljević (2009) respectively.

21 Such as Olga Dimitrijević, Tanja Šljivar, Vedrana Klepica, Rona Žulj, and Dino Pešut.

22 There is increasing evidence that Brechtian political effects can be achieved without the deployment of the Brechtian means, as I have shown in *Theatre-Making* (2013).

23 *Woman-Bomb* is prefaced as: '*A monologue for a woman-bomb, a nameless politician, his bodyguards and mistress, God, a choir of angels, a worm, Leonardo da Vinci's Mona Lisa, twenty friends of mine, my mother and myself*' (2010: 108).

24 It is significant, however, that the convention of stage directions was not used in Ancient Greek dramatic texts, they were subsequently added to ancient texts in the Middle Ages.

25 According to Sajko, this hybrid genre 'tests the border between the authoress and her character, while the strategies of writing become the strategies of performing' ('A–F' 2006: 12).

26 Another fascinating reading of *Barbelo* as an exploration of cultural identity via the mother–child relationship has been conducted by US scholar Melissa Rynn Porterfield (2013), with reference to Gnosticism rather than feminism.

27 Thanks to Andjelković for sending me this paper in Serbian.

28 The quotation is taken from an interview Sajko gave to Zagreb periodical *Zarez*, issue 99, in 2003, which is no longer accessible online.

29 Vujanović's periodisation is also aided by the fact that in the year 2000 the dramaturg Miloš Krečković began a project at the National Theatre in Belgrade called Nova Drama (NADA), which assembled new generations of writers, directors, and producers (recent graduates from the Faculty of Dramatic Arts) in a hopeful ('*nada*' means hope in Serbian) endeavour, modelled on the British new writing development model. Krečković also built links with Philippe LeMoine at the National Theatre Studio in London which enabled several exchanges and workshops of Serbian plays in English in the early 2000s.

30 For example, Elaine Aston (2013) re-reads *Blasted* by situating it instead within a genealogy of contemporary women's playwriting in Britain.

31 Sincere thanks to Lada Čale-Feldman for making this and several other key texts available to me.

32 This text appears in Serbian in Medenica's article. Srbljanović and Medenica did not respond to my request for the original text, and Ostermeier's office could not locate the original.

33 I would like to thank the editors for their patience and helpful comments. Also to Una Bauer, Lada Čale Feldman, Kristina Gavran, Melissa Rynn Porterfield, Vladimir Popadić, Jelena Popadić-Sumić, Ivana Sajko, and Ana Vujanović for relevant information, and to Bojana Janković, Maja Milatović-Ovadia, Andrej Mirčev, and Alexandra Portmann for their comments on drafts.

Works cited

'A-F' (2006) *Performance Research*, 11(3) [Special Issue: A Lexicon]: 1–60.

Andjelković, Sava (2008a) 'Didaskalijski tekst kao dijalog pisca sa vlastitom fikcijom (u dramama Biljane Srbljanović i Ivane Sajko)', manuscript version of conference paper presented at XIV Congress of Slavonic Studies, Ohrid

―――― (2008b) 'Le texte didascalique – Dialogue de l'auteur avec sa propre ficton dons les drames de Biljana Srbljanovic et Ivana Sajko', *Revue des Études slaves*, Paris, LXXIX: 1–14.

Aston, Elaine (2013) 'Feeling the loss of Feminism: Sarah Kane's *Blasted* and an experiential genealogy of contemporary women's playwriting', in Penny Farfan and Lesley Ferris (eds), *Contemporary Women Playwrights: Into the Twenty-First Century*, Basingstoke and New York: Palgrave Macmillan,.

Batinić, Jelena (2001) 'Feminism, nationalism, and war: the 'Yugoslav case' in feminist texts', *Journal of International Women's Studies*, 3(1): 1–23.

332 Duška Radosavljević

Beumers, Birgit and Mark Lipovetsky (2009) *Performing Violence: Literary and Theatrical Experiments of New Russian Drama*, Bristol and Chicago: Intellect.

Blažević, Marin (2006) 'Dying bodies, living corpses: transition, nationalism and resistance in Croatian theatre' in Joe Kelleher and Nicholas Ridout (eds), *Contemporary Theatres in Europe: A critical companion*, Abingdon: Routledge.

Boko, Jasen (2002) 'Nova europska drama u devedesetima; scenski odgovor na neuspjeh utopije 'Nova Europa', *Kazalište*, 9(10): 158–169.

Cavarero, Adriana (2005) *For More Than One Voice: Toward a Philosophy of Vocal Expression*, Palo Alto, CA: Stanford University Press.

Cvetković, Ljudmila (2015) 'Srbljanović: Žene u karijeri nailaze na stakleni plafon', Radio Slobodna Evropa, 6 March, https://www.slobodnaevropa.org/a/biljana-srblja novic-zene-u-karijeri-nailaze-na-stakleni-plafon/26885775.html

Čale Feldman, Lada (2005) 'Mediation of Medea', in *Femina Ludens*, Zagreb: Disput.

Diamond, Elin (1997) *Unmaking Mimesis*, Abingdon and New York: Routledge.

Gordy, Eric D. (1999) *The Culture of Power in Serbia: Nationalism and the Destruction of Alternatives*, State College, PA: The Pennsylvania State University Press.

Govedić, Nataša (2005) 'Trauma apatije: dvije dramatičarske postjugoslovenske Nigdine (Ivana Sajko i Biljana Srbljanović)', in *Etičke bilježnice: o revoltu i brižnosti*, Zagreb: Naklada Jesenski i Turk.

———— (2006) 'The trauma of apathy: two playwrights of post-Yugoslav Nowehereland', *Revue des Études slaves*, Paris, LXXVII(1–2): 203–216.

Horvat, Srećko and Igor Štiks (2015) *Welcome to the Desert of Post-Socialism: Radical Politics after Yugoslavia*, London, New York: Verso.

Jakovljević, Branislav (2016) *Alienation Effects: Performance and Self-Management in Yugoslavia 1945–1991*, Ann Arbor: University of Michigan Press.

Kesić, Vesna and Mladjenović, Lepa (2000) 'Laughter, tears and politics – dialogue: how women do it', in Marguerite Waller and Jennifer Rycenga (eds), *Frontline Feminisms: Women, War, and Resistance*, New York: Garland Publishers.

Lazin, Miloš (2007) 'Nova drama – nova gluma?', in Sava Andjelković and Boris Senker (eds), *Govor drame – govor glume: Zbornik radova sa simpozijuma Dramski tekst danas u Bosni i Hercegovini, Hrvatskojte Srbiji i Crnoj Gori*, Zagreb: Disput.

Lehmann, Hans-Thies (2004) *Postdramsko Kazalište*, trans. Kiril Miladinov, Zagreb-Beograd: Centar za dramsku umjetnost i Centar za teoriju i praksu izvođačkih umjetnosti.

Lipton, Briony and Elizabeth Mackinley (2017) *We Only Talk Feminist Here: Feminist Academics, Voice and Agency in the Neo-Liberal University*, Cham: Palgrave Macmillan.

Lóránd, Zsófia (2018) *The Feminist Challenge to the Socialist State in Yugoslavia*, Cham: Palgrave Macmillan.

Marjanić, Suzana (2009) 'Mitovi o majčinstvu, ili: 'Udana je i ima psa', *Kazalište*, Zagreb: Hrvatski Centar ITI.

Mazaj, Meta (2013) 'Marking the trail: Balkan women filmmakers and the transnational imaginary', in Radmila Gorup (ed.), *After Yugoslavia: The Cultural Spaces of a Vanished Land*, Palo Alto, CA: Stanford University Press.

McQueeney, Joan (2000) 'Theater; a voice for the outsiders', *The New York Times*, 2 July, http s://www.nytimes.com/2000/07/02/theater/theater-a-voice-for-the-outsiders.html

Medelić, Nenad (2010) 'Što ostaje nakon iluzije? Razgivor s Ivanom Sajko', *Slobodna Dalmacija*, 26 January, https://www.slobodnadalmacija.hr/kultura/clanak/id/86050/ sto-ostaje-nakon-iluzije-razgovor-s-ivanom-sajko

Medenica, Ivan (2007) 'Evropa ovde', *Vreme*, 3 May, https://www.vreme.com/cms/ view.php?id=497029

Miletić-Oručević, Tanja (2007) 'Strah golmana od jedanaesterca' in Sava Andjelković and Boris Senker, *Govor drame – govor glume: Zbornik radova sa simpozijuma Dramski tekst danas u Bosni i Hercegovini, Hrvatskoj i Srbiji*, Zagreb: Disput.

Miškovska-Kajevska, Ana (2017) *Feminist Activism at War: Belgrade and Zagreb Feminists in the 1990s*, London and New York: Routledge.

Munk, Erika (2001) 'Beginning to clean the air: two interviews from Belgrade, June 2000', *Theater* 31(1): 27–33.

Nikčević, Sanja (2005) 'British brutalism, the "New European Drama", and the role of the director', *New Theatre Quarterly*, 21(3): 255–272.

Pogačnik, Jagna (2012) 'Kraj feminizma i ženskog pisma', http://aquilonis.hr/dodaci/p isci_na_mrezi/pogacnik_zensko-pismo.pdf

Porterfield, Melissa Rynn (2013) 'Empty stomachs, empty wombs, and empty graves: gnosticism and the search for Serbian identity in Srbljanović's *Barbelo, on Dogs and Children,'* in Graley Herren (ed.), *Text & Presentation, 2012*, The Comparative Drama Conference Series 9, Jefferson, NC and London:McFarland & Company.

Puchner, Martin (2011) 'Drama and performance: toward a theory of adaptation', *Common Knowledge*, 17(2): 292–305.

Radosavljević, Duška (2005) 'Staging theatricalised reality: Yugoslav metatheatre and its political significance', in Birgit Haas (ed.), *Macht – Performanz, Performativitat, Polittheater seit 1990*, Wurzburg: Konigshausen & Neumann, pp. 283–302.

——— (2009) 'The alchemy of power and freedom – a contextualisation of Slobodan Šnajder's Hrvatski Faust (The Croatian Faust)', *Contemporary Theatre Review*, 19(4): 428–447

——— (2012) 'Sarah Kane's Illyria as the land of violent love: a Balkan reading of Blasted', *Contemporary Theatre Review* 22(4): 499–511.

——— (2013) *Theatre-Making: Interplay Between Test and Performance in the 21st Century*, Basingstoke: Palgrave.

Rafolt, Leo (2011) 'Fiziološko-hormonalna opremljenost za terorizam i radjanje', in *Priučen na tumačenje: Deset čitanja*, Zagreb: Zagrebačka slavistička škola.

Rancière, Jacques (1991) *The Ignorant Schoolmaster: Five Lessons in Intellectual Emancipation*, Paolo Alto, CA: Stanford University Press.

——— (2009) *The Emancipated Spectator*, London and New York: Verso.

Rosić, Tatjana (2013) 'Cheesecakes and bestsellers: contemporary Serbian literature and the scandal of transition', in Radmila Gorup (ed.), *After Yugoslavia: The Cultural Spaces of a Vanished Land*, Palo Alto, CA: Stanford University Press.

Russell-Omaljev, Ana (2016) *Divided We Stand: Discourses on Identity in 'First' and 'Other' Serbia*, Stuttgart: ibidem-Verlag.

Sajko, Ivana (2006) *Trilogija – Arhetip: Medeja; Žena bomba; Europa*, manuscript version.

——— (2010) 'Woman-Bomb', translated by Brek, Tomislav, *PAJ*, 94: 108–128.

——— (2011) *Trilogija o neposluhu – Uvod u disjunkciju; Rose is a rose is a rose; Prizori s jabukom; To nismo mi, to je samo staklo*, manuscript version.

——— (2018) Interview in *Teatrologike*, Radio Television Serbia.

Srbljanović, Biljana (2007) *Barbelo, o psima i deci*, manuscript version.

Sierz, Aleks (2001) *In-Yer-Face Theatre: British Drama Today*, London: Faber and Faber.

Vujanović, Ana (2008) 'From the myth of artistic independence to the myth of artistic engagement' in Dennis Barnett and Arthur Skelton (eds), *Theatre and Performance in Eastern Europe: The Changing Scene*, Lanham, MD and Plymouth: The Scarecrow Press.

——— (2010) 'Nova – postpolitička – drama', in Miško Šuvaković (ed.), *Istorija umetnosti u Srbiji*, 20. vek (prvi tom), Belgrade: Orion art.

18 debbie tucker green and Alice Birch

'Angry feminists' on the European stage

Marissia Fragkou[1]

Introduction

The beginning of the twenty-first century has seen a renewed energy in black and feminist writing in British theatre. During the first millennial decade, a handful of black British authors such as Kwame-Kwei Armah, Roy Williams, debbie tucker green, Rachel De-Lahay, and Bola Agbaje achieved mainstream visibility, having their plays staged at the National Theatre, Hampstead, the Royal Court Downstairs, and the West End. This 'Black British theatre Renaissance' was arguably owed to several initiatives, not least from the Arts Council, England, whose aim to redress institutional racism in British theatre played an important role in encouraging black arts to enter the mainstream and raise awareness about 'urgent contemporary social issues' (Goddard 2015: 14). This renewed interest in race relations in the theatre industry was followed by a revitalisation of feminism; a number of women theatre-makers such as Nic Green, Katie Mitchell, Alice Birch, Bryony Kimmings, and Laura Wade, among others, have contributed to a wider renewal in feminist discourse rehearsed in a range of international popular platforms (Gorman et al. 2018: 278–9). At the same time, the ongoing lack of access of women in the theatre industry continues to generate much discussion among institutions, scholars and theatre-makers with a number of initiatives for the advancement of gender equality in the theatre.[2] The two British millennial theatre voices that I deal with in this chapter, debbie tucker green and Alice Birch, have emerged from this distinct socio-cultural context. Sharing an acute interest in feminism and stylistic innovation, Birch and tucker green's feminist dramaturgies are fuelled by anger and indignation against gender and racial injustices and inequalities. They have both attracted much critical attention, received prestigious awards for their work,[3] and have seen their plays performed on national and international stages.

Playwright debbie tucker green made her professional debut on the British stage in 2000 with her short play *two women* (Soho Theatre) followed by two full-length plays in 2003: *dirty butterfly* (Soho Theatre) and *born bad* (Hampstead). She has since written several plays for the stage (four of which she also directed), as well as for radio, film, and television. She is the first black woman playwright to receive two premieres at the Royal Court Downstairs: *stoning mary* (2005) and *random* (2008). Her collaborators include directors Marianne

debbie tucker green and Alice Birch   335

Elliot (*stoning mary*), Kathy Burke (*born bad*), Rufus Norris (*two women* and *dirty butterfly*), and Sacha Wares (*trade*, 2005; *random*, 2008); in 2011, she made her directing debut with *truth and reconciliation* (Royal Court Upstairs) and has since directed four more plays: *nut* (National Theatre, 2013), *hang* (Royal Court, 2015), *a profoundly affectionate, passionate devotion to someone* (-noun) (Royal Court, 2017) and *ear for eye* (Royal Court, 2018).

At the heart of her oeuvre lies an interest in precarious life and social injustice on a local and global scale; her earlier work primarily focused on questions of violence, witnessing and responsibility (*dirty butterfly, born bad, random*) and global inequalities (*trade, stoning mary, generations*); she has since expanded those interests to further examine trauma through the lens of conflict (*truth and reconciliation*) and mental illness (*nut*). Race and gender play a chief role in her plays which feature strong black women at the epicentre. Her later work applies further pressure on the need to revisit legacies of racism and their contemporary relevance (*hang, ear for eye*). tucker green's plays are driven by emotions and their role in shaping human relationships (*a profoundly affectionate, passionate devotion to someone* (-noun)); her confrontational and contradictory characters often challenge traditional etiquette and implicate spectators as witnesses in ethically complex scenarios.

She has been recognised by critics as 'the most prominent and original black female playwright of her generation and [...] one of the most exciting playwrights around' (Cavendish 2018). British reviewers have noted the affective impact of her work, describing it as a 'machine-gun' (Johns 2005) and 'poetry laced with shards of broken glass' (Gardner 2006). And yet, they have criticised 'her subversion of conventional plot structures, highly stylised use of language and sparse stage design' (Abram 2014: 113) as well as her insistence on spelling her name in lower case. The lack of a recognisable social context has received negative criticism for plays like *hang, a profoundly affectionate, passionate devotion to someone* (-noun), and *stoning mary*, which, according to Goddard, confirms the 'predominance of expectations of social realism' in British theatre (2015: 132).

tucker green has also garnered much scholarly attention with several articles and book chapters in English, Spanish, and French examining her work. Particular focus has been paid to the affective registers and feminist attachments mobilised in her plays to address local and global inequalities (Aston 2010; Fragkou and Goddard 2013; Reid 2018; Fragkou 2019); the ethical and political implications/spectatorship/of her playwriting (Fragkou 2012; Aragay and Monforte 2013; Monforte 2015; Escoda 2017); as well as on the precision of her linguistic experimentation which Deidre Osborne terms 'dramatic-poetics' (2011) and Elisabeth Angel-Perez 'in-yer-ear solo symphonies' (2015). She has often been compared to other contemporary (white) British writers such as Sarah Kane, Samuel Beckett and Harold Pinter, yet the playwright herself cautions against such comparisons and notes her 'black influences' such as Afro-American playwright Ntozake Shange and Jamaican poet Louise Bennett among others (Gardner 2005). Theatre scholars have also paid particular attention to her position as a black British female writer while also drawing comparisons to other female playwrights; according to Goddard, 'debbie tucker green is undoubtedly the leading black British woman playwright of the early

336 *Marissia Fragkou*

twenty-first century' (2015: 69) while Osborne describes her as 'the most stylistically innovative, and uncompromisingly poetic, dramatist in contemporary British theatre' intricately combining 'African-diasporic and European-inflected inheritances' (2015: 163). In doing so, Osborne draws attention to her affinities with Afro-American playwright Susan Lori-Parks as well as tracing her lineage with other British women playwrights such as Pam Gems, Liz Lochhead, Winsome Pinnock, and Rebecca Prichard (2015: 163). For Elaine Aston, tucker green's experiential dramaturgy and linguistic innovation as well as her intention 'to dis-ease her spectators into viewing the dehumanizing effects of an inability to care for "others" locally and globally' (Aston 2011: 184) shares strong affinities with Caryl Churchill's oeuvre and 'is genealogically connected to experiential, socially aware women's writing' (Aston 2010: 588). Further, tucker green's work has received international recognition, unprecedented for a black British playwright (Goddard 2015: 69). Many of her plays have been staged in New York and Sydney,[4] Berlin, Madrid, and Strasbourg, while *born bad* and *stoning mary* have been translated into French as *mauvaise* (2012) and *lapider marie* (2015) by the renowned publishing house Maison Antoine Vitez.

While acknowledging the significance of race and Afro-Caribbean cultural heritage in tucker green's work, it is also important to examine how her oeuvre contributes to twenty-first-century feminist writing. In doing so, this chapter examines tucker green's work alongside Birch's as another significant contemporary feminist theatre voice. To date, Birch has written nine plays for the stage and the script of the feminist film *Lady Macbeth* (2016). Similar to tucker green, her dramaturgy articulates 'a politics of anger' (Fragkou and Goddard 2013: 152) around feminist concerns like paedophilia (*Many Moons*, 2011), the objectification of the female body through pornography (*We Want you to Watch*, 2015), the damaging legacies of postfeminism and neoliberalism (*Revolt. She Said. Revolt Again.*, 2014), the trauma of suicide haunting three generations of women (*An Anatomy of Suicide,* 2017) and the experience of marginalised female voices (*[Blank]*, 2018). Birch has written for new writing company Paines Plough as well as all-women theatre companies such as Clean Break and Rash Dash and for female directors such as Katie Mitchell and Erica Whyman; she has seen her work performed at several fringe and mainstream London venues such as the Orange Tree, Theatre 503, Royal Court, National Theatre, Donmar Warehouse, and the Barbican. Her work has further enjoyed several prestigious international stagings in Europe as well as the US, Australia, and New Zealand and has attracted a range of responses from critics. Her ongoing collaboration with Katie Mitchell in particular has allowed her work to be more widely seen on several European stages, particularly in France and Germany, while consolidating her identity as a feminist writer.[5]

Playwright Simon Stephens has often praised her as 'one of the most exciting playwrights in British theatre' (cited in Bowie-Sell 2011) and *The New York Times* critic Ben Brantley (2016) compares *Revolt. She Said.* to John Osborne's *Look Back in Anger* (1956) for its 'anarchic fury', as well as to 'the form-bending virtuosity of Caryl Churchill'. For the *Guardian*'s Michael Billington (2017b), 'Birch has a gift for radical experiment in the style of Caryl Churchill and Sarah

debbie tucker green and Alice Birch   337

Kane'. Scholarly attention to Birch's work is slowly growing with essays taking note of the significance of affect, vulnerability, feminist allegiances (Escoda 2018, forthcoming; Fragkou 2020) and her revolutionary language (Rebellato 2017).

In this light, Birch's affective attachments to anger and her dissonant voice, her stylistic innovation, linguistic precision, and strong commitment to the position of women in precarious social milieus, shares much common ground with tucker green. The following sections will each follow the staging and critical reception of a single play from each author across Britain and Europe.

debbie tucker green: *stoning mary*

tucker green's *stoning mary* opened at the Royal Court Downstairs (in collaboration with Drum Theatre, Plymouth) on 1 April 2005 and was directed by Marianne Elliott. This was the first time the work of a female black British playwright was presented on the main stage of the Royal Court. The play puts global issues at the centre of its enquiry by drawing connections with the locality of its audiences. As specified in the script, the play 'is set in the country it is performed in' and 'all characters are white' (tucker green 2005: 2). It is written as a series of short vignettes each comprising two characters in three different stories who mostly engage in an *agon* over life and its value: in one scene, Wife and Husband argue over a single AIDS prescription by competing about whose body most deserves the medication; in another, Mum and Dad bicker over who is responsible for the fact that their young son has been recruited as child soldier; in a third, Older Sister argues that her imprisoned Younger Sister does not deserve to get a new set of glasses since she is about to be stoned to death. As the play unravels, we realise that all three stories interlock revealing a complex network of relationships: the child soldier kills Wife and Husband and destroys their prescription; in an act of retribution he is killed by the couple's daughter, Younger Sister (Mary); it is for this reason that Mary awaits her execution by stoning which, the audience are led to believe, takes place directly after the lights go down following the final image: 'Mum picks up the first stone' (tucker green 2005: 73).

As a playwright who predominantly focuses on the experiences of black lives, the choice to only use white characters is deliberate; as she explains in an interview with Lyn Gardner (2005):

> I was interested in questioning what we don't see and hear. The stories of people who would be in the headlines every day if what was happening to them was happening to white people. It happens all the time. Look at Rwanda. It just fell out of the news. Or Zimbabwe. We're always hearing what is happening to the white farmers but what about the black political activists who are also being killed? Where are the news stories about them?

The strategy of changing the location of the events in order to bring them close to home echoes Brecht's dramaturgies of estrangement, drawing attention to

338   *Marissia Fragkou*

the differential grievability of black and white lives across the globe. In this sense, the play anticipates the global #blacklivesmatter movement which arose in response to the deaths of black people in US police custody in 2015. Further devices pay tribute to Brecht's legacy such as the introduction of scene titles and additional characters in the AIDS Genocide scenes named 'Wife Ego' and 'Husband Ego' who articulate and comment on the characters' inner thoughts. As Goddard notes, the use of 'Egos' works to speak to 'audience consciences about the lack of effective responses to global issues by drawing attention to the kind of defence mechanisms and diversionary or defiant behaviours that are used to avoid signing petitions' (2015: 129).

Director Marianne Elliott described *stoning mary* as an 'angry play' which 'is making a statement about our selfishness and our inability to touch each other' (*stoning mary* Post-Show Talk); this anger can be located in both 'the terrifying feeling of a world lost to a global tide of dehumanising values and a feeling for the loss of feminism' (Aston 2010: 588) that the play expresses. The playwright's anger towards the West's inability to care for geographically distant lives is channelled through two particular choices: the staging of selfish and cruel confrontational characters who refuse intimacy and fail to recognise each other as human beings (Fragkou and Goddard 2013: 151); and her acerbic commentary on the failure of feminism to inspire solidarity. In perhaps the most well-known excerpt from the play, Mary furiously delivers an angry speech against women who failed to sign the petition against her stoning, bringing into sharp focus a black feminist vehement critique of the white, middle-class feminism's lack of allegiance towards non-white women.

Like the majority of tucker green's plays, illustrative action is replaced with an emphasis on language as 'speech is the action of the drama' (Osborne 2007: 237), though this has not always been appreciated. Some critics admired the 'verbal stampede' (Segal 2005: 425) of *stoning mary*'s language but others found it more 'an acted poem than a fleshed-out play' (Billington 2005), more a 'brutal tone poem than conversation' (Johns 2005) containing 'inarticulate and manic speech patterns' (Bassett 2005). Some critics were perplexed by the play's transcultural approach to character; the *Daily Telegraph*'s Charles Spencer argued 'if Green [*sic*] had shown black Africans behaving so selfishly and cruelly in their distress, I suspect she would have been accused of racism' (Spencer 2005). Others found the play missing an emotional core: Spencer described the play as 'stubbornly unmoving' and Ian Johns (2005) found the inclusion of the 'Egos' more alienating than engaging.

In sum, the responses from the British press suggest a collective belief that tucker green's non-realist language, setting, and character represent a failure to stage a recognisable world, thus undermining the author's political intentions. These comments bring into sharp focus the play's complex spectatorial demands. Although most reviews fail to meet these demands, their complexity has been addressed by scholars and audiences alike: Keith Peacock argues that the play's dramatic devices serve to trigger empathy (2008: 60) and Fragkou and Goddard suggest that the play's Brechtian devices aim to produce astonishment in approaching the lack of caritas towards black lives (2013: 154–5). This impetus to mobilise astonishment and care for lives geographically distant from the West was particularly articulated through Ultz's stage design. The Royal Court's mainstage area was transformed, in Goddard's words, into 'an empty, horseshoe-shaped expanse covered in turquoise blue clay with stones placed around the edges as a constant visual reminder of Young Sister's impeding death' (2015: 127–8) (Figure 18.1). Seats from the stalls were also removed, thus allowing some audience members to stand very close to the action. The particular stage design and the cold light of the production alluded to both an African yard and an open non-specified geographical space (Elliott quoted in McLaughlin 2005: 6). This choice more directly implicated them in Mary's imminent stoning at the end of the play.

stoning mary's dramaturgical strategies underscore the 'need of representing black experience in such a way that it would reach the white, middle-class audiences traditionally forming the bulk of the theatre-going public in Britain' (Aragay and Monforte 2013: 100) and draws attention to power relations between the West and the so-called 'Global South'. Enric Monforte observes how the playwright's dramaturgy engages with the concept of the border: on the one hand, it 'exemplif[ies] the existence of tangible borders between [and within] Europe/the Western world and developing countries'; on the other, she occupies the border between the 'dramatic' and the 'postdramatic'. tucker green's 'dramaturgy of the border' explores the ethics of spectatorial engagement with the text (Monforte 2015: 320–1). In this

Figure 18.1 Cole Edwards, Peter Sullivan, and Emily Joyce in *stoning mary* directed by Marianne Elliott at the Royal Court Theatre, 2005. © Tristram Kenton

340   *Marissia Fragkou*

sense, tucker green's *stoning mary* is in line with the playwright's other work that seeks to produce ethical subjects by acknowledging 'collective responsibility for the "physical lives of one another"' (Fragkou 2012: 37).

stoning mary in Europe

tucker green's plays in Europe have attracted attention for their linguistic complexity and playfulness with character. For example, the French publisher of *mauvaise (born bad)* highlights its brutal and lyrical quality, which they describe as 'challenging for both the translator and the actor' but 'eminently theatrical language which demands to be spoken' (Vermande et al. n.d.). The translators for *lapider marie (stoning mary)* remark on the text's playfulness, theatricality and linguistic precision, describing the 'Egos' as a device that 'reinforces the violence of the dialogue' while also creating distance and theatricality (Gaillot et al. n.d.). In the play's 2008 Spanish premiere at Teatro Pradillo in Madrid directed by Vicente León, the 'Egos' wore latex masks that resembled the faces of the actors playing Husband and Wife, thus punctuating the scene's theatricality and investing it with 'a sinister and uncomfortable edge' (León 2020).

The most high-profile production of a tucker green play on a European stage to date is Benedict Andrews' *stoning mary* for Berlin's Schaubühne (2007) translated by Anja Hilling. The production was preceded by a rehearsed reading of *trade* and *stoning mary* a few weeks earlier as part of the theatre's international festival. Andrews had a track record of innovative productions of modern and contemporary plays on several international stages, including Sarah Kane's *Cleansed* for the Schaubühne in 2004, and 'spent years depicting the strangeness of our world in ever-changing, sometimes drastic images' (Mayenburg 2016). For *stoning mary*, Andrews followed a minimalist approach which placed emphasis on the power of words over stage action: 14 actors sat at the back of the stage waiting for their turn to speak in front of a set of four microphones placed downstage. The set further comprised 'steaming black rubber mats' on the floor (Meierhenrich 2007) and a bare concrete wall with brightly lit neon signs featuring the play's scene titles. As Katrin Bettina Müller (2007) of *Tageszeitung* observes, the characters looked like 'witnesses in court' or 'defendants in an interrogation'. Similar to the Royal Court production and echoing tucker green's emphasis on spectators as witnesses, the audience was directly implicated during the closing scene where actress Lea Draeger, playing Mary's sister, passed her ticket for the stoning to a spectator, saying the script's final line: 'Take my ticket. / ...I... don't wannit' before leaving the stage. The use of microphones complemented and amplified the harshness of the language and action; in scene 7, the actor playing the Child Soldier produced a strong crackling sound with his machete.

Reviewers were quite enthusiastic about the theatre's choice to introduce tucker green to German audiences. Contrary to British reviewers, a key point of focus seemed to be an appreciation of the playwright's use of language, the importance of voice, and how these reinforced the play's social significance. *Süddeutsche Zeitung*'s Christine Dössel (2007) welcomed the play's departure from 'kitchen-sink social realist tradition of the British well-made play' and described the play's linguistic landscape as 'a concert of polyphonic voices'. Max Glauner (2007) for *Freitag 18* called the characters 'the chorus of the forgotten' and suggested that the play's focus on language refuses the voyeuristic spectacle of precarious African lives as portrayed in the media. German critics, then, connected *stoning mary*'s formal innovations to its politics, the reviewer of *Nachtkritik* describing it as both a 'provocative thought experiment' and an 'angry curse-aria against the affluent society' (Peter 2007).

Some reviewers observed that the play might be better suited for radio, a point also raised by British reviewers in relation to the playwright's work; in the context of *stoning mary*'s German production this observation served more as a critique of the production than the play. The critic for the *Märkische Allgemeine* highlighted the pull of the play's language, arguing that 'acting offered the staging almost nothing. It is best to close your eyes and listen to the chorus of microphone-amplified voices. But then one may also forget the basic idea of the author' (Dietschreit 2007). Matthias Heine (2007) from *Welt* went as far as to state bluntly 'Andrews has refused to do his job'.

The German premiere of debbie tucker green's work demonstrates not only the relevance of *stoning mary*'s subject matter beyond British borders, but also the openness of German critics to new work by unknown playwrights using dramatic forms which depart from 'kitchen-sink social realism' – which still seems to be the preference of British reviewers.

Alice Birch: *Revolt. She Said. Revolt Again.*

In 2013, the RSC commissioned playwrights Timberlake Wertenbaker, E.V. Crowe, Abi Zakarian, and Alice Birch to each write a play for a feminist festival under the title 'Midsummer Mischief' performed at Stratford's The Other Place the following year. Their remit was to respond to feminist historian Laurel Thatcher Ulrich's provocation that 'well-behaved women seldom make history'. As Birch often mentions, this statement made her angry and propelled her to write *Revolt. She Said.* in three days (2016), a play which 'should not be well behaved' (RSC 2014: 45). One of Birch's key influences was Valerie Solanas's radical feminist *The SCUM Manifesto* which led her to consider how a manifesto might take on a theatrical form (Birch 2016). The outcome was a revolutionary play, or a 'feminist killjoy manifesto' (Fragkou 2020).

Originally written for a cast of six, the play is organised into four acts, further divided into shorter scenes. There is no indication of character; actors are encouraged to make visible the gap between actor and character and the offstage space is visible to the audience (RSC 2014: 45). Birch particularly notes that there should be 'at least one female character in each scene' and if 'a woman has to get a bit naked at any point, then the men should get naked also to redress the balance' (45). The first three acts appear as an instruction manual, with each scene beginning with an invitation for a revolutionary gesture: 'Revolutionize the World. (Do not Marry.)' (56); 'Revolutionize the World. (Don't Reproduce.)' (77); 'Galvanize' (86).

342   *Marissia Fragkou*

Act 1 comprises scenes focusing on language, reproduction, work, and the body, written as sections of a feminist manifesto. The first scene, entitled 'Revolutionize the Language (Invert It)', a woman questions her partner's phallogocentric phraseology in describing their prospective sexual act. The mischievous and playful tone of the first act is followed by moments of disillusionment and anxiety about the impact of feminism on the lives of women; set as a dinner scene among three generations of women (Grandma, Dinah and her daughter, Agnes), Act 2 stages a confrontation between Dinah and her mother caused by the lack of affection in their own relationship which has in turn damaged her relationship with Agnes. The scene ends with Grandma and Dinah performing a violent act of self-silencing as they chop their tongues out (85).

Act 3 constitutes 'the play's most radically experimental act [...] echoing the polyphonic, online nature of debate today' (Escoda forthcoming). It features an array of vignettes of overlapping voices which create a chaotic soundscape. Birch's precise typography, punctuation, and layout highlight the dynamic and the affective weight of the spoken word and angrily intervene in representations of women as victims. Structurally echoing Kane's *Blasted,* the scene ends with an explosion followed by a short final act where four women activists discuss the possibilities of revolt against patriarchy and neoliberal capitalism.

The incendiary quality of the writing was hailed by Simon Stephens (2017) as 'mark[ing] the arrival on the national stage of a writer of real confidence', declaring that the play 'sparkled with savage wit and formal explosion and culminated in one of the most viscerally anarchic scenes I've seen at the [Royal Court] Theatre Upstairs'. As Rebellato (2017) reported, the working title of Birch's play *Attempts on a Revolution* paid direct homage to Martin Crimp's *Attempts on her Life*, a play that similarly captures the political urgencies of the present by revolutionising dramatic form. Rebellato further situates the play within a wider turn in British theatre characterised by 'a profound withdrawal from realism and an imagination haunted by apocalyptic violence'. I would also suggest that *Revolt. She Said.* belongs to a feminist theatre canon utilising stylistic experimentation as a means to break patriarchal structures;[6] similar to tucker green, Birch forms part of the more recent 'experiential turn in women's writing' which records a feeling for the 'loss of feminism' (Aston 2010)[7] and articulates the urgent need to remobilise feminist politics in the public sphere as a 'caring' project (Fragkou 2020).

Following its premiere at Midsummer Mischief Festival at the RSC's the Other Place in 2014, Whyman's production of *Revolt. She Said.* transferred to the Royal Court Theatre Upstairs the same year; it was then presented again at The Other Place as part of the RSC's Radical Mischief Festival in 2016 before going on tour to Edinburgh Festival, the Traverse, and Shoreditch Town Hall in London. Perhaps surprisingly, there were very few negative comments about the play's radical feminist politics or stylistic experimentation which have often constituted frequent points of critique by British reviewers in relation to work by women playwrights.[8] Dominic Cavendish described Birch's play as 'a cluster-bomb of subversion' (2014) and singled it out from the accompanying pieces of Midsummer Mischief. Aleks Sierz (2016) also proclaimed Birch as 'one of the most exciting playwrights to have arrived in the last five years' and praised the play's 'enormous technical skill and sense of emotional truth'.

Madeleine Girling's set design comprised a glossy pristine black stage filled with a few chairs, several 'bright red fire buckets dotted across the stage, ready for when the production ignites' (Bano 2016), a fire extinguisher, red sand, red paint, and a watermelon. As the piece progressed, the space became messier with the actors splattering paint against the black wall, chopping the watermelon with an axe, and sifting sand on the floor. Some critics found Whyman's production a little too 'restrained' (Serratore 2016) and *The Stage*'s 'not messy enough' (Pringle 2016) to match the play's riotous third act. Serratore particularly compared the RSC production to that of New York's Soho Rep (which opened soon after the RSC run) where 'danger and surprise generated pulseracing anxiety'.

Revolt. She Said. in Europe

Birch's play has enjoyed significant popularity beyond British borders: it has been staged in France (2016), Luxembourg (2018), Germany (2018), and Denmark (2019) to wide critical acclaim. It has also played in New York (Soho Rep, 2016), Melbourne (Malthouse Theatre, 2017), and Auckland (Basement Theatre, 2017). One of the first theatre directors to take notice of Birch's text and stage it in continental Europe was Arnaud Anckaert, co-artistic director (together with Capucine Lange) of Théâtre du Prisme, based in Villeneuve, France. As Anckaert explains, British new writing, in his view, 'uses simple words to express complex ideas' and is 'unafraid of emotions' ('Table Ronde' 2016); he is also fascinated by its use of rhythm and its diverse and (often non-narrative) style which 'reveal both a way of writing and a way of thinking' (Anckaert 2016). Before encountering Birch's text, he had already staged Enda Walsh's *Disco Pigs* (2004), Dennis Kelly's *Orphans* (*Orphelins*, 2011), and Nick Payne's *Constellations* (2013).

Anckaert received the script for *Révolte* (*Revolt. She Said.*) from his collaborator and translator Séverine Magois who, in turn, discovered Birch through British author Matt Hartley ('Table Ronde' 2016). Anckaert describes it as a 'punk play', a 'striking and surprising, […] brutal and immediate piece of theatre […] a mosaic piece in the form of cabaret, a feminist manifesto' (Anckaert 2016). For him, the play's strong desire for a revolution is fuelled by finding the world incomprehensible (Anckaert 2016). Its French premiere (co-produced with Comédie de Béthune, CDN Nord Pas-de-Calais, and Le Théâtre de Rungis), opened at Villeneuve and then toured to Comédie de Béthune, Avignon Festival, and Theatre de Rungis outside Paris in 2016. During rehearsals, Anckaert worked closely with the actors and Magois, paying attention to the piece's musicality and verbal precision ('Table Ronde' 2016), linguistic playfulness and humour. The set design included a few chairs, a table, costumes, a drum kit, and other instruments; above, a luminous red sign presented the titles of each scene. This cabaret aesthetic was supported by live music during the scene changes.

344 *Marissia Fragkou*

The play and production were both enthusiastically received by the French press. Critics appreciated their dynamism and 'rock energy' (Favre and de Bonnay 2016) and its deconstruction of gender stereotypes (actors were also asked to swap gender roles 'in deference to Alice Birch's writing' [Naud 2016]). Gilles Costaz (2016) described the play as 'one of the most recent bombs of British theatre [...] raw, dirty, uncomfortable, sexualized, very suburban, unappealing and screaming with truth'. Yves Kafka (2016) admired Birch's writing style (noting its affinities with Martin Crimp), particularly observing how Birch 'dissects ordinary violence with a precision of an entomologist'.

Sarah Vermande's French translation of Birch's play was also used in Sophie Langevin's 2018 production at Théâtre du Centaure in Luxembourg which subsequently transferred to Avignon Off the following summer. The director acclaims Birch as a 'great writer' and argues that when she first read the text, she found it 'great but also crazy and did not know what to do with it' (Cimatti 2018). Langevin's staging explored the possibilities of a visual language suitable to the dynamic of Birch's piece; the director worked closely with visual artist and designer Sophie Van den Keybus, because she 'was looking more for a sculptural (*plastique*) than theatrical aesthetic as the writing has something performative' (*Révolte Dossier* 2016). The chosen stylised costumes became 'accessories' for the actors to play with: in long white shirts, thick socks and leggings, sleeveless plastic dresses and aprons, the actors' bodies were moulded and remoulded to capture the text's linguistic fluidity and were juxtaposed against sharply colourful backdrops onto which the scene titles were projected. Langevin's staging received praise for both the writing and the production. The piece was labelled as 'undoubtedly one of the most intense and superbly executed performances of the season' (Rodrigues 2018), a 'harsh feminist satire' which strikes like 'lightning' (Schinker cited in Révolte Dossier 2016).

Revolt. She Said. was staged alongside Marlene Streeruwitz's *Mar-a-Lago* at Berlin's Berliner Ensemble in 2018. The established Austrian playwright and novelist was specifically commissioned by the theatre to write a piece to be included as part of a theatre festival dedicated to gender. According to the theatre's website, this double bill 'radically dissect[s] the female perspective on the status quo between men and women, looking at the mechanisms and clichés of patriarchal structures in a highly entertaining manner' (Berliner Ensemble n.d.). The production strongly resonated with the international resurgence of feminist politics and the #MeToo movement which created much hype across different global platforms. Berliner Ensemble's intention to dedicate a season to gender was part of wider trend in Berlin which included a number of events in theatres such as Maxim Gorki and HAU (Hebbel am Ufer).[9] Streeruwitz's text, a direct allusion to Donald Trump's home in Palm Beach and the Weinstein scandal, revolves around five generations of actresses who are summoned by a famous director-producer, who had in the past sexually exploited each of them, to collectively play the role of Chairman Mao's widow.

debbie tucker green and Alice Birch 345

Both plays were directed by the Austrian-Bulgarian director Christina Tscharyiski who employed a trash-pop aesthetic, suffused with ironic humour, to execute Birch's demand that 'the play should not be well behaved'. Projections were used throughout to provide more of the feminist contexts that both plays navigate: for example, images of 'Disney's kneeling Cinderella, 1950s television spots with happy housewives, a beauty contest with sexy preschoolers, Mona Lisa with Botox lips, and a flying Wonder Woman' (Behrendt 2018). Tscharyiski's feminist agenda was further enhanced by references to protest; a tableau of women in a bright pink tent-like knitted hat demanding 'power to women now' and the live performance of feminist German-Turkish rapper Ebow whose songs spoke directly of female empowerment and feminist anger. The director also decided to interpolate Streeruwitz's text into Birch's, ending the performance with the final scene from *Revolt. She Said.,* thus highlighting the intricate connections between the two pieces. German reviewers were generally critical of Tscharyiski's approach, often arguing that her cartoon-aesthetic flattens the characters (Meierhenrich 2018), but read *Revolt. She Said.* in a more positive light than *Mar-a-Lago*; Barbara Behrendt (2018) argued that Tscharyiski's choices were much better suited to Birch's text enhancing its humour; she specifically labels the piece as a 'guide to feminist uprising' and 'an angry feminist text'.

The resonances with #MeToo were also present in the play's Danish premiere in Copenhagen's Husets Teater in 2018. Following the appointment of actor Jens Albinus as artistic director in 2016, the theatre's artistic portfolio began to include more experimental and contemporary work (Strømberg 2018). *Revolt. She Said.,* was part of a festival in response to #MeToo which included the #StopStilheden [Stop the Silence] initiative, a reading of a collection of texts by Danish women working in film, television, and theatre, who have experienced sexual harassment. Albinus and collaborator Marina Bouras shared the responsibility for design and direction and adopted a minimalist aesthetic which focused on voice and language: the stage comprised an ensemble of five actors, a piano, and several microphone stands placed close to each other. The performance maintained high energy with fast-paced dialogue addressed to the audience, deploying postdramatic theatre tropes which amplified the comic aspects of the play's attitude to gender conflict. The piece's opening punctuated Birch's intentions to juxtapose gendered uses of language; Albinus reluctantly tried to utter the play's first line 'I don't understand' with a series of 'uhs', which composer Hannah Schneider and the rest of the company then transformed into a soundscape for the rest of the performance ('Revolt. She Said.' 2018). As one critic noted, 'we are left with the feeling that this is what the modern man contributes in the #MeToo debate. A series of "uhs"' ('Revolt. She Said.' 2018).

From the number of productions discussed here, directors seemed to be welcoming the challenge of staging *Revolt. She Said.,* through reference to more postdramatic aesthetic choices such as placing emphasis on visual dramaturgies to complement the play's affective linguistic registers. The play's multiple stagings in continental Europe coincided with a wider visible resurgence of feminist politics particularly driven by the #MeToo movement which emphasised its contemporary relevance.

346 *Marissia Fragkou*

Conclusion

Although both playwrights are, in comparison to other writers in this volume, relatively young in their careers, they have already received wide recognition within and beyond British borders. Their positive reception on the European stage can, in part, be attributed to the popularity of other British writers like Caryl Churchill, Sarah Kane, and Martin Crimp, who have prepared the way for British playwriting distinguished by linguistic virtuosity and formal experiment. As I have shown through this chapter, feminist anger and stylistic experimentation run through both *stoning mary* and *Revolt. She Said.*, with a particularly intense sense of racial injustice in tucker green's work. This enables tucker green and Birch to explore alternative representations of female characters and to intervene in normalised perceptions of women as victims, as well as drawing attention to perennial gender and racial inequalities which continue to persist in the twenty-first century. As directors and critics have observed, it is this engagement with language and the need to actively listen to marginalised voices that mark both playwrights as important new voices on the contemporary stage.

debbie tucker green – four key productions

born bad. Directed by Kathy Burke. Stage design by Jonathan Fensom. Lighting design by Paul Keogan. Sound design by John Leonard for Aura. Cast: Jenny Jules, Nadine Marshall, Alibe Parsons, Nicholas Pinnock, Ewart James Walters, Sharlene Whyte. Hampstead Theatre, London, 29 April 2003.

stoning mary. Directed by Marianne Elliot. Stage design by Ultz. Lighting design by Nigel Edwards. Sound design by Ian Dickinson. Cast: Claire-Louise Cordwell, Heather Craney, Gary Dunnington, Cole Edwards, Emily Joyce, Martin Marquez, Claire Rushbrook, Ruth Sheen, Peter Sullivan, Alan Williams, Rick Warden. Royal Court Theatre Downstairs, London, 1 April 2005.

stoning mary. Directed by Benedict Andrews. Translated by Anja Hilling. Costume and stage design by Magda Willi. Dramaturgy by Maja Zade. Lighting design by Kathrin Kausche. Cast: Robert Beyer, Jule Böwe, Lea Draeger, Bettina Hoppe, Katrin Heller, Eva Meckbach, Christoph Gareisen, Rafael Gareisen, Islav Tillack, André Szymanski, Elza Marieke de Vos, Stefan Hufschmidt, David Ruland, Rafael Stachowiak. Schaubühne, Berlin, 28 April 2007.

random. Directed by Sacha Wares. Assistant Director: Gbolahan Obisesan. Costume Supervisor Iona Kenrick. Cast: Nadine Marshall. Royal Court Theatre Downstairs, 7 March 2008.

Alice Birch – four key productions

Revolt. She Said. Revolt Again. Directed by Erica Whyman. Assistant director: Joseph Wilde. Stage design by Madeleine Girling. Lighting design by Claire Gerrens. Sound design by Jonathan Ruddick. Dramaturgy by Sarah Dickenson. Cast: Robert Boulter, Scarlett Brookes, Ruth Gemmell, Mimi Ndiweni. Royal Shakespeare Company,

The Other Place, Courtyard Theatre, Stratford-upon-Avon, 14 June 2014. Transferred to the Theatre Upstairs, Royal Court, London, 15 July 2014.

Revolt. She Said. Revolt Again. Directed by Christina Tscharyiski. Stage design and costume by Verena Dengler and Dominique Wiesbauer. Sound design by Ebow. Video design by Dominique Wiesbauer. Lighting design by Steffen Heinke. Artistic consultation by Clara Topic-Matutin. Cast: Astrid Meyerfeldt, Lorna Ishema, Patrick Guldenberg, Sascha Nathan, Anita Vulesica. Berliner Ensemble, Berlin, 13 October 2018.

Anatomy of a Suicide. Directed by Katie Mitchell. Stage design by Alex Eales. Costume design by Sarah Blenkinsop. Lighting design by James Farncombe. Sound Design by Melanie Wilson. Music by Paul Clark. Cast: Gershwyn Eustache Jnr, Paul Hilton, Peter Hobday, Adelle Leonce, Sarah Malin, Jodie McNee, Hattie Morahan, Kate O' Flynn, Sophia Pettit, Vicki Szent-Kirallyi, Dickon Tyrrell. Royal Court Theatre Downstairs, London, 3 June 2017.

[Blank]. Directed by Maria Aberg. Stage design by Rosie Elnile. Lighting Design by Jess Bernberg. Sound Design by Carolyn Downing. Video Design by Heta Multanen. Cast: Ayesha Antoine, Shona Babayemi, Sophia Brown, Jackie Clune, Grace Doherty, Lucy Edkins, Zaris-Angel Hator, Zainab Hasan, Joanna Horton, Thusitha Jayasundera, Petra Letang, Leah Mondesir-Simmonds, Kate O'Flynn, Ashna Rabheru, Jemima Rooper, Taya Tower. Donmar Warehouse, Clean Break and National Theatre: Donmar Warehouse, London, 11 October 2019.

Notes

1 Quotes not in English are translated into English by the author. I would like to warmly thank Enric Monforte for providing me with useful information on the Spanish premiere of *stoning mary*. My thanks also go to Kristine Sommerlade and Clara Escoda for their help in translating extracts from German, Danish and Spanish.
2 See UK initiatives by Tonic Theatre (https://www.tonictheatre.co.uk) and Sphinx Theatre (https://sphinxtheatre.co.uk).
3 debbie tucker green's awards include the 2004 Olivier Award for Most promising Newcomer for *born bad*, the BAFTA TV award for Best Single Drama for her televised version of *random* (2011). Birch is the recipient of the 2014 George Devine award for Most Promising Playwright for *Revolt. She Said. Revolt Again.*, and the 2018 Susan Smith Blackburn Prize for *Anatomy of a Suicide.*
4 New York's Soho Rep presented *born bad* (2011) and *generations* (2014), Sydney's Red Stitch Theatre Company produced *dirty butterfly* (2003), and SWB Stables Theatre *stoning mary* (2008).
5 Her collaboration with Mitchell includes *Ophelias Zimmer* (2016), a feminist take on Shakespeare's *Hamlet* and an adaptation of Elfriede Jelinek's feminist text *Shadow (Euridice Speaks) [Schatten (Eurydike sagt)]* developed for the Schaubühne in 2016; *Anatomy of a Suicide* (Royal Court Downstairs, 2017); *La Maladie de La Mort* (Bouffes du Nord, 2018) and Virginia Woolf's *Orlando* (Schaubühne, 2019).
6 Some examples might include Ntozake Shange's *for colored girls who have considered suicide/when the rainbow is enuf* (1976) to Eve Ensler's *The Vagina Monologues* (1996), and Sarah Kane's *4.48 Psychosis* (1999).
7 Aston discusses plays by Sarah Kane, debbie tucker green, and Caryl Churchill.

348   *Marissia Fragkou*

8 See, for instance, reviews for Sarah Daniels' *Masterpieces* (1983), Phyllis Nagy's *Butterfly Kiss* (1994), Caryl Churchill's *The Skriker* (1994), and Timberlake Wertenbaker's *The Break of Day* (1995).
9 The Gorki theatre staged two world premieres focusing on gender that season: Yael Ronen's *Yes but No* and Suna Gürler's *You are not the hero of this story*. HAU celebrated the tenth anniversary of pop feminist *Missy Magazine* with lectures, concerts and a live show by Spanish performer Arantxa Martínez.

Works cited

Abram, Nicola (2014) 'Staging the unsayable: debbie tucker green's political theatre', *Journal of Contemporary Drama in English*, 12(2): 113–130.

Anckaert, Arnaud (2016) 'Avignon. Entretien/Arnaud Anckaert', *La Terrasse*, 26 June, https://www.journal-laterrasse.fr/revolt-she-said-revolt-again/

Angel-Perez, Elisabeth (2015) 'Du In-Yer-Face au In-Yer-Ear: les «solo-symphonies» de debbie tucker green', *Coup de théâtre*, 29: 175–192.

Aragay, Mireia and Enric Monforte (2013) 'Racial violence, witnessing and emancipated spectatorship in *The Colour of Justice, Fallout* and *random*', in Vicky Angelaki (ed.), *Contemporary British Theatre: Breaking New Ground*, Basingstoke: Palgrave, pp. 96–120.

Aston, Elaine (2010) 'Feeling the loss of feminism: Sarah Kane's *Blasted* and an experiential genealogy of contemporary women's playwriting', *Theatre Journal*, 62(4): 575–591.

———— (2011) 'debbie tucker green', in Martin Middeke, Aleks Sierz and Peter Paul Schnierer (eds), *The Methuen Drama Guide to Contemporary British Playwrights*, London: Methuen Drama, pp. 183–202.

Bano, Tim (2016) '*Revolt.She Said. Revolt. Again.*: Alice Birch's ferocious Odyssey finally hits London', *Time Out*, 31 August, https://www.timeout.com/london/theatre/revolt-she-said-revolt-again

Bassett, Kate (2005) 'Nice trick if only it worked', *The Independent*, 10 April, https://www.independent.co.uk/arts-entertainment/theatre-dance/reviews/stoning-mary-royal-court-downstairs-londonprofessor-bernhardi-arcola-londonamajuba-like-doves-we-5344129.html

Behrendt, Barbara (2018) 'Wer Penetriert hier wen?', *RBB*, 14 October, https://www.rbb24.de/kultur/beitrag/2018/10/theaterkritik-berliner-ensemble-revolt-she-said-revolt-again-mar-a-lago.html

Berliner Ensemble (n.d.) '*Revolt. She Said. Revolt. Again./Mar-a-Lago*', https://www.berliner-ensemble.de/en/production/revolt-mar-a-lago

Billington, Michael (2005) 'Review of *stoning mary*', *Guardian*, 6 April, https://www.theguardian.com/stage/2005/apr/06/theatre1

———— (2017a) '*a profoundly affectionate*... Review: Couple's rows are painful to watch', *Guardian*, 7 March, https://www.theguardian.com/stage/2017/mar/07/a-profoundly-affectionate-review-meera-syal-debbie-tucker-green

———— (2017b) 'Review of anatomy of a suicide', *Guardian*, 12 June, https://www.theguardian.com/stage/2017/jun/12/anatomy-of-a-suicide-review-royal-court-alice-birch-katie-mitchell

Birch, Alice (2016) 'Interview with Daisy Bowie-Sell', *WhatsOnStage*, 3 August, https://www.whatsonstage.com/edinburgh-theatre/news/alice-birch-interview-revolt-edinburgh_41421.html

debbie tucker green and Alice Birch   349

Bowie-Sell, Daisy (2011) 'Review: *Many Moons*', *Telegraph*, 1 June, https://www.tele graph.co.uk/culture/theatre/theatre-reviews/8550232/Many-Moons-Theatre503-London-review.html

Brantley, Ben (2016) 'Review: *Revolt. She Said. Revolt Again*. Captures the fury of modern womanhood', *New York Times*, 19 April, https://www.nytimes.com/2016/04/20/theater/review-revolt-she-said-revolt-again-captures-the-fury-of-modern-womanhood.html

Cavendish, Dominic (2014) 'Midsummer Mischief, The Other Place at the Courtyard Theatre, Stratford-upon-Avon, review', *Telegraph*, 22 June, https://www.telegraph.co.uk/culture/theatre/theatre-reviews/10917888/Midsummer-Mischief-The-Other-Place-at-the-Courtyard-Theatre-Stratford-upon-Avon-review.html

———— (2018) '*ear for eye* review, Royal Court: Beautiful theatrical invention meets crass identity politics', *Telegraph*, 2 November, https://www.telegraph.co.uk/theatre/what-to-see/ear-eye-review-royal-court-beautiful-theatrical-invention-meets/

Cimatti, Grégory (2018) 'Mesdames, Indignez-Vous!', *Le Quotidien*, 24 January, https://www.lequotidien.lu/culture/mesdames-indignez-vous/

Costaz, Gilles (2016) '*Révolte* d'Alice Birch: Radicalité féministe', *Webtheatre*, 19 July, https://www.webtheatre.fr/Revolte-d-Alice-Birch

Dietschreit, Frank (2007) 'Oratorium in der Todeszelle', *Maerkische Allgemeine.de*, 30 April.

Dössel, Christine (2007) 'Stimmen Africas', *Süddeutsche Zeitung*, 3 May.

Escoda, Clara (2017) 'Ethics, precariousness and the "inclination" towards the other in debbie tucker green's *dirty butterfly*, Laura Wade's *Posh* and Martin Crimp's *In the Republic of Happiness*', in Mireia Aragay and Martin Middeke (eds), *Of Precariousness: Vulnerabilities, Responsibilities, Communities in Twenty-First Century British Drama and Theatre*, Berlin: De Gruyter, pp. 187–202.

———— (2018) '"Her heart knows my heart for a brief moment": Mediated affect and utopian impulse in *Many Moons* (2011) by Alice Birch', *Performing Ethos*, 8: 19–34.

———— (forthcoming) '*Revolt. She Said. Revolt Again* (2014)', in Vicky Angelaki and Dan Rebellato (eds), *The Cambridge Companion to British Playwriting since 1945*, Cambridge: Cambridge University Press.

Favre, Frédérique and Lorène de Bonnay (2016) 'L'énergie rock de la mise-en-Scène finit par convaincre', *Les Trois Coups*, 25 July, https://lestroiscoups.fr/revolt-she-said-revolt-aga in-dalice-birch-la-manufacture-patinoire-a-avignon/

Fragkou, Marissia (2012) 'Precarious subjects: ethics of witnessing and responsibility in the plays of debbie tucker green', *Performing Ethos*, 3(1): 23–39.

———— (2019) *Ecologies of Precarity in Twenty-First Century Theatre: Politics, Affect, Responsibility*, London: Bloomsbury.

———— (2020) '"Feeling Feminism": politics of mischief in contemporary women's theatre', in Mireia Aragay, Cristina Delgado-Garcia and Martin Middeke (eds), *Speaking of Affect(s) in Twenty-First Century Theatre*, London: Palgrave.

Fragkou, Marissia and Lynette Goddard (2013) 'Acting in/action; staging human rights in debbie tucker green's Royal Court Plays', in Vicky Angelaki (ed.), *Contemporary British Theatre: Breaking New Ground*, Basingstoke: Palgrave, pp. 145–166.

Gaillot, Emmanuel, Blandine Pélissier and Kelly Rivière (n.d.) '*Lapider Marie*: Regard du Traducteur', Maison Antoine Vitez Website, https://www.maisonantoinevitez.com/fr/bibliotheque/lapider-marie-1080.html

Gardner, Lyn (2005) 'I was messing about: she's won awards and acclaim but still not sure if she is a playwright', *Guardian*, 30 March, https://www.theguardian.com/stage/2005/mar/30/theatre

350 *Marissia Fragkou*

——— (2006) 'Trade', *Guardian*, 21 March, https://www.theguardian.com/stage/2006/mar/21/theatre

Glauner, Max (2007) 'Hören-Sehen', *Freitag*, 18, 4 May.

Goddard, Lynette (2015) *Contemporary Black British Playwrights: Margins to Mainstream*, Basingstoke: Palgrave.

Gorman, Sarah, Geraldine Harris and Jen Harvie (2018) 'Feminisms now', *Contemporary Theatre Review*, 28(3): 278–284.

Heine, Matthias (2007) '"Stoning Mary" in der Berliner Schaubühne', 11 May, https://www.welt.de/welt_print/article865456/Stoning-Mary-in-der-Berliner-Schaubuehne.html

Johns, Ian (2005) '*Stoning Mary*', *The Times*, 7 April, https://www.thetimes.co.uk/article/stoning-mary-wc5rgxh5nkk

Kafka, Yves (2016) 'Revolt. She Said... Ondes de choc au pays du machisme et du feminisme ordinaires', *LeBruitOff*, 21 July, https://lebruitduoff.com/2016/07/21/revolt-she-said-ondes-de-choc-au-pays-du-machisme-et-du-feminisme-ordinaires/

Léon, Vicente (2020) Email to Enric Monforte. 8 January.

Mayenburg, Marius (2016) 'Introduction', trans. Maja Zade, in *Benedict Andrews: Collected Plays*, London: Oberon, n.p.

McLaughlin, Emily (2005) *stoning mary Education Resources*, London: Royal Court Theatre, pp. 1–14.

Meierhenrich, Doris (2007) 'Abgesänge auf das Sprechen Benedict Andrew inszeniert Debbie Tucker Greens Stück "Stoning Mary" an der Schaubühne', *Berliner Zeitung*, 30 April.

——— (2018) 'Premieren im HAU und im BE: Revolutionsperformance und Gendertheater', *Berliner Zeitung*, 15 October, https://archiv.berliner-zeitung.de/kultur/theater/premieren-im-hau-und-im-be-revolutionsperformance-und-genderthea ter-31443662

Monforte, Enric (2015) 'The Theatre of debbie tucker green: A dramaturgy of the border', in Núria Santamaria and Francesc Foguet (eds), *De fronteres i arts escèniques*, Lleida: Punctum, pp. 319–332.

Müller, Katrina Bettina (2007) 'Duelle der Demütigung', *Die Tageszeitung*, 2 May, https://taz.de/!287151/

Naud, Elisabeth (2016) 'Revolt. She Said. Revolt Again.', *Theatre du Blog*, 29 July, http://theatredublog.unblog.fr/2016/07/29/revolt-she-said-revolt-again/

Osborne, Deirdre (2007) 'Not "In-Yer-Face" but what lies in beneath: experiential and aesthetic inroads in the drama of debbie tucker green and Dona Daley', in R. Victoria Arana (ed.), *Black British Aesthetics Today*, Newcastle: Cambridge Scholars Publishing, pp. 222–242.

——— (2011) 'How do we get the whole story?: contra-dictions and counter-narratives in debbie tucker green's dramatic poetics', in Merle Tönnies and Christina Flotmann (eds), *Narrative in Drama*, Contemporary Drama in English, 18. Trier: Wissenschaftlicher Verlag Trier, pp. 181–206.

——— (2015) 'Resisting the standard and displaying her colours: debbie tucker green at the British theatre's vanguard', in Mary Brewer, Lynette Goddard and Deirdre Osborne (eds), *Modern and Contemporary Black British Drama*, London: Palgrave, pp. 161–177.

Peacock, D. Keith (2008) 'Black British drama and the politics of identity', in Nadine Holdsworth and Mary Luckhurst (eds), *A Concise Companion to Contemporary British and Irish Drama*, Malden, Oxford: Blackwell, pp. 48–65.

Peter, Anne (2007) 'Wo haben die sich hinverfickt?', *Nachtkritik.de*, 28 April.

Pringle, Stewart (2016) 'Revolt. She Said. Revolt Again', *The Stage*, 20 August, https://www.thestage.co.uk/reviews/2016/revolt-she-said-revolt-again-review-at-traverse-theatre-edinburgh-falls-short/

Rebellato, Dan (2017) 'Of an apocalyptic tone recently adopted in theatre: British drama, violence and writing', *Sillages Critiques* [*En ligne*], 22, http://journals.openedition.org/sillagescritiques/4798

Reid, Trish (2018) '"Killing Joy as a world-making project": Anger in the work of debbie tucker green', *Contemporary Theatre Review*, 28(3): 390–400.

'Revolt. She Said. Revolt Again.' (2018) *CPHCulture*, http://www.cphculture.dk/b412revoltshesaid.html

Révolte Dossier (2016) https://www.theatre-contemporain.net/images/upload/pdf/f-f66-5cd554a5d540d.pdf

Rodrigues, Fabien (2018) 'Theatre: être une femme', *Land*, 2 February, http://www.land.lu/page/article/835/333835/DEU/index.html

RSC (2014) *Midsummer Mischief: Four Radical New Plays*, London: Oberon.

Segal, Victoria (2005) 'Review of *stoning mary*', *Theatre Record*, 25: 425.

Serratore, Nicole (2016) 'Review: Revolt. She Said. Revolt. Again. at Traverse', *Exeunt*, 28 August, http://exeuntmagazine.com/reviews/review-revolt-said-revolt-traverse/

Sierz, Aleks (2016) 'Revolt. She Said. Revolt Again. Shoreditch Town Hall', *Aleks Sierz*, 2 September, http://www.sierz.co.uk/reviews/revolt-she-said-revolt-again-shoreditch-town-hall/

Spencer, Charles (2005) 'Thin play unworthy of its punchy production', *The Telegraph*, 7 April, https://www.telegraph.co.uk/culture/theatre/drama/3639955/Thin-play-unworthy-of-its-punchy-production.html

Stephens, Simon (2017) 'Alice Birch talks to Simon Stephens', Royal Court Playwright's Podcast, Season 2: Episode 1, *RoyalCourtTheatre.com*, https://royalcourttheatre.com/series/series-2/

stoning mary Post-Show Talk (2005) Royal Court Theatre, Available at the British Library's Soundserver.

Strømberg, Ulla (2018) 'Revolt. She Said. Revolt Again. Husets Teater', *Kulturkupeen*, 25 February, https://www.kulturkupeen.dk/revolt-she-said-revolt-again-husets-teater/

'Table Ronde avec Alice Birch, Arnaud Anckaert et Séverine Magois' (2016) *Vimeo*, https://vimeo.com/202923268

tucker green, debbie (2005) *stoning mary*, London: Nick Hern.

Vermande, Sarah, Gisele Joly and Sophie Magnaud (n.d.) 'Mauvaise: Regard du traducteur', Maison Antoine Vitez Website, https://www.maisonantoinevitez.com/fr/bibliotheque/mauvaise-773.html

19 Peter Handke

Inhabiting the world together

Hans-Thies Lehmann

At the entrance to the hall where a number of important, 'successful' contemporary theatre authors have here been gathered and arranged in pairs stands the solitary figure of Peter Handke. An older brother from another time, [he is][1] admired for the resoluteness with which he holds on to his idiosyncratic writing and his lifestyle far removed from the theatre industry; at the same time envied for his undeniable 'success' within this very industry. But do we not nowadays seem to recognise above all a particular warning for the younger ones in this gesture of turning away? For, a shared experience of this younger generation of authors, the majority of whom were born between the 1960s and 1980s and had their 'breakthrough' to a wider public response after 1989, is the following: that they found themselves confronted with the expectation that theatre had to be 'political', that it had to contribute to a critique of existing social conditions. Yet it is precisely the fact that Handke's work has always decidedly resisted this expectation which distinguishes him from most other authors. From the beginning to the end of his career he staunchly held on to one motif, namely to the relentless insistence on the tangible, the refusal of phrases and truisms, even of those that critique or that are intended to be critical. For him, this fight against trivialisation – page by page, day by day – is *the* task of the writer.

But it is precisely this [trivialisation] to which the 'political' degrades in his view when it wants to prove itself in the wrong terrain – within the realm of art. In fact, the authors soon found themselves confronted with the age-old and ever new problems of a political – or politically intended – theatre. All too easily the artist lowers his or her standards when trying to represent conflicts in a clarifying manner – which, according to Ernst Jünger, happens to anyone who provides a comment on their work. The investigation of the material's form often remains superficial, too often is such [political] engagement a transparent excuse for a lack of intellectual exertion, and the burningly topical issue is a result of an adaptation to the expectations of politically minded spectators. Of the authors represented in this volume we can certainly say that they strive to work vigorously against such difficulties. Yet the fundamental difficulty that will hardly ever cease to exist entirely is that any theatrical re-presentation of problems defined in reality as political has to regurgitate whatever has been qualified as 'political' in a preformed public discourse, especially mediatised public discourse. 'And does not theatre that aims to be politically effective inevitably have to adapt to the pre- and deformed habits of the spectators and thus reaffirm them, *precisely because it wants to be effective?*' (Lehmann 2012: 12 f.). Closely related to this problem is the danger of moralising and assuming a superior attitude:

> Moralism appeals to certainties in being able to differentiate between good and bad that are all too illusory. From the perspective of theatre, the decisive critique of moral discourse is, however, that it turns spectators into judges, instead of letting them experience the shaky premises of their own judging – which would be the real opportunity of aesthetic discourses.
>
> (Lehmann 2012: 19)

Grappling with Peter Handke's work should prove useful in achieving an increased awareness of the difficulties that theatre faces today. Admittedly, this presupposes the ability to allow oneself to be affected and made uncertain by an aesthetic piece, to experience oneself not only as the viewer, but also as the viewed – *ce que nous regardons ça nous regarde* – or in a more lyrical form: 'for here there is no place that does not see you. You must change your life' (Rilke 1995).

Such uncertainty was for example not possible for the group of protestors who showed up at the ceremony in Oslo where Handke was presented with the Ibsen Prize, rioting and raising absurd accusations against the author with chants and placards. Handke soon went outside to talk to them but this proved entirely impossible. Later he improvised a little speech, in which – in line with Nietzsche's 'The innocents are the downfall' – he caustically stated:

> You are entirely innocent. You evil men and evil women know – pretend to know – who is good and who is evil in this world. In doing so, you are only making the world more evil. [...] You are in hell, you are hell, you are the innocent devils of postmodern times.

I experienced this speech and was fascinated by how closely Handke's revulsion approached Heiner Müller (otherwise so far removed from him), who on multiple occasions said that the sight of the masses in a West German pedestrian zone literally caused him nausea. He simply could not stand the feeling of subjective innocence of these people, consumers, who of course were not guilty of anything that had happened in Germany. I was surprised, however, when the following year [Handke's] literary treatment was published as a play, entitled *Die Unschuldigen, Ich und die Unbekannte am Rand der Landstraße* (*The Innocents, Me and the Stranger at the Side of the Country Road*).[2] For, whoever expected a devastating critique of the innocents was disappointed. In the poetic process the hellish innocents had become a fairly normal crowd of people, who did not react uniformly either. Together with [the internal division of] the innocents, Handke has in this, his most recent play to date, realized a division [and] proliferation of the self that has hitherto not been seen.

For decades, the theatre has seen only a few poets who could design poetics that communicate with the profoundly changed and vastly expanded understanding of theatre. Despite and precisely because of his distance to theatre, Peter Handke belongs to those who have spurred a different way of thinking about theatre. What is special about his work is that he defines theatre beyond the dominance of the dramatic in a new and very idiosyncratic way, but always from the perspective of the *literary* author.

While more recent theatre is to a great extent postdramatic also in the narrower sense of pushing back the dimension of text and speech – especially the poetic dimension – and becoming visual dramaturgy, *Tanztheater*, performance, installation, exploration of urban spaces, approaching documentation and social action, Handke's theatre is postdramatic, too. However, it continues to refer emphatically to literature, not in the old sense of a 'literary' theatre of drama but as a theatre of language, as *Sprachtheater*. His texts are thus called *Sprechstück* (spoken piece) or *Dramatisches Gedicht* (dramatic poem). *The Hour We Knew Nothing of Each Other* returns as a silent play to the processes of *Kaspar* or *My Foot My Tutor*. Countless figures cross a square as a 'speaking' corporeal pantomime, passing each other, meeting each other, repeatedly, in all variations. Handke's theatre practice once more shows the enormous spectrum of postdramatic theatre texts.

Yet on hearing Peter Handke's name mentioned, nine out of ten readers will most certainly associate him with *Publikumsbeschimpfung* (*Offending the Audience*). This piece, his debut from 1966, is predominantly a funny, highly reflected, and at the same time circus-like, ridiculous 'language-play' (*Sprach-Spiel*). It represents a single great metaphor for that which was developing as performance and postdramatic theatre at the time and in the following decades. Just as Robert Wilson freed theatre from plot and the logic of the plot, from 'characters', from the embodiment of roles, and from securing dramaturgical frames with his visual poetry of the stage, so did Handke open the way for a theatre that did not provide any mimesis of a dramatic plot. It was a theatre in which the stage was thought of as space which metonymically extended the real theatre, and not as a symbolic stand-in for a different fictitious reality; and in which time was not presented as another fictitious time, but *exhibited* as the time of the performance itself. People appeared on stage who were trained actors but did not embody characters. The communicative situation of the theatre that was actually taking place became the primary source of energy – the recording of the performance in 1966 [directed by Claus Peymann], which still appears wonderfully fresh, demonstrates this very clearly. Handke had just made himself known with aplomb in the literary scene through his legendary performance at the conference of the Gruppe 47 (Group 47) in Princeton, when he, a then barely known budding author, accused the present literary giants in sparse words of an 'impotence of description' (*Beschreibungsimpotenz*).

After this chastisement of his colleagues, the public probably expected a form of performance that would aggressively attack the spectators, or possibly even abuse them. But here too it applies that many titles of Handke's theatre plays are misleading: *Prophecy* does not predict anything but explores linguistic images by transcribing them into the future tense. Self-accusation (*Selbstbezichtigung*) does not confess to a crime. *The Hour We Knew Nothing of Each Other* makes us think of the self-forgetting intimacy of a couple's togetherness, yet it shows a public space whose fascination stems from its non-intimacy. And similarly, offence or name-calling in the common sense is only the smallest part of *Offending the Audience*. Seemingly targeted at the audience, the following passage in truth makes fun of a list of clichés used by critics about theatre performances by applying them to the audience:

> [...] But you don't make an evening. You're not a brilliant idea. You are tiresome. You are not a rewarding subject. You are a theatrical blunder. You are not true to life. You are not theatrically effective. You don't send us [into another world]. You don't enchant us. You don't dazzle us. You don't entertain us fabulously. You are not playful. You are not sprightly. You have no tricks up your sleeve. You have no flair for the theatre. You have nothing to say. Your début is unconvincing. You are not with it. You don't help us pass the time. You are not addressing the human quality in us. You leave us cold.
>
> (Handke 1997: 14)

Not only is this funny but at the same time it is the precisely observed ideology of what theatre is supposed to be for fans of a kind of theatre that Brecht dismissed as 'the theatre of empathy' (*Einfühlungstheater*): an event on stage that enlivens the tired senses of a basically passive audience. Brecht's idea of theatre, that it was not to be imagined as a presentation *by* actors *for* the audience but as an event that is experienced together, where actors become 'delegates' of the audience and are commissioned to present the interests and problems that concern the audience for the purpose of a shared self-understanding, is much closer to Handke, who nevertheless kept his distance from Brecht and followed his methods with suspicious scrutiny. However, this engagement with Brecht only takes place 'à la cantonade' (to no one in particular), from behind the scenes. It is not verbalised, but *Offending the Audience* reads even more clearly today than at the time as a passionate speech against the bourgeois idea of the dramatic theatre of identification. It is therefore only logical when the above cited section is followed with the following depiction:

> This is no drama. No action that has occurred elsewhere is re-enacted here. Only a now and a now and a now exist here. [...] We are not acting out a plot. Therefore we are not playing time. Time is for real here, it

356   *Hans-Thies Lehmann*

expires from one word to the next. [...] The time here is *your* time. Space time here is your space time.

(1997: 14)

We are not playing ourselves in different situations. We are not thinking of the emergency. We don't have to represent our death. We don't have to represent our life. [...] We are speaking while time expires. We speak of the expiration of time. We are not acting as if [...] On the other hand we do act as if. We act as if we could repeat words. We appear to repeat ourselves. Here is the world of appearances. Here appearance is appearance. Appearance is here appearance.

(1997: 16)

At the end comes the description of the audience, who are going to leave the theatre:

You will push in an orderly fashion into the foyer [...] You will see yourselves in mirrors. You will help each other into coats. You will hold doors open for each other. [...] You will return into the everyday. You will go in different directions. [...] You will go to a restaurant. You will think of tomorrow. [...] You will lead your own lives again. You will no longer be a unit. You will go from one place to different places. [...] But before you leave you will be insulted. [...]

We will insult you because insulting is also one way of speaking to you. By insulting you, we can be straight with you. [...] While we are insulting you, you won't just hear us, you will listen to us. The distance between us will no longer be infinite. [...] We will contradict ourselves with our insults. [...] We will mean no one in particular. We will only create an acoustic pattern. You won't have to feel offended. *You* were warned in advance, so you can feel quite unoffended while we're insulting you. Since you are probably thoroughly offended already, we will waste no more time before thoroughly offending you, you chuckleheads.

(1997: 28)

What follows is a four-page actual attack on the audience that is as hilarious as it is drop-dead funny until the very end:

You crowned heads. You pushers. You architects of the future. You builders of a better world. You mafiosos. You wiseacres. You smart-alecs. You who embrace life. You who detest life. You who have no feeling about life. You ladies and gents you, you celebrities of public and cultural life you, you who are present you, you brothers and sisters you, you comrades you, you worthy listeners you, you fellow humans you.

(1997: 31)

Offending the Audience belongs to the theatre plays of which one can say that they were historically fortunate. It arrived in 1966 at the right time. The student movement was emerging and the audience was ready to accept even radical criticism of institutions such as the theatre. At the same time, the sense for literary quality was still more pronounced because for many the literary author was still considered the incarnation of the cultivated subject par excellence. The decay of literature's prestige had already begun but was not yet a resounding cultural reality. *Offending the Audience* became, in defiance of its dependence on the German language, an international success. Still today, one can observe that many students in Anglo-Saxon Drama departments choose to work on *Offending the Audience* for their independent practical projects, while every other year an established theatre produces a new production of the play.

Even in the 1960s, Peter Handke's interest was in theatre from the perspective of the writer – and that has not changed much since then. Therefore, it would be a misunderstanding to read his wordless plays or mimes like *Kaspar* or *The Hour We Knew Nothing of Each Other* merely as technical stage directions. They are poetic texts. Neither does the keyword 'epic' correctly characterise his theatre, which is distanced from Brecht. We have to think more of something like poetry, of a theatre that is almost as much scenic poetry as it is narration. One of his notes from 1982 reads: 'An epic made of haikus, which, however by no means appear as such individual things, without plot, without intrigue, without drama, but narrating nonetheless: that is what I imagine as the highest [achievement]' (52).

'Without drama': what disturbs Handke about theatre – and not only there, what he tries to avoid everywhere – is what he calls 'the dramatic'. Early on, he notes: 'To me, Aeschylus appears to be the most accomplished: no intrigue, only the power of the word; pure drama' (1982: 238). And further: 'In dramatic poems the persons should be able to turn to one another, like the heroes once turned to the gods: that would be natural dramaturgy, without the tricks of dialogue and action of the habituated theatre' (ibid.). The dialogue retreats behind the evocative and addressing dimensions of speaking, as in Aeschylus, who became the role model: 'In Aeschylus, everyone can continuously wish and curse, and that is what the drama consists of' (1982: 237). What fascinates Handke about Poussin is his 'classical de-dramatisation'. With respect to Cézanne he notes: 'When I look from van Gogh to Cézanne, his image emerges as reassurance, de-dramatisation, and at the same time on the threshold to seriousness' (1982: 183).

Despite (and because of) his disinclination towards the dramatic, writing for – one could also say: against – the theatre is a remarkable constant in Handke's work. Remarkable because one might think that his affinity towards a strictly self-involved, literarily formed reflexion; his understanding of poetry as a narrating, naming salvation of reality from idle talk and the inability to perceive; the chosen solitariness of his lifestyle – that all this would leave no room for the noisy, public, and in the best – but also most trivial – sense, ephemeral mass milieu of the theatre. As particularly the German theatre of the last few decades

358   *Hans-Thies Lehmann*

often appears loud, indecent, and deliberately rough, and rather wants to destroy a contemplative attitude, we could ask even more helplessly: where is there any space in this theatre for a hesitating consciousness, for Handke's unsettling way of writing that constantly questions the self and the surrounding world it encounters?

First of all, the following can generally be stated: Handke's writing is emphatically and specifically modern in that every word, every sentence, every text begins, time and again, with the probing doubt whether a linguistic 'form' could be possible that does justice to the experience of the world. In his early period and after the *nouveau roman* he initially searches for a self-reflective way of writing. In an interview, when asked about his readings during his youth, Handke highlights the positive influence of Alain Robbe-Grillet, who had taught him to believe in nothing else in literature but ever more precise description.

But even the texts after his so-called 'turn' (a question mark is to be put after this term) remain – variations included – experimental, provided that we understand this notion not as a random trial and error process, but as a form of literature that 'explores' the world, the self, and the possibility of their becoming language (*Sprachwerdung*). Handke does not have any illusions regarding the polemics that he can expect [from critics]: '[...] inevitably your linguistic recapturings of the world will at first be reviled as "harmonisation", the word itself will already suffice as scorn' (1982: 5). It is, however, simply about the – not so new – task of art to explore and expand human experience and ultimately the possibilities of human expression. The form is the actual proof of the depicted: 'It is only art when the how *shines* within what has been made' (1982: 158).

Countless texts by Handke that are written for his own self-understanding revolve around the question how in this writing two poles face each other. The one is his exceedingly attentive effort of description. But this always remains referred to the other pole: a painfully alert and distancing consciousness of the (de)scribing subject. Language and image, subject and object, experienced in a hostile polarity, are at the same time inseparable and forever separated from each other through the *chorismos* between words and things.

What looks at first sight like an immanently *literary* tension includes, sedimented with in it, an idea of *theatre*. Occasionally, the author's self-description also resorts to the image of theatre:

> How often am I painfully alone on the stage of my inner self, and then others join in, you and you, sometimes the peoples of the earth, and on my stage we then don't play but are simply together, and inside my chest it has become wide and warm.
>
> (1982: 13)

Theatre as a place of speaking is already inscribed into mute literary writing. 'Inside what I have written is probably me but my voice is missing. That's how it should be', writes Handke (1982: 134). What is good for the writing, however, shows a lack that becomes visible as soon as we understand that the longing for a solitary moment of experience through writing is kept in balance by a longing for addressing [someone] that is stressed time and again and which can be sensed in the texts, too. 'As if it would be a redemption to transfer all that is written into orality. I would only, sometimes, speak, not write anymore' (1982: 134). Theatre becomes a name for the moment in which the *voice* (which is latent, mute, and ambiguous in writing) addresses itself to someone. A drive of addressing the other, of communicating, declaring, also teaching (in a particular sense). Crucial for the image of theatre is a plurality, a 'gathering' (1982: 13), which is missing in the lonely silence of the script but indelibly inscribed into writing as longing. What is remarkable here is the priority in what is associated with theatre: more essential than the moment of presentational play in theatre is the [idea that] 'we are simply together'.

Theatre, this simply-being-together, could overcome the pain associated with the loneliness of the script, [and] is less a particular aesthetic practice rather than an image of longing for 'being-with' (*Mit-Sein*) or 'being-together' (*Zusammen-Sein*). Theatre becomes an *aluid* [alternative to or separating other] of the script. Admittedly, literature remains the irreplaceable possibility of language to stay entirely without an interpreting tone or indicating intonation, to fix neither duration nor rhythm nor speed of language and to allow for all kinds of interpretation to exist with and next to each other. Arthur Rimbaud replied once to his mother's question regarding the meaning of his text: '*J'ai voulu dire ce que ca dit, littéralement et dans tout les sens*' ('I wanted to say what this means, literally and in all its senses'). The preservation of these spaces for interpretation is what is meant in Hölderlin's '*Komm ins Offene, Freund!* (Come into the open, my friend!) and also in the '*Hiergelände*' (here ground) of which Handke speaks. Meanwhile, the chance of this – literal – indeterminacy remains bound up with an unresolvable [or unsublatable] loneliness. Surmounting it, even in a momentarily believed 'fiction', characterises theatre, its utopia.

That the theatre at least realises the fiction of the possibility of a community is not a commonplace in Handke's work. 'Togetherness' goes far, it would also connect the human species with animals, plants, stones:

> The *idea* of community appears to be over, even if many still continue in a dishonest-sad-desperate-bold manner. And still, the feeling of community is there, deeply in me, 'from the beginning', and sometimes becomes acute when listening to a trivial melody in a restaurant; then there is a feeling of community even with dogs.
>
> (1982: 47)

Writing is the persistent attempt to combine the fusion with the outside and the differentiation [or separation] of the subject. When Handke explains that a theatre play was, by contrast, 'the means of trying to construct at least a fiction

360 Hans-Thies Lehmann

of objectification' (Arnold 1978: 27), then the 'objective' here does not – as one might suppose – mean a generally accepted binding character of what is said. Rather it is a detachment of speech from within an interior space of the I towards a public and in this sense: an 'objective' situation in which the gestures and words of fictitious figures no longer (only) belong to the 'author-I' (*Autor-Ich*) but become a third medium for the sake of communication. Theatre becomes the epitome of a momentarily successful act with/in language. It can be realised in the mode of an 'addressing way of speaking' (*An-Sprache*), which in turn explains, from another perspective, why Handke hardly ever writes a 'normal', dramatically organised theatre play: it is precisely the constitution of a distinct fictive space for the drama that sets it apart as an autonomous 'playing space' (*Spielraum*) and so rather hinders the experience of theatre as a situation of 'being-together' (*Zusammensein*). 'He was unable to speak for so long that then, when he broke through the barrier after all and started to talk, it became a sermon (that was alright)' (1982: 45). Only in addressing [the other], do we perceive what in the practice of writing was likely the telos but also remained a utopian ideal: to *inhabit language* – and that simultaneously means *the world – together*, at least momentarily.

It is the word of the 'writer' that Handke wants to give back its great dignity.

Translated by Karen Jürs-Munby and Lisa Moravec

Handke's Nobel – a postscript

The unexpected award of the Nobel Prize in Literature for Peter Handke, which he received on 10 December 2019, has been followed – less unexpectedly – by a new round of almost habitual Handke bashing. This has, however, taken on such destructive and toxic forms that I could not possibly carry on as usual without including a note on this 'debate'.

Everything about this 'debate' is wrong; first of all, the seemingly compulsive repetition. For, nothing about these allegations against Handke is new, everything has been rehashed *ad nauseam*. The offences that led to his ostracisation have long been clarified – corrected by Handke himself or identified as mere defamation (his [alleged] denial of the war crimes of the Serbs or his [alleged] vilification of Muslims) – or can be disregarded as occasional outbursts. Equally wrong is the failed lens: the concentration on a single point in Handke's vast oeuvre: his speaking up for Serbia. Is it really about this? The blatant desire for punishment, which shows through in several of the contributions [to the debate], raises the suspicion that, now as then, it cannot be about a few real or imagined lapses with regard to Serbia. What is it, one wonders, that time and again brings Handke storms of denunciations and untenable accusations? Where does this rancour come from which wallows in the most spiteful interpretations of his sentences? Why the bucketloads of hatred and anger? At work in his writing and his person must be something like the unknown in us. Many seem to sense that they fell for conformism at the time. The non-conformist cannot be tolerated and is cast out precisely because he has triggered something like humiliation about it in us. There is no '*causa* Handke', at most there is the *causa* of conformism.

The spiteful denunciations should actually be given over to deserved oblivion on account of their factual baselessness. However, since [critics] consistently mobilise the heavy artillery of allegedly or actually morally dubious comments by the author in interviews, some defenders feel compelled to come to the defence of his writings against the author. This is right and necessary. Nevertheless, I would like to object. For, with this defence one moves too far towards accommodating the nonsense, if you will pardon my expression, above all the theoretical carelessness with which people draw most of the oppositions (author and text, aesthetics and politics, morality and art) that are prevalent here.

What seems forgotten is something one nevertheless knows: that anything an author describes has to have been experienced by him as a possibility for himself. What distinguishes great poets is precisely the courage to find the worst, the evilest, the most shameful in themselves. How would we understand a creation like Richard III if we were not willing to think that Shakespeare himself is Richard III as well? Handke has shown this courage time and again. I am thinking for example of the novel *The Chinaman of Pain* (*Der Chinese des Schmerzes*, 1983), in which he works himself up into the phantasy of a man who one day – apparently out of the blue – pursues someone who scrawls swastikas on walls, launches himself at him, and strikes him dead with a stone. And what is the greatness in Kafka's work, which Handke described as 'word for word the most significant' for his own, if not this ability: the radical courage to imagine to the extreme the absolute moral emptiness of one's own person.

Such questioning, however, which faces anyone who deals with literature, does not occur in the debate. Rather it is buried by killer verdicts, mostly in an abbreviated form suited to 'social' media, a 'twitterature' that is hardly prizeworthy, on the one side, and well-meaning but mistaken references to the difference between aesthetic formulation and real life, on the other.

Even the very idea that works of art, and thus also literary texts, were in principle open to a [kind of] hermeneutics that thinks of the work as such according to the model of a statement – an idea that is not questioned anywhere, as far as I can see – leads to mere superficiality. In truth, nothing is further from being self-evident. Literature is a praxis in language whose distinctive feature is that it renders all statements dubious. Its irreplaceable quality consists precisely in making possible an experience which in language goes beyond language into a realm where opinions and meanings hardly count anymore. What does [Goethe's] *Wanderers Nachtlied* (*Wanderer's Nightsong*) 'state'? '*Über allen Gipfeln / ist Ruh / in allen Wipfeln spürest du / kaum einen Hauch / die Vögelein schweigen im Walde. / Warte nur, balde / ruhest du auch*'. ('O'er all the hilltops / Is quiet now / In all the treetops / Hearest thou / Hardly a breath; / The birds are asleep in the trees: / Wait, soon like these /

362 *Hans-Thies Lehmann*

Thou too shalt rest'.). Or what would be the meaning of Hamlet? And did not Adorno – who was certainly no fan of Brecht's didacticism – state that it was 'hard to determine just what the author of [*The Life of*] *Galileo* or *The Good Person of Setzuan* himself meant, let alone broach the question of the objectivity of these works [*Gebilde*], which does not coincide with the subjective intention' (1997: 32)? Both assertions are simultaneously wrong and correct: poetry, the written artefact, is never identical with a statement of the empirical subject of the statement. At the same time the aesthetically formed artefact cannot simply be separated from the intentions of the author. Peter Handke, for instance, just to mention this one motif, articulates over and over a deep scepticism towards everything discursive. Whether in everyday speech, journalism, or science: an essentially predicative discourse cannot but subsume the singular, concrete, and individual under general terms, and in doing so marginalise and trivialise it. For Handke, the morality of the author's work thus does not consist in stating the morally correct but in resisting in his writing the temptations to generalise and universalise by insisting on the concrete individual thing.

One may say that Peter Handke's exorbitant life's work is testament to the attempt to live up to this expectation. In all its facets it shows an author who has dedicated his life to achieving a certain 'salvation' of external, concrete reality through its description. His special *écriture* comes as much from a tradition of classical narration as from modernity and postmodernity; it is a matter of 'literature in the age of experimentation'.

Closely related to the idea of the text as statement is the idea of the performative. As speech act theory has taught us, every linguistic act is an action. As such, it thus falls directly into the purview of ethics, morality, and politics. However, as artful linguistic formations elude the identification as a statement, i.e. as an action, they are to all intents and purposes only a mock performative; let us call it with reference to Werner Hamacher an afformative. Essentially, this insight goes beyond the question whether a linguistic act does something. What is attacked by literature is rather the certainty that one can know at all whether one does something or not.

Such considerations have nothing at all to do with relativising facts or political positions. And yet this accusation is constantly raised when one refuses to use texts as evidence for the (im)moral attitude of the author. The absurdity of this equation is not lessened but emerges in an even more conspicuously ugly form when critics attempt to assert a continuum between the author's poetic formulations, comments made by him in interviews, and his real acts.

Let me conclude with a remark on what is behind the question of how to assess Handke's solidarity with Serbia: the judgement about the intervention of NATO in the conflict. Handke did not share the assessment of the bombardment of Serbia as a justified 'humanitarian intervention', which in Germany is hardly ever seriously questioned. I have to admit that on this point I lean towards him: the reason for the war was likely the geo-strategical interests of the US and the West, who wanted to deactivate Serbia's regional supremacy (similarly to Iran's today) according to the maxim *divide et impera*, divide and conquer, not, in fact, humanitarian motives. In this light, Handke's solitary support for the Serbian position seems less abstruse. We can hardly hope for certainty in these questions within the foreseeable future. Yet, why the circumstance that Handke at the time took up this position should disqualify the artist, not to mention his grand work, from receiving the Nobel Prize remains entirely incomprehensible.

Translated by Karen Jürs-Munby

Notes

1 Translators' interpolations appear in square brackets throughout.
2 The play, whose subtitle is 'Schauspiel in vier Jahreszeiten' (Spectacle in Four Seasons), had its premiere on 27 February 2016 at the Burgtheater, Vienna, directed by Claus Peymann.

Works cited

Adorno, Theodor W. (1997) *Aesthetic Theory*, trans. Robert Hullot-Kentor, Gretel Adorno and Rolf Tiedemann (eds), London: Athlone, p. 32.

Arnold, Heinz Ludwig (1978) 'Gespräch mit Peter Handke', *Text + Kritik*, 24: 15–37.

Handke, Peter (1982) *Die Geschichte des Bleistifts*, Salzburg: Residenz.

——— (1997) *Plays: 1* [*Offending the Audience; My Foot My Tutor; Self Accusation; Kaspar; Lake Constance; They are Dying Out*], trans. Michael Roloff and Karl Weber, London: Methuen Drama.

Lehmann, Hans-Thies (2012) *Das Politische Schreiben: Essays zu Theatertexten*, Berlin: Theater der Zeit.

Rilke, Rainer Maria (1995) 'Archaic Torso of Apollo', trans. Stephen Mitchell, in *Ahead of All Parting: Selected Poetry and Prose of Rainer Maria Rilke*, Modern Library, https://poets.org/poem/archaic-torso-apollo

20 Jonas Hassen Khemiri
Writing out of the binary

Bryce Lease

Jonas Hassen Khemiri is one of the most important writers of his generation in Sweden. When his debut novel, *Ett öga rött (One Eye Red)*, was published in 2003, Khemiri's eccentric and imaginative prose made an enormous impact, reaching an audience far beyond traditional literary circles. The book-turned-phenomenon was awarded the Borås Tidning Award for Best Literary Debut Novel, selling over 200,000 copies in paperback – the most of any book in Sweden in 2004. Khemiri's second novel, *Montecore – en unik tiger (Montecore: The Silence of the Tiger)*, was awarded the prestigious P.O. Enquist Literary Prize, the Swedish Radio's Award for Best Novel, and was nominated for the August Award, the highest literary prize in Sweden. *Allt jag inte minns (Everything I Don't Remember)* was published in 2015 and Khemiri was awarded the prestigious August Prize in the category 'Best Swedish Fiction Book of the Year'. His novel *Pappaklausulen* (translated as *The Family Clause*) was published by FSG (US) and Harvill Secker (UK) in 2020. Khemiri is also a celebrated playwright, whose six plays have been performed by over hundred international companies on stages across Europe and in North America. His plays assault deep prejudices about identity, race, and language. He was awarded a Village Voice Obie Award for his first play *Invasion!*, which premiered in New York in 2011. *The Hundred We Are* received the Hedda Award for best play in Norway. Khemiri's most recent play *≈[Almost Equal To]* premiered at Dramaten in Stockholm in October 2014 and has been performed in Germany, Norway, Iceland, Denmark, and the US. Khemiri's writing has been translated into over twenty-five languages. In 2013, Khemiri's open letter to the Swedish Minister of Justice in response to the controversial police project REVA that promoted racial profiling was first published in *Dagens Nyheter* and rapidly became one of the most shared articles on social media in Swedish history.

This interview took place in Stockholm in April 2018.

BRYCE LEASE: As both a novelist and a playwright, could you discuss how you see the relationship between these forms? What does writing for the theatre teach you about writing novels and vice-versa?

JONAS HASSEN KHEMIRI: Books were always my thing. I spent endless hours in the library. I had two younger brothers and one of them was always the actor. In a family it is often the case that you divide the world between you and your siblings, so my brother had theatre and I had books. For me, it took a while to discover what a stage could be used for, and actually it wasn't until I was in my twenties that I started going to the theatre. I was a student and in my school we were allowed to attend performances that were not finished. I could go for free, which was important as I was a student and didn't have any money, and we could see rehearsals and run-throughs of plays that were not polished. We were always waiting for the director to intervene, to yell 'cut!' or 'let's do a retake', and then I began to understand theatre. That tension added something new that I hadn't seen before. There was something being created as I was watching it and it felt very clear to me why I was supposed to be in that physical space, taking part in a particular story. I felt very involved, which I hadn't before in the theatre. I had only felt like an observer. When you are that age it is very exciting to make such a discovery and then I went to see everything. One of the things I remember realising being in a theatre that I could not get from books was of course the physicality. I remember seeing a play by Swedish director and playwright Lars Norén, called *Sju Tre* (*7:3*) in which he put actual Nazis on stage. I saw this in Hallunda, a suburb south of Stockholm. They were trying to convince me of their ideology, and it was harsh to see that as well as experiencing the physicality of these men being present. I remember in one of the opening scenes this really buff dude enters the stage and he does 100 push-ups and I could sense his smell and his presence as he watched me, and he tried to convince me of the good things about Nazism. The physicality intrigued me. In 2003, I published my first novel, *Ett öga rött* (*One Eye Red*), and I was asked to write a play by the now sadly deceased Benny Fredriksson, the head of Stadsteatern, the city theatre in Stockholm. In our first meeting I had the impression that he wanted a specific story, that there were certain aspects of myself that he wanted me to tell. My first reaction was to turn down the commission because I didn't feel free. But I went away from that meeting and started thinking about a famous but now somewhat forgotten Swedish Romantic playwright and novelist called Carl Jonas Love Almqvist whom I had been reading at the time. I emailed Benny to say that if I am going to write a play it is going to be about the '1000 faces of Abulkasem', and that became the basis for my first play, *Invasion!*. The play starts out with a short excerpt of Almqvist's play *Senora Luna*. Some young people rebel against the historic language and kidnap the name Abulkasem from Almqvist, and start filling it with their own meaning. Abulkasem becomes a word that can mean anything, a limitless word, signifying a threat to some, and self-empowerment tool for others. In a way it's a play about a number of people trying, and failing, to free themselves from categorisation. I was very happy to write for the theatre and it was an amazing experience to see how the play changed when it started attracting a new kind of audience. But I see writing books as my main job. In Swedish we have a word, *växelbruk* (crop rotation). Every year or two you change the

366   *Bryce Lease*

grains to renew the soil. I think I use the theatre to experiment, similarly to why I write short stories or film scripts, but the grain that I need to survive is the novels. I need to have a novel brewing in order to be happy.

BL: I was curious about the way you construct character, and how this changes between your plays, *Invasion!* and *I Call My Brothers*, and your novel, *Everything I Don't Remember*, where dialogue is no longer attributed to particular characters. Part of the work of the reader is to solve character through the clues of language. In your playwriting, this is postdramatic and even anti-essentialist, because of the way actors move through multiple roles. Do you see a relationship between how you understand and how you create character in the plays and the novel?

JHK: I think it is rather ambiguous. Everything that I couldn't do in the novel that I could do in the play intrigued me. For instance, the ability to control time. It is tricky to do that in a book, but in the theatre I could have long pauses if I wanted them, or we could lock the doors to force the audience to stay. The magic of theatre is that you have the physicality, you have the bodies and voices present that you as the audience have to react to – and react to weirdly in some cases – but what I think drove me back to the novel form is that there is a peculiar intimacy when you are forced to create the body in your mind and hear the voice in your own head. *Everything I Don't Remember* found its form after having written a few plays where I was longing for the freedom to force the words to only be words. And interestingly the whole novel circles around that. How different can a certain sentence become when the reader has to decide who is saying it? It is not always 100 per cent certain who is speaking. When someone says, 'I loved him', and it is not obvious who is speaking then the meaning can change dramatically. I think this going back and forth between different crops or different modes of expression – the novel and the play – they seep into each other. It is also a way of keeping writing fresh and fascinating.

BL: Parody plays an interesting and also ambiguous role in your work. There are times when I am not sure if you are being parodic or not.

JHK: My gut feeling when I hear the word parody is that it is simple and cold. One of the things I have been intrigued by since starting to write is the different kinds of laughter it produces. There is simple laughter and dark laughter, and when I think my plays work best they have this kind of painful laughter where people are laughing but they are not really sure why they are laughing. And that is what I aim for. I really dig that laughter. When someone thinks 'Oh shit, I just laughed and I'm not really sure why I laughed, and can I take that back? Can I transform that laughter into a sigh or something?'. The laughter I have heard from seeing different versions of my plays is so dependent upon who is in the audience. During the first production of *I Call My Brothers*, the director said she had a run through and there was a lot of laughter, and then she had another run with a lot of teenagers who were from a social background that meant they were not used to going to the theatre and the director laughed at something the actor did. Some of the teenagers stepped up to her, defending the main character: 'Why are you laughing? This is not funny!'. There are of course humorous bits in my plays, but the moment I strive for is when the audience cannot decide between laughing and wanting to run for the exit.

BL: In Germany - and I am thinking particularly of Shermin Langhoff or Atif Hussein and Simone Dede Ayivior at venues such as the Ballhaus Naunynstraße and the Gorki Theater in Berlin and the work of playwrights like Marianna Salzmann - the term 'post-migrant' theatre is used to describe artists of second- and third-generation migrants. Wagner Carvalho said that there was no point having post-migrant texts in repertoire that are not performed by post-migrant artists (in Wildermann 2015). Do you also think about the politics of casting when you are writing?

JHK: No. My primary goal is to write interesting stories. In order to write well. I have to be honest and specific and it would feel bizarre and fake to write about contemporary Sweden in the old 'blue-eyed' way, and not include people from different backgrounds. To me it's just a natural consequence of trying to tell stories that matter. Then, in order to cast the plays, the directors have to find the best possible actors, and naturally they look for people whose thoughts and experiences relate to the script. I'm proud that many of the actors who started out in my plays are now performing roles that are not linked in any way to a specific political movement.

BL: Do you think your work has an impact on audiences, on who is coming to the theatre?

JHK: I think it has an impact, but one of the sure ways in my experience to fail in attracting a specific group is to directly aim at that group. Every time someone said to me when I was in school, 'This is a book that is good for your development', there was no way I was going to read it. I remember my mother had this big bookshelf and she would say, 'You can read it all if you want to, but there is just one book that I don't want you to read'. It was a kind of pseudo-pornographic 1970s novel called *Jack* by Swedish writer Ulf Lundell. She said that she wanted me to wait for this one. Ten minutes later I had read it, because it was not meant for me. In a way, it became dangerous. In that moment it became something that could threaten my being in the world, and I think that is much more of an interesting way of approaching the ambition of attracting an audience. With my own work, I have always been clear that these are adult plays directed for anyone who wants to come. They have never been framed in any way as being for young people, or people from certain backgrounds. The interesting thing is that those audience members found it thanks to the non-labelling. Word spread and we were very blessed to have audience members who were not used to going to the theatre.

BL: Astrid Trotzig has argued that ethnicity has become a lens through which Swedish writers of foreign decent are viewed. In Sweden, the term 'immigrant literature' is in general use, and Trotzig sees this as both discriminating and homogenising. The term 'immigrant' here does not refer to all forms of immigration; it is bounded by perceptions of race,

368   *Bryce Lease*

religion, and gender. Do you feel frustrated by this as a term that is constantly employed as a way of looking at your work? Do you feel it limits how people interpret your writing?

JHK: We had this debate 15 years ago when my first novel was published. Some critics used the prefix 'immigrant' literature, and I – with different levels of courtesy – tried to remind them that the main character was actually born in Sweden. This is a book about a Swedish character using racist and nationalist ideas to interrogate self-image, the invention of self through his life and through his diary. I've always resisted the term 'immigrant literature'. It is clear today that the term doesn't label anything. It's one of those words that can mean anything depending on your political ambitions, so to speak.

BL: One major aspect of your work is verb tense and the importance of memory and the elasticity of time, the movements and jumps between past and present. Also, characters often remember certain episodes differently, so versions of the past are often in conflict.

JHK: Yes, I keep coming back to the link between memory and words. How can you use text as a way to change your own memory, both to cling onto one version of the truth but also to slightly change who you are? In hindsight, this makes sense, because personally I've always had this feeling that my memory was not good enough and that I needed to write things down in order for them to be real. Whatever 'real' is. When I was a kid writing in my diary, I had this realisation I could slightly tweak the truth and it would change things. A feeling that words were linked with a sense of freedom, or I could use words to write myself out of ordinary life. In *Everything I Don't Remember*, I was curious about what kind of value words have when someone disappears. This is a theme I keep coming back to because it has been a big part of my life. I've had family members that for different political, economic reasons couldn't be present during my life. When they were not present physically, I could always write them back. I would write about them and they would be present. That intrigues me – how much of a person is possible to capture in words? In *I Call My Brothers*, we get to know a main character who is feeling very isolated but actually he consists of many voices, coming from people who are not physically present. But the main character has them in his mind. These voices become very dear to him. He's part of a network of voices. Even though he doesn't see them, he hears them and that is ultimately what saves him. I can relate to that in my own life. I have had the fortune of having these voices in my head; I have been able to write them and I have had the feeling that they've saved me.

BL: Truth is very difficult to attribute in your work. Selfhood is attached to memory but this is highly unstable.

JHK: Yes, it is in conflict with the outside world. In *I Call My Brothers* the main character starts doubting who he is when he sees himself in the reflection of a shop window. One could say he has been invaded by the outside gaze on him. He sees himself and sees a potential perpetrator or a criminal. One of the things that I have been fascinated with growing up is that I have encountered a lot of people who have wanted me to take sides either in political life, or in terms of ethnicity or nationality. They wanted a box to put me in. Resisting such binaries is what keeps coming back in my writing. One of the ways of resisting binary is to show that there is no easy version, that memory is always in some way tainted, but also that two versions can ultimately be true simultaneously. It is not a case of saying nothing is true, but rather that these two versions are true at the same time. Another way to depart from a binary is to use confusion. To force the audience to not be absolutely sure that this table is a table. There are different strategies for this. In *Invasion!*, the actors walking from the foyer up onto the stage causes a moment of confusion. Who are these people? Should I trust this? Which voice is the fictitious voice? If you are caught in a moment of confusion it is much more difficult to trust your preconceived ideas about the world.

BL: In *Invasion!* the actors come into the foyer before the play officially begins and interact with the audience. It is a very aggressive encounter. Was there ever a moment when actual violence erupted?

JHK: There were a number of incidents. In the first production in Stockholm the characters were dressed in costumes that were inspired by *Tintin*. They were wearing these comic book outfits that gave them no street credit and they looked really bizarre. But still their ethnicity and their language and age trumped that, so they were very quickly otherised by the rest of the audience. One of the main actors kept asking to bring a glass of water into the main auditorium and of course the guards said he couldn't. It was a mini confrontation about nothing, but the interesting thing was how the rest of the audience looked at them with judgment, like 'Oh now they even want water!'. These characters were reacting against Swedish history, against standard behaviour in the theatre. It took the audience quite a while to realise that they were actually actors, part of the fiction. Audience members got involved, trying to get these actors down from the stage. It was also interesting to hear the comments made when people could not be seen. All kinds of racial slurs being yelled in the dark, anonymously.

BL: In your novels and plays, the 'writer' often appears. Does autobiography play a significant role for you? Or is this a rhetorical strategy?

JHK: To be honest, I am not sure. In my first two novels there is always someone who could be the writer. The point is that this figure is not to be trusted. Maybe the presence of the writer is the only way I can be completely honest in the rest of the work. All of my characters are in some way me. In *Everything I Don't Remember*, Samuel is very much me. How many of Samuel's memories are my memories? In the beginning I was just dumping bad qualities on him, as you do. It is very easy to let your self-loathing come out when you just write one version of a character. One thing that made Samuel come to life was that I began doubting what I had spent so much of

370   *Bryce Lease*

my time doing. I am really fascinated by words, and I spend most of my time sitting in a room with no internet, just writing. One of the realisations I've had was that there are actual people beyond these words, and I really need to take care of them as well. The question that kept coming back was: how do you value words versus people? Words are everlasting and permanent, and people are always disappearing. My projects often start with questions that I don't have an easy answer to. Have I made a mistake spending so much of my life writing? This is the thing that has given my life such a sense of value. I wouldn't have survived without it. Everything that I feel unsure about seems to trickle down into the fiction, if it is an interesting project. The projects that I start when I know where they should finish are dead ends. Literally, they die before they are conceived.

BL: Intimacy, affiliation, and solidarity often arise as themes in your work. The word 'brother' frequently shows up in both your plays and novels. Those forms of loyalty are never easy. Characters have to be reminded of relationships and then they have to fight for them. There are also exciting potentials for queer moments where intimacy and affiliation are ambiguous.

JHK: I think this is fascinating – the limits of linguistic intimacy amongst men. It is very difficult, for example, to say 'I love you'. Growing up, a lot of the boys I knew said 'I love you' through insulting a friend's mother – there is a compliment in there somewhere. There is no way I can say it to you straight so I have to say it to you in other ways, and use different kinds of languages. Maybe just taking my physical body to you and being physically present, perhaps that is the only way that I can communicate intimacy.

BL: Is there more ambiguity in the novels than in the plays, which are explicitly physicalised?

JHK: You just need different strategies to keep the recipients alive. You have physical intimacy in the theatre; you can approach people. In my plays, the actors always share roles. They become someone and then they very quickly go out of that role. We are not always sure where we as beings end and where our surroundings begin. I am not really sure of what I consist. Do I consist of the words that I have written? Do I consist of the languages I speak? Do I consist of my memories? Not really, because they are really subjective and fleeting. Maybe I consist of what I leave behind in the way of memories. Maybe that is all we really are: what we leave behind and how we are remembered by the future. In one way that is sad, and in another way that is really powerful. We can exist as so many different versions in so many different people's minds after our physical bodies are gone. Those multiple versions I have tried to explore in my writing.

BL: You frequently use the same translator for English, Rachel Willson-Broyles. How has that relationship developed?

JHK: Rachel is an American who learned Swedish because she was an Ace of Base fan. She is a very talented translator. We have worked together on both plays and novels. I am very thankful for all of my translators. Normally, my translators do the work and ask me questions and I collect my answers in a growing document for each project. Every time there is a new translation my agent sends the translator this document with the questions that have been asked previously. There is a growing bank of queries. Translation is crucial when you write in a relatively small language like Swedish.

BL: *Invasion!* was reset in New York in the English translation. Was there a feeling that Stockholm would be too foreign for US audiences?

JHK: I am not sure. My general feeling is that something good happens when a text is kidnapped and collides with the vision of a director. If the play works it can stand the changes. In general, I am usually involved in the first production in Sweden and I only go to one run through. I never comment on the aesthetics. The only comments I make are sound based. I think she should be sadder when she says that, for example, or that should be lighter, or that should be darker. This is because my creative process is very similar to listening to voices.

BL: Many critics note your use of multilingualism as a strategy. What do they mean by this?

JHK: Maybe they mean that there is a continuous exploration of the many different kinds of Swedish in my work. This is the same in English – there is the English you speak in university, the English you speak with me, or the English you use when a friend calls, the English you use with your grandmother. All of these registers of language draw something out of you. You would not be the same person if a friend from high school called you as you are right now. In some way, you would be drawn back to the old version of yourself. And this is something that I play around with. There are many different registers of Swedish colliding. One way of creating different registers in Swedish is to use foreign languages. There is a hierarchy of languages. It is really fascinating to see how someone entering this café using Swedish with some English words sprinkled into the text is really high status. I would say even more high status than me speaking perfect Swedish. Another person speaking Swedish with Arabic words or Bosnian words gives them less power in a work place or in a negotiation. There are loan words from different languages in my writing to signify who is speaking.

BL: Stockholm is very vibrant in your fiction and plays. The cityscapes you write render deep social inequalities visible. Do you approach the question of writing site or space differently in the plays than in your fiction?

JHK: I don't think I approach it differently, but I think that one of the changes that my city has gone through in the last 10 to 20 years is that the economic boundaries have become so much more present and the difference between people who live in abundance to those who have scarce means has become much bigger. This trickles down into my writing in different ways. Stockholm is extremely segregated and there are very few places where people

372   *Bryce Lease*

from different areas and different generations meet. One of the intriguing things is that I can do that in my writing. For example, I can create places where people from different backgrounds can collide in a way that they wouldn't here, because they live in separate parts of the city.

BL: That is apparent in the final scene of *Everything I Don't Remember* when a tourist train is diverted from central Stockholm to the suburbs, and the recorded voice keeps naming the famous historical sites in the wrong places.

JHK: Yes, maybe names cannot be trusted. Maybe we need to separate the spoken words from what they are signifying, in order to see what is actually being said. I had a friend who had a job driving a tourist train, and he told me he hated his job. When I asked him why he said, 'Well, this is not my city. My past is not being told in this clichéd, superficial positive image of Stockholm'. He kept saying that one day he was going to kidnap the train and drive it to his area to make the tourists see it. 'Kidnapping the train', I thought that was a beautiful idea for a miniature rebellion against the official image of the city.

BL: Sweden is associated with welfare support, gender equality, peaceful civil society, and open democracy. Is the concept of nation and national identity important to you?

JHK: I think this stereotypical depiction of Sweden is really interesting. On the one hand this is true. Sweden might look like the perfect place for feminism and a place where equality reigns. A lot of people think that is the truth about our country. From another political angle, Sweden is being described as a country that has been ruined by immigration and that it is not safe to walk the streets anymore. Some people are afraid of coming here as tourists, because they think that they will get raped or robbed. This makes it really interesting to write about contemporary Sweden, because we know that both of these images are false. Is it possible to write yourself out of this binary? I'm not sure. But I don't think becoming silent is an alternative.

BL: In 2013, you wrote an open letter to Sweden's Minister of Justice, Beatrice Ask, proposing that you wanted to trade skins and experiences for a day. Within 24 hours, this was shared 120,000 times on Facebook and 250,000 times on *Dagens Nyheter*, the newspaper that published the letter. Why did you write this letter?

JHK: I wrote it in response to a radio interview made by our Minister of Justice at the time. When Swedish citizens complained about being racially profiled, our minister answered by comparing these worried citizens with paranoid ex-cons. In the letter I ask Beatrice Ask to switch bodies and memories with me. If I entered her body I would understand male privilege, and if she entered my body she would remember being followed in stores by security guards, being stopped in customs at airports, being stopped and put in the backseat of police cars, for no reason. These things happened to me, growing up. For a long time, I stopped myself from writing about these events, because I had friends from poorer backgrounds, who had much worse experiences with the police. But finally, I realised that it's a very efficient strategy from people in power to silence any demands for justice and equality by pointing to someone who has it 'worse'. So I wrote the text, and it went viral. A lot of people could relate to the feeling of not being seen as part of the official myth of their respective country, no matter their ethnic background or sexual orientation. And maybe it also spread because so many countries are in this position of not knowing who they are. What is the glue that holds us together?

Jonas Hassen Khemiri – four key productions

Invasion!. Directed by Lucy Kerbel. Translated by Frank Perry. Cast: Gregg Chillin, Chris Nayak, Raad Rawi, Viss Elliott Safavi, Soho Theatre, London, 11 March 2009.

≈ *[ungefär lika med]*. Directed by Farnaz Arbabi. Music by Anna Haglund. Scenography by Jenny Kronberg. Cast: Thérèse Brunnander, Ardalan Esmaili, Hamadi Khemiri, Marall Nasiri, Bahar Pars, Leonard Terfelt, Pablo Leiva Wenger. Dramaten, Stockholm, 23 October 2014.

I Call My Brothers. Directed by Erica Schmidt. Translated by Rachel Willson-Broyles. Set Design by Daniel Zimmerman. Costume Design by Jessica Pabst. Lighting Design by Jeff Croiter. Sound Design by Bart Fasbender. Cast: Dahlia Azama, Francis Benhamou, Damon Owlia, Rachid Sabitri. New Ohio Theatre, New York City, 22 February 2014.

Invasion!. Direction, design, and music by Jonas Holmberg. Dramaturgy by Ninne Olsson. Cast: Kimiya Faghih, Simon Mezher, Mariam Namow, Dennis Önder. Stadsteatern, Stockholm, 1 March 2019.

Works cited

Wildermann, Patrick (2015) 'Post-migrant theatre today: "We say loudly what doesn't suit us"', The Goethe Institut, https://www.goethe.de/en/kul/tut/gen/tup/20895444.html

21 Marie NDiaye

Eliding capture

Kélina Gotman

Marie NDiaye (b. 1967) may be France's most celebrated and controversial playwright, the only woman to have a work in repertory with the French national theatre, the Comédie-Française, and only the second woman to have a play in repertoire with the permanent company since its establishment in 1680 by royal decree. *Papa doit manger* (*Daddy Has to Eat*, 2003), produced with the company's first ever permanent black actor, Bakary Sangaré, like many of her other works, deals obliquely and powerfully with questions of race, coloniality, nation, language, exile, violence, family, and belonging. At once a playwright, novelist, screenwriter, essayist, and writer of children's fiction, NDiaye's first novel, *Quand au riche avenir* (*As to the Prosperous Future*, 1985) was published when she was 17 by one of France's two most prestigious publishers, Les Éditions de minuit, followed by a further 12 novels, seven of which have been translated into English at the time of writing, and four plays. She is the recipient of seven major international prizes, including France's two most important literary prizes, the Prix Femina (for her novel *Rosie Carpe*, 2001) and the Prix Goncourt (for her novel *Trois femmes puissantes* [*Three Strong Women*], 2009), making her the only recipient of both prizes concurrently. She is also the recipient of a Nelly Sachs Prize, recognising her contribution to international social life. As the present conversation makes clear, however, she is also adamant about her position as a writer first and foremost, and not as a political activist of any sort; she explicitly resists alignment with any recognisable trends in literature or politics, whether feminist, humanist, or postcolonial. As a writer of mixed black Senegalese and white French heritage born and raised in France, she frequently draws journalistic attention for the immaculate quality of her prose, a colonialist and quite patronising attitude that suggests unrelenting surprise at her mastery of a classically academic French language, and indeed her work appears to stage language itself as a site for the subtly but distinctly violent negotiation of position and propriety. Famously private, nearly silent with regard to her life or her writing, briefly self-exiled in Berlin, and now living and writing in rural France, away from Paris or the metropolises, NDiaye's hesitancy to explain or attempt to analyse her own work situates her in a critical zone of indeterminacy that powerfully also performs the very elision of capture her work enacts.

The present conversation explores a number of formal and thematic aspects in her work, as well as the relatively unusual relationship to theatricality that she describes, as a playwright of extraordinarily high stature who hardly sought out the theatre at all. As she explains, her intention is to write, rather than to write for a particular genre. While her novels combine elements of surrealism or supernaturalism, mysticism and transformation, with banal elements of family life, or are set in indefinite landscapes in Africa, France, or elsewhere, punctuated with detail that disorientate the reader just as she thinks she has found her way, destabilising any sense as to what type of 'reality' is taking place, her plays similarly present particular challenges for production. How concretely does one represent one of her dreamscapes, for example? NDiaye is clear on this point, as the conversation makes plain. Elements of hyper-reality (or surreality) are evocative only; they operate at the level of poetry, of language, rather than with the concretion of the theatrical object. While directors have aimed to represent the complexities of her characters' actions, and of the nearly magical, uncanny, and unsettling worlds they inhabit, she contends that theatre is powerful because it allows simple gestures and words to invite imagination of a world.

Questions of race are also addressed at times explicitly – at the level of narrative – and more casually, with regard to choice of character and setting. This presents challenges vis-à-vis representation and casting in an overwhelmingly white French theatrical culture. For NDiaye, aligning herself in this regard with Bernard-Marie Koltès (1948–89), a black character is unequivocally to be played by a black actor. Koltès was outraged at learning that a production of his play *Le retour au désert* (*Return to the Desert*) being prepared in 1988 at the Thalia Theatre in Hamburg, directed by Alexander Lang, featured two white actors cast in the parts of a Black African and an Arabic character respectively. As critic Katrin Sieg points out, the play 'portrayed ethnic tensions in postcolonial France'; part of what drove Koltès to write the play was his "'desire to see blacks and Arabs onstage'", he wrote. "'I do not accept the argument that you could not find any qualified actors for these roles. I would only need to cruise the discos for two days to bring you ten blacks who could play the black roles on the stage'". As Sieg further notes, for Koltès the situation of Turks in West Germany in the 1980s was like that of Arabs in France in the 1960s. That this parallel was not recognised was a further cause for outrage. Koltès wrote a searing critique in the daily *Der Spiegel*, launching a major debate in the West German theatre world (Sieg 2002: 1–2). Controversy erupted again more recently in 2007, when the same play entered the repertoire at the Comédie-Française, directed by Muriel Mayette, with the part of Aziz, the Algerian man, played by Michel Favory, a white actor; Mayette retorted that Favory is of Maghreban descent, and entirely credible in the role. Although Koltès died in 1989 at the age of 41, his brother François Koltès, who holds copyright, ordered the production stop after thirty performances, on the grounds that this went against his brother's very clear stipulation that Aziz's role should be played by an Arabic actor. The case proceeded to court, provoking a further storm of

376 *Kélina Gotman*

controversy. Although the first black actor joined the Comédie-Française troupe in 2002, Malian-born Bakary Sangaré, who played the father in NDiaye's *Daddy Has to Eat*, there are still no Arabic actors within the elite repertory company.[1]

As NDiaye's short story preface to the scholar (and her half-brother) Pap Ndiaye's groundbreaking work of black sociology *La condition noire* (*The Condition of Blackness*, 2008) attests, mixed race and otherwise racialised lives in France are still rarely addressed, almost invisible, elusive to a white majority in the everyday. At the same time, and in line with this, she carefully and consistently stops short of associating herself with any identitarian programme, and thus suffering yet another form of critical or cultural capture. In this regard aligned with the post-racial humanism described by Caribbean-British philosopher, novelist, and critic Sylvia Wynter, NDiaye's work nevertheless resists community and category – except, as she articulates it, that of the 'writer', the single term with which she deliberately and consistently identifies her life and work. Indeed, if NDiaye refrains from expressing party politics of any sort, as she argues below – anything pertaining to an 'ism' – it is clear that her work offers a radical attachment to, and grounding in, language as that which has the possibility of seeing and making the world around her. At the same time, in articulating this, such a stance powerfully and provocatively reveals her as an *ungovernable* writer, uncapturable, and in that sense inalienably autonomous: at once intensely present and unassailably free.

The following conversation took place in French on 7 February 2019 and was translated into English by Kélina Gotman.

KÉLINA GOTMAN: You are a novelist, but you also write for the theatre, for children. We discover in all your work supernatural, at times uncanny worlds; yet they are often partially anchored in quite concrete places. Where do you situate the work of playwriting in all of this? How do you approach the question of character, site, or scene in your plays?

MARIE NDIAYE: Every play I have written has been the result of an invitation, a commission. And every time, the plays are either commissioned for the radio – with the radio channel France Culture – or by a director, including the last play I wrote, which will be published in a month or two.[2] What this means is that my theatrical inspiration never originates in myself. I feel no need to write a play. I do not think I would ever have written one if I had not been invited to do so. And I write plays exactly as I write novels, that is to say that it is really the same gesture of writing. What changes is only the mode of presentation, the fact that everything is in the form of a dialogue; but this does not at all change the way I write, or the way I think about what I would like to do. And as I see very few plays – I go rarely to the theatre – I do not have any theatrical references as to what a theatre production, a *mise en scène*, really means. Writing plays for me is simply another way of presenting the work, another way of writing fiction.

KG: Have you seen any productions of your work that have stayed with you, perhaps affected your way of approaching playwriting? In connection with this, have you ever been present during the production process, either engaging in conversation with the director, for example, or working with dramaturgs or actors on the *mise en scène*?

MND: No. I have never done that. I have never attended or participated in the work of *mise en scène*. I consider that it is not really my profession; in a sense, I have nothing to say about this sort of work. In general, the plays that I have seen staged, I have encountered for the first time on opening night. It is not a very pleasant feeling. I think that if it were possible for me not to go, without this being offensive or rude, I would not. Every time, I have had the impression that everything done was unnecessary. I would find it just as unnecessary for someone to stand onstage and read my novels; it does not seem necessary to me for anyone to speak the words, or to act them. Perhaps to hear them spoken might not bother me quite so much. What bothers me is the acting, which seems to me so completely useless, in a sense. Of course I saw some work that was really very good. What bothers me often, in the end, is realism. For example, for the staging of *Daddy Has to Eat* at the Comédie-Française [Figure 21.1], there was a very realistic stage set: a bed, an armoire, chairs, everything that makes up a living room, a bedroom; and that shocked me, I found it so completely useless. [*Laughter*] Also, for the production of *Hilda* (1999) at the Théâtre de l'Atelier in Montmartre, it was so realistic that at one moment, when the characters are having a coffee, there was a coffee machine with water, with the coffee, and the actors were really drinking coffee. I found that so idiotic, when what is beautiful in the theatre is that when one says one is drinking coffee, one can just perform the gesture, or not even do that; what I mean to say is that it is not at all necessary.

KG: Some characters in your plays are clearly defined in terms of their socio-economic origin, others less so; some relationships are played out with direct reference to Africa or France, white or black, very dark skin or mixed heritages, and other times there is ambiguity, so that a character's origin might not be revealed at the start. It seems that in these cases, the casual revelations also constitute the fabric of your writing. From the point of view of theatre and the work of theatrical production, questions of casting are often very important and politicised, very difficult. Have you had surprises or thoughts concerning this question, or has seeing your work staged affected your way of approaching your characters in this regard?

MND: No, I don't think so. Of course, it's true that the only play in which I think this question exists clearly is *Daddy Has to Eat*, with the character of the father who is black. I can't think of any other play where the question of origins or of skin colour is posed.

KG: It is rather in your novels.

MND: Yes. I very much align myself with what Bernard-Marie Koltès had to say about this, when he absolutely refused to have a white actor play the part of a black character, since he had created this black character. And that was the opposite, in this regard, to a German production, which had sought to have the African character played by a white German, who would have been vaguely black-faced. Koltès was revolted by that, and he said, well, if you can't find any [black actors], you don't do the play, you do something else.

KG: Recently, there was a similar debate in Quebec and well beyond Quebec with Robert Lepage.[3]

MND: Yes, this all bothers me very much. I know that Ariane Mnouchkine, who invited the director [Lepage] and the show, finds the debate dangerous and absurd; but she retorts with an argument that seems to me completely wrong. She says it is as if every actor playing Hamlet should have to be a Dane, but it is not the same question at all.

KG: You went to live in Berlin for a while, during the presidency of [Nicolas] Sarkozy. Did German literary or theatrical culture provoke or inspire anything for you? In connection with this, do you feel any particular sense of kinship with a literary or dramaturgical generation or moment? That is to say, do you recognise a shared aesthetic, political, or cultural line of inquiry, perhaps a sense of common concerns with other writers, whether current or past?

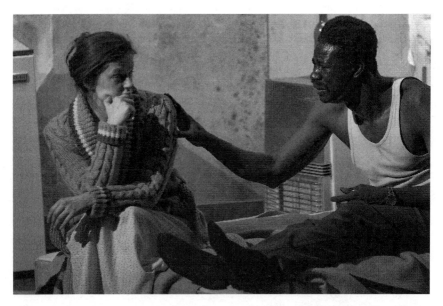

Figure 21.1 Catherine Sauval and Bakary Sangaré in André Engel's production of Marie NDiaye's *Papa doit manger* (Comédie-Française, Paris, 2003). Photograph © Cosimo Mirco Magliocca

MND: I went to the theatre a lot in Berlin, or in any case much more so than I was accustomed to doing in France, even though my German was quite poor; I could not really follow everything going on onstage. But I mostly went to the Volksbühne, when Frank Castorf was still there. And the particularity of what was going on at the Volksbühne I think is representative of everything going on in Germany at the moment. Plays are very rarely staged as they are written. The principle of taking a play written to be a play and saying the exact words onstage hardly exists there. What I saw at the Volksbühne was almost always mixtures, for example Castorf staged a three-hour show he called *Nord* (*North*, 2007). He took one of [Louis-Ferdinand] Céline's novels, cut up parts, reworked the whole; he even mixed in some fragments of [Antonin] Artaud's work, and he introduced a little bit of Molière I think, to create quite a surprising, very physical mixture onstage; there was video, there were dancers... but this is not what one would call a play. It is visually quite attractive and, from the point of view of what is said, quite seductive. It is also perhaps a little bit easy. I think that when one sticks fragments from the writings of great authors together, this always leads to quite beautiful things. But as a playwright, I had trouble with these sorts of practices.

In Hamburg last month, I saw an adaptation of Thomas Bernhard's *Extinction*, which is a novel, and not a play Bernhard wrote. The director [Karin Henkel] created a play after *Extinction*. But this bothers me, with regard to the author, that is to say that the author wrote plays and novels; he chose for *Extinction* to be a novel, not a play. And it seems pretentious to me for the director to say to herself, I am going to make out of this novel my play, and in spite of everything, it is presented as if it were Bernhard's work. People who are not really paying attention think that it is a play he wrote, whereas that is not at all the case.[4] I saw a lot of that in Germany, that is to say a fundamental questioning of the fact of writing plays, which would become useless, since the creative work belongs to the director. So this did not inspire me or shift any of my thinking, on the contrary. The same is happening in France as well, where there are fewer plays staged than collective creations based on films or novels. Naturally, as someone who writes plays, I find this grievous. At the same time, I can understand that young people want to engage in this sort of research, to create their own works based on what they have written, what they pilfer right and left; it is not in itself uninteresting. But it questions the very fact that a playwright [*un auteur*] should exist.

KG: I would like to return to this question of the contemporary moment, but I would also like to rest on the question of collaboration or collective work. How do you see this play out in the work of writing? You have collaborated with your husband [Jean-Yves Cendrey] on the quite surprising book, *Puzzle* (2007), which includes three plays – one of yours, one of his, and one you co-wrote. I was struck to see your film with Claire Denis

380   *Kélina Gotman*

also, *White Material* (2010). What place do these collaborations have in your life as a writer, and in your written work?

MND: These collaborations have quite a minor place, I would say. For me, it's a sort of game. The co-authorship with Claire Denis came from a wish I had in that moment to take a break between novels, and she came to me with her story. She was the one who had the characters, the site, in mind. We co-wrote it, but my role was more as an aid to the writing, it was not my story, these were not my characters; it was really not my film. And the play that I co-wrote with Jean-Yves, it was not even really co-authorship, because I took a text that he had written about his father, I cut it up, and I wrote the father's response. The son, who has good reasons to hate his father, writes him a letter. And it seemed interesting to me to have the despicable father's point of view. But for me, this was a sort of game.

KG: And then the decision to publish this along with your play, *Providence* (2007), that is also quite unusual – not so much in terms of co-authorship this time but in terms of the apposition of two writers, even if only physically, within the space of a single book. You have said that you see this as a sort of game, and the title of the two-author volume is *Puzzle*. How has it been received? If authors are typically touted for their singularity, this book destabilises that expectation; it creates a sort of authorial *mise en scène*.

MND: That particular book was hardly received: there were no articles, no surprises, no reactions. But yes, it is true, it was unusual. I had never really thought about it that way. But it is not really co-authorship, it is rather that each one wrote independently, and then we put these three plays together. It is a slightly artificial process, one might say, because it is true that when one sees the names on the cover, one might believe that this writing is intermingled, but in fact it is not.

KG: To come back to your work with Claire Denis. Were you involved at all in the filming, or in the lead-up to the filming?

MND: She filmed in Cameroun. I did not go.

KG: As with your plays, you send the work off like a raft … to be received.

MND: Yes.

KG: To touch again on this question of belonging or alienation with regard to a cultural or literary moment, do you sense any points of reference, present or past, or are there particular authors or artists whose work has marked you more than others, or relative to which you situate your writing – either in agreement, or in terms of rejection or refusal?

MND: Rather in terms of agreement and as a source of inspiration for the theatre, there is clearly [Jean] Genet. Genet, particularly *Les Bonnes* (*The Maids*, 1947), a play I have read many times. When I saw it staged once in Berlin, in fact, I regretted seeing it, because I did not like it at all, it brought me nothing. But no matter. I really prefer to read plays. Genet, also Koltès, [Jean-Luc] Lagarce, Martin Crimp.

KG: Playwriting in the UK has been famously opposed to the German culture of the director, with this *writer's theatre* [in English in conversation], this

Marie NDiaye 381

theatre that is really a theatre of and for writers. Your work in this sense really suits the British context, which favours writing as such, and which stages the writing, rather than foregrounding the *mise en scène*.

MND: Similar to what Lars Norén does; this has interested me for a long time. Again, this is theatre that foregrounds writing [*un théâtre d'écriture*].

KG: In a number of your works, including *Trois femmes puissantes* (*Three Strong Women*, 2009) or *Les grandes personnes* (*The Grown-Ups*, 2011), there is a sense of violence and rage, as well as extraordinary lucidity with regard to all kinds of acts of small-mindedness and meanness. It is arresting, sometimes quite shocking to read you. Given the preponderance of these strong emotions, and very difficult situations between characters, in your work, do you see your writing as seeking to jolt people who encounter it from complacency? Do you attend to the effects of your work on those who read or view it?

MND: No, I never think about that. I am always a little bit surprised when I encounter reader reports, because I never imagine what my writing might provoke; I am unable to represent it to myself. And I do not think about it. I do not want to think about it in fact, because that might transform the meaning of what I write, if I thought about what it might provoke in the reader. I write without thinking that what I write will be read.

KG: You wrote a very striking preface to Pap Ndiaye's book, *La condition noire* (2008) [*The Condition of Blackness*].[5] Had you been in dialogue with him about this at that point or did you read his work and think how to frame it? It is quite a striking juxtaposition, the short story that you offer, and the sociological and historical study that unfolds after that.

MND: I wrote it before reading his manuscript, as he had not finished it when the editor asked me to write a short work of fiction to set as a preface. He had, of course, told me about the principal through-lines, what he was aiming to achieve, and I enjoyed trying to interpret from a fictional standpoint what I thought I understood of his work. In fact, it is not at all the same story, it is not an interpretation of what he has done; it is rather something in the margins, which simply takes as a starting point the fact of being black.

KG: We spoke a little bit about the reception of your work, that is to say, the translation of your written work into theatrical productions. But from the point of view of its translation into other languages, your writing is so striking syntactically. Have you followed the journeys of your work into other languages, other cultures, other countries – that is to say, into other milieus, including in French, beyond metropolitan France?

MND: I follow very little of what happens with translations of my work. The only translator with whom I have worked for many years is my German translator, only because I always answer questions my translators pose – they are often women translators, for that matter. It is very rare for translators to pose questions, whereas Claudia Kalscheuer, my German translator, always has quite a long list of questions, and it is always very interesting, as she often

382   *Kélina Gotman*

puts her finger on minor errors in the text, small mistakes I have made out of inattention, or errors with regard to the meaning of the text, sentences that don't quite have the meaning I intended or errors in the storyline. For example, in one novel, a scene described at the start takes place in the spring, and the spring is clearly present: trees, flowers, what have you. And the same scene reappears 200 pages later. By that point, I had completely forgotten that I had set this in the spring, and I situate it in the autumn. She asked me if it was intended or not, and actually not at all, it was really an error that no one had picked up. Translators often pick up little things that usually pertain to the domain of error.

KG: Does this ever lead you to go back over your texts? Or, once written, they are there, and the error becomes a constitutive part?

MND: I think that if I were told that a re-edition of my work was going to come out in French, perhaps I might change this, but I am not sure. At the same time, it is an error that is of fairly little interest, it contributes nothing; it is like in a film, sometimes there are errors in the costuming, a character wears a pink shirt in the first shot, and it is blue in the second. It is better to avoid it, simply.

KG: You won the Nelly Sachs Prize in 2015 celebrating your work, but unlike the Prix Femina or the Prix Goncourt, awarded for literature, this prize is awarded in recognition of an author's social contribution, underlining their work as someone who shapes public opinion.[6] Do you experience, as a writer, a sense of carrying a public mantle or performing a larger role, or do you have a desire to say or to contribute a perspective on the world which might go beyond the comparatively more solitary work of writing that you do?

MND: No. I remember this prize is meant to reward what you say, an action, a sort of activism [*engagement*] through literature, but I do not see things this way at all. I strive most of all not to be an activist [*engagée*], since I write fiction. It would bother me to think one might be able, in reading me, to have an idea of the sort of citizen I am. I have the impression that this is not very interesting. I know very well that there are necessarily things that transpire through the writing, without one realising it; but I try to avoid this. It would bother me to think that one might know, in reading me, whether I am a left or a right-wing woman; or if I vote, or if I do not vote. It would really trouble me to think that one could say that what I write is feminist or humanist, or in any case anything that might pertain to an 'ism' would bother me.

KG: This is also what is so striking in your work, this feeling one has in reading you that your position is absolutely impermeable to being pinned down, circumscribed; that your writing resists this. The image that comes to mind is that of enclosing or encircling or framing [*cerner*]; this evokes a territoriality, as with all 'isms'. And your work strikes me as absolutely unsituable, in the same way as the worlds you depict are so often unsituable.

In your novels, and in your plays, there are sometimes sites [*lieux*] that are very precise, Brive-la-Gaillarde or Courbevoie; at the same time, there is often nearly an abstraction from site [*abstraction de lieu*]. It seems to me that this very willed imprecision is fundamental to the work's imaginary. What place does site [*lieu*] have in your work?

MND: Site has a really very important place. Even if I do not say where something is taking place, it is fundamental that I should know. It is the same for my novels; I have to know, even if I have never been there. For example, I have never been to Brive. What interests me at a given moment is the image I might have of this place – how I visualise it; sound is also important, everything the place evokes for me in terms of the sort of region or province it is, what this represents. Especially in France, where there is such a great divide between Paris and everything else – the provinces – everything that is not Paris is seen as an annex, reduced or belittled, less interesting, less beautiful, less important, though this is changing a little bit with Bordeaux [*laughter*], which has become the object of an extraordinary infatuation, even among Parisians. It has become the second most expensive city after Paris. That aside, the capital remains Paris, and the difference between the capital and everything else is intractable. And so, yes, site is very important for what it evokes for me of the characters; when you come from Brive, it is not the same as when you come from Marseille or Bordeaux. When you come from Brive, you are very far from Paris, and that also means that you make an effort to become respectable, in the eyes of the Parisians. But these are not things that exist in the plays; they help me imagine the characters. By the same token, I have to know what sort of childhood characters have had; I may not evoke their childhood, but I need to know where they are from, who they are, what world they grew up in.

KG: Do you engage in rewriting – refining or rarefying details, or adding details?

MND: I never rewrite.

KG: Do you find that for commissions – for example, *Rien d'humain* (*Nothing Human*, 2004), which you wrote for the Festival Temps de Parole and the Comédie de Valence – unlike for novels which come entirely from you, there might be an external starting point, a context, which determines the act of writing, story or set? Even if you do not become involved in the production process, there is a very concrete environment in which the play will be performed.

MND: I have never been asked to write about a particular theme. No, I am always completely free. The only constraint – and I quite like it, actually – is in terms of the number of characters, because it is connected to questions of budget. If I wrote a play for 20 characters that might be quite awkward, if there was not enough money for this. So I might be asked to write for three characters if possible, or five maximum, or eight. The last play I wrote was on the request of Stanislas Nordey, who runs the National Theatre of Strasbourg, and his request in terms of characters was around five to seven at most, and that there should be more women, because he

384   *Kélina Gotman*

prefers to work with women actors. And he added something that was not at all on the order of a request, but of a wish, and that was that it would make him very happy if it were possible for his mother to perform, as she had been an actress; at the time when he asked me this, she was 80 years old, so he hoped that there might be a role for an older woman. And I did this. I was very happy to do this. But she passed away before the play was finished. She will not be the one to play the part. Without her, I never would have had the idea for this character of an elderly mother.

KG: What is so striking for me in some of your work, for instance in *La sorcière* (*The Witch*, 1996) and to an extent in *Les serpents* (*The Snakes*, 2004) as well as in *Three Strong Women*, is that so many of your characters transform, perhaps reveal an engagement with or participation in aspects of magic. We spoke about *Nothing Human*, but there is also the more than human; there are zoomorphisms, transformations that present really powerful images. What place does this world – or set of worlds – have for you?

MND: I call these oneiric visions; this approximates what happens in dreams. In dreams, one can have a meeting between people who never would have met, because one of them is dead or because they do not belong to the same world. And you encounter these two people in the same place, for example, even though they belong to different temporalities. In dreams, there might also be a kind of physical transformation that does not actually exist, but which dreams enable. I have fairly often used dream images in my works, either from my own dreams, or from others'. I quite like this, the more or less perceptible sliding from strict reality to a reality that is slightly deformed.

KG: It is striking also when this nearly offers a sense of deliverance. I am thinking of the extraordinary scene in the last moments of *Three Strong Women*, when one becomes suddenly aware that this is a story about refugees attempting passage from Africa to France; and yet the dreamscape at the end – in the moment one abruptly realises that the protagonist is now flying overhead, looking down, right at the point of passing over a barrier, or not, it is unclear – twists and shatters the question of the refugee, subverting habitual narratives. Without revealing too much, what strikes me is that there is such a strong image of soaring, a near extraction from earthly concerns, from the mundanity of everyday life, even from the mundanity of death or escape; these become sublime. The story at once radically and almost imperceptibly shifts points of view, so that we are not at ground level anymore, but find ourselves up above. It is almost as if a moment of death takes place, and one is in it. This is destabilising, and very powerful. We often encounter birds in your work – and with this bird's eye view, there is an element of transcendence. 'Transcendence' is a big word, perhaps not accurate, but it seems to me there is quite a physical and emotional sensation – the word comes to me in English – of *entrapment*, of being caught or closed into a condition or situation, and emerging from it, soaring above – but it is not freedom, it is tragic also. This is very complex, completely unresolved, as a narrative; almost emotionless. We are left to experience the emotion – or perhaps the fact – of finding ourselves in a flash in the sky, looking down. It may not be that there are mostly birds in your work, but it seems to me that there is a strong recurrence of birds and of flight across your novels and plays.

MND: Yes. I saw a production of *The Grown-Ups* at the Théâtre de la Colline in 2011, and there again there was this strange need for realism. The director went to a lot of trouble to achieve this. He had a domestic falcon flying through the space at one point, so he must have had recourse to a bird tamer. This did not seem to me to be useful; that is to say that one does not need to see the bird. It is enough for the detail to be spoken. In fact, I am always surprised when in the theatre one tries to do the same as in film; with a film, it is difficult to avoid realism, as there is so much identification with the character that one really has to be inside it. I have the impression that in the theatre, this is not necessary.

KG: Have you seen plays – not your own, but other productions, perhaps – which from an aesthetic point of view, for example, demonstrate this quality of the unshown, of the visually unsaid, the eschewal of realism; and which struck you as touching on what theatre might be?

MND: I have never seen any, but I am certain that this must exist.

KG: One thing that is striking in your work is how one feels – one could say this of all writing, but I think it is exceptionally true with yours – at times inhabited, haunted, possessed by a world or by characters, which linger. You have spoken of dreams; with the theatre also, one might experience characters or situations that remain present, or else dissolve, or recur in moments or gestures, turns of phrase. Here I think of an expression that comes up in your play with Cendrey, *Toute vérité* (*All Truth*, 2007), of spitting: you say that when one writes, one spits, for instance one spits out a character, as if one were getting rid of that story. I think also of the Lady in Green [in the novel *Autoportrait en vert,* 2006], and how chilling the wearing of green clothing becomes with her – how this stays with you for days after reading. Do these characters stay with you, or once written, they are as if liquidated from your life?

MND: This all disappears, yes. Characters absolutely do not inhabit me. I forget them.

KG: Did they inhabit you before, or do you feel that in the moment of writing, they appear in the scene, on the page?

MND: It is in the moment of writing. I would not even say that they inhabit me, in fact, it's too much. I always have a sort of distance with them – that is to say that I never forget that they are characters. That is why it always seems absurd to me the comparison some people make between books and children. My old books do not interest me at all; my children – even when they are adult – interest me.

KG: Where are you with your writing at present?

MND: At the moment, I have just finished a dramatic monologue, on the request of an actress named Nicole Garcia. You may not know her, she is more than 70 years old. She acted in a lot of films and now she acts little, but she directs films. She wants to return to the theatre and she asked me to write her a monologue, which I have just finished. It will be presented at Avignon in July 2020. Otherwise, I am finishing a co-authored film project with a director and film editor. As with Claire Denis, it is a film we are writing; it is her idea. It is based on a news item that spilled a lot of ink a few years ago. It is a woman of Senegalese origin who was living in France for 15 or so years, and who left the Parisian *banlieue* where she was living, with her little 18-month-old daughter. They went to a beach in the north of France, it was November; she had looked at the schedule of tides, and in the evening around 11pm she set the little girl on the beach. She left and the sea came, and drowned the child. And this made a lot of noise of course, this story, on the one hand because it is horrible. And also, because infanticides in general are the result of abuse. A child dies under the blows of the stepfather, or the father, or the mother. Whereas here, this child was perfectly treated, pampered, nurtured, treasured, etc. And for a mother to kill a child whom she cherished is extremely original, I mean, it is even incomprehensible. So there, we are starting from this story. I have read everything I could find on infanticides – for the vast majority, in France in any case, these are mothers with very little education, whereas this woman is not only highly educated but also well-read, cultured, exceptionally intelligent. It is a fascinating story.

KG: What is striking in your work is that there is a narration of facts or – you have described this as a news item [*fait divers*] – an exploration of a situation without attempting to impose judgement, or any perspective other than that of a sort of wonderment or shock or recognition that this should be so banal and so extraordinary at the same time. It seems to me that this refusal to judge requires extraordinary strength, a desire for impartiality, a refusal of moralism. This comes back to the question of whether one aligns or affiliates oneself or not with this or that perspective. Your approach allows the event to become visible almost in its pure horror – or its simplicity nearly without horror. One goes beyond, one passes to the other side of affect or moralising or any other sort of judgement.

MND: Yes, it would bother me for there to be a moral outcome to what I write. Even if – it is not in my character – I do not believe that I write things that are immoral. I do not think so, though that might be very good, because immorality is troubling, also. It obliges one to think about the way one sees the world in general; but I do not think I am immoral.

KG: You allow space for a much larger reflection, all the more troubling because one does not have the usual recourse to chastisement, morality, to a perspective that one might feel self-satisfied with in regard to one's judgement; where one might feel self-congratulatory. That is, I think, what renders the intransigence; one is without points of reference. Do you have any thoughts pertaining to the question of theatre or playwriting [*dramaturgie*] that we have not discussed?

MND: No, I do not think so. I do not feel very competent. I only have competence as a reader. I do not have any dramaturgical competence in the German sense of the term; I do not know if it is the same in English. In French, '*dramaturge*' simply means the one who writes plays. In Germany, the dramaturg is the person who works with the director. So, I have no dramaturgical competence. I do not even know what a stage is. I do not know what theatre is, in fact [*laughter*].

KG: I think that your work on the contrary is all that is most theatrical, perhaps all the more so because it refuses theatrical conventions, and that therefore one is moved to ask the question what a play might be that might not seek to be one, might not seek the 'act' [*le jeu*].

MND: Yes, as I do not feel I have any particular aptitude such as to say to a director what to do, I write almost no stage directions, pertaining to staging or to tone. I count on the fact that it is up to the actors to find this, to feel it. I do not see myself writing that this or that should be said in a joyous or an ironic tone. I count on the reading they do of the text to inspire them to find tones and gestures.

KG: Might you nevertheless think of setting as a stage direction perhaps what you said to me earlier, that there is no need for realism?

MND: I would like to do this, but I will not, because people do as they wish.

Marie NDiaye – five key productions

Papa doit manger. Direction by André Engel. Assistant Direction by Jean Liermier. Dramaturgy by Dominique Muller. Set by Nicky Rieti. Costumes by Chantal De La Coste. Music by Alexandre Desplat. Cast: Clotilde de Bayser, Rachida Brakni, Christian Cloarec, Christine Fersen, Claudie Gillot, Catherine Salviat, Bakary Sangaré, Catherine Sauval. Comédie-Française, Paris, France, 22–23 February 2003.

Hilda. Direction by Christophe Perton. Assistant direction by Emilie Blon-Metzinger. Dramaturgy by Pauline Sales. Set construction by Gabriel Burnod and Didier Raymond. Costumes by Paola Mulone. Lighting by Guillaume De La Cotte. Cast: Emilie Blon-Metzinger, Ali Esmili and Claire Semet. La Comédie de Valence, Valence, France, 10 October 2005.

Les serpents. Direction by Georges Guerreiro. Assistant direction by Vincent Babel. Set design by Masha Schmidt. Lighting by Liliane Tondellier. Cast: Séverine Bujard, Marie Druc, and Geneviève Pasquier. Poche / GVE, Geneva, Switzerland, 21 February 2004.

Les grandes personnes. Direction by Christophe Perton. Assistant direction by Mirabelle Ordinaire. Set design by Christophe Perton. Costumes by Sylvie Skinazi. Sound by Frédéric Bühl. Lighting by Kevin Briard. Cast: Stéphanie Béghain, Christiane Cohendy, Roland Depauw, Évelyne Didi, Adama Diop, Vincent Dissez, Aïssa Maïga, Jean-Pierre Malo. Théâtre de la Colline, Paris, France, 4 March 2011.

388 *Kélina Gotman*

Honneur à notre élue. Direction by Frédéric Bélier-Garcia. Artistic collaboration by Caroline Gonce. Sets by Chantal Thomas. Costumes by Pauline Kieffer. Lighting by Roberto Venturi. Music by Sébastien Trouvé. Cast: Isabelle Carré, Patrick Chesnais, Jean-Charles Clichet, Claire Cochez, Romain Cottard, Jan Hammenecker, Jean-Paul Muel, Chantal Neuwirth, Agnès Pontier, Christelle Tual and the voices of Sarah Jane Sauvegrain, Sébastien Eveno, David Migeot. Théâtre du Rond-Point, Paris, 1 March 2017.

Notes

1 The Comédie-Française staged its first Arabic repertory play in 2013, with the late Syrian playwright Saadallah Wannous's *Rituel pour métamorphose* (*Ritual for Metamorphosis*); the title role of Mou'mia was played by French-born white actress Julie Sicard.
2 *Trois pièces (Délivrance – Berlin mon garçon – Honneur à Notre Élue)* is published by Éditions Gallimard, 2019. *Berlin mon garçon*, the second play in the collection, was commissioned by Stanislas Nordey, director at the Théâtre National de Strasbourg.
3 Québécois director Robert Lepage was similarly compelled to halt production following a storm of controversy surrounding his decision to cast a primarily white troupe for his piece *SLĀV*, which was based on slave songs from the black American south. See, for example, Bourgault-Côté (2018) and Lowen (2018).
4 NDiaye refers here to *Die Übriggebliebenen* [*The Remaining*], based on three novels by Thomas Bernhard: *Eve of Retirement; Ritter, Dene, Voss*; and *Extinction*. Directed by Karin Henkel, dramaturgy by Rita Thiele, produced at the Hamburg Deutsches Schauspielhaus (2019).
5 Pap Ndiaye's *La condition noire: essai sur une minorité française* (2008), with a preface by Marie NDiaye, is considered to be the first major work of Black Studies (or '*black studies*') in France, accounting for France's own minority black population in a historical and a postcolonial context.
6 The Nelly Sachs Prize is awarded biannually by the German city of Dortmund. It commemorates the Jewish dramatist, poet, and Nobel Prize winner Nelly Sachs, who fled Nazi Germany and escaped to Sweden. The prize is intended to recognise an outstanding contribution to literature and the promotion of understanding between peoples.

Works cited

Bourgault-Côté, Guillaume (2018) 'Robert Lepage fait son mea culpa', *Le devoir*, 29 December, https://www.ledevoir.com/culture/theatre/544487/polemique-sla v-robert-lepage-fait-son-mea-culpa.
Lowen, Claire (2018) 'Robert Lepage commits to changes as controversial SLĀV musical returns to stage', 28 December, Montreal, CBC News, https://www.cbc.ca/ news/canada/montreal/robert-lepage-slav-update-1.4960627.
Ndiaye, Pap (2008) *La condition noire: essai sur une minorité française*, Paris: Calmann-Lévy.
Sieg, Katrin (2002) *Ethnic Drag: Performing Race, Nation, Sexuality in West Germany*, Ann Arbor: The University of Michigan Press.

Afterword

The constructed space

David Greig

In 1970, the Scottish poet W.S. Graham wrote a poem called 'The Constructed Space'. In it, he imagines the poem itself as a conjuring up a space, almost like a balloon, suddenly inflated out of nothing. Inside this new space two beings encounter each other: 'you' and 'I'.

In the poem 'I' explains the miracle of this encounter,

> Anyhow here we are and never
> Before have we two faced each other who face
> Each other now across this abstract scene

For as long as the poem is read, 'you' and 'I' can experience ourselves in a new way, liberated from the 'disguise' of the mortal, fleshy, physical world and its limits. Inside the poem's gaps and silences we become free.

> And yet I say
> This silence here for in it I might hear you.
> I say this silence or, better, construct this space
> So that somehow something may move across
> The caught habits of language to you and me.

Inside the space of art, self and other dissolve, and we are briefly able to encounter each other with a liberatory empathy.

I believe that this way of understanding art, the model of The Constructed Space, is one that can be applied to all art, not just poetry. In particular I think it can be applied effectively to theatre.

Inside a poem, author and reader meet. But inside the space of a play many more encounters are possible: author meets character, character meets other character, character encounters actor, actor meets audience, and so forth – not to mention director, designer, and all the other myriad collaborators who make a play. With each of these encounters a 'self' has to understand the point of view of an 'other'; an 'I' has to listen for a 'you'. And, of course, when the play is on the stage, each new audience member in the room is having their own personal encounter not just with the

390   *David Greig*

characters and the actors, but with the reactions of the other audience members around them. The sheer volume of encounters multiplies exponentially.

A play is, in essence, a machine for manufacturing empathy on an industrial scale.

In this chapter I want to expand on W.S. Graham's poem and to propose that art in general, but theatre in particular, performs an important social function as a 'constructed space' of radical empathy. I want to propose that the power of this space applies as much to the actual physical building of a theatre and theatre company, as it does to the abstract space of a play in performance. Lastly, I want to propose that the presence of such constructed spaces of art are essential to the proper functioning of democracy in a city.

To explore all these ideas I will to refer to my experience of adapting and staging, at the Lyceum Theatre in Edinburgh, one of the earliest plays in human existence: The *Hikétides* (*The Suppliant Women*) by Aeschylus (Figure 22.1).[1] This is a play which contains both the birth of drama and the birth of democracy. It is also, I believe, a good model of how the constructed space of civic theatre can works in practice.

★★★

The Suppliant Women is the second oldest play in human existence. Written two-and-a-half-thousand years ago it tells the story of 50 young women from Egypt who flee forced marriages to the sons of King Aegyptos. To escape, the women build a boat, cross the Mediterranean and finally wash up on a beach in Greece where they claim asylum. Faced with the women at the gates of his city, the Greek king, Pelasgos, considers what to do for the best. To invite the women in may bring war to the city, but to bar the women will bring spiritual pollution and shame. Unable to decide, Pelasgos proposes that the citizens of Argos take a vote...

★★★

In order to make *The Suppliant Women*, the creative team and I immersed ourselves in Greek theatre. We wanted to learn exactly how the first audience would have experienced the play. We researched the original music, the structure of performance, the social conditions, and so on.

You may already be familiar with Greek theatre, but to briefly summarise: Greek theatre primarily took place at festivals, in particular the annual festival of Dionysos in Athens. The plays were performed with music and singing. To make the plays a small number of professional actors would work together with an amateur chorus of young men. In style, Greek plays are characterised by their use of music and rhythmic speech. They are also famous for their themes – power, violence, family, duty, sex – themes that go straight to the heart of what it means to be human. All the plays in a festival would be entered into a competition and the winning play and chorus would be honoured with prizes, garlands, and statues.

As I explored the Greek world I began to wonder if perhaps the Greeks, by inventing theatre, had also uncovered some of the key architectural principles which go into building the constructed space of art.

Those principles are:

Fiction
Choice
Empathy
Conviviality
Participation
Community
Transcendence
Excellence
Silence

Let's take each of those ideas one by one.

★★★

Fiction

Although *The Suppliant Women* is two-and-a-half-thousand years old, the events it describes are not contemporary to its performance. It is fiction, not journalism. Aeschylus took a myth held in common by the city and he re-imagined it. He made it a story and by doing so he created another world, as story must always bring into being its own world. The world it creates might resemble the real

Figure 22.1 The community chorus in Aeschylus's *The Suppliant Women* adapted by David Greig and directed by Ramin Gray at the Royal Lyceum, Edinburgh, 2016. © Stephen Cummiskey

392   David Greig

world. It might even parallel the real world. But if the story is any good, it will always be a world unto itself.

By offering us a fiction, Aeschylus allows us to enter a different world, and in so doing, he offers us the chance to see, as if for the first time, our own world.

The constructed space allows us to enter a different world.

★★★

Choice

Like most Greek tragedy, *The Suppliant Women* is centred around an impossible choice. If the city welcomes the women, they will bring war. But if the city does not welcome the women, it will bring shame. When these two aims are in conflict, what is the correct course of action? It's a classic Greek dilemma because it is insoluble. There can be no correct answer.

Wrestling with impossible dilemmas is, perhaps, a defining feature of being human. No person goes through life deliberately wishing to do the wrong thing. Perhaps the most common experience of us all is that of wishing to do right thing but nevertheless experiencing the fact that somehow everything still turns out wrong.

By taking a clear, rational eye to the most important issues of its day and then finding within those issues, not a lecture, nor an example, nor propaganda, nor an illustration, but instead a dilemma, a choice, Greek drama takes two hands to the surface of the world and wrenches open a space for the human.

The constructed space contains a choice.

★★★

Empathy

The Suppliant Women was written by Aeschylus at a time when Athens was undergoing a migrant crisis. The city was at the centre of a growing empire. Large numbers of foreigners were coming to live and work in the city. For the male citizens of Athens it was suddenly unclear who should be regarded as a 'citizen' and who should be consigned to second-class status.

In this context then, we see that at the centre of *The Suppliant Women* is an extraordinary act of empathy, because Aeschylus has made the central protagonist of his play a doubly marginalised group: migrant women.

Take for example this short fragment. In this moment all is lost. The city has not yet taken the women in, and from their sanctuary on a cliff-top they can see the sails of their tormentors speeding towards them. The women face capture or death. In a song the girls imagine their escape...

Oh Argos
Is there some summit,
A chair in the clouds,

A cliff-top I can climb to,
High up in the mountains,
A summit so high
Even goats cannot reach it?
Isolated
Overhanging
Mist turning to snow on my skin.
I will shiver
Look down
At the wings of the vultures
Wheeling below
Awaiting my fall.
Oh Argos
Will you watch
As I step into emptiness.
Will you witness my protest,
My thousand foot silence?[2]

Remember, of course, that this speech would have been spoken by a member of the chorus: a man. Aeschylus is requiring the privileged young men of Athens to put themselves into the shoes of frightened refugees. The male audience has been required to follow a drama whose protagonist is a group of women seeking asylum. Empathy courses through the drama.

Almost every act in the creation of a piece of theatre requires a person to imagine what it might be like to be in someone else's shoes.

The author must imagine being someone else.

The actors must embody someone else.

The director must imagine being an audience.

And finally, the audience, as they watch are invited think to themselves: 'Imagine, if I was that person, what would I do?'

As my friend the Scottish playwright Jo Clifford has said: 'Empathy is a muscle, theatre is the gym'.

The constructed space is a space of empathy.

★★★

Conviviality

All Greek theatre was dedicated to the god Dionysos. As well as being the god of theatre, Dionysos was also the god of wine. I don't think this is a coincidence. When *The Suppliant Women* was first performed at the festival of Dionysos, wine would be drunk and food would be eaten. The air would have been thick with the smell of barbecued meat.

This conviviality is a central plank of the Greek theatrical experience. By eating and drinking with our fellow citizens we are reminded that they are humans. We

394 *David Greig*

experience each other in our embodied forms: we laugh, we burp, we fart, we cry. We are human together.

In this atmosphere of conviviality, we feel welcomed and enabled to face the play on the stage and therefore to go deep into darkness, terror, complexity and rage. In the audience, we rub up against each other, hold hands, and draw strength from our shared humanity as we watch our own darkness played out before us.

In the constructed space we are convivial.

★★★

Participation

Bertolt Brecht said 'theatre is a transformative art, but those it transforms the most, are those who make it.' This was certainly a principle with which the Greeks were familiar.

Participation in a chorus was considered a religious duty for young men in Athens. It was almost a form of national service. Politicians would refer to their 'fellow chorus members' with the same affection of an old soldier thinking back to the men in his platoon.

(Personally, I think a very great deal of the problems of democracy might be solved if we were to introduce a system of compulsory national service but instead of going into the army, everyone would have to spend a year in a musical theatre chorus. It's not easy to be a fascist while performing in a kick line in *Oklahoma!*.)

The constructed space is built from participation.

★★★

Community

All male citizens of Athens would attend the festival of Dionysos. *The Suppliant Women* was performed in front of something akin to a football crowd. These plays were for *everyone*.

(Now, of course, they *weren't* for everyone. They weren't performed to women. This is a fascinating and difficult exclusion. It can't be ignored and it's something I will come back to, but for now, stay with me.)

The Greeks knew that the theatre's power was only fully released when it was attended by every citizen.

Everyone must have access to the constructed space.

★★★

Transcendence

Greek drama began as a religious ritual of music and dance: tragedy derives from the *trágos ōidé* or 'Goat Song'. The use of music, light, and rhythm to create transcendence is, of course, common to most spiritual traditions around

Afterword 395

the world. But the Greeks systematised this relationship in the figure of Dionysos, the god of Theatre, who is also the god of Dance and Trance.

In the wordless swirl of dance, trance, rhythm and light, we, as the audience, are lifted out of our mortal disguise and offered transcendence.

We enter the constructed space shorn of our daily selves: vulnerable and open.

★★★

Excellence

When we were making *The Suppliant Women* there were many arguments. Ramin, John, Sasha, and myself would argue about what the original performance might have been like. How should we approach the performance to achieve the right effect? And so on.

At one point we were having a very heated argument over 'what Aeschylus would have wanted'. The argument flew back and forth until Barnaby Brown, our *aulos* player, made a surprising comment. 'Aeschylus,' he said, '*would have wanted to win*'.

Barnaby comes originally from the world of Scottish piping. Scottish piping, like many traditional art forms, is artisanal rather than expressive and it often finds its artistic zenith in competition. Pipers compete at Highland games to win gold medals. Because of his background something was obvious to Barnaby which had passed the rest of us by.

Aeschylus would have wanted to win the competition.

By demonstrating excellence Aeschylus would have achieved two things. First, he would have honoured the gods with the very best he had to offer, and second he would demonstrated to his audience the greatness that lay within them.

The constructed space is a celebration of human excellence.

★★★

So we see that we find in the Greeks, the inventors of drama, the main planks of the constructed space: fiction, choice, empathy, community, conviviality, transcendence, participation, and excellence.

But I think there is still one quality missing: silence.

★★★

In W.S. Graham's poem he clearly states:

I say
This silence here for in it I might hear you.

★★★

Silence

Surely the constructed space must contain silence.

396   *David Greig*

There is between ourselves and the Greeks, two-and-a-half-thousand years of great silent darkness. That is surely silence enough in which to find ourselves. But still, I wonder. Where in their theatre did the Greeks find silence?

I do not know, for certain, how the Greeks built silence into their theatre but I know where I experience it.

In the mystery of the texts themselves.

There is a deep mystery at the heart of nearly every Greek play and it is this very unknowability which draws theatre-makers back to them time and time again. But whatever its source, I do know that this silence that is the most challenging thing for any artist to create. Silence is elusive. Silence is an accident. And yet surely, when we encounter any truly great work of art, it's the silence which most compels us to come towards it.

★★★

Of course, the moment we think about silence we also think about the excluded voices from Greek theatre; in particular, women. The festival of Dionysos was for men only.

The performers were male. The authors were male. The audience was male.

We do know, however, that women were aware of the plays. The comical Satyr plays performed at the end of the evening often satirise female reaction to particular authors or styles of drama.

It has been speculated that while the men were inside the open-air theatre there may have been women gathered outside, in the groves, on the grass, on roof-tops, or under the pines, listening to the words and songs drift from inside the theatre.

How, in amongst all this democracy and empathy, was it possible for the Greeks to exclude the voices of women? I can't answer that question. But it does throw up, for me, a couple of thoughts:

1   Who are we excluding now?
2   Imagine them, the women, standing in the darkness on a warm night in Athens, listening to these words from Aeschylus sung out from the stage –

> O Zeus
> Most blessed king of blessed kings
> Treasure bringer
> Blessing giver
> Mighty wave of power
> Use your force to
> Stop male violence.
> Take the hearts of men
> And plunge them
> Into a lake of blood
> Forever tether
> The black bull of madness
> To which men yoke their souls.[3]

Afterword 397

What space did those words open up on that night and what encounters were enabled to take place within the constructed space of those words?

★★★

I have discussed what 'The Constructed Space' is. Perhaps I ought to explore for a moment what the constructed space is *not*. It is *not*, for example, a 'safe space' (at least not in the sense that it is a comfortable space).

Inside the constructed space of art we encounter each other in our fully human forms and those fully human forms contain, for example, darkness, terror, violence and illicit desire.

I think here of the plays of Sarah Kane or Beckett. Such plays are unflinching and dark. But because and although the space they construct is bleak, these works allow all who access them to feel the full force of our shared humanity – author and reader, actor and audience – the discomfort of the darkness is shared, and sharing of the burden of the darkness becomes, in itself, a form of comfort.

★★★

When we add all these elements together, we see that the constructed space is a space which allows an encounter to take place, between 'you' and 'I'. But the architecture of the space means that this encounter is one which conjures another world, produces a dilemma, demonstrates empathy, community, conviviality, transcendence, participation, and excellence.

And so in art we encounter each other in our full humanity.

★★★

Which is all very nice. But a summer's day is nice. A delicious cake is nice. What is it about a work of art that makes it *vital*? What is it about the constructed space that *demands* our attention?

The Suppliant Women was performed the year before Athens underwent a democratic revolution. The play itself is focused around a vote. It is the first instance of a vote in any work of art. The play certainly contains the first instance of the use of the word 'democracy'.

When their father returns from Argos with word that the citizens have voted for them to be allowed to stay, the Chorus ask:

Father – tell us! How does it work this thing called democracy?[4]

In fact, my translation is a bad one. In the original, the word appears in the form of a typically Aeschylean mash-up:

Tell us father – how does it work this democra-handy-uppy thingy?[5]

It's interesting that what is, essentially, the first play also contains, essentially, the first mention of democracy.

398 *David Greig*

We are also told that the democratic process in Athens first took place in theatres. The constructed space and the democratic space were born at the same moment. This double birth seems to speak to a self-evident truth which is this: without access to the constructed space we cannot have true democracy.

Unless we are able to encounter each other within art, then any vote taken is taken in ignorance. Democracy becomes mob rule. Without the constructed space to restore us to humanity, democracy merely becomes another form of violence.

★★★

This, of course, is why the political realm is so wary of the constructed space. This is why authoritarians want to shut it down.

★★★

So, in these hastening, trying times, when it feels like democracy is becoming detached from empathy and rationality, when the polity feels afraid, surely this is the moment when it is most important for the constructed space to exist and for every citizen, and non-citizen, to be able to encounter themselves and others within it.

And is it not, therefore, on those of us who guard the constructed space, to defend our spaces against erosion? We must ensure our work opens up new worlds; we must ensure it opens up real dilemmas; we must ensure it allows access for the whole community. We must offer participation and community, but we must also aim for excellence. We must offer conviviality and encourage transcendence.

And perhaps most of all, we must construct within our programmes the silence in which 'I' might hear 'you.'

★★★

I am a runner. I like running hills and trails. One day recently I was on a run in the hills and I came across the ruin of a broch: a 10,000-year-old stone Pictish castle.

There was no signage on this ruin, no ropes to keep me away. It was simply there, present, on the hillside above the sea. I went in, ducking low under the lintel of the doorway and sitting on the grass at its centre.

In this space I sat for a moment in silence and I found myself feeling a deep curiosity about the makers of this broch, and the souls who had inhabited it. I imagined them, sitting where I was now sat, looking at the scene I was now seeing. How would it have been different? How would it have been the same?

On that damp afternoon high above Loch Shiel, sweating from my run, alone, I felt as profound a connection between 'you' and 'I' as I have felt reading any poem or seeing any play.

And so I ask myself, in what other realms might we find the constructed space? In Heritage? In Wilderness? What is the nature of the encounter between 'you' and 'I' in a ballet, or in a museum, or indeed when a walker stumbles across an ancient broch in the middle of a hillside?

★★★

Afterword 399

'The Constructed Space'

Meanwhile surely there must be something to say,
Maybe not suitable but at least happy
In a sense here between us two whoever
We are. Anyhow here we are and never
Before have we two faced each other who face
Each other now across this abstract scene
Stretching between us. This is a public place
Achieved against subjective odds and then
Mainly an obstacle to what I mean.

It is like that, remember. It is like that
Very often at the beginning till we are met
By some intention risen up out of nothing.
And even then we know what we are saying
Only when it is said and fixed and dead.
Or maybe, surely, of course we never know
What we have said, what lonely meanings are read
Into the space we make. And yet I say
This silence here for in it I might hear you.

I say this silence or, better, construct this space
So that somehow something may move across
The caught habits of language to you and me.
From where we are it is not us we see
And times are hastening yet, disguise is mortal.
The times continually disclose our home.
Here in the present tense disguise is mortal.
The trying times are hastening. Yet here I am
More truly now this abstract act become.

         W.S. Graham[6]

★★★

The constructed space offers a challenge to us all. It offers a challenge to artists and to curators. It is not enough to be beautiful. It is not enough to be funny or empathetic, or excellent, or apt. It is not enough simply to take us into another world. No, for a work of art to allow an encounter between 'you' and 'I' some space needs to be created: some silence.

The creation of that silence takes an heroic effort. It requires that, having transmuted ourselves into the abstract form of art, we, the artist, must depart the stage and allow our work speak for itself.

Having let ourselves become the poem, the play, the painting, the object, or even the conference speech, we, the author, must finally shut up.

Florence
December 2016

400   David Greig

Notes

1   [*All notes by the Editor*]: David Greig's version of *The Suppliant Women*, directed by Ramin Gray, with choreography by Sasha Milavic Davies, music by John Browne, design by Lizzie Clachan and lighting by Charles Balfour opened at the Royal Lyceum Theatre in Edinburgh on 1 October 2016. It subsequently played at the Royal Exchange, Manchester in March 2017 and at the Young Vic, London, in November 2017. The Chorus was always made up of young women volunteers from the city in which the show was being performed.

2   This is a version of lines 792–8 in the standard edition of *The Suppliant Women*. In Greig's published version of this play, the passage is slightly different, but may be found at Aeschylus, *The Suppliant Women*, in a version by David Greig (London: Faber & Faber, 2017), p. 36. All subsequent references will give lines in the standard edition and the equivalent passage in Greig's version.

3   *Suppliant Women*, ll. 524–30/p. 28.

4   *Ibid.*, ll. 603–4/p. 31.

5   Rather than use 'δημοκρατία' the usual word for 'democracy', Aeschylus uses a more roundabout phrase, 'δήμου κρατοῦσα χεὶρ ὅπη πληθύνεται' (l. 604), which refers to the people indicating a majority by show of hands.

6   'The Constructed Space' by W.S. Graham. From *New Collected Poems* (Faber and Faber, 2004). Copyright (c) the Estate of W.S. Graham, 2004. All rights reserved. Reproduced by permission of Rosalind Mudaliar, the Estate of W.S. Graham.

Index

absurdism 24, 31–6, 78, 87
acting 99, 117, 121–4, 157–8, 197, 230, 231, 232, 255–6, 284, 298, 300, 304, 327, 344, 377
actors 59, 69, 100, 113, 132–3, 140, 355
adaptation 69, 189, 269
Aeschylus 4, 357, 395; *The Suppliant Women* 390–7 *see also* Greek tragedy
Afrim, Radu 303–4, 305–6
agitprop 233
Aguilar, Andrea 1
Ahmad, Aijaz 5
Aktie Tomaat *see* Tomato Action
Albinus, Jens 345
Alföldi, Róbert 16
allegory 32, 33, 35, 139, 141, 181n2
Almqvist, Carl Jonas Love 365
America 50, 309
Anckaert, Arnaud 343
Andjelković, Sava 325
Andrews, Benedict 340–1
Angelaki, Vicky 18n1, 112, 118
animals 213–14, 359; animal rights 306
anti-Semitism 75n2, 100, 191–2
Apter, Emily 6
Argentina 215
Aristotle 215, 326
Arts Council, England 344 *see also* subsidy
Ask, Beatrice 372
Aston, Elaine 336
audience(s) *xviii–xx*, 22–3, 34, 38, 51, 80, 83–5, 97, 100, 105–7, 114–17, 121, 124, 132–3, 145–6, 155, 158, 161, 164, 215, 218–19, 235, 244, 253–4, 271, 284, 307–11, 323–4, 339–40, 355–7, 366–7, 369, 393
audience participation 12, 80, 84, 89–91, 284
Austria 14–15, 44–61

authorship 8, 40, 250, 257, 322, 328; co-authorship 379–80
autobiography 322–3, 369
avant-garde 47, 56, 68, 71, 163

bad conscience 1
Balkans 8, 86, 157, 158, 314–17, 325–7; Balkanism 10, 314–16, 328
Barker, Howard 14
Beckett, Samuel 32–6; *Waiting for Godot* 23–4, 33
Belbel, Sergi 17, 205–6
Belgium 37
Berg, Sybille 16
Berlin 136–7
Bernhard, Thomas 379
Bewältigung der Vergangenheit 22
Billington, Michael 106, 336–7
Birch, Alice 334, 336, 341–7; *Revolt. She Said. Revolt Again.* 341–6
Blancheteau, Annick 269
'Blood and Sperm' generation 150–64
borders 2, 5, 9, 10–14, 277
Bosnia 1, 27, 158, 315
Bosnian War 85, 151, 157
Boyd, Michael 233
Branco, José Mário *xviii–xix*
Braun, Volker 27
Brazil 87
Brecht, Bertolt 23–4, 36–8, 121–2, 321–3, 337–8, 355
Brexit 14
Britain 10, 23, 37, 150–2, 154–6, 159–61, 163–4, 194, 195, 271, 334–43, 346, 380
Brunkenm Thirza 56–7
Bulgaria 33
Butkovic, Vanda 54–5

402   Index

cannibalism 53, 231, 233
canon 67–9, 77, 189–90; canonisation
    11, 90
capitalism 5, 14, 130, 139, 142, 168, 196,
    198, 199, 226, 229, 305
Cărbunariu, Gianina 79
Casanova, Pascale 5–6
casting practices and policies 14, 53,
    132–3, 367, 375–6, 377–8
Castorf, Frank 379
Catholicism, *see* Christianity
censorship 7, 12, 28, 73, 219
characterisation 205, 250, 385
choice 392
chorus 46, 57–8, 394
Christianity 45, 73–4, 191, 250–2, 297
cinema 171, 198–9, 232, 248–9, 291,
    315, 379–80
class 32, 99, 130, 133, 136–7, 139, 142,
    154–5, 269, 172, 190–5
classics 29–30, 67, 139–40, 168, 170, 204,
    235, 262
clowning 36–7, 306
collaborations 6, 8, 9,40,68, 72, 81, 86,
    89, 120, 124, 164, 257, 300, 318–19,
    379–80; between writers and directors
    3, 87, 96–7, 99, 121–4, 134, 186–8,
    205, 208, 244, 255, 258, 320, 322,
    324, 336, 379; between writers and
    nations 16, 22, 25, 73–4, 205; between
    writers and theatres 87, 96, 100, 280
collective creation 7, 379
collecting societies *see* writers' guilds
colonialism 5, 23, 250, 374
comedy 36–7, 140, 142, 204, 205,
    207, 210, 218; black comedy 207;
    commedia dell'arte 310; romantic
    comedy 209;
commercial theatre 2, 204, 263
commodification 5, 62n10, 139
communication 238, 241
communism 7, 13, 14, 15, 25, 27, 29, 31,
    34, 39, 66, 82–6, 88, 90, 314 *see also*
    socialism
community 5, 359, 394
confrontational forms of writing 15
conviviality 393–4
Cooke, Dominic 177–8
Coonrod, Karin 81
corruption 137, 151, 210, 218, 229, 300
Crimp, Martin 4, 6, 112–19, 124–5;
    Attempts on Her Life 112, 114–17, 124,
    342; *The City* 117–19, 159; *Fewer
    Emergencies* 112

crisis 10, 15, 31, 58, 67, 68, 70, 72, 175,
    267, 269, 280, 291–2; European migrant
    crisis 58, 81
critics 48, 75n3, 96, 98, 102, 103, 104,
    106, 107, 124, 155–6, 163, 169, 186,
    194, 207, 254, 324, 335, 338, 341,
    343–4, 355
Croatia 315–29
cultural memory 12, 68, 77–8, 80, 83–4,
    199, 271
cultural privilege 15
Czechoslovakia 26, 34

Damrosch, David 5–6
dance 257
Dante, Emma *xx*, 296–8, 299–302,
    306–8, 310–11; *The Macaluso Sisters*
    297, 301–2; *The Monkey* 297; *Parasite
    Dogs* 297; *Trilogy of the Sicilian family*
    297, 299–301, 307–8; *The Whores* 297
Dejmek, Kazimierz 26
Delgado, Maria 30, 266
Demirski, Paweł 185–92, 195–6,
    199–200; *Battle of Warsaw* 195;
    Forefathers' Eve. Exhumation 189; *In the
    Name of Jakub S.* 190; *Long Live the
    War!* 195; *There was a Pole, Pole, Pole
    and the Devil* 189–90; *Un-divine
    Comedy, I WILL TELL GOD
    EVERYTHING!* 190–2, 193
democracy 12, 16, 32, 37, 84, 161,
    192–3, 212, 239, 390, 394, 396–8;
    failures of 2; radical democracy 325
Denis, Claire 379–80
Denmark 8, 345
design, theatre 25, 32, 54, 85, 99, 104,
    106, 107, 121, 144, 152, 177–8, 179,
    187, 206, 207, 217, 267, 302, 303,
    320, 335, 339, 343, 345, 377
devising practices 8, 186
dialect *xx*, 9, 48, 55, 56, 245, 296–7,
    300–1, 307–8, 310
didacticism 36, 321, 363
didaskalia 323–4, 328 *see also* stage
    directions
direct address 58–9, 246, 322–4
director(s)/directing 8, 16–17, 21, 30,
    56–7, 66–74, 76, 90, 98, 101, 102,
    107, 117, 120–3, 152–3, 174, 177,
    18–86, 205, 226, 255, 257, 258,
    262–3, 273, 285, 287, 305, 316, 324,
    327, 365, 371, 377, 379, 380–1, 387
directors' theatre 21, 107, 205, 262–3,
    316 *see also* Regietheater

Index 403

director-writer partnerships 3, 17, 87, 96–7, 99, 121–4, 134, 186–8, 205, 208, 244, 255, 258, 320, 322, 324, 336, 379
diversity 194, 375–6, 377–8
documentary theatre 25, 78, 171, 226–7, 235
Donbas, war in 228, 233, 235–7
Dramatic Studio (Denmark) 8
dramaturg 7, 8, 66, 68–70, 80, 96, 98, 187–8, 386–7
dramaturgy 4, 12, 21, 28, 32, 36, 55, 73, 113, 117, 131, 137, 139, 145, 169, 171, 179, 226–7, 262, 264, 315, 322, 339, 345, 354, 386–7; Barrack Dramaturgy 80, 88–90; fragmentary dramaturgy (*fragmentarna dramaturgija*) 316, 318, 324, 326–7, 330n9
dreams 384
Dvoretski, Ignatii 27–8

ecology 78
economic recession 4, 58, 145, 319; economic recession post-2007 in Spain 204, 209–10, 239; in Greece 10, 14, 253, 277–8, 280; in Italy 299, 305, 309; in Ireland 253, 255
écriture féminine 40, 316, 324, 328
editing process 216
Egan, Jennifer 1
Ekaterinburg 169–70, 172–3
Elliott, Marianne 338
elliptical theatre 6, 17, 29
emancipation 317, 323, 328
empathy 392–3
entertainment *xxi*, 103, 168, 261, 301
environmentalism 36
epic theatre 24, 36–8
Esslin, Martin 31–2
Estonia 255
Europe *see also* European Union 1–18, 21–41, 45–6, 50, 53–4, 56, 70, 76, 84, 86, 88, 112–14, 117, 120, 124–5, 137, 145, 151, 163–4, 180, 212–13, 253, 258, 271, 277, 283, 303, 306–7, 316–17, 325–7
European Capital of Culture 253
European Common Market *see* European Union
European Union 9, 14, 22, 255
Euskadi Ta Askatasuna (ETA) 209–10, 218
evasion 199, 219
existentialism 15, 22, 24, 34, 102, 104, 119, 174–5, 229, 230, 238, 239
expressionism 26, 187

fable 31, 208, 213
fake truth(s) 2
Fall of the Berlin Wall 130, 151
family 306–7
farce 209
fascism 15, 16, 27, 32, 34, 55–6 *see also* National Socialism
feminism 71–2, 313–14, 316, 319–20, 324, 328, 334–6, 338, 341–2, 344–5 *see also* gender politics
festivals 5, 9, 11, 68, 80, 98, 390; Adelaide Festival 143; Analogio Festival 278; Belgrade International Theatre Festival [BITEF] 157, 317; Berliner Theatertreffen 11, 103, 106–7, 153; Bonner Biennale Festival 129, 325; Brighton Festival 85; Dionysia 390, 394, 396; Dublin Theatre Festival 248; Edinburgh Festivals 5; EUROKAZ Festival 317; Festival d'Avignon 5; Festival Couperin 269; Festiwal Festiwali 68; Festival OFF d'Avignon 80; Festival Temps de Parole 383; Heidelberg Stückemarkt 282; Ibsen Festival 98; International Greek Festival 282; International Martin McDonagh Theatre Festival 248; Liubimovka New Play Festival 226; Midsummer Mischief Festival 341, 342–3; Montpellier Festival 269; Mühlheimer Theatertage 134; Royal National Theatre Connections festival 298; Saison Russe festival 187; Sibiu International Theatre Festival 80; Theater der Welt Festival 58; TR/PL Festival 193
fiction 391–2
film noir 123, 208
financial crisis, *see* economic recession
Finburgh, Clare 271
First World War 69–70
Fo, Dario 36
Fosse, Jon *xx*, 6, 95–6, 97–8, 101–2, 105–9; *The Child* 97, 102, 107–8; *Death Variations* 105; *Dream of Autumn* 102, 105, 106–7; *Nightsongs* 105–6; *Somebody is Going to Come* 97, 102, 105
Foyer, Donya 96
France 23, 37, 104, 261–74, 343–4
Frank, Anne 156
Frayn, Michael 112
Fredriksson, Benny 365
freedom of expression 13, 74, 78
Fukayama, Francis 14

404   *Index*

Galceran, Jordi 203–10, 218, 219–20; *Burundanga* 204, 209–10; *Cancún* 208; *Credit* 208–9; *Dakota* 204; *The Grönholm Method* 2, 203–8; *Killing Words* 204
gameplay 208
gaming 131, 198
García, Rodrigo 17
gaze 16, 198–9, 314–15, 317, 327–8, 368–9
Gémier, Firmin 5
gender politics 70–2, 174, 334–5, 344–5 *see also* feminism
Genet, Jean 32, 380
genocide 1, 85, 151, 215, 314
Germany 14–15, 22–3, 27, 38, 102–4, 106, 120, 129–146, 151–5, 159–63, 340–1, 344–5, 353, 357–8, 362, 375, 378–9
Guénoun, Denis 261
globalisation 133, 136–8, 145
Global South 13,339
Goddard, Lynette 336, 338
Gogol, Nikolai 174
Gombrowicz, Witold 31, 69
Gorin, Grigory 35
Gosch, Jürgen 134
Göttingen 134
Govedíc, Nataša 325
Graham, W.S. 389–90
Greece 10, 36, 37, 277–93
Greek tragedy 4, 47, 57, 58, 390–7 *see also* tragedy
Greig, David 4, 9, 389–400
grotesque 33, 35, 49, 52, 139, 142, 170, 174, 178, 297
Grotowski, Jerzy 71

Hampton, Christopher 12, 271–2
Handke, Peter 1–2, 114, 352–63; *The Chinaman of Pain* 361; *The Hour We Knew Nothing of Each Other* 354–5; *The Innocents, Me and the Stranger at the Side of the Country Road* 353–4; *Prophecy* 355; *Offending the Audience* 354–7
Hare, David 187
Harrower, David 16–17
Havel, Václav 33
historical memory, see cultural memory
historical injustice 2
historical revisionism 13
Holocaust 156, 190, 191–2, 199
Holodomor 233–5
Holoubek, Gustaw 67

Holter, Lars Erik 179
humanity *xviii–xxi*, 72, 85, 291, 394, 397–8
humour *see* comedy
Hungary 16, 28–9, 77, 80–1, 90

identity 3, 40, 71–2, 90, 139, 191–3, 196, 237, 283, 364; black British 23; European 22, 86, 145, 151; gender identity 50; Greek 282; national 14, 26, 189, 237, 255, 309, 372; Polish 189; post–Soviet 180, 230, 231; Sicilian 306–8; theatre of identity 308
Illyés, Gyula 28
improvisation 3, 39, 69, 88, 199, 256, 284, 300, 318
'In Yer Face' theatre 11, 130, 141, 248, 278, 325–6
individualism 25, 37, 39–40, 57–8, 99, 115–16, 119, 139, 142, 191, 306, 323, 327
intellectualism 7, 24, 26, 32, 77, 83, 90, 137
International Criminal Court (ICC) 121
internationalism 5
internet 131, 313
intertextuality 140, 318
Ionesco, Eugène 32, 35, 83, 87
Iraq 45–6, 159
Ireland 244–59
Islam 162
Italy 23, 296–311
Ivaškevičius, Marius 13, 16

Jakimiak, Agnieszka 66, 68, 70
Jarry, Alfred 30, 121
Jarzyna, Grzegorz 194, 196–8
Jelinek, Elfriede *xx*, 44–50, 55–60, 61–2; *Burgtheater* 55–6; *Charges* 58; *Rod, Staff and Crook – a Handicraft* 56–7; *Sports Play* 45, 57–8; *What Happened after Nora Left Her Husband; or, Pillars of Society* 47
Jewish; Judaism 68, 191–2, 215

Kane, Sarah *xx*, 6, 150–9, 162–5; *4.48 Psychosis* 156–7; *Blasted* 150, 154–5, 157, 342; *Cleansed* 154, 156–7, 163–4
Karaca, Abdullah Kenan 52
Kelly, Dennis 17
Kerbrat, Patrice 265, 267
Khemiri, Jonas Hassen 7, 13, 15, 364–73; *Everything I Don't Remember* 364, 366, 368, 369, 372; *I Call My Brothers*

366–7, 368–9; *Invasion!* 364, 365, 369, 371; *Montecore: The Silence of the Tiger* 364; *One Eye Red* 364
Kirchner, Alfred 103
Kitsopoulou, Lena 278–86, 291–2; *Antigone – Lonely Planet* 281; *Athanasios Diakos – The Return* 282, 285; *Austras or The Weed* 282–3; *Bats* 279; *Cry* 281–2, 284; *M.A.I.R.O.U.L.A.* 279, 281; *My Green Dress* 282; *N-Euro-se* 284; *The Price* 284; *Red Riding Hood or The First Blood* 284; *Remember the Sabbath Day and Keep It Holy* 279–80
Koliada, Nikolai 170, 172
Koltès, Bernard-Marie 23, 375, 377–8
Krakowska, Joanna 188–9
Kühnel, Tom 129
Kulenovic, Skender 27
Kunzru, Hari 7–8
Kwaśniewska, Monika 191
Kyiv 232–3, 235 *see also* Ukraine

Labanauskaitė, Gabrielė 16
Langevin, Sophie 344
language 49, 51, 55, 115–16, 132, 212–3, 246–7, 338, 340, 346, 354, 357–62
Laskowska, Wanda 71
Lease, Bryce 52
Lehmann, Hans-Thies 3, 10–11, 46, 115–16, 164, 183n23, 185, 316
Lepper, Johannes 52–4
LGBTQ 192–3 *see also* queer
librettos 2, 280
Liddell, Angélica 17
Lima, Andrés 270
linguistic dexterity 4
literary agents 11
Loher, Dea 16
Lorraine, Melissa 81, 89–90
love 238–9, 284
Lupa, Krystian 52
Luxembourg 344

Madách, Imre 26
Maidan Revolution 233, 235
Major, John 151
market *see* capitalism; globalisation
Marxism 4–5
masculinity 174, 180
Masłowska, Dorota 13, 186, 193–201, 201n6; *A Couple of Poor, Polish-Speaking Romanians* 193–5; *No Matter How Hard We Tried* 196–8; *Other People* 194, 197–8

Mavritsakis, Yannis 278–9, 286–93; *Blind Spot* 288; *Fucking Job* 289; *The Invocation of Enchantment* 291; *Quasar* 290–1, 292; *Vitriol* 289–90; *Wolfgang* 287, 288–9;
Mayenburg, Marius von 129–30; 138–46; *Bang* 143–4; *Fireface* 140–2, 144; *Martyr* 143; *Moving Targets* 143; *Parasites* 142; *Plastic* 143; *Turista* 139; *The Ugly One* 138–9, 142–3;
Mayorga, Juan 12, 203–4, 210–20; *A Dog's Word* 213; *The Boy at the Back* 211, 216–18; *The Cartographer* 203, 214–15, 216; *Darwin's Tortoise* 212–13, 216, 221n22; *The Good Neighbour* 216; *Hamelin* 219; *Intensely Blue* 216; *Love Letters To Stalin* 211; *The Magician,* 216; *More Ash* 211; *Nocturnal,* 211; *Perpetual Peace* 216, 219; *The Scorched Garden* 211, 212, 216, 219; *Snowflake's Last Words* 213–14; *Way to Heaven* 215
Mazaj, Meta 315–16, 328
McDonagh, Martin 2, 244–50, 253–9, 283; *A Behanding in Spokane* 250; *A Very Very Very Dark Matter* 250, 255; *The Beauty Queen of Leenane* 244–6, 247, 248; *The Cripple of Inishmaan* 250; *Hangmen* 250; *The Lieutenant of Inishmore* 253–5; *The Pillowman* 249–50
Meirelles, Márcio 87
Melander, Björn 99
memory 195, 197, 368 *see also* cultural memory
Mickiewicz, Adam 26, 189
migration 3, 10, 76, 86, 162, 376–8, 392–3
migrant(s) 3, 17, 86, 131–3, 193–4, 282, 367–8, 392
Mijač, Dejan 324
Miletić-Oručević, Tanja 326–7
Miškovska-Kajevska, Ana 314
mise en scène 7, 90–1, 131, 135, 320, 376–7, 380
Mitchell, Katie 105–6, 116–17, 121–2, 125, 163–4, 336; *Attempts on Her Life* 116–17; *The City* 117, 119; *Cleansed* 163–4; *Nightsongs* 105–6; *The Trial of Ubu* 121, 125
modernity 302
Montenegro 315
Moretti, Franco 5
Moscow 170, 173–4, 228
Mrożek, Sławomir 33, 34–5, 68–9
Mühe, Ulrich 154
Müller, Heiner 353

406   *Index*

Müller, Ida 17
Multiculturalism 12, 13, 79, 162
multilingualism 371
multimedia 131, 197, 345
music 11, 46, 47–8, 56, 142, 206, 228–9,
    232, 246, 252, 257, 284, 321–2, 343,
    390, 394–5
musical(s) 2, 150–1, 249, 394
Muskała, Monika 1
Mustafić, Dino 319

narrative 14, 15, 16, 17, 70, 71, 78, 101,
    131, 136, 153, 173, 175, 176, 198,
    203, 217–18, 226–7, 230, 234–8, 241,
    271, 287, 305, 384; narrator 114, 173,
    215, 231, 236, 302, 321
National Socialism 45, 55–6, 100 *see also*
    fascism
nationalism(s) 1, 10, 12, 14–15, 16–17,
    26, 130, 137, 192, 199, 313, 315
naturalism 119–20, 121, 164, 178–9, 271;
    hypernaturalism 50, 375
NDiaye, Marie 7, 13, 374–88; *All Truth*
    385; *As to the Prosperous Future* 374;
    Daddy Has to Eat 374, 376, 377; *The
    Grown-Ups* 385; *Hilda* 374; *Nothing
    Human* 383, 384; *Providence* 380; *Three
    Strong Women* 384; *White Material*
    379–80
Ndiaye, Pap 381
neoliberalism 14, 54–5, 139, 142,
    197, 305
Nestbeschmutzer 8, 44
Netherlands 39, 40
New Drama 325–7; New Russian Drama
    168–81, 226–41
Nikčević, Sanja 158, 325
Nobel Prize for Literature 1–2, 360, 362
Norén, Lars 6 95–7, 98–104, 107–9; *A
    Horrible Happiness* 97; *Blood* 104; *Chaos
    is Neighbour of God* 98–9; *The Courage
    to Kill* 96; *Demons* 100, 102–4; *Dust*
    104; *The Human Circle 3:1* 100, 365;
    The Last Supper 103; *Night is Mother of
    the Day* 98–9; *Orestes* 96; *The Prince's
    Bootlicker* 96; *Seven Three* 100; *Shadow
    Boys* 100
Norway 95–6, 97–8, 101
novelist(s) 194, 268, 285–6, 287–8,
    364–6, 379
Nübling, Sebastian 119–20, 122–4

open borders 2, 10, 14
Orbakaite, Christina 170

Örkény, István 33
Osborne, Deirdre 335–6
Osborne, John 25
Osten, Suzanne 97
Ostermeier, Thomas 103–4, 119, 129,
    139, 140–2, 151–5, 159–60, 162, 268,
    325, 327; *Bella Figura* 268; *Blasted*
    154–5; *The City* 119, 159–60; *The Cut*
    159–60; *Demons* 103–4; *The Human
    Circle 3:1* 103; *The Name* 106, *Parasites*
    142; *Shopping and Fucking* 152–3, 162

painting *see* visual arts
Pankov, Vladimir 172
Paravidino, Fausto 296, 298–9, 302–6,
    308–11; *Genoa 01* 298, 308, 310;
    Giobbe's Butchery 299, 305–6; *Mariapia's
    Journal* 305; *The Meaning of Emma's Life*
    308; *The M Family Illness* 298, 302–4,
    309; *Peanuts* 298; *Still Life in a Ditch*
    298, 304–5; *Two Brothers – Chamber
    Tragedy in 53 Days* 298, 302
Paris 39
participation 394
patriarchy 27, 45, 250, 342
Perceval, Luk 106–7, 142
perestroika 170, 172, 172, 183n5
Peymann, Claus 102, 160–2
physicality 123, 142, 246, 247, 300, 304,
    365, 366
Pinter, Harold 32
play creation, methods of 8
play publication 264, 281
plot 36, 46, 59, 84, 107, 112, 136, 139,
    142, 208, 230, 239, 266, 301, 306,
    309; dismantling of 6, 188, 335,
    354, 357
poetry 354, 357–8, 362, 389
Poland 10, 16, 26, 30–1, 34–5, 52,
    66–75, 81, 156–7, 185–201
political; political violence 2, 12, 258;
    political theatre 37, 187–8, 194
'poor theatre' 3, 156, 298
popular theatre 21, 36
populism 9, 16, 45, 50, 53, 55, 56
Portugal *xviii*, 38
Poschmann, Gerda 46
postcolonialism 5, 37, 66, 87, 316, 327
postcommunist 66, 82–4, 85, 86, 88,
    90, 151, 159, 168, 199, 231 *see also*
    post-soviet
postdramatic theatre, *see* Lehmann,
    Hans-Thies
post-identity politics 3

postmodernism 88
Powell, Kersti Tarien 255
power 5, 30, 32, 45, 48, 73, 192,
    211, 213, 250, 289, 306, 322;
    self-empowerment 15, 365;
    technologies of power 289, 291
'Prague Spring' 39
postwar 4, 6, 7, 8, 13, 21–3, 25, 29, 32,
    45, 47, 55, 190
Presniakov, Oleg and Vladimir 169–171,
    174–81; *Playing the Victim* 171, 175–9;
    Sexual/floor covering 180; *Terrorism*
    174–5, 177, 179;
process 59, 68, 80, 113, 120–3, 125, 138,
    187, 216, 245, 255–8, 279, 285, 321,
    326, 371, 377, 383–4
protectionism 9
Provo movement 39
Putin, Vladimir 180

queer 71–2 *see also* LGBTQ
de Quinto, José María 25

racism 334–9, 341, 375, 376, 377
Radosavljević, Duška 157–8
Rambert, Pascal *xx*, 17
Rancière, Jacques 317, 323–4, 328
Rau, Milo 18
Ravenhill, Mark 6, 150–3, 158–62,
    163–5; *The Cut* 159–60; *Shoot/Get
    Treasure/Repeat* 160–2; *Shopping and
    Fucking* 150, 152–3;
Real Academia Española (RAE) 203
realism 24–31, 106, 117, 119, 131, 141–2,
    145, 152–3, 157, 171–2, 174, 180,
    255, 317, 335, 341 377, 385; grotesque
    realism 170–1; poetic realism 3;
    psychological realism 94, 102, 168;
    socialist realism 25–31; social realism
    174, 335, 341; *see also* naturalism
Rebellato, Dan 117, 342
Regie 8
Regietheater 153, 154 *see also* directors'
    theatre
Reza, Yasmina 261–2, 264–73; *Art* 2, 206,
    265–8, 271–2; *Babylone* 268; *Bella Figura*
    268; *Conversations After a Burial* 265; *God
    of Carnage* 267–8; *Hammerklavier* 268; *Life
    X 3* 267; *Winter Crossing* 265
refugees 58–9, 162, 235, 392–3
rehearsals 3, 54, 70, 97, 100, 113, 121,
    122–3, 179, 187, 298, 343, 365
religion 251–2
remembering 214

Renaude, Noëlle 17
research 69, 132, 187, 216, 379, 390
rhetoric 122, 189, 193, 196, 321
ritual 53, 58, 89–9, 101, 241, 289, 297,
    301, 306, 394–5
Rodrigues, Tiago *xvii–xxi,* 17
roles 8, 17, 69, 286, 354; distribution of
    323–4; gender roles 72, 344
Romania 10, 27, 29, 67–92, 195, 306
Romanticism; Polish Romanticism 26,
    29, 187, 189
Rosso, Beppe 89
Royal Court International Writer's
    Programme 11
Różewicz, Tadeusz 34, 69, 71
Rudnev, Pavel 230, 232
Russia 8, 10, 25, 27–8, 168–81, 226–42
    see also Soviet Union
Russo, Letizia 17
Ryan Report 252
Šafránek, Ota 25
Sajewska, Dorota 69–70
Sajko, Ivana 16, 315–25, 327–9; *An
    Orange in the Clouds* 318; *Archetype:
    Medea/Woman-Bomb/Europa* 318, 319,
    323, 324; *It's Not Us, It's Just Glass*
    319, 321, 323; *Rose is a rose is a rose is a
    rose* 318
Salzmann, Mariana 17
samizdat 7
Sartre, Jean-Paul 22, 206
satire 25, 31, 32, 33, 79, 83, 115–16, 190,
    196, 233, 253–4, 281–2, 284, 344
scenic writing 139
scenography *see* design
Schimmelpfennig, Roland 129–38,
    145–6; *Arabian Night* 135–6; *Before/
    After* 134; *The Eternal Mary* 135; *The
    Golden Dragon* 131–3; *On Greifswalder
    Street* 136; *Peggy Pickit Sees the Face of
    God* 137; *Push Up 1–3* 134, 135–6;
    Winter Solstice 137
Schleef, Einar 57–8
Schuster, Robert 129
Schwab, Werner 44–55, 60; *Anti-Climax*
    45; *Comedies of Kings* 54; *Dead at Last,
    At Last No More Air* 54; *OVER-
    WEIGHT, unimportant, MISSHAPE: A
    European [Last] Supper* 52–4; *Schwabisch*
    48; *The Presidents* 51–2
science fiction 290
Scotland 14
sculpture 49
Second World War 22, 136, 196

408   *Index*

secularism 74; postsecularism 278, 291
Serbia 315–29, 360, 362–3
Serebrennikov, Kirill 173–4, 177
sexuality 53, 191–3
Shakespeare, William 29, 31, 67, 83, 139,
  263, 287; *Hamlet* 176–7, 185, 248,
  347n5, 362, 378; *Julius Caesar* 30;
  Midsummer Night's Dream 135; *Much
  Ado About Nothing* 140; *Richard III* 54,
  361; *Sonnet 30* xvii; *Troilus and Cressida*
  46; *Twelfth Night* 140; see also *Hamlet-
  machine* 38; *Lady Macbeth* 336; *Richard
  III Will Not Take Place*, 83–4
Sicily 298, 300–2, 306–8, 310
Sierz, Aleks 11, 115, 326
Sigarev, Vasilii 169–174, 177–181; *Black
  Milk* 172–3, 179, *Plasticine* 171–2,
  173–4, 177–8
silence 95, 101, 105–8, 123, 178, 203,
  219, 303–4, 314, 328, 395–6
Slavkin, Viktor 35
Smolensk 231
Socialism 27, 35, 37–8 see also
  communism
Solanas, Valerie 341
solidarity 12, 89–90, 370; Solidarity
  (Polish trade union) 186
Sorescu, Marin 29
Soviet Union 10, 16, 27–8, 35, 83, 168,
  211, 226, 230, 233–4; post–Soviet
  168–70, 172, 175–7, 180, 226–31
Spain 14, 29–30, 38, 203–220
Spanish Civil War 211–2
spirituality 15, 102, 172–3, 175, 177, 180,
  238, 394–5
sports 45, 57–8, 189–90, 192–3
Sprachkritik (language critique) 47, 115–16
Srbljanović, Biljana 16, 315–25, 327–9;
  America, Part Two 318, 324; *Barbelo: On
  Dogs and Children* 320, 322, 324; *The
  Belgrade Trilogy* 317; *Family Tales* 317;
  Neck Made of Glass 319; *Someone Else's
  Heart: Or a theatrical tract about borders*
  319; *This Grave is Too Small for Me*
  318–19
stage directions 320–5 see also didaskalia
Stalinism 83, 211–12
state of the nation play 37–8
Stemann, Nicolas 58–9
Stephens, Simon 6, 112–13, 119–26;
  Carmen Disruption 112, 113; *Herons*
  119–20; *Pornography* 112, 113; *Three
  Kingdoms* 6, 122–4; *The Trial of Ubu*
  121–2

Štivičić, Tena 315
Stockholm 371–2
Stokfiszewski, Igor 192
storytelling 37, 145, 218, 245,
  249–51, 253
Streeruwitz, Marlene 344–5
Strzępka, Monika 186–7, 189–92
subsidy 22, 73–4, 113–14, 262–3
subtext 28, 29, 249
Sweden 13, 15, 39, 95–109, 362–73
Szczawińska, Weronika 18, 66–75
Székely, Csaba 79

Tarantino, Quentin 158, 218, 245 see also
  cinema
television 130–1
terrorism 175, 219, 254
theatre prizes and awards: Anti-Booker
  Award 171, 182n10; Ernst Toller Prize
  317; Eureka Prize 229; Evening
  Standard Awards 177; Hedda Award
  364; Ibsen Prize 353; Ignasi Iglesias
  Prize 204; International Playwright's
  Award (Heidelberg Stückemarkt) 282;
  Kleist Prize 140; Marin Držić Award
  318; Molière Award 265; Nelly Sachs
  Prize 382; New Theatrical Realities
  European Prize 328; Polityka Passport
  Prize 66; SACD Award 265; Stanley
  Thomas Johnson Foundation Prize
  265; Sterija Festival Award 317, 330n7;
  Tondelli Award 298; Village Voice
  Obie Award 364
theatres and theatre companies: A.C.T.I.
  Teatri Independenti Torino 89; Actors
  Touring Company 132–3;
  Akademietheater 254; l'Atelier in
  Montmartre 377; Baracke 151–4;
  Barbican 154; Beogradsko Dramsko
  Pozorište 32–3, 157–8; Berliner
  Ensemble 160–1, 344–5; Catalan
  National Theatre 205; Centre
  Dramatique National 263; Centre for
  Playwriting and Dramaturgy 171;
  Centro Dramático Nacional [CDN]
  211, 219; Chekhov Moscow Arts
  174–5, 176; Comédie-Française 14, 16,
  304, 374, 375–6, 377; Compagnia Sud
  Costa Occidentale 297, 299, 306–7;
  Cross–Channel Theatre 272; Deutsches
  Schauspielhaus 57, 113, 122, 134,
  140–1; Deutsches Theater 13, 151–2;
  Divadlo Na zábradlí 35; Draamateater
  255; Drolatic Industry 89; Druid

Theatre 244, 245–6; Grupo de Teatro Realista 25; Hackney Empire 132–3; Hamburger Kammerspiele 154; Hampstead Theatre 121–2; Husets Teater 345; Giljotin Theatre 105; Just a Must Theatre 54; Komuna Warszawa 73–4, 186; Lyceum Theatre 390; Lyric Theatre 122–4; Maravillas Theatre 210; Marquina Theatre 206; Maxim Gorki Theatre 129; Menier Chocolate Factory 208–9, 270; Münchner Kammerspiele 106–7, 122–4; National Theatre see Royal National Theatre; National Theatre of Greece 279–80; National Theatre of Strasbourg 383–4; New Ambassadors Theatre 150; Old Vic Theatre 105–6; Onassis Cultural Center 281; Piccolo Teatro 217; Poliorama Theatre 205, 206; Print Room 14; Realistické Divadlo 25; Realistiko Theatro 25; Riksteatern 100–1; Romea Theatre 205; Royal Court Theatre 8, 11, 129, 177–9, 211, 215, 226–7, 233, 298, 309–10, 334, 337, 339, 341; Royal Dramatic Theatre (Dramaten) 96, 107–8; Royal National Theatre [NT] 116–17, 163–4; Royal Shakespeare Company [RSC] 13–14, 233, 341, 342, 343; Saarländisches Staatstheater 54; Saint Gervais Theatre 281; Schaubühne Theatre 11, 103–4, 117, 119, 139, 142–3, 196, 310, 340–1; Schauspiel Essen 162; Secret Theatre 124; Signa 17; Slovak National Theatre 29; Soho Theatre 194, 272; Stavros Niarchos Foundation Cultural Center 280; Szybki Teatr Miejski 187; Teater NO99 122–4; Teatr.doc 187, 227; Teatr Dramatyczny 71, 73; Teatr Narodowy 25; Teatr Nowy 80; Teatro Biondo 297, 298; Teatro della Corte di Genova 254; Teatro Kamikaze 238–9; Teatro Nacional D. Maria II xviii; Teatro Pradillo 340; Teatro San Martín 215; Teatro Stabile di Torino 299; Teatro Valle 298–9; Teatr Polski 189; Teatr Powszechny 73; Teatr Praktika 232; Teatrul Dramaturgilor Români 76; Teatr Współczesny 156; Teatr Wybrzeże 186; Theater am Turm [TAT] 129; Théâtre de la Colline 385; Théâtre de la Tempête 215; Théâtre de Nanterre–Amandiers 105; Théâtre des Champs-Elysées 265–6; Théâtre des Mathurins 269; Théâtre du Centaure 344; Théâtre du Rond-Point 263; Théâtre Garonne xvii–xxi; Théâtre Gérard–Philipe 263; Théâtre Hébertot 270; Theater Oberhausen 253; Theatre of Displaced People 235–6; Théâtre Ouvert 263; Théâtre Paris-Villette 265; Timisoara National Theatre 303–4; Trap Door Theatre 86; Traverse Theatre 122, 235; TR Warszawa (Teatr Rozmaitości) 156, 185, 193; Vienna Burgtheater 57–8, 103, 162; Volksbühne 379; Werkteater company 39; Wooster Group 320

theatre training institutions: Aleksander Zelwerowicz Theatre Academy 66; Drama School of the Greek Art Theatre Karolos Koun 279; Ekaterinburg State Theatre Institute 169–70; Ernst Busch Theatre Academy 129; Jacques Lecoq Theatre School 265; National Theatre Drama School (Greece) 286; Otto Falckenberg Theatre School 134–5; Royal Court Theatre's Young Writers Programme 8; Warsaw Theatre Academy 71

theatres of memory 214 see also cultural memory

theatricality 32, 46, 54, 90, 142, 245, 254, 340, 375; metatheatricality 86, 88, 118, 131, 179, 256–7, 284

ticking clock scenario 203

time, treatment of 102, 118, 134, 135, 136, 139, 187, 198, 203, 208, 214, 216, 240–1, 354, 355–6, 366, 368, 384

Thorpe, Chris 12

thriller 122, 204–5, 208, 210

Tomato Action 39

tourism 194, 282–3, 372

Townsend, Tamzin 205, 206

Tscharyiski, Christina 345

tragedy 132, 177, 194, 238–9, 254, 301, 304–5 see also Greek tragedy

transcendence 394–5

translation 9, 12, 76, 178–9, 194, 205, 272, 307–8, 326, 340, 371–2, 381–2 see also untranslatability

transnationalism 315

Transylvania 79

trauma 325, 326

Treaty of Trianon 3–4

tucker green, debbie xx, 334–6, 337–41, 346; born bad 340; stoning mary 337–41

Turkey 254

410   *Index*

Turrini, Peter 187
Tynan, Kenneth 32

Ukraine 228, 230, 232–6, 241
Ulrich, Laurel Thatcher 341
Unions 7; Equity 132–3; Union of Polish
  Writers 7
United Kingdom *see* Britain
unity of time, place and action 203, 208
untranslatability 6, 56, 307 310 *see also*
  translation
universal 67, 68, 72, 78–9, 84, 89, 188–9,
  193, 199; universality 239, 296, 297, 307
urbanisation 136, 303

Vampilov, Aleksandr 27
verbatim theatre *see* documentary theatre
Verdichtung (poetic concentration) 132
verse 25, 40, 176
video *see* multimedia
Viennese Actionism 49–50
Vinge, Vegard 17
violence 5, 11, 15, 24, 39, 44–5, 53, 120,
  123, 150, 155, 164, 175, 205, 226,
  231–2, 234, 246–7, 249–50, 251–3,
  257–8, 262, 265, 282–4, 335, 337–8,
  340, 344, 369, 381, 398; political
  violence 2, 12, 15, 32, 213, 258
Visky András 77–8, 80–3, 84–5, 89–91;
  Disciples 89; *I Killed My Mother* 84; *Juliet*
  81; *Porn* 82; *Stories of the Body* 81
Visniec, Matéi 3, 13, 76, 77–8, 79, 80,
  81–92; *Beware of Old Ladies Gnawed by
  Solitude* 89; *The Body of a Woman as a
  Battlefield in the Bosnian War* 85, 87;
  *Decomposed Theater or The Human
  Trashcan* 88–9; *The Extraterrestrial that
  Wanted some Pyjamas as a Keepsake*
  86; *How to Explain the History of
  Communism to Mental Patients* 83; *The
  Last Godot* 87; *Richard III Will Not Take
  Place, or Scenes from the Life of Meyerhold*
  83–4; *Why Hecuba?* 88
visual arts 49–50, 66, 74, 85, 137, 160,
  170, 173, 197, 215, 249, 257, 266, 269
  324, 344
voice 16, 56, 80, 106–7, 114, 197, 304,
  323, 327, 340–1, 342, 345, 359, 366,

368–9, 372; giving voice 57, 79, 213,
  237, 336, 346
Volksstück 9, 52
Vorozhbyt, Natalia 227–8, 229–31,
  232–7, 240–2; *Bad Road* 236–7;
  Cyborgs 236; *The Grain Store* 233–5;
  The Khomenko Family Chronicles 233;
  Take Out the Rubbish, Sasha 237
Vyrypaev, Ivan 15, 227–32, 238–42;
  Delhi Dance 238; *Euphoria* 232; *Genesis
  No. 2* 239; *Illusions* 238–9; *July* 231–32;
  Oxygen 228–9

Walsh, Enda *xx*, 244–53, 255–9; *Arlington*
  257; *Ballyturk* 256; *bedbound* 248; *Disco
  Pigs* 244, 246–8; *Fishy Tales* 244;
  Hunger 249; *Misterman* 251–2; *The New
  Electric Ballroom* 251, 252; *Penelope*
  252–3; *Sing Street* 252; *The Walworth
  Frace* 256
Warlikowski, Krzysztof 156–7
Warsaw 194
West End 2, 150, 248
Williams, Faynia 85
Wilson, Richard 178
Witkacy (Witkiewicz), Stanisław 30–1
Wittgenstein, Ludwig 47
Wojcieszek, Przemysław 193
wordplay 3, 47, 140, 205, 208
world literature 4–6
writers' guilds 7
Whyman, Erica 342–3

xenophobia 9, 45, 53–4, 56, 282–3

Yugoslavia 1, 10, 27, 32–3, 157–8, 313–20,
  324, 328 *see also* Bosnian War

Zeller, Florian 261–2, 264, 268–74; *The
  Father* 270–2; *Hary Janos* 269; *The
  Merry-Go-Round* 270; *The Mother* 270;
  The Other 269; *The Truth* 270; *She's
  Waiting for You* 270
Zuckmayer, Carl 23

#blacklivesmatter movement 338
#MeToo movement 344, 345